Computers and Applications

Second Edition

COMPUTERS & APPLICATIONS

AN INTRODUCTION TO DATA PROCESSING

Daniel L. Slotnick

Evan M. Butterfield
George Washington University

Ernest S. Colantonio
University of Illinois

Daniel J. Kopetzky
Supercomputing Research Center

Joan K. Slotnick

D. C. HEATH AND COMPANY

Lexington, Massachusetts   Toronto

To the memory of Dan Slotnick.

Acquisitions Editor: Peter C. Gordon
Developmental Editor: Katherine T. Sheehan
Production Editor: Jill E. Hobbs
Designer: Cornelia L. Boynton
Production Coordinator: Mike O'Dea
Photo Researcher: Martha L. Shethar
Text Permissions Editor: Margaret Roll
Cover: Sharon Green/The Stock Market
Inset: Cray Research, Inc.

Published simultaneously in Canada.

Printed in the United States of America.

International Standard Book Number: 0-669-19938-9

Library of Congress Catalog Card Number: 88-82326

10   9   8   7   6   5   4   3   2   1

Preface

The second edition of *Computers and Applications* is designed to reflect the changes in the technology and use of computer systems since the publication of the first edition. These changes in the software, hardware, and applications of computer systems are exciting. The end user can revel in the power, flexibility, and productivity gains made available at an increasingly modest price by these new systems.

It is for the end-user that this book was written. As with the first edition, the approach remains one of learning and application. This practical approach will appeal to a broad spectrum of students. Readers of this text may be enhancing their career prospects, looking for ways to utilize their personal computer systems, fulfilling a requirement, or simply satisfying their curiosity. Whatever the readers' goals, our goal in writing this book was to present enough detail about the actual working of computer system hardware and software and their uses to dispel the mystery without overwhelming readers with more technical detail than is needed for competency. Competency is a first step to confidence and enthusiasm for the subject. We hope that readers will enjoy learning information from this text as well as developing skills useful in academic, home, or business endeavors.

Text Content and Organization

This text has been carefully designed for use in any first course in computer data processing or for any individual who is learning more about computers. It meets or exceeds most of the requirements for an introductory course as proposed by the Data Processing Management Association (DPMA); the American Assembly of Collegiate Schools of Business (AACSB); and the Association for Computing Machinery (ACM). It is also intended to prepare students in two-year colleges who plan to transfer to curricula in four-year institutions, as well as those taking courses offered at four-year schools.

Variety As evidenced by the table of contents, the text lends itself to a wide range of courses, from those that deal only lightly with programming to hands-on applications courses and more traditional surveys, from the business-oriented to the technical. Note, too, that the materials in the text require neither computer skills nor mathematical skills beyond high school algebra.

Flexibility As with the previous edition, the text has been organized for maximum flexibility. Its 18 chapters are divided into six modules that can, with some exceptions, be taught in any order. We recommend covering Part 1, Overview (Chapters 1 and 2) first. After that, Part 2, Hardware (Chapters 3 through 6); Part 3, Software (Chapters 7 through 10); Part 4, Systems (Chapters 11 through 13); Part 5, Applications (Chapters 14 through 16); and Part 6, Implications (Chapters 17 and 18) can be read in any order. Those teaching the course in combination with an applications software or programming laboratory may wish to cover Part 3 earlier.

Text Learning Aids

Computers and Applications, second edition combines a relaxed writing style with an outstanding array of pedagogical features to facilitate understanding and encourage reader enthusiasm.

Chapter Preview and Review Materials Since we believe that repetition of key ideas in preview and review materials helps a student to learn more effectively and to study for exams, we have structured each chapter around such materials. Each chapter opens with *In This Chapter,* a preview outline of the chapter's headings annotated with easily remembered study phrases. These study phrases are then repeated for guided study in the text margins. Finally, the chapter *Summary* is structured for review around the same outline of chapter headings.

Computer Use and Users Each chapter opens with a *Focus* on a real-world situation closely related to the chapter content. These selections have been chosen from popular computer magazines and from other nonfiction views of the computer world. They are designed to give the reader a taste of the real, if somewhat eccentric, world of the computer literate.

Boxed Features Chapters include *Issues in Technology* boxes within the running text to encourage the student to pause and reflect, and to take a stand on an ethical question related to the chapter content.

Case Studies At the end of 12 chapters of the text are vignettes where applications software is used to tie the text concepts to a real world application. These *A Closer Look* features are a natural extension of the theme of the text.

Readability The text's engaging writing style ensures that concepts are explained clearly and simply. To ensure accessibility for students, the reading level has been carefully monitored by the editors, course instructors and reviewers.

Design and Illustrations Students prefer a textbook that will hold their interest. Since today's students are part of a visually-oriented society, we have created a full-color design that reflects the excitement and dynamism of the field. We have made a studied effort to illustrate the second edition liberally with actual screen illustrations that are both realistic and instructive.

End-of-Chapter Materials A carefully graded set of chapter review materials is provided at the end of each chapter. First, *Computer Concepts* review vocabulary, providing page references to the chapter's boldfaced glossary terms. From 15 to 20 *Review Questions* follow, providing a rote review of the chapter's major topics and paralleling the chapter outline. New to this edition are *True or False* and *Multiple Choice* questions designed specifically to help the students prepare for examinations. *A Sharper Focus* questions challenge students to apply what they have learned. Finally, special *Projects* encourage students to stretch their learning beyond the chapter content.

Career Guidance Because many readers will be interested in job opportunities in the computer industry, Appendix B, Careers in Technology, provides a number of job descriptions, qualifications, and outlooks, as well as suggestions for career paths and some basic help on résumé preparation.

Glossary and Index A complete glossary includes clear definitions for the bold-faced terms in the text. In addition, an extensive index provides a handy reference for both student and instructor.

Changes to this Edition

Many of you who used the first edition of this text will note that substantial changes have been made to this edition. These changes reflect the changing technology, use, and availability of smaller, yet more powerful, systems. These changes also reflect the increasing influence of end-users in determining their own information and equipment needs.

Microcomputer-Integrated The reader will notice that the material in Part 5 of the first edition, called "The Miraculous Micro," is now integrated throughout all chapters and is greatly expanded. The text properly treats all aspects of both large and small systems in parallel.

Text and Chapters Consolidated We have resisted the temptation common in text revision to expand the length without concern for the students or the instructor. Instead, the number of chapters has been reduced from 23 to 18, with two appendices. This decision was made for two reasons. First, 18 chapters fit the length of most courses better. Second, students' increasing familiarity and exposure to computers makes some of the topics previously included of less critical import. The more manageable length now matches the ideal recommended by users and reviewers for a text of this type.

Other changes that may be of particular interest are the following. Every effort has been made to include the most up-to-date information possible.

Chapter 3: The CPU and Memory
Material on data representation moved to the appendix.
Expanded coverage of workstations.
Microcomputer perspective expanded.

Chapter 4: Input and Output
Now approached from a device viewpoint rather than a process viewpoint.
Separate first edition chapters 4 and 6 (Input and Output) consolidated.

Chapter 5: Secondary Storage and File Organization
More emphasis on disk storage.

Chapter 6: Data Communication
Expanded coverage of LANs and WANs.

Chapter 7: Program Development
Increased emphasis on pseudocode.

Chapter 8: Programming Languages
New coverage of Modula-2.

Chapter 9: Application Packages
Expanded coverage of all major applications, including word processing, spreadsheets, data bases, graphics, and communications.

Chapter 10: Operating Systems
New coverage of OS/2 and expanded material on UNIX.

Chapter 12: Data Base Systems
New material on SQL.

Chapter 14: Computers in the Office
New coverage of desktop publishing.

Chapter 17: Privacy, Security, and Other Concerns
New coverage of viruses and vaccines.

BASIC and Pascal Programming Texts Users and reviewers suggested that no appendix can give adequate coverage of a programming language. These appendices can also add to the length and expense of a book. In practice, it appears that most instructors who teach programming have their students purchase a separate text. Therefore, we have deleted the BASIC appendix, offering instead separate—and more complete—texts on BASIC and Pascal to introduce students to these programming languages.

Applications Software In the first edition, application software packages were covered in one chapter (Chapter 10). Coverage of these very powerful tools has been radically expanded. In addition to a full chapter of coverage (Chapter 9) in the second edition, application software case studies called *A Closer Look* have been added. These features offer realistic demonstrations of some of today's most popular application packages. They include: Using CROSSTALK (Chapter 6), Prototyping (Chapter 7), Applications Generators (Chapter 8), Lotus 1-2-3 (Chapter 9), MS-DOS (Chapter 10), Microsoft Project (Chapter 11), dBASE III PLUS (Chapter 12), VP-Expert (Chapter 13), and WordPerfect 5.0 (Chapter 14).

More Applications Software for Your Laboratory Today's students must be conversant with a wide variety of applications and many packages in order to be fully computer literate. Additionally, the school and the instructor, faced with limited resources, may not always have the variety of software tools the interested student may desire. Therefore, in order to allow maximum flexibility, we are also offering inexpensive laboratory supplements that cover 14 commonly used software tools.

Supplements

An extensive supplements package is offered with the text to help both student and instructor cover the material. Each supplement has been prepared by an experienced teacher/author.

Software Supplements The *Heath Software Guide Series* includes the following student software laboratory manuals, most available with software:

Word Processing
- Using WordStar 5
- Using WordPerfect 5.0
- Using PC-Write
- Using PC-Type+

Spreadsheet

- Using SuperCalc5
- Using Lotus 1-2-3
- Using VP-Planner Plus
- Using PC-Calc+

Expert Systems

- Using VP-Expert

Data Base

- Using PC-File+
- Using dBASE III PLUS

Communications

- Using PC-Dial

Macintosh Software

- Using Macintosh Software

Operating Systems

- Using PC/MS-DOS and OS/2

These manuals provide the student with instructions, examples, and exercises to get them started using microcomputers quickly and confidently. Each begins with a DOS or Macintosh Operating System tutorial.

Study Guide Prepared by Fred L. Head of North Orange County Community College District, and Richard E. Morel and Beth H. Morel, the *Study Guide* has been designed as a thorough review and self-test of text concepts and information. Included for each chapter are:

- Learning objectives written especially for the guide.
- *Making the Chapter Work:* Learning and study tips for making the most of each chapter.
- *Chapter Review:* A summary of the chapter organized by text headings and written from a new angle.
- A variety of exercises, including a true-false pretest and a multiple-choice posttest. Each chapter has an average of 118 exercises.

Instructor's Supplements The supplements designed for instructors include an *Instructor's Guide* with transparency masters, a *Test Item File, HeathTest+* (a computerized test generator), and *Transparencies.*

- **Instructor's Guide.** Prepared by Marilyn Meyers of Fresno City College, the *Instructor's Guide* includes a wealth of materials for busy instructors. For each chapter, we provide learning objectives, a chapter overview, annotated lecture outlines, answers to text questions, additional classroom and lecture materials, and transparency masters.
- **Test Item File.** A new *Test Item File* developed by Richard E. Morel includes approximately 3000 test questions: 40% true-false, 50% multiple choice, and 10% fill-in.
- **HeathTest+.** A computerized test generator for microcomputers is also available. Instructors can produce chapter tests, mid-terms, and final exams easily and accurately. The instructor can also edit existing questions or add new ones as desired, or preview questions on screen and add them to the test with a single keystroke.
- **Transparencies.** The transparency package includes 50 transparency acetates.

Acknowledgments

The number of individuals contributing to a textbook like this is, of course, countless. We do want to give special thanks to C. Brian Honess of the University of South Carolina for his significant contributions to the end-of-chapter projects and to Gayle M. Ross of Copiah-Lincoln Junior College for her ideas.

We would also like to thank our colleagues who reviewed the second edition manuscript: Mike Brown, Clemson University; Anthony C. Connor, Clemson University; Louise Darcy, Texas A & M University; Henry Etlinger, Rochester Institute of Technology; Dennis Guster, St. Louis Community College at Meramec; Grace Hertlein, California State University, Chico; Betty Jehn, University of Dayton; Antonio M. Lopez, Jr., Loyola University; Donna McClelland, Montana State University; Marilyn Wertheimer Meyers, Fresno City College; Mike Michaelson, Palomar College; Randy Molmen, University of North Dakota; Marlon Sampson, Southeast Community College; Paul Ross, Millersville University; Ken Walter, Weber State College; and Ron Willard, Bowling Green-Firelands.

Finally we would like to thank the hundreds of instructors and thousands of students who used the first edition. Many of your comments have been incorporated in this edition to create a better, more exciting book.

About The Authors

Daniel L. Slotnick

Before his death in 1985, Dr. Daniel L. Slotnick was a Professor of Computer Science at the University of Illinois at Urbana-Champaign. His early academic experience included participation in the development of the IAS machine, the earliest general purpose computer, from 1952 to 1954.

Evan M. Butterfield

A professional writer and editor, Evan Butterfield brings to *Computers and Applications* a strong background in both writing and teaching. He is currently teaching writing at George Washington University.

Ernest S. Colantonio

Ernest Colantonio brings combined teaching, technical, and writing skills to this textbook. Currently a professional textbook author, he also works as a consultant and programmer for the University of Illinois Department of Psychology Instructional Computer Laboratory.

Daniel J. Kopetzky

Daniel Kopetzky is currently employed at the Supercomputing Research Center, a major institution in the research, development, and applications of supercomputers.

Joan K. Slotnick

Joan Slotnick, an experienced textbook author and project coordinator of this text.

Brief Contents

Contents

2 The Evolution of Computers

Part 2 Hardware

3 The Central Processing Unit and Memory

Part 3   Software   203

7   Program Development   204

Part 4   Systems   **373**

Part 5   Applications   469

14   Computers in the Office   470

OVERVIEW

In a sense, this entire text is only an overview of the vast topic of computers and their applications. While no one book can possibly cover all computer topics, this text will help you face a world in which the role of computers is being continuously expanded. Part 1 presents the conceptual and historical background you need to study the various components, systems, applications, and implications of today's computers. Chapter 1 briefly describes why you should study computers, what they are, how they are used, what they actually do, the role they play in our lives, and what they aren't. Chapter 2 is a historical survey designed to give you some perspective on how and why today's computers evolved as they did.

1

Computers in Our Lives

Focus On

Computers and Applications

The America's Cup has become the ultimate computer game. San Diego's John Marshall, a firm believer in the message of the machine, doesn't lament this in the least. As he explains, "Computers are the tools of the current artists. You can't really conceive of doing creative work in the modern world without computers. With a computer you can substantiate your intuition, you can lay down some quantification of why you should do what you would do anyhow. So you can still have a Michelangelo without a computer, but how would a Michelangelo get something built in today's world? It's hard to get anything new built today if you can't document it first. I think without a computer, it is hard to avoid mediocrity. Without a computer there is enormous pressure to avoid risk. That doesn't win the America's Cup, I'll tell you that."

"We lost the America's Cup in 1983 because our boat, *Liberty*, was a creative failure," offers Marshall, who sailed aboard the U.S. boat as tactician. "Simply stated, the Australians made a commit-

ment to a computational approach to design, and America concluded that progress in boat design was unlikely; in any case, it wouldn't be made by people playing games with computers. It would be made by hands-on sailors, intuitively modifying and adjusting. And I'll tell you what, the number crunchers won."

Sailing in the America's Cup race changed from an art to a

science—a computer science—in 1983.

What has followed has been an unparalleled commitment to computer-aided design (CAD), which centered on yacht design and also touched upon complex areas such as sail making, weather as it affects boat design and race strategies, and tactical decisions on the water.

A boat's keel might be thought of as a sailboat's underwater wing. Weighted with lead, it serves two purposes: it changes the sideward force of the sails into a forward force, and it balances the heeling forces of the sail plan.

A computer program, called a velocity prediction program (VPP), was used in the Dutch national aerospace laboratory to evaluate the efficiency of lifting surfaces and was modified to test the efficiency of the lifting surfaces on sailboats—keels, in particular.

In the 1988 race, the yacht from New Zealand was a huge monohull. The other, from the United States, was half its size, but it was a catamaran, with two hulls instead of one and a solid-wing sail rather than the familiar soft kind.

Even before the two boats raced head-to-head, the outcome had been predicted correctly based on the established computer models. Stars and Stripes, the catamaran sailing from the San Diego Yacht Club, was significantly faster, winning the two races by margins of 18 and 20 minutes.

While the court fights continue over the rules of this particular race, it is clear that both boats embody advances in sailboat technology that have developed from a powerful mix of two forces: brilliant design and big-time computer power. In post-1983 America's Cup competition, it seems, you can't have one without the other.

The most striking feature of our time is not so much the wonderful scientific and technological advances that have occurred, but the rate at which they continue to occur and the profound impact they have on our lives.

In another era it was possible for a person to assimilate new concepts at a measured pace. Scientific and technical breakthroughs were less common and certainly less widely reported and implemented. It was also possible for a person to ignore those ideas and devices that did not conform to their needs or wants. Social decisions could be made with reference to a set of clear, well-defined rules. This set of rules, or framework, for understanding appropriate social behavior was learned from parents, friends, teachers, books, magazines, and many other sources.

Today we learn from even more sources. The facts come to us faster, with greater intensity, and with more variety than ever before. It is no longer possible for a person to ignore the impact of scientific and technological developments, especially those in computer technology. We have the tremendous opportunity to use computers to enrich our lives.

In this text we provide a framework for understanding the impact of computer technology and a working knowledge of the components of computer systems. This knowledge will help you make informed decisions about using computers in your life and career. In short, our goal in this text is to make you an *informed user* of computer systems.

In this first chapter you'll have an opportunity to organize in your mind those things about computers that you may already know to be true and to learn some new things.

Throughout this book, words that are printed in **boldface** are key terms, vital to understanding the material. They are collected at the end of each chapter for review and are also listed alphabetically in the glossary. In this first chapter, however, most technical terms will be defined very briefly or only in context. You should try for only a general understanding in this chapter—don't worry about mastering the specifics yet. Important terms will be defined more rigorously in later chapters, after you have read additional background material.

COMPUTERS: WHY STUDY THEM?

Computers have been getting a lot of press lately. We hear about them almost every day and we see them all around us. But what can they do for you? Why should you spend the time and effort to learn more about computers? Why did you take this course?

Various reasons for learning more about computers

You could simply answer that this course is required by your department or perhaps it is a prerequisite for some other, more advanced course that you want to take. There are, however, more profound reasons why you should study computers. A few of them have to do with education, employment, productivity, capability, and fun.

Education

You cannot have a well-rounded education without learning *something* about computers. Computers affect all of our lives, whether we realize it or not. They are used in banks, offices, stores, factories, schools, governmental agencies, military installa-

You can't have a well-rounded education without knowing something about computers

tions, and just about any other organization you can imagine. Tiny specialized computers are built into many modern appliances, machines, and vehicles. All kinds of advanced equipment from cameras to jet aircraft are utterly dependent on computer technology. Unless you learn a few fundamental computer concepts, it will be difficult to understand many of today's and tomorrow's technological issues. Just as more and more people had to learn to use the telephone in the early twentieth century, more and more people will have to learn to use computers in order to function in our increasingly complex society.

This is especially true for college students. Computer use on campuses has been growing at a phenomenal rate. According to a report in the *Chronicle of Higher Education*, colleges spent $800 million and students spent another $1 billion on computer products in 1987 alone. At many colleges, courses in a wide range of subjects now require students to use computers (see Figure 1.1). In some cases, faculty members are designing their own ways for students to use computers in their studies. For example, the philosophy department at Carnegie-Mellon University offers a computerized course to help students learn the principles of symbolic logic at their own pace. Students who already know how to use a computer may find it easier to adapt to these types of courses (Hayes 1988).

Employment

Computer knowledge helps you compete in today's workplace

Since most businesses and other organizations routinely use computers, employers need workers who are at least familiar with these machines. Knowing how to use a computer certainly won't guarantee you a job, but it can help you to be more competitive in today's labor market. At Northwestern Mutual Life, for example, computers are essential tools. The company has sold over 2000 computers to its 6000 independent insurance agents. Agents working in the same office generally share computers, so every agent has access to a computer. According to Mark Lichtenberger, a technical planning officer at Northwestern Mutual, "An agent can't do business without a PC [personal computer]. Without one, he or she has no access to sales-illustration charts, which are impossible to calculate manually." Some life insurance policies now offered by Northwestern Mutual are so complex

Figure 1.1 Computers In Education
Many schools now require students to use computers in some of their classes.

that agents need a computer to demonstrate the advantages to potential customers (Zarley 1988).

Another indication that students with computer skills do better in the job market comes from an informal survey done by Barbara Kurshan, former director of academic computing at Hollins College. A cross section of students was questioned, including 100 who had taken at least two computer courses at Hollins. Kurshan found that 70 percent of the students who had taken computer courses were routinely using computers in their jobs. These individuals generally thought that they got their jobs and were paid more because of their computer experience (Hayes 1988). (Appendix B describes many of these jobs and their growth prospects in the near future.)

Productivity

A compelling reason for learning to use a computer is that it can help you do certain jobs better and more efficiently. For example, a common application of computers is **word processing** (see Figure 1.2), which allows you to produce documents, such as letters and reports, with a computer. Once you learn how to do this, it is easier, faster, and more flexible than using an ordinary typewriter. Since you can correct errors before committing your work to paper, word processing can also produce much cleaner final documents. Most word processors even have a built-in *spelling checker* (an electronic dictionary) to help you eliminate spelling errors, and a *word finder* (an electronic thesaurus) to help you increase your word power.

Computers can help you be more efficient

The fact that word processing is more efficient than ordinary typing in an office environment has been known for a long time. For example, a 1979 study suggested that word processing could eliminate up to 70 percent of the time spent on conventional typing (Haider 1979). And today's word processors are much more sophisticated, more powerful, and easier to use than those of 10 years ago.

Besides word processing, many other computer applications can save you a great deal of time and effort in your routine work. We'll have much more to say

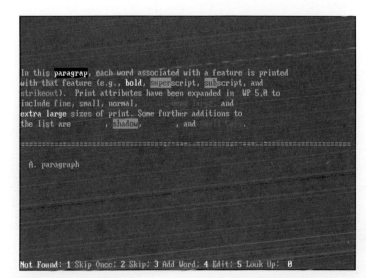

Figure 1.2 Word Processing

Word-processing packages, such as WordPerfect, help you prepare documents such as letters, reports, articles, and even books. Most have handy features such as a built-in spelling checker, which can significantly reduce typographical errors.

about these computer applications later in this chapter and throughout the rest of this book.

Capability

Computers can help you do jobs that might otherwise be impossible

Computers not only perform some everyday tasks better and more efficiently, they often allow you to tackle jobs you otherwise wouldn't be able to do at all. We've already mentioned the presentation of sales-illustration charts by Northwestern Mutual Life insurance agents. Another example is a computer-simulated chemistry lab at the University of Illinois (see Figure 1.3), which lets students mix hazardous chemicals and see the results without endangering themselves or the building. Actually, students don't mix real chemicals; they just tell the computer what they would mix. The computer then displays on a screen prerecorded video sequences of the results that would occur if those chemicals were actually mixed. Although computer-simulated explosions aren't quite as exciting as real ones, they are much safer for students and less destructive to equipment and facilities.

Fun

Computers can be enjoyable and entertaining

Once they learn to use a computer, most people find that they enjoy it. It's fun to work with such an interactive and attentive device. Give the computer the correct command and it will leap into action, often performing the task much quicker than you thought possible. Although working with a computer can sometimes be frustrating, you usually get a feeling of accomplishment after successfully completing a task. A computer can open up whole new worlds of information, communication, productivity, and entertainment (see Figure 1.4).

Figure 1.3 Computer Chemistry Lab
At the University of Illinois, computers enable students to simulate mixing dangerous chemicals without blowing themselves up.

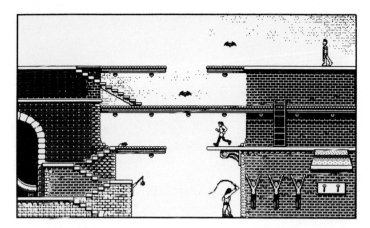

Figure 1.4 Computer Entertainment
Microcomputers are often used to play games and pursue other entertaining activities. This screen shows Dark Castle, a popular adventure arcade game for the Apple Macintosh computer that uses realistic graphics, sounds, and voices.

COMPUTERS: WHAT THEY ARE

Now that you appreciate some of the reasons for learning about computers, let's begin by defining just what they are. Basically, a **computer** is an electronic device, made up of several distinct components, that can be instructed to process, or manipulate, data in some manner. **Data** are numeric representations of quantities, measurements, characters, pictures, sounds, facts, events, objects, and just about anything else you can imagine that can be symbolized in some way by numbers. Before we go on to discuss exactly what computers do and just how they process data, we'll describe the major types of computers and then examine the primary components of a **computer system:** hardware, software, and users.

Defining the computer

Types of Computers

Computer systems vary widely in performance and price as well as in size and appearance. To give you some idea of just how wide the price range is, a very simple computer might sell for as little as $100, while an extremely sophisticated computer can easily cost more than $20 million. The upper limit is around 200,000 times the lower one. In contrast, car prices run from roughly $5000 to $100,000; the upper limit is only 20 times the lower one. All cars have the same general purpose—transportation. Despite the enormous price differences, computers, just like cars, all have the same basic purpose—data processing. There are, however, a few distinguishable, albeit somewhat overlapping, categories of computers. These include microcomputers, workstations, minicomputers, mainframes, and supercomputers.

Common classifications include microcomputers, workstations, minicomputers, mainframes, and supercomputers

Microcomputers

Microcomputers are the smallest, cheapest, and by far the most popular computer systems. Thanks to their economy and small size, millions of people have purchased these **personal computers,** as they are also called. The part of a microcomputer that does the actual data processing is the tiny **microprocessor,** a marvel of miniature electronic engineering. Microcomputers vary in size from handheld models as small as a checkbook, to floor-standing models as big as a suitcase.

Figure 1.5 Microcomputer
This photograph shows a typical desktop microcomputer, the IBM Personal System/2 Model 30, which sells for around $2,500.

Figure 1.5 shows a typical desktop microcomputer, the IBM Personal System/2 Model 30.

Workstations

A **workstation,** sometimes called a **supermicro,** is a small, yet powerful, computer generally used by only one person at a time. Similar to top-of-the-line floor-standing microcomputers, workstations have been traditionally used by scientists and engineers as tools for drafting, design, and map-making. They are superior to most microcomputers in their speed, storage capacity, and abilities to perform complex calculations, to display colorful detailed pictures, and to communicate with other computers. Figure 1.6 shows a typical workstation, the Sun-3/60.

Minicomputers

Minicomputers make up the middle class of computer size and power. The largest, called *superminis*, are the size of a few file cabinets, and the smallest can fit on a desk top. Since minicomputers generally have no special environmental or personnel requirements, such as for air conditioning or data-processing staff, they are particularly popular with small and medium-sized businesses. They are also sturdy

Figure 1.6 Workstation
Workstations are powerful small computers frequently used by scientists and engineers for drafting and design. This one is a Sun-3/60, which sells for around $12,900.

Figure 1.7 Minicomputer
Minicomputers often serve several users or control automated equipment. The DEC VAX 8200 is a typical minicomputer. It can serve up to 20 users and costs around $100,000.

enough to withstand the rigors of the industrial and military environments in which they are frequently employed. Figure 1.7 shows a Digital Equipment Corporation VAX 8200.

Mainframes

A **mainframe** is a big, powerful, fast, expensive computer. Mainframes typically serve hundreds of users at the same time, execute many millions of instructions per second, and cost anywhere from $100,000 to $20 million. A mainframe computer may be as small as one or two file cabinets or large enough to fill an entire room. Some mainframes must be kept in carefully controlled environments to keep them cool and as dust-free as possible. Mainframe computers are generally used by large businesses and organizations for high-volume data processing, such as the preparation of thousands or even millions of paychecks, bills, orders, and mailing labels. A typical mainframe is the IBM 3090/600, shown in Figure 1.8.

Figure 1.8 Mainframe
Mainframes are big, powerful, fast, expensive computers. This IBM 3090/600, for example, can serve hundreds of users at the same time and costs $10.3 million.

Figure 1.9   Supercomputer
Supercomputers are extremely fast mainframes. This $20 million Cray Y-MP, for example, is one of the fastest computers ever made.

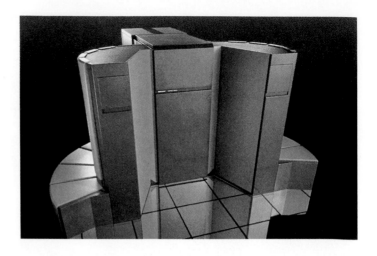

Supercomputers

A **supercomputer** is an extremely fast mainframe. These computers typically execute billions of instructions per second, can serve hundreds of users simultaneously, and cost millions of dollars. Although there are only a few hundred supercomputers operating today in the entire world, they perform many vital tasks which would simply take too long to complete with ordinary mainframes. Supercomputers are used mostly in scientific, industrial, and military research. The Cray Y-MP, shown in Figure 1.9, is one of the most powerful computers ever made, equivalent to the computing power of tens of thousands of microcomputers.

The Physical Components: Hardware

The electronic and mechanical equipment that make a computer work

As Figure 1.10 shows, a functional computer system is really made up of three basic elements: hardware, software, and users. The **hardware** of a computer system is the electronic and mechanical equipment that make it work. Like a stereo system, computer hardware generally consists of several distinct components built into metal or plastic cabinets and connected by cables. Figure 1.11 shows the basic hardware components of a typical microcomputer system:

- *Display.* Similar in many ways to an ordinary television and also called a **monitor,** this screen is used to present text and **graphics,** which are simply any kind of pictures, drawings, charts, or diagrams.

- *System unit.* This central component houses the computer's "brain" or **central processing unit (CPU),** the control circuitry, memory, and disk drives. In a microcomputer, the CPU consists of a single microprocessor (see Figure 1.12). **Memory** is a computer's internal storage, used to hold temporarily data and the instructions that tell the computer what to do. A **disk drive** is a piece of equipment that can read and write data and computer instructions on magnetic disks. A **magnetic disk** is a semipermanent storage medium that can be erased and written on over and over again. From the outside, the system unit looks like a shallow box about the size of a portable typewriter.

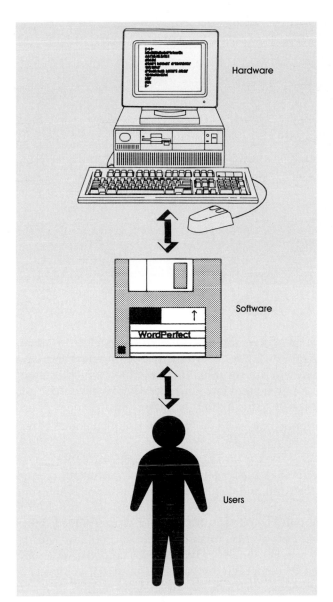

Figure 1.10 The Computer System

A functional computer system is really made up of three elements: hardware, software, and users.

Figure 1.11 Typical Microcomputer Hardware

The four basic hardware components of a microcomputer system are the display, system unit, keyboard, and printer. The display is a screen to present text and graphics. The system unit (not shown) contains the central processing unit (CPU), control circuitry, memory, and disk drives. The keyboard is the primary device for entering commands and data, but many microcomputers also use a mouse. Finally, the auxiliary printer is used to produce text and graphics on paper.

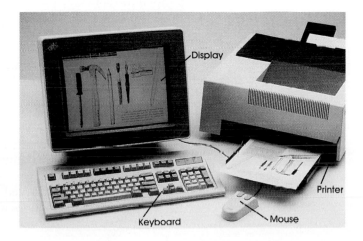

Figure 1.12 Microprocessor

In a microcomputer, the CPU consists of a single integrated circuit chip known as a microprocessor. This is a
typical microprocessor, the Intel 8088, which was used in
the original IBM Personal Computer and in many other
similar microcomputers. It's about two inches long, a half-
inch wide, and a quarter of an inch thick. The forty pins
sticking out and bent down from the two longer sides are
electrical connections that plug into a socket or are soldered into a larger circuit board. In fact, the black rec-
tangle you see is not actually the microprocessor itself,
but rather a ceramic or plastic case within which the microprocessor is permanently and completely sealed.

- *Keyboard.*   Descended from the typewriter, this is the primary device for entering data and telling the computer what to do. Many microcomputers also have
  an auxiliary input device known as a **mouse.** This little box, which is glided
  across the table top, allows you to manipulate objects on the display screen and
  select actions to be performed by pressing one or more buttons.

- *Printer.*   This auxiliary component is used to produce permanent copies of text
  and graphics on paper.

There are, of course, several common variations to this typical microcomputer arrangement. Sometimes the system unit and display are joined in a single housing.
In other cases, the system unit and keyboard are combined. Computers that serve
multiple users, such as minicomputers and mainframes, are also arranged differently. In these systems, each user sits at a **terminal,** which is a monitor with an
attached keyboard (see Figure 1.13). Terminals are where users enter data and view
results, and they are connected to computers by cables. The actual computer is
housed in its own separate cabinet, which can be rather large in the case of a
mainframe. Quite frequently, terminals and the computer running them are located
in different rooms, or even in different buildings.

The Conceptual Components: Software

*The step-by-step instructions
that tell a computer how to
perform a task*

By itself, computer hardware is useless. Programs are needed to operate the hardware. A **program** is simply a sequence of instructions that tells a computer what to
do. **Software** is a general term that refers to any single program or group of
programs. In contrast to hardware, which is constructed from physical materials
like metal and plastic, software is built from knowledge, planning, and testing. A
person who creates programs is called a **programmer.** Programmers use their
knowledge of how a computer works to plan sets of instructions that accomplish
useful tasks. These instructions are entered into the computer and repeatedly tested

Figure 1.13 Terminal
A terminal is an input/output station consisting of a display screen and an attached keyboard. Terminals are connected by cables or other communication links to a computer system that serves several users at the same time. Each user works at their own terminal, but the actual data processing takes place in the multiuser computer, which may be in the same room, a nearby room, a different building, or even very far away.

and modified until they achieve the desired results. As we said before, programs and data are generally kept on storage media such as magnetic disks, where they can be retrieved and used over and over again. One common type of magnetic disk, the **floppy disk,** is quite inexpensive and can be removed from the computer's disk drive when not in use (see Figure 1.14). Note that the disks themselves aren't the software, they're just the medium on which software is stored.

Figure 1.14 Floppy Disks
The floppy disk is a commonly used medium for storing computer programs and data. The two most commonly used sizes are 5 1/4-inch and 3 1/2-inch disks.

As an analogy, think of a stereo system again. The amplifier, compact disc player, and speakers are the hardware. The amplifier is like the central processing unit and memory, the compact disk player is like a disk drive, and the speakers are like the display, except that they present audio instead of video output. The music, which is stored on compact discs, is like software, which is stored on floppy disks. Just as you can amass a huge music collection by buying more compact discs, you can build a bigger software library by purchasing additional programs on floppy disks. The stereo system is of little use without the compact discs, and the compact discs are useless without the stereo system. Similarly, a computer system is useless without software, and software is useless without a computer system on which to run it.

Just as there are different types of hardware, there are also different types of software. The three basic categories are:

- **System software.**   This type of software handles the many details of managing a computer system (see Figure 1.15). One example of a small portion of system software is a program that identifies which key you've pressed, determines the character that corresponds to that key, and forms that character on the display screen. Another example is a program that lets you erase the contents of a magnetic disk. Some system software is built into the computer, while other system software comes on magnetic disk and must be purchased separately. We'll have more to say about operating systems in Chapter 10.

- **Programming languages.**   Computer programs are developed with programming languages. A programming language consists of a set of symbols and rules to direct the operations of a computer (see Figure 1.16). Many different programming languages are in general use, each designed to solve certain types of problems. As we will discuss in Chapter 8, a few of the most popular programming languages are FORTRAN, COBOL, BASIC, Pascal, Modula-2, C, Ada, and RPG.

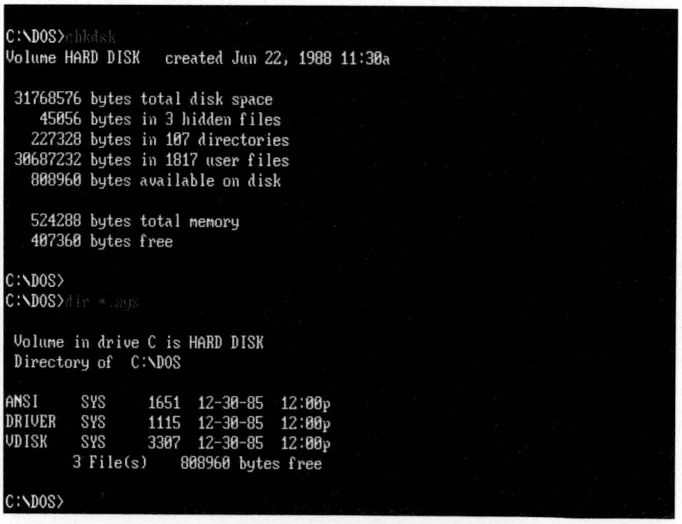

```
C:\DOS>chkdsk
Volume HARD DISK    created Jun 22, 1988 11:30a

31768576 bytes total disk space
   45056 bytes in 3 hidden files
  227328 bytes in 107 directories
30687232 bytes in 1817 user files
  808960 bytes available on disk

  524288 bytes total memory
  407360 bytes free

C:\DOS>
C:\DOS>dir *.sys

Volume in drive C is HARD DISK
Directory of  C:\DOS

ANSI      SYS      1651  12-30-85  12:00p
DRIVER    SYS      1115  12-30-85  12:00p
VDISK     SYS      3307  12-30-85  12:00p
        3 File(s)    808960 bytes free

C:\DOS>
```

Figure 1.15 System Software

System software, such as the MS-DOS operating system for IBM microcomputers and similar machines, controls the many details of managing a computer's hardware and software resources.

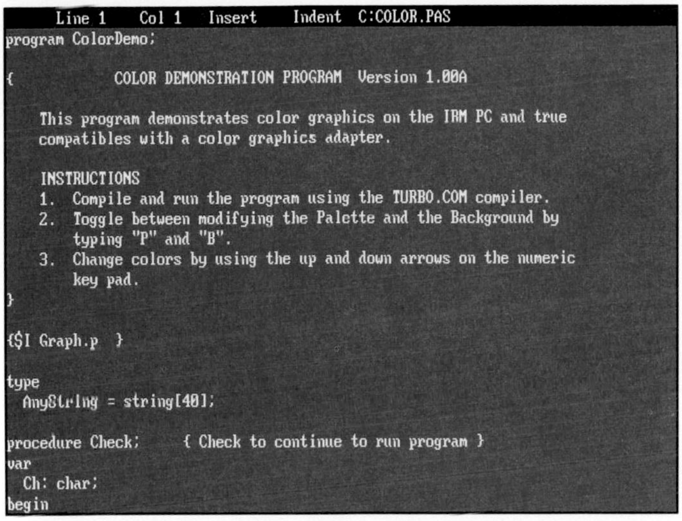

```
    Line 1    Col 1    Insert    Indent  C:COLOR.PAS
program ColorDemo;

{           COLOR DEMONSTRATION PROGRAM  Version 1.00A

  This program demonstrates color graphics on the IBM PC and true
  compatibles with a color graphics adapter.

  INSTRUCTIONS
  1.  Compile and run the program using the TURBO.COM compiler.
  2.  Toggle between modifying the Palette and the Background by
      typing "P" and "B".
  3.  Change colors by using the up and down arrows on the numeric
      key pad.
}

{$I Graph.p }

type
  AnyString = string[40];

procedure Check;     { Check to continue to run program }
var
  Ch: char;
begin
```

Figure 1.16 Programming Languages
This screen shows a program being written in a popular microcomputer programming language, Turbo Pascal.

- **Application software.**   This software applies the computer to useful tasks such as helping you create documents, figure your taxes, maintain mailing lists, and draw charts. Also called **application packages,** or simply **applications,** these programs are the real reason most people buy and use computers. Many types of application software are available. We've already mentioned word-processing programs, which are application packages that help you prepare documents, such as letters and reports. Other examples of application software include: a **spreadsheet package,** for manipulating tables of numbers; a **data base management package,** which helps you organize and retrieve large quantities of information; a **communications package,** which lets your computer "talk" to other computers; a **graphics package,** for producing pictures and charts; a **desktop publishing package,** which allows you to combine the results of word processing and graphics to produce documents of near typeset quality; and an **accounting package,** which lets you manage the finances of a business. We'll have much more to say about these and other types of application software in Chapter 9.

The Human Components: Users

It might seem obvious, but hardware and software don't do anything without users. A **user,** sometimes called an **end-user,** is a person who runs software on a computer to accomplish some task. Just as there are different kinds of hardware and software, there are also different kinds of users. A beginning user is often called a **novice.** Somewhat unfamiliar with computers, novices need a little extra help to perform some tasks. Many computer programs are developed with the novice in mind. These easy-to-learn programs are sometimes described as **user-friendly** because they can be run by people who don't necessarily have a lot of computer experience.

The people who run computers

At the other end of the user spectrum are those who have a great deal of computer experience. An **expert,** sometimes called a **power user,** is someone who feels quite at home using computers. Although programmers are generally experts, every expert is not necessarily a programmer. A person can become an expert at running particular application programs without knowing how those applications were actually developed in the first place. To use an analogy, a race car driver is certainly an expert automobile user. A good race car driver, however, does not need to be an auto mechanic or engineer.

COMPUTERS: HOW THEY ARE USED

Computers are tools that help people perform many different kinds of tasks. It's difficult to think of an activity that hasn't been profoundly affected by computers since their first appearance about 40 years ago. It would take more pages than this book could hold to list all the current applications of computers or to count the ways they interact with us in our daily lives. Nevertheless, one way to gain an appreciation for what computers can do is to see how some "real" people use them in their daily lives. Although by no means a comprehensive list of everything that computers can do, the following sections describe a few specific examples of indi-

Examples of how real people use computers in their lives

viduals who use computers to improve their personal productivity, to manage information, to communicate with others, to make presentations, and to help them learn.

Personal Productivity

Dr. Robert Hendersen, the acting head of the psychology department at the University of Illinois at Urbana-Champaign, uses computers, especially microcomputers, nearly every day. He has an IBM Personal Computer AT in his office on campus and an identical system at home. When he travels to conferences he often takes a small, battery-operated portable microcomputer, the IBM Convertible. Word processing is probably Dr. Hendersen's most frequently used microcomputer application. He uses a commercial application package called WordPerfect to prepare scientific articles, classroom lectures, student handouts, research specifications, and letters. Budgets, grant proposals, and other numeric tables are created, manipulated, and printed by Dr. Hendersen with a program called Lotus 1-2-3, which is an example of a popular spreadsheet package (see Figure 1.17). Many of the graphs and figures Dr. Hendersen includes in his articles and lectures are prepared on his computer with graphics packages such as Energraphics and AutoCAD. He even used AutoCAD to design the landscaping of his yard at home.

Helping with routine tasks

Dr. Hendersen also uses his computers for much of his routine correspondence with colleagues. From home with his Personal Computer AT or from a hotel room with his Convertible, Dr. Hendersen can call up and tap into the Harris mainframe computer housed in the Psychology Building on campus. He can read **electronic mail** messages sent to him by other faculty members and send them instantaneous replies. For regular phone and mail correspondence, Dr. Hendersen maintains a list of associates' telephone numbers and addresses with a program called SideKick. This same program also provides an on-screen calculator and notepad for jotting

```
B8: +B6+B7                                                    READY

        A           B          C          D          E          F
                        Income Statement 1989
1
2
3      Item      Jan-Mar    Apr-Jun    Jul-Sep    Oct-Dec     Total
4
5    INCOME
6  Sales Income $10,523.50 $13,459.25 $17,752.00 $11,543.50 $53,278.25
7  Labor Income  $7,987.25 $11,208.00 $15,489.50 $10,653.00 $45,337.75
8     Total     $18,510.75 $24,667.25 $33,241.50 $22,196.50 $98,616.00
9
10  EXPENSES
11 Rent          $1,500.00  $1,500.00  $1,500.00  $1,500.00  $6,000.00
12 Telephone       $750.00    $625.45    $589.32    $782.50  $2,747.27
13 Utilities       $425.67    $398.25    $450.68    $410.25  $1,684.85
14 Advertising     $625.00    $625.00    $625.00    $625.00  $2,500.00
15 Insurance       $500.00               $500.00             $1,000.00
16 Vehicles        $712.52  $1,020.50  $1,200.25    $945.67  $3,878.94
17 Payroll       $7,200.00  $7,200.00  $7,200.00  $7,200.00 $28,800.00
18    Total     $11,713.19 $11,369.20 $12,065.25 $11,463.42 $46,611.06
19
20  Net Profit   $6,797.56 $13,298.05 $21,176.25 $10,733.08 $52,004.94
22-Jun-88  11:36 AM
```

Figure 1.17   Spreadsheet Software

One of the most common applications of a microcomputer is a spreadsheet package. This screen shows Lotus 1-2-3, one of the most popular spreadsheet packages of all time.

down ideas. Finally, because many psychology classes and research projects require microcomputers, Dr. Hendersen uses his machines to test and demonstrate software that is developed by teaching assistants, research assistants, and other faculty members. In short, the psychology department at the University of Illinois would probably be run much less efficiently if Dr. Hendersen didn't use microcomputers.

Information Management

Computers are excellent tools for managing large quantities of information (see Figure 1.18). Just ask Ron Wubker, a partner at Western Freezers, a company based in Fremont, California, that sells ice cream machines. Wubker uses an IBM Personal Computer and a program called Prodex to keep track of staff, suppliers, and

Helping organize large quantities of information

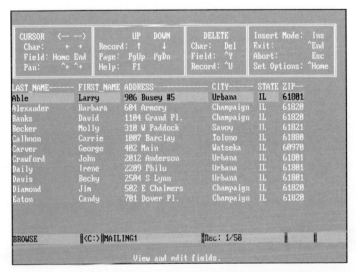

Figure 1.18   Information Management

Computers are frequently used to manage large quantities of information. This screen shows dBASE III PLUS, a popular package for storing, retrieving, and manipulating data bases.

other contacts. Once he entered the name, address, phone number, and a few brief notes about each of his 200 contacts into the computer, Wubker was able to maintain and retrieve this information much more efficiently than he could with a Rolodex. The Prodex program allows him to organize his list of contacts by last name, first name, company, or recall date. If he wants to make a call to one of his contacts, Wubker can tell the program to have the computer automatically dial the phone. Instead of taking a card file of contacts with him on business trips, Wubker simply prints out the entire list on paper. It's a lot less frustrating, Wubker claims, than spending half the night in a hotel room reorganizing his card file after accidentally spilling the cards out all over the floor (Diamond 1987).

Communication

Combining the benefits of computers and telephones

The telephone and the computer are two of our most useful tools. Combine them with an electronic device called a **modem** and you end up with a powerful communication system. Many people use their computers, modems, and telephones to call **on-line information services.** These services allow computer users to retrieve vast quantities of information, read the latest news, shop, bank, buy stocks, make travel arrangements, and send instant electronic mail to other users all over the world. Many information services also allow users who share special interests to participate in interactive electronic forums, or **teleconferences.**

For example, CompuServe is the largest on-line information service in the world. One of its many special interest groups is MedSIG, the Medical Special Interest Group (see Figure 1.19). MedSIG recently sponsored an on-line conference about an anti-inflammatory drug called Zomax. According to Dr. John Sheppard, a general practitioner in Vermont who operates MedSIG, one of the members of the group started the conference because "He believed people were dying from the drug, and he wanted to see what kinds of experiences other doctors were having after prescribing the drug for their patients." This electronic conference was one of the first organized discussions about problems with the drug Zomax. Other doctors,

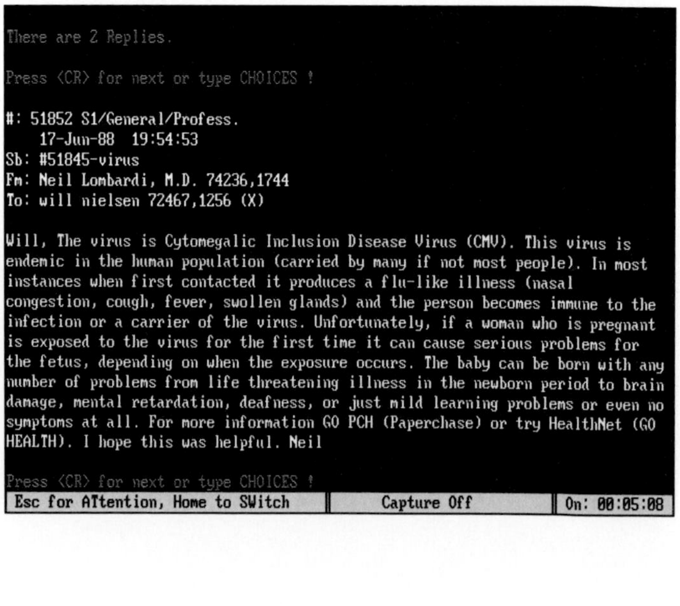

Figure 1.19 Teleconferencing

This screen shows a computer session with CompuServe's Medical Special Interest Group (MedSIG).

it seemed, were also having bad results with Zomax. One of the conference participants happened to be a member of the Food and Drug Administration. Eventually, Zomax was withdrawn from the market. The FDA was so impressed with the MedSIG conference that it is investigating ways to use an internal on-line information service (Fersko-Weiss 1987).

Presentation

Microcomputers are frequently used to present graphs, charts, and other figures at meetings, lectures, and demonstrations (see Figure 1.20). For example, when Secretary of the Interior Donald Hodel presented his $5 billion 1989 budget proposal at a press conference, he used a microcomputer to project images on a 20-foot screen. The secretary began his presentation by saying, "To those of you who are cost-conscious and think this looks sophisticated, it's an off-the-shelf technology using a $49.95 software package called Hypercard on the Macintosh II." Hodel went on to describe his department's annual budget proposal for managing park lands, Indian reservations, and wildlife protection programs. Sue Masica, budget analyst for the Department of the Interior, controlled the projected images from the Apple Macintosh II microcomputer sitting next to the podium. "Budget numbers are always changing at the last minute," said Masica, who had just learned to use the Macintosh three months before. "Hypercard is wonderful in that it gives us the ability to make sure things are correct right up until the last minute. We didn't have to send out to get our slides made. We had complete control of the process right here in the office." As Hodel said to his audience, "We're using a new technique, different from slides. Not only can we show images in sequence, but if a question arises, we can go back or pick out images to help answer them." Apparently, the presentation was a success. According to New York Times correspondent Phil Shabbacoff who was in the audience, "[Hodel] could push a button and go immediately to a line item that someone was asking about. I had never seen that before. I found his ability to flash those numbers on the screen very impressive" (Silverstone 1988).

Using the computer in meetings, lectures, and demonstrations

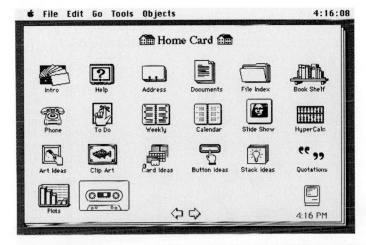

Figure 1.20 Presentation Graphics
Secretary of the Interior Donald Hodel used an Apple Macintosh II microcomputer and a program called Hypercard to present his 1989 budget proposal.

Education

Helping students learn all kinds of subjects

As you probably know by now, microcomputers are widely used in schools, especially at colleges and universities. Drexel University in Philadelphia, Pennsylvania, for example, made an early commitment to microcomputers. Starting in 1984, all freshmen were required to have access to an Apple Macintosh, and most students bought their own from Drexel at less than half the full retail price. Students were enthusiastic, and the program has continued with each incoming freshman class. Today there are more than 12,000 Macintoshes on the Drexel campus.

Many faculty members at Drexel create Macintosh programs to help their students learn difficult subjects. Allan Smith of the chemistry department, for example, developed the Molecular Editor, which students can use to build complex molecules on the screen (see Figure 1.21). Atoms of any element in the periodic table can be combined, manipulated, and analyzed without using expensive laboratory equipment. The Molecular Editor includes an animation of a chemical reaction in three dimensions and ready-made samples of organic molecules, inorganic molecules, and crystals. Undoubtedly, the Molecular Editor has made chemistry a little more understandable to students at Drexel (Osgood 1987).

COMPUTERS: WHAT THEY DO

The basic operations that all computers perform

As we have seen, computers can be used for many different tasks. At the lowest level, however, all computers perform the same basic operations (see Figure 1.22). In simple terms, all general-purpose computers do the following fundamental activities:

1. Accept input data
2. Process data into information
3. Present output information

Let's examine each one of these functions in more detail. But again, you must realize that *programs* are needed to instruct a computer to do all of these things.

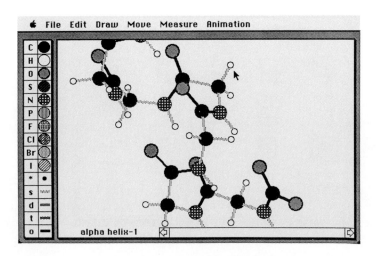

Figure 1.21 Computer Chemistry

The Molecular Editor was developed by Allan Smith of Drexel University to allow students to build molecules on the Apple Macintosh screen and rotate them in three dimensions.

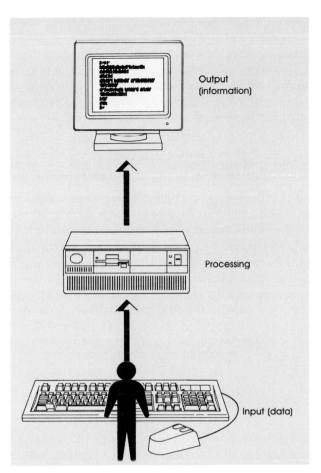

Figure 1.22   What Computers Do
At the lowest level, all computers perform the same basic operations: accept input, process data into information, and present output.

Accept Input Data

As we said before, all computers process data or **input.** These are the raw facts and figures that a user enters into a computer under the direction of a program. Several different types of data and various kinds of input devices can be used to enter those data into a computer. Word-processing programs, for example, primarily accept *textual input*. The letters, digits, punctuation, and other symbols that comprise the body of text in a document are usually typed directly at a keyboard. But text may also be entered from a **scanner,** an input device that can optically "read" text right from a printed or even handwritten page. Textual input may also come from a magnetic disk, where it has been previously stored by some other program. Finally, the textual input can even come from a **voice recognition module,** which actually interprets human speech in a limited fashion and enters it into the computer just as if it had been typed at a keyboard.

Many programs, such as spreadsheet packages, primarily accept *numeric input*. These data also usually come from a user typing at a keyboard, but they can sometimes be obtained from other sources. Stock figures, for example, can be transmitted from an on-line information service over a telephone line and entered directly

Getting the raw facts and figures

into a spreadsheet program. Numeric data are also frequently obtained from disk storage where they have been placed previously by other programs.

Many programs also accept *graphic input*, pictorial data that are entered from input devices such as a mouse. For example, a type of graphics package called a **painting program** lets you use a mouse to draw pictures on the screen. Entire pictures can also be entered as input from devices such as graphics scanners and video cameras that are connected to computers.

Process Data into Information

Calculating, comparing, and manipulating the input

As we have said, a program lets you enter input data, which can consist of text, numbers, pictures, and even sounds. The program then instructs the computer to process the data by doing calculations, comparisons, and other manipulations. Sometimes, the program merely stores the data, either temporarily in memory or more permanently on a disk, so that it can be retrieved and processed at a later time. Ultimately, however, the obtained data are processed. The final result is **information,** a more organized and useful form of the original input. This information produced by the computer is called **output.** Like input, output can take the form of text, numbers, pictures, and sounds. Keep in mind that there is no magic here—a program is needed to tell the computer what to do, and the output information is only as valid as the input data.

Present Output Information

Returning the results

Ultimately, the information produced by the computer program from the original input is presented back to the user. In most cases, output information consists of text and pictures displayed on a screen. Another common form of output is **hard copy,** which may consist of just text, or text and pictures that are printed on paper with a printer. In some cases, hard copy output such as blueprints, diagrams, and graphs are produced with a device known as a **plotter,** which actually uses one or more pens to draw precisely on paper. Output can also be copied to a disk for later use instead of being presented directly to the user. Finally, output can even take the form of sounds, music, and synthesized speech in appropriately equipped computer systems.

COMPUTERS: THEIR ROLE

Reasons we use computers

In all the specific activities we might list, no matter how many there are, the computer would be employed for the same fundamental reasons: to increase speed, to reduce costs, and to improve quality. Although individuals and enterprises have always aspired to these goals, the opportunity to achieve them has never been so great. The computer stands alone as a means of reinvigorating old industries and creating entirely new ones. Whoever fails to take advantage of its unique capabilities can be sure that others will not (as the Swiss discovered in 1980, when their 90 percent share of the international watch market was cut to 30 percent, largely due to the widespread availability of less expensive computerized quartz watches). Competition at both international and corporate levels is fierce; companies are pouring money into research and development to come up with faster circuits, larger memories, and more effective applications. This intense rivalry produces rapid change and a lot of computers—all the more reason to take a closer look at the basic three-part role the computer plays in our lives.

Increased Speed

Computers are incredibly fast machines. But, more specifically, here are a few examples of how computers can speed up some of our daily activities:

Computers help us work faster

- In Detroit, Chrysler's computerized automation efforts have increased productivity by 20 percent.

- It is estimated that the average secretary spends more than a quarter of each work day ''holding'' on the telephone; electronic mail can eliminate much of that wasted time.

- Sixty billion checks are processed annually by the nation's banks. Trying to manage this enormous volume of paperwork without computers would bring the whole financial world to a standstill. With them, more than $100 million per second moves through the Federal Reserve's electronic Fedwire system.

- In seconds, a computer can figure the payroll for a medium-sized company, score 3000 SAT tests, or evaluate 100 electrocardiograms.

- At the supermarket, the electronic check-out system can read and interpret the bar code on an item (see Figure 1.23), transfer the necessary information from scanner to computer to check-out terminal, do the calculation, and print both the item's description and price on the tape in less time than it would take a clerk to locate a printed price on an item and punch it into a cash register.

Figure 1.23 Computerized Supermarket Check-Out System
(a) The Universal Product Code (UPC) identifies each item for the computer. (b) The computer "looks up" the price of the item identified by the code and then transmits the information back to the point of sale. (c) The bar code also provides assistance in inventory management. Using a hand-held scanner, a clerk enters the UPC code from the shelf and counts the number of items. The computer, with this information, can determine when items should be reordered to restock the shelves. It can also verify that the number of items present matches what inventory and sales records say ought to be there.

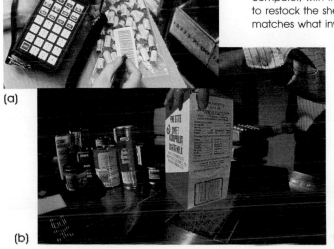
(a)

(b)

(c)

Reduced Costs

*Computers help us work less
expensively*

Even though computer prices have been constantly decreasing, they still *seem* relatively expensive. In many cases, however, computers can dramatically reduce the costs of getting the job done. Here are a few specific examples:

● Crash testing a prototype car can take more than two weeks and cost an automobile manufacturer more than $30,000. Through the use of computer simulation (see Figure 1.24), an unlimited number of tests can be run under very different conditions at a fraction of the cost, and with no mess to clean up later. Modifications in the design can also be made on the computer, drastically reducing the number of expensive and time-consuming rebuildings of the traditional clay model.

Figure 1.24 Computer Simulation
The high costs of real-life crash testing can be reduced by performing preliminary computer simulated tests.

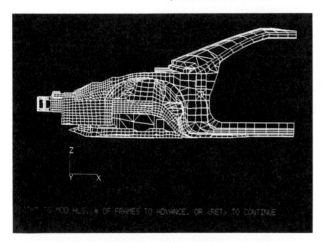

(a)

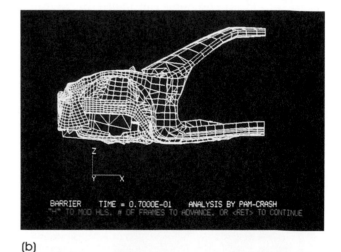

(b)

(c)

(d)

- In 1965, a typical communications satellite held about 240 telephone circuits at a cost of $22,000 each; such satellites now carry 100,000 circuits for only $30 each, largely due to the use of more sophisticated computers. These plummeting costs opened the door to numerous telecommunications activities, from international phone conferencing to pay-TV movies.

- The cost of keeping an exploratory drilling crew on an oil rig in the North Atlantic can be tens of thousands of dollars per day, and many holes are ''dry.'' The indispensable help of the computer in exploratory decision making increases the likelihood of payoff and minimizes the risk.

- The wages of supermarket checkers and stock clerks have increased by a factor of approximately 10 during the 40-odd years in which the computer's cost has decreased by a factor of roughly 100,000. The clerk's wages are still increasing; the computer's cost is still decreasing.

- Because an automated assembly line can operate 24 hours a day without breaks, a major investment in automation can pay for itself within one or two years.

Improved Quality

Because computers, in some manufacturing situations, operate more reliably and precisely than the most skilled human workers, their use can often significantly improve the quality of goods and services.

Computers help us work better

- A robot at General Dynamics makes 30 parts for the F-16 fighter plane every shift, with no rejects; human workers average six parts per shift, with a 10 percent rejection rate.

- Computer-based management information systems provide fast, reliable, and accurate statistics on sales, marketing, financial, and personnel activities, thus potentially helping executives make better decisions. Information networks help professionals in financial, legal, scientific, and other fields keep up with current issues, trends, and discoveries, which makes them better qualified to solve complex problems in a constructive and profitable way.

- Contrary to all the jokes and horror stories about computer errors, computers can perform billions of complex calculations 24 hours a day, every day, and—for the most part—make very few mistakes.

COMPUTERS: WHAT THEY AREN'T

Even this brief discussion of computers begins to clarify just what they are and what they can do. Computers often produce such impressive results that we need to remind ourselves from time to time that all they're really able to do is process raw data, which must be symbolized by numbers, into more useful information. Computers are not ''thinking machines,'' nor are they ''electronic brains.'' The analogy to human thought processes and intellect is vastly simplistic at best. Computers don't decide how they will be used. That decision is our responsibility alone. Computers can't perform the research and analysis that capture the essence of problems, and they don't write the programs that attempt to solve them. They don't enter the

Exposing the myths

input data, and they don't make policy decisions based on the results. These are our jobs, our responsibilities. Computers can't anticipate the economic or social side effects of an application. This, too, is our responsibility. Only through an enlightened understanding of what computers are and how they work can we possibly expect to use their capabilities as effectively and as widely as we should.

Issues in Technology

A computer simulation for the Bay of Fundy in Canada has been developed to help assess the fuel economies possible with various tidal-power/dam configurations at different points in the Bay. The model shows that fuel savings of 23 million barrels of oil per year are possible on the Atlantic Coast of the U.S. and Canada (not to mention a possible drop in acid rain because the source is clean). Nevertheless, the model also indicates that tide levels would be raised as far away as Boston. The effects of the higher tides must be dealt with by people, however, and not by the computer, which can only indicate where the higher tides may occur—not which effects are acceptable politically and economically. What other types of decisions must be made by people and not by computers? Is the list likely to change? If so, how will we be affected by those changes?

Summary

Computers: Why Study Them?

There are several reasons why you should spend the time and effort to study computers.

Education You cannot have a well-rounded education without learning something about computers.

Employment Knowing how to use a computer can help you be more competitive in today's labor market.

Productivity A computer can help you do certain jobs better and more efficiently.

Capability Computers often allow you to do jobs you otherwise might not be able to do at all.

Fun Computers can be enjoyable and entertaining to use.

Computers: What They Are

A computer is an electronic device, made up of several distinct components, that can be instructed to process, or manipulate, data in some manner.

Types of Computers Commonly accepted categories of computers include microcomputers, workstations, minicomputers, mainframes, and supercomputers.

The Physical Components: Hardware The electronic and mechanical equipment of a microcomputer system, for example, consists of a display, system unit (with a CPU, memory, and disk drives), keyboard and possibly a mouse, and a printer.

The Conceptual Components: Software A software program is a sequence of instructions that tells a computer what to do. Three basic software categories include system software, programming languages, and application packages.

The Human Components: Users Users are people who run computer programs, from novices to experts.

Computers: How They Are Used

Computers are tools that help people perform many different kinds of tasks.

Personal Productivity Computers are frequently used for many routine activities such as preparing documents, creating budgets, drawing graphs, and corresponding with colleagues.

Information Management Computers are excellent tools for managing large quantities of information such as mailing lists.

Communication Many people use their computers and telephones to call on-line information services and participate in electronic forums and teleconferences.

Presentation Computers are frequently used to present graphs, charts, and other figures at meetings, lectures, and demonstrations.

Education Computers are widely used in schools to help students learn all kinds of subjects.

Computers: What They Do

At the lowest level, all computers perform the same three fundamental tasks.

Accept Input Data The raw facts and figures must be entered by the user under the direction of a program; any of several different input devices can be used depending upon the type of data, but the keyboard is by far the most common.

Process Data into Information Input data may be merely stored, but calculations, comparisons, and other manipulations are usually performed, resulting in output information.

Present Output Information The results of processing must be returned to the user, usually in the form of text and graphics displayed on a screen or printed on paper.

Computers: Their Role

Ultimately, computers are generally employed for three basic reasons.

Increased Speed   Computers are incredibly fast machines that can speed up many routine activities.

Reduced Costs   Thanks to their efficiency and constantly decreasing prices, computers can significantly reduce the costs of performing certain activities.

Improved Quality   Because computers can frequently operate more reliably and precisely than the most skilled workers, they can significantly improve the quality of certain goods and services.

Computers: What They Aren't

Computers aren't thinking machines, nor are they electronic brains. All they can do is process raw data into information.

Computer Concepts

As an extra review of the chapter, try defining the following terms. If you have trouble with any of them, refer to the page number listed.

word processing *7*
computer *9*
data *9*
computer system *9*
microcomputers (personal computers) *9*
microprocessor *9*
workstation (supermicro) *10*
minicomputers *10*
mainframe *11*
supercomputer *12*
hardware *12*
display (monitor) *12*
graphics *12*
system unit *12*
central processing unit (CPU) *12*
memory *12*
disk drive *12*
magnetic disk *12*
keyboard *14*

mouse *14*
printer *14*
terminal *14*
program *14*
software *14*
programmer *14*
floppy disk *15*
system software *16*
programming languages *16*
application software (application packages, applications) *17*
spreadsheet package *17*
data base management package *17*
communications package *17*
graphics package *17*
desktop publishing package *17*
accounting package *17*

user (end-user) *17*
novice *17*
user-friendly *17*
expert (power user) *18*
electronic mail *18*
modem *20*
on-line information services *20*
teleconferences *20*
input *23*
scanner *23*
voice recognition module *23*
painting program *24*
information *24*
output *24*
hard copy *24*
plotter *24*

1. From the point of view of your education, why is it important to study computers?
2. In terms of employment opportunities, why is it important to study computers?
3. What are some of the advantages of word processing over using an ordinary typewriter?
4. What are the primary components of a computer system?
5. What are the categories of computers?
6. What are the main characteristics of each category?
7. Where or how is each category typically used?
8. What are the four basic hardware components of a typical microcomputer?
9. What is the function of each component?
10. What are computer terminals?
11. Define the term *software*.
12. Contrast computer hardware and software.
13. List and describe briefly what the three basic categories of software do.
14. Give six examples of applications software other than word-processing software.
15. For whom are user-friendly programs designed?
16. What activities do on-line information services allow computer users to perform?
17. What are the three fundamental activities that all general-purpose computers do?
18. What are four ways of entering textual input?
19. What is a hard copy?
20. List the three fundamental goals to which users of computers aspire.

True or False

1. Most word processors have built-in spelling checkers.
2. The part of a microcomputer that does the actual data processing is the microprocessor.
3. Minicomputers require carefully controlled environmental conditions.
4. Magnetic disks can be erased and rewritten.
5. A floppy disk is a type of magnetic disk.
6. A person who runs software on a computer to accomplish a task is called an end-user.
7. Spreadsheet packages primarily accept graphical input.
8. Output is information produced by a computer.
9. Wages of supermarket checkers have dropped as the use of computers has increased.
10. In some manufacturing situations computers work more reliably and precisely than skilled human workers.

Multiple Choice

1. Computers can be purchased for as little as:
   (a) $1000   (b) $100   (c) $1500

2. The ultimate purpose of computers is:
   (a) programming   (b) word processing   (c) data processing

3. One of the most powerful computers ever made is the:
   (a) IBM 3090/600   (b) MicroVAX 3600   (c) Cray Y-MP

4. A computer's main internal storage is its:
   (a) disk drive   (b) CPU   (c) memory

5. A terminal is a:
   (a) monitor and attached (b) CPU and control   (c) a monitor and
       keyboard   circuitry   a display

6. A sequence of instructions that tells a computer what to do is called a:
   (a) microprocessor   (b) program   (c) modem

7. COBOL, FORTRAN and Ada are:
   (a) application software (b) systems software   (c) programming languages

8. The raw facts that a user enters into a computer are called:
   (a) output   (b) input   (c) hard copy

9. A painting program is a type of package that accepts:
   (a) numerical input   (b) textual input   (c) graphical input

10. A plotter is used to:
    (a) input data   (b) draw graphic output (c) rewrite magnetic disks

A Sharper Focus

1. What major questions about computers did you have before you read this chapter? Now that you have completed this chapter, has your list of questions changed? How or why not?

2. Students at some colleges are concerned that increased use of computers on campuses leads to depersonalization. There are some people who think that the upsurge in the use of personal computers has created this effect. What is your opinion and what evidence supports it?

Projects

1. Make a list of specific situations in which you come into contact with computers. What benefits (or drawbacks) do you find personally? Try to determine how the functions you list were handled before computers. How have things improved?

2. Investigate your campus or a local business to find out what jobs have been created or changed since the advent of computers.

3. Consider your daily routine and make a list of activities in which computers do not (or apparently do not) play a role. Do you see any way in which computers would improve these activities? How?

4. Do you expect computers to play a significant role in the career you have chosen? Research one of the leading firms or institutions in your field and determine how they use computers now and how they expect to use them when you graduate.

References

Diamond, Sam. "People Tracking." *Personal Computing* (December 1987): 133–139.

Fersko-Weiss, Henry. "On-line Contacts." *Personal Computing* (January 1987): 83–91.

Haider, R. "New Frontiers in Office Automation." *Proceedings of the Infotech State of the Art Conference, Vienna, Austria* (1979).

Hayes, Jack. "Do Computer Skills Make College Grads More Marketable?" *Family & Home Office Computing* (April 1988): 26–28.

Osgood, Donna. "The Difference in Higher Education." *Byte* (February 1987): 165–178.

Silverstone, Stuart. "Hypercard Helps Hodel Present Budget Proposal." *MacWeek* (March 8, 1988): 42–44.

Zarley, Craig. "PCs an Essential Tool For Insurance Sales." *PC Week* (March 15, 1988): 47–53.

2

The Evolution of Computers

In This Chapter

Focus On

The Early Days of Computers

Despite the illusion that personal computers have been around a long time, there was a fairly recent era when you had to build your own or do without. Stephen Gray, contributing editor to *Creative Computing* magazine, reminisces:

Twenty years ago, while I was the computers editor of *Electronics* magazine at McGraw-Hill, I realized there was much I could learn from building a computer. It didn't take long to find out how difficult it was just to get started. There were no kits, no "cookbooks." Computer textbooks usually contained partial schematics, but none told how to connect the various sections.

After several years of trying to build a digital computer in my spare time, I began to realize how difficult it must be for other hobbyists. . . .

Back in the mid-sixties, to build a simple computer accumulator, which could do no more than add successive inputs, using toggle switches for input

and lamps for output, cost several dollars per bit. To build an extremely simple "computer" with four-bit words and without memory, and which divided the easy way (by repeated subtraction without shifting), could cost two or three hundred dollars. . . .

Building one's own computer was such a complicated undertaking that very few were ever completed, and nearly all of those were built by electronics engineers working in the data processing industry.

The main problem in building a computer was (and still is) the many technologies involved. Computer companies had specialists in logic, input/output, core memory, mass memory, peripherals, and other areas. To build one's own computer required learning a great deal about each one.

If the computer hobbyist was an electronics engineer working for a computer manufacturer, he could drop in on a friend down the hall or in the next building and ask what kind of drivers might be needed for a core memory with such-and-such specs. Most hobbyists had no such resources.

In addition to having to learn a great deal about computer electronics, the hobbyist also had to get into mechanical areas such as packaging, back-plane wiring, metal working, plastics, and many others.

Eventually, the young personal computer industry began to market kits, then kits *or* completed computers, and finally finished products.

Computers are the logical end product of centuries of humanity's pencil-breaking frustration with having to add things, subtract things, and perform other feats of arithmetic derring-do. "Make it easier; make it more accurate; make it faster!" has been the universal cry, and an ever-progressing technology has been the response. From portable notched bones (themselves a large technological leap forward from the bulky, hard-to-carry cave wall) to the abacus, from unwieldy mechanical adding machines to the silicon chip, from no numbers at all to magnetic spots on plastic disks, technological developments have answered the demand that computations be made faster, better, and easier. It's a long way from the cave wall to the silicon chip, but this chapter will trace the major steps that led from then to now.

The main thread of the story concerns the sequence of ever-improving calculating and computing machines created by a succession of inventive geniuses. Each of these inventors used the technology, that is, the parts and tools, available in his or her era. Frequently, the existing technology was the determining factor in whether or not an idea for a machine would actually work or could be built for a price anyone was willing to pay.

THE ORIGINS

What would life be like without numbers? What if there were no words for numbers, no symbols for numbers, in fact, no concept of number at all? How could we engage in agriculture or plan the hunt to meet the needs of a tough winter if we couldn't count our population or reckon the passage of time? How could we even define or describe "a tough winter" without using some kind of numerical measurement? Without numbers, how could we manufacture or build? How could we buy or sell or trade?

The concept of number

It's obvious that the concept of number must have coincided with the earliest advances of civilization. At first, the concept covered no more than the distinction between one and many. Later, one, two, and many were distinguished—a vital step forward. Then came the realization that there is a concept of "twoness" that is the same whether it refers to two rabbits or two trees. Further generalization and application of this idea, over the millennia, gave rise to the words and symbols that enable us to record and communicate numbers.

The idea and the symbol came together with the first calculation— counting. The earliest surviving records unearthed by archeologists are notched bones about 30,000 years old. Two notches in a bone or stick stood for two head of cattle; a third notch was added when a calf was born. This type of counting tool persisted for thousands of years, marked by a transition to counting in groups of five (the Romans) and ten (in eastern India and Arabia) and the development of *positional notation*, which is illustrated in Figure 2.1.

Symbols for numbers

The first counting "machine," shown in Figure 2.2, was the *counting board*, dating back about 3000 years. More than 1000 years went by before the stones in a column of the counting board evolved into the "high-tech" beads on the wires of the *abacus*. The origin of this first calculator is obscured in Chinese, Arabic, European, and Egyptian antiquity. The abacus shown in Figure 2.3 is clearly lighter and more portable than the counting board, and it enables addition to be done more rapidly and accurately.

The earliest aids to counting

As the centuries passed, an influential merchant class arose in Europe, the sign of a growing international and even intercontinental commerce. The more complex social and economic system called for elaborate account keeping, with calculations of interest and currency exchange. Science awakened to computation; mathematical theories concerning the motions of the earth, moon, planets, and sun used equations to compute planetary positions and daily variations in daylight and tides. Seasonal effects were estimated more accurately, increasing agricultural productivity and creating the food surpluses necessary to feed a burgeoning urban population. Government clerks calculated tariffs and other taxes. In 1642, Galileo died, Newton was born, and the French mathematician Pascal built the first gear-driven mechanical calculator.

EARLY MACHINES

The first mechanical calculating machine

Blaise Pascal (1623–1662), the son of a mathematically gifted tax official, spent long hours with his father adding columns of figures. He later became an entrepreneur who built and sold 50 of the far-from-perfect mechanical calculators he invented. Figure 2.4 shows his *Pascaline*, a gear-driven machine that performed addition and subtraction. Pascal's calculator was **digital;** that is, like the abacus, it dealt with whole numbers and produced precise results. Another class of instruments and calculators, such as certain surveying and astronomical instruments, was **analog;**

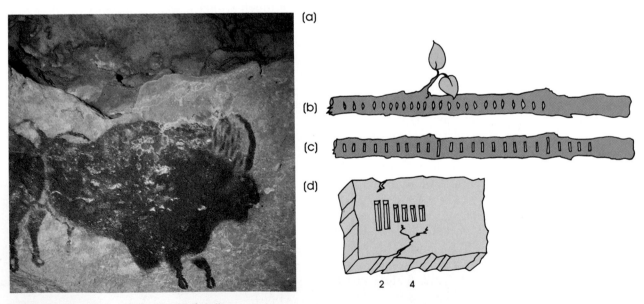

Figure 2.1 Counting and Positional Notation

(a) Before anyone had thought of numbers, in order to represent, for example, a herd of cattle, someone had to draw the actual number of cows in the herd on a cave wall. (b) Sticks (the first great counting innovation) are portable, unlike cave walls, and it was easier to make notches than to draw portraits. But the notches often became too numerous, making it difficult to grasp the number at a glance or to compare the number of notches to the number of cattle. (c) A great leap forward occurred when every tenth notch was made longer, greatly facilitating record keeping. (d) It was then just a small step to positional notation, in which each big notch represents 10 and each little notch stands for 1. The notches shown here correspond to 24 in our number system.

Figure 2.2 The Counting Board

The counting board, a great advance over a heap of stones, depends on positional notation; each column of the board represents a digit position. More than ten stones in a position result in a carry: one stone to the next higher position and the removal of 10 stones from the position that caused the carry. Unlike the notched stick, the counting board was "erasable." It was undoubtedly a precursor of the abacus.

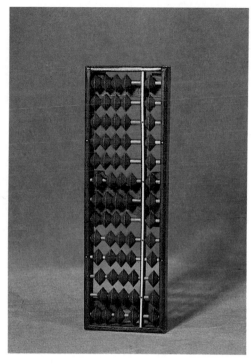

Figure 2.3 The Abacus

The Japanese abacus *(soroban)* appeared late in the sixteenth century and is completely harmonious with decimal notation. The beads on each wire can represent all nine digits. When pushed to the bar, the bead at the right stands for a value of 5. When pushed to the bar, the beads to the left of the bar each count for a value of 1.

Figure 2.4 The Pascaline

Pascal's mechanical calculator performed addition and subtraction. Each digit was entered manually by turning the appropriate gear. This turning also carried out the operation and produced the display of the result in the window.

Figure 2.5
Analog and Digital

(a) The traditional clock presents an analog indication of the time and is capable of representing every possible value. However, it provides only an approximation of the true value, perhaps to two or three reliable digits.
(b) The digital clock gives precise readings to as many digits as are required.
(c) The analog slide rule was the universal calculator of engineering students before the invention of (d) the digital electronic calculator. After centuries of use, slide rules are no longer manufactured.

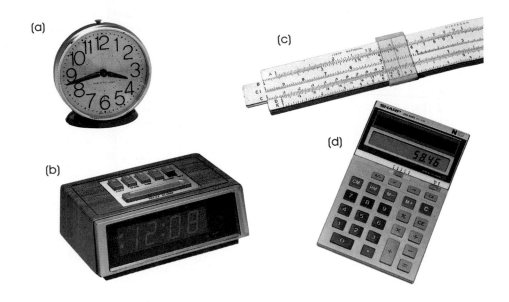

these machines, like the conventional mechanical wristwatch, gave only a visual depiction of the result, in contrast to the precise read-out of a digital watch (see Figure 2.5).

Later in the seventeenth century, the German mathematician *Gottfried Wilhelm von Leibniz* (1646–1716) built the first calculator designed to do multiplication and division as well as addition and subtraction. The complexity of this machine was, however, somewhat beyond what could be effectively built out of the contemporary mechanical gears and levers, and the machine, shown in Figure 2.6, was not very reliable.

In the nineteenth century, the British inventor and mathematician *Charles Babbage* (1792–1872), who had very little practical success, achieved the intellectual

Figure 2.6 Leibniz's Calculator

Leibniz's calculator not only added and subtracted but also multiplied and divided. The complicated and unreliable mechanism formed products by adding the multiplicand first to itself and then to the preceding subtotal, as many times as indicated by the value of the multiplier. To multiply 23 by 8, for example, it added 23 to itself and then added 23 to 46, and so on. This is essentially the method used in modern computers, although countless refinements have been made.

triumph of clearly anticipating most of the logical principles on which the modern computer is based. Babbage designed his *analytical engine* (Figure 2.7) as a result of his boredom with long calculations and his distress at the inherent errors they involved. He incorporated a mechanical memory in his design to store intermediate calculated results so they wouldn't have to be copied onto paper and subsequently reentered—a process that was one of the principal sources of error. He also provided for the entry of both numbers and calculation steps on punched cards. He adapted this idea from *Joseph Jacquard* (1752–1834), who, late in the eighteenth century in France, had built a weaving machine that used punched cards to select the threads to be incorporated into a pattern. However, Babbage's steam-powered analytical engine proved too complex for him to build: his idea was ahead of the currently available technology.

A precursor to the modern computer

It is largely due to the efforts of *Augusta Ada*, Countess of Lovelace (1816–1852), daughter of the romantic poet Lord Byron and now generally regarded as the first computer programmer, that we remember the work of Babbage today. A mathematical prodigy, the Countess of Lovelace became interested in Babbage's idea, and in 1842, at the age of 27, she translated a description of Babbage's machine from French into English. She added some of her ideas about programming to the translation and corrected Babbage's errors. Ada Lovelace is credited with developing the programming loop (see Chapter 8), in which a sequence of operations is repeated within a program.

Not until 1886 did *William Seward Burroughs* (1855–1898) introduce the first commercially successful mechanical adding machine. A million Burroughs Adding

(a)

(b)

Figure 2.7 Babbage's Analytical Engine and the Jacquard Loom
(a) A model of Babbage's analytical engine, built from his plans. The machine read data and programs from cards adapted from (b) the Jacquard loom, which used holes in a sequence of cards to control which threads were picked up by hooks and inserted into a woven pattern.

and Listing Machines (Figure 2.8) were sold by 1926, and Henry Ford even produced a car, the Burroughs Special, with a rack designed to carry the popular device.

At about the time that Burroughs was building his mechanical adder, another important development occurred in the United States. There had been a census in 1880, and manual tabulation of the data had taken seven years. Since the population was growing rapidly and more information was to be included on the census forms, it was clear that the data from the 1890 census wouldn't be compiled before it was time to start on the 1900 census. *Dr. Herman Hollerith* (1860–1929) was an employee of the Census Office when he recognized this problem. He struck out on his own and developed the first electromechanical punched-card tabulator, shown in Figure 2.9. Data were represented by the position of punches on cards that were fed into the tabulator. (In Chapter 4, we'll describe the Hollerith code, which is still in use today to represent data on punched cards.) The tabulator then automatically totaled the data from selected parts of the card.

Hollerith took another major step. He recognized that the punched data could be "sorted" to determine how many people had more than two children, or non-English-speaking family members, or any other attribute on which data had been collected. He built a sorting machine powered by electricity rather than muscle or steam to do this automatically. As a result of Hollerith's work, the tabulation of the 1890 census was completed in three years, and vastly improved analysis and use of the data had been made possible.

The Tabulating Machine Company, founded by Hollerith on the basis of his machines, proved to be a profitable venture. *Thomas J. Watson, Sr.* (1874–1956) joined this company in 1914. After an initial period of less-than-perfect harmony, the technical genius of the founder was subordinated to the business mastery of his successor. In 1924, with Watson as its president, it was renamed the International

Punched cards and the beginning of IBM

Figure 2.8 The Burroughs Adding and Listing Machine

Each column of keys corresponds to a decimal digit position. Numbers were entered and then accumulated into the total by pulling down on the handle.

Figure 2.9 Hollerith's Tabulating Machine

This is the historic machine that was the basis for what today is the IBM Corporation.

Business Machines Corporation (IBM), and the Hollerith card became the IBM card. In 1914, the company had 1300 employees; today, more than 380,000 people work for the $54-billion-a-year firm. Watson's commercial vision led to his sponsorship of another technical pioneer, Howard H. Aiken, whose work was instrumental in the development of the modern computer.

DAWN OF THE COMPUTER AGE

The Harvard Mark I

By the end of the 1930s, the production of punched-card tabulating equipment based on Hollerith's initial inventions had turned IBM into a large and profitable company. These machines served many routine business needs, with unmatched accuracy and speed. In 1939, Professor *Howard H. Aiken* (1900–1973) of Harvard University sought backing from Watson, who had established IBM's policy of enlightened corporate self-interest and demonstrated it by generous gifts to universities. Aiken wanted to design and construct a computer that, like Babbage's, could be programmed to execute an entire sequence of instructions automatically. Watson responded with financial support of nearly a million dollars and the assistance of some of IBM's best technical people.

IBM and Aiken

The *Harvard Mark I*, as the computer came to be known, became operational in 1944 (see Figure 2.10). It employed electromechanical devices called **relays** (originally employed in telegraph systems), which consisted of an electromagnet and a switch. Hollerith had already used electricity rather than muscle power to move the mechanical parts in his machines. The inclusion of the relay was the next big step in the advance of early twentieth-century computing technology; it soon entirely replaced the gear.

Relays

(a)

(b)

Figure 2.10 The Mark I and ENIAC
(a) The Mark I executed a sequence of instructions automatically. It was built out of electromechanical relays.
(b) ENIAC, though not yet a general-purpose computer, used fully electronic components to achieve its then unparalleled speed.

Harvard Mark I's relays were much quicker than mechanical gears; each switch took only a few thousandths of a second to open or close. This seemed like a very short time indeed, but three seconds had elapsed by the time all the thousands of relays required to multiply two numbers had operated. The process was held up by the fact that some of the relays couldn't start operating until others had finished (for example, those responsible for making "carries" from one digit position to the next). Some of the calculations performed by the Harvard Mark I involved many thousands of multiplications. There are 3600 seconds in an hour, enough time for the Harvard Mark I to do only 1200 multiplications, so the total time per calculation sometimes ran to many hours.

ENIAC

With its 51-foot length and 500 miles of wire, the Harvard Mark I was a significant accomplishment, but it was to be eclipsed in 1946 by the first of the totally electronic machines, *ENIAC* (Electronic Numerical Integrator and Computer), shown in Figure 2.10. Development of ENIAC began during World War II under Army sponsorship. It was designed to compute the numerical tables used to target artillery, that is, it calculated the ballistic trajectories of artillery shells and of the first generation of U.S. military rockets.

The machine

The principal designers of ENIAC were *John Presper Eckert, Jr.* (b. 1919) and *John W. Mauchly* (1908–1980) of the Moore School of Electrical Engineering at the University of Pennsylvania. ENIAC wasn't a general-purpose computer by our current standard; substantial manual set-up (plugging units together and setting switches) was required to vary even its rather narrow repertoire of calculations. But ENIAC started a revolution in arithmetic speed by doing away with the electromechanical relay altogether. Instead, ENIAC employed an electronic switch, the

Vacuum tubes

vacuum tube, which was used at that time in radio and radar equipment. The relay, in which an appreciable mass must move a finite distance, completes its task in *milliseconds* (thousandths of a second); the vacuum tube, in which only electrons move, operates in *microseconds* (millionths of a second).

ENIAC was an enormous machine: it was 100 feet long, 10 feet high, and 3 feet deep, and it weighed 30 tons. It contained 18,000 vacuum tubes, 70,000 resistors, and 6000 switches, and required 140 kilowatts of power to operate. But it carried out a multiplication operation in 3 milliseconds—a thousand times faster than the Mark I!

Eckert, Mauchly, and Atanasoff

Assigning credit for initiating the electronic computer age to the designers of ENIAC is open to question. In 1941, two years before the start of the ENIAC project, Mauchly visited the laboratory of *John V. Atanasoff* (b. 1903) at Iowa State University. Atanasoff had already built a specialized computer to solve systems of linear equations. Although Atanasoff's computer employed vacuum tubes and was not as flexible or as powerful as ENIAC, nonetheless it was fundamentally an electronic computer. Atanasoff sued Mauchly and his associates when they tried to patent what he claimed were his ideas. A federal court finally decided in 1974 that his claim was valid. This controversy, however, had little impact on ENIAC's development or its significance in the evolution of computer technology.

It must also be pointed out that in two important ways ENIAC itself did not qualify as a modern electronic computer: it worked with decimal rather than binary numbers, and its calculations could be varied only by tedious manual altering of its set-up rather than by simply changing a numerically coded program. But, all disclaimers aside, ENIAC was certainly of great historic importance. For one thing, the principals of the ENIAC project stayed in the forefront of the developing computer field. Eckert and Mauchly went on to found the company that built *UNIVAC*, the first commercial electronic computer. John von Neumann, one of the world's leading scientists, was a consultant to the project, and he would later bring the computer age into full flower.

The IAS Computer and the Binary Number System

John von Neumann (1903–1957), of Princeton's celebrated Institute for Advanced Study (IAS), the academic home of Albert Einstein and many other great scientists, was a true scientific genius. He had a virtually photographic memory, was a prodigious mental calculator, and made broad and fundamental contributions to science. He was a consultant to the U.S. government and was actively involved in the World War II atomic weapons research at Los Alamos. Consulting on the ENIAC project was only the start of his work on computers. Before the ENIAC was complete, von Neumann formulated plans with Eckert and Mauchly for a new computer, *EDVAC* (Electronic Discrete Variable Automatic Computer), which was to store programs as well as data as numbers in memory, just as is done by computers today.

John von Neumann

Von Neumann abandoned the decimal system, once and for all. He reasoned (as had Atanasoff) that the switches out of which computers were built had two states: on and off (or conducting and nonconducting for the vacuum tubes he employed). Using such switches to represent decimal digits (the numbers from 0 through 9) is somewhat inefficient and complicates the arithmetic circuitry as well. Rather naturally, von Neumann concluded that the **binary system** of notation, in which the digits indicate what powers of 2 (1, 2, 4, 8, 16, etc.) a number contains, would be better suited to computers. In the binary system, since the base is 2, each digit can have a value of either 0 or 1. One binary digit (either a zero or a one) is called a **bit.** The two possible values of a bit are represented by the two possible states of a switch.

The binary system

In 1945, long before EDVAC's completion in 1950, von Neumann went on to direct his own computer project. The machine produced at Princeton, the *IAS computer* (Figure 2.11), unlike the solely military EDVAC, was the immediate precipitant of the explosion of computers onto the commercial scene. At Princeton, von

The IAS computer

Figure 2.11 The IAS Computer
The first truly general-purpose electronic computer was built at the Institute for Advanced Study in Princeton, New Jersey, by a group headed by John von Neumann. Compare its size to that of the Mark I or ENIAC. It was vastly more powerful than the others.

Neumann created not only a computer but an intellectual environment in which the application of computers was the focus of broad and deep investigation.

Unlike its predecessors, the IAS computer possessed the hallmark of the truly general-purpose computer—the ability to turn instantly from one program to another. For example, it could solve equations of atmospheric motion one second and those describing nuclear detonations the next. The versatility of the IAS machine meant that it had more than one use. Although its major role was to design U.S. nuclear weapons, it ran hundreds of other pioneering programs written at Princeton, from the simulation of genetic processes to the first electronic checker player.

After the IAS computer and EDVAC, things began to move quickly. In 1951, Eckert and Mauchly delivered UNIVAC I to the U.S. Bureau of the Census, and a year later IBM unveiled its first computer. The computer age had begun.

FOUR GENERATIONS OF COMPUTERS

Traditionally, the years from the delivery of the first UNIVAC in 1951 to the present have been separated into four periods. Each is identified primarily by the hardware components used during that particular *generation*. In the latter part of the 1980s, however, the development of hardware and software has been so rapid that the idea of generations and categories of computers has become blurred. The original generations are usually defined like this:

Generation	Dates	Hardware
First	1951–1958	Vacuum tubes
Second	1959–1964	Transistors
Third	1965–1971	Integrated circuits
Fourth	1971–Present	Large-scale integration/very large-scale integration

With each generation, costs decreased, performance improved, utilization became easier, and the computer industry continued its rapid growth.

The First Generation (1951–1958)

The first commercial electronic computers

The first generation began with Eckert and Mauchly's UNIVAC I (Figure 2.12) and IBM's 701. These machines were the first computers to be used by businesses, mostly for accounting functions such as payroll and billing. Previous computers had been used mainly for military and scientific computation.

Hardware

Many thousands of vacuum tubes were required to build a single first-generation CPU. Vacuum tubes were notoriously unreliable because of, among other factors, the heat generated in using them and the imperfection of the vacuum (enough air remained inside the glass to slowly burn up the metallic parts). The aging of the seal between the glass body of the tube and its metal and plastic base accelerated this process. A dedicated maintenance effort, checking and replacing aging tubes, was necessary to keep a first-generation computer operating.

Figure 2.12 UNIVAC I
The UNIVAC I is being used by CBS and Walter Cronkite to predict the outcome of the 1953 presidential election.

Relatively few numbers could be stored using a vacuum tube to represent each binary digit. Although several other electronic storage techniques were used during the first generation, most of these have since become extinct. The lasting contribution of the first generation to modern computer technology was the use of magnetic storage media.

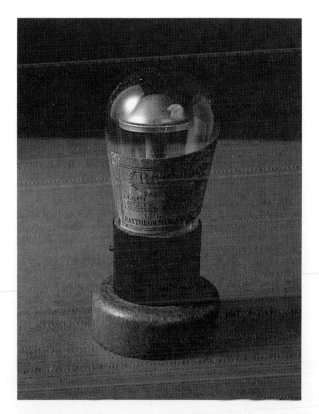

Figure 2.13 The Vacuum Tube
Vacuum tubes were a primary component of the first-generation computer CPU.

Magnetic drums (cylinders with a magnetizable outer surface) were used as internal memory for many of the first-generation computers. Programs and data were usually first punched on IBM cards. Since reading and punching IBM cards is a slow process, the data were, upon input, transferred to a magnetic drum. The drum was the internal memory, or **primary memory** (sometimes also called the **primary storage unit**); that is, it was directly connected to the ALU (discussed in Chapter 3) and control unit and held the active data and program. Intermediate results were written on and retrieved from the drum. No slow card punching and reading were necessary. Although magnetic drums were very slow by today's standards, they were still much faster to access than punched cards, which were the first generation's secondary storage. **Secondary storage** refers to memory with higher capacity but slower accessibility; data to be processed are transferred from secondary storage to the primary storage unit.

Even though they represented an improvement in speed, drums did have a limited capacity; only a few thousand or tens of thousands of numbers could be held on a drum. To augment this capacity, secondary storage on magnetic tape was developed toward the end of the first generation. The amount of data that can be stored on tapes is virtually limitless, but the price for this high capacity is paid in terms of the longer time it takes to access the data. If the data you want to use were recorded in the middle of a tape, you might have to wait several minutes until that spot unreels under the *read head*, where an electromagnet converts the magnetic spots on the tape into the electronic impulses handled by the processor. (Of course, if the reel of tape is on a shelf in another room, the time it will take to access the data will be even longer.) Like data on cards, specific data on magnetic tape secondary storage were transferred to a magnetic drum primary storage unit to be processed.

Software

Keeping first-generation hardware running was tedious and exacting, but programming for it was even worse. The first programs were expressed in the long strings of binary digits that the machine dealt with. That is, the program instruction we encountered in Chapter 1:

ADD wage income and interest income

might have looked like this:

110001101001101011001110100100100111001

where the first 12 digits instructed the machine to add and the remaining digits described the locations in memory of the numbers to be added. Arranging the digits in groups of three or four, in ways we'll explain in Chapter 3, made the programming task somewhat easier, but not much. Writing programs in **machine language** consisting of long sequences of such instructions was error-prone, and checking page after page of ones and zeros tested many a programmer's endurance.

The first big software breakthrough was the development of **assembly language.** An assembly language allowed programmers to use *mnemonics* (easily remembered names) for operations and symbols for variables. An assembly language instruction looked like this:

ADD A and B

where A and B are symbols representing variables. Programs were written in assembly language and punched on cards; then each instruction was converted by the computer itself under the direction of a program called the **assembler** into the string of zeros and ones that the machine could manipulate. Assembly language was a definite improvement over machine language, but it was still hard to work with. Had programming remained at that level of difficulty, there's no question that we'd still be in the dark ages of computers.

The Second Generation (1959—1964)

The second generation was defined by two advances that produced fundamental changes in the manufacture and use of computers: the invention of the transistor and the development of programming languages that were more like English.

Hardware

At Bell Telephone Laboratories in 1948, three men changed the young world of computing. *John Bardeen, Walter H. Brattain* and *William B. Shockley* invented a new electronic device, the **transistor.** In 1956 they were jointly awarded the Nobel Prize in physics for this achievement. Transistors could be made of solid material and were consequently more mechanically rugged than the delicate assemblies of vacuum tubes. They were also small and lightweight and employed no heater. Because of their cool operation, they had a long life. By 1959, when they were being produced in volume and thus at a relatively low price, transistors were the dominant component of the typical CPU.

The transistor

Primary memory was also radically transformed during the second generation. Powdered magnetic material was pressed into tiny doughnut-shaped (*toroidal*)

Figure 2.14   The Transistor

The transistor was lighter, smaller, more reliable, and lasted much longer than vacuum tubes.

Magnetic cores and disks

magnetic cores, which were strung together on wires. Each tiny core can store one bit. Memories built out of magnetic cores have a striking advantage over those using drums and tapes: the data are instantly available. There is no waiting for a part of a drum or tape to arrive under a read head. No physical motion at all is involved in the accessing of a magnetic core memory.

The magnetic tape of the first generation was joined in the second generation by the **magnetic disk,** a large, flat, stereo-record-like magnetic storage surface. With magnetic disk secondary storage (which we will discuss in greater detail in Chapter 5), less time is required to move data into primary memory for processing. Disks rotate rapidly; each item on a disk passes under the read and write heads every 30 or 40 milliseconds—a great improvement over the many seconds, or even minutes, it could take for data on a tape to reach the heads.

During the second generation, computer hardware in general became smaller, more reliable, and more easily maintainable. Components were "packaged" onto **printed circuit boards,** each of which could easily be removed and replaced with a nondefective spare. While the faulty part on the removed board was located and replaced, the system went right on working. **Diagnostic programs,** which test the machine and locate faulty parts quickly (the computer is patient and doctor simultaneously), were developed and improved during the second generation.

Software

High-level languages

The second generation ushered in **high-level languages,** programming languages that resemble written English in vocabulary and syntax. They were essential to the proliferation of computers in every walk of life. We will have much more to say about high-level languages in Chapter 8; here we say that, with their help, programming changed from writing the long strings of digits that are meaningful to computers to writing statements that can be understood by other humans, such as

LET C = A + B

The job of translating such a statement into the zeros and ones on which the computer depends was performed by a complex computer program called a **compiler,** or **translator.** A compiler had to be written only once. It then served to compile, or translate for the computer, any program written in the language it was designed to handle.

The two earliest high-level languages, which are both still widely used today, were *FORTRAN* (FORmula TRANslator), designed for scientific problems, and *COBOL* (COmmon Business-Oriented Language), created for business use. (These languages will be described in Chapter 8.) In addition to making programming efforts far less strenuous, high-level languages had another important impact on computer technology: they made possible the **portability** of programs between computers of different manufacturers. In other words, a single high-level language program (or **source program** as it is called) can be translated by different compilers into various **object programs,** or **machine codes** ("code" is a freqently used synonym for "program"). Each compiler is designed to translate from a particular high-level language into a specific machine language.

At the beginning of the era of high-level languages, however, things weren't that straightforward. Different manufacturers used their own **dialects,** or versions of a language, which meant there were difficulties in conversion. Different machines, then and now, work with numbers of different lengths (numbers of digits). This, and the details of each machine's handling of input/output, added to the difficulties. It wasn't until later, with the establishment of industry-wide standards, that the promise of portability became a reality.

The Third Generation (1965–1971)

The economy and reliability of transistors made computers available to entirely new classes of users. High-level languages made it easier to write programs for business users, enabling them to apply computers to their jobs. A period of explosive growth in the computer industry was taking place within a generally buoyant economy. It was common for a business to buy a computer and then quickly outgrow its capacity. Buying a more powerful computer usually meant that many of the company's existing programs had to be scrapped, all of the ones written in assembly language, for example, and perhaps even the high-level language source programs. The necessity for program conversion was definitely a negative factor to any organization that was contemplating changing computers.

IBM made a $5 billion bet on an answer to this problem when they developed a compatible *family* of computers. IBM's 360 product line started at its low end with a relatively small and economical computer and progressed through half a dozen others to a large, ultra-high-speed machine. The family possessed **upward compatibility:** any program written for one of these machines could be run, without change, on any larger machine in the series. IBM was offering users a means to

IBM and compatibility

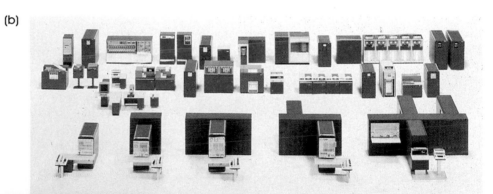

(b)

(a)

Figure 2.15   The IBM 360
(a) The IBM 360 was the first compatible family of computers.
(b) This is a scale model of the entire system.

cope with growth without having to convert most of their programs. The business of manufacturing computers was permanently changed. From this time on, companies built product lines rather than just a single model.

Hardware

During the third generation, the manual assembling of transistors and other components on printed circuit boards gave way to the mechanized manufacturing of small solid pieces of silicon that contained all these components, as well as all their necessary interconnections.

Integrated circuits

These new **integrated circuits** were much smaller, more efficient (in terms of power consumption), more reliable, and ultimately far cheaper than their slower second-generation counterparts. The resulting increases in computing speed were also dramatic. It became necessary to think in terms of a new time unit, the *nanosecond* (a billionth of a second). Soon after, an even less comprehensible unit of time, the *picosecond* (a trillionth of a second), had to be added to the general computer vocabulary.

Memory technology was transformed by integrated circuits. By 1969, approximately 100 transistors could be built on a single piece of silicon (a *silicon chip*), making the transistor primary memory, in which a transistor circuit is used to store each bit, more competitive in price with magnetic core memory. Magnetic core memory does have one advantage over transistor memory: it is *nonvolatile*, that is, the information remains stored even if the power is shut off. Even the most reliable electric power systems have momentary outages that, in the absence of special safeguards, will destroy the information in a transistor memory. In situations where it is vital that the contents not be lost, magnetic primary memories remain in use today.

Integrated circuits and miniaturized core memories made low-cost minicomputers possible. These small, rugged machines are generally used for a single application, or at most a small set of applications, as opposed to the mainframes, or large computing-center machines, which do hundreds or even thousands of different tasks every day.

The human user was linked more directly to the computer with the development of the *terminal*. Instead of punching cards on some off-line device, then giving them to an operator who would, some time later, place them in a card reader for processing, programmers could now type their programs directly into computer memory, and check them on the printed output. Terminals were also perfect for data entry and the operation of minicomputers; they continue to play a large role in communications between humans and computers.

Magnetic disks represented an increased percentage of the volume memory market in the third generation. **Disk packs** became prevalent. These are like other rotating disks but with removable disk storage surfaces. This gives a disk unit the same ability as a tape unit to make rooms full of data accessible to the computer, while maintaining the speed advantages of the disk.

Software

Software became more sophisticated during the third generation. The number of high-level languages continued to grow. Languages adapted to more specific applications began to make their appearance: *RPG* (Report Program Generator) for generating business reports; *APT* (Automatically Programmed Tools) for fabricating parts on automatically controlled machine tools; and *BASIC* (Beginner's All-purpose Symbolic Instruction Code) for easy programming.

The expanded power of the CPU and the increased quantity and variety of input/output equipment with which it was surrounded created a need for more efficient management of these complex and costly resources, some worth several million dollars. A new class of computer program, the operating system, answered this need. In the first and second generations, jobs were run successively under the supervision of a human operator. The computer's efficiency was greatly improved by placing its resources under the control of an **operating system,** a program that could match the jobs that needed to be done with the equipment that was available. With an operating system, much more work can be accomplished by the same equipment.

A natural extension was **time sharing** of an operating system. The CPU is so fast that it can keep up with many users communicating with the system from a number of terminal keyboards. In fact, in time sharing, the operating system parcels out successive connection times of a few milliseconds' duration to several users. Unless traffic is particularly heavy, each user has the illusion of having sole and immediate access to the computer.

Time-sharing operating systems

The Fourth Generation (1971–Present)

During the third generation, computers penetrated deeply and permanently into the fabric of industry, commerce, government, and higher education. In the fourth generation, computers have reached beyond these institutions to the individual at work, at school and at home. Two innovations that have enabled this extension of the techonology are the microprocessor (the hardware means by which the power of the computer was delivered to virtually everyone) and user-friendly software (the means by which the complexities of using the machine were made easily comprehensible).

Hardware

Technology has progressed from the abacus to gears, vacuum tubes, transistors, and the integrated circuits of the third generation. These advances did not mark the end of an era, but another starting point instead.

In the early 1970s, integrated circuit technology, by which a dozen or so transistors were included on a single chip, was supplanted by the techniques of *large-scale integration (LSI)*. LSI chips could be manufactured containing a few thousand transistors. By the mid-1970s, an even more powerful technology, *very large-scale integration (VLSI)* was used to produce a chip containing an entire **microprocessor,** or microcomputer CPU.

VLSI and the microprocessor

The Intel Corporation, founded by Robert Noyce (a student of Shockley) introduced its first microprocessor, the Intel 4004, in 1971. Credit for the development of this first microprocessor is given to Ted Hoff and several other scientists from Intel. The Intel team had been working on a project begun in 1969 with a design contract from the Japanese calculator manufacturer Busicom. Although Busicom no longer exists the results of this work have had a profound effect on the computer industry (see Figure 2.16).

The Intel 4004 possessed a limited capacity, but it was quickly followed by more powerful and flexible designs, including the Intel 8008 and 8080. There were

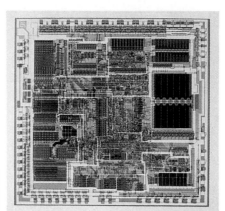

(b)

(a)

Figure 2.16 Intel Microprocessor

(a) The Intel 4004 microprocessor. Newer, more powerful Intel chips include the 80286 (b) and the 80386 (c).

(c)

a number of companies at this time competing to produce even faster and more reliable microprocessor chips. Among the important competitors in this race were Motorola, Texas Instruments, Zilog, and Fairchild Semiconductor. These early microprocessors and their successors incorporated the computing power of many larger machines into a tiny package, with the additional benefit of greatly increased reliability at a greatly reduced price. The first microprocessors cost a little over $400, but by 1974 they had dropped to around $100, and the price continued to fall.

Personal computers

In 1974 the Intel 8080 microprocessor was packaged as part of a kit to build the Altair 8800, the first **personal computer** (PC). It was an immediate success with electronics buffs who put together their own microcomputer systems. In 1977 two of these electronics buffs, Steve Wozniack (an engineer) and Steve Jobs (a high school student), created their own personal computer kit and started selling the Apple I kit from a garage. The limited market for kit sales encouraged the development of a new product, the Apple II (see Figure 2.17). The Apple II was preassembled, and it included a disk drive and a simple visual operating system.

The Apple II

The extraordinary success of the Apple II was soon followed by machines from Tandy/Radio Shack, Atari, Commodore, and others. The early sales advantage went to Radio Shack, which had a large network of established retail outlets. These early machines were extremely popular with hobbyists, game players and educators. Some major players in the large computer markets adopted a conservative strategy

(a)

Figure 2.17 Apple Computers
(a) The original Apple II. (b) Apple Computers' Macintosh II.

(b)

and did not attempt to compete for several years. When IBM, in particular, did enter the personal computer market in 1981 with its IBM Personal Computer, it quickly became a major supplier of personal computers to the business market pioneered by Tandy/Radio Shack (see Figure 2.18). Soon many companies began to manufacture microcomputers that worked just like, or even better than, **IBM's**

(a)

Figure 2.18 IBM Personal Computers
(a) The IBM-PC. (b) IBM's PS/2 family.

(b)

Personal Computer. These so-called **"clones"** or **"IBM-Compatibles"** have become a major force in reducing prices and making powerful microcomputers widely available.

One consequence of VLSI was the virtual replacement of magnetic core memory with transistor memory. Single memory chips now contain up to a million bits and an upper limit to their capacity is still not in sight. The number of transistors on today's VLSI chip is enough to build 20 ENIACs. Secondary storage has grown to a capacity large enough to contain all the data needed to operate a big corporation or a major government agency. Each generation of computers has featured its largest, fastest, and generally scientifically-oriented computers—the *supercomputers.* These supercomputers have played a special role in a variety of fields which will be discussed in later chapters.

While the cost of this computer hardware was dropping quickly and the power of the systems was increasing rapidly, the development of VisiCalc, an electronic spreadsheet software tool, was similarly important in bringing the personal computer to the desks of many people in business. Developments in other areas of software have continued to make these machines very user-friendly.

Software

The VLSI techniques that created ever more powerful machines allowed increasingly sophisticated and complex problems to be solved. The need to manage efficiently the machines and the enormous quantity of data that could be manipulated by them led to the development of more sophisticated operating systems.

Microcomputer operating systems

The first commercially successful operating system for microcomputers was Digital Research's *CP/M.* When IBM decided to license a version of the Microsoft

Figure 2.19   MC88100

New chip architectures promise even greater speed and power.

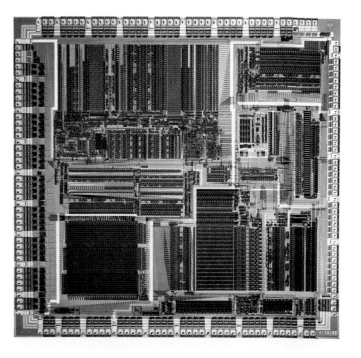

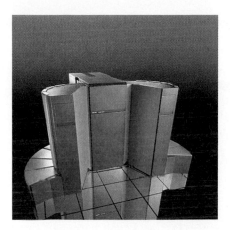

Figure 2.20 Cray Supercomputer
Enormously powerful and specialized, supercomputers help forecast our weather and advance our scientific understanding.

Corporation's operating system program to accompany its PC upon the PC's release in 1981, many claimed a standard had been developed: *PC-DOS (Personal Computer Disk Operating System)* for IBM's personal computers and *MS-DOS (Microsoft Disk Operating System)* for compatibles. More recently, AT & T's *UNIX* operating system has been proposed as a highly efficient system and is gaining popularity. The most sophisticated models of the new generation of IBM microcomputers, the PS/2 line, have adopted a new operating system co-developed by Microsoft and IBM, called *OS/2*. We will discuss various new operating systems in more detail in Chapter 9.

Figure 2.21 Lap-top Computers
Portability and power in a package that can weigh less than 10 pounds.

Figure 2.22   The Macintosh Operating System
The user-friendly operating system of the Apple Macintosh personal computer displays icons on the screen to represent systems functions. The user selects a function with a mouse-directed cursor.

Apple Computers, which introduced its very successful Macintosh microcomputer in 1984, adopted a different standard. The Macintosh operating system is mostly built into the machine and is accessed via simple screen commands activated by a mouse, rather than through keyboard commands (see Figure 2.22). This very easy method of communicating with the computer has been largely responsible for the Mac's popularity.

For both large machines and personal computers, the growing scope and complexity of programming efforts has meant that greater and greater intellectual discipline and organization must be imposed on what are frequently large programming

Structured programming

teams. A set of techniques called **structured programming** has made an important contribution to the standardization of such efforts. It is a vital underpinning of the complex fourth-generation software (discussed in detail in Chapter 8). The advent of structured programming techniques has encouraged some programmers to leave the first language of the microcomputer revolution, BASIC, in favor of more structured languages such as Pascal or Modula-2. New structured versions of BASIC, including TRUE BASIC, have recently appeared.

The **application package** may be the most important software development of the fourth generation. It is a software program or collection of related programs that lets a user perform a specific task or tasks. The application package allows users with no programming experience to perform numerous functions previously re-

User-friendly software

stricted to programmers. These user-friendly programs have been a driving force behind the installation of computers in offices and in the home. These packages are also having an important effect on large-computer programming. We will explore this topic further in Part 3.

The pioneering microcomputer application program VisiCalc, developed by Dan Bricklin and Dan Fylstra, was released in 1979. VisiCalc was a spreadsheet analysis program that allowed business people and other users to view and evaluate sometimes complex alternative financial scenarios on the Apple computers in their offices. Before VisiCalc, this would have required a mainframe computer and a programmer; after the development of this software, an Apple computer was all that was required.

VisiCorp has since been purchased and merged into Lotus Development Corporation (founded in 1982). Visicalc is no longer an important program but its effect on business has been profound. Lotus 1-2-3, a spreadsheet program developed by Mitch Kapor, is now the leading business application program. The success of this application package, and the release of additional programs such as Symphony (an integrated software package), has brought Lotus into the forefront, with Microsoft, of microcomputer software suppliers (see Figure 2.23).

In 1978 Seymour Rubinstein founded MicroPro to market a word-processing package called WordStar (see Figure 2.24). WordStar was the first commercially successful package of its kind. Since its introduction, many alternative packages have become available. We will discuss these further in Chapter 9.

Bill Gates and Paul Allen founded Microsoft Corporation in 1974. Their first product was a version of the BASIC programming language adapted for microcomputers. The variety and success of the Microsoft products created since then has been staggering. The operating systems for many of the most popular microcomputers are Microsoft's MS-DOS and PC-DOS. Microsoft also offers versions of popular programming languages for microcomputers including BASIC, Pascal, C, FORTRAN, and COBOL. Microsoft Word, a word-processing program, holds a major portion of its market, and other Microsoft products include EXCEL (a spreadsheet), WORKS (an integrated package), Windows, and OS/2, the operating system for the new generation of IBM personal computers.

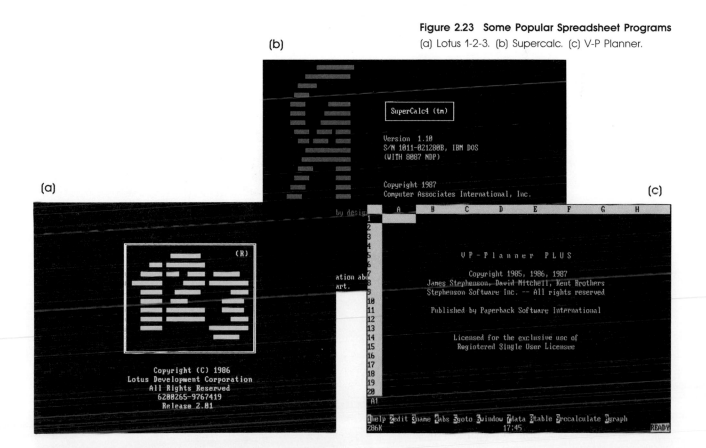

Figure 2.23 Some Popular Spreadsheet Programs
(a) Lotus 1-2-3. (b) Supercalc. (c) V-P Planner.

**Figure 2.24 Some Popular
Word-Processing Programs**

(a) Microsoft Word. (b) WordPerfect.
(c) WordStar.

(b)

```
                    ┌─────────────────────┐
                    │     WordPerfect     │
                    ├─────────────────────┤
                    │     Version 5.0     │
                    └─────────────────────┘

                   (C)Copyright 1982,1988
                     All Rights Reserved
                   WordPerfect Corporation
                      Orem, Utah  USA




NOTE: The WP System is using C:\WP50
```

(a)

(c)

```
Microsoft ®



        Microsoft Word
          Version 4.0
  Serial Number 034099-400-0474216



        Copyright (c) Microsoft Corporation, 1983-1987.
All Rights Reserved. Microsoft is a registered trademark of Microsoft Corp.
  Word Finder Copyright Microlytics, 1986, 1987. All rights reserved.
```

```
WordStar Release 4.00  Serial #FYT0091H   027
Copyright (C) 1979, 1987 MicroPro International Corporation.
All rights reserved.

IBM PC Compatible
IBM Proprinter XL24


▌▌▌      WordStar Professional
by MicroPro

CorrectStar copyright (C) 1983, 1987 MicroPro International Corp.
Spelling licensed under U.S. Pat. No. 4,580,241.
Spelling licensed under Canadian Pat. No. 1,283,916.
Copyright (C) 1985 Houghton Mifflin.  All rights reserved.
Based on the American Heritage Dictionary.
_
```

Ashton-Tate was founded in 1980 by George Tate and Hal Lashlee. Its first product, a data base management software package known as dBASE II, was one of the hottest software products in the personal computer marketplace. In 1988, the company released dBASE IV, an enhanced version of its very successful dBASE III PLUS. Ashton-Tate also produces MultiMate (a word processor), Framework (an integrated package) and ByLine (a desktop publishing system) (Figure 2.25).

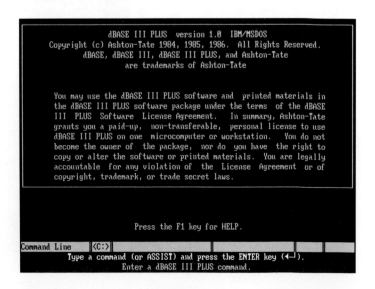

Figure 2.25 dBASE III PLUS

Ashton-Tate's popular data base management package for microcomputers.

In little more than 40 years, computer technology has moved through four generations. Computers commonly available today were almost inconceivable 40 years ago. Is this technology moving too fast for society to assimilate the changes it brings?

Issues in Technology

Epilog and Prolog

The fourth generation is not the end of the story. As we said at the beginning of this chapter, hardware and software development is proceeding at such a rapid pace that distinctions between categories of computers are, at the least, indistinct, and in some cases are essentially nonexistent. New materials (such as gallium arsenide) are being used for chips that increase speed and capacity beyond what was imagined only a few years ago. Part 2 will explore aspects of computer hardware.

The fifth generation

New applications software packages have also been created to aid in decision making; these new packages are called expert systems. Other packages produce elaborate printed documents in a process called desktop publishing. Parts 3 and 4 will look at new software developments and the application of computer systems in several systems.

Computer control of robots in manufacturing has already been achieved. This development and the production of designs, art, and music will be discussed in Part 5. Computers in education will also be examined at that time.

Current research into the area of *artificial intelligence* may bring about completely new types of computers (a fifth generation) in the 1990s. We will have more to say about these research efforts, as well as some potential problems with AI, in Part 6.

Summary

The Origins
The computer story begins with the concept of number. With the use of symbols for numbers came the earliest aids to counting, which culminated in the first calculator, the abacus.

Early Machines
The mathematician Pascal developed the first mechanical calculator. Pascal's machine was digital, which distinguished it from earlier analog instruments. Leibniz built a more ambitious calculator that performed multiplication and division. Charles Babbage's analytical engine anticipated the main principles underlying the modern computer. William Seward Burroughs developed the first commercially successful calculator. Herman Hollerith invented punched-card tabulating machines for the 1890 census. Thomas J. Watson joined the company Hollerith founded and later renamed it the International Business Machines Corporation.

Dawn of the Computer Age
The Mark I With financial and technical support from IBM, Howard Aiken of Harvard built the Mark I using relays, electromechanical devices that replaced the purely mechanical gears of earlier machines.

ENIAC   John Presper Eckert and John W. Mauchly built ENIAC at the University of Pennsylvania. The U.S. Army sponsored the project in order to achieve faster and more accurate calculation of artillery and rocket trajectories. ENIAC was built with vacuum tubes, purely electronic switches that replaced relays. Eckert and Mauchly later went on to produce UNIVAC I, the first commercial electronic computer.

The IAS Computer and the Binary Number System   John von Neumann took the vital step of representing program steps numerically and storing them, together with data, in the computer's memory. He was also responsible for making the binary system, whose two digits perfectly match the on or off state of a switch, the basis of computer arithmetic and logic.

Four Generations of Computers

The year 1951 marked the start of commercial production of computers. From then until the late 1980s, machines have been grouped into four generations, defined mainly by the hardware components used to build them.

The First Generation (1951–1958)   The first UNIVAC and the early IBM machines had vacuum tube CPU's and magnetic drum memories. Programs were written in numerical machine language until the development of assembly language, which brought the first significant reduction in programming labor.

The Second Generation (1959–1964)   As a result of the replacement of vacuum tubes with transistors, computers became smaller and cheaper, more powerful, and more reliable. Magnetic cores were used increasingly to build primary memory, and magnetic disks were the common form of secondary storage. The first high-level languages, FORTRAN and COBOL, were developed. Portability thus became possible, and program conversion was less of a nightmare.

The Third Generation (1965–1971)   IBM developed the first upward-compatible family of computers, the 360 series. Integrated circuits produced further performance increases and cost reductions for mainframe computers and made minicomputers possible. High-level languages continued to proliferate, and operating systems and time sharing appeared.

The Fourth Generation (1971–Present)   The computer's decreasing cost and improving performance extended its range of application into the home. Techniques of LSI and VLSI ultimately produced the microprocessor, the single-chip CPU of the personal computer. The needs of a rapidly growing community of users are served by user-friendly software. The greater size and complexity of programming undertakings are managed more efficiently with structured programming.

Epilog and Prolog   Fading of clear distinctions between classes of computers has occurred, even as artificial intelligence and new approaches to computing have been researched.

Computer Concepts

As an extra review of the chapter, try defining the following terms. If you have trouble with any of them, refer to the page number listed.

digital *38*	primary memory (primary storage unit) *48*	magnetic cores *50*
analog *38*		magnetic disk *50*
relays *43*	secondary storage *48*	printed circuit boards *50*
vacuum tube *44*	machine language *48*	diagnostic programs *50*
binary system *45*	assembly language *48*	high-level languages *50*
bit *45*	assembler *49*	compiler *50*
magnetic drums *48*	transistor *49*	translator *50*

Review Questions

1. What were some of the first counting devices?
2. What was Blaise Pascal's contribution to the development of computers?
3. Name some digital and analog devices you use every day.
4. Who built the first calculator designed to do multiplication and division?
5. What was the principal advantage of Charles Babbage's analytical engine?
6. In terms of computer development, what is the significance of the 1890 U.S. census?
7. What electromechanical device was used by the Harvard Mark I?
8. Name two ways ENIAC differed from a modern computer.
9. Who is credited with the idea of using binary notation to represent numbers in computers and with storing program and data in memory?
10. What were the first computers to be widely adopted for business use?
11. What is the lasting contribution of first generation computer technology to modern computers?
12. Why is assembly language considered a significant breakthrough in software development?
13. How did the transistor make the succeeding generations of computers possible?
14. In second generation software, how did advances in higher languages make computers more accessible?
15. What hardware device was introduced in the third generation that made communication between user and computer easier?
16. What two innovations in the fourth generation led to the proliferation of computers?
17. Why did the development of ever more sophisticated operating systems become necessary?
18. What was the first high-level language introduced for microcomputers?
19. Why is the application package sometimes called the most important software development of the fourth generation?
20. What was the pioneering spreadsheet package that permitted business people to use their personal computers to do complex analyses?
21. What area of contemporary research is leading to new approaches in how computers solve problems?

True or False

1. Counting boards were among the first counting machines.
2. Pascal's calculator was an analog machine.
3. Leibniz's calculator was the first to do all four arithmetic operations.
4. The first programming loop was invented by Ada Augusta, Countess of Lovelace.
5. Before the first generation, computers used electromechanical devices called relays.
6. The second generation is defined by the invention of the transistor and high-level languages.

7. Upward compatibility among computers means a program that can run on one manufacturer's machines can run on other manufacturers' machines.
8. The microprocessor was introduced in the fourth generation.
9. The first high-level language for a microcomputer was BASIC.
10. Time sharing was a natural extension of an operating system.

Multiple Choice

1. The first counting machine was:
   (a) the abacus   (b) the counting board   (c) the Pascaline
2. The first calculator to contain a memory was invented by:
   (a) Pascal   (b) Leibniz   (c) Babbage
3. The first computer programmer was:
   (a) Wilhelm von Leibniz (b) Ada Augusta, Countess   (c) Lord Byron
                               of Lovelace
4. The first fully electronic computer was developed by:
   (a) Mauchly   (b) John Atanasoff   (c) John von Neumann
5. One of John von Neumann's principal contributions to the development of computers was the introduction of:
   (a) the decimal number (b) octal notation   (c) the binary system
       system
6. The lasting contribution of the first generation was:
   (a) magnetic storage   (b) vacuum tubes   (c) the relay
7. The invention that helped define the second generation was:
   (a) magnetic cores   (b) machine language   (c) the transistor
8. The first commercially available personal computer was:
   (a) the Altair 8800   (b) Apple II   (c) the IBM PC
9. The technology that made the microcomputer possible was:
   (a) the vacuum tube   (b) printed circuit boards   (c) the microprocessor
10. A software development in the third generation that enabled many users to communicate simultaneously with the same computer is:
   (a) an operating system (b) CPU   (c) high-level languages

A Sharper Focus

Now that you've completed this chapter, you should be able to answer the following questions about the chapter.

1. Do you think that computer technology is moving too fast for society to respond to the changes it brings? What is your evidence?
2. In view of the continuing blurring of distinctions between the three basic computer types, do you think you will be using a single-user supercomputer within the next five years?

1. Consider some of the mechanical and electronic devices you use or come in contact with every day. Are any of them analog? Do you expect them to be converted to digital displays in the near future?

2. Research some of the capabilities of UNIVAC I, the first commercial electronic computer. Compare its features (size, memory capacity, speed) with those of the newest personal computers available on campus or in a local computer store.

3. How has the use of computers changed on your campus over the last ten years? the last twenty years?

4. Ask faculty members how the use of computers has changed life on your campus during the last decade. How do these changes relate to project #3?

Part

2

HARDWARE

Computer hardware—the physical parts of a computer system—varies widely in performance, price, size, and appearance. The structure and function of the central processing unit, the numerous peripheral devices, and the various media for the input, storage, and output of data are essential to data processing. Part 2 covers these physical aspects of computers.

Chapter 3 focuses on the parts common to all computers, the central processing unit (CPU) and memory. Chapter 4 moves outside that central core, to cover the devices and media that accept input data as well as those devices that present the results of processing, or output, to the user. Chapter 5 shows how the data are organized and stored. Finally, Chapter 6 discusses data communications, that is, sending data back and forth between separate computers.

3

The Central Processing Unit and Memory

In This Chapter

Putting Chip Designs on Silicon

Ten years ago, Carver Mead, Professor of Computer Science at California Institute of Technology, and Lynn Conway, computer scientist at Xerox, launched a new way of designing chips that closed the gap between chip customers and chip producers. Two years later one of Mead's Caltech students, David Johannsen, used this method to develop a new invention called the silicon compiler.

The silicon compiler integrates an array of computerized chip design tools into one powerful program. The program can produce a chip layout pattern from a systems designer's idea of what he wants the chip to do. The designer does not have to know how to manufacture a chip, just as an author does not have to know how to print a book. When the pattern is complete, the designer can take his design to a chipmaker and have it produced.

This technique is revitalizing the semiconductor industry. In 1981, Mead and Johannsen formed a new company, Silicon Compilers, to produce and sell the silicon compiler. A rival firm, started by two more of Mead's students, was formed somewhat later; in 1987 the two firms merged to form Silicon Compiler Systems Corp., which recently announced new programs to help test chips.

Other firms have since been started by former students and colleagues of Mead. In fact, in the last five years 99 new semiconductor firms have been formed. A higher proportion of this generation of new companies has thrived than in any previous startup wave in the industry.

The new technologies are increasing the number of chip designs from a little over 10,000 in 1985 to 25,000 in 1987 and well over 100,000 by 1991. Each of these chips is designed to perform a designated task, such as operating automobile lighting systems, VCR remote controls or portable cellular telephones.

Another breakthrough, announced in February 1988, allows systems designers to produce chip designs and inscribe those designs on actual chips, a form of desktop printing on silicon. These new technologies are expected to revolutionize the semiconductor industry just as desktop publishing has done in the publishing industry.

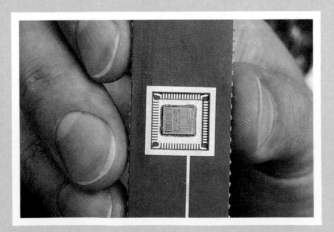

Thirty years or so ago, people unfamiliar with computers often referred to them as "electronic brains." Today, people are more sophisticated about computers and are no longer astonished by their computational abilities. Most of us know that computers must be programmed in order to do anything and that there are many limitations on what they can do. So where did that "electronic brain" label originate, and why does the attitude it represents persist today?

The labeling of computers as "brains" is based on a certain limited similarity between the two complex entities, one organic and the other electronic. The comparison is faulty at best—like comparing apples with oranges because both are round and both are fruit. The weak analogy is drawn from certain superficial similarities between brains and computers: a computer's central processing unit resembles a brain in that both are places where input is transformed into output and where the control of the peripheral equipment (arms and legs, or terminals and printers) is centered. Also, without a brain or a CPU, a body or a computer is useless.

The first two chapters in this book introduced the modern computer—its operation and role and its origins and development. This is sufficient conceptual background for a more detailed study of the machine itself. In this chapter, we begin to see what's inside a computer, how a computer really works, and what makes it such a unique and capable machine.

THE COMPUTER REVEALED

Let's remove the cover from a typical microcomputer and look at its internal structure. Figure 3.1(a) shows the system unit of an IBM Personal System/2 Model 50 taken apart. Inside we find that there are several major components. We'll briefly examine each of these parts, and then go on to delve into the ones that are most important for understanding how a computer processes data. The components you see in Figure 3.1(a) include:

A look inside a typical microcomputer

- *Chassis.*   The **chassis** is a frame, constructed of metal and high-impact plastic, that houses all of the internal components of a computer. This particular computer also has a plastic subchassis, which helps secure the disk drives and extra circuit boards. When all the parts are assembled, the chassis is covered by a plastic case coated on the inside with conductive silver paint to reduce radio frequency emissions.

- *Motherboard.*   The **motherboard** or **system board** is the main circuit board of a computer [see Figure 3.1(b)]. Among other components, the motherboard holds the computer's CPU, some memory, and much of its control circuitry. Although not all computers are constructed with a motherboard in this fashion, it's a popular arrangement used in most microcomputers.

- *Memory.*   In this particular computer, most of the primary storage consists of chips mounted on their own small circuit boards that plug into special sockets on the motherboard. Many computers, however, have their primary memory chips plugged or soldered directly into the motherboard.

- *Power supply.*   The delicate circuits that make up any computer require a refined source of electrical power. The **power supply** plugs into an ordinary outlet, but contains a transformer to lower and regulate the voltage level of the

Figure 3.1 Inside the IBM Personal System/2 Model 50
(a) This photograph shows the system unit broken down into its major components. (b) Here is a closeup of the **motherboard** or **system board.**

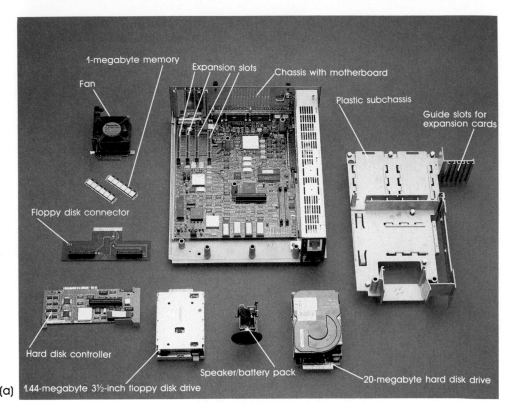

(a)
- Fan
- 1-megabyte memory
- Expansion slots
- Chassis with motherboard
- Plastic subchassis
- Guide slots for expansion cards
- Floppy disk connector
- Hard disk controller
- 1.44-megabyte 3½-inch floppy disk drive
- Speaker/battery pack
- 20-megabyte hard disk drive

(b)
- Four expansion slots
- Parallel port (printer)
- Mouse port
- Serial port (modem)
- VGA display controller
- Floppy disk controller
- Floppy disk connector
- Socket for Intel 80287 math coprocessor
- Intel 80286 microprocessor (CPU)
- Four 32K ROM chips
- Socket for 1 megabyte of RAM

electricity provided to the computer. The power supply often represents a significant amount of space, weight, and cost in a computer. Unfortunately, it can also be a source of problems in many machines. In Figure 3.1(a), the power supply occupies the entire right-side length of the chassis. The red toggle at the front end is the power switch that turns the computer on and off.

- *Expansion slots.* An **expansion slot** is an internal connector that allows you to plug an additional circuit board into the motherboard. This particular computer has four expansion slots, although some computers come with eight or more. A circuit board that plugs into an expansion slot is called an **expansion board, card,** or **adapter.** Such circuit boards make it possible to connect a wide variety of auxiliary peripheral equipment to a computer, thus expanding its capability.

- *Device controllers.* A **device controller** is a set of chips or a circuit board that operates a piece of computer equipment such as a disk drive, display, keyboard, mouse, or printer. Some device controllers are so complex that they are, in actuality, computers unto themselves. Recently, a trend toward building device controllers onto microcomputer motherboards has emerged. In Figure 3.1(a) for example, the device controllers for the display, keyboard, mouse, and floppy disk drives consist of chips mounted on the motherboard. The hard disk controller, on the other hand, is a separate circuit board that plugs into one of the expansion slots. By having the hard disk controller on a removable expansion board, the computer can be easily upgraded with a faster or higher capacity hard disk.

- *Disk drives.* As we said in Chapter 1, a disk drive is a piece of equipment that can read and write data on magnetic disks. Most microcomputers now have two basic kinds of disk drives. A *floppy disk drive* works with floppy disks, which are inexpensive flexible magnetic disks encased in plastic. Floppy disks can be inserted and removed from their disk drives. The standard IBM Personal System/2 Model 50 comes with one floppy disk drive, which can accept $3\frac{1}{2}$-inch floppy disks that hold up to 1.44 megabytes of programs and data. (We will formally define a *megabyte* later in this chapter. For now, realize that it is approximately equal to one million characters.) This computer also comes with a 20-megabyte **hard disk drive.** Unlike floppy disk drives, a hard disk drive has its magnetic disks permanently sealed inside. These rigid magnetic disks are much faster and have a much greater capacity than a floppy disk.

- *Other components.* Most computers have various other components inside. This particular computer, for example, also has a speaker, a battery pack, a fan, and a floppy disk connector. The speaker is used for emitting "beeps," musical tones, and other sounds. The battery pack is used to maintain power to a few special memory chips that hold the current date, time, and various equipment settings. The fan keeps the sensitive computer circuits from overheating. In this particular computer, the floppy disk connector is needed to plug floppy disk drives into their device controller on the motherboard.

As you can see, there are many components in a computer, even a fairly simple one such as the IBM Personal System/2 Model 50. A few parts, however, stand out as being the most important from the perspective of understanding exactly how a computer processes data into information. This chapter concentrates on those key computer components inside the system unit: the central processing unit, primary storage, and the bus (see Figure 3.2).

Figure 3.2 The Key Computer Components

The key components of any computer are the central processing unit (CPU), primary storage, and the bus that connects them to each other and to the input and output device controllers.

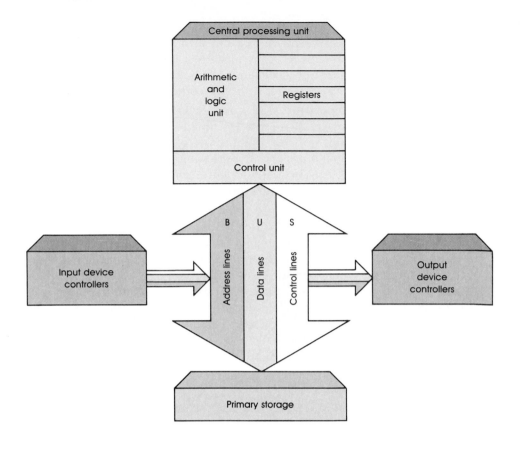

THE LANGUAGE OF COMPUTERS

How computers encode numbers and text

Before we discuss these three key components of a computer and how they operate, let's first consider the way in which instructions and data are represented electronically. The vast majority of contemporary computers deals only with the zeros and ones of the **binary** (base 2) number system, which correspond to the on and off states of an electronic switch. The number system we are most familiar with, the decimal system, uses 10 symbols (the digits 0 through 9) to represent numerical quantities; single digits represent quantities smaller than 10, and groups of two or more digits represent quantities larger than 9. Computers take an even simpler view of numbers since the only digits that are processed are 0 and 1.

Each digit in a decimal number stands for 10 times as much as its neighbor to the right. Reading backward from right to left gives digits multiplied by the sequence 1, 10, 100, 1000, and so on. A binary number, on the other hand, has each binary digit counting for only twice as much as the right neighbor. Here the sequence of multipliers goes 1, 2, 4, 8, 16, and so on. These numbers are the powers of 2, some of which are shown in Figure 3.3. More information on the different ways computers store numbers can be found at the end of this book in Appendix A.

2^0	=	1
2^1	=	2
2^2	=	4
2^3	=	8
2^4	=	16
2^5	=	32
2^6	=	64
2^7	=	128
2^8	=	256
2^9	=	512
2^{10}	=	1024
2^{11}	=	2048
2^{12}	=	4096
2^{13}	=	8192
2^{14}	=	16,384
2^{15}	=	32,768
2^{16}	=	65,536

Figure 3.3 Powers of 2

Just as the decimal number system uses successive powers of 10 (that is, 1, 10, 100, 1000, . . .), the binary system uses successive powers of 2. Some of these powers and their decimal equivalents are listed here.

Coding Systems

Textual information is processed in a computer by associating each character with a separate number. There are two dominant coding schemes used in the computer industry that uniquely match numbers with characters. The most prevalent code is the **American Standard Code for Information Interchange** or **ASCII.** In this code, for example, the decimal numbers 65 through 90 (binary 1000001 through 1011010) represent the capital letters from *A* through *Z*. Other numbers are assigned to punctuation marks, lowercase letters, and digits. There are also various control codes for input, output, and communication devices that signal such events as when a new line of printing should be begun or a fresh page of output started. Although the original ASCII code uses only 7 data bits to represent a character and can therefore encode 128 different characters, some ASCII variations now in common use have 8 bits per character and can encode 256 different characters. Appendix A contains the 128 7-bit ASCII codes and a popular 8-bit variation developed by IBM for use in its microcomputers.

ASCII and EBCDIC schemes for representing characters

　　Extended Binary Coded Decimal Interchange Code or **EBCDIC** is the other dominant computer coding scheme. Used primarily in IBM mainframes, it has 8 bits per character. In EBCDIC, for example, the capital letter *A* is represented by the number 193 (11000001 binary) and the letter *Z* is represented by 233 (11101001 binary). Appendix A compares EBCDIC codes with ASCII codes.

Bits, Bytes, and Words

How binary digits are grouped

In Chapter 2 we introduced the bit: 0 or 1, off or on. This is the fundamental unit of data processing, since all data handled by today's digital computers are ultimately reduced to bits. The **byte** is usually defined as a group of 8 bits, the amount of memory needed to store a single character or a number from 0 to 255. Occasionally, you encounter the term **nibble** (or **nybble**) which is half of a byte (4 bits), and one example of the computer scientists' sometimes whimsical sense of humor.

A computer **word** is a group of adjacent bits that are generally manipulated and stored as a unit. The number of bits in a word depends on the computer and is a key element of the computer's design. As we'll see later in this chapter, the smallest computers handle 8-bit words, and the largest can deal with words of 128 bits. The most common word lengths, however, are 16, 32, and 64 bits. For the most part, the larger a computer's word length, the more powerful the computer. There are three basic reasons why this is so:

- A large word length means that a computer can manipulate more data at a time, making it faster than a computer with a smaller word length. For example, a computer with a 32-bit word length can generally process data at least twice as fast as a computer with a 16-bit word length.

- The larger the word length, the greater the potential primary storage capacity of the computer. Each memory location must be uniquely identified by a different number, or **address,** that must usually fit within one or two computer words. Consequently, a computer with a larger word length can address more memory than a computer with a smaller word length.

- Computer instructions, like data, are represented by numbers. In many computers, the code number that identifies an operation must fit within a single word. Therefore, a larger word length means that more instructions can be built into the computer, usually resulting in a more powerful computer.

THE CENTRAL PROCESSING UNIT

Where data are turned into information

The actual data processing takes place in the central processing unit. In a microcomputer, the CPU consists of a single microprocessor chip. In larger computers, the CPU may be physically constructed from several different chips and circuits. In either case, there are three major conceptual components. As Figure 3.2 shows, these are the arithmetic and logic unit, registers, and the control unit.

The Arithmetic and Logic Unit

Where calculations and comparisons are carried out

The **arithmetic and logic unit (ALU)** is the part of the CPU where calculations and logical operations are carried out. Calculations performed by the ALU usually involve just the four elementary **arithmetic operations:** addition, subtraction, multiplication, and division. Some ALUs are quite simple and only have the built-in capability to do addition and subtraction. In these simple ALUs, multiplication, division, and other more advanced mathematical operations must be performed by programs that cleverly employ just addition and subtraction. Other ALUs are more complex and have the built-in ability to do all four of the basic arithmetic operations.

Logic operations performed by the ALU basically consist of comparing or combining two numbers in some manner. This allows the computer to evaluate situations and take alternate courses of action. The comparison capabilities of the ALU make a computer more than just a calculator. In a payroll program, the computer can compare the total number of hours an employee worked in a week with the number 40. If that employee's hours are greater than 40, then the payroll program applies the overtime hourly pay rate to those hours that exceed 40.

For example, let's say that you have two numbers, A and B. All ALUs can perform the following three basic comparison operations:

$A > B$ (Is A greater than B?)
$A = B$ (Is A equal to B?)
$A < B$ (Is A less than B?)

In addition, some ALUs can also perform these handy compound comparisons:

$A >= B$ (Is A greater than or equal to B?)
$A <= B$ (Is A less than or equal to B?)
$A <> B$ (Is A not equal to B?)

ALUs can also combine comparisons in various ways with other logical operations sometimes called **logical connectives.** There are two basic logical connectives: AND and OR. In addition, there is another essential logic operation that operates on only one number: NOT. These three logical operations are each formally defined by a **truth table,** (see Figure 3.4). Each truth table gives all of the possible results of applying these logic operations to binary inputs.

When put together with comparisons, logical connectives and NOT can be used to create **logical expressions.** For example, a payroll program might have the logical expression:

$(A > 40)$ AND $(A < 80)$

Here A stands for the number of hours an employee worked in a week. This logical expression might be used as follows to determine the overtime pay rate:

If hours worked is GREATER THAN 40 AND hours worked is LESS THAN 80, then overtime pay rate equals 1.5 times regular pay rate.

How can the ALU work with logical expressions such as this when we've said that it can only deal with numbers? Obviously, the inputs and outputs of logical expressions must be symbolized by numbers. The answer "TRUE" or "YES" is symbolized

Figure 3.4 Truth Tables for AND, OR, and NOT

Given binary inputs, all of the possible outcomes of the logical operations AND, OR, and NOT are defined by these three truth tables.

AND

A	B	A AND B
0 (false)	0 (false)	0 (false)
0 (false)	1 (true)	0 (false)
1 (true)	0 (false)	0 (false)
1 (true)	1 (true)	1 (true)

OR

A	B	A OR B
0 (false)	0 (false)	0 (false)
0 (false)	1 (true)	1 (true)
1 (true)	0 (false)	1 (true)
1 (true)	1 (true)	1 (true)

NOT

A	NOT A
0 (false)	1 (true)
1 (true)	0 (false)

by 1 and "FALSE" or "NO" is represented by 0. Interestingly, by choosing 1 to represent TRUE and 0 to represent FALSE, the logical AND operation turns out to be the same as multiplication, and the logical OR operation is the same as taking the maximum value of two expressions.

The Registers

High-speed storage locations inside the CPU

The ALU can only manipulate one or two inputs to produce an output. The CPU's **registers** are the special high-speed storage locations that temporarily hold inputs and outputs for the ALU. In addition, registers also hold program instructions and data merely being transferred from one place to another. Although registers are memory circuits, they are considered part of the CPU and *not* part of primary storage. Registers are much faster, but they also possess much less capacity than primary storage. Most CPUs possess several different types of registers, including:

- **Accumulator.** Sometimes considered part of the ALU, this register is primarily used to hold the results of ALU computations and logic operations. Some CPUs have more than one accumulator, while others have no particular register designated as the accumulator.
- **Data register.** One or more of these registers is used to hold data just transferred to or from primary storage.
- **Address register.** One or more of these registers indicates the location of data to be stored or retrieved from primary storage.
- **Program counter.** This register always holds the primary storage address of the next instruction to be executed. It is sometimes considered to be part of the control unit.
- **Instruction register.** This register holds the instruction that is about to be executed. Like the program counter, the instruction register is sometimes considered to be part of the control unit.
- **Status register.** This register contains individual bits, called **flags,** that signal the results of logic operations or indicate other computer conditions.
- **General-purpose registers.** These registers can be used by programmers to store data, memory addresses, intermediate results, and sometimes even instructions.

Some CPUs actually contain only a few of these registers. Other CPUs have even more types of registers. The arrangement of a CPU's registers in relation to its ALU and control unit is often referred to as its **architecture.** Figure 3.5, for example, depicts the architecture of a simple accumulator-based CPU. Although this figure is an oversimplification of most contemporary CPUs, it does represent the architecture proposed by von Neumann and his colleagues for the IAS computer. Most CPUs designed since then have been based, at least in part, on this classic architecture. As you can see, the accumulator is considered to be part of the ALU, and the program counter and instruction register belong to the control unit. The lines and arrows indicate the flow of instructions, data, primary storage addresses, and control signals between the various components.

Finally, you should see that an important aspect of a CPU's architecture is the size of its registers. The size of a CPU's registers basically defines its word length. Consequently, register size is also given in bits, with the most common sizes being

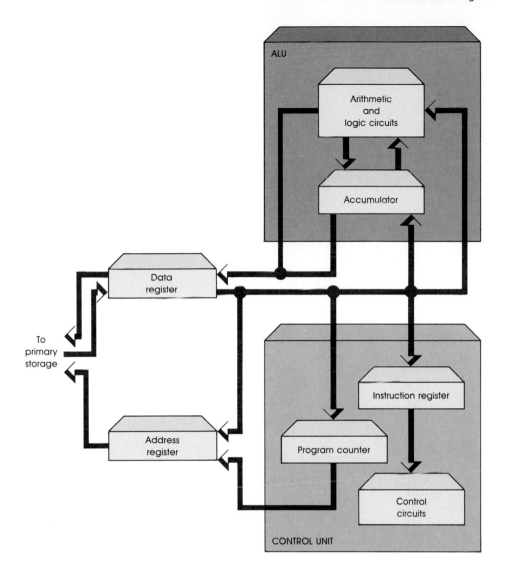

Figure 3.5 CPU Architecture
The relationship between the components of a simple accumulator-based CPU are shown here. This architecture represents the classical von Neumann machine and has been the basis, at least in part, for most CPUs designed after the original IAS computer (see Chapter 2).

8, 16, 32, 64, and 128 bits. Figure 3.6, for example, depicts the registers of the Motorola 68000 microprocessor, the CPU used in low-end Apple Macintoshes and several other microcomputers and workstations. Except for the 8-bit status register, all of the other registers in this CPU are 32 bits long.

The Control Unit

The **control unit** directs the operation of the CPU by interpreting program instructions, telling the ALU to carry out those instructions, and communicating with primary storage and input and output device controllers. In other words, the control unit is a collection of circuits that orchestrates the functioning of all the computer system's components. Based on program instructions it takes from primary storage, the control unit causes data to be transmitted back and forth between the

Coordinating the entire system

Figure 3.6 Motorola 68000 CPU Registers

The Motorola 68000 microprocessor is the CPU used in several popular microcomputers, including the low-end Apple Macintoshes. This figure depicts the registers of the 68000 chip from the programmer's point of view. Each little box represents one bit. As you can see, bits in registers are customarily numbered from right to left, starting with zero. Except for the status register, all of the registers are 32 bits long.

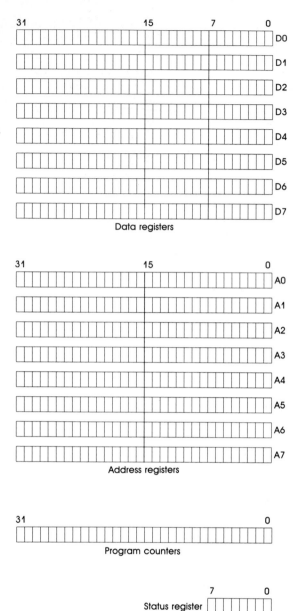

ALU, registers, primary storage, and input/output devices, and it tells the ALU what operations are to be performed. The control unit is the part of a computer system that makes it a system; like the captain of a drill team, it gets a collection of individual components to perform their various roles in a precise and constructive way.

PRIMARY STORAGE

Short-term memory for programs and data

Primary storage, also called **main memory,** is where input, program instructions, intermediate calculations, and output are held just before or just after they are processed by the CPU. Main memory locations differ from registers in that they are separate from the CPU, slower, and much more numerous. Registers, for example, can hold at most a few dozen numbers. Memory, on the other hand, can hold hundreds of thousands, millions, or even billions of numbers in some computer systems. It is important to realize that primary storage holds programs and data only temporarily. As we will discuss in Chapter 5, **secondary storage** is where programs and data are kept permanently or semipermanently, usually on some form of disk or tape. Secondary storage is generally slower, but has a much greater capacity than primary storage.

The Two Basic Functions of Primary Storage

One basic function of primary storage is to hold the program that is being executed. In Chapter 2 we emphasized the importance of the idea that computer instructions, which describe actions to be carried out by the computer, could be represented numerically. This means that a program, which is nothing more than a sequence of instructions, is handled as a list of numbers that can be held in primary storage just as if it were a list of prices or any other data. The instructions, of course, are used by the computer much differently than data are used: the instructions determine what the computer does with data to produce the desired results. (We will look at instructions in more detail later.)

Holding programs and holding data

The other basic function of primary storage is to hold the data that are required by the program being executed. In an extensive calculation, the results of carrying out the instructions using the input data are usually twofold: there are some intermediate results, which are used in subsequent calculations; and there are final results, which are to be presented as output. Primary storage thus includes working storage (space to hold the intermediate results) as well as space for input data and the final results (see Figure 3.7).

The Logical Structure of Primary Storage

Figure 3.8 illustrates the relationship of primary storage to the other storage components in a computer system. There are several factors to consider in understanding the logical structure of primary storage: its capacity, the fact that it is random access, and its volatility.

Memory capacity, access methods, and transient chips

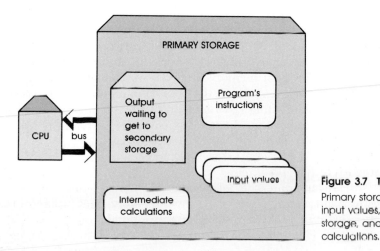

Figure 3.7 The Functions of Primary Storage
Primary storage is used to hold instructions, input values, output destined to secondary storage, and the values from intermediate calculations.

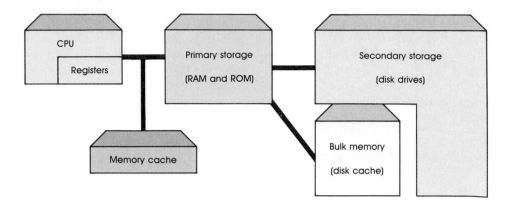

Capacity of Primary Storage

At any given time, several programs and their data may be in secondary storage awaiting the availability of the CPU and space in primary storage. One feature of primary storage that distinguishes it from secondary storage is that its contents can be transmitted very rapidly to the CPU for processing. Also, its physical size is relatively small compared to that of secondary storage since it must be both close to the CPU and built out of fast (and therefore expensive) memory chips. For these reasons, the overall capacity of primary storage remains limited compared to the slower, less expensive, and physically larger secondary storage.

As we've implied, the capacity of primary storage is always a major concern. In most computers, the amount of primary storage to some extent determines which programs can be run. Large, complex, and powerful programs generally require more primary storage than smaller programs. Sometimes, the amount of primary storage also affects the quantity of data that can be processed. At the very least, less primary storage means that a program will have to access the slower, but higher-capacity, secondary storage more frequently, resulting in slower data processing. Finally, the capacity of primary storage is especially important in computer systems that run multiple programs or serve multiple users at the same time, since each program or user must be allocated some memory. In these systems, less primary storage means fewer programs or users can be handled at the same time.

For a variety of historical reasons, the number 1,024, or 2^{10} (as shown in Figure 3.3), has become the basic measure of memory size. The total size of some early computer memories, it later made up the number of bits on a single LSI (Large-Scale Integration) memory chip. Nowadays the memory size 1,024 bytes is somewhat imprecisely called 1K or one **kilobyte** (*kilo* means thousand). For example, 64K bytes of memory does not mean 64,000 bytes, but rather 64 times 1,024 or 65,536 bytes. This is the number of different bytes that can be specified by a memory address that is 16 bits long ($2^{16} = 65,536$ different addresses).

As we discussed in Chapter 2, the entire history of the computer industry has been characterized by constantly increasing memory capacities. With the transition from LSI to VLSI (Very Large-Scale Integration) has come the need for the unit **megabyte** (the prefix *mega* stands for million). One megabyte is equal to 2^{20} or 1,048,576 and represents the number of different bytes that can be accessed with a 20-bit address. Nowadays, even larger memory capacities must often be described. One **gigabyte** (*giga* means billion) corresponds to a 30-bit address space, and a

terabyte (*tera* means trillion) refers to a 40-bit address space. These prefixes are summarized in Figure 3.9. At the end of this chapter, we will discuss the typical primary storage capacities found in today's microcomputers, workstations, minicomputers, mainframes, and supercomputers.

Random Versus Sequential Access

An important characteristic of primary storage is that it takes the same amount of time to retrieve a byte from any location. Since any randomly selected location in primary storage can be accessed in the same amount of time, this feature is known as **random access memory (RAM)**. In contrast, **sequential access** is characteristic of some secondary storage media such as magnetic tape, which we will discuss in Chapter 5. The time required to retrieve data from a tape clearly depends on the location of that data, since it takes time for the tape to be physically rewound or advanced to the proper position. Figure 3.10 illustrates this critical distinction between random and sequential access.

Volatility

In most computers, the majority of primary storage can hold its contents only as long as the computer is turned on. In other words, most RAM chips are *volatile*. Removing the electrical power from these chips for as little as one hundreth of a second will cause all of their memory locations to be erased. The most commonly used chips, **dynamic random access memory (DRAM)** chips, must be periodically refreshed with additional boosts of electricity. Another type of chip, the **static random access memory (SRAM)** chip, must be constantly supplied with a tiny electrical charge. Although SRAM chips require simpler support circuitry and work somewhat faster in a computer system, they are also more expensive and have less capacity than comparable DRAM chips. While both of these types of RAM chips are volatile, some computers can be equipped with a battery backup system to keep the data in primary storage intact for hours, days, or even longer.

In contrast, secondary storage mainly uses magnetic and optical media to store data. Unlike volatile memory chips, these media can indefinitely hold data intact, without the need for constant or periodic electrical power.

Communicating with Primary Storage

Before leaving the subject of primary storage, let's examine how it interacts with both secondary storage and the CPU, paying close attention to techniques used to make primary storage operate more efficiently in many of today's computers.

Unit Prefix	Traditional Meaning	Computerese
kilo	1,000	$1,024 = 2^{10}$
mega	1,000,000	$1,048,576 = 2^{20}$
giga	1,000,000,000	$1,073,741,824 = 2^{30}$
tera	1,000,000,000,000	$1,099,511,627,776 = 2^{40}$

Figure 3.9 Prefixes for Units Used with Computers
This table summarizes a few of the prefixes used for specifying computer storage capacities.

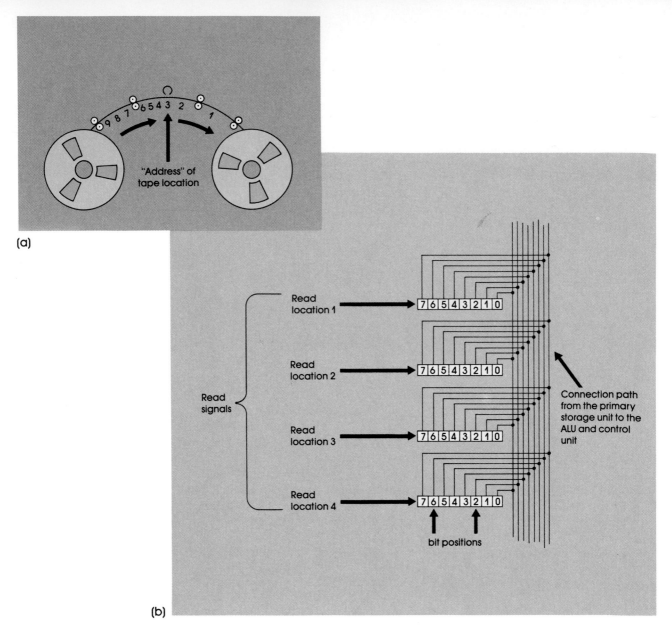

(a)

(b)

Figure 3.10 Sequential Versus Random Access

(a) The information at location 3 on the tape is available immediately, since it is directly beneath the place where data can be read. The data at location 9 will have to be brought into proper position before it can be accessed. Data on a typical magnetic tape can take many seconds (even minutes, depending on where on the tape it is) to reach the position where it can be accessed—virtually an eternity of computer-measured time. (b) Each of the locations in the primary storage unit (four 8-bit locations are shown here) has its own, independent connection to the bus (the pathway that connects primary storage to the ALU and the control unit). The data item in any randomly selected location is available in the same amount of time as the data in any other location.

Communication Between Primary and Secondary Storage

For the entire computer system to operate most efficiently, all of its parts must work at or near their maximum speeds. But, as we've seen, different subsystems often work at different speeds. Although it has much less capacity, primary storage operates much more rapidly than secondary storage does—typically more than 1,000 times as fast. Avoiding delays while transferring programs and data between primary and secondary storage remains a problem. These delays can significantly slow overall computer performance because the CPU depends on primary storage for both programs and data.

Part of the solution involves minimizing the frequency and maximizing the efficiency of communication between primary and secondary storage. Complex programs monitor the operation of the computer system and ensure that programs and data are loaded into primary storage as they are needed and in a sequence that permits efficient operation. For example, if a program loaded from secondary into primary storage is to perform operations on certain data, then those data are also loaded at the same time.

Another part of the solution is to use existing or additional hardware cleverly to reduce delays when transferring programs and data between primary and secondary storage. A type of memory with a size and an access speed that are between those of primary and secondary storage, called **bulk memory,** is sometimes used. One specific example of bulk memory is the **disk cache.** This is an area of primary storage or some additional memory set aside for temporarily holding data from a disk drive. In Figure 3.8, bulk memory is positioned between secondary and primary storage. Blocks of data, often several kilobytes in length, are transferred between primary storage and the disk cache. The overall computer system is controlled by software in such a way that when necessary program instructions or data are not already in primary storage, they are usually held in the disk cache. This eliminates idle periods for primary storage, which would have to wait while data are transferred from secondary storage. On some machines data transfers between the disk cache and primary storage are performed during periods when the CPU is busy with another task and is not accessing primary storage. Because the memory chips used in the disk cache are much faster than even the fastest disk drive, the overall performance of the system is significantly improved.

Bulk and cache memory

Communication Between the CPU and Primary Storage

Just as a disk cache mediates between primary and secondary storage, a **memory cache** is sometimes used to bridge the gap between primary storage and the faster circuits in the CPU. A memory cache works by watching and remembering which memory locations the CPU has been using most frequently (see Figure 3.8). When the CPU reads a primary storage location, the memory cache holds on to that value. Then, at a later time, if the CPU again asks for the contents of that same location, the memory cache circuitry quickly supplies the answer without tying up (or waiting for) primary storage. A well-designed memory cache system can intercept primary storage requests over 90% of the time. This allows a faster CPU to be used more efficiently with slower primary storage.

A good example of a memory cache system can be found in the Compaq Deskpro 386/20 microcomputer. In this machine, the Intel 80386 CPU gets its program instructions and data from a small (32 kilobyte) area of very high-speed SRAM. For example, a number can be retrieved from this memory cache in approximately 35 **nanoseconds** (35 billionths of a second). As long as the requested data item is in the memory cache (a condition known as a *hit*), the CPU gets it very quickly without having to wait. If, on the other hand, the data item is not currently in the memory cache (called a *miss*), then the CPU must wait while the item is retrieved from the slower (100 nanoseconds) DRAM chips that comprise the bulk of primary storage. Although primary storage is slower than the memory cache, it has a much greater capacity (from 1 to 16 megabytes). Compaq claims that this memory caching system has a hit rate of 95 percent, thus significantly improving computer performance.

Disk and memory caching schemes are both examples of **buffer storage:** units inserted between two different forms of storage in order to synchronize their activities and make them operate more efficiently.

RAM, ROM, PROM, EPROM, and EEPROM

Understanding the memory acronyms

It's almost impossible to read about computers without eventually encountering at least some of these acronyms. Unfortunately, they are sometimes a source of confusion. We've already discussed RAM, which stands for random access memory. Although virtually all memory chips used today are truly random access memories, the term RAM has come to mean a type of chip that can both store and retrieve data, over and over again. This is especially true in the context of microcomputers. A RAM chip is one that you can write data to and read data from as many times as you like. For this reason, most of a computer's primary storage is made up of some kind of RAM chips, allowing you to load your own programs and data. This type of storage is also called *read/write memory.*

Read-only memory (ROM), on the other hand, is also quite different. Although a ROM chip is a random access device, it is loaded only once, at the factory. After a ROM chip has been manufactured, the programs and data stored on it can only be retrieved. In other words, the contents of a ROM chip can *never* be altered. Furthermore, unlike a RAM chip, a ROM chip is nonvolatile and thus keeps its contents intact even when the electrical power is shut off. While ROM chips are also used as part of primary storage in most computers, they have a very limited function. They generally hold certain critical operating system programs and data that will never change. For example, the operating system routine that determines which key you've pressed and displays the appropriate character on the screen is usually kept in ROM. Similarly, the patterns that make up the characters that are drawn on the screen are also stored in ROM. In most computers, fundamental programs and data such as these are permanently held in the ROM chips that make up a relatively small part of primary storage.

PROMs, EPROMs, and EEPROMs are all special types of ROMs. The contents of a basic ROM are loaded by the manufacturer and are thereafter essentially unalterable. In contrast, the user may initially load the contents of a **programmable read-only memory (PROM)** with a special tool called a *PROM burner.* Ordinary ROMs that must be loaded by the manufacturer are generally prohibitively expensive unless they are ordered in lots of 10,000 or more. PROM chips allow hardware designers and research scientists to avoid this expense and circumvent the long delays usually associated with ordering preloaded ROMs from manufacturers.

Since the programs and data stored in ROM chips are often complex, programming errors of some kind are possible, and in fact, are quite likely to occur. For this reason, **erasable programmable read-only memory (EPROM)** and **electrically erasable programmable read-only memory (EEPROM)** chips were developed. Their contents can be completely erased and then new programs and data can be written that correct the errors. The EPROM can only be erased by exposing the chip to a strong ultraviolet light for several minutes. Such alterations can't be done while an EPROM chip is still inside the computer, so under normal circumstances the EPROM chip remains securely nonvolatile. As can be seen in Figure 3.11 the erasing light enters through a window in the top of the chip. Even though this reprogramming process is time-consuming, it's certainly more cost-efficient than programming a new PROM and discarding the old one.

Unlike an EPROM chip, an EEPROM chip can be erased with an electrical charge while it is still in the computer. There is a limit, however, to the number of times that an EEPROM can be erased.

THE BUS

The **bus** is a set of wires and connectors that link the CPU to primary storage (see Figure 3.2). It is also the pathway that data and information travel between memory and various input, output, and secondary storage device controllers. The bus gives a computer flexibility to expand memory, accommodate alternate input, output, and secondary storage devices, and add interfaces to control and interact with other machines.

Connecting the internal computer components

Bus Structure

The group of wires that make up a bus is generally divided into three subgroups: address lines, data lines, and control lines. Address lines carry signals indicating which memory locations are to be read from or written to. Figure 3.12 shows how address lines can select between different memory banks. Data lines carry instructions and data to and from primary memory. Control lines convey directives such as which operation (read or write) is to be performed in memory. Other subsystems connect the bus to controllers for input, output, and secondary storage devices.

Address, data, and control lines

The number of address lines in a bus determines how much primary memory a computer can address. A machine with 24 address lines, such as a microcomputer that uses the Intel 80286 microprocessor, theoretically can access up to 16 megabytes of memory. The number of data lines available determines how fast data can

Figure 3.11 An Erasable Programmable Read-Only Memory

The contents of this type of PROM chip can be erased by shining ultraviolet light through the window on top.

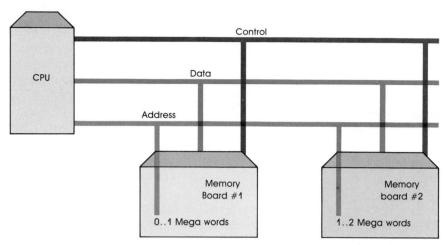

Figure 3.12 The Bus
The bus carries all the information necessary for the CPU to exchange data with other computer components. The two memory boards shown here compare values found on the address bus to values set by configuration switches to determine which one should respond and send back data.

be transferred between primary storage and the CPU. Simple microprocessors, such as the Intel 8088 used in the original IBM Personal Computer, have only 8 data lines. If the program calls for reading a 32-bit value from memory then four separate transactions will be needed. Higher performance systems use 16 to 32 data lines, and mainframes and supercomputers use 64, 128, or more data lines.

The System Clock

Synchronizing computer components

Directly connected to the CPU and also tied into the control lines of the bus is an essential component of any computer known as the **system clock.** This clock consists of a chip containing a crystal that vibrates, or *ticks*, at a certain frequency, typically several million times per second. It serves the function of synchronizing the operation of many computer components. In some respects, the system clock acts like a musician's metronome by pacing the work of the CPU and the devices connected to it over the bus.

The speed of the system clock helps determine how fast a computer can execute instructions. This speed is gauged by the number of ticks or **clock cycles** per second and is usually expressed in a unit of frequency measure known as the *hertz*. One hertz (Hz) equals one cycle per second. Since most system clocks tick several million times per second, their speeds are usually given in **megahertz.** One megahertz (MHz) equals one million clock cycles per second. Today's computers exhibit a wide range of clock rates. For example, the system clocks in many low-end microcomputers such as the original IBM Personal Computer operate at a leisurely 4.77 MHz, while those in high-end machines such as the IBM Personal System/2 Model 70 can run as fast as 25 MHz.

Examples of Buses

In many microcomputers, the bus is accessible through a series of connectors, or *expansion slots*, that accept plug-in circuit boards with extra components. The IBM Personal System/2 microcomputers, for example, have expansion slots that allow users to add boards containing additional disk controllers, more memory, interfaces to printers or boards controlling color graphics monitors, modems, and other optional hardware devices.

As we have said, on most microcomputers the CPU, memory, bus, and other vital components are collected together on a single large circuit board called the motherboard or system board. Several different bus designs are used in today's microcomputer system boards. Two of the newest and most advanced bus designs are the Micro Channel Architecture bus of the high-end IBM Personal System/2 microcomputers and the NuBus architecture used in the Apple Macintosh II.

Micro Channel and NuBus architectures

In contrast with microcomputers, larger systems, from minicomputers to supercomputers, generally implement the bus as a separate entity called a **back plane.** Computers with a back plane bus can usually be configured with different types of processors but identical memory and device controllers. Consequently, low-end back plane machines can be upgraded easily to create much more powerful systems.

HOW PROGRAMS ARE EXECUTED

Now that we've discussed the key components inside a computer's system unit, let's see how they work together to carry out program instructions. We know that a program and its data must be loaded into primary storage in order to be executed. We also know that the sequence of operations listed in the program is carried out on the specified data in the ALU. Let's trace the steps in the execution of a simple ADD operation, assuming that the instruction and data that make up this operation are already in primary storage. As Figure 3.13 shows, there are two major phases to the process of carrying out a computer instruction: the fetch cycle and the execution cycle. Together, these are called the **machine cycle.**

The machine cycle

The Fetch Cycle

To be executed, an instruction must first be retrieved or *fetched* from primary storage. You will recall that the *program counter* is a special register in the CPU that always holds the address of the next instruction to be executed. The control unit uses the address in the program counter to locate and copy the next instruction from memory into the instruction register. This is the first step of the **fetch cycle,** shown in Figure 3.13.

Retrieving and decoding the instruction

The second step of the fetch cycle determines what instruction is being requested. This is known as *decoding* the instruction. All computer instructions have one or more parts. The first part is a code number that specifies the **operation** to be performed. Computer programmers call this part the **op-code,** and each instruction that can be performed by a particular computer has a different op-code. All of the op-codes of a computer make up its **instruction set.** In the decoding

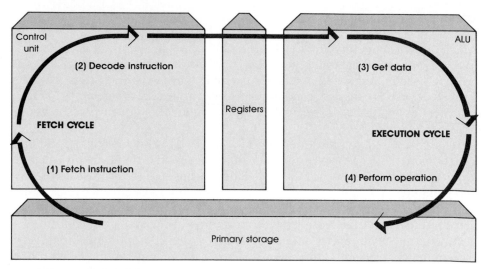

Figure 3.13 The Machine Cycle
The machine cycle is the process by which a computer completes a program instruction. This cycle can be broken down into two phases. The fetch cycle consists of retrieving the next instruction from primary memory and decoding it. The execution cycle consists of retrieving any necessary data from registers or memory and actually completing the arithmetic or logic operation.

procedure, the control unit looks up the op-code in special type of ROM known as the **operation decoder.** Once the op-code has been decoded, the control unit can then call for the retrieval of any needed additional data and direct the ALU to perform the operation.

Depending on the operation being requested, the instruction can have other parts that specify the location of data and the destination for the results. These other parts of the instruction are called **operands.** Figure 3.14 depicts our two-operand instruction, which will ADD the contents of memory location 37 with the contents of register number three.

Operands are needed only when an instruction has to make a choice about where to get data or where to place results. Consequently, the two most frequently used types of operands are memory addresses, which uniquely identify memory locations, and register numbers, which uniquely identify CPU registers. Some machines have been built with very complex instructions that require five or more operands; at the other extreme are machines in which most instructions have no operands. Input data and output results are sent to a central data structure called a **stack.** One can envision a stack as a deck of cards. Reading input corresponds to taking cards from the top of the deck; writing a result is like placing a fresh card on top of the deck.

The Execution Cycle

Retrieving the data and completing the operation

In our example, the instruction stored in binary form at memory location 17 is ADD 37,r3, which means add the value at memory location 37 to the number currently in register three. Once this instruction has been retrieved and decoded during the fetch cycle, it can then be actually carried out in the **execution cycle.**

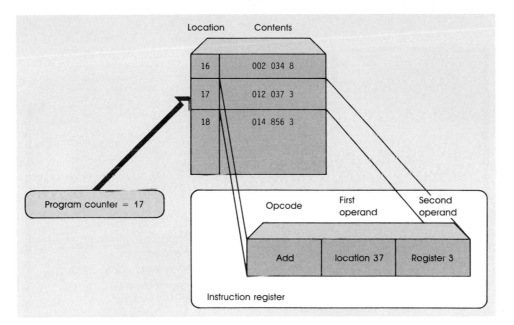

Figure 3.14 Op-codes and Operands
The primary storage address of the next instruction to be executed is always in the program counter register. The first step in executing an instruction is transferring the value at that address into the instruction register. A computer instruction is made up of an operation code and possibly one or more operands. This particular ADD instruction has two operands, the register containing one addend, and the address of the memory location that contains the other addend.

The first step of the execution cycle is to get the necessary data from memory. The address 37 is transmitted on the address bus to primary storage, accompanied by a *read* signal from the control unit. This read signal informs the primary storage unit to send the value held at address 37 to the ALU for processing.

During the next step of the execution cycle, the control unit sends another signal to the ALU informing it to do an ADD operation with value it will receive next from primary storage. One register, in this case register three, is selected from the register bank and its value is also sent to the ALU. When the ALU has received both the word stored at address 37 and the current contents of register three it adds them together and transmits the result to back that register (see Figure 3.15).

As you can see, several steps make up the machine cycle of even a simple instruction such as this ADD operation. In other words, a machine cycle instruction is typically comprised of several subinstructions called **microinstructions.** Taken together, the microinstructions that make up a computer's instruction set are called its **microcode.** Each microinstruction requires at least one system clock cycle to complete. Therefore, in most computers, the majority of CPU instructions take several clock cycles to finish.

The Program Counter and Branching

In our description of the execution of an instruction, we began by assuming that the instruction was stored at the memory location identified by address 17 and was transmitted to the control unit when it was time for it to be executed. In fact, in

Incrementing versus loading the address of the next instruction

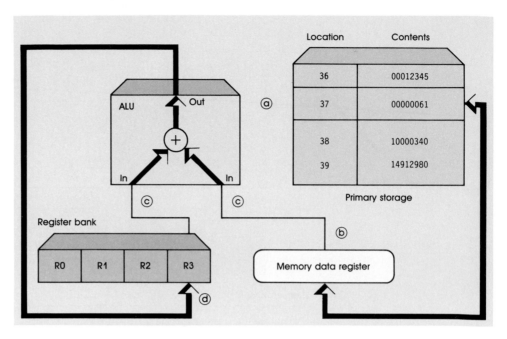

Figure 3.15 Executing an Instruction

(a) The control unit schedules a read operation from memory location 37. (b) The result is placed in the memory data register. (c) The values in register 3 and the memory data register are sent to the ALU along with a command to perform an addition. (d) The resulting value is written back into register 3.

addition to controlling the execution of each instruction, the control unit also determines the sequence in which the instructions are executed.

Recall that the program counter contains the address of the instruction that is about to be executed. Returning to our earlier example, let's assume the program counter contains 17. This causes the instruction stored in the primary storage unit at the memory location with address 17 to be transmitted to the instruction register for execution.

When writing a program, consecutive addresses are assigned automatically to each successive instruction. The instructions are executed sequentially, in the order of their assigned addresses. That is, execution of program starts with the address of its first instruction in the program counter. After that instruction has been executed, the instruction at the next consecutive address (obtained by adding 1 to the contents of the program counter) is executed, and so on, until all of the program's instructions have been executed.

If computers were limited to executing instructions in a single, fixed sequence, their applications would be few and uninteresting. Computers, however, can be programmed to use input data or calculated results to determine which of several alternative paths to take. For example, consider a computer program to handle a company's payroll. If an employee has worked more than 40 hours in a week, they are entitled to overtime pay. The program that calculates paychecks must alter the normal sequence of instructions to handle this exceptional condition. In other words, the payroll program would have to **branch** to an alternate instruction. At the machine level, this is accomplished by having the program load the program counter with the address of the alternate instruction, instead of merely *incrementing* (increasing) the contents of the program counter by a fixed number. Figure 3.16 shows how the result of a comparison operation can be used to change the contents of the program counter, and hence alter the normal sequential execution of instructions stored successively in memory. Few really useful programs could be written without this ability to go through different sequences of instructions (or *branches*) based on the values of input data or calculation results.

Further details of how branching is actually accomplished in computer programming are discussed in Chapters 7 and 8. For today's programmers, advanced programming languages eliminate the need to be concerned with the numerical contents of the program counter. The notion of branching, however, remains one of the most important concepts in understanding how computers process data.

COMPUTER TYPES REVISITED

In Chapter 1, we classified computer systems according to size, price range, and function. Now we can elaborate on those classifications in a much more meaningful way—based on the speed and capacity of the computer and the types of functional units that make up the computer. Here, it is primarily CPU architecture that establishes a system's place in the classification. Note that these classifications are not static. The size and cost of electronic components may continue to decrease, so that today's mini becomes tomorrow's micro, and so on.

Comparing speed, capacity, and structure

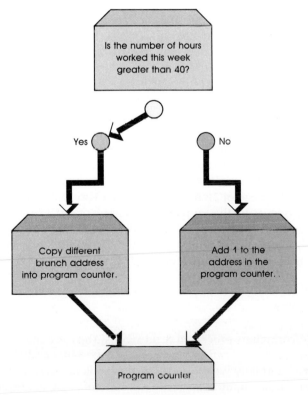

Figure 3.16 The Program Counter and Branching

The result of a comparison instruction, such as this one which might be found in a payroll program, is used to determine whether to increment the program counter by one (the normal case) or to load in an entirely new branch address from another source.

Microcomputers

Word lengths of 8, 16, or 32 bits and megabytes of memory

The first microcomputers handled 4-bit words, but this word length soon grew to 8 bits and 16 bits. Most top-of-the-line microprocessors, such as the Motorola MC68030 and the Intel 80386, handle 32-bit words. Memory capacities of microcomputers range in size from 100 kilobytes up to 16 megabytes, and their memory access times are about 100 nanoseconds, a ten millionth of a second. Most microcomputers can be equipped with a disk cache, forged out of a portion of primary memory. Many high-end models incorporate an SRAM memory cache as well.

The types of peripheral equipment available for microcomputer systems are multiplying rapidly, but their sophistication is limited by the relatively simple architecture of microprocessors. In general these machines are characterized by an emphasis on cost reduction. The simplest, slowest, least expensive hardware is brought together to make a system suited to mass production. Successful microprocessor systems sell millions of machines.

Workstations

Increased emphasis on performance and graphics, and the use of RISC architecture

Like microcomputers, workstations are computers that are designed to be used by a single person. They offer high performance as a distinguishing characteristic. These machines can rapidly display complex graphical images on screens where 1 million pixels (dots on the screen) represents a minimum capability. Several megabytes of primary storage are typically available, and secondary storage is usually measured in hundreds of megabytes.

Many workstations produced today incorporate a relatively new type of CPU architecture known as **reduced instruction set computer (RISC)** technology. A RISC CPU keeps the number of fundamental instructions that can be performed to a minimum—often around 120 or so, which is less than half that of a traditional or **CISC (complex instruction set computer)** CPU with comparable capabilities. But even more noteworthy than the reduced instruction set, RISC CPUs execute most of their instructions in a single clock cycle. This is in marked contrast to most CPUs that require several clock cycles for the majority of instructions. Consequently, even though RISC CPUs may require more complex machine-level programming, they generally result in faster overall program execution.

One example of a RISC workstation is the IBM RT PC. This computer is based on a proprietary 32-bit microprocessor that has only 118 different instructions, 84 of which execute in a single clock cycle. This efficient RISC design, coupled with the RT PC's clock speed of 22 MHz, results in a very fast computer. Although there is some controversy in the computer industry over the relative merits of RISC versus CISC architecture, the RISC philosophy of optimizing the instruction set has profoundly influenced many modern CPUs, including those used in minicomputers, mainframes, and even supercomputers.

Minicomputers

Scaled-down versions of mainframes

The first minicomputers processed 8-bit words; the most advanced minicomputers today, the so-called *superminis*, such as the Vax 8840 and the Gould NP1, have hardware that normally works with 32-bit words but can do some operations on 64-bit words. Minicomputers typically have memory capacities of up to 128 megabytes, and those that use sizable memory caches can maintain average access times of 50 nanoseconds.

A wide range of conventional peripheral equipment is available for minicomputers. Also available is a large assortment of special peripheral devices that facilitate the incorporation of minicomputers into automatic monitoring and control systems. These minicomputers are often shared by a group of individuals.

Mainframes

The word length used by mainframes usually ranges from 32 to 64 bits. Extremely fast CPUs are standard equipment in mainframes. Many of these machines excel in the areas of managing large secondary storage and data communication systems. Well-developed business software makes these machines attractive for satisfying the data processing needs of an entire company. The IBM 3090 VF is an example of a recently introduced mainframe.

The workhorses of the computer industry

By incorporating large memory caches, mainframes routinely achieve primary storage access times of 15 nanoseconds. Many have memory capacities in excess of 128 megabytes. Their architectural features include the ability to attach from two to four ALUs and main control units to the same primary memory, with hardware and software features that keep them all working productively. The peripheral equipment available for mainframes is virtually endless, as we will see in later chapters.

Supercomputers

A word length of 64 bits is the standard for supercomputers, the fastest of all computers. They can also handle 128-bit words, but at reduced speed.

The fastest of the fast

Today, the fastest U.S.-built supercomputer is the Cray Y-MP. Under ideal conditions, with its eight processors working together, the Y-MP can perform from two billion to four billion arithmetic operations per second. Using cache memories, supercomputers such as this can typically achieve primary storage access times of less than 10 nanoseconds.

Supercomputers often have multiple ALUs and separate specialized units that work simultaneously to perform the different arithmetic operations. In comparison with other types of computers, however, supercomputers tend to have more primitive operating systems, fewer programming languages from which to choose, and very few off-the-shelf application packages.

Summary

The Computer Revealed

A typical microcomputer, the IBM PS/2 Model 50, has these components inside its system unit: chassis, motherboard, memory, power supply, expansion slots, device controllers, and disk drives.

The Language of Computers

The vast majority of computers use the binary number system.

Coding Systems   Textual data is processed in a computer by associating each character with a separate number. The two most prevalent schemes are ASCII and EBCDIC.

Bits, Bytes, and Words   A bit is a 0 or 1. A byte is a group of 8 bits. A word is a group of adjacent bits generally manipulated and stored as a unit.

The Central Processing Unit

In a microcomputer, the CPU is a single microprocessor chip. In larger computers, it may be composed of several distinct parts. Conceptually, the CPU is made up of the ALU, registers, and the control unit.

The Arithmetic and Logic Unit   This part performs mathematical calculations, such as addition, subtraction, multiplication, and division. The ALU also does logical comparisons, such as $>$, $<$, $=$, as well as AND, OR, and NOT operations.

The Registers   These special high-speed storage locations inside the CPU include the accumulator, data register, address register, program counter, instruction register, status registers, and general-purpose registers.

The Control Unit   This unit directs the operation of the CPU by interpreting instructions, telling the ALU what to do, and communicating with other computer components.

Primary Storage

Main memory is where input, program instructions, intermediate results, and output are temporarily held.

The Two Basic Functions of Primary Storage   Primary storage holds programs and holds data.

The Logical Structure of Primary Storage   The capacity of primary storage is measured in kilobytes, megabytes, gigabytes, or terabytes. Primary storage is random access rather than sequential access, and it is volatile in the sense that it loses its contents when the power is turned off.

Communicating with Primary Storage   Additional hardware in the form of bulk memory (such as a disk cache) is sometimes used to increase the efficiency of communication between primary and secondary storage. Similarly, a memory cache is sometimes used to increase the efficiency of communication between primary storage and the CPU registers.

RAM, ROM, PROM, EPROM, and EEPROM   The term RAM has come to mean read/write memory (all memory chips are really random access devices). ROM chips are written at the factory with programs and data and can only be read thereafter. PROM, EPROM, and EEPROM are various types of do-it-yourself ROMs.

The Bus

The bus is a group of wires that link the CPU to memory, and to various input, output, and secondary storage device controllers.

Bus Structure   A bus is made up of address lines, data lines, and control lines.

The System Clock   This vibrating chip synchronizes the operation of many computer components including the CPU. Clock speeds are usually measured in megahertz (MHz), or millions of cycles per second.

Examples of Buses   In many computers, the bus emerges from the motherboard in a series of expansion slots that can be used to add auxiliary components. Some computers employ a back plane instead of a motherboard.

How Programs Are Executed

Two major phases make up the machine cycle, during which a computer executes an instruction.

The Fetch Cycle   During this phase, the control unit fetches the next instruction from memory and decodes it.

The Execution Cycle   In this phase, any necessary data is obtained and the operation is actually completed by the ALU.

The Program Counter and Branching   The normal sequence of a program gets successive instructions from consecutive primary storage addresses by simply incrementing the program counter after each fetch. Branching allows the computer to deviate from this sequence by loading a completely new address into the program counter.

Computer Types Revisited

The various types of computers can be examined from the viewpoint of speed, capacity, and architecture.

Microcomputers   These machines generally have 8-, 16-, or 32-bit word lengths, up to 16 megabytes of memory, and memory access times of about 100 nanoseconds.

Workstations   These high performance graphics machines come with several megabytes of memory and often hundreds of megabytes of secondary storage. Many use reduced instruction set computer (RISC) architectures.

Minicomputers   Normally minicomputers handle 32-bit words, but some minicomputers can handle 64-bit operations. Memory capacities range up to 128 megabytes and access times average around 50 nanoseconds.

Mainframes   The word lengths used by mainframes range from 32 to 64 bits. Memory capacities often exceed 128 megabytes and access times of 15 nanoseconds are common. Many mainframes incorporate several ALUs and control units.

Supercomputers   A word length of 64 bits is standard for a supercomputer, but some supercomputers can handle 128-bit operations at reduced speed. These machines have multiple processors working together to achieve speeds of up to four billion arithmetic operations per second and can often access memory in 10 nanoseconds or less.

Computer Concepts

As an extra review of this chapter, try defining the following terms. If you have trouble with any of them, refer to the page number listed.

chassis 71
motherboard (system board) 71
power supply 71
expansion slot 73
expansion board (card, adapter) 73
device controller 73
hard disk drive 73
binary 74
American Standard Code for Information Interchange (ASCII) 75
Extended Binary Coded Decimal Interchange Code (EBCDIC) 75
byte 76
nibble (nybble) 76
word 76

address 76
arithmetic and logic unit (ALU) 76
arithmetic operations 76
logic operations 77
logical connectives 77
truth table 77
logical expressions 77
registers 78
accumulator 78
data register 78
address register 78
program counter 78
instruction register 78
status register 78
flags 78
general-purpose registers 78
architecture 78

control unit 79
primary storage (main memory) 80
secondary storage 81
kilobyte (K) 82
megabyte 82
gigabyte 82
terabyte 83
random access memory (RAM) 83
sequential access 84
dynamic random access memory (DRAM) 84
static random access memory (SRAM) 84
bulk memory 85
disk cache 85
memory cache 85
nanoseconds 85

buffer storage *86*
read-only memory (ROM)
  86
programmable read-only
  memory (PROM) *86*
erasable programmable
  read-only memory
  (EPROM) *86*
electrically erasable
  programmable read-only
  memory (EEPROM) *86*

bus *87*
system clock *88*
clock cycles *88*
megahertz (MHz) *88*
back plane *89*
machine cycle *89*
fetch cycle *89*
operation *89*
op-code *89*
instruction set *89*
operation decoder *90*

operands *90*
stack *90*
execution cycle *90*
microinstructions *91*
microcode *91*
branch *92*
reduced instruction set
  computer (RISC) *94*
complex instruction set
  computer (CISC) *94*

Review Questions

1. What are the major components of a typical microcomputer?
2. How does a hard disk drive differ from a floppy disk drive?
3. What is the difference between the binary and decimal systems?
4. What are the two dominant coding schemes used in the computer industry?
5. Describe the computer terms *byte*, *nibble*, and *word*.
6. Give three reasons why a larger computer word length usually means a more powerful computer.
7. What are the most common computer word lengths?
8. List the three major conceptual components of a central processing unit.
9. In the statement "If you have a bone and a carrot and some water, then you can make soup," what are the basic logical connectives?
10. What are the two basic functions of primary storage?
11. Why is the capacity of primary storage a major concern?
12. What units are used to express the memory size of primary storage?
13. What are the two most commonly used RAM chips?
14. What are some differences between a ROM and RAM chip?
15. Describe three special types of ROM variants and how they work.
16. What are the three subgroups of wires that make up a bus? What are their functions?
17. What is a system clock and what is its function?
18. What two elements make up the machine cycle?
19. What are the first and second steps in the fetch cycle? In the execution cycle?
20. How is branching accomplished at the machine level?

True or False

1. The chassis is the main circuit board of a computer.
2. Each memory location must be uniquely identified by an address.
3. The ALU can manipulate an unlimited number of inputs to produce an output.
4. Primary storage is also called main memory.
5. The contents of primary storage cannot be rapidly transferred to the CPU.
6. SRAM chips are faster and more expensive than DRAM chips.
7. A memory cache is sometimes used to bridge the gap between primary storage and the faster circuits in the CPU.
8. ROM chips usually make up the bulk of primary storage.
9. All of the op-codes of a computer make up its instruction set.
10. RISC CPUs are generally faster than CISC CPUs.

1. The ALU is part of the:
   (a) disk drive   (b) CPU   (c) register

2. The special high-speed storage locations that temporarily hold inputs and outputs for the ALU are:
   (a) truth tables   (b) logic units   (c) registers

3. Operation of the CPU is directed by:
   (a) the control unit   (b) primary storage (c) the instruction register

4. Primary storage includes space for input data, final results and:
   (a) working storage   (b) architecture   (c) bulk memory

5. Primary storage typically operates how many times faster than secondary storage?
   (a) 10   (b) 100   (c) 1000

6. Disk and memory caching schemes are both examples of
   (a) bus structures   (b) buffer storage (c) fetching cycles

7. The bus is a set of wires that link the CPU to:
   (a) truth tables   (b) registers   (c) primary storage

8. The microinstructions that make up the instructions of a computer are called its:
   (a) truth tables   (b) microcode   (c) stack

9. Minicomputers typically have memories of up to:
   (a) 128 megabytes   (b) 100 kilobytes (c) 256 bits

10. The standard word length for supercomputers is:
    (a) 16 bits   (b) 32 bits   (c) 64 bits

1. If you were shopping for a microcomputer, what questions would you want to ask about the CPU and memories of competing brands?
2. What questions would you ask about the other major components?

1. Discuss with the staff at your computer center the types of computers available to you and to other people on campus. What is the standard word length each type handles? Write a description of what is available and what tasks are carried out by each type.

2. Visit a local microcomputer service shop and ask if they will show you an uncovered computer. Find out what expansion slots are available with a few micros and what can be added to upgrade each; write a report on a variety of these micros.

3. Select a paragraph from a newspaper, magazine, or a text for another course that contains a discussion of several alternatives. Discuss sentences from the paragraph in terms of logical connectives and logical comparisons.

4. Some organizations provide every person in certain departments with a microcomputer, allowing those people to communicate with each other. Other departments may share a minicomputer through individual terminals. If your campus administration or your employer has such an arrangement, find out from the users how convenient each type is and do a report discussing the merits of each in a given office environment.

4

Input and Output

In This Chapter

High-Powered Graphics

At Martin-Marietta Aerospace in Denver, Colorado, the software engineering team uses several Apple Computer [Macintosh] systems for a variety of graphics tasks. According to departmental staff engineer Jerry Simonson, the graphics systems have paid off in a number of ways. Staff drawing time is reduced, illustrations are finding their way into more documents and presentations for improved communications, and there's a substantial cost savings. While software engineers aren't involved in the drafting work of mechanical or electrical engineers, they do use block diagrams and flowcharts to visualize the programs they're working on.

"Before we got the [Macintosh] systems," Simonson says, "we used to send out diagrams to the art department or do them on a big CAD/CAM [computer-assisted design/computer-assisted manufacture] system. We allocate our costs for expensive equipment to individual departments," he says, "and with our $500,000 CAD/CAM system, we figured flow dia-

grams were costing about $200 a page to produce."

With several software engineers doing flow diagrams constantly, the costs added up quickly. The introduction of [the new systems] into the department quickly converted the engineers from the CAD/CAM system. With the [systems] and an Apple printer, flow diagrams can be produced at a

fraction of the cost. Now that the . . . systems are available, some of the engineers haven't used the CAD/CAM system in months. Ease of use is an important feature that allows users of all levels to get up on the system quickly. "We had a new person," Simonson says, "and we showed him the . . . system on a Friday night. He came in and played with it on Saturday, and did 10 to 12 viewgraphs for a meeting on Tuesday."

In addition to block and flow diagrams that are photocopied for distribution or made into transparencies for overhead projection at meetings, the department also creates organizational charts and timelines. These documents are stored . . . and when changes are made, it's easy to recall the file and edit the chart. With the organizational charts, for example, individual boxes can simply be moved to new locations during a reorganization.

The power of graphics to make a point has been shown again and again in the department. "For example," Simonson says, "I was doing facilities planning for some of our software engineers. We wanted to partition everybody in their own space to give them more privacy. We were going back and forth with the facilities people about how big each space should be, and I finally sat down and drew the desk, table, and computer terminal in each module to scale so they could see how a 6' × 8' cubicle wasn't big enough. It was amazing how easily they could see the problem once I showed the graphic. Otherwise, I could have spent quite a few days or months arguing, and they probably would have gone ahead and committed to a smaller space."

This chapter deals with the devices and methods of interacting with computers—probably one of the most important concepts you'll come across in your study of computers. Input is the very foundation of the Information Age, of high tech, of Silicon Valley—of practically everything related to computers. Whether it's the Cray Y-MP, capable of carrying out nearly a billion operations per second, or a desktop microcomputer that processes words, a computer is just an expensive place to set your coffee cup unless someone makes it work. And if the necessary data aren't entered correctly, all of the computer's programmed wizardry may as well not exist.

INTERACTIVE SYSTEMS

This section focuses on the devices that humans use to interact with computers. Interaction means that the computer receives some sort of input and immediately generates a response. The response may be as simple as showing on the display screen the last key pressed or as complex as redrawing a three-dimensional model of next year's car.

Devices that allow humans to interact with computers

The phrase **computer terminal** stands for a wide variety of devices that collect input from a user, send the data to a computer, receive information from the computer, and generate a display of that information. (Chapter 6 will investigate the computer-to-terminal communication path.)

Computer Terminal Keyboards

Terminals have keyboards similiar to but more elaborate than those of an ordinary electric typewriter. In addition to the standard roman alphabet, punctuation, and numerals, many other optional specialized keys are often found. The meaning of these extra **function keys** can depend on the program that is reading the keyboard input. A key labeled with an arrow pointing down may move a program's attention to a spreadsheet cell or cause a word processor to skip down a paragraph. Computer keyboards also have at least one extra key that behaves like the shift key on a typewriter. This key, usually labeled CONTROL, is used in conjunction with the keys that ordinarily send a printable character. For example, CONTROL and the S key send a message that most computers understand as *pause*; output to the screen ceases until another key is pressed. Although the alphabetic keys of these keyboards are almost always in the same positions (as on a typewriter), each manufacturer seems to have unique ideas about how many other special function, special character, and numeric keys should be on a keyboard and how they should be arranged (see Figure 4.1).

Additions to the standard typewriter keyboard, CONTROL shift keys, function keys

Terminals are classified as dumb, smart, or intelligent. A **dumb terminal** can be used to send data to and receive them from a computer. A **smart terminal** has its own microprocessor and some internal storage, enabling it to do some data editing prior to transmission. An **intelligent terminal** is a smart terminal that can be programmed by the user to perform certain simple processing tasks independently of the computer to which it is connected.

Figure 4.1 Terminal Keyboards
This montage of photographs of keyboards reveals the nonstandardization of their layouts.

Types of Computer Displays

Displaying information on demand

The types and uses of display screens vary. A unit consisting solely of a display screen is called a **monitor.** Display screens are either cathode ray tubes or flat panels. The display may be **monochrome** (of one color) or multicolor, alphanumeric or graphic. Sizes range from the one-line, 12-character display screen of the smallest portable pocket computer to the full-page, 80-character-per-line, 66-line display screen of a word processor.

The Cathode Ray Tube

An inexpensive, versatile output device

The majority of computer display devices currently in use are built around the **cathode ray tube (CRT),** in which a raster-scan technique produces images on a screen. In a raster-scan, a beam of electrons moves rapidly back and forth, from top to bottom, across the phosphor-coated backing of the display screen. The phosphor coating glows wherever it is hit by the beam. The computer controls precisely when the electron beam is on or off, thus causing images to be formed on the screen. This is essentially the same process used to produce television images; picture tubes in television sets are cathode ray tubes.

Monochrome CRT displays are produced when only one electron beam hits phosphor that glows in a single color. Multicolored displays contain triplets of phosphor dots that glow red, blue, or green when hit by one of three electron beams. Furthermore, the electron beams may be partially turned on to yield a variety of colors.

CRTs have been produced for so long and in such high volume that they are relatively inexpensive. They consume much more power than all the other components in a terminal or microcomputer, are moderately heavy, yet somewhat fragile.

The Flat-Panel Screen

Another type of computer display screen currently in use is the **flat-panel screen.** Although CRTs are still the dominant type of display screen, flat-panel screens are the focus of a great deal of current research and have already found a place in several specialized applications. Far less bulky than CRTs, flat panels are ideal for the popular pocket-, notebook-, and briefcase-sized portable computers (their major area of application), and have also been incorporated in a few types of terminals. Current flat-panel screens may be one of three general types: liquid crystal, electroluminescent, and plasma.

A low-power, lighter, smaller alternative to CRTs

The technology of the **liquid crystal display (LCD)** has been used in watches, calculators, and other small electronic devices for years. More recently, LCDs have been used in tiny television sets and many portable computers. These displays consist of a thin layer of a liquid crystalline material between two polarized sheets of glass, in which thin wires are embedded. The wires in one sheet run horizontally, and in the other they run vertically. When current passes through a wire in each sheet, the crystals at the intersection align themselves in a certain angle to be seen clearly. An LCD screen with a capacity of 24 lines of 80 characters each costs about twice as much as a comparable CRT. However, this type of display consumes very little power, making battery-powered computers practical. The LCD screen also weighs less and is comparatively flat, being less than 1 inch thick (see Figure 4.2). Because they generate no light of their own, LCD displays are easy to read in brightly lit areas.

An **electroluminescent display (ELD)** has an image composed of orange and yellow dots. A thin layer of zinc sulfide and manganese is sandwiched between glass panels; parallel wires running through one panel are perpendicular to those in the other. When current is passed through a wire in each panel, a glowing dot is produced in the sandwiched layer at the point where the wires cross. Although they are used in some portable computers, ELDs aren't as popular as LCDs, probably because of their considerably higher cost.

The **plasma display panel (PDP),** on the other hand, is a relatively new type of flat-panel screen that is already commercially viable. As in the other flat panels we've discussed, glass sheets criss-crossed with wires are used to sandwich some material, in this case, neon gas that glows orange at the points where current is

Figure 4.2 A Liquid Crystal Display
The Zenith portable computer uses a liquid crystal display (LCD) screen that can present 24 lines of 80 characters each.

flowing through intersecting wires. PDPs are currently used in mainframe computer terminal screens and in some touch-sensitive screens.

Display Operations

Producing more than characters

As we have noted earlier in this chapter, computer displays are capable of forming characters on a screen. In its simplest mode of operation the display generates one image for each character it receives. A special nonprinting control character is used to signify that a fresh line of characters should be started. When the bottom line on the screen has been filled, a new line is obtained by moving all the other lines up one position. This operation is called **scrolling.**

Special Operations

Escape operations, moving characters, highlighting

Certain characters have a special effect on the display. Some of these characters have an immediate effect. The **newline** code is one such charater. Others introduce an **escape sequence.** This allows several characters to be combined to produce the parameters for an operation; for example, the place where new characters are added to the screen can be moved. The visual appearance of part of the screen can be modified by requesting underlining, reverse video, blinking, or other forms of **highlighting.** Other codes can selectively erase or move characters from one part of the display to another.

Protected Fields

Electronic forms display

When computer terminals are used for data entry, some areas of the screen will be set to simulate a paper form. These areas usually take on a distinctive appearance, possibly presenting characters that are dimmer than normal. The terminal's user can type whatever is desired on the areas of the screen that have normal characters. The protected areas cannot be modified from the keyboard. When enough of the form has been filled, a single keystroke causes the terminal to transmit only the modified areas back to the computer.

Graphics Displays

Drawing pictures, scaling text

The least expensive display terminals are limited to a fixed number of characters (for example, 25 rows of 80 characters), evenly spaced across the screen. Graphics terminals allow the computer to access each dot (or *pixel*, short for picture element) on the screen. Drawing commands, for example, rendering a curved line through a set of points, filling in a group of rectangles with a selected color, and drawing characters in different sizes and orientations are some of the operations a graphics terminal provides, in addition to those capabilities expected of an ordinary character-only terminal.

Additional Interactive Input Devices

The output capabilities of a graphics terminal are often accompanied by some form of **graphic input** device. The information collected from such a device must be reduced to a numeric form that is often transmitted to the computer over the same data path as the keyboard characters. A number of different input devices are shown in Figure 4.3.

A **digitizer,** also called a **graphic tablet,** is a flat surface that the user draws on with a special stylus. The tablet senses each location where the stylus touches it, produces signals communicating the x and y coordinates of the contact points and inputs these coordinates to the computer. A digitizer can be used to trace over a picture, converting it into a series of xy coordinates that represent, to the computer, a digital map of the points comprising the picture.

A **light pen** is a light-sensitive pen (usually attached to a cable) that is used with special graphics terminals. Touching the light pen to the display screen of such a terminal creates a photoelectric current which the terminal uses to identify the contact point as an xy coordinate. With such a system, the user can draw any image on the display screen, and it is converted to digits and stored.

Another input device, the **mouse,** has become increasingly popular since its adoption by many user-friendly microcomputer systems. Mechanical mice consist of a small plastic box, with two wheels or a ball roller, that produces electrical pulses when rolled around on a flat surface. The wheel or ball rotations are converted to xy coordinates that are stored as numbers. Optical mice use light beams to sense motion over a reflective grid. The mouse is used to direct the movement of a *cursor*, a small figure (often a + sign) indicating a particular position on the screen. With the mouse, a user can point the cursor at symbols (also called *objects* or *icons*) representing the available activities.

Obtaining graphical information from tablets, light pens, mice, trackballs, and touch screens

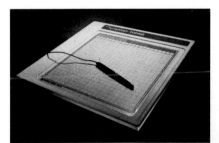

(a)

(b)

Figure 4.3   Graphic Input Devices

(a) A digitizer is used to enter data from photographs, drawings, diagrams, and illustrations. (b) A light pen is used to input data in the form of positions on images presented on visual display screens. (c) The mouse is used to enter instructions for the control of hardware and software and software functions. (d) The trackball performs operations similar to those of a mouse and takes up less desk space.

(d)

(c)

Figure 4.4 Touch-Panel Screen

The touch-panel screen allows the user to input data by simply touching an area of the display. These data are usually an instruction concerning some hardware or software function. The Hewlett-Packard HP 150 micro-computer utilizes a touch-panel screen.

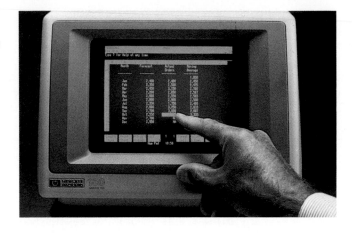

The **trackball** could be considered an enlarged mechanical mouse turned upside down. It generates the same information that a mouse can and uses similar circuitry to do it. The difference is that the trackball housing remains stationary; the user's fingers roll the captive ball in the direction they want the cursor to go. Trackballs take up less desk space than mice and are sometimes integrated into the same housing as the keyboard.

Touch-panel screens (Figure 4.4) employ either a pressure-sensitive surface or crisscrossing beams of infrared light to enable the user to enter data. The computer is programmed to display instructions or items to be manipulated on the touch-panel screen. The user instructs the computer to perform a specified action simply by touching the appropriate place on the screen. Because the touch panel can detect where it is touched, these data can be relayed to the computer, which completes the desired action. Although touch panels are a relatively recent innovation, they have already been applied fairly extensively in education and with user-friendly microcomputer systems. Since users simply point to what they want the computer to do, touch panels reduce the use of the keyboard and thus the time required to learn how to operate the computer. They are unacceptable as a drawing device because most devices can only resolve a few hundred different points on the screen. Most computer screens display more than a quarter million pixels at a minimum.

OTHER INPUT SOURCES

Obtaining data for later processing

Computers can receive input data from places other than terminal keyboards. The devices introduced in this section, while sometimes requiring human intervention, primarily generate input data for the computer.

Business Information Gathering

Data acquired from point-of-sale terminals, optical character recognition, bar codes, and magnetic strips

Point-of-sale (POS) registers are specialized terminals located at check-out counters in retail stores. They are classified as intelligent terminals. A hand-held wand or fixed bar code reader forms an integral part of the POS register, in addition to the sophisticated cash register keyboard. These terminals pass along item identification codes to a store computer, which updates sales inventory figures and sends

Figure 4.5 Machine-Readable Characters

Optical character-recognition (OCR) devices can read characters printed with regular ink. The characters, however, must conform to certain standards. The most commonly used typeface for optical character recognition is OCR-A. Some OCR devices can read carefully formed handwritten characters.

back price information. Some POS terminals can also process credit card transactions by checking customers' credit status and updating their credit accounts (see Chapter 15).

The POS terminals use **optical character recognition (OCR)** to read alphanumeric characters from price tags. Machine-printed characters are produced in a standard typeface, called **OCR-A,** which can be easily read by OCR techniques. However, machines are available that can read well-defined, carefully formed handwritten characters. Figure 4.5 illustrates machine-readable characters.

Bar code recognition reads the familiar black and white stripes of the **Universal Product Code (UPC)** that appears on most supermarket items and even books and magazines (Figure 4.6). **Bar codes,** which were first used by railroads in the

Figure 4.6 Bar Code Recognition

The most common bar code is the Universal Product Code (UPC) printed on virtually every item in today's supermarkets. The device most often employed to read these codes is a fixed bar code reader that scans the surfaces of products with laser beams.

(a)

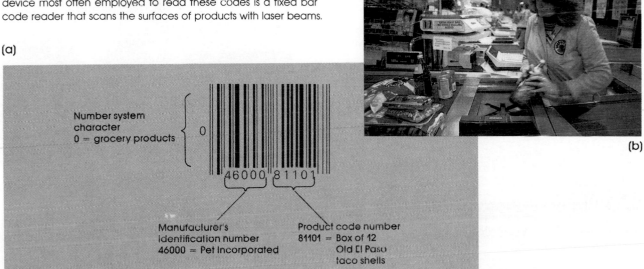

(b)

1960s to track freight cars, represent data as a series of light and dark marks. The UPC bar codes identify the manufacturer and product and are read either by wands or by **fixed bar code readers.** As items are scanned, the identification data are transmitted to a store's computer, which finds the current price, updates inventory and receipts, and sends the price back to the check-out counter. The use of bar codes in supermarkets has resulted in more accurate prices, faster check-out, decreased training and labor costs, and easier inventory control (see Chapter 15). Because of this success, bar codes are being adapted for such applications as library books and student identification cards.

Magnetic strips are the short lengths of plastic-covered, magnetizable coating that are often found on the backs of credit cards, bank cards, identification cards, and security badges (see Figure 4.7). Magnetic strips are encoded with confidential data such as account numbers, personal identification numbers, privacy codes, and access codes. The data encoded on a magnetic strip can be read and input into a

Figure 4.7 Magnetic Strips

Magnetic strips are used to encode confidential data. Special devices are required to read this data. (a) A bank card with a magnetic strip (the dark band across the back). (b) Automated teller machines are programmed to read the data encoded on the magnetic strips of bank cards.

(a)

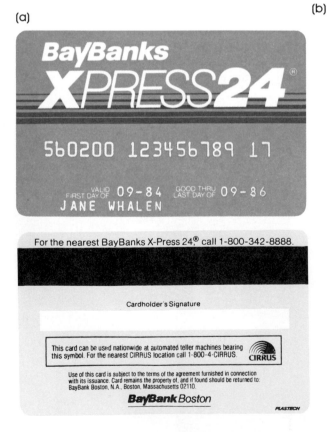

(b)

computer by a special machine equipped to accept such cards from users. If the data on the strip coincide with predetermined standards, the user gains access to his or her account or receives some type of entry authorization.

Magnetic strips are not human-readable, and they can hold much more data than could be printed in the same space. As a result, they are excellent for holding data that must be kept confidential or that must be entered often, quickly, and conveniently. Magnetic strips, however, have the disadvantage of being susceptible to damage by magnets, fingerprints, scratches, and bending.

Optical mark recognition (OMR), or **mark sensing,** is widely used in the scoring of test forms, such as the SAT answer sheet shown in Figure 4.8. A pencil is used to mark a box or other space representing the selected answer. Test forms are scored by an optical mark sensing device that uses light beams to convert the presence of pencil marks into electrical signals that can be input into a computer.

Magnetic Ink Characters

Magnetic ink character recognition (MICR) is an input method that utilizes characters printed with magnetizable ink to make them machine-readable. If you have a checking account, you've probably noticed the chunky black numbers

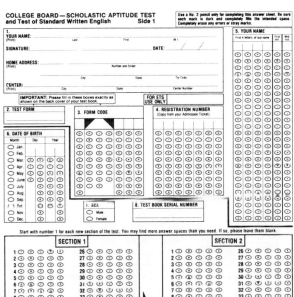

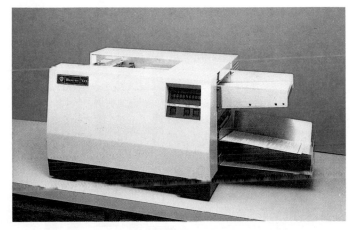

(b)

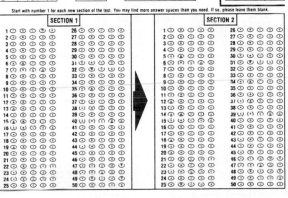

(a)

Figure 4.8 Optical Mark Recognition

(a) Optical mark recognition (OMR) is often used for scoring answer sheets for multiple-choice tests such as the Scholastic Aptitude Test (SAT). A pencil mark must fill the oval designating each desired answer. (b) An optical mark-sensing device is used to read the pencil marks and to input the data to a computer.

How banks keep track of checks

printed along the bottom of your checks (see Figure 4.9). Those symbols, consisting of the 10 decimal digits and four special characters, allow a MICR reader-sorter unit to process up to 2600 checks per minute. The MICR input method is widely used by banks to process the large numbers of checks written every day.

When you pay for something with a check, an operator at the first bank to receive your check after it's cashed will print the amount, in magnetizable ink, in the lower right-hand corner of the check and batch it with other checks received that day. These batches are placed in the *input hopper* (a tray or shallow bin that

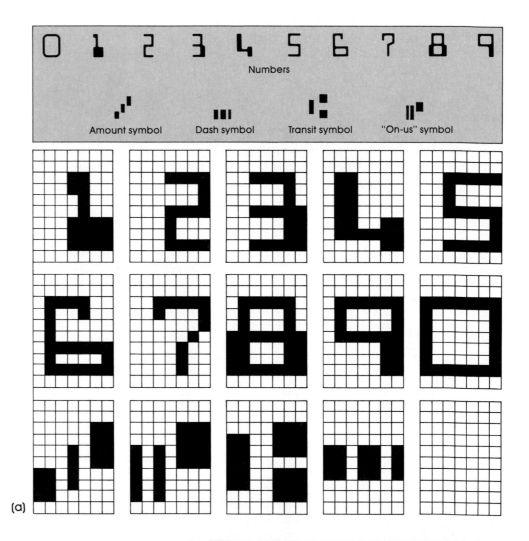

(a)

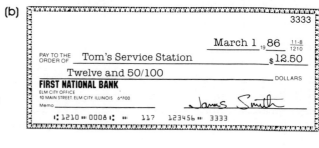

(b)

Figure 4.9 MICR Characters

MICR characters are printed with magnetizable ink in a special typeface and are easily machine-readable. These characters are most commonly seen on personal checks. (a) The magnetic ink character set, with its underlying grid pattern, (b) A check with MICR characters.

neatly holds the checks) of an **MICR reader-sorter unit.** One at a time, the checks are passed through a magnetic field that magnetizes the iron oxide particles in the special ink. The MICR characters on your check can then be detected by read heads that can "interpret" these magnetic symbols in a way similar to how data are read from tapes or disks. The data can be input directly into a computer or placed on magnetic tape for later processing. The reader-sorter unit also sorts all the checks according to their identification codes, and eventually your check ends up back at your bank.

The advantages of using MICR include:

- *MICR characters are not easily damaged.*   Checks can be folded, wrinkled, written on, and stamped. Character recognition is magnetic, so minor mutilation will usually not affect the accurate reading of data.

- *MICR allows faster input and processing.*   Because the data are directly entered from source documents, input speeds are not limited by an operator's typing abilities.

- *MICR reduces errors.*   Inaccurate input due to human keying mistakes is largely eliminated.

- *MICR characters are human-readable.*   Only the four special characters require any getting used to.

The chief disadvantage to using MICR is that it's limited to 14 characters. No alphabetic characters are available.

Image Processing

Computers can process and display pictures. These pictures are acquired from two types of devices. Video cameras convert a picture into an electronic signal by scanning the picture from left to right and from top to bottom. The scanning order is identical to that used by the CRTs in your television set and computer displays. Video cameras send 60 pictures each second. A device called a **frame buffer** captures one of those images as a string of numbers. Larger numbers are associated with brighter parts of the picture, while zero is used to indicate black. Pictures acquired this way have moderately low resolution, usually 320 pixels horizontally and 200 vertically.

Computers can read pictures

Page scanners can copy an image from a printed page using technology similar to that in facsimile (fax) machines. The machine slowly pulls a page past a reading station that converts it into a digital representation. Although the whole process takes several seconds, the machine can typically distinguish 300 pixels per inch. If the scanner in Figure 4.10 processed an 8- by 10-inch photograph, the output would record more than 7 million pixels!

Voice and Sound

Computers can also have interface systems that use sound as a communications media. **Touch-tone devices** send input data, in the form of sounds of varying pitch, over telephone lines from remote locations to a central computer. Touch-tone devices are by no means full-fledged alphanumeric terminals; they have lim-

Touch-tone telephone input, voice recognition, and computer-generated voice reply

Figure 4.10 A Page Scanner
Artwork and photographs are turned into digital images by a page scanner. The images can be enlarged, enhanced, and cropped by computer and later incorporated directly into printed output.

ited capabilities and are generally used only for specialized tasks, such as verifying credit card transactions or updating warehouse inventories. These devices use the pushbuttons of a touch-tone telephone as a keyboard.

Voice Input

Wouldn't it be convenient if users could simply tell the computer what to do and forget about learning how to use keyboards, tablets, mice, or touch panels? To some extent, voice input is already a reality. Although it will probably be decades before effective vocal dialogues with computers are possible, some **voice-recognition modules (VRMs)** have been developed that can recognize from 40 to 200 isolated sounds, words, and phrases. To be understood, however, words spoken to these devices must be distinctly and slowly pronounced, for example: "print" (pause) "trans" (pause) "ac" (pause) "tion" (pause) "file." Such devices, which convert voice input into the digital codes acceptable to computers, are being employed in a limited number of applications involving small vocabularies.

Speaker-dependent systems are the most prevalent types of voice-recognition module. The individual user repeats required words such as "run" or "print" to the system several times to create **templates,** the speech patterns against which the computer compares all subsequent voice commands when spoken by other users if their pronunciations closely resemble those of the template maker. Most manufacturers of speaker-dependent systems claim an accuracy rate of better than 90 percent for their machines. In other words, the user's commands will be recognized at least nine times out of 10 (unless his or her voice is distorted by a cold or sore throat).

The less common **speaker-independent systems** can theoretically recognize the words in their vocabularies no matter who says them. Such systems have an accuracy rate of 95 percent, due to the many built-in templates for each word. Their drawback, however, is their very small vocabularies—some are limited to "yes," "no," and the digits "zero" through "nine."

Currently, VRMs are used in voice-activated executive computer systems (for the executive who has everything), nonflight controls in sophisticated aircraft, automated inventory systems and assembly lines that require input from workers who are using their hands to move stock or build components, certain phone-answering machines that handle requests for information or service, and robots that carry out simple tasks for the physically disabled.

Voice Output

Computer-generated voice output, like graphic displays, has been growing in popularity in recent years. Voice-output capabilities are now incorporated into many general-purpose computer systems and are available as an option for most home computers (for some machines, additional interface hardware must be purchased).

Voice-output devices convert data into spoken words using either prerecorded speech samples or computer-synthesized words. The technology behind such devices is not that complicated, so they are relatively inexpensive and widely applied. For example, voice output emanates from children's toys, automobile dashboards, cash registers, video games, telephones, vending machines, and greeting cards. A less trivial application of voice output is a reading machine for the blind that can scan printed text and pronounce the words aloud.

PAPER OUTPUT SYSTEMS

Paper is by far the most popular permanent medium for computer output. Also called *hard copy,* paper output is produced using many different kinds of paper and is presented in many ways. Text, tables, reports, graphs, charts, and drawings are some of the typical formats of paper output, as Figure 4.11 illustrates. Two major types of devices are used to produce paper output: printers and plotters.

The most popular output medium

Printers

A **printer** is a machine that outputs on paper letters or numbers that humans can read. The size, speed, cost, and operation of the devices classified as printers vary widely. For example, speeds range from 10 cps (characters per second) for character printers to more than 60,000 cps for the most advanced laser printers. Also, cost varies from less than $100 for the cheapest thermal printers to as much as $300,000 for laser printers with built-in minicomputers. Printers are usually categorized according to how much they print at one time and how they produce characters.

Character printers print a single character at a time, one after another, across the paper from margin to margin. As you might guess, this is the slowest class of printer, with printing speeds ranging from 10 to 400 cps. Character printers are

Output formed a character at a time, a line at a time, or a page at a time

Figure 4.11 Paper Output
Paper output, or hard copy, may be presented as text, tables, reports, graphs, charts, or drawings.

used either where *letter-quality text* (like that produced on a good electric type-writer) is required or where slowness is acceptable (because the price is right). Consequently, character printers are often used in word-processing systems and in microcomputer systems. Character printers can be further subdivided according to printing method: daisy wheel and dot matrix printers use an impact method; and inkjet, thermal, and electrostatic printers employ nonimpact methods.

Line printers have a hammer for each character position across a page. They use the impact method of printing and can therefore print on multipart forms.

Page printers compose an entire page of output before it is printed. Examples of these printers include the fastest, most expensive ($300,000) monsters down to laser printers that cost little more than an office copier.

Impact Methods

Producing an image by striking the paper

Impact methods of printing work similarly to typewriters in the sense that an object is struck against an inked ribbon and the paper in order to produce an image of a character. Since they use physical pressure to produce output, impact printers can make simultaneous multiple copies with carbon or pressure-sensitive paper (nonimpact methods cannot). For this reason, impact printers are often chosen for applications that require extra file copies.

Daisy wheel printers (Figure 4.12) have a printing mechanism with solid raised characters embossed on the ends of arms that are arranged like the spokes of

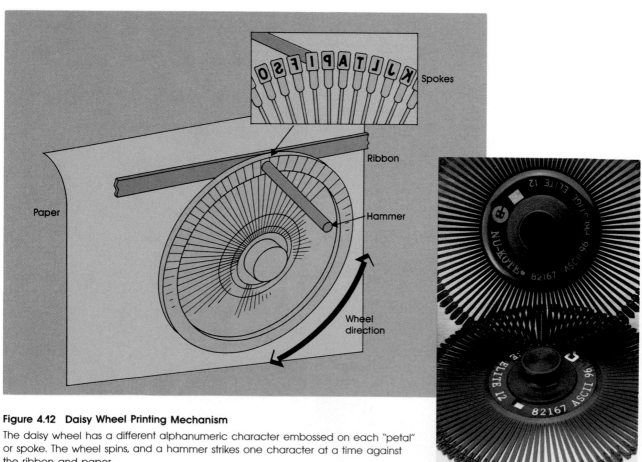

Figure 4.12 Daisy Wheel Printing Mechanism
The daisy wheel has a different alphanumeric character embossed on each "petal" or spoke. The wheel spins, and a hammer strikes one character at a time against the ribbon and paper.

a wheel or the petals of a daisy. As the wheel spins, a tiny hammer strikes the back of the proper character as it passes. The impact of the hammer bends the spoke and forces the embossed character against the ribbon and paper. Daisy wheel printing is rather slow, not that much faster than typewriting, but the print is of a high quality.

Dot matrix printers are cheaper and faster than daisy wheel printers. The print quality, however, isn't as good. The dot matrix *printhead* constructs the character images by means of a vertical column of from seven to nine pins that is struck repeatedly against the ribbon and paper. Electrical signals cause the appropriate pins to be pushed out to form the successive columns of dots that make up a character's image. Each column of the character is struck in its turn against the ribbon and the paper until the complete image has been formed (see Figure 4.13).

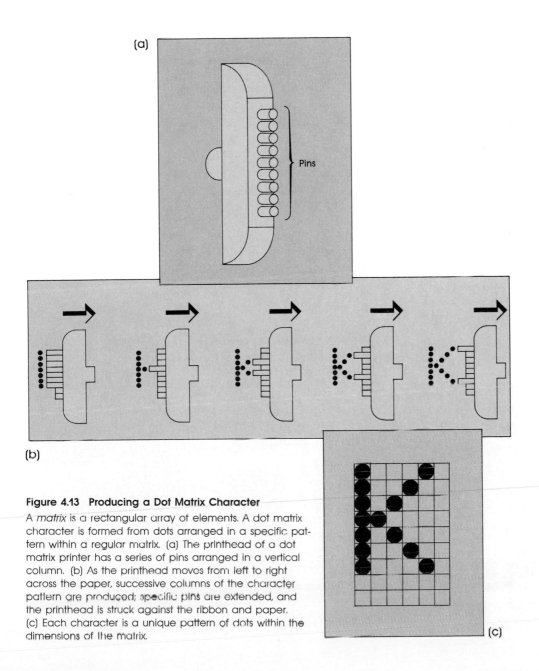

Figure 4.13 Producing a Dot Matrix Character

A *matrix* is a rectangular array of elements. A dot matrix character is formed from dots arranged in a specific pattern within a regular matrix. (a) The printhead of a dot matrix printer has a series of pins arranged in a vertical column. (b) As the printhead moves from left to right across the paper, successive columns of the character pattern are produced; specific pins are extended, and the printhead is struck against the ribbon and paper. (c) Each character is a unique pattern of dots within the dimensions of the matrix.

Dot matrix printers are used primarily when speed is the most important consideration and when the aesthetic appeal of the output is less important.

The size and number of pins used in the printhead governs the quality of its output. Because the characters are formed by carefully timed signals (instead of preformed stamps), the range of characters that can be printed is virtually limitless. Characters for other languages, Greek letters for mathematical equations, and all sorts of symbols can be sent from the computer to the printer. Furthermore, the computer can take over complete control of the printing process to produce artwork ranging from simple graphs to shaded pictures.

Line printers, which print an entire line at a time, are often part of larger minicomputer or mainframe systems. Since the print quality is usually poorer than that of typewriters, line printers are often used for producing output whose appearance is not important, such as internal reports, rough drafts, and hard copies of computer programs. Line printers print from 300 to 3000 lines per minute and can be subdivided into band and drum printers.

Band printers have a printing mechanism consisting of a scalloped steel band with five sections of 48 characters each and an array of hammers, one hammer for each position in the line. Printers that support both upper- and lower-case letters have fewer sections with more characters in each section. As the band moves at high speed, the hammers are timed to hit the paper and ribbon against the proper characters as they pass by (see Figure 4.14). Band printers can print as many as 3000 lines per minute.

Drum printers have a solid metal cylinder embossed across its outside surface with rows of characters—as many as there are character positions in a line. Behind the paper, at each print position, is a small hammer. As the drum rotates at high speed, each hammer strikes the paper against the ribbon and drum as the appropriate character moves into position. Figure 4.15 shows the arrangement of hammers and characters. For example, all the A's in the line are printed, then all the B's, and so on until all of the characters included on the drum have been rotated past the array of hammers. Thus a complete rotation of the drum is required to print each

Figure 4.14 The Band Printer

(a) A band printer. (b) The printing mechanism of a band printer is a moving steel band on which characters are embossed. A hammer at each character position of the line strikes against the paper, ribbon, and band just as the proper character arrives at that position.

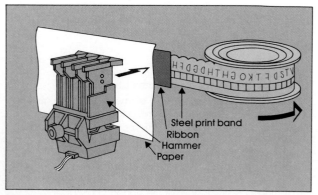

Steel print band
Ribbon
Hammer
Paper

(a)

(b)

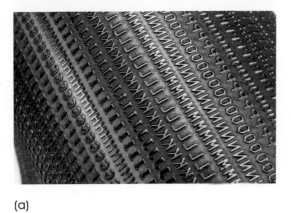

(a)

Figure 4.15 The Drum Printer

(a) The drum is a metal cylinder with horizontal rows of characters embossed across the outer surface. (b) The drum rotates at high speed, and a hammer at each print position strikes the paper exactly when the appropriate character is in place.

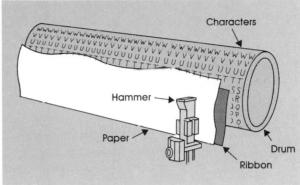

(b)

line. Although this might sound like a time-consuming process, drum printers work at rates as fast as 3000 lines per minute.

Nonimpact Methods

Nonimpact methods of character printing employ inkjet, thermal, laser, or electrostatic processes to form alphanumeric images on paper.

Electronic and inkjet methods of marking the paper

Inkjet printers have a mechanism that shoots tiny, electrically charged droplets of ink out of a nozzle; the droplets are guided to their proper positions by electrically charged deflection plates (see Figure 4.16). Ink that isn't used for a particular character is recirculated. Although inkjet printers are fast and quiet and produce high-quality print, they are more expensive than dot matrix and daisy wheel printers. Inkjet printing is well suited for offices where the noise of impact methods would be distracting and where speed and high-quality print are important.

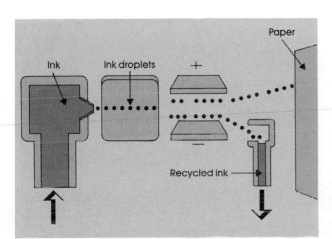

Figure 4.16 Inkjet Printing

This nonimpact method of printing produces characters using a stream of tiny ink droplets shot out of a nozzle and guided to their proper positions by electrically charged deflection plates.

Two types of printers produce output that is literally "hot off the presses." **Thermal printers** use heat to produce characters, which look like dot matrix characters on special heat-sensitive paper. The printing mechanism resembles that of a dot matrix printer, except that the pins produce the columns of dots by heating up *near* the paper instead of actually striking it. An improvement of the thermal process transfers heat-sensitive dye from a special ribbon to the paper. This permits the use of ordinary paper as well as multicolor ribbons for color output. **Electrostatic printers,** on the other hand, use static electrical sparks to burn away aluminum from special aluminum-coated, black-backed paper. Thermal printers that use heat-sensitive paper are the least expensive of the character printers, but they produce poor-quality output. Furthermore, the special papers they use are expensive, the image degrades when exposed to sunlight, and the distinctive appearance of the output limits its uses.

Figure 4.17 shows some of the types of character printers that we've described.

High-speed page printers, which print entire pages at a time, are the most sophisticated and expensive paper output devices. Their very high-speed, nonim-

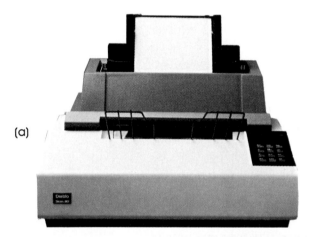

(a)

Figure 4.17 Examples of Character Printers

(a) This daisy wheel printer, the Diablo 630, can print from 32 to 40 characters per second. (b) The Epson LQ-850 and LQ-1050 dot matrix printers print from 73 characters per second for a letter-quality copy, and 330 characters per second for a draft copy. (c) The Hewlett-Packard Paint Jet, a thermal color-graphics printer, prints 67 characters per second on special chemically treated paper.

(b)

(c)

pact printing methods are based on either xerographic (like Xerox copy machines) or laser technology. Such printers are necessary equipment at installations where large volumes of paper output must be produced every day. The quality of the print produced by page printers is quite good, but their very high cost (as much as $300,000, or more) limits their use to organizations such as large law firms, central government agencies, and major publishers, which produce so much paper output that speed is a vital factor. The most advanced page printers are capable of producing more than 60,000 lines per minute.

Laser printers represent the most advanced printing technology. They are much faster than character printers but slower than a good line printer. Laser beams are reflected from spinning disks onto electrically charged paper. The reflected beams form electrostatic images on a light-sensitive drum. The drum passes through powdery ink that sticks to the charged areas. Next, paper is pressed against the drum, picking up the still powdery ink. Finally the paper is passed over a source of heat that binds the ink to the paper.

Laser printers make output with light

Inexpensive laser printers can produce 8 to 16 pages of output per minute if the output is simple enough. Laser printers form characters using the same scanning process that goes on inside a CRT or a dot matrix printer. The characters consist of individual dots spaced 300 to 600 to the inch (see Figure 4.18). Some laser printers emulate character printers. They have a fixed number of typefaces and character sizes. When printing only characters, their output is roughly 600 lines per minute. The output speed plummets when graphic images are printed because of the communication time involved in sending pictures to the printer. Other printers use a special language, *PostScript*, to describe what a page should look like. Characters can be as small as an unreadable 1/300 of an inch high up to a single character taking up the entire page. Here the speed of printing a page is limited by the complexity of what is being drawn. For ordinary output the PostScript printers have the same speed as other laser printers.

Plotters

Plotters are computer-controlled drawing machines used to produce paper output in the form of maps, graphs, charts, or illustrations.

Drawing lines on paper

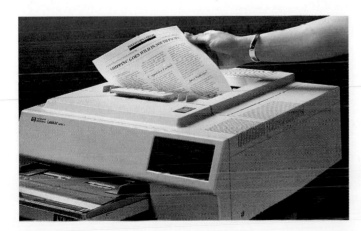

Figure 4.18 The Laser Printer
The LaserJet Series II printer from Hewlett-Packard offers publication quality printing for the office environment. This fast, quiet, high-quality office printer can merge text and graphics for desktop publishing needs.

Graphic output from plotters can be used to clarify complicated statistics or to make dry material more interesting. A recent study by the Wharton Business School found that presentations that used graphics were 10 percent more persuasive than those that did not. Graphics can be very effective communicators, and computer-generated graphics are particularly neat, clear, and professional. Architects, artists, and sales departments also use computer-generated color graphics to clarify ideas. Outside the business world, seismologists studying earth tremors rely on computer-generated graphic output, as do engineers performing stress tests on various materials, and obstetricians monitoring fetal heartbeats and the strength of contractions during delivery.

Inkjet plotters (such as that shown in Figure 4.19) produce an image by spraying droplets of different-colored inks on paper rolled over a rotating drum. The computer to which the inkjet plotter is connected controls the movement of both the drum and the ink jets, which are mounted on a carriage above it. Inkjet plotters can produce complicated multicolored drawings quickly, quietly, and accurately. Consequently, they are often used for drawing large, detailed, and colorful maps.

Pen plotters produce images in a way similar to manual drawing—a pen or pens move across the paper's surface. Useful for graphing, charting, and diagramming, pen plotters are often used to present statistical data in graphic form. They are most often used in engineering and manufacturing applications (as will be discussed in Chapter 15), but many medical and research organizations employ them as well. The two basic types of pen plotters are flatbed and drum.

Flatbed plotters have one or more pens suspended from a carriage above a horizontal surface. On some models, a sheet of paper remains stationary on the flatbed while the computer-controlled carriage moves the pens forward and backward, left and right, and on and off the surface. This is shown in Figure 4.20(a). Other flatbed plotters, such as the popular Hewlett-Packard desktop models shown in Figure 4.20(b), have a smaller horizontal drawing surface. The sheet of paper moves in and out while the pen, which is perpendicular to the paper, moves from side to side along a fixed carriage. In both cases, the plotter can draw over the entire surface of the page.

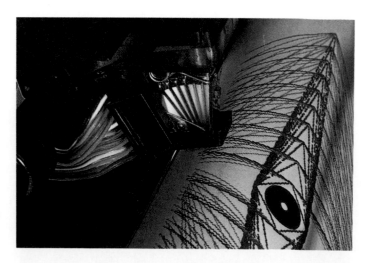

Figure 4.19 The Inkjet Plotter
An inkjet plotter produces pictures by spraying droplets of different-colored inks on paper wrapped tightly around a drum.

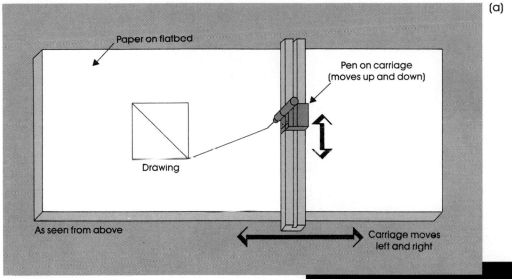

(a)

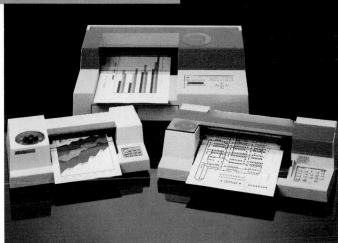

(b)

Figure 4.20 The Flatbed Plotter

(a) A flatbed plotter has a pen or pens suspended from a carriage above a stationary sheet of paper. (b) Hewlett-Packard makes several desktop plotters which can produce multicolored drawings.

In **drum plotters,** a continuous sheet of paper rolls over a cylinder (the drum) beneath one or more pens (see Figure 4.21). The drum can move the paper forward and backward by rotating in either direction, while the pen or pens can move back and forth perpendicular to the paper's motion, and can also be retracted from the paper's surface. Both drum and pen movements are controlled by the computer; various combinations of movements yield a full range of lines, curves, and shapes.

One final note: pen plotters aren't limited to drawing on paper. Some flatbed plotters have light-emitting "pens" suspended over light-sensitive Mylar sheets. Such plotters produce images on the Mylar sheets, which are used as transparencies for overhead projectors. The high-precision technology used for two-dimensional control in pen plotters has also been applied in certain industrial processes (which we'll discuss in Chapter 15) that employ devices very much like pen plotters as cutting tools. For example, a laser can be used to cut patterns from fabric in much the same way as a pen can be used to draw them.

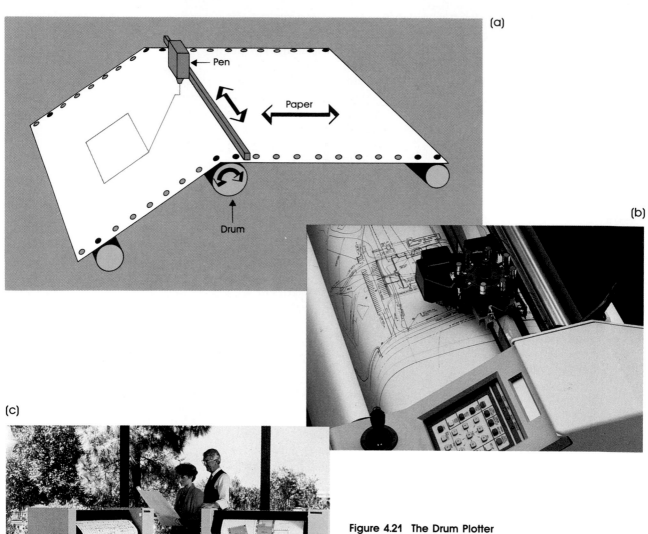

Figure 4.21 The Drum Plotter

(a) The paper in a drum plotter rolls over a cylinder and under a pen or pens suspended above. The paper moves forward and backward, and each pen can move in either direction perpendicular to the movement of the paper, as well as on and off the surface of the paper. (b) This large drum plotter employs several pens of various colors. (c) The Hewlett-Packard DraftMasters series of drafting plotters is used for CAD applications.

MICROFILM AND MICROFICHE OUTPUT

Reducing costs and volume by using film instead of paper

Sometimes paper isn't the most desirable medium for output. In large quantities, it is heavy and bulky, taking up a lot of file cabinet or shelf space. Although rather expensive, individual sheets are easily defaced, lost, or destroyed. Fortunately, an alternative medium exists for situations in which these disadvantages are significant.

Computer-output microfilm (COM) consists of either rolls or sheets (called **microfiche**) of thin plastic film on which output text is reproduced photographically at greatly reduced size. Computer-output **microfilm** is a much more sensible form than paper output for organizations that handle very large quantities of information. Banks, insurance companies, and public utilities can store their massive accounting, billing, and personnel records in a few small file drawers rather than in warehouses. A single 4 × 6-inch sheet of microfiche holds as much information as hundreds of pages of computer paper. The information is more quickly accessible and relatively inexpensive to produce (at least for high-volume users). For example, it costs about eight times as much to print a 1000-page report on paper as to output it on microfilm. Also, microfilm is more durable than paper.

Let's look at how computer output microfilm is produced. The information to be output is transmitted from an on-line or off-line device and read into a *microfilm recorder*, where it is displayed sequentially on the screen of a CRT (which we'll describe more completely in the next section). A high-speed camera (loaded with 16-mm, 35-mm, or 105-mm photographic film) in the recorder snaps a picture of each full screen of displayed material, at recording speeds of up to 32,000 lines per minute. The photographic film is then developed, in either the microfilm recorder or a separate machine.

After being developed, the microfilm or microfiche can be viewed at a *viewing station*, which is basically a magnifying slide projector. Some COM systems require that the user search manually for the particular frame (screenful or page). Other, more sophisticated systems utilize *computer-assisted retrieval (CAR) techniques* (see Figure 4.22) to speed up the accessing of information. Each document is cataloged in an index along with its exact location on a roll or sheet. A small computer stores the index, presents it on request, and automatically retrieves the selected document so that it can be viewed. Whether the search is manual or automatic, it is important to note that users must have a special machine to read the output on microfilm or microfiche.

Figure 4.22 Kodak KAR-6600 Information System

In the computer-output microfilm process, data from either an on-line or off-line device are read into a microfilm recorder. The output text is displayed on a CRT, photographed a screenful at a time, and reduced. After the film is developed, it can be viewed at a viewing station and can also be printed from to produce a paper document.

ENSURING THE QUALITY OF DATA

Hardware and software means for keeping data accurate both inside and outside the computer system

Computers can only process numbers; in fact, as we discussed in the last chapter, they can only process numbers represented by patterns of electrical signals. Somehow raw data, the collected facts and figures that are to be processed, must be converted into this machine-readable form before the computer can accept and manipulate them. *Data entry* is the process of gathering a specific type of factual material, converting it to machine-readable form (if necessary), and either storing it temporarily or presenting it directly to the central processing unit (CPU).

Given the wide range of tasks performed by computers, it isn't surprising that input data come from an equally wide variety of sources. In the business world, data are collected from sales, inventory, and payroll records, customer orders, or market research reports. Data collected by government agencies such as the IRS are taken from forms filled out by individuals and corporations.

Regardless of the source, the facts and figures must be correctly transcribed and transmitted or the results of processing them will be useless. Let's consider this clearly essential characteristic of input—accuracy.

Hardware Checks on the Accuracy of Data

Operations that keep data accurate when it is stored or transported

Unfortunately, even computers aren't perfect; computer errors do occur. For example, a bit of data can be lost or altered during transmission within or between computers. Such losses, although rare in relation to the enormous numbers of computations and data transfers that take place, happen often enough to cause concern. Dust, moisture, magnetic fields, and equipment failures are the most frequent source of machine errors. We must have some way of detecting machine errors, of pinpointing when and where they have occurred. Furthermore, the means to check for, and if possible correct, these errors should be built right into the computer hardware. Two of the most common built-in means of maintaining the accuracy of data are parity checks and redundancy checks.

Parity Checks

The **parity bit** is an extra bit that is added to a machine code for error-detecting purposes. For example, with the ASCII 7-bit code for the letter A (1000001), the parity bit is added to the leftmost position, resulting in an 8-bit code. If a computer uses *even parity*, the added bit is whichever bit produces an even number of ones in the 8-bit code. Similarly, *odd parity*, used by some computers, adds the binary digit that makes the total number of ones odd. With odd parity, the 8-bit code for A is 11000001. With even parity, the correct 8-bit code for A is 01000001.

The parity bit is generated by the computer circuitry before data transmission. Upon reception, the computer circuitry checks each byte to see whether it has an even (or odd) number of ones. If it does, it is accepted as correct. If it doesn't, at least one of its bits must have been changed during transmission; the data transfer is tried again. If the error persists, a serious problem exists, and the computer informs the user.

Notice that, although the parity bit is used successfully to detect one erroneous bit in a byte, two erroneous bits in the same byte will cancel each other out and thus will not be caught. This might sound like a serious setback for computer designers, but in fact it isn't—the probability of machine errors occurring twice in the same byte is very small. The parity check also cannot detect when data have been entered incorrectly. We'll discuss how to catch those kinds of errors in the section on software checks.

Redundancy Codes

The parity check employs one redundant bit per word, the parity bit. **Redundancy codes** use additional redundant digits. To give a simple example, storing a given 3-bit code for one and another 3-bit code for a zero provides some powerful error-detection capabilities. It might seem wasteful to store 3 bits for every single bit of input data, but in fact it pays off handsomely.

Let's say that 111 is stored for every bit that is a 1, and 000 is stored for every bit that is a 0. So, for example, the 7-bit ASCII code for the letter A is stored as 21 bits:

111   000   000   000   000   000   111   Redundancy code for A

1   0   0   0   0   0   1   ASCII code for A

What is gained by using redundancy codes? First, a single-bit error in any of the triplets is immediately detectable since all of the triplets should consist of three identical bits. If, after transmission, the leftmost bit is 011, 101, or 110, it is obvious that some error has occurred in that bit. Furthermore, it is *automatically* corrected. Thus, unlike the parity bit, the redundancy code can be used to eliminate all single-bit errors automatically. Not only is it an error-detecting scheme but, in the case of single-bit errors, it is an error-correcting scheme. Also, unlike the parity bit, the redundancy codes can be used to determine if two bits in a byte are erroneous. In practice, other more complex redundancy codes are used because expanding the amount of data transferred by a factor of three is unacceptable.

Software Checks on the Accuracy of Data

Even perfectly functioning computer hardware is limited by the reliability of what is input. Given correct data and programming, computer processing is predictable and reliable. But computers cannot evaluate the quality of the data they're given. For all their technological sophistication, if you provide them with inaccurate data, they will produce erroneous results. The programmer's phrase *garbage in, garbage out (GIGO)* says it all: the computer's output is only as good as the input data it is given. The vast majority of the "computer errors" people are so fond of citing are not hardware malfunctions at all, but rather the result of mistakes made in programming or data entry—two essentially human responsibilities. Blaming such mistakes on the computer is a little like putting apples in a food processor and then complaining to the manufacturer that a "food processor error" produced applesauce instead of tomato purée.

Software and procedural methods of obtaining accurate data

The two main types of input errors are: (1) those due to the incorrect collection or recording of data; and (2) those due to mistakes made in entering or keying in the data. Quite a few techniques for detecting input errors have been developed. Although often performed manually, these checks are most successful if they are programmed into the software that controls data input. Because the computer is well suited to the repetitive task of checking details, it can play a major role in the process of ensuring the accuracy of its own input data.

These are some of the accuracy-checking techniques that are included in computer software:

- *Checking for correct data types.*   If a letter or punctuation mark turns up within a particular data item that is supposed to consist only of numbers, an input error has occurred. Many programs that are used for inputting mailing addresses can check for such errors. For example, such a program would identify the zip code 606A2 as invalid (because it includes a letter of the alphabet) and would alert the operator accordingly.

- *Checking for reasonable data values.*   It is often possible to predetermine what range of input values will be acceptable. Checks to see if particular data items are reasonable can be included in input software to avert certain inaccuracies. For example, programs that input data concerning people's ages can be designed to recognize that three-digit numbers above 110 are unreasonable values for a person's age in years. Similarly, some types of data have very specific ranges of acceptable values, and software can reflect this. For example, there are only 12 months in a year, so 14 should be rejected as out of range for a month value.

- *Checking for data consistency.*   Two separate data items may be related in some way that can be used to check their accuracy. An item that seems correct when viewed on its own may really be invalid when viewed in relation to some other item. For example, software that inputs data on educational histories might check high school graduation dates against college graduation dates. A high school graduation date of 1983 and a college graduation of 1979 for the same person would mean that at least one date is probably incorrect.

- *Checking control totals.*   Input data often consist of columns of numbers. One way to help ensure the correct entry of such numbers is to use **control totals,** or sums that are computed twice: by hand before input and by computer afterwards. If the two totals match, the numbers were probably entered correctly. For example, software that inputs the daily number of hours an employee works may use control totals to see if the number of hours entered matches the total number of hours reported.

- *Using a check digit.*   The digits themselves can be used to help ensure the accuracy of numeric input data. Through the use of some predefined mathematical formula, an additional **check digit** is calculated for a number to be input and appended on that number. After input, the same calculation is performed again to see if the same check digit is obtained. If it isn't, then some error has occurred during input. This method, which is usually built into the input software, is similar to the parity check we discussed previously. It is often part of customer account numbers.

Summary

Interactive Systems

In an interactive system the computer receives some form of input and generates a response.

Computer Terminal Keyboards

Computer keyboards have many keys in addition to ones that produce printable characters. Control keys and function keys can perform different operations in different programs.

Types of Computer Displays

Computer displays are built from cathode ray tubes (CRTs), liquid crystals, electroluminescent displays, and plasma panels. All of them form characters by creating images out of closely spaced dots. CRTs are inexpensive but power hungry. The other types of displays have specialized uses. For example, liquid crystals are used in battery-powered equipment.

Display Operations

Special character sequences cause a display to perform operations like moving characters from one place on the screen to another.

Escape sequences pass along the information needed to perform the operation. The visual aspect of characters can be modified.

Protected fields are used when a computerized version of a paper form is being filled out.

Terminals capable of drawing graphic images allow access to each dot of the display. They have commands to draw lines and fill in areas of the screen.

Additional Interactive Input Devices

Graphical input can be obtained from several drawing and pointing devices.

A *digitizer* converts coordinates into numbers using a special stylus.

Using a *light pen*, you can draw directly on the screen.

A *mouse* senses motion over a surface using either a rolling ball or beams of light.

A *trackball* is an upside-down mechanical mouse. The user's fingers move the ball and device itself remains stationary.

Touch panels can be used to sense pressure against a limited number of points on a screen.

Other Input Sources

Business information can be gathered at its source with *point-of-sale* (POS) terminals. Data is read from price tags using *optical character recognition* (OCR) devices or is scanned from bar codes. Information can be read from magnetic strips on the backs of credit cards. Student's tests and consumer survey forms with check-the-box entries can be read with *optical mark recognizers* (OMR).

Magnetic Ink Character Recognition (MICR) is commonly used to encode banking information on the bottom of checks.

Image Processing   Computers can input pictures, process the images, and incorporate them into printed output.

Touch-Tone Input   Touch-tone devices employ telephone pushbuttons and lines to send data, in the form of sounds, to a central computer.

Voice Input   Voice-recognition modules enable computers to accept a limited number of vocal commands from users. Voice-input systems are either speaker-dependent or speaker-independent.

Paper Output Systems

Paper is by far the most popular permanent medium for computer output.

Printers   A printer is a machine that outputs alphanumeric characters on paper. Character printers print one character at a time, by impact or nonimpact methods. Impact methods are used in daisy wheel and dot matrix printers. Nonimpact methods are used in inkjet, thermal, and electrostatic printers. Line printers print an entire line at a time and can be subdivided into wheel, drum, band, and chain printers. Page printers print an entire page at a time, by means of xerographic or laser technology.

Plotters   Plotters are computer-controlled drawing machines used to produce paper output such as maps, graphs, charts, and illustrations. Inkjet plotters produce images by spraying droplets of ink on paper rolled over a rotating drum. Pen plotters produce images by moving one or more pens across paper and can be classified as either flatbed or drum plotters.

Microfilm and Microfiche Output

Computer output microfilm (COM) is either rolls or sheets (microfiche) of thin plastic film on which text is reproduced at reduced size. Microfilm recorders are used to produce COM, which must be read at a viewing station. Sophisticated COM systems utilize computer-assisted retrieval (CAR) techniques to improve the speed of microfilm access.

Ensuring the Quality of Data

All computer input consists of numbers, but it originates from various sources.

Hardware Checks on the Accuracy of Data   Parity bits or redundancy codes are used to detect and correct data errors caused by hardware malfunctions.

Software Checks on the Accuracy of Data   The accuracy of computer input is critical—garbage in, garbage out. Error detection is accomplished by checking for correct data types, reasonable data values, or consistency of data or by using control totals or check digits.

Computer Concepts

As an extra review of the chapter, try defining the following terms. If you have trouble with any of them, refer to the page number listed.

1. How do dumb, smart, and intelligent terminals differ?
2. What are some devices in which the technology of LCDs is used?
3. How is the *mouse* related to the *trackball*?
4. How does a touch panel screen reduce the time required to learn how to operate the computer?
5. What do point-of-sale terminals do?
6. What are magnetic strips? Where are they commonly found?
7. What are some advantages of using magnetic ink character recognition (MICR)?
8. What do voice output devices do?
9. What are some of the typical formats of paper output?
10. Describe the different types of printers.
11. What types of applications are most suitable for character printers?
12. What are the different types of impact printers?
13. What types of applications are most suitable for line printers?
14. What are some nonimpact methods of character printing?
15. What are plotters? How can they be used?
16. What kinds of organizations would use microfilm effectively?
17. What is data entry?
18. What are parity bits?
19. What are the two main types of input errors?
20. Name five error-detecting techniques that can be used to minimize input errors.

True or False

1. Computer keyboard terminals are not similar to the keyboards of electric typewriters.
2. A display unit consisting solely of a display screen is called a monitor.
3. Electroluminescent displays (ELDs) are more expensive than liquid crystal displays (LCDs).
4. A digitizer is a graphic tablet that can be used to trace a picture and communicate the contact points to a computer.
5. Bar codes represent data as a series of numbers.
6. Magnetic strips are not suitable for holding data that must be entered often and kept confidential.
7. Speaker-independent systems are more accurate than speaker-dependent systems.
8. Pen plotters can draw only on paper.
9. A disadvantage of microfilm is that it is more expensive to use than paper for high-volume users.
10. Two of the most common built-in means of maintaining the accuracy of data are parity checks and redundancy checks.

Multiple Choice

1. The dominant type of display screen is
   (a) LCD   (b) CRT   (c) PDP

2. Flat panel screens that use neon gas are:
   (a) PDPs   (b) LCDs   (c) ELDs

3. A mouse is an input device used to direct the motions of a:
   (a) stylus   (b) digitizer   (c) cursor

4. Specialized terminals located at check-out counters in retail stores are called:
   (a) touch panels   (b) point-of-sale (POS)   (c) protected fields
                              registers

5. Optical mark recognition (OMR) is used to:
   (a) score test forms   (b) read characters from   (c) update sales
                              price tags

6. An input method that uses characters printed with magnetizable ink is:
   (a) UPC   (b) ELD   (c) MICR

7. Devices that send input data in the form of sounds of varying pitch over telephone lines to a central computer are called:
   (a) speaker-independent   (b) touch-tone devices   (c) voice-recognition
       systems   modules

8. Output from computers printed on paper is called:
   (a) hardcopy   (b) postscript   (c) data type

9. Most computer errors are:
   (a) due to hardware   (b) unavoidable   (c) due to errors in pro-
       malfunctions   gramming or data entry

10. Sums that are computed twice, one by hand before input and once by computer afterward, are called:
    (a) data values   (b) control totals   (c) check digits

A Sharper Focus

1. How would everyday activities, such as shopping and banking, be more difficult without the aid of computers and computing systems?
2. Having read this chapter, how would you be better prepared to deal with a situation in which you were the victim of a computer error?

Projects

1. Write a report on the various types of input devices available to you in the computers you use routinely, such as the computer(s) at your campus computer center, your bank ATM, or the various stores where you shop.

2. Visit a local computer store and discuss with the sales people what type of computer you might find useful for your personal use. Report on what types of input and output devices are available with that computer, including what types of printers would be compatible and the relative costs of each type.

3. Visit your campus or municipal library. Find out what types of documents are maintained on microfilm or microfiche and write a report discussing the advantages of buying and storing these documents in microfilm (or microfiche) form versus paper form.

4. Contact one of the departments on campus where large data bases are kept and updated or where fairly long programs are input into computer systems. Discuss with the programmers what types of error checking techniques they use; write a report on your discussions.

5

Storage Devices and File Organization

In This Chapter

Focus On

Cataloging a Library

The main card catalog at the Library of Congress—the rows and rows of massive wooden cabinets that hold 23 million well-thumbed index cards—is gradually becoming obsolete as the library moves toward automation.

Traditionalists worry that they are losing a cherished national institution, a place where scholars can make serendipitous discoveries among the cards and where more than a few romances have started from chance encounters.

Library officials, on the other hand, assert that the evolving computerized catalog is a physical necessity at the world's largest library, which has to add two million index cards each year. The general collection's card catalog, which dates back to 1800, occupies several rooms—about the size of half a city block—and has 22 trays of cards on Shakespeare alone.

Even with increasing automation, the old card catalog will not be abandoned after renovation, according to library spokesman Craig D'Ooge, mostly because the cards are being microfilmed. "And it's for certain that as long as there's a need for it, it will be accessible [to] scholars," he said. In 1981, the catalog was "frozen" so that books obtained after January 2, 1981, were recorded only in the computerized files. And by the end of 1984, virtually all of the library's English-language books were cataloged in the automated system and available to researchers through 40 terminals in the library's reading rooms, according to John W. Kimball, head of the automation and reference collections section in the general reading rooms.

The automation has proceeded on two fronts. Since 1968, the library has cataloged new acquisitions in its machine-readable cataloging (MARC) computer system, and recently the library converted its 1979 list of 5.5 million books into computer format to cover pre-1968 items, in what is called the Pre-MARC (PREM) system. The PREM system also contains serials, maps, and music. The MARC system is updated every two weeks; PREM is not updated, but there are plans to complete and edit it as well.

A researcher looking for English-language books on Shakespeare, for example, now could use a computer terminal to find at least 90% of the library's books on the subject, Kimball said. . . .

The library has about 71 million items now that could be cataloged. About 7.5 million books (in English and many other languages) are currently in machine-readable form.

To handle the huge data base, the library is currently using IBM 3033 and 3084 mainframes to process on-line requests. However, there are plans to replace these soon. The automation projects will continue as the library undergoes a major renovation, to be completed by 1992. According to Linda Arret, assistant to Mr. Kimball, by 1989, when the renovated main reading room will reopen, the number of public terminals will increase to between 75 and 100. The entire system includes about 3,000 terminals or printers in the Library and in Congressional offices.

Computers perform more than 25 trillion calculations a day just in the United States. The federal government holds dozens of computer files on every individual, and the 1980 census gathered more than 5 billion facts about Americans. In business, medicine, education, finance—in practically any field—people constantly create new data for computers to analyze. But just as you can't remember everything you've read in books, magazines, and newspapers, no computer can hold in its primary memory all the data it will need to process to carry out the variety of jobs that it is asked to do. That's why computers need secondary storage.

A variety of media can be used to store data. Once the data are stored, a number of methods are available for organizing them into useful, quickly accessible pieces of information. The choice of organizing method depends in large part on the storage medium being used. And the choice of a storage medium is based on a careful analysis of how quickly and how often the data need to be accessed, how frequently they will be changed, whether copies are necessary; in other words, it depends on how the data should be filed.

In this chapter, we'll look at the various media and devices used to store data— at the strengths and weaknesses of each and at the methods for organizing the data they hold.

THE NEED FOR SECONDARY STORAGE

In Chapter 3, we learned that in order to do any processing a computer must have both a program and the data required by that program in its primary memory. **Secondary storage,** also called **auxiliary storage,** supplements primary memory by providing a place to keep programs and data when the computer isn't processing them. Secondary storage may be either **on-line** (controlled by the CPU and ready to operate, for example, a disk pack mounted and spinning) or **off-line** (requires some manual intervention to begin access, for example, fetching a tape from a tape vault and threading it on a drive). Accessing secondary storage usually involves some mechanical operation, such as waiting for tape to wind or waiting for read/write heads to move. It is much slower than accessing primary memory, which involves no moving parts. Despite its access advantage, primary memory has several shortcomings that make secondary storage a necessity:

Why primary memory isn't enough

- *Most primary memories are volatile.*   When the power is shut off, the contents of most types of primary memory disappear. Because secondary storage is usually magnetic rather than electronic, its contents remain unaffected by power loss.

- *Primary memory has a limited capacity.*   Even though technological advances have produced a steady increase in the amount of primary memory that can be installed in computers, the upper limit is still far less than most users need for all of their programs and data. Furthermore, for a particular computer, the number of address wires in its interconnection bus restricts the amount of primary storage that may ever be added. The amount of secondary storage a system can have is virtually unlimited.

- *Primary memory is expensive.*   Technological advances are steadily reducing the cost of primary memory, but secondary storage remains less expensive.

- *Primary memory is nonportable.*   The contents of a computer's primary memory cannot be transferred to another computer or device unless a communications link exists. Many forms of secondary storage can be transported between machines.

MAGNETIC TAPE STORAGE

Magnetic tape is a recording medium used extensively for computer batch input and data storage. It consists of a long strip of thin, tough plastic called *Mylar*, which is coated on one side with a film of an easily magnetizable substance such as iron oxide. Magnetic tape can be reused many times because recording new data automatically erases the data previously recorded in that location.

As a secondary storage medium, tape has been a vital element of mainframe computer systems for years. Today, magnetic tape storage remains an efficient, economical, and reliable method for keeping backup copies of large quantities of data. Whether the system is a word processor or a supercomputer, some type of magnetic tape unit can be incorporated in it as a valuable component. To see exactly how magnetic tape storage is utilized in computer systems, let's examine how data are represented and organized on tape.

Computer magnetic tape resembles that used for audio recording. The major differences are that data tapes are usually of much higher quality and are often packaged differently than sound tapes. Data tapes have three basic physical formats (shown in Figure 5.1).

(a)

(b)

(c)

Figure 5.1 Magnetic Tape
Magnetic tape is packaged in three formats: reels, cartridges, and cassettes. Reels are generally used when high capacity and interchange between different computers is important. (a) Reels are up to 10½ inches in diameter and hold 2400 feet of ½-inch-wide tape. (b) Cartridges hold 450 feet of ¼-inch-wide tape. (c) Cassettes hold 300 feet of 1/8-inch-wide tape.

- **Tape reels,** commonly used with mainframes and minicomputers, are 10½ inches in diameter and typically hold 2400 feet of ½-inch-wide tape (300-foot, 600-foot, and 1200-foot lengths are also used). The **data density** (number of bytes per given area) for such tape can be as high as 6250 **bytes per inch (bpi),** giving a full reel a capacity of 150 megabytes.

- **Tape cartridges,** commonly used with minicomputers, are plastic cases enclosing small reels that typically hold 140 to 150 feet of ¼-inch-wide tape. Data densities of 400 bpi are common.

- **Tape cassettes,** commonly used with microcomputers, look just like those used in audio cassette recorders. These ⅛-inch-wide tapes are 150 or 300 feet long. The data density is usually about 200 bpi.

Each type of tape container has a mechanism that can tell the computer not to overwrite the tape. Tape reels use a **write-protect** ring that fits into the underside of the reel near the hub. If the ring is absent, the tape can only be read. Cartridges use a small plastic slider near the front of the tape box.

Data Organization on Tape

Data are represented on magnetic tape by tiny, invisible, magnetized spots. Once recorded, these magnetic spots persist until they're either erased or written over by new data. A spot magnetized in one direction represents a binary one, and a spot magnetized in the opposite direction, a zero. The tape's surface has a gridlike organization, with short vertical columns called *frames* and long horizontal rows called *channels*, or *tracks*. The most common ½-inch tapes have nine tracks. One character is stored in a frame; there is one track for each of the eight bits in a byte of memory and an extra track for a parity bit, which is used by the computer to see if an error has occurred in the storage, transmission, or copying of a character. (Chapter 4 contains more information on how parity bits are used to ensure data integrity.) Tape is a sequential access medium, in which characters are stored one after another along the length of the tape. A decision to use magnetic tape for data storage must take into account the limitations imposed by its sequential nature. Figure 5.2 shows how data are represented on magnetic tape.

How data are represented on tape

Magnetic tape as a sequential access medium

Unfortunately, it usually isn't possible to store characters one after another for the entire length of a tape. If it were, the tape's data density and length would be the only factors needed to calculate its maximum capacity. Data density varies with the quality of the tape and the equipment used to read from and write on it. The usual data density is 6250 bpi, but some ½-inch-wide magnetic tape is recorded at a density of 1600 bpi or 800 bpi. Very high density systems, such as the IBM 3480, can record tapes at 38,000 bpi.

Adjacent characters are usually arranged in consecutive groups called **fields,** each of which holds some particular data category. A Social Security number, for instance, could be stored in a field nine characters long. Fields are further grouped into **records,** each of which is a collection of adjacent fields treated as a unit. For example, a mailing list record could consist of three fields: a name, a Social Security number, and an address.

How data are grouped into records

Sometimes it's necessary for the records stored on a tape to be individually accessible. Because the starting and stopping of the tape motion by the tape drive requires some leeway, a blank space, or **interrecord gap (IRG),** must then be left to separate adjacent records. If the records are short, these gaps (usually about ½-inch long) can easily take up more space on the tape than the data do.

Figure 5.2 Data Representation on Tape

Data are stored on tape in the form of spots magnetized in one direction or the other. Here, arrows pointing up represent binary ones, and arrows pointing down represent zeros. Each vertical column, or frame, is made up of 9 bits and contains one 8-bit character and a parity bit. The 9 horizontal rows are called tracks, or channels.

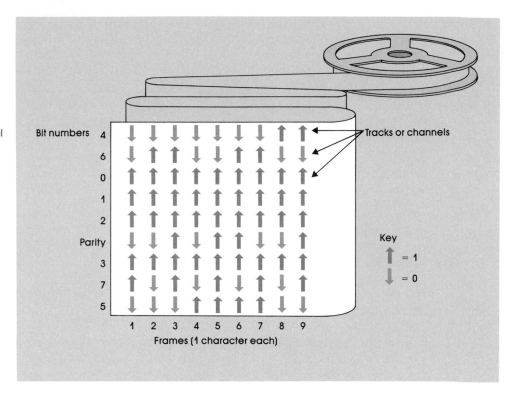

To avoid this waste of tape, records are often grouped into **blocks,** also known as **physical records.** The individual records are then called **logical records.** The fixed number of logical records that make up a block is known as the **blocking factor.** The blocking factor must be chosen carefully to optimize overall processing. As you can see in Figure 5.3, when records are blocked, interrecord gaps aren't necessary. However, an **interblock gap (IBG)** must follow each block. With interblock gaps, fewer gaps fill the tape, and thus less space is wasted. Furthermore, since entire blocks of records are written to or read from the tape at once, storage and retrieval speeds are significantly improved. However, the programs that use tapes on which records have been blocked must reserve enough primary memory to hold entire blocks and must perform the blocking and deblocking of records.

Storing Multiple Files on Tape

Tape labels and the volume table of contents

A group of records that contain related information is often called a **file.** It is possible to write data records directly onto a tape. More often, several files are written onto a single tape. As shown in Figure 5.4, the tape is divided into separate sections, first recording a **label,** then the **volume table of contents (VTOC),** and finally the data files. Each section is separated from its neighbors by a special **end-of-file (EOF)** marker.

The tape label gives a name to the tape, as well as containing other information about where and when the tape was written. The system's software checks the

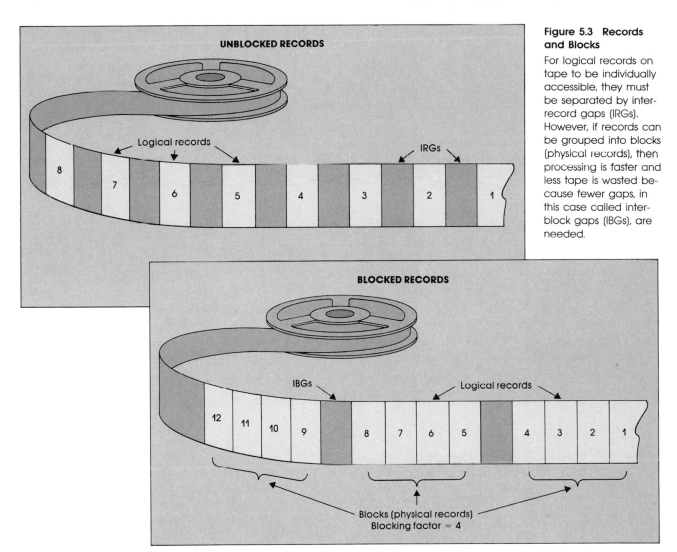

Figure 5.3 Records and Blocks

For logical records on tape to be individually accessible, they must be separated by inter-record gaps (IRGs). However, if records can be grouped into blocks (physical records), then processing is faster and less tape is wasted because fewer gaps, in this case called inter-block gaps (IBGs), are needed.

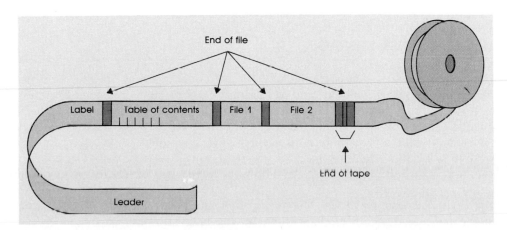

Figure 5.4 Multiple Files on One Tape

A standard tape is recorded with a label, table of contents, and multiple data files. A special End of File (EOF) marker separates each. A pair of EOF markers signify that the logical end of the tape has been reached.

tape's name to verify that the proper tape has been threaded on a drive. The name of the tape is also written on the outside of the tape reel for the benefit of operators and data librarians.

The VTOC holds information about all the files that are recorded on the tape. Each file has a name, size, ownership data, and other information that is used to identify what has been recorded on the tape.

Advantages and Disadvantages of Magnetic Tape Storage

How magnetic tape is best used

The use of magnetic tape as a storage medium has both advantages and disadvantages, all of which determine how it is best used. Its strengths include:

- *Magnetic tape is inexpensive, reusable, and easily handled.*
- *Magnetic tape has a high data density, can be read from and written on very quickly, and can hold records of different lengths.*
- *Magnetic tape is nonvolatile.* Magnetic tape is widely utilized for making off-line backup copies of important data just in case some unforeseeable erasure of on-line data occurs.
- *Magnetic tape is standardized.* The recording format for tapes usually follows strict standards so that tapes (particularly ½-inch reel tapes) can be exchanged between computers made by different manufacturers.

The weaknesses of magnetic tape as a storage medium include the following:

- *Magnetic tape can only be accessed sequentially.* Tape isn't an acceptable storage medium for data that must be accessed in an unpredictable sequence; thus it is not useful for such applications as the storage of airline or hotel reservation information that must be constantly accessible to any number of users. It is useful, however, for holding large quantities of data that will be accessed in order and only periodically, such as payroll, billing, and personnel files.
- *Magnetic tape is vulnerable to dust and extremes of temperature and humidity.*

MAGNETIC DISK STORAGE

The magnetic disk is the most popular on-line secondary storage medium for microcomputers, minicomputers, and mainframes. Superficially, disks look like phonograph records; they have the same circular shape and they rotate on a spindle in the disk drive. However, a phonograph record has a spiraling groove that starts at the outside edge and ends near the center, and a magnetic disk stores data in separate concentric rings, or *tracks,* of magnetic spots. Magnetic disks can be used over and over again—new data are simply recorded over the old data. However, unlike magnetic tape, which is a **sequential access medium,** the magnetic disk is a **direct access medium.** This means that any particular piece of data on a disk can be read at any time, without having to go through all the preceding data.

Hard Disks

Hard disks make up the major secondary storage medium for most mainframes, minicomputers, and all but the least expensive microprocessor systems. Several different kinds and arrangements of hard disks are in common use today. Hard disks are either *fixed* (that is, permanently installed) or *removable*. A single side of one disk, both sides of one disk, or a group of as many as 12 disks may be used as a unit. A group of disks that can be mounted and removed as one unit is called a *disk pack*. One double-sided 5¼-inch hard disk can store 40 megabytes of data. Large disks packs have capacities of hundreds of millions of bytes.

Secondary storage for microcomputers, minicomputers, and mainframes

Floppy Disks

Floppy disks, also called diskettes, are presently the most prevalent secondary storage medium used with microcomputers. Their name comes from having the recording surface bonded to flexible Mylar. **Single-density diskettes** hold 3200 bits of data per inch, and **double-density diskettes** can accommodate 6400 bits per inch. **Quad-density** uses recording tracks that are narrower than normal, therefore packing even more information in the same space. In addition, floppy disks are either *single-sided* (data can be recorded on one side only), or *double-sided* (both sides can be used). As an example of floppy disk capacity, a 5¼-inch, double-sided, quad-density floppy disk used with a typical personal computer can hold 1.2 megabytes of data.

The transportable storage medium for microcomputers

Another packaging of a floppy disk uses a hard plastic shell 3½-inches wide, which is equipped with a metal shutter that protects the disk's surface when it is outside the computer. Up to 1.44 megabytes of data are recorded on its two surfaces.

Figure 5.5 shows examples of each type of floppy disk. The primary advantages of floppy disks are that they are removable, inexpensive (some cost less than 25 cents each when purchased in large quantities), and convenient to transport or mail.

Disk Drives

The machines that record and retrieve data on magnetic disks are known as *disk drives*. Disk drives, like disks, have different sizes and capacities. The operating principles, however, are generally similar for all disk drives, both hard and floppy. The primary differences are in precision, speed, and capacity.

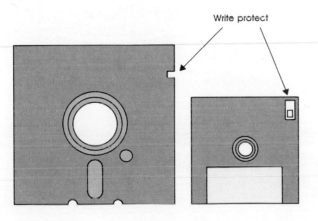

Write protect

Figure 5.5 Floppy Disks
5¼-inch disks have a write-protect notch that must be left open in order to write on the disk. The recording surface is normally exposed and is protected by a paper or Tyvek envelope when the disk is outside the drive. With 3½-inch disks, a sliding plastic block write-protects the disk. A metal shutter closes over an access window when the disk is removed from the drive.

General Operating Principles

How the devices that write onto and read from disks work

Inside the disk drive, each disk is spun on a spindle. For a hard disk the speeds may exceed 3600 rpm (about 150 mph at the outer edge). Read/write heads mounted on **access arms** move in and out across the surface of the disk (see Figure 5.6), creating and detecting magnetic fields on it. The heads in floppy disk drives actually touch the disk surface, but those in hard disk drives do not. The combination of disk rotation and access arm movement allows a head to be positioned over any spot on any track of a disk. The disk drive must have an access arm for each disk surface. Thus, if a disk pack containing four double-sided disks is to be used in a disk drive, the drive must have eight access arms.

The classic challenge for designers of disk drives is how to achieve higher data densities and faster storage and retrieval speeds. Two factors that directly affect the data density that can be achieved are the closeness of the read/write head to the disk surface and the precision of the access arm movements. Higher data densities are possible with closer heads, and more precise arm movements can be achieved by using smaller magnetic spots and tracks that are placed closer together (thus more of them can fit on a disk). Another factor influencing data density is the

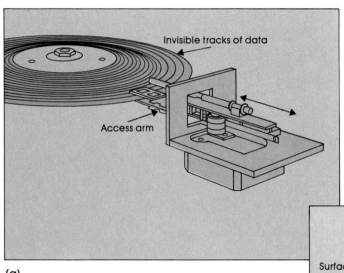

Figure 5.6 The Disk Drive
The disk drive spins (a) a disk or (b) a group of disks (a disk pack) on a spindle at a very high speed. Access arms, one for each disk surface, position the read/write heads that create and detect the magnetic spots.
(c) Seagate Technology hard disk drive.

quality of the disk's magnetizable coating. Achieving faster storage and retrieval is mainly a matter of improving the speed of moving the disk heads or reading data from several heads simultaneously.

Hard disk drives outperform floppy disk drives in all areas except cost. Hard disk drives have more precise access arm movements, and their heads fly very close to the disk surface. Also, coatings of the hard disks are of higher quality than those of floppy disks. As a result, a disk pack containing 11 hard disks (a popular format) can hold 600 million characters, a feat that would require 500 floppy disks! Because hard disks are rigid, they can be spun faster than their flexible counterparts (centrifugal force would eventually bend and damage a floppy disk that was spun too rapidly).

Hard disk drives, however, are rather expensive. They must be carefully sealed because of the disks' sensitivity to contamination by dust, smoke, and fingerprints. If a hard disk drive's read/write head collides with one of these minute obstructions as it glides 20 millionths of an inch above a disk spinning at 150 mph, the resulting **head crash** can destroy the data, disk, and read/write head all at once (see Figure 5.7). Floppy disk drives are less susceptible to such mishaps, even though the heads actually come into contact with the floppy disks. Floppy disks can be damaged by contaminants, but their flexibility and slower rotation speeds of 300 rpm minimize the consequence of collisions. In general, floppy disk drives are less expensive and more rugged than hard disk drives.

The Winchester

In the early 1970s, in an effort to increase the storage capacity, access speed, reliability, and economy of hard disks, IBM developed the **Winchester disk drive.** Its access arms and read/write heads, as well as the hard disk or disks, were completely enclosed in a sealed, airtight housing (see Figure 5.8). This arrangement virtually eliminated contamination from airborne particles and dramatically increased both access speed and storage capacity (to 70 million bytes on four 8-inch disks). The result was hard disk storage that was much more reliable and much less expensive. Prior to 1980, the most common medium for high-speed disk storage was large, removable disk packs. Since then, Winchester disk drives have become more popular and have increased the power of affordable small computer systems.

The Winchester disk

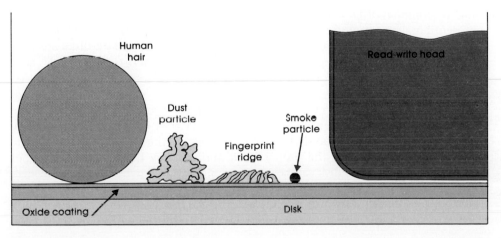

Figure 5.7 Head Crash
This illustration depicts the extreme sensitivity of hard disks to contamination. That smoke particle, only 250 millionths of an inch in diameter, is about to collide with the read/write head, which is only 20 millionths of an inch above the surface of the disk.

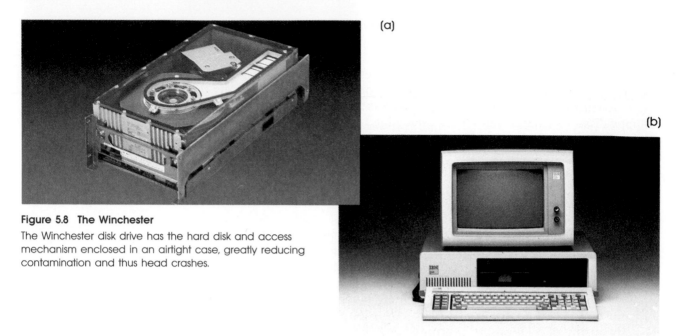

(a)

(b)

Figure 5.8 The Winchester
The Winchester disk drive has the hard disk and access mechanism enclosed in an airtight case, greatly reducing contamination and thus head crashes.

Removable Hard Disks

Removable hard disks

Recent advances in disk-packaging technology have allowed removable hard disks to return to popularity. A single small metal platter is housed in an airtight plastic cartridge. With a capacity that can exceed 45 megabytes, these disks offer fast data access, transportability, unlimited storage (by using multiple disk cartridges), and finally data security. Sensitive information can be kept in locked file cabinets when it isn't needed on-line. This type of disk can also be paired with a much larger fixed disk. The removable disk is used as a backup medium. It collects duplicates of all the files that are changed each day.

Data Organization on Disk

How data are arranged on this direct access medium

Data are stored on disks as they are on tape, in the form of tiny magnetic spots that represent binary zeros and ones. However, only a single channel is used to record the data, in contrast to a tape's nine channels. Characters stored on disks are usually grouped into records—again, as they are on tape. But there the similarities end.

As we said earlier, data on a disk are arranged in concentric rings called tracks, which are numbered from 0, starting at the outer edge (see Figure 5.9). One side of a disk may have as few as 35 tracks (on some floppies) or more than 800 (on some hard disks). For all but a few floppy disks, regardless of its circumference, every track on a particular disk holds the same number of characters. By moving the access arm in or out over the proper track and rotating the disk to the proper position, any record on a disk can be read or written. This is why the magnetic disk is a direct access medium. Any record on a disk can be accessed directly, as long as its position is known. The records on a disk can also be accessed sequentially, another way in which magnetic disks are similar to phonograph records.

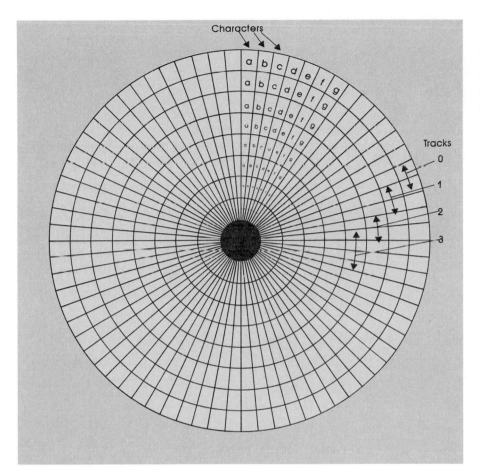

Figure 5.9 Disk Tracks
Data are recorded on disks in concentric rings called tracks, which are numbered starting with 0 at the outer edge. Each track, regardless of its circumference, holds the same number of characters.

Each of the physical records on a disk, called **disk blocks,** holds the same number of bytes. Even the positions for all of the records are preassigned. This allows a disk drive to overwrite each disk block at any time without corrupting the next disk block. Tapes, with their variable length records, cannot have inner records updated. Additions can only be made to the end of a tape. Some floppy disks indicate where each record should fall by a series of holes punched in the center near the hub. These are called **hard-sectored** disks: the number and size of the disk blocks are permanently fixed. **Soft-sectored** disks have only one index hole. The size and number of sectors can be adjusted by a software operation called reformatting.

The Sector Method

The **sector method** is the approach to data organization that is used on virtually all floppy disks. The disk surface is divided into shapes like slices of a pie, called *sectors*. A record on a disk organized by the sector method is located by its *address*. Such a record's address has three components: the *surface number* (if there are two sides), the *track number* on the surface, and the *sector number* within the track. Figure 5.10 shows how these three parts of an address identify the exact location of a record.

Pie slices called sectors

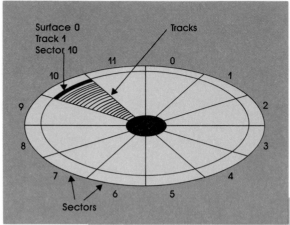

Figure 5.10 The Sector Method

The sector method subdivides the disk surface into areas shaped like wedges of a pie, which are called sectors. Accessing a given record requires the surface number, the track number, and the sector number.

Figure 5.11 The Cylinder Method

The cylinder method, used only with multiple disks, is based on the grouping of all tracks having the same number to form a cylinder. A stack of disks has as many cylinders as each disk has tracks. Accessing a record requires the cylinder number, the surface number, and the record number.

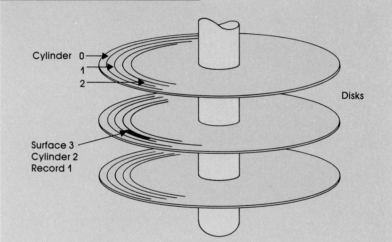

The Cylinder Method

Cylinders for multiple disks

Another approach to the organization of data on disks, the **cylinder method,** is used only for disk packs. All disks in a pack are fixed to the same spindle, and for each surface there is a read/write head on an access arm. All of the access arms move in concert. Since the disks are stacked, each track on a surface lines up with the same track on all the other surfaces. Thus, all the tracks with the same number make up a *cylinder;* that is, each set of vertically aligned tracks forms one of a series of nested cylinders, as shown in Figure 5.11. A stack of disks has as many cylinders as the number of tracks on each individual disk; all access arms are positioned at the same cylinder at any given time. The location of a record stored on a disk pack is specified by an address made up of the *cylinder number,* the *surface number,* and the *record number* within the cylinder.

Clearly, the cylinder method of data organization offers an advantage with disk packs. When the access arms are in position at the appropriate cylinder, they don't have to be moved again until all the data on that cylinder have been accessed. If the data to be accessed are on one cylinder, this shortens the **access time,** or how long it takes for data to be written on or read from the storage medium. To speed up the storage and retrieval of data, this time must be kept as short as possible. (Keep in

Disk access time: how long it takes

mind that access time is measured in milliseconds and usually adds up to only 10 to 60 milliseconds for hard disks and 100 milliseconds or more for floppy disks.)

Access time for disks can be broken down into three segments that represent three separate events in the data storage and retrieval process. **Seek time,** the longest segment, is how long it takes for the access arm to position its read/write head over the proper track or, on disk packs organized by the cylinder method, to position the read/write heads at the proper cylinder. **Rotational delay** is the time it takes for the turning motion of the disk to bring the desired record under the read/write head once the access arm is in position. **Data transfer time,** generally the shortest of the three segments, is how long it takes for the data to be transmitted to or from the computer.

Storing Multiple Files on Disks

Disk drives do not have a single standard format like that used for nine-track, ½-inch tape systems. Often it is necessary to completely erase a disk pack and re-record its sector assignments if the pack is to be moved to a different computer system. Normally, disks hold multiple files.

File systems record multiple files but consume disk space

The operating system (the software in charge of a computer) uses the space on a disk drive to record a **file system.** Files are accessed and created using names that a program specifies. Empty space is allocated to new files. If a file grows to exceed its initial allocation, then more space is found and added to the allocation. The file names and the information needed to find all the blocks associated with a file are recorded in a **directory** or **catalog.** Implementing the file system can sometimes consume over 5 percent of the disk's space.

Advantages and Disadvantages of Magnetic Disk Storage

Magnetic disks also have advantages and disadvantages as a storage medium, which affect the ways in which they can be effectively used. The advantages of magnetic disk storage include:

How magnetic disks are best used

- *Magnetic disks can be accessed directly or sequentially.* This makes disks more flexible than magnetic tape.

- *Magnetic disks can be read from and written to very quickly.* The fastest hard disk drives can transfer more than 15 million characters per second to primary storage.

- *Magnetic disks have high data densities.* Magnetic disk storage, especially hard disk storage, is very compact. Hard disks can hold 750 characters per inch of track and may have 400 tracks per inch of diameter.

- *Magnetic disks are portable.* Removable hard disks and floppy disks can be taken off-line and are easily transported.

The disadvantages of magnetic disk storage include:

- *Magnetic disks are relatively expensive.* Although magnetic disks are becoming more economical, they still cost more per byte than magnetic tape. The higher cost makes disks less suitable than tape for storing large quantities of periodically accessed off-line data.

- *Magnetic disks are easily damaged.*   Fixed-disk units are fragile, and removable disks and floppy disks can be damaged by heat, dust, and magnetic fields.

These characteristics indicate that magnetic disks are applicable for general, on-line secondary storage. Magnetic disk storage is best suited to situations where data must be accessed directly and in no particular order.

OTHER TYPES OF SECONDARY STORAGE

Although magnetic tapes and disks are the most common, you may encounter some other types of secondary storage. These are either currently being used or promise to become important in the near future.

Bulk Memory

An intermediary between primary memory and disks

The access time for magnetic disk storage lies somewhere between that for primary memory and that for sequentially accessed magnetic tapes. On high-performance computers, the difference between the access time for primary memory and that for high-speed disks constitutes an opening for another type of storage called *bulk memory* (see Chapter 3), which can be accessed faster than disks, but is as much as 10 times slower than primary memory. Bulk memory is often accessible only in blocks, rather than as individual bytes. The data transfer time between bulk memory and primary memory is about the same as that for accessing the faster disks. However, accessing bulk memory involves no seek time or rotational delay. Also, data transfers from most disk drives must start at a sector boundary, and there is no way to transfer only part of a sector to the CPU. When data are in bulk memory, any byte or group of bytes can be transferred into primary memory.

Bulk memory is sometimes configured as *disk cache memory*. In other words, when access to a particular disk sector is required, the entire track or cylinder on which the sector resides is transferred into bulk memory as a cache (pronounced ''kash,'' meaning literally a container for safekeeping). If a program requires data from a sector that is among those just transferred, the request may be satisfied without having to return to the disk. This eliminates most of the seek time and rotational delay associated with disk access.

Microprocessor software must be written to run on small machine configurations. Programmers have learned to fit their applications into these environments by sending intermediate results to disk to free up some primary storage. Although this allows the creation of more complex programs, performance suffers. Furthermore, some machines have a moderate number of address wires, which limits the amount of primary memory the machine can address. Extended memory is often identical in speed to a microprocessor's main memory. However, special commands must be given to set up an access to a block of extended memory. Software can treat extended memory as a very fast disk drive called a **RAM (random access memory) disk.** Disk-bound software can have spectacular performance improvements when a RAM disk substitutes for a floppy disk. Because this memory is volatile, RAM disks are best used for storing copies of programs or temporary files that are ordinarily deleted after a program finishes running.

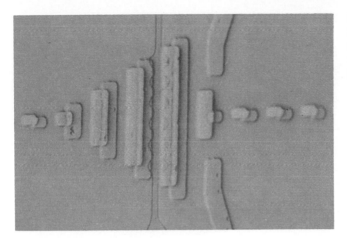

Figure 5.12 Magnetic Bubble Storage
In magnetic bubble storage, solid-state chips store thousands of tiny magnetic fields. This nonvolatile type of memory is used in some portable computers.

Magnetic Bubble Storage

Secondary storage without moving parts

Magnetic bubble storage utilizes thousands of tiny floating magnetized areas (the "bubbles") induced on chips of synthetic garnet (a hard, glasslike mineral), as shown in Figure 5.12. The presence of a bubble indicates a binary one, and its absence, a zero. The magnetic bubbles can be moved across the chip to be read, written on, or erased. An important feature of this type of storage is that, like tapes and disks, it keeps its magnetic configuration even after the power is turned off. However, its biggest advantage (and the characteristic that differentiates it from magnetic tape and disk storage) is its solid-state nature. Magnetic bubble chips operate completely by electromagnetic forces, and thus magnetic bubble storage systems have no mechanical or moving parts. Because of this, magnetic bubble storage systems are potentially much more reliable than magnetic tape or disk storage systems, which typically have many moving parts. Magnetic bubble storage is used in a variety of portable computers, intelligent terminals, robots, and communications equipment.

Introduced and widely utilized in the late 1970s, magnetic bubble storage was heralded as the future replacement for magnetic disks. However, the relatively slow access speeds and the high cost of the chips, in conjunction with recent phenomenal advances in hard and floppy disk technology, makes this changeover seem much less likely today.

Optical Disks

Storing data using light

Optical storage is a promising means for storing massive amounts of data inexpensively. The **optical disk,** also known as the **laser disk,** is a circular platter covered with a thin metallic film beneath a layer of glass or plastic, as shown in Figure 5.13. Optical disks provide great durability and reliability because the metallic film is protected by the plastic and isn't as easily damaged by extremes of temperature or humidity, scratches, or dust. Compared to magnetic media, optical media are relatively indestructible; they can easily last 10 years or more.

Optical disks are similar in principle to the laser-driven videodisks that were introduced in 1979. To store data on an optical disk, a laser is used to either burn

Figure 5.13 Optical Disk Storage
Optical disks are a possible answer to the need for inexpensive storage of huge quantities of data. An optical disk is a platter coated with metallic film that is covered with glass or plastic.

holes or raise blisters in the metallic film. The presence of a hole or blister represents a binary one, and the absence, a zero. Another, less powerful, laser reads the recorded disk by detecting the differing amounts of reflected light caused by the presence or absence of holes or blisters. The biggest advantages of optical disks is their high data densities: the holes can be made so tiny that 100 of them could fit into a space the diameter of an eyelash. Many optical disks currently being marketed have capacities of from 1 to 4 gigabytes (recall from Chapter 3 that a gigabyte is 1 million kilobytes). Some research labs have reported achieving a data density of 1 gigabit per square centimeter. At this density, the entire contents of the 18 million volumes in the Library of Congress could be recorded on just 100 optical disks!

Mass-produced read-only optical disks, called **CD-ROM,** are identical to the 4¼-inch audio compact discs (see Figure 5.14). Although they have a 550 megabyte capacity, CD-ROM disk drives have slow access times. The disks are produced using the same mechanical stamping process as audio CDs. They are suited for publishing information that is not very volatile, for example, a dictionary and thesaurus. Because of their high capacity and low manufacturing cost, the CD-ROM promises to be an exciting new media for the publishing industry. Although the

Figure 5.14 Compact Disc
Hitachi's 4¼-inch audio CD and CD player.

physical aspects of a CD-ROM have been standardized, no universally acceptable data format has emerged. The data format needs to define how files are recorded, the names of all files, and even the meaning of the data that are held in each file. For example, a file could contain printable text, pictures, sound, or even computer programs.

Many currently available optical storage systems can only be used to read stored data and write new data; previously written data cannot be erased. Thus, they have been given the acronym **WORM,** which stands for *write once read many*. Unlike the CD-ROM, WORM disk formats have not been standardized. Disks recorded on one manufacturer's system won't be readable on another system. However, much research is being directed toward the development of erasable optical disks, and at least one company has marketed a model. Such disks are made of plastic that is coated with special materials (known as *amorphous glasses*) which change state when hit by laser light. As a result, lasers can be used to write, read, and erase spots in these materials. This general concept was hit upon by self-trained physicist Stanford Ovshinsky more than 15 years ago and has since been successfully incorporated into the Optical Document File System of the Japanese company Matsushita. The end-product of a $600-million-a-year research program at Matsushita, this system stores 10,000 documents on 8-inch optical disks that hold 700 megabytes each.

Despite the development of erasable optical disks, current applications of optical storage systems are mainly limited to the holding of large quantities of data that must be read but are not expected to change. For example, libraries and other archives can use optical disks to store more compactly much information that is now in paper form. NASA, the Air Force, and the Library of Congress have all instituted pilot programs to test the use of optical storage systems.

FILE ORGANIZATION

All secondary storage media hold collections of data that need to be maintained outside a computer's primary memory. These collections, generically known as *files*, are characterized by their relative permanence and large size. They exist independently of the programs that create, modify, and use them. Files hold data that will not fit into primary memory or that should remain intact after the computer is shut off.

Arranging data into fields, records, and files

A file is a collection of records. Each record is subdivided into fields, which are groupings of characters. For example, a record built to contain mailing addresses would have fields for name, street address, city, state, and zip code. In the following sections, we will look at three different ways to organize files: sequential, direct access, and indexed sequential.

Sequential Files

A **sequential file** is organized so that one record follows another in some fixed succession, as shown in Figure 5.15. This format is forced on a tape but is sometimes used on disks because of its simplicity. To access a particular record, it is necessary to search through the file from the beginning until the desired item is reached. Also, new records can be added only at the end of the file. Keeping large

One record after another

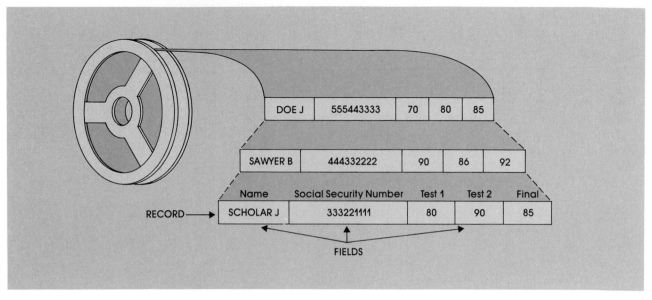

Figure 5.15 The Sequential File
This file of student grades is a sequential file. Note that the characters are grouped into fields and the fields into records, and that the records follow one another in a specific order in the file.

sequential files *sorted*, that is, keeping them in a predictable ascending or descending order (like the names in a phone book, for example), is crucial to their efficient use and maintenance. To achieve this end, a particular field in each record is chosen as the **key,** or item on which the sorting will be based. If, for example, the name field is chosen as the key in the student grades file in Figure 5.15, the records can then be sorted in alphabetical order by name.

The importance of sorting   This sorting of files, seemingly an obvious thing to do, is an extremely important aspect of data processing. Most computer resources are devoted to data processing, and most data processing consists of sorting, searching among, and combining files. Many business and organizational applications of computer hardware and software, such as inventory control, customer billing, and payroll accounting, depend on these processing operations. As a result, computer science professionals devote a lot of time and effort to developing efficient methods of sorting files, searching them for particular records, and *merging* them (combining them in order) with other already sorted files.

The maintenance of sequential files involves keeping them sorted in the proper order and keeping the records up to date. Additions, deletions, and changes to be made are known as *transactions* and are temporarily batched into **transaction files.** Transaction files are sorted, then merged at regularly scheduled intervals with the files to be updated, known as **master files.** Sequential files are often used for payroll, billing, and statement preparation, and for check processing by banks.

The advantages of sequential files include the following:

- *Sequential files have a simple organizational principle.*
- *Sequential files have a range of applications.*

- *Sequential files are an efficient storage method if a large number of records must be processed.*

- *Sequential files are inexpensive to use.* Magnetic tape is an inexpensive medium.

Some of their disadvantages are:

- *Sequential master files must be completely processed and new ones created every time records are updated.*

- *Sequential files must usually be kept sorted.*

- *Sequential files are hard to keep current.* The master file is up to date only immediately after the transaction file is merged with the master files.

- *Sequential files cannot be accessed directly.* Individual records of a sequential file can only be accessed by checking the key in all preceding records of the file.

Direct Access Files

A **direct access file** (also called a **random access file**) consists of records stored on a direct access medium, such as a disk, according to some addressing scheme (see Figure 5.16). If the address of a record is known, that record can be accessed directly, without going through the records preceding it. The address, or *location*, is determined in some way from the record itself. Either the address is one field in the record or the address is obtained through some transformation of the record key—a method known as **hashing,** or **randomizing.** For example, using the Social Security numbers of bank customers as addresses at which to store their savings account records on a disk wouldn't work because Social Security numbers have nine digits, and the disk would have to have 1,000,000,000 locations to correspond to all the possible different Social Security numbers. Not many disks have such a large

Locating records by their addresses

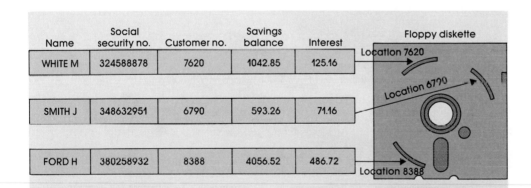

Figure 5.16 The Direct Access File

This savings account file is a direct access file. Each record is stored on the disk according to its address, which is obtained through some manipulation of the customer's Social Security number (hashing) and is stored as part of the record (the customer number). The records need not be sorted, and any one can be accessed without going through the preceding ones. If the disk locations are numbered sequentially from 0000 starting at side 0, then the customer number can be used directly to access the disk.

capacity, and, besides, using such a long address would be a great waste of disk space. However, since every possible Social Security number isn't actually used, the nine-digit Social Security number could be reduced to four or five digits. Figure 5.17 describes one way this hashing might be done.

Direct access files should be used if a few records must be updated frequently. These files also help in situations in which additions, deletions, and changes must be made immediately on the master file (such as an airline flight's seat availability list) or for situations in which transactions cannot be batched. Besides being used for bank account files (as shown in Figure 5.16), direct access files are employed for factory production records and for processing travel, hotel, and car rental reservations.

Direct access files have several advantages:

- *Direct access files eliminate the need for separate transaction files.* Transactions are processed as soon as they occur.
- *Direct access files do not have to be kept sorted.*
- *More efficient processing is possible with direct access files.* Only the portion of the file that needs to be changed is processed.
- *Retrieval of data stored in direct access files is fast.* It takes essentially the same time to access any record in a file, no matter where it is.
- *Several direct access files can be updated at the same time.* Because transactions are processed as soon as they occur, without using separate transaction files, more than one file can be immediately updated from a single transaction.

Some of their disadvantages are:

- *Backup files may need to be kept.* Records are modified by being written over; thus the old data will disappear forever unless they have been copied.
- *Available storage space may be used less efficiently with direct access files than with sequential files.*
- *More complex hardware and software are needed to implement direct access files.*

Indexed Sequential Files

The best of both methods

The **indexed sequential file** (Figure 5.18) combines the best features of the sequential file and the direct access file. Records are kept sorted so that transactions can be processed in batches, but an index is also used to speed up access when

Figure 5.17 Hashing

Hashing is the transformation of a record key into a number that can be used as a storage address. For example, a nine-digit Social Security number is divided by a prime number (a number that is evenly divisible only by itself and 1) that is close in value to the largest desired result, and the remainder is used as the address.

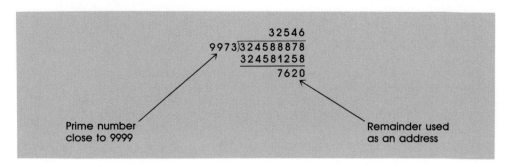

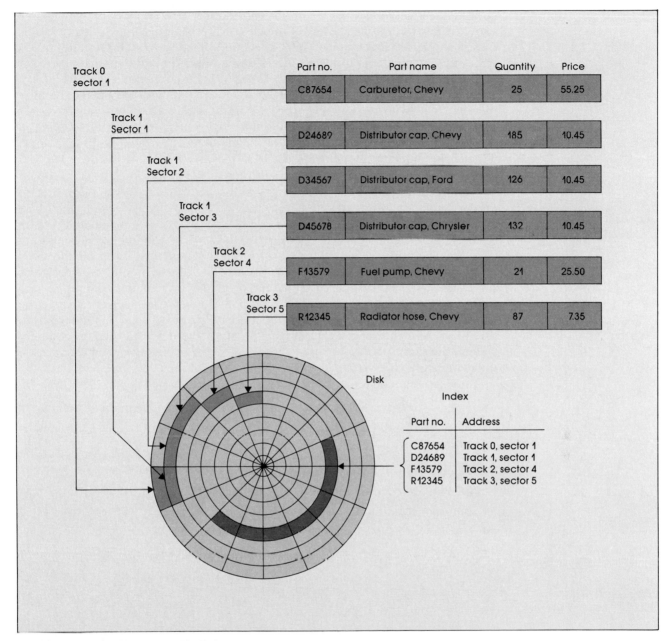

Figure 5.18 The Indexed Sequential File

This parts inventory file is an indexed sequential file. The index, stored on the same disk as the file, is a table of selected record keys and their addresses. The index is searched first, which speeds up the retrieval of records. Indexed sequential files, however, must be sorted.

records are updated one at a time. An **index** consists of a table of selected record keys with their corresponding addresses that is stored on the same disk as the file. To locate a specific record, the index is first searched to get an idea of its approximate location. The sequential search for the desired record starts at an indexed record that precedes it slightly, rather than at the beginning of the whole file. Figure 5.18 illustrates the concept of the index.

For example, to find the record for part number D34567, the index would be searched first to find the address of the closest preceding record. In this case, this record is that for part number D24689, found at track 1, sector 1. The disk is searched sequentially from there, one sector at a time, until the desired record for part number D34567 is found at track 1, sector 2. With indexed sequential files, a given record can be accessed more quickly than with purely sequential files because there is no need to examine every record on the disk preceding the desired one.

Indexed sequential files are useful when both batch and on-line updating of records are necessary. Their applications therefore include inventory files that must be used by different departments (such as the one shown in Figure 5.18) and customer billing files that are also used for credit checks.

For very large files, the index grows to the point where it cannot be held in primary storage. Both searching a large index and making additions to the index become time-consuming. A search through a large index can be facilitated by constructing an index to the index. For example, the cards in a library's card catalog are its index. The labels on the fronts of the drawers that hold those cards are the index to the index! Adding information to an indexed file can be simplified by reserving some disk space at the end of each data run pointed to by an index. As long as space is available at the end of such a block, adding the new data does not change the values of any of the indices and would require only moving some of the records in that block to make room at the proper place for the new record. In our library system, the extra space is the room at the ends of the bookshelves and the backs of the card catalog drawers.

Indexed sequential files have certain advantages, for example:

- *Indexed sequential files are well suited to both batched and individual transactions.*
- *With indexed sequential files, access to any particular record is faster than with sequential files.*

Disadvantages of indexed sequential files include the following:

- *Access is not as rapid as with direct access files.*
- *Some extra storage space is required to hold the index.*
- *Complex hardware and software are required to implement indexed sequential files.*
- *Making additions and deletions from the file will eventually require the index to be recomputed.*

The Need for Secondary Storage   # Summary

Because primary memory is limited in capacity, expensive, volatile, and nonportable, secondary storage is necessary.

Magnetic Tape Storage

Magnetic tapes have proven to be an efficient, economical, and reliable back-up storage medium for all computer systems.

Data Organization on Tape   Data on tape are represented as tiny magnetized spots. The tape's surface has a gridlike pattern of channels and tracks. Characters on tape are grouped in a sequential fashion into records, and records are usually grouped into blocks.

Storing Multiple Files on Tape   Several files can be combined and written on one tape. The files are separated by a special end-of-file (EOF) marker. A label is written at the beginning of a tape. It is followed by a table of contents.

Advantages and Disadvantages of Magnetic Tape Storage   Magnetic tapes have high data densities and are reusable and transportable; and variable record lengths are possible. However, they are accessible only sequentially and are physically vulnerable.

Magnetic Disk Storage

The magnetic disk is the most important on-line secondary storage medium for all types of computer systems.

Hard Disks   Hard disks have very high data densities. Because they are rigid, they can be spun, and thus accessed, very quickly. They may be fixed, removable, or Winchester, or packaged in disk packs.

Floppy Disks   Floppy disks (diskettes) are the most prevalent secondary storage medium used with microcomputers.

Disk Drives   A disk drive reads and writes data on magnetic disks. Read/write heads mounted on access arms can access any location on a disk surface. Hard disk drives surpass floppy disk drives in both access speed and precision.

In the Winchester disk drive, the access mechanism and the hard disk are completely enclosed in an airtight housing.

Data Organization on Disk   Data are recorded on disks in the form of tiny magnetic spots arranged in concentric tracks. Because of this arrangement, disks are a direct-access storage medium. All records on a disk hold the same number of bytes. Hard-sectored disks have the size and number of disk blocks assigned when the disk is manufactured. Soft-sectored disks can reassign disk records by reformatting the disk.

With the sector method, each disk surface is divided into sectors resembling pie slices. The cylinder method, used with disk packs, has all tracks on the various disks arranged into cylinders.

Access time is how long it takes to store or retrieve a piece of data. It includes seek time, rotational delay, and data transfer time.

Storing Multiple Files on Disks   The space on a disk drive is organized into a file system. A directory holds the information needed to access a file by name.

Advantages and Disadvantages of Magnetic Disk Storage   Magnetic disks can be used as a direct or sequential access medium, are very fast, have very high data densities, and can be transported. However, they are more expensive than tape and are physically vulnerable.

Other Types of Secondary Storage

Besides tapes and disks, other forms of secondary storage are becoming more common.

Bulk Memory   Bulk memory is a type of electronic storage used to speed up the transfer of data to primary memory.

Magnetic Bubble Storage   Magnetic bubble storage employs solid-state chips to hold data in the form of tiny magnetized bubbles. It is used in a variety of specialized systems.

Optical Disks   Optical storage systems utilize lasers to create and detect tiny holes or blisters in metallic film. They have great potential because they can store large volumes of data that can be accessed very quickly. However, most systems available today use nonerasable disks called CD-ROM.

File Organization

Files are collections of records stored on secondary storage media.

Sequential Files   Sequential files have their records organized in a fixed order. They must be kept sorted and cannot be accessed out of order. With sequential files, a master file is usually updated from transaction files.

Direct Access Files   The records in direct access files are stored according to their addresses, which are often determined by hashing. These records can be accessed in any order.

Indexed Sequential Files   Indexed sequential files share certain characteristics with both sequential files and direct access files. They employ an index to store the locations of selected records.

Computer Concepts

As an extra review of the chapter, try defining the following terms. If you have trouble with any of them, refer to the page number listed.

1. What limitations of primary memory make secondary storage necessary?
2. How are data represented and organized on magnetic tape?
3. How are fields related to records? Give an example.
4. Why is blank space left on magnetic tape?
5. Why are records grouped into blocks on magnetic tape?
6. What are four advantages of using magnetic tape?
7. Why can multiple files be stored on one tape?
8. How are magnetic disks similar to phonograph records? How are they different?
9. Name and describe three data densities available on floppy disks.
10. What are disk drives? Primarily, how do they differ?
11. Why are floppy disks less susceptible to head crashes than hard disks?
12. What prompted the development of the Winchester disk drive?
13. Name some advantages of a removable hard disk.
14. What is the approach to data organization used on virtually all floppy disks?
15. What is an advantage of the cylinder method of data organization in terms of access time?
16. What are some advantages of disk storage?
17. Why is bulk memory faster to access than magnetic disks?
18. Why hasn't magnetic bubble storage been as widely used as was originally expected?
19. What is the biggest advantage of optical disk storage systems?
20. In general, what advantageous features of sequential files and direct access files are combined by indexed sequential files?

True or False

1. Data density of magnetic tape can be expressed as bytes per inch.
2. The blocking factor is the fixed number of records that make up a field.
3. Magnetic tape is useful for airline and hotel reservation services.
4. A group of hard disks that can be mounted and removed as a unit is called a disk pack.
5. Hard disk drives outperform floppy disk drives in all areas except data density.
6. Access time can be broken down into seek time, rotational delay, and data transfer time.
7. Laser disks are circular platters also known as optical disks.
8. Files cannot exist independently of the programs that use them.
9. Sequential files are often used by banks for processing checks.
10. A direct access file is also called a random access file.

Multiple Choice

1. Secondary storage is also called:
   (a) off-line   (b) on-line   (c) auxiliary

2. One weakness of magnetic tape storage is:
   (a) that it is volatile   (b) that it can only be   (c) that it is expensive.
                              accessed sequentially

3. Read/write heads are mounted on:
   (a) floppy disks   (b) spindles   (c) access arms

4. Data are stored on disks on
   (a) one channel   (b) six channels   (c) nine channels

5. The location of a record stored on a disk pack is specified by an address made up of the surface number, the record number, and the:
   (a) stack number   (b) cylinder number   (c) track number

6. Disadvantages of magnetic disks include:
   (a) they cannot be   (b) they are not portable   (c) they are easily
       accessed directly   damaged

7. To keep records in a sequential file sorted, a particular field in each record is chosen as the:
   (a) master file   (b) key   (c) transaction file

8. Among the advantages of sequential files is that:
   (a) they can be accessed   (b) they are easy to keep   (c) they are inexpensive to
       directly   current   use

9. Direct access files:
   (a) must be kept sorted
   (b) are useful where changes must be made immediately on the master file
   (c) are used where transactions must be batched

10. Indexed sequential files:
    (a) cannot access data as rapidly as direct access files
    (b) are not suited for batched transactions
    (c) access data more slowly than sequential files

A Sharper Focus

1. If you wanted to store on a floppy disk data that included the birthdays, anniversaries, names and addresses of friends and relatives, how would you set up your files, records, and fields?
2. If you were starting work in a computerized office, what questions would you ask initially about their storage devices and file organization?

1. Survey your campus or several local businesses to determine where floppy disks or hard disks are being used. Why did users choose one instead of the other?

2. Suppose data are written on magnetic tape at a density of 1600 characters per inch, and records are 80 characters long. Between each pair of records is a blank space (the inter-record gap) that is ½ inch long. A tape reel holds 2500 feet of usable tape. What percentage of such a tape is blank? How many records can be written on it?

3. Find out what files are stored on magnetic tape at your school or company. What criteria are used to determine what files are put onto magnetic tape and when? Are tape files eventually disposed of, or do they just keep accumulating?

4. Find out which file organization method is used at your school for student records. Why was this method originally chosen? About how many times is a typical record accessed during a school year?

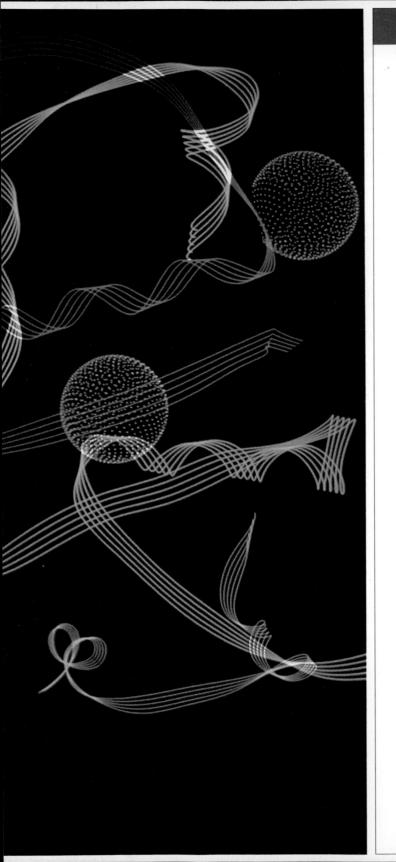

6

Data Communications

In This Chapter

Applications of Data
Communications

Information Services	*Networking of home computers.*
Electronic Mail and Bulletin Boards	*Messages sent via computer.*
Electronic Funds Transfer	*Money moved via computer.*
Computer Conferencing	*Conferring via computer.*
Telecommuting	*Working at home using a computer.*

Components of Data
Communications Systems

Communications Hardware	*The equipment used to construct systems.*
Terminals	*Input/output devices at the ends of communications lines.*
Modems	*Devices that enable computers to send and receive data over telephone lines.*
Interface Units	*Devices that coordinate data transmission and reception: multiplexers, concentrators, message switchers, and front-end processors.*
Computers	*Machines that process data.*
Communications Software	*The programs used to control data flow through systems.*
Communications Channels	*Pathways for data.*
Physical Structure	*Channels made of wire cables, microwave systems, and fiber optic cables.*
Transmission Speed	*How much data can be sent at one time: narrowband, voiceband, and broadband channels.*
Transmission Direction	*Allowed direction of data transmission: simplex, half-duplex, and full-duplex channels.*
Transmission Mode	*How data are sent over channels: asynchronous and synchronous transmission.*
Line Configuration	*How channels connect terminals to computers: point-to-point and multidrop lines.*
Leased Versus Switched Lines	*Weighing factors of access and cost.*
Protocols	*Rules and procedures governing data communications.*
Common Carriers	*Companies licensed to transmit data.*
Distributed Data-Processing Networks	*Decentralized processing of data.*
Network Configurations	*Basic designs of DDP networks: star, ring, and hierarchical networks.*
Advantages and Disadvantages of Distributed Data-Processing Networks	*Benefits and drawbacks of DDP network.*
Local Area Networks	*Connecting nearby computers.*

Focus On

Computer CBs

One of the surest measures of public acceptance of a technology is its integration into popular culture. Subscribers to various on-line information service such as CompuServe, GEnie, and The Source can access a service called CB Simulator. Using a computer, a modem, and communication software, a link can be established between a subscriber, the information service, and other subscribers. This allows the CompuServe subscribers to use their computers to "talk" to each other in much the same way as Citizen's Band (CB) radio operators use their radios to communicate. The primary difference is that computer CBers transmit to each other by keying in their messages. The message is output on the receiver's screen.

Just like CB radio enthusiasts, computer CBers use "handles" to identify themselves. Donald Trivette, a journalist for *PC Magazine* describes the importance of choosing an interesting handle.

"Selecting a good CB 'handle,' or alias, is important. It's got to be sexy and clever enough to make people want to talk to you, but not so provocative that it turns them off or frightens them. Neither Ace nor V-8 (my first two tries) attracted much attention, but after considerable experimentation I found one that worked for me.

"Some of the better handles on CompuServe put mine to shame; they include Gentle Moose, SwEtsoX, Alaska Dan, and JET JOCK.

"A few talented CBers have incorporated graphics in their handles. Flex signs on as !FLEX! and President Aviator includes --o=O=o-- in his handle."

With rates that approximate $6/hr off-peak and $12/hr during high-demand periods, the price is certainly right when compared to an equivalent telephone charge. Different channels cater to different age and interest groups. Young adults congregate on one channel, senior citizens on another, and teens on yet another. Other services offer alternative features and rates, such as GEnie, which offers LiveWire CB, and The Source, which offers Chat.

CBers have a lingo all their own. Some examples:	
bcnu	be seeing you
cu l8tr	see you later
gr8	great
oic	oh, I see
rehi	hi, again
/wrist	I am depressed
[]	hugs
:)	smiley face (sideways)
;)	winking smiley face (sideways)
<o><->	wink
=:0	surprise (sideways)

Computers were first linked across distances in 1940, when Dr. George Stibbitz sent data over telegraph lines from a computer at Dartmouth College in New Hampshire to a calculating machine at Bell Laboratories in New York City. That event marked the birth of **data communications,** the sending of data between geographically separated computers.

Since 1940, advances in computer and communications technology have resulted in vast communications networks and a worldwide explosion of data communications. Data are sent over telephone lines, bounced off satellites, and carried through the air by microwaves. Any business or home with a telephone and a computer (and there are more than 25 million computers in the United States) has easy access to a multitude of data communications services ranging from electronic mail and stock reports to retail catalogs and games. A $100-billion-a-year industry, data communications is clearly here to stay.

In this chapter, we'll look at the physical aspects of data communications—how (and why) networks are set up and what hardware and software resources are involved—and at some of its most significant applications of data communications.

APPLICATIONS OF DATA COMMUNICATIONS

Applications of the principles and technology of data communications are rapidly transforming society. Let's look at some of the many ways data communication is being used today.

Information Services

Information services offer interactive networking to users who have an inexpensive terminal or a personal computer. These easy-to-use services can be accessed with most types of microcomputers. The multitude of services includes:

Networking of home computers

- information retrieval (news, weather, home education, financial data, sports, and so forth)

- electronic mail (discussed in the next section)

- computing (computer languages, application packages, computer games)

- telemonitoring (home security systems)

- home shopping and banking

- travel, theater, restaurant, and sports reservations

The two largest information services in the United States are The Source and CompuServe (see Figure 6.1). The Source, now owned by *Reader's Digest*, was the first information service in the United States. News, financial data, games, electronic mail, and other options are available nationwide to home computer users who subscribe to The Source. CompuServe, owned by H & R Block, offers news, games, want ads, travel reservations, and financial data, among other services.

Figure 6.1 Information Services
A wide variety of options is available to home computer users who subscribe to one of the large information services such as CompuServe or The Source.

Electronic Mail and Bulletin Boards

Messages sent via computer

Electronic mail is a data communications service that employs computers and telecommunications lines to store and send messages that would otherwise be sent in memos, telephone calls, or letters. Electronic mail is one of the "hot" new business services. Nearly one third of all U.S. businesses use some form of electronic mail, paying nearly $2 billion annually for the services. Electronic transmission of business messages accounts for more than 20 percent of all business mail in the United States.

Similar communications services, known as **electronic bulletin boards (BBS),** have become quite popular among home computer users and hobbyists. These systems provide a means for their users to exchange messages, programming tips, advice, comments, and software. To access an electronic bulletin board, all one needs is a microcomputer (almost any kind), a modestly priced communications device known as a modem, and a telephone. The machine running the BBS generally consists of a personal computer with a hard disk that is equipped to answer a telephone automatically and to allow callers to link up their own computers. Once communication has been established between two computers, callers can "post" messages or read messages left for them by other users. Costing as little as $500 for a complete system (personal computer, modem, software, and phone), electronic bulletin boards have proven to be an entertaining and educational way for computer enthusiasts to "get together" and trade notes.

Electronic Funds Transfer

Money moved via computer

Electronic funds transfer (EFT) is the electronic movement of money into, out of, and between bank accounts. EFT systems are a very important application of data communications. By the end of 1989, half of all financial transactions in the United States may be handled electronically. One of the most obvious signs of the growth of EFT has been the proliferation of the **automated teller machine (ATM).** Operating 24 hours a day, ATMs are programmed to perform many of the functions of human tellers—to dispense cash, receive deposits, and report account balances. To use an ATM, a bank customer must have a specially coded plastic card and a personal identification number that maintains security and privacy.

Computer Conferencing

Data communications can be applied in ways that eliminate the need for a certain amount of travel, resulting in significant savings in travel costs and time. In **computer conferencing** a link joins distant computers and terminals so users can exchange information or messages directly and immediately, in effect, having a meeting. Thus, computer conferencing is a convenient, economical alternative to business travel.

Conferring via computer

Telecommuting

Enormous amounts of energy and time are spent every day by people commuting to work. The combination of microcomputers, data communications networks, and computer conferencing techniques makes **telecommuting,** or working at home using a computer, a feasible alternative to traditional work patterns. Companies such as Control Data Corporation, Walgreen, McDonald's, and Mountain States Telephone & Telegraph have limited telecommuting projects allowing professional, managerial, and clerical employees to work at home.

Working at home using a computer

COMPONENTS OF DATA COMMUNICATIONS SYSTEMS

We've seen that various data communications systems have become an essential facet of modern life. What elements make up such systems? Although their complexity and configuration vary widely, systems such as the one illustrated in Figure 6.2 basically involve some arrangement of the following components:

- *Video display terminals* and *printing terminals* are both widely utilized in data communications systems, as are other input/output devices.

- *Interface units* are the hardware components that enable data to be transmitted over communications lines. They include such devices as modems and data communications interface units.

- *Communications channels* (also called data links or communications lines) are the means by which data are sent to and from a computer. They include telegraph and telephone lines, various types of cables, and microwave and satellite systems.

- *Computers* ranging from microcomputers to supercomputers are an essential element of data communications systems. A system may have one large central computer, a number of small scattered computers, or both.

- *Communications software* consists of the programs used by the computers in data communications systems to control, coordinate, and monitor the data transmissions.

COMMUNICATIONS HARDWARE

The equipment that makes up the hardware of data communications systems includes various types of terminals, modems, interface units, and computers.

The equipment used to construct systems

Figure 6.2 Components of a Typical Data Communications System

The principal components of a typical data communications system are terminals, interface units, some communications channels, at least one computer, and communications software.

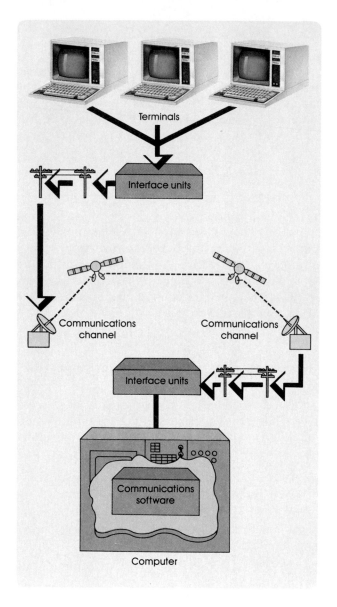

Terminals

Input/output devices at the ends of communications lines

In Chapter 4 we discussed the computer terminal as both an input and an output device. All types of terminals are used in data communications systems: dumb, smart, and intelligent terminals, and video display and printing terminals. In fact, any input/output device can be used in a data communications system. Printers, plotters, and even voice input/output devices may be part of such a system. When used in this context, such devices are called terminals since they are at the ends (or terminal points) of communications lines. This usage of the label *terminal* can be extended even further to encompass other computer systems. A small microcomputer system can act as a terminal when it transmits data to and receives data from another system like itself or a larger, centrally located computer. Data communications systems that employ full-fledged computers as terminals have the ability to do local processing at the terminal sites.

Modems

A **modem** is an interface unit that enables a computer or terminal to transmit and receive data over telephone lines. Both computers and terminals employ *digital signals* consisting of discrete low and high voltages that represent zeros and ones. Ordinary telephone lines, however, are designed to carry *analog signals* with continuous voltage ranges which represent the sounds of human voices. Digital signals must be converted to analog signals before they can be sent over phone lines. Such conversion is called **modulation.** At the other end, where the data transmission is received, the analog signals must be converted back into digital signals. This is called **demodulation.** A modem acts as both a modulator and a demodulator (see Figure 6.3). Modems are necessary only when analog communications channels (for example, normal telephone lines) are used. Recently, phone companies have started installing lines and equipment specially designed to carry digital signals. An international cooperative effort is building the Integrated Services Digital Network (ISDN). As such digital channels become more widely available, the need for modems will decrease.

Several types of modems are available. **Intelligent modems** can simultaneously transmit both voice and data, automatically dial telephone numbers, automatically answer incoming calls, and test and select transmission lines. **Acoustic modems** work with audio signals that are transferrred through a telephone receiver cradled in rubber cups. Acoustic couplers are often used to connect portable terminals to telephone lines. Their transmission speed is limited to a maximum of 300 **baud** (pronounced "bawd", equivalent to bits per second). That corresponds to sending 30 characters per second. **Direct-connect modems** attach themselves to the phone system through the same standard modular connector that ordinary telephones use. The data being sent remain in an electronic form and are sent at rates up to 19,200 baud. Figure 6.4 shows an external modem compatible with microcomputers. Internal modems are built to fit right inside the computer and are less expensive than their external counterparts.

Devices that enable computers to send and receive data over telephone lines.

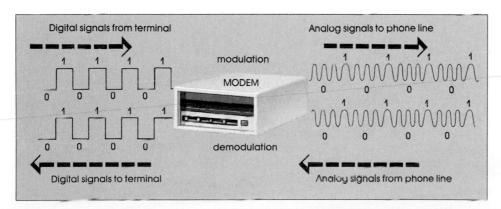

Figure 6.3 The Modem
The modem's name reflects its dual role; it modulates, or converts digital signals from a terminal into analog signals to be sent over telephone lines; and it also demodulates, or converts analog signals from telephone lines into digital signals to be sent to a terminal.

Figure 6.4 A Direct-Connect Modem
This Hayes modem can send information at up to 19,200 bits per second by using data compression techniques.

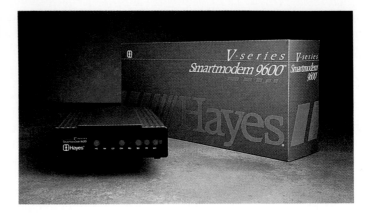

Interface Units

Devices that coordinate data transmission and reception: multiplexers, concentrators, message switchers, and front-end processors

Many data communications systems employ interface units that coordinate various aspects of data transmission and reception. These units greatly increase the overall efficiency of the systems in which they are used. Such devices include multiplexers, concentrators, message switchers, and front-end processors.

Multiplexers

A **multiplexer** combines the signals from several terminals into a single transmission that can be carried by one communications channel. Because communications lines almost always have a greater capacity than can be filled by transmission from a single terminal, the use of a multiplexer ensures that this carrying capacity isn't wasted. In essence, a multiplexer treats a high-speed communications line as if it were multiple low-speed lines, resulting in a much more economical use of these expensive channels. Note in Figure 6.5 how the multiplexer *interleaves* the data streams from different terminals one character at a time so that one combined stream can be sent over a single line.

Concentrators

A **concentrator** is a minicomputer or microcomputer that combines the data from a number of terminals onto a single high-speed line to a central computer. While similar to a multiplexer, a concentrator is a more sophisticated piece of equipment that often has an internal memory. This gives the concentrator the ability to store data temporarily until enough is collected to forward significant chunks to the computer at high speed. A concentrator also differs from a multiplexer in that it waits until a group of characters is collected from each terminal, instead of interleaving the data streams character by character (see Figure 6.6). Transmissions from several terminals are collected and compressed, one after another, into a continuous, high-speed stream. Again, more efficient use of expensive communications channels is the main reason for employing concentrators.

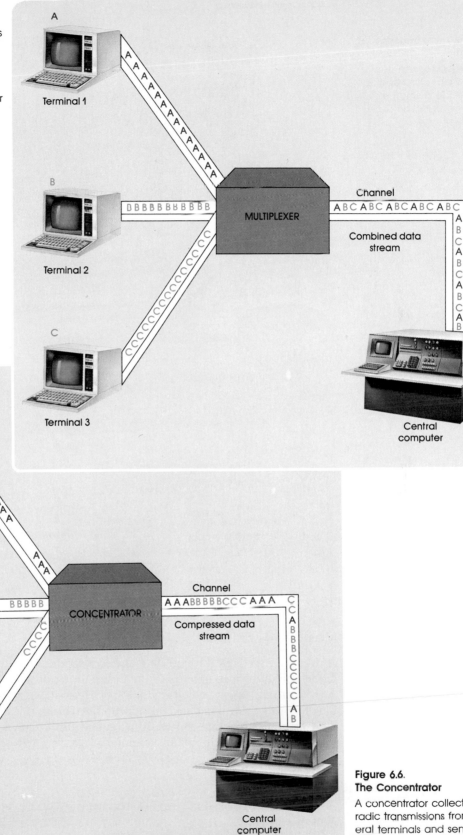

Figure 6.5 The Multiplexer
A multiplexer combines the signals from several terminals into a single transmission. Here, terminal 1 is sending A's, terminal 2 is sending B's, and terminal 3 is sending C's. Note how the multiplexer combines these data streams.

Terminal 1

Terminal 2

Terminal 3

MULTIPLEXER

Channel
ABCABCABCABCABC
Combined data stream

Central computer

Terminal 1

Terminal 2

Terminal 3

CONCENTRATOR

Channel
AAABBBBBCCCAAA
Compressed data stream

Central computer

Figure 6.6.
The Concentrator
A concentrator collects sporadic transmissions from several terminals and sends them on as a single, continuous data stream.

Figure 6.7 The Message Switcher

Entire messages are stored and relayed to the appropriate destination when time and communication availability allow.

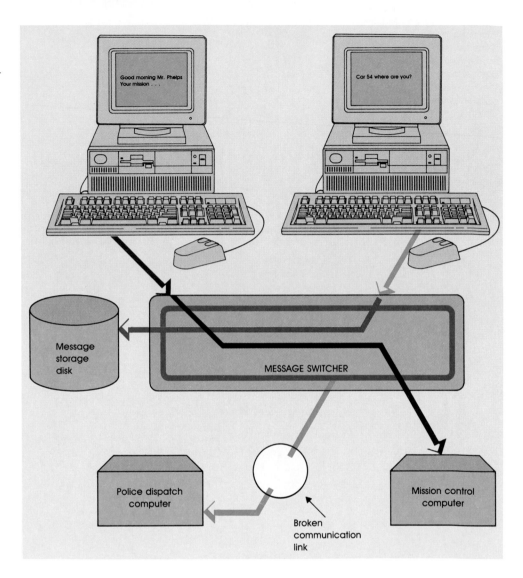

Message Switchers

A **message switcher** accumulates a complete message (for example, an electronic letter), analyzes it to determine the destination and proper routing, and then forwards it to the appropriate locations (see Figure 6.7). Message switchers are capable of storing transmissions if the appropriate communications lines aren't immediately available. Message switchers increase the efficiency of a data communications system by relieving the main computer of routing responsibilities.

Front-End Processors

A **front-end processor** is a computer that is usually located in the same site as the central computer in a data communications system. Its function is to relieve the central computer of routine transmission-oriented tasks. This leaves the central computer free for processing other programs, typically increasing the amount of processing that can be accomplished in a given amount of time by more than 30 percent. Front-end processors can be programmed to do message switching, error checking, data translation, and transmission coordination and control. They can also keep logs, compile statistics concerning data communications activities, and maintain security by limiting access to authorized users (see Figure 6.8).

Computers

The computers in data communications systems vary widely in size and capabilities. The ultimate purpose of any system is to transmit and process data. Data are usually sent from terminals to some computer for processing and then sent from that computer back to the terminals. When a single computer is designated as the central processing component of a data communications system, it is called the **host computer.**

Machines that process data

COMMUNICATIONS SOFTWARE

Host communications software consists of the programs that enable the host computer or front-end processor to establish, coordinate, monitor, and control the flow of data through data communications systems. Some of the tasks accomplished by such programs include:

The programs used to control data flow through systems

- *Opening and closing communications lines.* Certain programs direct the computer to establish the correct connection to make a transmission and to break that connection when the transmission has ended. These programs may also maintain banks of phone numbers for establishing such connections.

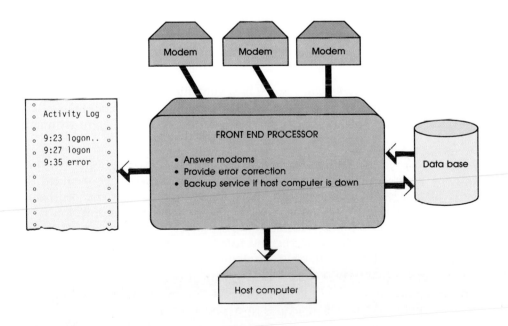

Figure 6.8 The Front-End Processor

A front-end processor is a computer that contains communications software that enables it to relieve the central computer of many routine data communications tasks.

- *Finding and correcting transmission errors.*   Data may be garbled or bits may be lost during transmission. There must be programs that can determine if errors have occurred and that cause the data to be retransmitted if necessary.

- *Coordinating multiple use of communications lines.*   When several terminals must share communications channels to a computer, programs that coordinate data transmissions are needed. **Polling** is one technique for maintaining a smooth flow of data in which each connected terminal is "asked" if it has data to send. With another similar technique, called **contention,** each terminal is instructed to "listen" to see if any other terminal is transmitting and, if so, to wait.

- *Routing data transmissions.*   Data must be sent to the appropriate destination. Programs that handle routing may also perform *queuing,* or ordering transmissions into some sequence or priority, if more than one are to be sent to the same place. In larger data networks, messages may be sent through several intermediary computers on their way to the final destination.

- *Keeping statistics.*   Some programs compile useful facts about system performance, such as the number of errors that have occurred and how many transmissions have been sent.

The microprocessor user also needs communications software. For many host computers, a microprocessor-based system performs the same tasks as an ordinary terminal. In fact, the software running on the microprocessor is often called a **terminal emulator** program. Some of the operations that terminal emulator programs perform include:

- *Select type of modem.*   The operation of the various modems, while usually similar, may require some customization. The terminal program relieves the user from having to know these differences.

- *Utilize data base of phone numbers.*   Commonly used phone numbers, log-in identification information, and other control data are recorded in a data base. Therefore, the user can simply issue a command to connect to a particular service by selecting a name rather than manually issuing the sequence of phone numbers, transmission speed selection commands, and other operations that are used to establish a connection.

- *Emulate a variety of terminals.*   Some host computers can be used with only a few types of terminals. Often a certain terminal will perform better than others. A terminal program can pretend to be any one of several different terminals, effectively matching the microcomputer to the host computer.

- *Transfer data files.*   Entire files of data can be transferred between two machines. Because transmission errors are very common on telephone lines, the information is divided into small groups of characters and is encoded before being sent. For all those blocks received with errors, a retransmission is requested. Microcomputer error-correcting protocols currently in use have names like *Kermit, MNP, XModem,* and *YModem.* For very short files that consist of printable information (in contrast to binary programs), the user may choose to forego error correction and simply have the data displayed on both screens and copied to the user's printer.

COMMUNICATIONS CHANNELS

Communications channels, also called communications lines or data links, are the pathways over which data are sent. They connect the various hardware components of a communications system. Communications channels are classified in various ways, each based on a particular characteristic, for example, physical structure; speed, direction, and mode of transmission; line configuration; and whether lines are leased or switched.

Pathways for data

Physical Structure

Communications channels can consist of wire cables, microwave systems, or fiber optic cables.

What channels are made of: wire cables, microwave systems, and fiber optic cables

Wire Cables

Ordinary telegraph and telephone lines are cables comprised of bundles of **twisted pairs** of copper wires that carry information in the form of analog electrical signals; they are widely used for data communications. Since a worldwide network of these lines already exists, they have the advantages of economy and accessibility. The telephone system, however, was intended to handle voice transmission and isn't the ideal medium for transmission of digital signals. Its analog nature and its susceptibility to electromagnetic interference limit the transmission speeds that can be achieved. During phone calls, you can often hear faint conversations in the background caused by *crosstalk,* a phenomenon in which high-speed transmissions to one pair of twisted wires interfere with those in nearby pairs. Although crosstalk is merely a nuisance with voice communications, it seriously impairs the high-speed transmissions necessary for some sophisticated types of data communications.

Communication by twisted pairs can send up to 4 million bits per second over a limited distance. However, data rates achieved through the telephone system are usually under 56,000 bits per second. At higher data rates the wires are usually confined to a single building. Many microcomputer networks use twisted pairs as their physical communication channel because of its low cost.

Invented in 1929, **coaxial cables** are efficient transmission lines developed primarily to combat crosstalk. They consist of a central cable completely surrounded by, but insulated from, a "tube" of outer wires (see Figure 6.9). This outer layer of wires shields the inner cable and thus helps to reduce electromagnetic interference. Coaxial cables are widely used in data communications systems because they allow signals to be sent faster and with less interference than do ordinary twisted wire cables. They can be laid underground and underwater and are often used in local area networks. Data can be communicated through coaxial cables at a rate of up to 500 million bits per second.

Microwave Systems

Microwaves are radio signals with high frequencies that can be used to transmit any kind of data. Microwave systems transmit data over the earth's surface by transferring them to and from relay stations on tall buildings, towers, and mountains. Such stations must be located about every 30 miles or so because microwave

Figure 6.9 Coaxial Cable
This cross-section of a coaxial cable shows the special shielding used to reduce transmission distortion.

transmissions are line-of-sight signals—they won't bend to follow the earth's curvature. Microwave systems may also utilize *communications satellites,* which relay microwave transmissions from one earth station back to another earth station at some distance from the first (see Figure 6.10). Many such satellites are presently orbiting the earth 22,300 miles above the equator at the same speed at which the earth rotates. Due to this matching of the earth's rotational speed, such satellites appear stationary with respect to earth stations. Initially used for voice and video transmissions, communications satellites can relay very large quantities of data rapidly. The data rate for microwave systems usually falls in the range of 10 to 100 million bits per second range. However, a single microwave installation normally serves several users simultaneously mixing voice, data, and video traffic.

Fiber Optic Cables

Fiber optic cables are used throughout the world to transmit voice, television, and data signals. A fiber optic cable consists of very thin glass filaments that transmit light (see Figure 6.11.). Lasers generate the off-and-on pulses of light that carry binary data over fiber optic cables. Instead of electrons moving through metallic wires to carry signals, light waves travel through tiny glass fibers to accomplish the same purpose.

The greatest advantage of fiber optics lies in the extremely wide bandwidth of light transmission. **Bandwidth,** which we will discuss further when we talk about transmission speed, refers to the range of frequencies that can be accurately transmitted. Light has a wide range of frequencies, so an immense volume of information can be sent over a single circuit at very high speed. Light does not travel much faster through fiber optic cables than electrons do through wires; the speed advantage results primarily from the fact that light can be turned on and off more rapidly than can electricity. Some single optical fibers can transmit 2 billion bits per second—the equivalent of 27,000 simultaneous telephone calls.

Fiber optics also offers other significant advantages. Lightweight cables with very small diameters are formed from the hairlike optical fibers. For example, 900

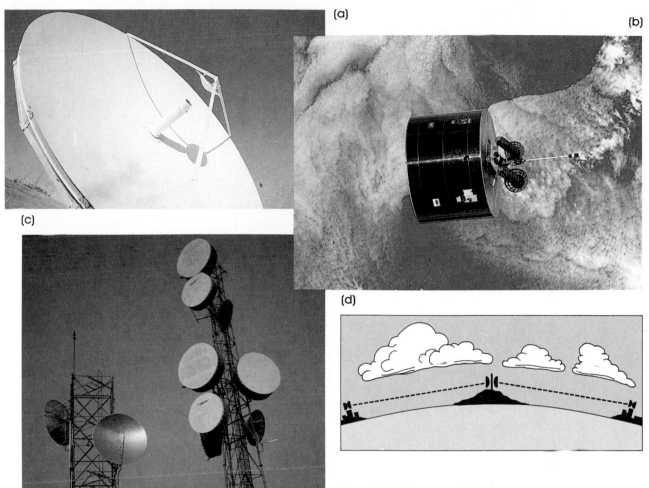

Figure 6.10 Microwave Systems

Microwave systems employ earth stations and communications satellites or relay stations to transmit messages over great distances. Data encoded in microwaves are beamed from earth stations up to orbiting satellites. The satellites relay the microwave transmissions back down to other earth stations. (a) An earth station aimed at a satellite. (b) A communications satellite. (c) A microwave relay station high atop a mountain. (d) The line-of-sight arrangement necessary for microwave relay stations.

pairs of copper wires in a bundle 3 inches thick can be replaced by a fiber optic cable 0.005 inch in diameter in a 1/4-inch jacket. Also, crosstalk remains negligible even when many fibers are cabled together. Because optical fibers are immune to electrically generated interference (such as that caused by lightning and nearby electric motors), error rates are as much as a million times lower than they are with metallic wires. (Optical fibers do not produce undesirable electromagnetic interference either.) Since it is almost impossible to wiretap optical fibers, data transmission over fiber optic cables is much less liable to security breaches. Finally, fiber optic cables are safer (no electrical sparks to cause fires or explosions) and last longer (no corrosion).

Figure 6.11 Fiber Optic Cable
Fiber optic cables consist of very thin glass filaments that transmit light pulses generated by lasers. This photograph shows a thin fiber cable contrasted with a thick wire cable cross-section.

Fiber optic cables do have disadvantages, of course. They are somewhat difficult to handle and install, and they require complex, expensive interface units. These drawbacks of fiber optics are mostly due to its relative newness. Although the technology has proven to be cost-effective for long-distance voice and video communications, it is still somewhat expensive for data communications applications. Nonetheless, fiber optics has the potential to play a major role in the data communications systems of the near future.

Transmission Speed

How much data can be sent at a time: narrowband, voiceband, and broadband channels

The transmission speed of a channel refers to how much data can be sent over that channel in a given time. This rate is dependent on the bandwidth (also called *grade*) of the channel. For example, your ears differentiate the frequencies of sound wave vibrations as tones of distinct pitches. All the tones a person can normally hear make up the bandwidth of audible sound, which is the range from about 20 to 20,000 *hertz* (or cycles per second). One can send a block of digital information by choosing a group of tones (one tone per bit). If the tone is on, it represents a 1 bit. With this method, the amount of information that we can send in a fixed amount of time can be increased by adding more tones. Computer hardware, just like our ears, needs to have those tones spaced far enough apart so that they are distinguishable. The greater the bandwidth, the greater the amount of information that can be simultaneously sent in a given time period and the greater the transmission speed. Channels are classified by bandwidth into narrowband, voiceband, and broadband.

Narrowband channels have a bandwidth of less than 2000 hertz and a transmission rate between 7 and 30 characters per second. Telegraph lines are examples of narrowband channels. Such channels are too slow for most modern data communications, but they have been widely used for low-speed data transmission to devices such as news service teletype machines.

Voiceband channels have a bandwidth of about 3000 hertz and transmission rates of up to about 960 characters per second. These channels were so named because they are commonly used for voice communication (telephones use voiceband channels).

Broadband channels have a bandwidth up to several hundred million Hertz and transmission rates of several 40 million characters per second. Coaxial cables, microwave systems, and fiber optic cables are all broadband channels. In terms of transmission speed, these three types rank as follows: the fastest by far are fiber optic cables, followed by coaxial cables, and then by microwave systems. Broadband channels are primarily used for high-speed, high-volume data transmission between computer systems.

Transmission Direction

Channels can be classified according to the direction in which they allow transmission. There are three directional classifications: simplex, half-duplex, and full-duplex (see Figure 6.12).

Allowed direction of data transmission: simplex, half-duplex, and full-duplex channels

Simplex channels allow transmission in one direction only. Devices connected by simplex channels can either send or receive, but not both. Simplex channels are rarely used for data communications. They are found only in a few one-way applications such as weather and news wire service teletype lines.

Half-duplex channels allow transmission in either direction, but not simultaneously. Devices connected by half-duplex channels can send or receive, but not at the same time. A pair of walkie-talkies serves as a good analogy to a half-duplex

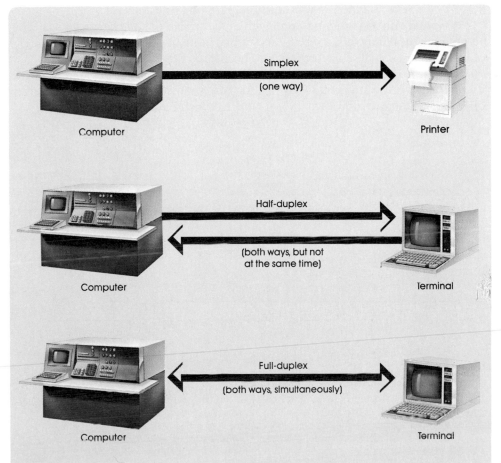

Figure 6.12 Simplex, Half-Duplex, and Full-Duplex Channels

The classifications of simplex, half-duplex, and full-duplex refer to the direction of transmission allowed for a channel.

channel; although both users can talk and listen, only one can talk at a time. Half-duplex channels are commonly used to connect remote terminals, printers, and other peripheral devices to computers. Because the receiving unit must wait until the transmitting unit has finished sending and then switch over to its transmitting status to send a reply, these channels are characterized by a certain amount of delay between the transmission of a message and the reception of a reply.

Full-duplex channels allow simultaneous transmissions in both directions. A telephone line, for example, is a full-duplex channel because the two parties can both talk and listen at once (although such a conversation would be confusing). A full-duplex channel is very efficient because signals can flow in two directions at the same time. This ability to carry constant two-way "traffic" means that full-duplex channels are ideal for high-speed, high-volume computer-to-computer communications.

Transmission Mode

How data are sent over channels: asynchronous and synchronous transmission

Channels can also be classified according to the way in which data are transmitted over them. Inside computers and terminals, data are handled in parallel fashion, that is, a byte at a time. Over communications channels, however, data must be transmitted in a serial fashion, or one bit after another. Two common modes of serializing data are asynchronous and synchronous transmission.

Asynchronous transmission involves the sending of one character at a time. To separate the characters, a *start bit* and one or more *stop bits* are added to each end of the individual 8-bit character codes. This means that for each character at least 10 bits are actually sent. The start bit is a signal to the interface unit that a character is coming next; the stop bits signal the end of a character. A 1 bit is sent continuously when there is no other information to send. For example, Figure 6.13(a)

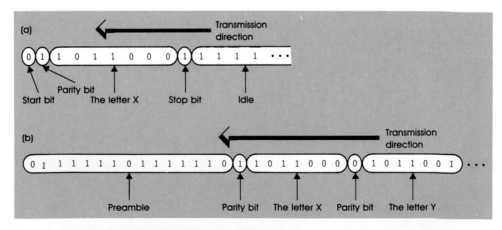

Figure 6.13 Asynchronous and Synchronous Transmission
Channels can be classified according to how data are sent over them. (a) With asynchronous transmission, one character is sent at a time, preceded by start bits and followed by stop bits and idle time. (b) With synchronous transmission, a single preamble tells the receiver that data will arrive, and then groups of characters are sent without start and stop bits. The transmissions are carefully timed so that the interface unit can "recognize" the individual characters.

shows how the letter *x* would be sent asynchronously. The ASCII code for *x* (101100) is preceded by one start bit (0) and followed by a stop bit (1). Asynchronous transmission is appropriate for devices that communicate at peak rates from 30 to 240 characters per second but are sometimes idle. Typing at a keyboard certainly fits within this model. Consequently, it is quite adequate for, and is commonly employed in, channels that connect terminals to computers.

Synchronous transmission involves the sending of blocks of characters, sometimes called *frames,* or *packets.* These groups of characters are sent without start and stop bits, as shown in Figure 6.13 (b). Transmission of a block of data begins by sending a distinctive pattern of bits called a *preamble* whose purpose is to tell the receiver precisely when the first data bit will arrive. The transmissions are carefully timed (or synchronized) so that interface units "know" that each 8 bits is another character. If 100 8-bit ASCII characters are sent synchronously, the message will be not much more than 800 bits long (it would be 1000 bits with asynchronous transmission). Because fewer bits are sent, synchronous transmission is more commonly used than asynchronous transmission for sending high volumes of data at rates exceeding 480 characters per second. Therefore, synchronous transmission is most often used in the channels that connect mainframe computers.

Line Configuration

Channels that connect terminals to a computer have two principal line configurations: point-to-point and multidrop (see Figure 6.14).

Point-to-point lines connect each terminal directly to the computer by a separate line. Because point-to-point line configurations are expensive (each terminal must have its own channel and interface unit), their use is generally limited to situations in which each terminal must have uninterrupted access to a computer.

Multidrop lines, on the other hand, connect several terminals to the computer via a single channel. Such a configuration is more economical because communications channels and interface units are shared by more than one terminal. Although multidrop lines allow several terminals to receive data simultaneously, only one terminal at a time can send data. Earlier, we described how the techniques of polling and contention enable communications software to coordinate data transmissions over multidrop lines.

How channels connect terminals to computers: point-to-point and multidrop lines

Leased Versus Switched Lines

Finally, some channels can be classified according to whether they are leased or switched. **Leased lines** (also called *private lines* or *direct lines*) connect a computer to fixed destinations. If you had a private telephone line that ran directly to your best friend's house, it would be similar to a leased line in that you could call no one but your friend. A **switched line,** in contrast, can connect a computer through switching centers to any of a number of destinations. This type is like an ordinary telephone line—you can call up anyone who has a phone connected to the telephone system. Because their use is limited to transmissions between two fixed end points, leased lines are more expensive than switched lines. However, leased lines are always available to their users and in some cases can be enhanced, or *conditioned,* to increase the transmission rate.

Weighing factors of access and cost

Figure 6.14   Point-to-Point and Multidrop Lines

Point-to-point lines connect each terminal directly to the computer. Multidrop lines connect several terminals to the computer via a single channel.

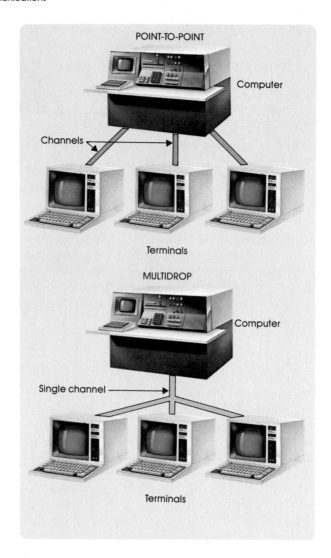

POINT-TO-POINT

Computer

Channels

Terminals

MULTIDROP

Computer

Single channel

Terminals

PROTOCOLS

Rules and procedures governing data communications

As you've probably concluded by now, data communications systems are complex entities. Setting up a working system requires the careful consideration of many hardware and software options. Contributing to this complexity is the fact that manufacturers and data communications professionals employ a variety of transmission techniques. In a move toward standardization, various national, international, and industrial groups have attempted to set up guidelines to which data communications hardware and software should conform. One result has been the establishment of several **protocols,** or sets of rules and procedures spelling out how to initiate and maintain data communications. These protocols are intended to enable the components of data communications systems to work together harmoniously.

A necessary function of protocols is to define the rules by which receivers can properly interpret transmitted messages. Without protocols to guide the orderly exchange of data between components of communications systems, messages would be impossible to decode. Protocols determine who transmits when, how transmissions are made, how errors are detected and handled, and how received messages are interpreted and decoded. Protocols establish operating standards for data communications systems and have greatly increased the efficiency with which messages can be sent and received. Examples of protocols include teletypewriter (TTY), binary synchronous communication (BSC), synchronous data link control (SDLC), and high-level data link control (HDLC).

COMMON CARRIERS

Although some private data communications systems have been established by large government agencies and business firms, most data communications are handled by common carriers. A **common carrier** is a company licensed and regulated by the state or federal government to carry the property of others at approved rates. In the context of data communications, common carriers are organizations licensed to transport data belonging to others. The two largest such carriers in the United States are American Telephone and Telegraph (AT&T) and Western Union, but there are more than 3000 others.

Companies licensed to transmit data

In the United States, communications are regulated by the Federal Communications Commission (FCC) and various state agencies. Since 1968, the FCC has allowed companies to compete with AT&T (which previously had a virtual monopoly over data communications) by producing equipment (such as modems) that could be interfaced with AT&T's telephone network). In 1982, the U.S. government agreed to drop an antitrust suit against AT&T if the company divested itself of the 22 local telephone companies making up the Bell System. At the same time, AT&T became free to enter areas from which it had formerly been barred, such as data processing and computer equipment manufacturing.

An important result of the increased competition in the communications industry has been the rise of specialized common carriers and value-added carriers. **Specialized common carriers,** such as MCI Communications Corporation and ITT World Communications, offer a limited number of data communications services in and between selected metropolitan areas. These carriers often employ microwave systems or communications satellites.

Value-added carriers are companies that lease channels from common carriers and add extra services beyond the basic ones provided, such as error detection or message storage. Such a carrier thus creates a **value-added network (VAN).** Some value-added networks, such as Tymnet, Inc. and GTE's Telenet, are **packet-switching networks;** that is, large messages are chopped apart into smaller packets. Packets from several customers are combined and transmitted as a unit at high speed. That block of data is disassembled into the various messages at the carrier's office closest to their final destinations. Customers use local leased or switched lines to get their messages from this office.

More and more businesses are finding that value-added networks are a faster and economical means for data transfer. The two largest of these networks, Tymnet, Inc. and Telenet, share more than 80 percent of the total market. Tymnet serves 750 U.S. and Canadian cities, interconnects with similar networks in 70 foreign countries, and handles data transmitted among thousands of computers and hundreds of thousands of terminals. Telenet is somewhat smaller.

DISTRIBUTED DATA-PROCESSING NETWORKS

Many data communications systems consist of remote terminals connected via channels to a central host computer. Such systems, with one computer and many distant terminals, are often called **teleprocessing systems** (a combination of tele-communications and data processing). Teleprocessing systems operate under either a time-sharing or a batching scheme. *Time sharing,* involves dividing the host computer's capacity among many users. In **remote job entry systems,** the host computer receives tasks to be processed from distant terminals and batches them. Both of these types of systems have problems, however, which have led to the development and rapid growth of distributed data-processing networks.

Decentralized processing of data

Instead of a single computer and many remote terminals, **distributed data-processing (DDP) networks** have several widely dispersed computers that are interconnected to form a data communications system. Thus, there is not one host computer, but several computers with independent processing capabilities. Although DDP networks may have a computer that is designated as the central computer to do generalized processing, each of the outlying computers can do much of its own processing.

Many private and public organizations use DDP networks. In a move to auto-mated information collection K-Mart completed the installation of a $500 million project to link all of its stores to its headquarters in Troy, Michigan. Data gathered from computerized checkouts help to expand their market share. Texas Instruments has an equally complex network of hundreds of different-sized computers and over 7000 terminals scattered throughout Europe, South America, Asia, and the United States. At least 20,000 computers, ranging from minicomputers to supercomputers, at universities and research institutions in the United States and Europe are part of a collection of networks called the Internet. Some of the larger networks in this system are the U.S. Defense Department's ARPANET (Advanced Research Projects Agency Network) and MILNET (Military Network). Finally, air-line reservation networks such as the Apollo system of United Airlines and the Sabre system of American Airlines give thousands of travel agencies up-to-the-minute access to flight schedules and rates and allow them to make car rental and hotel reservations as well as to print out tickets and itineraries.

Network Configurations

Basic designs of DDP networks: star, ring, and hierarchical networks

Three basic designs are used for distributed data-processing networks, each with its own advantages. These configurations are commonly known as the star network, the ring network, and the hierarchical network.

The **DDP star network** consists of several computers connected to a central computer, as shown in Figure 6.15(a). This central computer, usually located at an organization's headquarters, controls the communications to and from the outlying computers. The star network is well suited to organizations that must centrally control and coordinate the operations of distributed branch outlets (such as banks).

In a **DDP ring network,** several computers are connected directly to each other; there is no central, dominant computer, as is shown in the diagram in Figure 6.15(b). Messages travel from node to node until they reach their destination. In some ring network designs, the loss of any node breaks the entire network. For this reason, ring networks are often implemented with a pair of rings, one for messages circulating clockwise, the other for messages circulating counterclockwise. The fail-

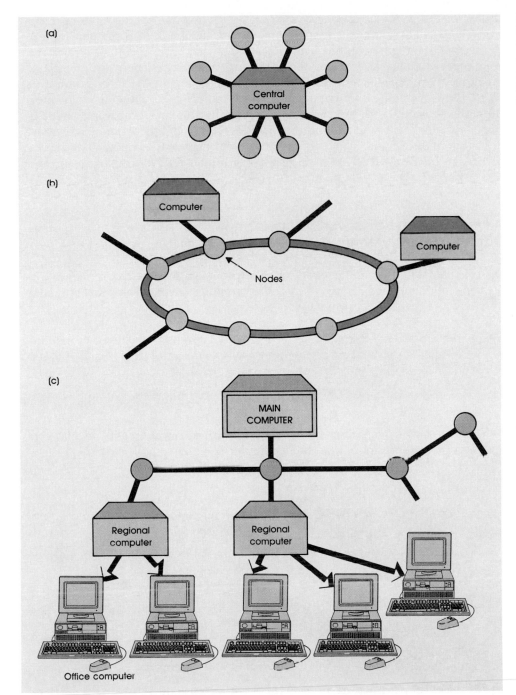

(a)

Central computer

(b)

Computer

Nodes

Computer

(c)

MAIN COMPUTER

Regional computer

Regional computer

Office computer

Figure 6.15 Star, Ring, and Hierarchical Networks
The three basic designs of distributed data-processing networks are (a) the star, (b) the ring, and (c) the hierarchical network.

ure of a single link still leaves an alternate communication path. In a star network, on the other hand, the failure of the central computer effectively crashes the whole network.

The **DDP hierarchical network** reflects the chain-of-command type of management structure found in many organizations. Computers are connected together in a pyramidlike arrangement, reflecting their relative levels of importance, as shown in Figure 6.15(c). The *root computer* at the top of the hierarchy exercises control over all of its immediate subordinates. This highest-level computer communicates with computers on the level beneath it, which in turn communicate with computers on the level beneath them. The Texas Instruments network mentioned previously is arranged in a hierarchical fashion. At the top are five large mainframes that serve as corporate information and control centers. Next in the hierarchy are a number of medium-sized mainframes responsible for data processing at major manufacturing plants and administrative offices throughout the world. Below these are many minicomputers that serve the computing needs of individual departments. At the lowest level are the intelligent terminals used by employees for routine tasks.

Advantages and Disadvantages of Distributed Data-Processing Networks

Benefits and drawbacks of DDP network

Distributed data-processing networks are very popular, largely because they alleviate some of the problems inherent in single-computer teleprocessing systems. DDP networks are favored because they:

- *Decentralize the system work load.*   The central computer is relieved of the burden of being the only processing unit available to all of the users in the network.

- *Speed up response times.*   Because there are more computers to do the work, it gets done faster.

- *Provide access to more users.*   Vital computer resources are readily available to more users since more than one computer is employed.

- *Allow flexibility.*   Hardware configurations can be customized, so individual user needs can be met.

- *Reduce communications costs.*   Many jobs can be performed locally and do not have to be sent to the central computer for processing.

- *Increase system reliability.*   If one computer or some communications lines go down, processing can still be done by the computers at local sites.

DDP networks also have their drawbacks, however, including the following:

- *Limitations of the local computers.*   Each site is to some extent dependent on its computer's processing capabilities, memory, and software. A centralized host computer facility is generally better staffed and equipped.

- *Incompatibility between local computers.*   Equipment and software used at one local site may not work smoothly with the equipment and software at other local sites. This is usually the result of employing different protocols.

- *Increased complexity of the system.*   The bigger the network, the more complications that inevitably arise.

- *Difficulties in ensuring the confidentiality and integrity of user programs and data.*   These important issues of privacy and security are dealt with in Chapter 17.

Local Area Networks

The increasing technological sophistication and decreasing costs of microcomputers and minicomputers have brought about significant growth in the application of data communications systems in the office environment. A lot of what we've described in this chapter concerns data communications systems as a means of exchanging information over relatively long distances. Businesses and other organizations have discovered, however, that as much as 80 percent of their communications occur across relatively short distances, such as within a large office, between offices in a building, or among a group of neighboring buildings. The result has been the rapid rise of the branch of data communications known as local area networking.

Connecting nearby computers

A **local area network (LAN)** basically consists of two or more computers physically connected together with some type of cable that forms a path over which data are transmitted (see Figure 6.16). Anything from twisted-pair to coaxial or fiber optic cables and specialized interface units are used to transmit data. Once established, an LAN enables all of its users to exchange programs, data, and essential information at high speeds. In addition, LANs allow expensive equipment, such as large-capacity hard disk drives and laser printers, to be shared more efficiently by users within the same organization. This can promote greater productivity, as well as encourage individuals to use available computer resources more effectively.

Hardware

Local area networks are comprised of several physical components. The key pieces of network hardware include:

- *Workstations.* In most cases, a **network workstation** is an ordinary microcomputer used to run software, transfer files, and send messages. Some companies sell less expensive microcomputers uniquely adapted to be network workstations. These specialized terminals have a microprocessor and memory to run microcomputer software, but they lack the disk drives, serial interfaces, and parallel interfaces needed for stand-alone computing. The actual number of workstations that can be connected together depends on the specific hardware and software, but it can be as few as two or as many as several hundred to more than 1,000 workstations per network.

- *Servers.* A **network server** is a workstation that handles special chores. For example, a **file server** is used to store shared program and data files on a large-capacity, high-speed hard disk; a **print server** is used to control a printer shared by other workstations on a network; and a **communications server** lets network users communicate with computers outside the network via serial ports and a high-speed modem. Sometimes a workstation is reserved solely for one or more of these chores, in which case it is called a **dedicated server.** Small networks may have only one server, while large networks may have many servers.

- *Media.* The **network media** is what connects the various workstations. Usually, the media is either twisted-pair wire, coaxial cable, or fiber-optic cable. These media were discussed earlier in this chapter.

- *Interfaces.* Each workstation is linked to the network by a **network interface.** In most cases, this device is a network adapter with a connector for the appropriate media. As we said in Chapter 1, a network adapter is usually a circuit board that fits into one of the computer's expansion slots. Besides the connector, the network adapter has a specialized microprocessor and other integrated circuits that perform communications and data processing tasks.

- *Bridges.*   Only a limited number of computers should be connected on a single network. Adding too many increases contention for the available network capacity and can lead to unacceptable delays in sending messages. Two smaller networks can be joined with a device called a **bridge.** The bridge listens to the

Figure 6.16   A Local Area Network

An organization can increase its efficiency by linking small computers and peripheral devices into a local area network.

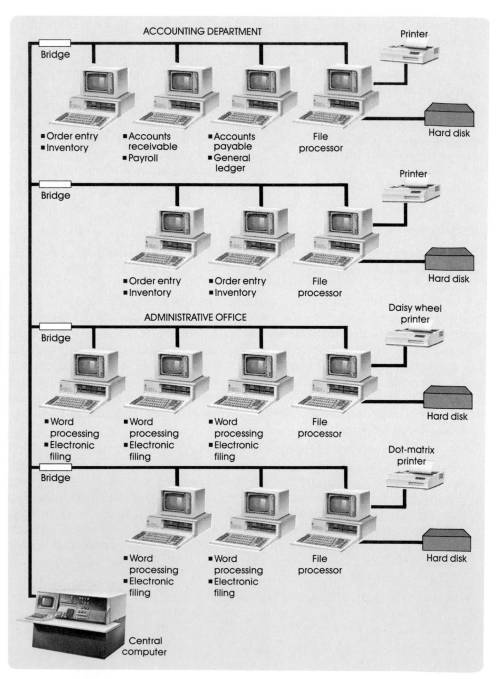

traffic on both networks. It actively transports messages from one network that are addressed to computers on the other. Neither network sees messages that can be delivered within a network.

- *Gateways.* A more complex network joiner, the **gateway,** performs a similar operation but with networks of different types. The gateway must cope with different addressing schemes, varying limits in the size of messages, and choosing the routes over which the messages are sent.

Topology

The arrangement of these hardware components in a network is called the **topology.** The three fundamental network topologies are the bus, the ring, and the star. Figure 6.17 on the following pages shows an example of each of these arrangements. In a **LAN bus network,** each workstation is connected to a single cable running past all the workstations. A **LAN ring network** is similar to a bus network, except that the two ends of the central cable are hooked together. The **LAN star network** has an individual cable run from a central server to each workstation.

The topology of a network affects its efficiency, reliability, and cost. For example, a bus network requires less wiring than a star network, so it costs less. A star network, however, is easier to troubleshoot if a problem occurs. You can simply unplug each workstation in a star network to see which one is causing the problem. On the other hand, ring networks are more reliable than star networks. If a central server in a star network breaks down, the whole network is disabled. If any one of the workstations in a ring network breaks down, however, the remaining functional workstations can still communicate.

Protocols

A protocol is a set of rules that governs how computers communicate. Networks also have protocols. For the most part, you need not be too concerned with these network protocols, unless of course, you are an engineer designing a network. Nevertheless, protocols are often mentioned in books and articles about networking, and it helps to be familiar with the concept.

The most commonly used protocols in local area networks are polling, carrier sense multiple access, and token-passing. With polling, a controlling workstation sends messages to the other workstations on the network, asking each one in turn if it has any messages or data to transmit. In contrast, the **carrier sense multiple access (CSMA)** protocol requires each workstation to listen before sending messages. Like people on a party line telephone, workstations using CSMA only transmit messages or data if they sense that the line is clear. Since two workstations can potentially begin transmitting at the same instant, their messages may "collide" and become garbled. Variations of the basic CSMA protocol have been developed to detect and avoid these collisions. For example, CSMA/CD (the CD means "collision detection") and CSMA/CA (the CA means "collision avoidance") are commonly used network protocols. Finally, the **token-passing** protocol uses a control signal called a *token* that determines which workstation is allowed to transmit data. The token is passed from workstation to workstation, and complex rules prevent any one user from "hogging" the system. Token-passing is generally used with ring networks. For example, the IBM Token-Ring Network is one of the most popular LANs for IBM-compatible microcomputers.

**Figure 6.17   Local Area
Network Topology**

(a)   **Bus network**

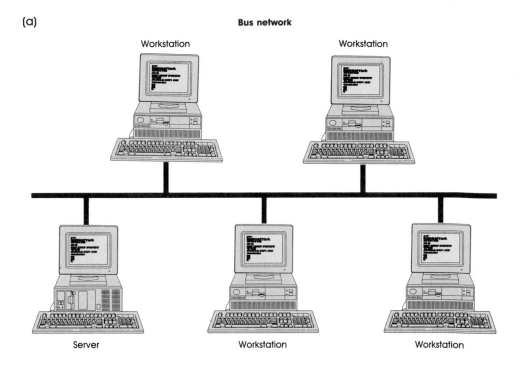

(b)   **Ring network**

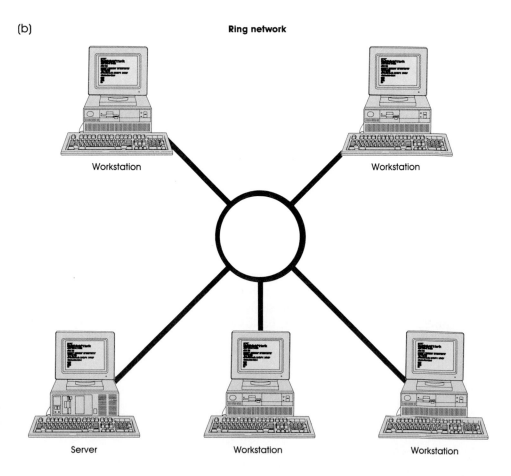

(c)

Star network

Figure 6.17 (continued)

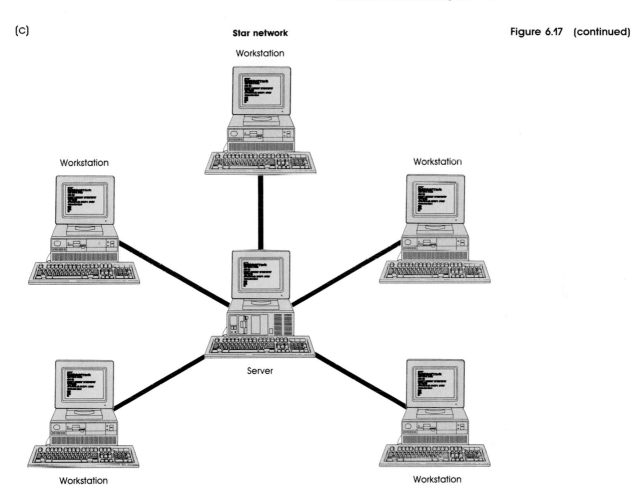

One of the best-selling commercial communications packages available for IBM-compatible microcomputers is CROSSTALK XVI from MicroStuf, Inc. This program allows you to set various parameters for controlling the manner in which your computer and modem communicate with another computer. It also dials the phone and lets you transfer files to and from a distant computer. These capabilities are essential for tapping into any of over 3,000 on-line information services in the United States alone. Most of these services offer access to specialized data bases aimed primarily at business, academic, and scientific researchers. Others are targeted at more general educational and home markets. To subscribe, all you need is a microcomputer, a modem, a telephone line, communications software such as CROSSTALK, and a credit card. Without leaving your home or office, you can perform the following types of activities with an on-line information service:

- Access electronic versions of popular encyclopedias.
- Search *Books in Print* and *The Reader's Guide to Periodical Literature*.
- Check the latest weather report for almost any place in the world.
- Read up-to-the-minute news from major wire services.
- Obtain stock quotes and buy and sell stocks.
- Plan a vacation, review airline schedules, and book tickets.
- Exchange electronic mail.
- "Converse" with other on-line subscribers.
- Obtain free software.
- Get answers to questions from other subscribers about computer hardware and software.
- Browse through electronic shopping malls.
- Play computer games.
- Join special interest groups.
- Participate in electronic forums.

CompuServe, based in Columbus, Ohio, is the premier on-line information service. First established in 1969, CompuServe now has more than 380,000 subscribers all over the world. There is an incredible variety of individual activities offered by CompuServe, including all of those we just listed.

It's a simple matter to subscribe to an information service such as CompuServe. All you do is call their toll-free number and provide your name, address, and credit card number. CompuServe then sends you a starter kit that includes your user identification number, password, a manual, and some other handy refer-

A Closer Look

Using CROSSTALK to Call CompuServe

ence guides. At publication time, it cost $39.95 to initially subscribe to CompuServe plus additional charges for the time you actually spend using the system. These charges, assessed per minute like long-distance telephone charges, usually range from $6.25 to $12.75 per hour depending upon the time you call, the transmission speed you use, and which CompuServe number you are calling.

As a good example of practical microcomputer communications, let's use CROSSTALK to call CompuServe and access one of its most popular services, the Grolier's on-line *Academic American Encyclopedia*. Let's assume you've already subscribed to CompuServe and have a copy of CROSSTALK installed on your computer, which is connected to a modem capable of transmitting and receiving at 1200 bps (bits per second). First you turn on your modem (if it is an external model) and then activate the CROSSTALK program by typing *XTALK* and pressing the Enter key. The initial copyright message pops up on the screen, followed by any one of a number of humorous quotes, as seen in the next screen.

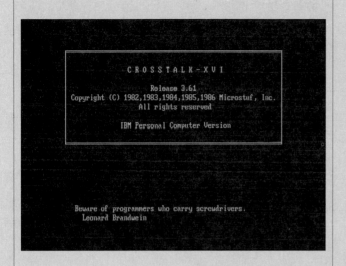

After giving you a few seconds to appreciate the authors' wit, CROSSTALK displays its default *status screen*, which looks like this:

```
┌───── CROSSTALK - XVI Status Screen ─────┐        Off line

NAme   CROSSTALK defaults                    LOaded   C:STD.XTK
NUmber                                       CApture  Off

┌── Communications parameters ──┐        ┌── Filter settings ──┐
SPeed 1200   PArity None   DUplex Full    DEbug   Off   LFauto   Off
DAta 8       STop  1       EMulate None    TAbex   Off   BLankex  Off
POrt 1                     MOde  Call      INfilter On   OUtfiltr On

┌──── Key settings ────┐                  ┌── SEnd control settings ──┐
ATten  Esc            COmmand ETX (^C)    CWait  None
SWitch Home           BReak   End         LWait  None

┌──────── Available command files ────────┐

1) CIS      2) HARRIS     3) MCIMAIL     4) STD

┌─────────────────────────────────────────┐
Enter number for file to use ( 1 - 4 ): _
```

The status screen serves two functions. First, it displays all of CROSSTALK's major options, along with their current settings. Second, it is a menu of some of the commands available. The first two letters of every command on the screen appear in bright capitalized letters. Although you may enter the entire name of a command, this isn't strictly necessary. You need only enter its first two letters.

At this point, CROSSTALK is prompting you to enter the number of a file to use. In other words, CROSSTALK is asking you if you want to use any of the existing command files available on your disk. A *command file* is simply a list of CROSSTALK commands stored as text in a disk file. CROSSTALK can load a command file from disk into memory and perform the commands it contains just as if you had manually entered those commands from the keyboard. Command files are handy for performing frequently used sequences of commands. For example, if there is a particular host computer or information service you often call, you can set up a command file to automate the specific operations necessary to make the connection. There are several ready-made command files provided by MicroStuf along with CROSSTALK. By default, the one named STD.XTK is automatically loaded into memory and executed whenever you start CROSSTALK. This command file initializes all of CROSSTALK's standard default settings. These default settings are sufficient for many operations, including calling CompuServe. Since you don't need to load in any other command file, you can just press the Enter key in response to the prompt on the screen.

After you do this, CROSSTALK displays the *Command?* prompt in the reverse video bar across the bottom of the screen. This *command line* is where you enter CROSSTALK commands. Whenever you see the command line at the bottom of the screen, you know that you can enter a CROSSTALK command. The command line disappears from the screen when you are interacting with a host computer. Right now, you are not yet connected to a host computer and the command line is on the screen, so you are free to enter a CROSSTALK command.

In order to call another computer, you must first tell CROSSTALK the relevant telephone number. CompuServe publishes and constantly updates a list of its many local telephone numbers. You must look up the one closest to you or call CompuServe to find out the proper number. In Champaign, Illinois, for example, the local number is 352-0041. To tell CROSSTALK that this is the number you want to call, you would enter the command *NU 352-0041* as seen in the following screen.

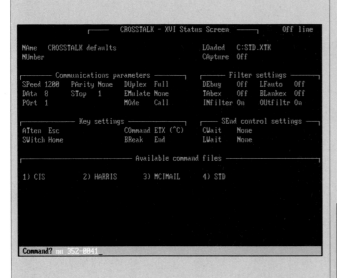

CROSSTALK inserts the number you enter into its status screen. To have CROSSTALK place the call, simply enter *GO*:

Assuming your modem is turned on and correctly connected to your microcomputer, CROSSTALK automatically will dial the number. You should hear the tones or pulses through the modem's speaker as CROSSTALK dials the phone number and waits for a connection. On the other end of the line, another modem connected to a CompuServe computer answers the call with a special tone. Once the connection has been established, CROSSTALK tells you to proceed. Simply press the Enter key, and CompuServe initiates its *log on* procedure. You now specify the system you are calling, iden-

tify yourself as a valid subscriber, and enter your secret password. CompuServe asks for the Host Name, and you enter *CIS* (for CompuServe Information Service). Then it asks for your user identification number and password, which were sent to you in the starter kit after you subscribed. As this screen demonstrates, the password doesn't actually appear on the screen, even after you type it (this is a security measure found in most multiuser systems to prevent someone from looking over your shoulder and seeing your password):

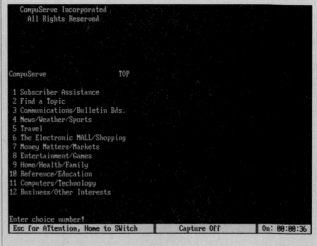

Finally, you are connected to CompuServe. The service presents its copyright message and then displays its main or *TOP* menu:

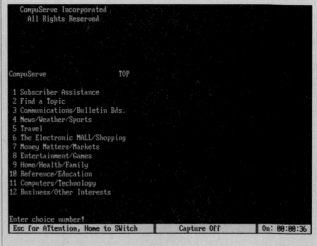

CompuServe uses a combination of menus and direct commands to let you access its many varied services. The menus are especially nice for beginners because they can be used with very little instruction. There is also an on-line tutorial that teaches new subscribers (at no charge) the basics of navigating through CompuServe's menus. After awhile, however, the menus can become tiresome. It begins to seem as if most of your time (and money) is spent waiting for menus to scroll across your screen. Since CompuServe has many levels of menus, just reaching the service you want to use can take several minutes. Fortunately, CompuServe also lets you jump directly to any service with the *GO* command. If you know exactly which feature you want to use, you can save a great deal of time with the *GO* command. An index of services and the equivalent *GO* commands is given in the CompuServe documentation and is periodically updated in the *Online Today* magazine sent to all subscribers. For example, to go directly to the Grolier's on-line *Academic American Encyclopedia*, simply enter the command *GO AAE*:

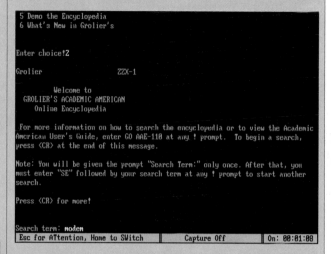

The Grolier's *Academic American Encyclopedia* is one of CompuServe's most popular services. Updated and revised four times each year, this is one of the most current encyclopedic references you're likely to find. It has more than 32,000 articles, fact boxes, bibliographies, and tables. Although there is an additional subscription charge ($7.50 for one month, $29.95 for six months, and $49.95 for one year at present), many CompuServe subscribers gladly pay to use the Grolier's encyclopedia for help with research, homework, speeches, travel plans, trivia answers, and other reference needs. And unlike most libraries, CompuServe never "closes."

As an example, let's look up the word *modem* in the on-line encyclopedia. Assuming that you have already subscribed to the encyclopedia service, you select item 2 to look up a topic. CompuServe gives you some brief instructions and then prompts you for the *search term:*

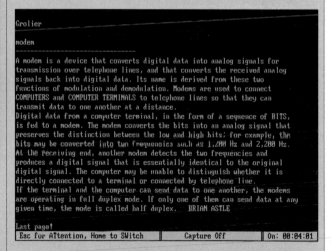

As this screen shows, to look up *modem* simply type that word and press the Enter key. Here is the result:

At this point you can continue using the on-line encyclopedia researching other topics. You can also go back to CompuServe's main menu by entering the *TOP* command at any time, and then proceed to access any of its other many services. When you are finished with CompuServe, you use the *BYE* command to disconnect from the service. Finally, you can terminate the CROSSTALK program by entering the *Quit* command.

Summary

Applications of Data Communications

Data communications has changed many aspects of modern life.

Information Services   Information services offer interactive networking to users who own inexpensive terminals or personal computers.

Electronic Mail and Bulletin Boards   Electronic mail employs computers and communications lines to enable users to send and receive messages. Electronic bulletin boards serve as a means of electronic message exchange between home computer users.

Electronic Funds Transfer   EFT systems use data communications to move money among bank accounts.

Computer Conferencing   Computer conferencing enables users to interact directly and immediately.

Telecommuting   Telecommuting utilizes microcomputers and communications channels to allow people to work at home.

Components of Data Communications Systems

The components of most data communications systems are communications hardware, communications software, and communications channels.

Communications Hardware

The devices that a data communications system includes are terminals, modems, interface units, and computers.

Terminals   All types of input/output devices can be used as terminals in data communications systems. Small computers can act as terminals when they send data to and receive data from other computers.

Modems   A modem (modulator/demodulator) is an interface unit that enables a computer to send and receive data over telephone lines. Intelligent modems, direct-connect modems, and acoustic couplers all convert digital signals to analog signals for transmission and convert received analog signals back to digital signals.

Interface Units   These devices coordinate data transmission and reception. Multiplexers combine signals from several terminals into a single transmission that can be carried by one channel. Concentrators collect data transmissions from several terminals and compress them, one after another, into a continuous high-speed stream. Message switchers route transmissions from several terminals to their proper destinations. Front-end processors are computers that relieve the host computer of many routine data communications tasks.

Computers   Several computers or a single host computer of any size may be used in a data communications system.

Communications Software

Communications software consists of programs that coordinate, monitor, and control data transmission, routing, and reception.

Communications Channels

Channels are the communications lines or pathways over which data are sent.

Physical Structure   Channels can consist of wire cables (twisted pairs or coaxial), microwave systems (possibly involving satellites), or fiber optic cables.

Transmission Speed   How much data can be sent over a channel in a given time is determined by the bandwidth of the channel. Channels are classified as narrowband, voiceband, and broadband.

Transmission Direction   Simplex, half-duplex, and full-duplex are the channel classifications that describe the direction of allowed transmissions.

Transmission Mode   Data are transmitted over channels one character at a time (asynchronous transmission) or in groups of characters (synchronous transmission).

Line Configuration   Two principal ways of connecting terminals to a computer are with point-to-point lines (a direct connection exists between each terminal and the computer) and with multidrop lines (several terminals share a single channel).

Leased Versus Switched Lines   Leased lines connect the computer to a limited number of fixed destinations, and switched lines connect the computer via switching centers to a large number of destinations.

Protocols

Protocols are sets of rules and procedures that govern the initiation and maintenance of data communications.

Common Carriers

Most data communications are handled by companies licensed and regulated by state and federal governments. Specialized common carriers offer data communications services in and between certain metropolitan areas. Value-added carriers lease channels from common carriers and provide special services via value-added networks or packet-switching networks.

Distributed Data-Processing Networks

Instead of one host computer, several computers, each with processing capabilities, can be interconnected in a distributed data-processing network.

Network Configurations   The three basic designs for distributed data-processing (DDP) networks are the star network, the ring network, and the hierarchical network.

Advantages and Disadvantages of Distributed Data-Processing Networks   DDP networks decentralize the computer workload, speed up response times, provide more users with ready access, allow flexibility, decrease communications costs, and increase system reliability. However, local computer capabilities may be limited, resources at different sites may be incompatible, system complexity is usually increased, and data confidentiality and integrity may be compromised.

Local Area Networks   Local area networks link the small individual computers in organization. Bridges join two similar networks by transporting messages on one network to destinations on the other network. Gateways join dissimilar networks.

Computer Concepts

As an extra review of the chapter, try defining the following terms. If you have trouble with any of them, refer to the page number listed.

Review Questions

1. List ways in which data communications are being used today.
2. List the components of a typical data communications system.
3. What advantage is there to using a full-fledged computer as a terminal in a data communications system?
4. What does a modem do and why is it a necessary component of many data communications systems?
5. What do interface units do in data communications systems?
6. What is a multiplexer? How does a multiplexer differ from a concentrator?
7. How does a message switcher increase the efficiency of a data communications system?
8. How does a front-end processor increase the amount of processing that can be done by the central computer in a data communications system?
9. What kinds of tasks does host communications software perform?
10. What are some operations performed by terminal emulator programs?
11. What role do communications satellites play in microwave systems?
12. What are half-duplex channels commonly used for?
13. What are full-duplex channels commonly used for?
14. In terms of sending data, how do synchronous and asynchronous transmissions differ?
15. Why are point-to-point lines usually more expensive than multidrop lines?
16. What are the two largest common carriers of data in the United States?
17. What has been an important result of increased competition in the communications industry?
18. Why are DDP ring networks generally more reliable than DDP star networks?
19. In what ways are distributed data-processing networks better than single computer teleprocessing systems?
20. What constitutes a local area network?

True or False

1. Electronic bulletin boards are used primarily by large businesses.
2. The conversion of digital signals to analog signals is called modulation.
3. Message switchers cannot store transmissions.
4. Polling and contention are both techniques for maintaining a smooth flow of data.
5. Kermit is the name of a microcomputer error-correcting protocol.
6. Microwaves can be used to transmit only limited kinds of data.
7. Transmission speed refers to how fast data travels along a communications channel.
8. Protocols are sets of rules and procedures spelling out how to initiate and maintain data communications.
9. A star network consists of a single computer connected to a series of CRTs.
10. Networks of different types can be joined by a gateway.

Multiple Choice

1. One of the two largest information services available to home computer users in the United States is:
   (a) AT&T (b) CompuServe (c) IBM
2. The need for modems will decrease as:
   (a) multiplexers become more sophisticated (b) host communications software improves (c) digital channels become more widely available
3. A single computer designated as the central processing component of a data communications system is called the:
   (a) front-end processor (b) host computer (c) concentrator
4. A transmission line developed to combat crosstalk is:
   (a) coaxial cable (b) twisted-wire cables (c) central cable
5. The speed advantage of fiber optic cables over wire cables in transmitting information is primarily due to the fact that:
   (a) light travels faster than electricity
   (b) optical fibers are immune to electrical interference
   (c) light can be turned on and off more rapidly than electricity
6. Coaxial cables, microwave systems and fiber optic cables are all:
   (a) broadband channels (b) voiceband channels (c) narrowband channels
7. A system that interconnects several widely dispersed computers to form a data communications system is called a:
   (a) remote job entry system (b) time-sharing system (c) distributed data processing network
8. A computer network in which computers are connected in a pyramid-like arrangement that reflects their relative importance is:
   (a) a star network (b) a ring network (c) a hierarchical network
9. In a hierarchical network the highest level computer is called the:
   (a) mainframe computer (b) the root computer (c) the star computer
10. One drawback of DDPs is that they:
    (a) slow down response times
    (b) depend in part on the limitations of local computers
    (c) are not flexible

A Sharper Focus

1. If you were subscribing to an information service and could pick only three kinds of services, which three would you select? Why?
2. Do you think data communications technology makes consumer goods more or less expensive? How?

Projects

1. Prepare a report on one of the large value-added networks (such as Telenet or Tymnet). What do they offer their users, and what kinds of organizations do they serve?

2. Most large libraries have access to data retrieval networks. Investigate the typical costs and features of these systems and prepare a report of your findings.

3. Modems, even those used with small home computers, differ significantly in features and price. Prepare a report delineating available features and corresponding costs.

4. Find out the exact roles data communications plays at your school or company. To supplement your written report, draw diagrams showing all the communications channels used and indicating the type of channel, transmission mode, and transmission speed. Also, explain why data communications is used for each application, what other possibilities are available, and why they aren't being used.

Part

3

SOFTWARE

To imagine a world without computers isn't difficult; to imagine a world with computers and without software, without the programs that tell the hardware what to do, is impossible. Just as a computer needs electricity, it needs software in order to do anything. In Part 2, we looked at the computer's various component devices. In Part 3, we'll discover what makes them work.

Chapters 7 and 8 discuss the concepts and tools programmers use to write software. Chapters 9 and 10 focus on two of the most significant types of software: commercial application packages that let even nonprogrammers put computers to work and the operating systems that oversee program execution.

7

Program Development

Focus On

The New Frontier

The Los Alamos National Laboratory has been a pioneer computer user, going back to 1945 when they began to use the ENIAC (see Chapter 2). In 1952 the lab built MANIAC, a machine based on a design of John von Neumann.

Los Alamos has always wanted and taken advantage of the computer industry's latest, most powerful products. That led to the purchase in 1966 of the CDC 6600, designed by Seymour Cray, and his CDC 7600 in 1970. In 1972 Cray had founded his own company in Chippewa Falls, Wisconsin and was planning to introduce an innovative new computer early in 1976.

Cray Research knew that the first customer for this new machine had to have considerable expertise. The company knew that the first installation was a do-or-die proposition. There were possibly a dozen potential customers who would be able to handle it. Los Alamos was certainly one of those, and the Lab wanted the new machine. The architecture of the Cray system, vector processing, was a feature that people at Los Alamos had wanted, and the new computer seemed to fit the bill.

Problems arose with the budgetary allotment for the new computer in 1976. Los Alamos had budgeted for a new system in 1977, and getting funds in advance from the government is never an easy proposition. Also, because of problems with a previous vector processing machine, some people involved in the procurement process were nervous about buying another. These financial considerations were problematical for Cray Research and for Seymour Cray personally. So, in typical fashion he made a bet; he offered his system to Los Alamos as a loan for six months with certain restrictions. If the system did what Los Alamos wanted, the Lab would pay Cray. If not, they could return the machine.

Unfortunately for Cray, the government is not designed to grab quickly at an innovative offer and run with it. Procurement requirements were such that competitive bids had to be solicited. The system was shipped in March 1976 for a six-month demonstration and evaluation; at the end of that time, a competitive procurement was to be conducted. Los Alamos was offered a minimum-risk option that was within government restrictions. Cray, however, had laid its last card on the table—the Cray-1 was their only asset; all their venture capital had been used up.

The first system was delivered without software. However, Los Alamos was accustomed to developing their own software—a process that has continued to the present. They developed a time-sharing system and a mass storage program for Cray computers, both of which are now in the public domain. In 1976 a million words was a very large memory. The Lab suggested an error correction and detection process in main memory that utilized memory more accurately, and it was incorporated in the subsequent Crays built.

At the end of six months, Cray Research and two other vendors entered into competitive bidding. Cray won, the money came in October, and Seymour Cray's bet paid off.

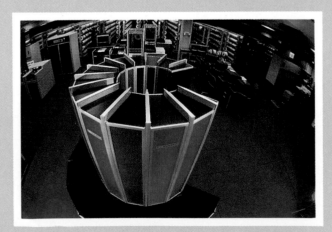

We've covered the essential facts about all kinds of hardware, and now we can shift our emphasis to what makes that hardware work—software. In this chapter, we'll discuss how software is created, that is, the program development process, and the role of the computer programmer. Since computers are nothing more than machines, the process of developing a program basically involves systematically formulating a detailed sequence of instructions to solve a concrete, real-life problem (such as organizing a company's payroll records or tracking the paths of satellites). Thus, a **computer program** is a precise, ordered group of statements that tells a computer how to execute a well-defined task.

The words *precise* and *ordered* are crucial. A computer cannot tolerate ambiguity, nor can it generalize or infer. It does *exactly* what it is told to do. Consequently, computer programming is often difficult and frustrating. The more complex the program, the more likely it is to contain erroneous statements that tell the computer to perform unintended operations. Because many programs are quite complex (consisting of hundreds of thousands of lines in some cases), the process of developing computer programs must be disciplined and systematic if the results are to be useful and correct.

THE PROGRAM DEVELOPMENT PROCESS

Recognizing that a computer can be used for a certain task is a far cry from having a useful program. The **program development process** is the series of activities necessary for the creation of a successful computer program. Before examining these activities, let's list the characteristics of a successful computer program.

How successful programs are created

correct	it does what it's supposed to do
usable	it's easy to use
reliable	it works without failing
understandable	it can be easily comprehended
modifiable	it can be enhanced and updated
maintainable	it can be corrected when errors are found
flexible	it can be modified to supply other information as required
general	it isn't overly specialized
efficient	it doesn't waste computer resources

As Figure 7.1 shows, the program development process can be divided into seven stages: (1) defining the problem; (2) developing the software requirements; (3) designing the program; (4) coding the program; (5) testing the program; (6) installing and maintaining the program; and (7) documenting the program.

Following these steps won't guarantee that a program will be successful. Unless the program is very simple, however, not following these steps is likely to detract from the program's quality. To illustrate the process of developing a program, let's go through these steps to accomplish a fairly simple task: writing a program to compute your grade-point average.

Defining the Problem

The programmer's first task is to determine just what the problem is and how to solve it. This can often be accomplished by simply talking with the people who are requesting the program, learning what they need, and how they want the program

Pinpointing what needs to be done

Figure 7.1   The Program Development Process
There are seven basic stages of developing a computer program.

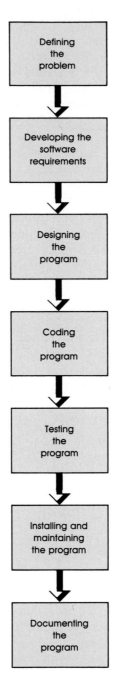

to work. The programmer sometimes receives only vague or generalized verbal descriptions of what's needed; in that case, he or she will have to help determine what the program should do. Even then, it's not uncommon for both beginning and experienced programmers to end up with a program that bears no resemblance to what was originally intended. It is vitally important to view the whole project at the outset, so that the problem is clearly defined and understood. Because they can have a bearing on how the problem is defined, the other stages of the program development process must also be considered at the beginning. Although we've presented the program development process as a sequence of distinct steps, the stages are interrelated, and all must be kept in mind throughout the entire process.

Our example program will calculate a grade-point average. Although this is a fairly simple task, it's still important to formally define the problem to be solved. In our case, defining the problem is easy. Given your grades and the number of semester hours for each course you have taken, the program is supposed to calculate your grade-point average. Note that the problem definition does not explain the detailed steps of solving the problem. The details will be formulated later.

Developing the Software Requirements

Software requirements specify exactly what a program should do without giving any details concerning how it should be done. This second stage produces the program *specifications*. From specifications, the program can be designed. If the solution to the problem is very complex, the specifications may be expressed in a *software requirements document (SRD)*, a set of precisely stated constraints that the finished program must satisfy. If the program satisfies these constraints, we consider it an acceptable solution to the problem.

Prototyping is another way to specify software requirements that involves constructing a working model of the proposed program. A prototype resembles a rough draft of the program, demonstrating the layout of display screens and giving an idea of how the program will work when finished. While the prototype doesn't do everything the final program will do, it does allow the programmer to demonstrate an understanding of how the program should work. The prototype can be shown to the program requestor to make sure it yields the desired results. If the prototype doesn't correctly represent the proposed program, it can be modified and refined until it does. Since prototyping is much easier than programming, it can save a great deal of time and effort in the long run. In practice, prototyping is usually done with a *prototyping software package*. A Closer Look, at the end of this chapter, examines the use of a popular prototyping package for microcomputers, Dan Bricklin's Demo II.

Software requirements documents and prototyping are generally reserved for fairly large programming projects. Most simple tasks, such as our grade-point-average program, can be developed without them. Nevertheless, programmers must still specify the exact form of the output to be produced by the program, the necessary input, and the types of processing that must be done to convert the input data to output information.

Specifying the output, input, and processing

Desired Output

Because the output is the whole reason for developing a program in the first place, specifying the output is as important as defining the problem. The following characteristics of the output must be determined:

- *Content.* What information must the output convey? How detailed should this information be? The answers to these questions depend on the problem definition.

- *Format.* How is the information to be presented? What output devices are to be used, and how is the information to be arranged? For example, if the output is to appear on a display screen, how it will look, where it will be placed, and what color it will be are some of the factors to be considered.

- *Timing.* When is the information to be presented? Is the information to be output immediately or batched and output periodically?

In our grade-point-average program, the output is very simple. It consists of a small table like the one shown in Figure 7.2 to be presented on the display screen. This table shows the total grade points, total semester hours, and computed grade-point average. As for the timing of the output, this table will be displayed on the screen immediately after all input data have been entered. Specifying the final form of the output in this manner shows exactly what the proposed program is supposed to accomplish.

Required Input

Since the output of a program represents the results obtained from the processing of the input, a careful analysis must be made of the input data. The programmer must know what data are needed, whether they are available and accessible, and how they are formatted:

- *Necessary data.* What data are needed in order to get the desired output? A thorough list of all data that must be input is a very important part of developing software requirements.

- *Availability and accessibility of data.*   Where will the necessary data come from? Are the input data already stored somewhere, or must they be gathered? Will the data be obtained directly from on-line input devices or from secondary storage media such as magnetic or optical disks? In other words, will the user have to enter the data immediately or will the data be read from a previously created file?

- *Format of data.* What is the physical arrangement of the input data? If a program receives data in a format it was not designed to handle, it may fail or yield unpredictable results.

The grade-point-average program will require the user to directly enter the input data. For each course, this data will consist of the course name, number of semester hours, and the letter grade received. To be even more specific, the course name should be less than 20 characters in length, the number of semester hours must be

```
            Total Grade Points = 68

            Total Semester Hours = 16

            Grade-Point Average = 4.25
```

Figure 7.2 The Desired Output
This table shows what the final output of the grade-point-average program should look like. The actual numbers would depend on the particular input data that were entered.

a whole number between 1 and 5, and the only acceptable letter grades are A, B, C, D, and F. The user will simply enter these data for each course to be included in the grade-point average. A grade-point average can be computed for a single semester, the whole year, or even several years.

Necessary Processing

The computer operations indicated in the program perform the processing of input into output. The software requirements must list the processing tasks to be executed, define the way users will communicate with the program, and designate the necessary equipment:

- *Processing data.* What operations must be performed to process the data? For example, input data may have to be sorted or mathematical calculations may have to be carried out. The software requirements should specify exactly what is to be done with the input data.

- *User interface.* How will the user interact with the program? The **user interface** is the means by which a person using the program communicates with it. How this interface should work largely depends on the intended users. If the users are to be computer professionals, familiar with the equipment and programming, the user interface may be fairly simple, allowing much to be done quickly with only a few commands. If, on the other hand, the users are novices, the interface should be **user-friendly;** that is, it should be easy to learn to use the program. In practice, a user-friendly interface is much more sophisticated and difficult to create because it must help guide those people who don't already know how to use the program.

- *Necessary equipment.* Exactly what computers, peripheral equipment, and other programs will be needed to run the program? The software requirements should list the hardware resources that must be available if the program is to run successfully. For example, a program may be designed to run only on one computer model with a specific kind of monitor and disk drive. On the other hand, some programs are designed to run on a number of machines with a variety of peripheral equipment.

The grade-point-average program performs several simple processing tasks. First it reads from the keyboard the course name, semester hours, and letter grade of a course to be included in the average, and it checks these data to make sure they are valid. In other words, the program must make sure that the user doesn't enter a letter grade of Z or 15 semester hours for a single course. If the data are valid, then the program computes the grade points for that course. This is done by multiplying the number of semester hours by a certain point value for each letter grade. The point values are: A = 5, B = 4, C = 3, D = 2, and F = 1. For example, if you received a B in a 3-semester-hour course, your grade points for that course would be 4 points times 3 hours, or 12. To compute the actual grade-point average, the program must read in data from each course, compute its grade points, sum all of the grade points, sum all of the semester hours, and divide the total grade points by the total semester hours. Because this is a simple program, the user interface need not be sophisticated. The program will just ask the user for the necessary input data. When the user is finished entering data, the program displays the table shown in Figure 7.2 and then terminates. No extra equipment is needed, just the standard keyboard and monitor.

Designing the Program

Once the programmer has determined *what* the program must do, the next step is spelling out *how* it will be done, designing the problem solution. Before instructing the computer in detail specifically how to perform a task, the programmer must develop a step-by-step method for getting from input to output. This set of steps is called an **algorithm.** Drawing up the algorithm, which specifies a particular method for solving a problem or performing a task, is the first step of program design.

As any programmer will tell you, good algorithms don't grow on trees. Finding a suitable algorithm for the task at hand can be something of a challenge, which is sometimes made even trickier by the fact that there may be more than one algorithm that will do the job. For example, let's say we want to sort a list of names into alphabetical order. There are a number of different algorithms that will let us accomplish the same result. We might pick out all the names beginning with A, then those beginning with B, and so on. Alternatively, we could start with one name and place other names one by one into their proper relative positions.

The search for the right algorithm may be made less difficult by the fact that for tasks like sorting, which have been done many times before, workable algorithms have been collected and printed in reference books. On the other hand, for tasks that are new or somehow different from what has been done before, original algorithms must be developed. This part of the job tests a programmer's problem-solving and puzzle-working abilities, skills that are very difficult to teach. Sometimes mathematical skills are also needed to develop a working algorithm, while other solutions may come from outside sources: coworkers, friends, or other projects may supply new approaches to a problem.

Once the general algorithm that best solves the problem has been chosen or developed, the programmer must express it clearly in words, diagrams, charts, or tables. The means for doing this is a **program design aid,** a tool for building a computer program. A design aid either outlines the program's overall organization or gives some of the specific steps of the program. We will introduce a few of the more established methods: pseudocode, flowcharts, decision tables, and structure charts.

Pseudocode

Pseudocode is an informal, yet structured, expression of a program algorithm, using words, phrases, and mathematical symbols. This program design aid allows the programmer to specify the problem solution with enough precision that it can later be translated almost directly to a formal programming language. Pseudocode is a "pidgin" computer language; it includes statements and grammar borrowed from various computer languages along with ordinary English phrases. The informality of pseudocode and its lack of standardized rules free the programmer to concentrate on the general structure and flow of the program without getting bogged down in the specific requirements of a particular programming language.

Pseudocode is a very popular design aid for simple to moderately complex programs. Compact, easy to write, easy to revise, and easy to convert into an actual program, pseudocode is employed by most programmers. In some cases, however, pseudocode may not be as suitable as other program design aids, such as flowcharts and decision tables, for depicting algorithms with very complex logic.

Although a great deal of individual variation is possible with pseudocode and there are no "official" standards, much pseudocode appears to be similar because a few widely accepted formatting rules exist. Some of these rules are as follows:

- Capitalize key words and phrases, such as READ, COMPUTE, and DISPLAY.
- Use indentation to show the logical structure of the program.
- Use BEGIN and END to bracket a set of operations to be performed in sequence.
- Represent a decision between two alternatives as follows:

    IF (some condition is true) THEN
        one or more operations
    ELSE
        one or more operations
    END IF

- Represent the repetition of a sequence of instructions, or **loop,** in one of the following two ways:

    DO WHILE (some condition is true)
        one or more operations
    END DO

    (This tests to see if the condition is true *before* performing the operations each time, at the beginning of the loop.)

    DO UNTIL (some condition is true)
        one or more operations
    END DO

    (This tests to see if the condition is true *after* performing the operations each time, at the end of the loop.)

Figure 7.3 illustrates a pseudocode representation of the algorithm for our grade-point-average program. The program is a sequence of instructions bracketed by BEGIN and END. The user is asked to supply input data, and those data are read from the keyboard. After checking the data to make sure they are valid, the program begins a loop. Inside the loop, the number of grade points for a course is computed according to its semester hours and letter grade. (In computer notation, the * (asterisk) stands for multiplication and the / (forward slash) stands for division.) A running total, or **accumulator,** records the grade points, while a second accumulator tallies the semester hours. The loop repeats as long as the user continues entering valid data for another course. When no more data are entered, the loop terminates and the program computes the grade-point average. Note that the program makes sure that the total number of semester hours is greater than zero before trying to divide by that number. Dividing a number by zero is undefined and usually results in an error message from the computer. Finally, the total grade points, semester hours, and grade-point average are displayed in a table on the screen.

Flowcharts

A **flowchart** is a graphic form of an algorithm. Standard symbols, such as the ones shown in Figure 7.4, represent the operations that must be performed by the program. Lines with arrowheads on them, called flowlines, show the order in which

Diagramming the algorithm

Figure 7.3 Grade-Point-Average Program Pseudocode

Pseudocode is perhaps the most commonly used design aid for simple to moderately complex programs, such as this grade-point-average program. Note how key words are capitalized and how indentation is used to reflect the structure of the program. Also note the use of the IF . . . THEN . . . ELSE . . . END IF construct for decision-making and the DO WHILE construct for looping.

```
BEGIN (Grade-Point-Average Program)
   DISPLAY "Please Enter course name, semester hours, letter grade:"
   READ course name, semester hours, letter grade
   CHECK course data for validity
   DO WHILE (course data has been entered and is valid)
      IF (letter grade = 'A') THEN
         COMPUTE grade points = semester hours * 5
      ELSE IF (letter grade = 'B') THEN
         COMPUTE grade points = semester hours * 4
      ELSE IF (letter grade = 'C') THEN
         COMPUTE grade points = semester hours * 3
      ELSE IF (letter grade = 'D') THEN
         COMPUTE grade points = semester hours * 2
      ELSE
         COMPUTE grade points = semester hours
      END IF
      COMPUTE total points = total points + grade points
      COMPUTE total hours = total hours + semester hours
      READ course name, semester hours, letter grade
      CHECK course data for validity
   END DO
      IF (total hours > 0) THEN
         COMPUTE grade-point average = total points / total hours
      END IF
      DISPLAY "Total Grade Points = " total points
      DISPLAY "Total Semester Hours = " total hours
      DISPLAY "Grade-Point Average = " grade-point average
END (Grade-Point-Average Program)
```

these operations are to be performed. In other words, a flowchart is a diagram of the sequence of steps that a program must follow to produce the desired output.

Flowcharts are one of the oldest program design aids and are still quite popular. By graphically depicting the structure of a program, a flowchart clearly shows the sequence of steps that must take place to convert input data into output information. Unlike pseudocode, flowchart symbols and guidelines for their use have been standardized by the American National Standards Institute (ANSI). A few of the suggested flowcharting guidelines follow:

● Always use the ANSI symbols; don't make up your own.

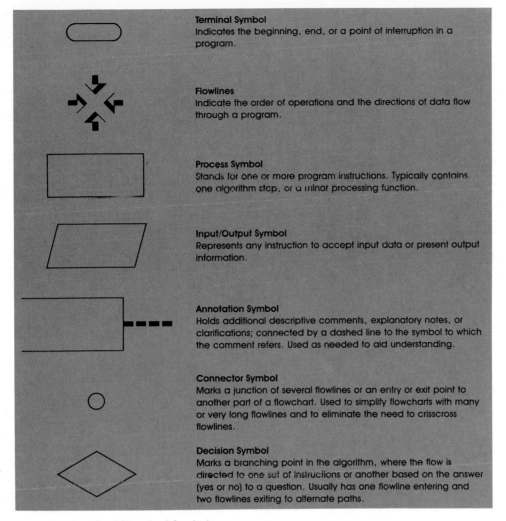

Terminal Symbol
Indicates the beginning, end, or a point of interruption in a program.

Flowlines
Indicate the order of operations and the directions of data flow through a program.

Process Symbol
Stands for one or more program instructions. Typically contains one algorithm step, or a minor processing function.

Input/Output Symbol
Represents any instruction to accept input data or present output information.

Annotation Symbol
Holds additional descriptive comments, explanatory notes, or clarifications; connected by a dashed line to the symbol to which the comment refers. Used as needed to aid understanding.

Connector Symbol
Marks a junction of several flowlines or an entry or exit point to another part of a flowchart. Used to simplify flowcharts with many or very long flowlines and to eliminate the need to crisscross flowlines.

Decision Symbol
Marks a branching point in the algorithm, where the flow is directed to one set of instructions or another based on the answer (yes or no) to a question. Usually has one flowline entering and two flowlines exiting to alternate paths.

Figure 7.4   Standard Flowchart Symbols
The symbols used in flowcharts include geometric shapes, lines with arrowheads, words, phrases, and mathematical expressions. The widespread use of flowcharts by computer programmers has led to the adoption by the American National Standards Institute (ANSI) of a set of Standard Flowchart Symbols for Information Processing. Here are a few of the most commonly used ANSI standard flowchart symbols for programs.

- Construct your flowcharts to read from top to bottom and from left to right, as much as possible.
- Don't cross flowlines (use labeled connectors, if necessary), and use arrowheads to indicate direction of flow.
- Make the messages and labels inside the flowchart symbols direct and descriptive.
- Strive for neatness, clarity, and simplicity. If necessary, break down a large flowchart into two or more smaller flowcharts using labeled connectors. Use a *flowcharting template* to trace uniform symbol outlines and print clearly to ensure legibility.

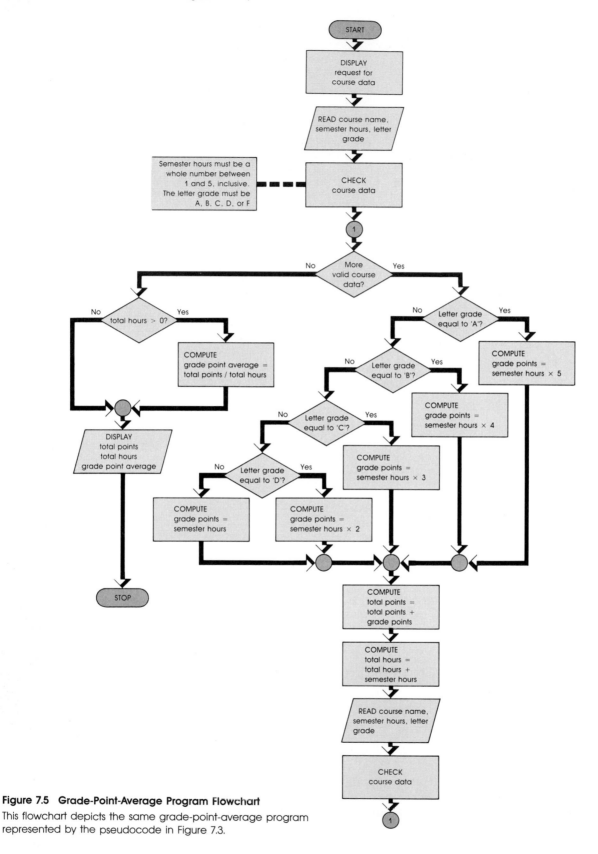

Figure 7.5 Grade-Point-Average Program Flowchart
This flowchart depicts the same grade-point-average program represented by the pseudocode in Figure 7.3.

Figure 7.5 depicts a flowchart of the grade-point-average program represented by the pseudocode in Figure 7.3. As you compare these two program design aids, you might notice some of the disadvantages of using flowcharts. They can be quite difficult and time-consuming to draw by hand, although there are several application packages available that let you more easily draw flowcharts with a computer. Furthermore, flowcharts can be unwieldy, especially for very large or complex programs. They can fill up many pages of paper, which sometimes makes them difficult to read and understand. Finally, flowcharts are generally more difficult to modify than pseudocode, since you usually have to rearrange and redraw several symbols, if not the entire flowchart, just to make an addition or deletion. Despite these disadvantages, flowcharts can still be quite useful for designing certain critical sections of a program.

Decision Tables

The **decision table** is a program design aid used for specifying complex logical conditions and actions. Most often employed in conjunction with other aids, decision tables help a programmer verify that every possible outcome has been considered and provided for. A programmer is often faced with problems that have multiple combinations of conditions and possible actions. By constructing a decision table for each portion of a program that will handle this complex decision-making process, the programmer ensures that no likely combination has been omitted. Decision tables give the programmer a clear, concise way of enumerating every possible case and therefore reduce errors in finished programs.

Clarifying complex logic

Figure 7.6 offers a simple decision table that might be used in designing a computer program that takes action after student grade-point averages have been calculated. The *condition entries* are based on students' academic and disciplinary records. A condition entry of Y means the answer to the question in the same row is yes, N means it is no, and — means the question doesn't apply or the answer doesn't matter. The *action entries* indicate what should be done for each combination of conditions. An X indicates that the action in the same row is to be taken in response to the combination of conditions entered above in the same column. Each rule ties a specific action or actions to a given set of conditions. Rule 3 on the decision table in Figure 7.6, for example, indicates that any student with a grade-point average less than 3.0 who isn't already on academic or disciplinary probation should now be placed on academic probation and should not be allowed to graduate this semester.

A series of criteria that is fairly complicated to put into words is relatively easy to express in a decision table. Figure 7.6 shows a very simple decision table. More complex tables with greater numbers of condition and action rows and rule columns are usually necessary.

Structure Charts

The **structure chart** is a program design aid that helps the programmer organize large, multipart programs. It shows the overall structure of a complex program and illustrates the relationships among its various parts, called modules. A **module** is a relatively independent, identifiable group of related program statements that can be treated as a unit. The structure chart shows how the modules of a program are interrelated but does not reveal any details about how they work. A structure chart

The big picture

HEADING

Allowing Graduation	RULES			
	1	2	3	4
Grade point average less than 3.0?	Y	Y	Y	N
On academic probation?	—	Y	N	—
On disciplinary probation?	Y	N	N	—
Allow graduation				X
Put on academic probation			X	
Suspend graduation		X	X	
Expel from college	X			

CONDITION STUB — ACTION STUB (left side labels)
CONDITION ENTRIES — ACTION ENTRIES (right side labels)

Figure 7.6   The Decision Table

Decision tables help the programmer allow for every possible case in a problem with a number of conditions and corresponding actions to be taken. This example shows a procedure that might be followed in a computer program that decides what actions should be taken after student grade-point averages have been calculated.

presents the broad picture—the overview of a program's organization. Like decision tables, structure charts are usually used in conjunction with other design aids.

The typical structure chart is arranged in a hierarchical (ranked by level) fashion and looks like an upside-down family tree or a corporate organizational chart (see Figure 7.7). Labeled boxes represent the program modules, and the connecting lines indicate which modules control, or are controlled by, others. There is usually a single module at the top that controls the entire program much as a president runs a corporation. This module directly controls the modules just beneath it, which in turn control the ones beneath them. The modules at the very bottom of the chart are the ones that do the "real" work, the specific tasks required to get the job done.

As we'll discuss later when we talk about structured programming and top-down design, very large or complex problems are best solved by such a "divide-and-conquer" approach. Thus, a structure chart is useful for showing the overall layout of very large programs, but it must be supplemented by other design aids that detail the lower level modules.

HIPO Charts

The **HIPO chart** (Hierarchy plus Input-Process-Output chart) was originally developed at IBM as a tool for documenting programs. A HIPO chart clearly displays what a program does, what data it uses, and what output it creates. For many programs, HIPO charts are easier to read than flowcharts. They are highly detailed, yet flexible and easy to modify and maintain.

Diagrams showing the three levels of detail

Producing a HIPO chart requires constructing three types of diagrams: the visual table of contents (VTOC), overview diagrams, and detail diagrams.

The *visual table of contents* is very similar to the structure chart, as you can see by comparing Figure 7.8(a) with Figure 7.7 The only difference is that each module is given a reference number that reflects its place in the hierarchy. A *legend* listing these numbers along with a short description of each module's purpose accompanies the VTOC. The VTOC shows the overall structure of the program and gives a general impression of what it does. The use of the sequence numbers and the legend allows lower level design details to be referenced and located.

Figure 7.7 The Structure Chart
This simple structure chart shows the overall organization of a variation of our grade-point-average program that produces a summary report of the grade-point averages of a whole group of students. The boxes, which represent modules, are connected by lines that indicate the flow of control. Higher modules control the modules directly beneath them. Note the lack of detail, even in the modules on the lowest level. The idea is to give a broad picture of the structure of the whole program.

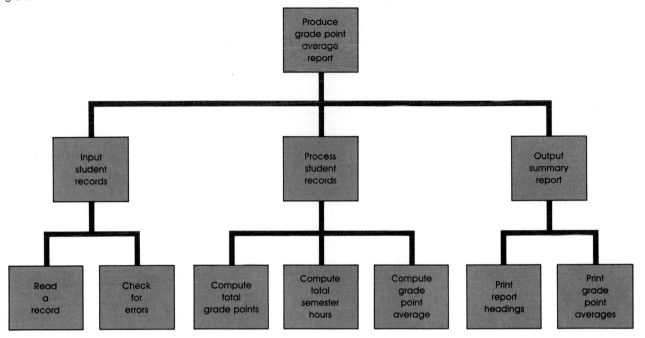

The second type of diagram in the HIPO chart, the *overview diagram*, presents a general summary of the input, processing, and output done in each module identified in the VTOC. If there are 12 modules, 12 overview diagrams exist. The overview diagram for one module of the VTOC in Figure 7.8(a) is shown in Figure 7.8(b). Again, this diagram does not go into great detail. The major logical divisions are shown, and the flow of data through the module is indicated by arrows.

The third type of diagram in the HIPO chart, and the most specific, is the *detail diagram*, which further describes the logical flow of data through the modules and contains complete details about the processing to be done. Each module has a single overview diagram but complex modules may have more than one detail diagram. Figure 7.8(c) is a detail diagram for one of the modules in Figure 7.8(a). The programmer translates detail diagrams almost directly into program instructions in a programming language.

Coding the Program

Once an algorithm has been developed and its design completed, the next step is to code the program. **Coding** is the process of expressing the fully detailed algorithm in a standard programming language. This stage of the program development

Expressing the detailed design in a standard programming language

Figure 7.8 The HIPO Chart

This HIPO chart depicts the same program illustrated in Figure 7.7—a variation of our grade-point-average program that produces a summary report of the grade-point averages of a whole group of students. A HIPO chart consists of three types of diagrams: (a) a visual table of contents (VTOC) (the number in the lower right-hand corner of each VTOC box reflects the hierarchical position of that module and enables it to be specifically referenced in overview and detail diagrams); (b) an overview diagram for each module; and (c) one or more detail diagrams for each module.

(a)

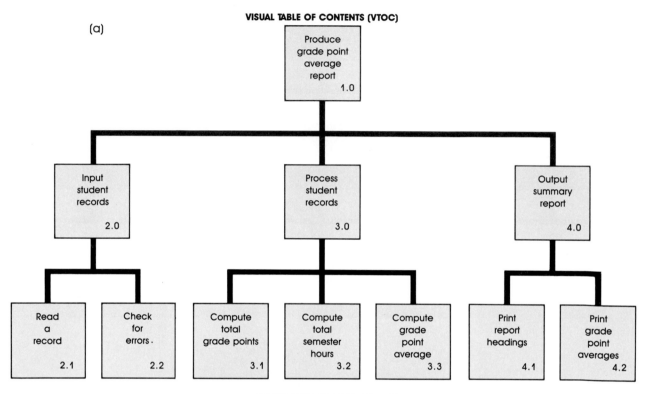

VISUAL TABLE OF CONTENTS LEGEND

REF. NO.	DESCRIPTION
1.0	Produces summary report of grade point averages
2.0	Reads in grade records of all students
3.0	Computes the necessary totals and grade point averages
4.0	Formats and prints out summary report
2.1	Reads in a single student record
2.2	Checks for no more students or invalid data values
3.1	Computes each student's total grade points
3.2	Computes each student's total semester hours
3.3	Computes each student's grade point average
4.1	Prints the headings of the summary report
4.2	Prints each student's name and grade point average

process requires strict adherence to the specific rules of format and **syntax** (vocabulary, grammar, and punctuation) of the language being used. A programmer who has researched the details of the design thoroughly and is familiar with the chosen

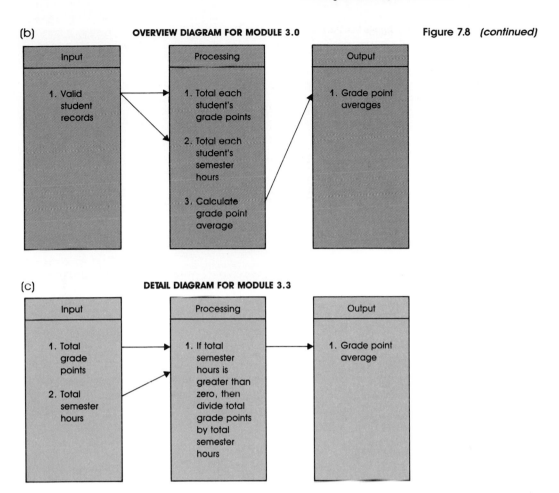

(b)   **OVERVIEW DIAGRAM FOR MODULE 3.0**   Figure 7.8   *(continued)*

Input	Processing	Output
1. Valid student records	1. Total each student's grade points 2. Total each student's semester hours 3. Calculate grade point average	1. Grade point averages

(c)   **DETAIL DIAGRAM FOR MODULE 3.3**

Input	Processing	Output
1. Total grade points 2. Total semester hours	1. If total semester hours is greater than zero, then divide total grade points by total semester hours	1. Grade point average

language should have little trouble in the coding stage. In fact, coding is usually the easiest and least time-consuming of the seven stages of program development.

Because there are a number of programming languages, as we'll see in Chapter 8, the first task of program coding is to decide which language to use. (Actually, the choice of language is often made before the program development process begins and in that case will affect the program design.) Different languages have been developed to answer the different needs of specific applications, so the particular job at hand may dictate the choice of a language. On the other hand, a particular language may be chosen because of its availability, standardization, or manufacturer support.

The program expressed in a programming language, or **source code,** must be entered into the computer. Source code is generally keyboarded into the computer with a **text editor** (see Figure 7.9). This program allows you to type text consisting of letters, numbers, and punctuation into a computer file, which is then stored on a disk. Once the source code has been entered in a text file, it can be reviewed, modified, and even printed on paper.

As a program is being coded, care should be taken to make it as clear as possible for the benefit of subsequent programmers. Understandable programs are

Figure 7.9 Coding the Program with a Text Editor

Source code is an expression of a program in a real programming language. A text editor is generally used to type source code into a computer file for later processing. This screen shows a program being entered into a computer file with IBM's Personal Editor, a text editor for IBM-compatible microcomputers. The program is being coded in the Pascal programming language, which we'll be discussing further in Chapter 8.

```
== Top of file ==
(* GRADE POINT AVERAGE PROGRAM *)

(* This program calculates a student's grade point average, given a list of *)
(* course names, semester hours, and letter grades.                         *)

PROGRAM Grade_Point_Average (INPUT, OUTPUT);

VAR
    course_name         : STRING [20];  (* This is the section that declares *)
    semester_hours      : INTEGER;      (* the data type of each variable to *)
    letter_grade        : CHAR;         (* be used in the program.           *)
    grade_points        : INTEGER;
    total_points        : INTEGER;
    total_hours         : INTEGER;
    grade_point_average : REAL;

BEGIN (* Grade_Point_Average *)

    total_points := 0;   (* Initialize the accumulators to zero. *)
    total_hours  := 0;

c:\slotnick\chap08\gpa.pas                              1    1 Replace
```

not only easier to maintain, but they are also easier to test and are more likely to be initially correct. With complex programs, even the original programmer can get confused or forget what certain sections of source code are supposed to do. Simply following the explicit rules of a particular programming language is no guarantee that a program will be easy to understand by any programmer, including the original author. Techniques used by good programmers to make their source code more understandable include:

- *Meaningful variable names.*   In a computer program, a *variable* is a named storage location that holds one or more pieces of data. For example, in our grade-point-average program, the sum total of a student's grade points might be stored in a variable called TOTAL_GRADE_POINTS. Choosing a descriptive variable name, such as this one, instead of a short, cryptic name such as X, helps make program source code much clearer. Programs that contain only meaningful variable names are sometimes said to be *self-documenting* because they can often be understood with few additional explanations.

- *Indentation.*   Look back at the pseudocode in Figure 7.3. Notice how indentation is used to help show the underlying structure of the program. Indentation is a simple, yet powerful, tool for helping make source code more understandable.

- *Blank Space.*   One way to make any piece of writing, including program source code, difficult to understand is to crowd it all together. Blank space costs nothing to add to source code, and most modern programming languages let you freely insert empty spaces between words and lines. Like indentation, blank space is a simple, yet powerful, tool for making source code more understandable.

- *Comments.*   Virtually all modern programming languages let you add comments to source code. A *comment* is simply an explanatory note in the source code that is totally ignored by the computer when the program is translated and executed. Comments can explain, clarify, and otherwise describe what is going on in a program, especially in sections that are particularly complex or unusual. Well-written and strategically placed comments help make even so-called self-documenting source code more understandable.

Testing the Program

After the program has been coded and entered comes the moment of truth: does it work? Testing a program to see if it does what it's supposed to do is usually the hardest, longest, and most frustrating stage in the program development process. It has been estimated that testing takes from 50 to 90% of total program development time. Program testing is the stage in which the programmer is tested as well; the task of perfecting source code so it is accepted by the computer can take on immense proportions. Emotionally, programmers want (and secretly expect) their programs to be completely correct and to run without a hitch the first time. Intellectually, they should realize that this is extremely unlikely, especially if a program is at all complex.

Testing a program completely requires three separate activities: desk checking, translation, and debugging.

Making sure the program works: proofreading it for errors, submitting it to the computer for checking, finding and fixing mistakes

Desk Checking

Desk checking, also called **hand checking,** means just what it says: it's the process of sitting at a desk and checking the source code, proofreading for obvious syntax errors, and looking for not-so-obvious logic errors. *Syntax errors* are violations of the rules of the specific programming language being used; they can be the result of an error in entering the source code or a misinterpretation or unawareness of a syntax rule. An example of a syntax error might be inserting a comma where a period is required. Syntax errors can be easily uncovered by careful proofreading and can be reduced if the programmer looks up new or unfamiliar language features in a reference manual. *Logic errors* are mistakes in the algorithm, or program design, and are much more difficult to spot during desk checking. An example of a logic error is forgetting to make sure that a division by zero doesn't occur anywhere in a program.

Besides proofreading a program for syntax and logic errors, another desk-checking technique is to pretend that you are the computer and go through each step by hand. This requires first formulating *test data* and using them to execute the program manually. If the expected results don't occur, you know that there is an error in the program. The fabricated test data should include the following:

- *Typical data.* These data represent a normal processing scenario. For example, typical test data for our grade-point-average program might be:

```
BIOLOGY 100, 3, B
MATH 100, 3, A
ENGLISH 100, 3, C
HISTORY 100, 3, A
PSYCHOLOGY 100, 3, B
PHYS ED 100, 1, A
```

These data should yield the results shown in Figure 7.2 if the program is correct.

- *Unusual data.* These data are rare, but could occur, and are nonetheless valid. In our grade-point-average program, for example, input data consisting of only a single course would be unusual, but perfectly valid:

```
BIOLOGY 100, 3, B
```

In this case, the program should produce 12 total grade points, 3 total semester hours, and a grade-point average of 4.0.

- *Invalid data.*   These data are erroneous, incomplete, or inappropriate, but they might be encountered. Invalid data are tested to see how the program handles potential error situations. Here are some examples of invalid data for our grade-point-average program:

BIOLOGY 100, B
MATH 100, 25, A
ENGLISH 100, 3, E

Desk checking is a monotonous chore that many programmers would like to avoid. As boring as it can be, skipping it only postpones the frustration of discovering errors that must be corrected before the program can be used with confidence.

Translation

Translation is the conversion of the source code to the internal instructions that the computer requires. This process is carried out by the computer. During translation, another computer program (the *translator*) checks for and finds all syntax errors. If the programming language has been used improperly or entered incorrectly, the translation may be ambiguous or impossible to complete. The computer then issues *diagnostic messages*. Having a comma where a period should be, for example, might yield the message "PERIOD MISSING" or "INCOMPLETE STATE-MENT." (We'll have more to say about translation in Chapter 8.)

Translation is not a check of the logic of a program; that is, it will not reveal whether the program will work the way it was intended. Consequently, logic errors will remain undetected by the translation process. The translator only checks that all of the syntax rules of the programming language have been followed; it has no way of checking a program for illogical structures or of ensuring that it won't produce garbage as results.

Debugging

Debugging is the process of detecting, locating, and correcting logic errors (or *bugs*) by submitting a translated program to the computer for execution and seeing what happens. As we said before, some test data are tried by hand during the desk-checking stage. To completely debug a program, however, the programmer must actually run it with a comprehensive set of test data that simulates as many as possible of the real-life conditions under which the program will be run. This means that the test data should include typical, unusual, and invalid items to reveal their effect on the program. The results obtained from the computer must then be compared with the correct results, which have been precomputed by hand or with a calculator. For very complex programs, it is often impossible to test all of the possible variations in data and conditions. Consequently, many programs in daily use have hidden bugs just waiting to appear at some inopportune moment, such as the one that nearly kept Apollo 14's lunar module from descending or the one that made Voyager II's computer refuse to carry out a number of orders from Mission Control.

Besides trying test data, other techniques are also used for debugging programs. For example, some programming languages have a *trace* feature that can be activated to display automatically the contents of selected variables after each step in a program. This provides the programmer with a picture of the program's actions during execution. When using programming languages without a trace feature, programmers can achieve essentially the same results by adding additional statements to display on the screen or print on paper the contents of selected variables.

Just as diagnostic messages are issued by the computer to indicate syntax errors during the translation of a program, *error messages* are generated by the computer to signal the occurrence of certain errors during the execution of a program. These are a special type of logic error called *runtime errors*. Not all logic errors cause the computer to issue error messages. For example, if you mistakenly divide total semester hours by total grade points in an attempt to calculate the grade-point average, the computer has no way of telling that this is incorrect. It does not "know" that grade-point average is defined as total grade points divided by total semester hours. On the other hand, if you attempt to do something that is mathematically undefined, such as dividing by zero, the computer will recognize this as a mistake and issue a runtime error message. Unfortunately, runtime error messages are not always easy to interpret. In addition, it can be difficult to determine exactly which program instructions are causing the runtime error. Debugging is often a confusing, frustrating, and time-consuming activity.

Installing and Maintaining the Program

Once the program has been as thoroughly tested as possible, it must be *installed*, or put into everyday operation at the site where it will be used. This involves making sure that it will work properly with the particular equipment at the designated site. If a program has many unique features or complicated operating procedures, installation may also involve training the personnel who will use it. If it is supposed to replace an old program currently in use, that old program may need to be kept around until users adapt to the change.

Setting up the program and keeping it useful

Program maintenance is the ongoing process of correcting bugs discovered during operation, upgrading the program to accommodate new hardware and software, and introducing minor improvements. Essentially, it is the correction, expansion, updating, and improvement of a program after its installation. The environment in which most programs are used constantly changes because of factors such as new company policies, revision of laws or government regulations, and new equipment. Therefore, regular maintenance is essential to the continued usefulness of a program. And proper maintenance depends on the existence of complete documentation.

Documenting the Program

Documentation is a detailed description of a program's algorithm, design, coding method, testing, and proper usage. Documentation is a necessity for the users who will rely on the program on a day-to-day basis, as well as for the programmers who may be called on to modify or update it.

Describing the program to others

Creating and collecting documentation should be an ongoing activity throughout all stages of program development. No programmer's memory is good enough to hold all the important facts about a program's development or proper use. Also, the original programmer may no longer be available. Therefore, written records should be kept during all stages of the program development process.

No universally accepted standards concerning what should be included in a program's documentation exist. Although the contents will vary somewhat depending on the complexity of the program, in general, comprehensive documentation consists of the following:

- A description of what the program is supposed to do, such as the software requirements document.

- A description of the problem solution (the algorithm) in general terms.

- A description of the program's design, including any aids used (pseudocode, flowcharts, decision tables, structure charts, and/or HIPO charts).

- A description of the program-testing process, including the test data used and the results obtained.

- A description of all corrections, modifications, and updates made to the program since it was put into operation.

- A *user manual*, or set of instructions telling the average user how to work with the program.

STRUCTURED PROGRAMMING

Disciplining the job of software development

Structured programming refers to a set of software development techniques that includes many important concepts. Although it has had a major impact on data processing, structured programming is difficult to define succinctly. Originating in the latter half of the 1960s, structured programming was basically a response to two problems: the productivity of programmers was unacceptably low, and nearly all programs of any complexity were filled with bugs and almost impossible to maintain. This "software crisis" was at least partly due to the widespread perception of computer programming as a mysterious, esoteric art rather than a systematic, definable task. Programmers strove to be clever, tricky, and very concise, and thus produced cryptic source code that was often unintelligible to other programmers. Programming projects were difficult to keep on schedule because low productivity made estimations of completion dates notoriously unreliable. In short, the state of the art of computer programming was near chaos.

The objective of structured programming, then, was to bring order to this unsettled scene. Specifically, structured programming techniques have produced the following results:

- *Greater productivity.*   More code can be written by fewer programmers in less time.

- *Increased economy.*   The costs (in time and dollars) of producing software are reduced.

- *Better programs.*   Programmers develop software with fewer bugs.

- *Decreased debugging time.*   Errors that do occur are easier to locate and correct.

- *Clearer source code.*   Structured programs can be readily understood, modified, and maintained by people other than the original programmer.

- *Longer software lifetimes.*   Programs that can be easily modified, updated, and maintained are more flexible and can remain in service for longer periods of time.

Control Structures

The central principle of structured programming calls for the construction of all programs from just three basic control structures, symbolized in both pseudocode and flowcharts in Figure 7.10. A **control structure** is a pattern for the flow of logic in a computer program; in other words, it is a framework that indicates the order in which operations are to be performed. The three control structures of structured programming, the sequence, selection, and iteration control structures, have one important characteristic in common. Each has one entry point and one exit point, which makes structured programs much easier to understand, debug, and maintain.

Three basic formats for logical structures

The **sequence control structure** simply lists one operation after another in a stepwise fashion. This structure, shown in Figure 7.10(a), is represented in pseudocode as a sequence of instructions bracketed by BEGIN and END.

The **selection control structure** offers a way to choose between two alternative paths. This is the IF-THEN or IF-THEN-ELSE structure of pseudocode, shown in Figure 7.10(b). The IF-THEN structure is just a special case of the IF-THEN-ELSE, in which nothing is done if the condition is false.

The **iteration control structure** is simply a loop, a sequence of operations that is performed repeatedly until a certain condition is fulfilled. As Figure 7.10(c) shows, there are two basic versions of the iteration control structure: DO WHILE and DO UNTIL. The repetition of a DO WHILE loop ceases when a condition tested at the start becomes false. The DO UNTIL structure is a variant of the DO WHILE that is also acceptable in structured programming but is not strictly necessary. It has been proven mathematically that any computer program can be constructed using just sequence, selection, and DO WHILE iteration structures. The DO UNTIL iteration structure is used because in some circumstances it is more convenient.

In the DO WHILE structure, the condition is tested *before* the operations are performed, and, in the DO UNTIL structure, the condition is tested *after* the operations are performed. In other words, the test for exiting is at the top of a DO WHILE loop, but at the bottom of a DO UNTIL loop. This means that the operations in a DO WHILE loop will not be performed at all if the test condition is initially false. In contrast, the operations in a DO UNTIL loop will always be executed *at least once*, because the test condition follows them.

Conditions in iteration control structures must be carefully considered. If for some reason the condition never changes, the program will become stuck in an *infinite loop*, repeating certain operations over and over again like a broken record. To avoid this undesirable event, a programmer must make sure that an operation within a loop somehow changes the value or values being tested.

Originally, structured programming simply meant the use of these three basic control structures. Pseudocode that uses only these control structures is often called **structured pseudocode.** Similarly, flowcharts that contain only the control structures shown in Figure 7.10 are called **structured flowcharts.** These one-entry, one-exit control structures make even complex programs easier to design, code, debug, understand, and maintain. Structured programming, however, has gradually come to include a number of related concepts and techniques. As the benefits of these innovations have become apparent, structured programming has not only been widely accepted but has become synonymous with proper programming. A few of these techniques are especially relevant to our discussion of structured programming: the avoidance of GOTO statements, top-down design, modularity, egoless programming, structured walkthroughs, and the chief programmer team.

SEQUENCE CONTROL STRUCTURE

(a)

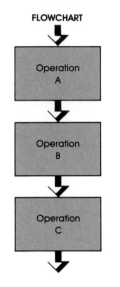

SELECTION CONTROL STRUCTURE

(b)

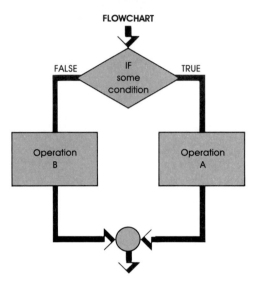

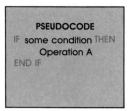

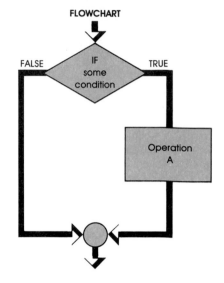

(c)

ITERATION CONTROL STRUCTURE

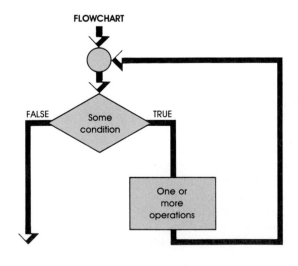

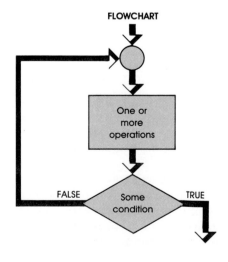

Figure 7.10 The Three Control Structures
Structured programming employs only three types of control structures, all of which
have a single entry point and a single exit point: (a) the sequence control structure,
(b) the selection control structure, and (c) the iteration control structure.

Avoiding GOTO Statements

Many programming languages include a **GOTO statement** that causes an unconditional jump from one part of a program to another. In other words, a GOTO
statement enables a programmer to go from one point in a program to any other
and continue from that point on. Before the advent of structured programming
techniques, most programs were characterized by many GOTO statements that
broke up the sequential flow of operations.

 One of the motivations for the development of structured programming techniques was the realization in the late 1960s that the excessive, undisciplined use of
GOTO statements often resulted in programs that were overly complicated, difficult
to understand and modify, and likely to contain errors. In short, GOTO statements
can alter the logical flow of processing in a very unstructured way. This conclusion,
however, was not universally accepted: a great controversy arose among computer
professionals. Those accustomed to using GOTOs as much as they pleased resisted
the notion of limiting this use in any way. Ultimately, the foes of the GOTO won
out. It's now generally accepted that the indiscriminate use of unconditional jumps
is poor programming practice. Most experts agree that sticking to the three basic
control structures results in the best programs. A few programming languages still
lack built-in expressions for selection and iteration control structures, and, in these
cases, it is acceptable to use GOTOs to build your own selection and iteration
control structures.

Limiting unconditional branches

Top-Down Design

The technique of **top-down design** is a divide-and-conquer approach that involves breaking down a large task into successively smaller subtasks, organized
hierarchically. The design process starts with the highest level and proceeds
through the middle levels to the lowest level. Higher levels control the lower levels.
Structure charts and HIPO charts are direct reflections of this design strategy.

 Top-down design entails three steps:

1. Define the output to be produced, the input required, and the major processing
   tasks that must be performed to convert input to output.

2. Break down each major processing task into a hierarchy of independent modules.

3. Create the algorithm for each module, starting with the top one (or *main module*) and proceeding downward.

This approach forms a major component of structured programming. It requires
that the problem be clearly defined and that software requirements be explicitly
stated before the design process can begin. This systematic manner of handling the
design process makes program development more efficient. Coding is much easier,
and testing takes less time because there are fewer errors. Finally, programs de-

The divide-and-conquer approach

signed from the top down are much easier to maintain than those designed in a less organized fashion.

Modularity

A module, as we stated earlier, is a set of related program statements that can be treated as a unit. The desirability of breaking down a large program into modules, or small *subprograms*, has been acknowledged for years. The concept of program modularity, however, takes this recommendation one step further by being concerned with how modules are constructed and the relationships between them. To be useful, a module should be not merely a collection of related statements but a well-defined program segment. It should have a name and carry out a specific program function. Furthermore, like a control structure, a module should have only one entry and one exit. Although there is no limit to the number of statements a module can contain, it is generally accepted that a module should not be too large. About 50 lines (or one page) of source code is considered an appropriate size.

Coupling

One of the terms describing the relationship between modules is **coupling,** a measure of the strength of interconnection between two modules. Basically, two modules are coupled if one controls the other in some way or if they pass data back and forth. The greater the extent of this control or data sharing, the higher the degree of coupling. *Highly coupled modules* are strongly interconnected; in fact, they are interdependent—to understand one, we must also understand the other. *Loosely coupled modules*, on the other hand, have little dependence on each other. Modules are said to be *decoupled* if they are completely independent, with no interconnections. Programs with loosely coupled modules are the easiest to understand, debug, and maintain because one module can be studied or changed without having to know very much about any of the other modules in the system. If modules are highly coupled, changes in one will very likely lead to changes in another.

Cohesion

Cohesion is a structured programming term used to describe the closeness of the relationships among the elements within a module. Ideally, the components of a module should be very closely related and directed toward achieving a single function. A highly cohesive module contains only those statements necessary for performing a single, well-defined task. Cohesion can be thought of as the glue that holds a module together. The clearest examples of program modules with high levels of cohesion are those that perform mathematical functions. For example, a module to compute a square root is certain to be highly cohesive. Nothing will be included that is not directly related to the single function of computing a number's square root.

As you may have guessed, coupling and cohesion are related. In general, the greater the cohesion of individual modules, the looser the coupling between them. Programmers who strive to make modules functionally cohesive will find that the resulting program demonstrates minimal coupling, which generally means easier maintenance.

Egoless Programming

We've been looking at some structured programming techniques that programmers can use to achieve the desirable end of well-designed, understandable, error-free programs. But what about the programmers themselves? Are there personality traits that facilitate good programming practice? In 1971, Gerald Weinberg published *The Psychology of Computer Programming*. In this book, Weinberg explored the relationship between programmers' attitudes and the quality of the programs they produced. He found that programmers and their employers often think of programming as a rather asocial job. This fosters the image of programmers as mysterious loners, working privately to find hidden solutions to esoteric problems. As a result, many programmers, though proud of their skills, are secretive or defensive about their work. Some are reluctant to share their techniques with others, afraid that their weaknesses may be uncovered and their images as software wizards destroyed. In short, Weinberg proposed that many programmers are egotistical about their work.

It's fairly obvious that such an attitude leads to the production of many programs that contain costly, hidden errors or that are difficult for others to understand. As the software industry grew and the scope of projects became greater, secretive, lone-wolf programmers became more and more of a liability. Weinberg suggested the practice of **egoless programming** as an alternative. According to this model, programming is a social activity, open to and benefiting from the inspection of colleagues, who check each other's work for errors in a constructive rather than a negative, fault-finding way. Complex programming is virtually impossible to do without making mistakes, but review by other programmers at all stages of program development can catch most of them and thus results in programs with significantly fewer errors. The emphasis is on the program rather than on who produces it, and the software product is seen as a team achievement.

Cooperation rather than confrontation

Programmers are not criticized for making errors (errors are seen as unavoidable), but they are praised for discovering them. In addition to minimizing the occurrence of errors in programs, the practice of egoless programming produces a more pleasant and effective working environment. (See Figure 7.11.)

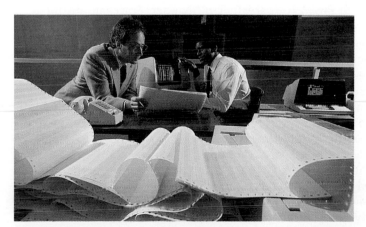

Figure 7.11 Egoless Programming
The concept of egoless programming rejects the notion of the programmer as a lone-wolf artist. Instead, it promotes programming as a social activity in which colleagues constructively work together to develop more error-free software.

Structured Walkthroughs

Step-by-step peer reviews

One specific way of implementing the practice of egoless programming is to schedule **structured walkthroughs,** peer reviews of the design or coding of a computer program. Structured walkthroughs are one of the most effective ways to improve the quality of computer programs. Typically, a walkthrough consists of a meeting of the members of a programming team, each member taking a specific role. For example, one member presents the design or code, another coordinates the activities, another takes notes, and others point out implications for future maintenance, standardization, and user needs. Usually, no managers or bosses attend because their presence might inhibit honest evaluation of the program.

The basic purpose of a structured walkthrough is to detect errors, not to correct them; suggestions for better algorithms or justifications for the existing design or code have no place in a walkthrough. It's also important that all participants keep in mind that the program, not the programmer, is being reviewed. Ideally, if the proceedings follow formal guidelines no one's feelings will be hurt. Some data-processing managers aren't convinced of the value of structured walkthroughs. Perhaps structured walkthroughs aren't applicable to every programming situation, but they do serve as another tool in the useful kit of structured programming.

The Chief Programmer Team

The coordination of a large programming project may require more than the general principles of egoless programming or the use of structured walkthroughs. The greater the number of people working on a program, the more likely it becomes that the design will suffer from too many contributions. What such a group undertaking needs is *conceptual integrity*; that is, the design appears and is developed as a unit instead of as a collection of disjointed ideas. The best way to achieve conceptual integrity is to have one person in charge of the design, thus ensuring consistency of purpose. This realization led to the implementation of chief programmer teams.

An organizational means for achieving design unity

A **chief programmer team** is a collection of specialized personnel directed by a chief programmer, who prepares the software requirements, designs the overall structure of the program, and oversees all of the lower level activities of the entire program development process. The team consists of several specialists with roles defined so that work will progress in an efficient manner. For example, the team may include an assistant administrator, a documentation editor, a code tester, a programming language specialist, and a secretary. Although each member of the team has responsibility for certain lower level decisions, the chief programmer makes all major decisions. This organizational division helps to ensure communication among the personnel.

The chief programmer team seems to work well for large programming projects. In some ways, however, this model violates the principles of egoless programming. The chief programmer is sometimes perceived (and often self-perceived) as a superprogrammer. Since one person at the top is making all the important decisions, the potential for egotism may detract from the quality of the product. The situation by definition is not democratic, and, if the chief programmer decides to review all the code personally rather than delegating some of the responsibility or making it a group activity, the result may well be confrontation instead of cooperation.

A Closer Look

Using a Prototyping Package

A *prototype* is a working model of some new construction, engineering, or design project. In most cases, a prototype is at least partially functional. Developing a prototype, or *prototyping*, is a cost-effective way to work out preliminary design features in the early stages of a project. This helps to avoid mistakes and omissions that could present serious problems later. Prototyping is frequently employed in the development of medium-to-large software programming projects.

Dan Bricklin's DEMO II is a popular prototyping package for IBM-compatible microcomputers. Selling for $195 from Peter Norton Computing, it features Dan Bricklin's name conspicuously to emphasize his role as the legendary software wizard who developed VisiCalc, the very first spreadsheet program. Thus, when the prototyping package was released in late 1985, the microcomputer industry took immediate notice.

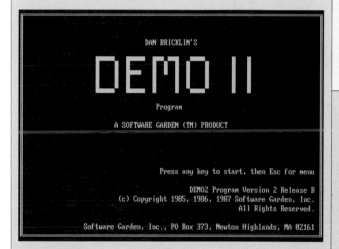

Demo II is an extremely versatile software package billed as a professional tool for producing program prototypes, demonstrations, and tutorials. Using the analogy of a slide show, it allows you to develop a working model of a program quickly and easily, without having to use a programming language. DEMO II is especially useful for designing the screen layouts of a program because it includes a *full-screen editor*. This editor lets you enter ordinary text, draw various types of lines and boxes, produce special IBM graphics characters, and set the *display attributes* of items on the screen. These attributes include qualities such as color, brightness, reverse video, blinking, and underlining. Each screen image

you create with the DEMO II editor corresponds to a single slide, and many slides can be created and arranged in any order you like. DEMO II possesses a wide range of features for controlling the switch from one slide to the next. By creating slides that show the output of a proposed program, instructing DEMO II to accept user input from the keyboard, and specifying the criteria for changing slides, you can cleverly mimic the actions of a real program.

The following figures, for example, show a series of slides that represent a prototype of a simple program to present your course grades and grade-point average on demand. This prototype is slightly different from the grade-point-average program described throughout this chapter. Instead of entering your course names, semester hours, and letter grades, all you have to do is enter your name. The prototype simulates a grades program that already has all of your grade data stored in a disk file. After you enter your name, the prototype displays a screen that shows a typical lising of courses, grades, and the grade-point average. Note that the prototype doesn't actually look up your grades and calculate your real grade-point average. It just presents a fictional screen to show you an example of what the proposed program will display.

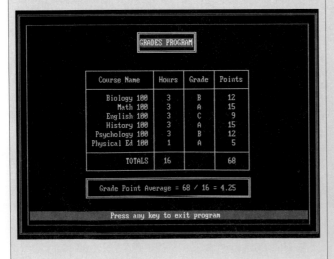

The first screen pops up on the display when the prototype is started. The directions on this first screen say to press any key to begin. When the user does this, DEMO II rapidly and smoothly switches to the second screen. The user then enters a name. After the name has been entered, the final screen pops up, showing the fictional grade listing.

The three slides that make up this prototype were created with the DEMO II screen editor. Special instructions were given to tell DEMO II when to switch from the first slide to the second, and from the second slide to the third. The prototype was tested and refined until it was suitable. Then the prototype was stored on a disk in its own file. To run the prototype, all you have to do is start up the DEMO II program and load this prototype file. Although the prototype does nothing but present previously created slides, it gives you an idea of how the grades program will work when it is actually finished. Because prototyping is much easier and quicker than programming, it allows you to refine the details of a program's user interface before the program is even written.

Summary

The Program Development Process

The program development process is the series of activities that is necessary to create a successful computer program.

Defining the Problem   This crucial first step involves determining exactly what needs to be done.

Developing the Software Requirements   This process involves drawing up exact specifications of the desired output, the required input, and the processing for converting input to output.

Designing the Program   This very important step is the determination of how the requirements are to be fulfilled. An algorithm is developed, and one or more program design aids are employed to express the logic of the computer program. Pseudocode, flowcharts, decision tables, structure charts, and HIPO charts are some of the most commonly used aids.

Coding the Program   Once the design is complete, it must be expressed in a programming language before it can be entered into the computer.

Testing the Program   The finished computer program must be thoroughly tested to make sure that it does exactly what it was intended to do. Testing includes desk checking, translation, and debugging.

Installing and Maintaining the Program   The tested program must be put into everyday operation, and any overlooked bugs must be fixed. Modifications, updates, and improvements may also occasionally need to be made.

Documenting the Program   Compiled throughout the entire program development process, documentation is a detailed description of the program's algorithm, design, coding method, testing, and proper usage.

Structured Programming

Structured programming is a set of techniques for program development; it is a discipline that has produced greater productivity, increased economy, fewer errors, decreased debugging time, clearer source code, and longer software lifetimes.

Control Structures   Structured programming minimizes complexity by using only three basic control structures: sequence, selection (IF-THEN or IF-THEN-ELSE), and iteration (DO WHILE or DO UNTIL).

Avoiding GOTO Statements   The overuse of GOTO statements (unconditional branching statements) in computer programs results in complex, error-prone code. Programmers should stick to the three basic control structures.

Top-Down Design   This design approach involves breaking down large tasks into hierarchically organized, smaller subtasks. Then the subtasks, or modules, are designed from the top, or the highest level, down to the lowest.

Modularity   Modules should be well-defined program segments with one entry and one exit. Coupling, or the degree to which modules are interdependent, should be minimized. Cohesion, or the degree to which the statements within a module reflect a single function, should be maximized.

Egoless Programming   This practice recommends that programming be viewed as a social activity, open to and benefiting from the involvement of colleagues.

Structured Walkthroughs   Structured walkthroughs are formally organized sessions for peer group review of program design or coding. Their purpose is to discover errors.

The Chief Programmer Team   A large programming project may best be carried out by a collection of specialized personnel directed by a chief programmer, who prepares the software requirements, designs the overall structure, and oversees all the aspects of development. Having a single person in charge helps ensure that a large program will have conceptual integrity.

Computer Concepts

As an extra review of the chapter, try defining the following terms. If you have any trouble with any of them, refer to the page number listed.

computer program *207*
program development
  process *207*
software requirements *209*
prototyping 209
user interface *211*
user-friendly *211*
algorithm *212*
program design aid *212*
pseudocode *212*
loop *213*
accumulator *213*
flowchart *213*
decision table *217*
structure chart *217*
module *217*

HIPO chart *218*
coding *219*
syntax *220*
source code *221*
text editor *221*
desk checking (hand
  checking) *223*
translation *224*
debugging *224*
program maintenance *225*
documentation *225*
structured programming
  226
control structure *227*
sequence control structure
  227

selection control structure
  227
iteration control structure
  227
structured pseudocode *227*
structured flowcharts *227*
GOTO statement *229*
top-down design *229*
coupling *230*
cohesion *230*
egoless programming *231*
structured walkthroughs
  232
chief programmer team
  232

Review Questions

1. Describe the characteristics of a successful computer program.
2. List the seven stages of the program development process.
3. What do the three main parts of the software requirements specify?
4. What factors must be determined in specifying a program's output?
5. What factors must be considered in specifying a program's input?
6. What must the software requirements say about a program's processing tasks, user interface, and necessary equipment?
7. What is the first task of program design?
8. Why has pseudocode become a very popular alternative to flowcharts?
9. How do decision tables help in the design of logically complex programs?
10. How is a structure chart like a corporate organizational chart?
11. What are the three types of diagrams in a HIPO chart?
12. What factors may influence which computer language is chosen for coding a program?
13. What is usually the most difficult and time-consuming stage of program development?
14. What are the three phases of thorough program testing?
15. Why do programs have to be maintained?
16. When should program documentation be compiled?
17. In the 1960's, what problems instigated the development of structured programming?
18. Why should GOTO statements be avoided?
19. What are the three steps of top-down design?
20. How cohesive should a module be, and why?

True or False

1. The process of development of a computer program can be divided into seven stages.
2. Specifying the output is not a major concern in program development.
3. The user interface permits the person using the program to communicate with it.
4. A set of steps to get from input to output is called an algorithm.
5. Repetition of a sequence of instructions in a program is a loop.
6. A flowchart is another name for a program.
7. A comment is an instruction in a program which tells the computer to do something.
8. If a programmer has followed the necessary steps accurately, it is extremely unlikely that testing of a program is necessary.
9. There are three separate steps in checking a program.
10. Documentation is essential for current and future users and modifiers of a program.

Multiple Choice

1. Pseudocode is another term for:
   (a) a programming language
   (b) a repeated sequence of instructions in a program
   (c) a structured expression of a program algorithm

2. A HIPO chart is:
   (a) a tool for documenting a program
   (b) a program for entering text into a computer
   (c) a list of variables

3. Translation of a program is:
   (a) a check of the program's logic
   (b) conversion of source code to the internal code of the computer
   (c) a diagnostic message

4. One of the three basic control structures of structured programming is:
   (a) a flowchart
   (b) sequence control structure
   (b) documentation

5. A GOTO statement is:
   (a) a statement that causes a jump from one part of a program to another
   (b) an important step in structured programming
   (c) part of the debugging process

6. The process of detecting and correcting logic errors is:
   (a) program maintenance
   (b) debugging
   (c) documentation

7. A divide and conquer approach to program design is:
   (a) desk checking
   (b) sequence control structure
   (c) top-down design

8. A set of related program steps that can be treated as a unit is called:
   (a) a loop
   (b) a couple
   (c) a module

9. An approach to programming that emphasizes working with colleagues in a social setting is:
   (a) egoless programming
   (b) cohesion
   (c) modularity

10. A chief programmer team is directed by:
    (a) a structured walkthrough
    (b) a group of programmers
    (c) a chief programmer

A Sharper Focus

1. If you were a programmer with an assignment to develop a program to calculate and distribute grade-point averages to students, faculty, and administrators, who would you contact during the program development process? What questions would you ask them?

2. What modules of the HIPO chart in Fig. 7.8 do you think would be affected most by the answers to your questions? Why?

1. Most of us encounter algorithms daily; they weren't invented just for the computer. For example, there is probably an algorithm on the back of your bank statement, showing how to balance your checking account using the checks and deposit slips that were returned. List and briefly describe five more algorithms that you frequently use.

2. Write a program in pseudocode for balancing your checking account. Now do a flow-chart. Which do you prefer?

3. Assume you are debating taking a full-time job next semester (or summer) vs. taking more courses. Draw up a decision table listing factors to be considered in each case, "what if . . ." scenarios, etc.

4. Make a structure chart of all your activities in a typical week of this semester. Would such a system help you plan your available time better? Using the structure chart, try to develop a simple program that would guide you most efficiently through a week (including recreation).

8

Programming Languages

In This Chapter

One type of applications software which is finding a place with business managers is project management software. These are programs which enable a manager to handle all phases of a project in order to see it to completion in the shortest time and at the lowest cost possible. For example, the facilities manager of M. D. Anderson Hospital and Tumor Institute in Houston, a leading cancer research center, realized that the hospital's physical plant needed to change and expand. Using a project management program, he was able to plan the expansion from new construction to remodeling floors to door repairs. He could monitor costs, progress and schedules. As a new office building and outpatient clinic opened, he was able to update the 40 doctors and administrators involved in moving without causing undue hardship for them (or, therefore, the patients).

Until recently project management software has not been used by many managers because it was traditionally construction-oriented and, therefore, was considered out

Focus On

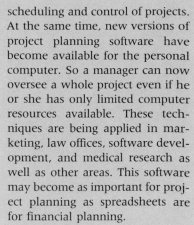

Project Management

of the realm of data processing people. Also, it was perceived as available only for projects using large computers. Early programs were not powerful enough to be useful and were clumsy for casual use. Also, managers did not initially perceive the need to think scientifically about the projects they manage.

Now, however, managers have begun to develop the planning,

scheduling and control of projects. At the same time, new versions of project planning software have become available for the personal computer. So a manager can now oversee a whole project even if he or she has only limited computer resources available. These techniques are being applied in marketing, law offices, software development, and medical research as well as other areas. This software may become as important for project planning as spreadsheets are for financial planning.

The project management technique is most useful in cases where a schedule must be revised often, as happens when a number of groups are involved in a project. For instance, an aquarium was designed for a newly developed area in a city on the east coast of the U.S. The project manager had to work with the construction firm, the zoo authority of a nearby city (in another state), who will handle the animal management, and the resident state's sports authority, who will handle the recreation management of the facility. The project went smoothly because the project manager was able to coordinate schedules, see where everything was in relation to the original plan and budget, and let all parties know what was happening.

Among the attractive features of the new software are the ability of the manager to make clear to all participants each one's accountability to the whole group, the capacity of the newest programs to report to different levels of management with appropriate levels of detail, and, most important, the conditioning of managers to think of planning in more scientific terms. The new products will not replace managers—just make them better.

In Chapter 7, we looked at the general process of program development. In this chapter, we examine some of the most popular and important languages that programmers employ to do their job.

During the past 30 years, the development of a new programming language has been a fairly common event. Today, more than 100 languages are being used for programming computers, and new ones are still being introduced every year. This abundance contrasts sharply with the fact that most programmers don't attempt to use more than a few languages. In the face of so many widely different choices, how do programmers know which ones to learn in the first place? Just how does one decide which language is best suited for a given purpose? To answer these questions, in this chapter we present an overview of the characteristics and applications of programming languages in general and examine several of the most important high-level ones in detail.

PROGRAMMING LANGUAGES IN GENERAL

A language, as you know, is a means of communicating, usually via human speech or written symbols. A computer **programming language** is a set of symbols and usage rules employed to direct the operations of a computer. Just like any human language, a programming language consists of a set of symbols (an alphabet and punctuation); rules of *syntax* or *grammar* governing how those symbols are combined; and *semantics*, or meanings associated with certain symbol combinations. Unlike human languages, however, programming languages have very limited vocabularies and very specific functions. Human languages are used to express the vast, rich world of human experience and thus are full of colorful, context-dependent words and ambiguous rules. The single purpose of programming languages is the construction of computer programs.

What a programming language is

Characteristics of Programming Languages

Although there are many different programming languages, each designed to solve certain types of problems, all of them have the basic function of directing the operations of a computer. Therefore, general classes of instructions are present in every programming language, which can be categorized as follows:

Instructions found in every language

- *Instructions for input and output.* These instructions tell the computer to get data and present information. They usually provide details indicating which input or output device to use, where the data or information is stored, and what formatting rules to use.

- *Instructions for calculations.* These instructions direct the computer to perform common mathematical operations such as addition, subtraction, multiplication, and division.

- *Instructions for transfer of control.* These instructions allow deviations from the normal sequential processing of operations. A deviation may be based, for example, on the value of a computed result or the existence of some specified condition. These instructions are used to transfer program control (to *branch*) to an instruction other than the one immediately following. (The selection and iteration structures we introduced in Chapter 7 are examples of how control is transferred based on the outcome of some logical or arithmetical comparison. The GOTO statement, also introduced in Chapter 7, is an example of an unconditional transfer of control.)

- *Instructions for data movement, storage, and retrieval.* These instructions cause the movement, storage, and retrieval of data in primary memory. For example, a data item may be copied from one location to another, the result of a computation may be stored at a specified location, or an intermediate result may be retrieved from a given location.

All programming languages must be able, in one way or another, to perform the above types of operations. As we'll see, however, there are marked differences in how the various languages accomplish these things.

In addition to these kinds of statements, almost every computer language includes some provision for programmers to insert explanatory notes within their programs. Known as **comments,** these descriptive sections of text are ignored by the computer during program translation and execution. Different languages denote and delimit comments in different ways.

Levels of Language

Four general categories of languages

Although there are many different computer languages, most fall under one of four broad categories. These groups are also known as *levels* of language because they can be arranged hierarchically. The lowest level in this hierarchy is occupied by those languages that are closest to the binary zeros and ones used by computers. The highest level is occupied by languages that make it easy for people who aren't necessarily trained programmers to develop computer applications. Going from the lowest to the highest level, the classifications are:

Machine languages

Assembly languages

High-level languages

Application generators

MACHINE LANGUAGES

The languages of zeros and ones

The only language that can be directly used by a particular computer is its own machine language. A machine language program consists of binary numbers that represent the instructions, memory locations, and data necessary to solve a specific problem. Thus any machine language consists entirely of zeros and ones, but their arrangement differs for each model of computer. A machine language instruction generally consists of two parts. The first part is a binary code representing the operation to be performed. Each computer has such an **operation code,** or **opcode,** for every operation it can perform. The second part of the instruction specifies the **operand,** that is, the number on which the operation is to be performed. In some cases, there may be no operands or there may be several operands. When an operand is present, it is usually a piece of data itself or the address of a memory location in which a piece of data is stored. For example, the machine language instruction to add 8 to the value in the accumulator looks like this for IBM-compatible microcomputers (it might be helpful to review Chapter 3, particularly the discussion of what the accumulator is):

$$\underbrace{00000101}_{\text{ADD}} \quad \underbrace{00001000}_{\text{8 (in binary)}}$$

In the very early days of computing, all programming utilized machine languages. Since every instruction, memory location, and piece of data had to be specified in strings of zeros and ones, machine language programming was extremely difficult, time-consuming, and error-prone. People weren't very happy, accurate, or efficient when forced to write zeros and ones all day. As a result, languages that are easier for people to use have been developed. Programs written in any of these other languages are translated by other computer programs into machine language after they are entered into the computer. While machine languages are now rarely used for programming, it's important to realize that programs written in any other language must ultimately be translated into machine language before they can be executed by a computer.

ASSEMBLY LANGUAGES

At a higher level than that of machine languages, but still on a fairly low level, are assembly languages. An assembly language consists of easy-to-remember abbreviations, or **mnemonic symbols,** that represent the zeros and ones of machine language. For example, an assembly language might use ADD, MUL, and STO instead of the binary codes for the computer's addition, multiplication, and storage operations. **Symbolic addressing,** or the practice of using representative names instead of numeric memory addresses, is usually allowed when using assembly languages. That means a programmer can call a memory location TOTAL, rather than 00001001. In doing this, the programmer creates a *variable*, a meaningful abstraction for a given memory location. In addition to symbolic addressing, most assembly languages allow programmers to use decimal, octal, or hexadecimal numbers for data values instead of only binary numbers. All of these factors make assembly languages much easier to use than machine languages.

Machine-specific symbolic languages

Figure 8.1 presents a simple example of an assembly language program for IBM-compatible microcomputers, which use the Intel 8088, 8086, 80286, or 80386 microprocessors. Assembly languages, like machine languages, are specific to particular machines; that is, the assembly language shown here for IBM-compatibles isn't the same as the assembly language for the Apple Macintosh. As in machine language, the individual assembly language instruction isn't very powerful. Many instructions may be needed to perform even the simplest task.

Unlike a machine language program, an assembly language program must be translated before it can be executed. A special program called an **assembler** translates the assembly language for a particular computer into that computer's machine language. As stated in the previous chapter, a program in the form in which it's written by a programmer is known as *source code*. After the source code (the assembly language program) has been converted by the assembler (or other translator program) to machine language, it's referred to as **object code.**

Although much more efficient than machine language programming, assembly language programming is still rather tedious and error-prone because of the tremendous amount of detail necessary. The use of assembly language is, however,

Figure 8.1 An Assembly Language Program

This very simple example shows an assembly language program for IBM-compatible microcomputers. Assembly language is often used for programs or parts of programs that must execute very efficiently or must deal intimately with some machine-dependent task. Each computer model or family has its own unique assembly language. This program doesn't have any practical use; it is intended to be extremely elementary, so you can get a feel for what assembly language programming is like. All it does is calculate the sum of two numbers that have been placed in primary memory, subtract a third number, and place the result in another memory location. Note the use of *comments* (any text to the right of a semicolon) to annotate the program.

```
; This program calculates the sum of two numbers, subtracts a third number
; and stores the result in memory.
;
;
;
DATA      SEGMENT                    ; Define the data to be used.
;
NUMBER1 DW      20                   ; Store the 1st number (20) in memory.
NUMBER2 DW      35                   ; Store the 2nd number (35) in memory.
NUMBER3 DW      12                   ; Store the 3rd number (12) in memory.
RESULT  DW      ?                    ; Reserve a place in memory for the result.
;
DATA      ENDS
;
;
CODE      SEGMENT                    ; Describe the processing steps.
          ASSUME  CS:CODE,DS:DATA    ; Tell computer where to find code and data.
;
          MOV     AX,NUMBER1         ; Move the 1st number into the accumulator.
          MOV     BX,NUMBER2         ; Move the 2nd number into the BX register.
          ADD     AX,BX              ; Add the two and place result in accumulator.
          MOV     BX,NUMBER3         ; Move the 3rd number into the BX register.
          SUB     AX,BX              ; Subtract 3rd number from previous sum.
          MOV     RESULT,AX          ; Move the result from accumulator into memory.
;
CODE      ENDS
          END
```

worth the extra effort when the unique characteristics of a particular computer must be considered or when the most efficient use of computer resources is a crucial factor. Because assembly language gives programmers control of the internal functioning of the computer at a very basic level, it is often used when peripheral devices are to be interfaced, or connected, to the computer. Also, because of this control, assembly language can be used by skillful programmers to produce programs that run faster and take up less space in memory. Thus assembly languages have a significant role in the programming of certain types of machine-dependent tasks.

HIGH-LEVEL LANGUAGES

By far the most utilized category of programming languages is the high-level languages, whose statements more closely resemble human language or mathematical notation than machine or assembly languages. High-level languages were developed to help programmers focus their attention on the task to be performed and pay less attention to machine-specific details. More abstract than low-level languages, these languages make it easier for programmers to express complex data-processing operations using fewer statements. We'll describe each of the important high-level languages a bit later. First, let's deal with some important general aspects that affect their application.

Abstract languages to describe procedures or solve specific kinds of problems

Compilers and Interpreters

Like assembly language programs, high-level language programs must be translated into machine language before execution by a computer. Unlike assembly languages, however, most high-level languages have the advantage of **machine-independence** or **portability;** that is, programs written in a high-level language can be run on any computer that has the applicable translator program.

Most high-level languages are translated, or *compiled*, into machine language by special programs known as **compilers.** Compilers are to high-level languages what assemblers are to assembly languages: they translate the language into computer-usable form. In other words, compilers translate high-level language source code into machine-specific object code.

Programs that translate high-level languages

High-level language source code is for the most part machine-independent or portable. For example, you can write a Pascal program on an IBM-compatible computer that can be recompiled and run on an Apple Macintosh computer. Borland International sells a Turbo Pascal compiler for IBM-compatibles and also a Turbo Pascal compiler for Macintoshes. If you develop a Turbo Pascal program that doesn't use unique features of one computer or the other, you can easily compile and run the same program on both machines.

Some high-level languages can also be translated into machine language by programs called **interpreters.** A compiler translates an entire high-level language program all at once, producing a complete, executable machine language program; an interpreter translates and executes one statement at a time as it's entered into the computer. This ongoing translation allows a programmer to try out ideas or make changes to programs and see the results almost immediately. Consequently, an interpreter provides a more interactive programming environment, which can make it easier to write programs. Although they can speed up program development, interpreters often produce translated programs that run slower or take up more memory space than they would if they had been compiled. Once a program has been compiled, the compiler is no longer needed to run it because it has been fully translated into machine language. An interpreter, on the other hand, must be used each time the high-level language program is run because the translation isn't stored. You might see a compiler as analogous to a human translator who is given a book written in English and returns the Russian version of the whole text. Once the book has been translated, the translator's job ends. An interpreter is like a worker at the United Nations who converts English into Russian as it is being spoken—he or she must be present for every English speech.

Some high-level languages have both compilers and interpreters available for program translation. BASIC, for example, is usually translated by an interpreter, but BASIC compilers are also commonly used.

The Advantages of High-Level Languages

High-level languages offer many advantages over assembly and machine languages: they are easier to learn, write, correct, and revise. Furthermore, because of their greater degree of abstraction, they allow programmers to pay more attention to the problem at hand and to be less concerned with machine-dependent details of processing. As a result, very large, complex programs can be written in high-level languages (it would still be a demanding job but a much less difficult one than with lower-level languages). Programming errors are easier to avoid when high-level languages are used and easier to find when they do occur. It's also easier to follow the principles of structured programming with high-level languages, which offer all the advantages we discussed in Chapter 7. Finally, the machine-independence of high-level languages means that the same programs can be run on vastly different types of computers. This not only makes programs much more useful, it frees programmers from having to learn a different language for each computer with which they work.

MAJOR HIGH-LEVEL LANGUAGES

Now that we've placed high-level languages in the general hierarchy of computer languages, let's look closely at several of the most important ones in use today: FORTRAN, COBOL, BASIC, Pascal, Modula-2, C, Ada, and RPG. Each of these languages is noteworthy because of its widespread use or profound influence. If you use computers, it's very likely that you'll hear about or even learn at least one of these high-level languages.

We'll briefly examine some important aspects of each of these languages, including features, program format, data types, and control statements. By *features*, we mean those characteristics that make a language useful, as well as those that limit its use. The program format specifies what elements a program written in a particular language must contain and how these elements must be arranged. The **data types** of a computer language are the kinds of data that can be processed using that language; they indicate what applications the language accomplishes best. **Control statements** show how the flow of program logic is determined and reveal how structured a language is. Finally, we include a brief example of a program written in each of these languages (except RPG). For continuity, we show the same grade-point-average program (introduced in Chapter 7) throughout.

FORTRAN

FORTRAN, or FORmula TRANslator, was developed by IBM and introduced in 1957. Designed with scientists, engineers, and mathematicians in mind, it was the first commercially available high-level language. To this day, FORTRAN is the most widely used programming language in the scientific community.

Features

FORTRAN's most outstanding feature is the ease with which it enables programmers to express complex computations. Because of its mathematical orientation, efficient execution, and numerical precision, it is the top "number-crunching" language. Noted for its simplicity and conciseness, FORTRAN is one of the most highly standardized computer languages. These factors, along with its familiarity, have made it a favorite of many mathematically inclined users. In addition, it is commonly and effectively used on all types of computers, from microcomputers to supercomputers.

A number-crunching language

The original American National Standards Institute (ANSI) FORTRAN standard, FORTRAN 66, was not particularly adept at handling alphabetic data or performing file-processing tasks. It didn't have a wide variety of data types or control statements. Furthermore, the logic of FORTRAN-66 programs was often difficult for users to follow. Programming errors occurred frequently and were difficult to find and correct. In general, FORTRAN wasn't particularly well suited to business applications, which typically require extensive manipulation of files containing nonnumeric data.

These drawbacks have been addressed, however, with more recent FORTRAN standards and dialects. FORTRAN 77, FORTRAN 80, and WATFIV-S are modern versions of FORTRAN in widespread use. Despite some incompatibilities between these different versions, they all provide some structured programming features that allow FORTRAN to perform a wide variety of tasks effectively.

Figure 8.2 shows our grade-point-average program written in Microsoft FORTRAN 77 for IBM-compatible microcomputers.

Program Format

FORTRAN was originally developed when punched cards were the dominant input medium. Consequently, FORTRAN programs have a fixed format of 80 characters per line. A FORTRAN program consists of a series of statements that begin in predefined line positions. Every program is concluded with an END statement. Statements to which other statements branch must be preceded by line numbers so that they can be referenced. Variables are introduced as needed and often lack an explicit declaration of what type of data they hold. Large programs are usually subdivided into subprograms, of which FORTRAN has two types: subroutines and functions. A **subroutine** is a sequence of statements, or module, that performs a particular processing task and can be called from various locations in the main program. A **function** resembles a subroutine except that it returns a single value (for example, the square root of a number) to the main program.

Data Types

The data types that FORTRAN programs can process reveal its mathematical orientation. Integer (fixed-point), real (floating-point), and complex (containing the square root of -1) numbers can be processed, as well as logical values (also called *Boolean values*), that consist of true and false. FORTRAN offers a *double-precision capability*, which means results can be calculated to twice as many significant digits as there are in regular real numbers (in other words, results are very accurate). Modern versions of FORTRAN include a character data type that facilitates the processing of alphanumeric characters. FORTRAN also allows the use of **arrays,** ordered sets or lists of data items identified by a single name.

Figure 8.2 A FORTRAN Program
This simple Microsoft FORTRAN-77 program implements a version of the grade-point-average program we introduced and designed in the previous chapter. The program asks you to supply a course name, the number of semester hours, and your letter grade. To keep the example programs in this chapter short, simple, and more understandable, we do not check the input data for validity. If this were a program to be used on a routine basis, it would be vitally important to make sure the data entered by the user are valid. After the data for each course are obtained, the program computes the grade points and updates accumulators for the total grade points and total semester hours. Then it attempts to read more data and keeps looping through this whole process until you make blank entries by simply pressing the Enter key in response to the prompts. Finally, the program computes and displays on the screen your total grade points, total semester hours, and grade-point average. The rest of the example programs in this chapter work in the same manner.

```
C   GRADE POINT AVERAGE PROGRAM
C
C   This program calculates a student's grade-point average, given a list of
C   course names, semester hours, and letter grades.
C
        INTEGER HOURS,POINTS,TPOINTS,THOURS
        REAL GPA
        CHARACTER CNAME*20,GRADE*1
C
        TPOINTS = 0
        THOURS = 0
C
        WRITE (*, 10)
10      FORMAT (' ', 'Please enter course name, semester hours, and',
       +' letter grade:')
        WRITE (*, 20)
20      FORMAT (' ', 'Course name: '\);
        READ (*, 25) CNAME
25      FORMAT (A20)
        WRITE (*, 30)
30      FORMAT (' ', 'Semester hours: '\);
        READ (*, 35) HOURS
35      FORMAT (I1)
        WRITE (*, 40)
40      FORMAT (' ', 'Letter grade: '\);
        READ (*, 45) GRADE
45      FORMAT (A1)
C       In a routinely used program, these data should be checked for validity.
C
C       An IF and GOTOs are used to construct the equivalent of a WHILE loop.
50      IF (CNAME .EQ. '                    ') GOTO 60
C       In other words, WHILE CNAME is not blank, do the following:
            IF ((GRADE .EQ. 'A') .OR. (GRADE .EQ. 'a')) THEN
                POINTS = HOURS * 5
            ELSEIF ((GRADE .EQ. 'B') .OR. (GRADE .EQ. 'b')) THEN
                POINTS = HOURS * 4
            ELSEIF ((GRADE .EQ. 'C') .OR. (GRADE .EQ. 'c')) THEN
                POINTS = HOURS * 3
```

Figure 8.2   (continued)

```
             ELSEIF ((GRADE .EQ. 'D') .OR. (GRADE .EQ. 'd')) THEN
                POINTS = HOURS * 2
             ELSE
                POINTS = HOURS
             ENDIF
             TPOINTS = TPOINTS + POINTS
             THOURS = THOURS + HOURS
             WRITE (*, 20)
             READ (*, 25) CNAME
             WRITE (*, 30)
             READ (*, 35) HOURS
             WRITE (*, 40)
             READ (*, 45) GRADE
C            Again, these data should be checked for validity.
          GOTO 50
60        CONTINUE
C
          IF (THOURS .GT. 0) THEN
             GPA = FLOAT (TPOINTS) / THOURS
          ELSE
             GPA = 0
          ENDIF
C
          WRITE (*, 70) TPOINTS, THOURS, GPA
70        FORMAT ('0', 'Total Grade Points   = ', I3/,
         +        ' ', 'Total Semester Hours = ', I3/,
         +        ' ', 'Grade Point Average  = ', F4.2)
C
          STOP
          END
```

Control Statements

Originally, FORTRAN had only three major control statements: the GOTO statement (an unconditional transfer of control), the IF statement (a conditional transfer), and the DO statement (a *counted loop* structure that executes a specified number of times). This rather limited collection of simple control structures made it somewhat difficult to apply the principles of structured programming with FORTRAN (and was due to the fact that FORTRAN was invented before structured programming). Newer and more commonly used versions of FORTRAN, however, such as FORTRAN 77, FORTRAN 80 and WATFIV-S, do have enhanced control structures. WATFIV-S, for example, has a WHILE-ENDWHILE loop which tests the exit condition at the beginning, and a LOOP-ENDLOOP structure that can contain the exit condition anywhere inside.

COBOL

*The business-as-usual
language*

COBOL, which stands for COmmon Business Oriented Language, was introduced in 1960, after having been developed by the Conference on Data Systems Languages (CODASYL), a committee of government and industry representatives assembled by the Department of Defense. COBOL was the first high-level language suitable for business data processing, its use greatly encouraged by the U.S. government. Consequently, it has been applied extensively throughout business and industry and may well be the most widely known and used computer language in the world.

Features

COBOL's outstanding features include its ready handling of the input and output of large volumes of alphanumeric data, its machine-independence, and its Englishlike vocabulary and syntax. Business data processing usually involves a great deal of input, output, and file manipulation, with few and relatively simple mathematical computations. COBOL functions well in such an environment. Another strength of COBOL lies in its specifically designed machine-independence. This means that COBOL programs can be run on different computer systems with few modifications, so COBOL programs generally have both portability and longevity. Finally, COBOL is noted for its Englishlike statements that often make programs understandable even to nonprogrammers. For this reason, COBOL is sometimes called a *self-documenting language*.

This self-documenting capability, however, also serves as the source of much of the criticism directed at COBOL. COBOL programs are quite wordy—it's next to impossible to write a "short" one. A long list of **reserved words** (words with set meanings that aren't available for programmers to use as data or variable names) frequently frustrates programmers. In addition, COBOL requires a relatively large and sophisticated compiler, which can make it difficult to implement on some small computers. Although there are COBOL compilers for microcomputers, they tend to be expensive and slow and to use a lot of space in memory. Despite these drawbacks and its unsuitability for complex computations, COBOL is likely to remain a very important language in the business world for the foreseeable future because so much COBOL business software already exists.

Figure 8.3 shows our grade-point-average program written in COBOL.

Program Format

All COBOL programs have a specified, uniform format. The basic unit of a program is the *sentence*, which ends with a period. Sentences make up *paragraphs*; paragraphs make up *sections*; and sections make up *divisions*. Every COBOL program must have four divisions. The *IDENTIFICATION DIVISION* contains the name of the program and its author, the date it was written, and other documentation details. The *ENVIRONMENT DIVISION* specifies the computer on which the program is to run and lists the names of the input and output files to be used by the program. The *DATA DIVISION* lists and describes the exact formats of all variables, records, and files that the program will use. Finally, the *PROCEDURE DIVISION* contains the instructions that perform the data processing.

Figure 8.3 A COBOL Program

Here is the same grade-point-average program expressed in COBOL. Note that
comments in COBOL are preceded by an asterisk.

```
        IDENTIFICATION DIVISION.
        *  This division contains general documentation details.

        PROGRAM-ID.        GRADE-POINT-AVERAGE.
        AUTHOR.            ERNEST COLANTONIO
        DATE-WRITTEN.      JANUARY 1, 1989.
        REMARKS.           THIS PROGRAM CALCULATES A STUDENT'S GRADE-POINT
                           AVERAGE GIVEN A LIST OF COURSE NAMES, SEMESTER
                           HOURS, AND LETTER GRADES.



        ENVIRONMENT DIVISION.
        *  This division contains computer-specific details.

        CONFIGURATION SECTION.
        SOURCE-COMPUTER.        IBM.
        OBJECT-COMPUTER.        IBM.



        DATA DIVISION.
        *  This division describes the data formats.

        WORKING-STORAGE SECTION.
        01   COURSE-NAME          PIC X(20).
        01   SEMESTER-HOURS       PIC 9.
        01   LETTER-GRADE         PIC X.
        01   GRADE-POINTS         PIC 999.
        01   TOTAL-POINTS         PIC 999.
        01   TOTAL-HOURS          PIC 999.
        01   GRADE-POINT-AVERAGE  PIC 9V99.



        PROCEDURE DIVISION.
        *  This division contains the actual processing instructions.

        MAIN-PROGRAM.
            MOVE 0 TO TOTAL-POINTS.
            MOVE 0 TO TOTAL-HOURS.

            DISPLAY 'Please enter course name, semester hours, and letter
        -           ' grade:'.
            DISPLAY 'Course name: '.
            ACCEPT COURSE-NAME.
            DISPLAY 'Semester hours: '.
            ACCEPT SEMESTER-HOURS.
            DISPLAY 'Letter grade: '.
            ACCEPT LETTER-GRADE.
        *   In a routinely used program, these data should be checked.
```

Figure 8.3 (continued)

```
        PERFORM PROCESS-INPUT
           UNTIL COURSE-NAME = '                              '.

        IF TOTAL-HOURS > 0
           COMPUTE GRADE-POINT-AVERAGE = TOTAL-POINTS / TOTAL-HOURS
        ELSE
           MOVE 0.00 TO GRADE-POINT-AVERAGE.


        DISPLAY 'Total Grade Points   = '  TOTAL-POINTS.
        DISPLAY 'Total Semester Hours = '  TOTAL-HOURS.
        DISPLAY 'Grade Point Average  = '  GRADE-POINT-AVERAGE.
        STOP RUN.


    PROCESS-INPUT.
        IF LETTER-GRADE = 'A' OR LETTER-GRADE = 'a'
           COMPUTE GRADE-POINTS = SEMESTER-HOURS * 5
        ELSE
           IF LETTER-GRADE = 'B' OR LETTER-GRADE = 'b'
              COMPUTE GRADE-POINTS = SEMESTER-HOURS * 4
           ELSE
              IF LETTER-GRADE = 'C' OR LETTER-GRADE = 'c'
                 COMPUTE GRADE-POINTS = SEMESTER-HOURS * 3
              ELSE
                 IF LETTER-GRADE = 'D' OR LETTER-GRADE = 'd'
                    COMPUTE GRADE-POINTS = SEMESTER-HOURS * 2
                 ELSE
                    COMPUTE GRADE-POINTS = SEMESTER-HOURS.
        ADD GRADE-POINTS TO TOTAL-POINTS.
        ADD SEMESTER-HOURS TO TOTAL-HOURS.
        DISPLAY 'Course name: '.
        ACCEPT COURSE-NAME.
        DISPLAY 'Semester hours: '.
        ACCEPT SEMESTER-HOURS.
        DISPLAY 'Letter grade: '.
        ACCEPT LETTER-GRADE.
*       Again, these data should be checked for validity.
```

Data Types

A central rule of COBOL is that all data are internally stored in character form unless they are explicitly declared to be numeric. This reflects COBOL's data-processing orientation and simplifies the handling of common items like names, addresses, identification numbers, inventories, and dollar amounts. COBOL allows the use of simple single variables, as well as more complex hierarchical record structures and tables. All data must be defined and their exact formats specified in the DATA DIVISION.

Control Statements

COBOL has three major control statements: the GOTO statement, the IF-ELSE statement, and the PERFORM statement. As in FORTRAN, the GOTO is an unconditional transfer of control, and the IF-ELSE a conditional transfer of control. The PERFORM statement serves both as a looping structure and as a call to execute a named set of instructions (that is, a module). COBOL, like FORTRAN, was developed before the principles of structured programming became accepted. Nevertheless, the combination of COBOL's control statements and its sentence-paragraph-section-division format generally produces structured, modular programs.

BASIC

BASIC, or Beginners' All-purpose Symbolic Instruction Code, was developed by Dr. John Kemeny and Dr. Thomas Kurtz at Dartmouth College in 1965. Originally designed as a simple, instructive, interactive language for use with time-sharing computer systems, BASIC has become the most widely used high-level language for microcomputers.

A popular beginner's language

Features

BASIC's most striking feature is its simplicity: it is very easy to learn and to use. Users can often begin to write and run functional programs after only a few hours of instruction and practice. Derived from both FORTRAN and ALGOL, BASIC resembles a somewhat simplified version of FORTRAN. As an interactive language by design, BASIC is most often translated by small, compact interpreters. Nevertheless, BASIC compilers are also quite common. Applicable to both computational and alphanumeric data-processing tasks, BASIC has been extensively employed by users of all types of small computers. Very suitable for microcomputers, pared-down versions of BASIC are even available for notebook and pocket-sized computers.

Heading the list of BASIC's negative features is its lack of standardization; there are several different versions, or dialects, of BASIC. The most popular are probably Microsoft's BASIC and Quick BASIC, Borland International's Turbo BASIC, and True BASIC, a powerful, structured version of BASIC from its originators, Kemeny and Kurtz. Fortunately, a core of certain BASIC features is common to almost every version, but program transportability is often a problem. Also, BASIC's very simplicity can be a drawback when it limits BASIC's power. Furthermore, this simplicity makes it difficult to write very long or very complex programs in some versions of BASIC. Finally, the ease of programming in BASIC is often offset by slower running times and less efficient programs.

Figure 8.4 shows our grade-point-average program in Microsoft BASIC.

Program Format

The format of BASIC programs is quite simple and unrestrictive. A program consists of a series of statements terminated by an END statement. Statements are entered in a free format, one or more to the line. Some versions of BASIC require that all lines be numbered. BASIC programs can be subdivided into subprograms, but in some dialects this capability isn't as sophisticated as it is in most other high-level languages.

Figure 8.4 A BASIC Program

This is a version of our grade-point-average program written in Microsoft BASIC. The
lines that begin with REM (short for REMark) are BASIC comments.

```
010 REM GRADE-POINT-AVERAGE PROGRAM
020 REM
030 REM This program calculates a student's grade-point average, given a list
040 REM of course names, semester hours, and letter grades.
050 REM
060 PRINT "Please enter course name, semester hours, and letter grade:"
070 INPUT; "Course name: ", COURSE.NAME$
080 INPUT; "   Semester hours: ", SEMESTER.HOURS%
090 INPUT "   Letter grade: ", LETTER.GRADE$
095 REM In a routinely used program, these data should be checked for validity.
100 REM
110 WHILE COURSE.NAME$ <> ''
120    IF (LETTER.GRADE$ = "A") OR (LETTER.GRADE$ = "a") THEN
          GRADE.POINTS% = SEMESTER.HOURS% * 5: GOTO 170
130    IF (LETTER.GRADE$ = "B") OR (LETTER.GRADE$ = "b") THEN
          GRADE.POINTS% = SEMESTER.HOURS% * 4: GOTO 170
140    IF (LETTER.GRADE$ = "C") OR (LETTER.GRADE$ = "c") THEN
          GRADE.POINTS% = SEMESTER.HOURS% * 3: GOTO 170
150    IF (LETTER.GRADE$ = "D") OR (LETTER.GRADE$ = "d") THEN
          GRADE.POINTS% = SEMESTER.HOURS% * 2: GOTO 170
160    IF (LETTER.GRADE$ = "F") OR (LETTER.GRADE$ = "f") THEN
          GRADE.POINTS% = SEMESTER.HOURS%
170    TOTAL.POINTS% = TOTAL.POINTS% + GRADE.POINTS%
180    TOTAL.HOURS%  = TOTAL.HOURS% + SEMESTER.HOURS%
190    INPUT; "Course name: ", COURSE.NAME$
200    INPUT; "   Semester hours: ", SEMESTER.HOURS%
210    INPUT "   Letter grade: ", LETTER.GRADE$
220    WEND
230 IF TOTAL.HOURS% > 0 THEN GRADE.POINT.AVERAGE = TOTAL.POINTS% / TOTAL.HOURS%
240 REM
250 PRINT
260 PRINT "Total Grade Points  = "; TOTAL.POINTS%
270 PRINT "Total Semester Hours = "; TOTAL.HOURS%
280 PRINT "Grade Point Average  = "; GRADE.POINT.AVERAGE
290 REM
300 END
```

Data Types

Although the data types that are acceptable vary somewhat depending on the version of BASIC, all BASIC dialects handle real numbers and *strings*, or groups, of characters. And almost all BASIC dialects support arrays of real numbers and arrays of character strings. The small set of data types was intentional; it was designed to emphasize BASIC's overall simplicity. Most manufacturers have augmented the original set with such additions as integers and double-precision numbers.

Control Statements

BASIC's control statements resemble those found in FORTRAN: a GOTO statement, an IF-THEN statement, and a FOR-NEXT loop. Most modern versions of BASIC also have WHILE-WEND loops and can be considered structured programming languages. A good example is True BASIC. Introduced in late 1984, it retains all the strengths of the original language but is faster, more powerful, more portable, and contains many new features that allow structured programming as well as sophisticated graphics, mathematics, and text processing.

Pascal

Pascal was invented by the Swiss computer scientist Niklaus Wirth, who named the language in honor of the seventeenth-century French philosopher and mathematician Blaise Pascal. Introduced in 1971, it was originally intended as a high-level language for teaching the concepts of structured programming and top-down design. Pascal's simplicity, elegance, and embodiment of structured programming principles have made it quite popular with computer scientists and students, scientific programmers, and microcomputer users.

A structured programmer's dream

Features

Among all the computer languages currently in widespread use, Pascal is one of the best for demonstrating structured programming. Simple, straightforward, and easy to learn, Pascal imposes rules that encourage good programming habits. In addition, Pascal is a versatile and powerful language that helps users avoid programming errors. Consequently, large, complex, relatively error-free programs are easier to write in Pascal than in many other languages. Furthermore, Pascal can be translated by small compilers. As a result, Pascal has become a popular alternative to BASIC on microcomputers as well as being commonly used on larger computers.

Pascal's main shortcoming is its limited input/output and file manipulation capabilities. This makes Pascal somewhat unattractive to business users, and it has not been utilized much in traditional data-processing applications. Designed to be a teaching language, Pascal was not originally intended to be employed outside of educational institutions. Its limitations, however, have been addressed to some extent by vendors selling extended versions of Pascal that incorporate additional features. These extensions constitute another negative feature for Pascal—there are many different versions being sold. Even though there are standards, such as Wirth's original specifications and an ISO (International Standards Organization) set, vendors haven't consistently followed them. Two of the most popular implementations of Pascal for microcomputers are Microsoft Pascal, which runs on IBM-compatibles, and Borland International's Turbo Pascal, which comes in versions for both IBM-compatibles and Apple Macintoshes. Despite its problems, Pascal is a very influential language, especially in educational environments, and is a strong competitor of FORTRAN and BASIC.

Figure 8.5 shows our grade-point-average program in Turbo Pascal.

Program Format

Pascal has a very well-defined program format. The program name comes first, followed by the data descriptions, then any subprograms used, and finally the body of code representing the main program. The internal organization of each subpro-

Figure 8.5 A Pascal Program

Here the grade-point-average program is expressed in Turbo Pascal, from Borland
International. In Pascal, comments are enclosed between these characters: (* and *).

```
(*   GRADE POINT AVERAGE PROGRAM   *)

(*  This program calculates a student's grade-point average, given a list of *)
(*  course names, semester hours, and letter grades.                         *)

PROGRAM Grade_Point_Average (INPUT, OUTPUT);

VAR
   course_name         : STRING [20];   (* This is the section that declares *)
   semester_hours      : INTEGER;       (* the data type of each variable to *)
   letter_grade        : CHAR;          (* be used in the program.           *)
   grade_points        : INTEGER;
   total_points        : INTEGER;
   total_hours         : INTEGER;
   grade_point_average : REAL;

BEGIN   (* Grade_Point_Average *)

   total_points := 0;    (* Initialize the accumulators to zero. *)
   total_hours  := 0;

   WRITELN ('Please enter course name, semester hours, and letter grade:');
   WRITE ('Course name: ');          READ  (course_name);
   WRITE ('  Semester hours: ');     READ  (semester_hours);
   WRITE ('  Letter_grade: ');       READLN (letter_grade);
   (* In a routinely used program, these data should be checked for validity *)

WHILE course_name <> '' DO
   BEGIN  (* WHILE *)
      CASE letter_grade OF
         'A','a' : grade_points := semester_hours * 5;
         'B','b' : grade_points := semester_hours * 4;
         'C','c' : grade_points := semester_hours * 3;
         'D','d' : grade_points := semester_hours * 2;
         'F','f' : grade_points := semester_hours;
      END;    (* CASE *)
      total_points := total_points + grade_points;
      total_hours  := total_hours + semester_hours;
      WRITE ('Course name: ');          READ  (course_name);
      WRITE ('  Semester hours: ');     READ  (semester_hours);
      WRITE ('  Letter_grade: ');       READLN (letter_grade);
      (* Again, these data should be checked for validity *)
END;    (* WHILE *)

 IF total_hours > 0 THEN
    grade_point_average := total_points / total_hours
 ELSE
    grade_point_average := 0;
```

Figure 8.5 (continued)

```
WRITELN;
WRITELN ('Total Grade Points   = ', total_points);
WRITELN ('Total Semester Hours = ', total_hours);
WRITELN ('Grade-Point Average  = ', grade_point_average:4:2);

END.   (* Grade_Point_Average *)
```

gram, of which Pascal has two types (procedures and functions), mirrors this program format. The basic units of Pascal programs are statements, which can be entered in free format but which must be separated by semicolons.

Data Types

Pascal provides users with a full range of simple and structured data types, in addition to supporting programmer-defined ones. Pascal's built-in simple data types include integers, real numbers, Boolean values (true and false), and characters. Its structured types include arrays, sets, records, and files. Programmer-defined data types are user-constructed, custom-made types that significantly contribute to Pascal's power and versatility.

Control Statements

Pascal is richly endowed with the control structures that exemplify structured programming. To handle conditional transfers of control, it has the old standby, the IF-THEN-ELSE statement, as well as the multiple-choice CASE statement. Pascal has three kinds of looping structures: the WHILE statement, the REPEAT-UNTIL statement, and the FOR statement (which sets up a *counted loop* that executes a specified number of times). Although Pascal does have a GOTO statement, it seldom appears in well-designed programs.

Modula-2

Modula-2, which is an acronym for MODUlar LAnguage-2, was developed in 1978 by Niklaus Wirth as the successor to his previous creation, Pascal. Although there are many similarities between the two languages, Pascal was originally designed to be only a teaching language. Wirth designed Modula-2 for the professional software developer. Modula-2 includes features not found in Wirth's original implementation of Pascal that make the newer language more powerful, versatile, and better suited to the development of large software systems, such as operating systems, programming language compilers, and application packages. When commercial Modula-2 compilers first became available in 1980, many colleges and other organizations began using it as an alternative to Pascal, C, and Ada. Today, Modula-2 is available for most popular microcomputers and some minicomputers and mainframes.

Pascal's descendant

Features

Modula-2 is quite similar to Pascal in many ways although there are several important differences. The name *Modula-2* refers to the most important feature of the language, the module. This separate section of code has a specific purpose and is treated as a unit. In Modula-2, a program consists of one or more modules. This encourages the top-down, divide-and-conquer approach that facilitates the development of large programming projects. In Wirth's original Pascal, a program is a single **compilation unit** that is compiled all at once and must be entirely recompiled whenever any part of the source code is changed. In Modula-2, modules can be compiled separately. You can build libraries of modules that can be reused in different programs. If changes must be made, you need only recompile altered modules. Since modules can be developed and compiled separately, Modula-2 is much better than Pascal for team programming projects.

Another improvement over Pascal is Modula-2's built-in ability to control low-level hardware functions. Modula-2 is suitable for some tasks otherwise possible only with assembly language. This makes Modula-2 ideal for developing operating systems, programming language compilers, and programs that control the operation of electronic equipment.

Unlike Wirth's original Pascal, Modula-2 can also be used to program coroutines and interrupt handlers. A **coroutine** is a special subprogram that can execute concurrently with another coroutine, rapidly switching back and forth from one to the other so as to appear to run simultaneously. An **interrupt** is a signal, usually generated by a hardware device, that indicates a high-priority job must be taken care of immediately. An **interrupt handler** is a program that temporarily suspends the current program to process one of these high-priority requests. The ability to program coroutines and interrupts is especially important for the development of operating systems.

Modula-2's main disadvantage stems from usage less frequent than most other high-level languages. Although Modula-2 compilers are available from a number of companies, the dominant language developers, such as Microsoft, IBM, and Borland International, have not yet released Modula-2 compilers. As with most high-level languages, a few slightly different versions of Modula-2 being sold are somewhat incompatible with each other.

Figure 8.6 shows our grade-point-average program in Modula-2.

Figure 8.6 A Modula-2 Program

Now the grade-point-average program expressed in FTL Modula-2 from Workman & Associates. Note the similarity to the Pascal program in Figure 8.5.

```
(*   GRADE POINT AVERAGE PROGRAM   *)

(*  This program calculates a student's grade-point average, given a list of *)
(*  course names, semester hours, and letter grades.                         *)

MODULE Grade_Point_Average;

FROM MyInOut IMPORT
     String, Read, ReadInt, ReadString, WriteString, WriteInt, WriteReal;
```

Figure 8.6 (continued)

```
VAR
    course_name          : String;        (* This is the section that declares *)
    semester_hours       : INTEGER;       (* the data type of each variable to *)
    letter_grade         : CHAR;          (* be used in the program.            *)
    grade_points         : INTEGER;
    total_points         : INTEGER;
    total_hours          : INTEGER;
    grade_point_average  : REAL;


BEGIN  (* Grade_Point_Average *)

    total_points := 0;     (* Initialize the accumulators to zero. *)
    total_hours  := 0;

    WriteString ('Please enter course name, semester hours, and letter grade:');
    WriteString ('Course name: ');         ReadString (course_name);
    WriteString ('Semester hours: ');   ReadInt (semester_hours);
    WriteString ('Letter_grade: ');      Read (letter_grade);
    (* In a routinely used program, these data should be checked for validity *)

WHILE course_name <> '' DO
    CASE letter_grade OF
        'A','a' : grade_points := semester_hours * 5; ¦
        'B','b' : grade_points := semester_hours * 4; ¦
        'C','c' : grade_points := semester_hours * 3; ¦
        'D','d' : grade_points := semester_hours * 2; ¦
        'F','f' : grade_points := semester_hours;
    END;   (* CASE *)
    total_points := total_points + grade_points;
    total_hours  := total_hours + semester_hours;
    WriteString ('Course name: ');          ReadString (course_name);
    WriteString ('Semester hours: ');    ReadInt (semester_hours);
    WriteString ('Letter_grade: ');       Read (letter_grade);
    (* Again, these data should be checked for validity *)
END;  (* WHILE *)


IF total_hours > 0 THEN
    grade_point_average := total_points / total_hours;
ELSE
    grade_point_average := 0;
END  (* IF *)

WriteString ('Total Grade Points  = ');
WriteInt (total_points, 3);
WriteString ('Total Semester Hours = ');
WriteInt (total_hours, 3);
WriteString ('Grade Point Average  = ');
WriteReal (grade_point_average, 4);

END Grade_Point_Average.
```

Program Format

The general structure of a Modula-2 program consists of a main program module and possibly one or more library modules. The program must begin with the reserved word MODULE, followed by the name of the program. Next come the *import lists* that contain the names of data objects to be used in the program but that are defined in other modules. After the import lists are the data declarations, just like in Pascal. Any subprograms follow, along with the body of source code representing the main program module. Finally, the Modula-2 program is terminated by the reserved word END followed by the name of the program and a period. As in Pascal, the basic instructions of Modula-2 are statements, which can be entered in free format but which must be separated by semicolons.

Data Types

Like Pascal, Modula-2 possesses a rich set of data types. In fact, Modula-2 even has a few more data types than Pascal. There are numeric data types, including cardinal numbers (whole numbers from zero on up), integers, long integers (very large integers), real numbers, and long real numbers (very large real numbers). Modula-2 also has characters and Boolean values (true and false). Like Pascal, its structured types include arrays, sets, and records. Unlike Pascal, no built-in type for files exists. Files and input/output operations are provided in standard library modules that come with the compiler instead of being built into the language itself. This enables Modula-2 to be a more machine-independent language than Pascal.

Control Statements

Modula-2 has the same basic control statements as Pascal, with a few handy improvements and one notable exception. Slight changes to the IF-THEN-ELSE, CASE, WHILE, and FOR statements make them easier to use in some instances. Modula-2 has a LOOP statement not found in Pascal. This statement allows intentional infinite loops (for certain programs that always run, such as operating systems), loops that have an exit in the middle, and loops with multiple exit points. Finally, Modula-2 is the ultimate language for avoiding the GOTO statement; it doesn't have one. The EXIT, HALT, and RETURN statements, along with the rich set of control statements, eliminate the need for an unconditional GOTO statement.

C

A versatile language for systems and applications

A concise, general-purpose programming language, C was originally developed at Bell Laboratories as part of the UNIX operating system (about which we will have more to say in Chapter 10). Dennis Ritchie designed and implemented C in 1972 on a DEC PDP-11 minicomputer. He intended C to supplant assembly languages as a tool for developing operating systems. The versatile and portable C allows users to perform tasks that are normally only achievable with assembly languages. Similar to Pascal in its compatibility with structured programming techniques, C has become quite popular with microcomputer users and is also commonly used on larger computer systems.

Features

C differs from most high-level languages in that it doesn't divorce the programmer from the internal workings of the computer's hardware and software. In fact, C encourages programmers to use their knowledge of the computer's functioning. Because of this, C gives programmers great power, and is therefore often described as being "robust." C has a diversity of operations and commands that makes it a favorite general-purpose language. At the same time, it is also clear, pragmatic, and concise. One of its most desirable attributes is portability; it's easy to take software written in C and adapt it to other computer systems with very little modification. Especially on microcomputers, C has become the language of choice for many professional programmers who develop operating systems, programming language compilers, and application software such as word processors, spreadsheets, and data base managers.

Even C's best features, however, have a negative side to them. The great power C provides to programmers makes it easy to create hard-to-find logic errors when writing programs. The conciseness that is characteristic of C programs sometimes means that users who aren't highly skilled programmers can find them difficult to understand. In addition, documentation, error messages, and even expository books written about C tend to be short and cryptic. Although some novice programmers do learn C without difficulty, it isn't considered to be a particularly user-friendly language. Despite these drawbacks, C produces fast, compact programs, and it's one of the most versatile programming languages available for microcomputers.

Figure 8.7 shows our grade-point-average program written in Microsoft C.

Program Format

A C program consists of a main module that must be named "main" and a number of subprograms called functions. The main module and each function must begin with a description of all the data items that are used within. Following these data descriptions is the list of statements that actually direct the processing. Each statement must end with a semicolon. Functions can be placed after the main module in any order.

Data Types

C's fundamental data types are characters, integers, real numbers, double-precision real numbers, and pointers. A *pointer* is a value that indicates the storage address of a data item. C also supports arrays and special constructs called *structures*, which allow data items of different types to be grouped together.

Control Statements

C control statements are similar to those in Pascal. C has an *if-else* statement and a multiple-choice *switch* statement (parallel to Pascal's CASE statement) for conditional transfers of control. Also present, but not recommended, is the *goto* statement for unconditional transfer of control. Loop structures consist of the *while, do while* (identical to Pascal's REPEAT-UNTIL), and *for* statements (the latter is a counted loop). All the key words in C, as you may have concluded, must be entered in lower-case letters.

Figure 8.7   A C Program

This is a Microsoft C version of our grade-point-average program. Comments are
the text situated between /* and */ characters.

```
/*   GRADE POINT AVERAGE PROGRAM   */

/*  This program calculates a student's grade point average, given a list   */
/*  of course names, semester hours, and letter grades.                     */

#include <stdio.h>

main ()
{
   char   course_name [20];
   char   letter_grade;
   int    semester_hours;
   int    grade_points;
   int    total_points = 0;
   int    total_hours = 0;
   float  grade_point_average = 0.0;

   printf ("Please enter course name, semester hours, and letter grade:");
   printf ("\nCourse name: ");
   scanf   ("%[^\n]", course_name);
   if (course_name[0] != '\0') {
      printf ("Semester hours: ");
      scanf   ("%d", &semester_hours);
      printf ("Letter grade: ");
      scanf   ("%1s", &letter_grade);
      letter_grade = toupper (letter_grade);
   }
   /* In a routinely used program, these data should be checked for validity.*/

   while (course_name[0] != '\0') {
      switch (letter_grade) {
         case 'A' : grade_points = semester_hours * 5; break;
         case 'B' : grade_points = semester_hours * 4; break;
         case 'C' : grade_points = semester_hours * 3; break;
         case 'D' : grade_points = semester_hours * 2; break;
         case 'F' : grade_points = semester_hours;
      }
      total_points += grade_points;
      total_hours  += semester_hours;
      getchar ();
      printf ("\nCourse name: ");
      scanf   ("%[^\n]", course_name);
      if (course_name[0] != '\0') {
         printf ("Semester hours: ");
         scanf   ("%d", &semester_hours);
         printf ("Letter grade: ");
         scanf   ("%1s", &letter_grade);
         letter_grade = toupper (letter_grade);
```

Figure 8.7 (continued)

```
    }
    /* Again, these data should be checked for validity. */
}

if (total_hours > 0)
    grade_point_average = (float) total_points / (float) total_hours;

printf ("\nTotal Grade Points   = %d", total_points);
printf ("\nTotal Semester Hours = %d", total_hours);
printf ("\nGrade Point Average  - %4.2f", grade_point_average);
}
```

Ada

A new language for large software systems

Named for Augusta Ada Byron, Countess of Lovelace, "the first programmer" (of Babbage's analytical engine), Ada was introduced in 1980. Commissioned by the U.S. Department of Defense (the world's largest software consumer), Ada is a powerful, comprehensive language applicable to a wide range of problems. Many organizations now employ Ada on all kinds of computers.

Features

Ada was specifically designed to be a universal computer programming language. It is a structured language, encompassing the principles of modular, top-down program design. In fact, many of the concepts in Ada were derived from Pascal and are similar to those of Modula-2. Like both these languages, Ada requires all data items to be explicitly declared, so it helps the programmer to develop programs with fewer bugs. Ada resembles Modula-2 more closely, however, in its applicability to almost any kind of programming task. For example, Ada was specifically designed to be effective for the programming of **embedded computers.** These computers are part of larger, electromechanical systems such as sophisticated weapons, aircraft, ships, space vehicles, rapid transit networks, and message switching systems. Like Modula-2, Ada can be used to program coroutines and interrupt handlers. Ada was also designed to be used as a data-processing language, like COBOL. The vast amount of time and effort spent on its design has resulted in Ada's two most outstanding features: its power to accomplish almost any task, and its wealth of programming structures.

Some experts, however, characterize Ada as a very "big" language. In other words, Ada has a great many features, and because of this it can be difficult to learn. Presently, there are fewer Ada compilers available than there are for most other high-level languages. This is probably the language's major weakness. The situation is expected to improve steadily because the Department of Defense (DOD) has made an exclusive commitment to Ada. For the most part, it refuses to accept any new software that isn't written in Ada. The DOD is such a major software consumer that developers are hustling to produce Ada compilers and software so they will not miss out on lucrative defense contracts. The DOD has even registered Ada as a trademark so that it can have the final say regarding what constitutes an acceptable Ada compiler. A few Ada compilers are now available for microcomputers, but Ada isn't expected to achieve the popularity of BASIC, Pascal, and C among users of small machines.

Figure 8.8 shows our grade-point-average program written in Ada.

Program Format

In its simplest form, an Ada program has two parts: a *declarative part* that describes the data, and a *statement part* that describes the computations and processing. The declarative part lists the names and types of the variables that will be used in the program. The statement part, which is bracketed by the reserved words "begin" and "end," lists the operations to be performed. Ada, like Pascal, has two types of subprograms: *procedures* and *functions*. Ada also has two other program units known as *packages* and *tasks*. Packages are either separately compilable modules that contain collections of common data, or groups of related subprograms that collectively carry out some activity. Tasks are similar to packages, except that they can be executed concurrently with other program units. Really coroutines, Ada tasks help in programming operations that must be carried out simultaneously with other operations, such as the concurrent functioning of multiple input/output devices in a large computer system.

Data Types

Ada has all the built-in simple types that are found in other languages: integers, Boolean values, characters, real numbers, and double-precision real numbers. In addition, Ada also supports arrays, character strings, records, files, and programmer-defined data types. As you can see, Ada is fairly similar to Pascal in the types of data it accommodates, with a few important additions. And, as with Pascal,

Figure 8.8 An Ada Program
Here is our grade-point-average program written in Ada. Again, note the similarities
to the Pascal and Modula-2 programs in Figures 8.5 and 8.6, respectively.

```
--  GRADE POINT AVERAGE PROGRAM

--  This program calculates a student's grade-point average, given a list of
--  course names, semester hours, and letter grades.

with TEXT_IO;

procedure GRADE_POINT_AVERAGE_PROGRAM is

    use TEXT_IO;
    package INT_I_O is new INTEGER_IO (INTEGER);
    package FLOAT_I_O is new FLOAT_IO (FLOAT);
    use INT_I_O, FLOAT_I_O;
```

Figure 8.8 (continued)

```
        COURSE_NAME              :  STRING (1..20);
        SEMESTER_HOURS           :  INTEGER;
        LETTER_GRADE             :  CHARACTER;
        GRADE_POINTS             :  INTEGER;
        TOTAL_POINTS             :  INTEGER;
        TOTAL_HOURS              :  INTEGER;
        GRADE_POINT_AVERAGE  :  FLOAT;
        LENGTH                   :  NATURAL;


begin
     TOTAL_POINTS  := 0;
     TOTAL_HOURS   := 0;

     PUT_LINE ("Please enter course name, semester hours, and letter grade:");
     PUT ("Course name: ");         GET_LINE (COURSE_NAME, LENGTH);
     PUT ("  Semester hours: ");  GET (SEMESTER_HOURS);
     PUT ("  Letter grade: ");    GET (LETTER_GRADE);
  -- In a routinely used program, these data should be checked for validity.
     NEW_LINE;


     while LENGTH > 0 loop
        case LETTER_GRADE is
           when 'A', 'a' => GRADE_POINTS := SEMESTER_HOURS * 5;
           when 'B', 'b' => GRADE_POINTS := SEMESTER_HOURS * 4;
           when 'C', 'c' => GRADE_POINTS := SEMESTER_HOURS * 3;
           when 'D', 'd' => GRADE_POINTS := SEMESTER_HOURS * 2;
           when 'F', 'f' => GRADE_POINTS := SEMESTER_HOURS;
           when others   => null;
        end case;
        TOTAL_POINTS := TOTAL_POINTS + GRADE_POINTS;
        TOTAL_HOURS  := TOTAL_HOURS + SEMESTER_HOURS;
        PUT ("Course name: ");         GET_LINE (COURSE_NAME, LENGTH);
        PUT ("  Semester hours: ");  GET (SEMESTER_HOURS);
        PUT ("  Letter grade: ");    GET (LETTER_GRADE);
     -- Again, these data should be checked for validity.
        NEW_LINE;
     end loop;

     if TOTAL_HOURS > 0 then
        GRADE_POINT_AVERAGE := FLOAT'(TOTAL_POINTS) / FLOAT'(TOTAL_HOURS);
     else
        GRADE_POINT_AVERAGE := 0.0;
     end if;

     PUT ("Total Grade Points  = ");  PUT (TOTAL_POINTS);          NEW_LINE;
     PUT ("Total Semester Hours = ");  PUT (TOTAL_HOURS);           NEW_LINE;
     PUT ("Grade Point Average = ");  PUT (GRADE_POINT_AVERAGE);  NEW_LINE;

end GRADE_POINT_AVERAGE_PROGRAM;
```

this variety in data typing gives programmers the flexibility and versatility to solve many different kinds of problems.

Control Statements

Like Pascal, Ada has the basic control statements necessary for structured programming. These statements include IF-THEN-ELSE (for conditional transfer), CASE (for selection among multiple choices), WHILE (for loops), and FOR (for counted loops). It does not have an exact counterpart to Pascal's explicit REPEAT-UNTIL statement. Ada does, however, have an EXIT statement that can be used to exit a loop based on a condition tested at the loop's end. These straightforward control statements provide the programmer with the basic tools of structured programming.

RPG III

RPG (Report Program Generator) was introduced by IBM in 1964; an updated form of the language, RPG II, was released in 1970, and in 1979 RPG III became available. Unlike the other high-level languages we've described, RPG III is not really a general-purpose language. Its major function is the production of business reports. Originally designed for use with punched cards on minicomputer systems, RPG III has evolved into a modern, interactive, information-processing tool.

Features

A convenient language for certain business tasks

The main attraction of RPG III is the ease with which it enables users to handle straightforward business tasks such as accounts receivable, accounts payable, file updating, and accessing a data base. The user "programs" in RPG III by filling out special coding forms presented on the display screen. The detailed *specification forms* require the user to describe the files to be used, the format of any input, any calculations to be performed, and the desired format of the output report. The user does not have to worry about the logical procedures actually involved in producing reports. Thus users need not be programmers. Because RPG III is so easy to learn and use, it is quite popular with businesses that operate minicomputer systems.

RPG III's specialization limits the types of tasks it can perform. It works well for those simple data-processing tasks for which it was designed, but it has neither the power nor the versatility of a general-purpose language such as COBOL. Its restricted mathematical capabilities make it not applicable to scientific problems. Finally, RPG III is not a standardized language, although the versions produced by IBM tend to dominate the market.

Program Format

An RPG III program consists of three or four specification forms. These forms give the RPG III translator the information it needs to produce the desired report:

- *File description specification*, which identifies the input and output files to be used.
- *Input specification*, which describes the exact format of the data contained in the input file.

- *Output specification*, which describes the exact format of the output report.
- *Calculation specification*, which describes any mathematical computations to be performed.

Each line is entered into the computer through the keyboard. The user must stick to a fixed format because the RPG III translator requires that entries be placed in predefined columns. If this is done, however, the translator takes care of everything else.

Other Important High-Level Languages

There are several other high-level languages that are not as prevalent as the ones we've just discussed, but are important enough to be worthy of brief mention.

Some less common but significant languages

ALGOL

ALGOrithmic Language, or ALGOL, was developed in the early 1960s after long study by an international committee. No other computer language has had such a far-reaching influence on the design of subsequent languages. Designed with the scientific community in mind, ALGOL is noted for its clarity, elegance, and excellent control structures.

APL

APL, or A Programming Language, was introduced by IBM in 1968, although it was conceived by Kenneth Iverson in 1962. Expressly designed to be an interactive language, APL is especially well suited to handling data arrays and to performing mathematical computations quickly. It is characterized by the use of many special symbols, which requires a special APL keyboard.

APT

APT is short for Automatically Programmed Tools. This extremely specialized language is used for describing the operations involved in machine-cutting metal parts. Developed at the Massachusetts Institute of Technology (MIT) in the late 1950s, APT is a good example of a special purpose language. Industries employing automated manufacturing methods comprise the main audience for APT.

Forth

Invented by Charles Moore in the late 1960s, Forth is a powerful, yet flexible combination of programming language and operating system. Although somewhat difficult for beginners to understand and use, Forth is unique in allowing users to define their own new commands. This capability gives Forth programmers much creative freedom and is mainly responsible for the growing number of Forth fans.

LISP

Developed by a group headed by John McCarthy at MIT and introduced in 1960, LISP (for LISt Processing) was designed to manipulate lists of abstract symbols. Often used interactively, LISP is noted for being almost tailor-made for applications such as game playing, robot control, pattern recognition, mathematical proofs, and artificial intelligence.

LOGO

LOGO was derived from LISP and was developed at MIT by Seymour Papert. It is an interactive programming language with graphics output. LOGO was designed to combine the theories of artificial intelligence with the learning theories of famed psychologist Jean Piaget. The result is a language often used to teach children to program and also used to develop artificial intelligence applications. Children can draw pictures on the terminal screen by moving a little triangular pointer, informally referred to as the "turtle." This simple-to-use language lets users form statements by grouping commands together; the results of their instructions are immediately visible on the video display.

PL/I

PL/I, or Programming Language I, was sponsored by IBM and introduced in 1965. Intended as a general-purpose computer language applicable to both science and business, PL/I combines the best features of three earlier languages: FORTRAN, COBOL, and ALGOL. Even though it's an excellent language, for some reason PL/I has never achieved the popularity of FORTRAN and COBOL.

PROLOG

PROLOG, an acronym for PROgramming LOGic, was invented by Philippe Roussel at the University of Marseilles in the early 1970s. It now rivals LISP as the premier artificial intelligence language. PROLOG's strength lies in defining and manipulating logical relationships between pieces of data.

Smalltalk

Sometimes classified as an *object-oriented language*, Smalltalk was invented at Xerox's Palo Alto Research Center by Alan Kay. It makes extensive use of the mouse, which, as you'll recall from Chapter 4, is a graphic input device in the form of a little box the user moves about on top of a desk or table. Many of the concepts used in Smalltalk became the basis for today's user-friendly graphical operating systems, such as that of the Apple Macintosh.

SNOBOL4

Developed at Bell Laboratories during the 1960s, SNOBOL4 is a powerful language for processing character strings. Its major application is to problems in which substantial amounts of data in character-string form must be processed in complex ways. SNOBOL4 is often used in the development of text editors, word processors, and high-level language translators.

APPLICATION GENERATORS

Application generators are the most abstract type of programming language. These systems are also known as *fourth generation languages (4GLs), very high-level languages*, and *nonprocedural languages*. Application generators attempt to make it as easy as possible for users to tell the computer what to do by eliminating many of the strict rules characteristic of high-level programming languages. With an application generator, the user typically concentrates on specifying the necessary input and the desired output instead of giving the computer explicit procedural instructions on how to convert input to output. Some application generator programs resemble human languages such as English. Others look like high-level languages, such as Pascal, but they have fewer format, syntax, grammar, and punctuation rules.

Application generators are sophisticated development tools designed to help end-users, who aren't necessarily expert programmers, produce their own application software. Many application generators are integrated systems that include everything you need to develop large application packages: source code editor, screen editor, report generator, prototyping facility, data base management system, compiler, and debugging aids. *A Closer Look* at the end of this chapter examines the use of a popular microcomputer application generator called the Clarion Professional Developer.

Query languages are another type of abstract, nonprocedural programming language similar to application generators. A query language enables users to interrogate and access computer data bases by means of Englishlike statements. For example, a user request in a query language might look like this:

> Get sales and personnel files and print names and salaries by department and highest salary.

Users can learn to use a query language with very little instruction. (We'll have more to say about query languages in Chapter 12 when we talk about data base systems.)

Application generators and query languages are becoming more popular as computer hardware and software systems become increasingly sophisticated. They offer many advantages, especially to the end-user who may not be trained as a programmer. Even professional programmers often find these nonprocedural languages easier to use than traditional high-level programming languages. One particularly important advantage of application generators is that they often significantly cut the time it takes to develop application software. For some organizations, this reduction in development time can be more important than any other consideration. Some industry experts predict that application generators and query languages will gradually replace conventional high-level programming languages as tools for software development.

For now, however, there are still some disadvantages to application generators and query languages. Many of them are invented and sold by only one company. With a few notable exceptions, such as Structured Query Language (SQL) which we will discuss in Chapter 12, there is little industry standardization. Application generators generally cannot offer the same degree of control over low-level hardware functions as can Modula-2, C, and Ada. Consequently, application generators are typically not suitable for the development of operating systems and programs that control electronic devices. In many cases, programs created with application generators execute less efficiently than programs created with high-level languages

End-user computing

such as Modula-2, C, and Ada. Application generators are often more expensive and require more memory and disk space than high-level language compilers. Finally, high-level languages are still widely used to develop the great majority of application packages. This means that a lot of users and programmers who are already familiar with conventional high-level languages are hesitant about learning an entirely new development system, even if it would ultimately prove to be easier to use and take less time to create software.

WHAT MAKES A LANGUAGE GOOD?

Criteria for choosing a programming language

This section could also be entitled "How to Choose a Language." Since we've described or mentioned several popular computer programming languages and there are others as well, the task of choosing any particular language for a problem at hand might seem bewildering. In fact, programmers often have no choice—the decision regarding what language is to be used has already been made by management. Whether the decision is made by management or programmer, the following characteristics should be taken as the criteria for judging the programming language:

- *Suitability to the problem.* For example, because of its limited computational capabilities, COBOL is much less appropriate than FORTRAN for a program to compute a rocket's trajectory.

- *Clarity and simplicity.* A language with straightforward concepts and a simple program structure can help the user think about the solution before the program is even written and can help reduce errors discovered during and after development.

- *Efficiency.* Ideally, a language should allow (1) efficient program execution (it runs fast), (2) efficient program translation (it compiles fast), (3) efficient memory use (it takes up little room), and (4) efficient program development (programs can be written quickly).

- *Availability and support.* Is there a translator program available for the language for your computer, and can you get help using the language? Sometimes this factor winds up being the deciding one. Many organizations have only one or a few language translators and can't afford to purchase a new one for a specific application.

- *Consistency.* Many organizations have a policy that all their software must be written in a single language or in one of a small number of languages. Besides being easier for programmers, who only have to know one or a few languages, this policy means that new programs will work with already existing ones. A language is often chosen because it has been successfully and extensively used in the past.

A Closer Look

Using an Application Generator

Application generators allow users to create their own software without many of the tedious format, syntax, grammar, and punctuation rules of conventional high-level programming languages. Because application generators are more abstract and less procedural, users can better concentrate on specifying *what* they want the computer to do instead of exactly *how* the computer should do it.

Clarion Professional Developer from Clarion Software is a popular application generator for IBM-compatible microcomputers. This system, which currently sells for $695, can slash total development time and effort for many common business and data-processing applications. In many cases, entire application packages can be developed without having to write any source code at all.

The Clarion Professional Developer primarily develops programs by designing data files, menus, output screens, and reports. The data files hold collections of related facts, while the menu contains a list of available program options. An output screen displays the application's results on the terminal, with a report being printed on paper. After specifying the data files, menus, output screens, and reports of an application, you can tell Clarion what to do with them. This process is similar to prototyping, except that the Clarion Professional Developer automatically generates structured source code in the Clarion programming language directly from your prototypes. In other words, the Clarion Professional Developer allows you to eliminate prototyping as a preliminary step, making it an integral part of program design. Program design and coding are done concurrently, so you can create applications with much less time and effort than when you use a conventional high-level language.

To give you an idea of what it's like to use the Clarion Professional Developer, let's create a simple application. This application will display, maintain, and print a computerized telephone directory. Once you set up the application and initially enter the names, addresses, and phone numbers of your acquaintances, you can use the directory to look up any of this information. New data can be added and old data deleted from the directory. Finally, the entire directory can also be printed. All this will be done via an attractive, user-friendly menu.

The first step is to start up the Clarion Professional Developer program by entering the word *CLARION* into a computer on which the system is installed. Clarion's main menu will appear on your screen, as shown at right.

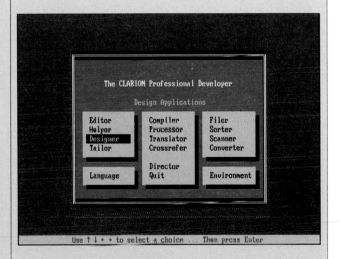

The Designer allows you to convert your ideas into source code automatically. After starting up the Clarion system, you simply select the Designer from the main

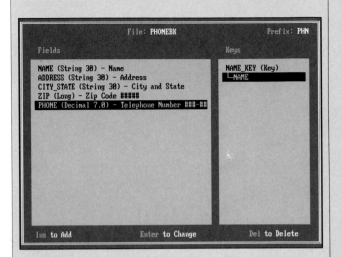

```
                    File: PHONEBK                    Prefix: PHN

  Fields                                    Keys

  NAME (String 30) - Name                   NAME_KEY (Key)
  ADDRESS (String 30) - Address               └─NAME
  CITY_STATE (String 30) - City and State
  ZIP (Long) - Zip Code #####
  PHONE (Decimal 7.0) - Telephone Number ###-##


  Ins to Add              Enter to Change              Del to Delete
```

menu. You can then define your data files and specify the actions your application will perform.

In the Clarion development system, an *application* consists of files and procedures. Files contain data, while procedures process screens, edit data files, print reports, and direct any other operations the application must perform. The first step of designing an application is to define its files. The screen above, for example, shows the Clarion File Worksheet for specifying the contents of the phone book data file.

The next step is to define each of your application's procedures. Clarion has five types of procedures:

Menu	Selects another procedure for execution
Table	Displays the contents of a data file on the screen

Form	Allows you to update the contents of a data file
Report	Prints a report
Other	Performs other operations, written in Clarion language

The first procedure in our telephone directory application is a menu that simply lists the three available options. When it is finished, our menu will have the appearance of the screen at bottom left.

Each menu in an application is designed with a Menu Screen Worksheet. The Menu Screen Worksheet is essentially a full-screen editor that lets you specify the exact appearance of a menu. Our telephone directory has only one menu. The following three screens illustrate how this menu is designed with a Menu Screen Worksheet:

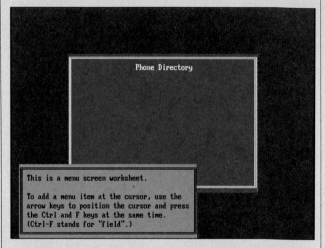

```
                    Phone Directory




  This is a menu screen worksheet.

  To add a menu item at the cursor, use the
  arrow keys to position the cursor and press
  the Ctrl and F keys at the same time.
  (Ctrl-F stands for "field".)
```

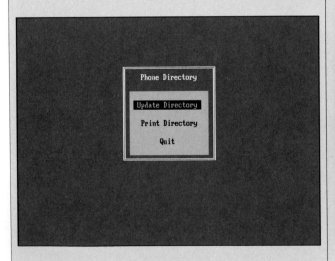

```
                    Phone Directory

                  Update Directory

                   Print Directory

                        Quit
```

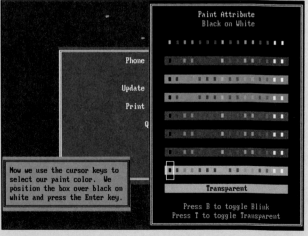

```
                                        Paint Attribute
                                        Black on White

                          Phone

                          Update

                          Print

                          Q

                                          Transparent

  Now we use the cursor keys to
  select our paint color. We        Press B to toggle Blink
  position the box over black on     Press T to toggle Transparent
  white and press the Enter key.
```

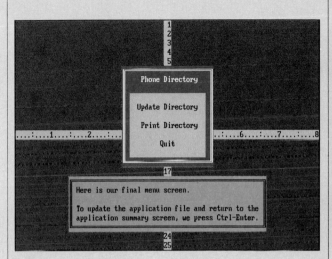

Here is our final menu screen.

To update the application file and return to the application summary screen, we press Ctrl-Enter.

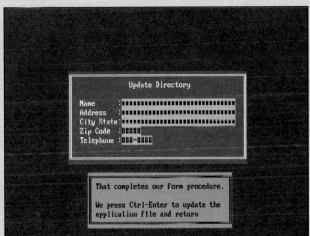

That completes our form procedure.

We press Ctrl-Enter to update the application file and return

After the menu screen is designed, you can define the other procedures in the telephone directory application. These will include a table procedure to display the telephone directory on the screen, a form procedure to let you update the telephone directory, and a report procedure to print out the entire telephone directory. The following screens illustrate this process. The final screen is the Application Summary Screen, which is automatically updated as you build your application and shows all of the files and procedures.

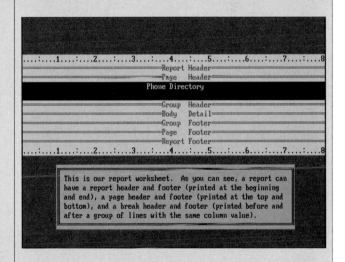

This is our report worksheet. As you can see, a report can have a report header and footer (printed at the beginning and end), a page header and footer (printed at the top and bottom), and a break header and footer (printed before and after a group of lines with the same column value).

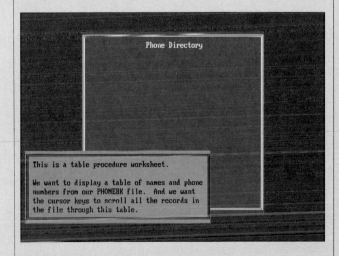

This is a table procedure worksheet.

We want to display a table of names and phone numbers from our PHONEBK file. And we want the cursor keys to scroll all the records in the file through this table.

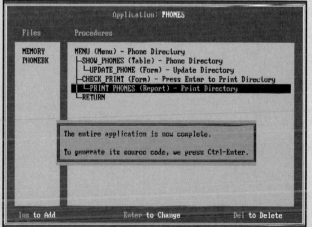

The entire application is now complete.

To generate its source code, we press Ctrl-Enter.

Once the entire application has been specified, you can have the Clarion Professional Developer automatically generate structured source code in Clarion's own language. The source code is then compiled and tested. The final result is a stand-alone application package that displays, maintains, and prints a telephone directory. The three screens at right, for example, show what happens when you select the Update Directory option from our newly created Phone Directory application.

Once the Phone Directory application has been thoroughly tested to see that it works correctly, it can be used on a routine basis. After the application has been compiled, you do not need to run the Clarion Professional Developer to use the Phone Directory. This actual application program has been developed by simply filling in a series of Clarion Designer worksheets, without writing a single line of source code in a high-level language.

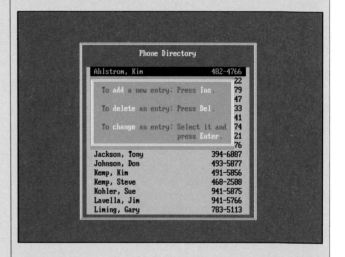

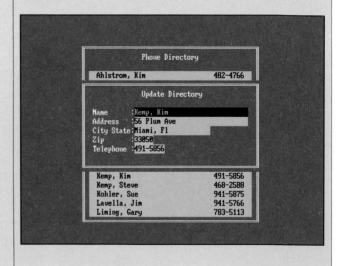

Summary

Programming Languages in General

A programming language is a set of symbols and usage rules employed to direct the operations of a computer.

Characteristics of Programming Languages Every programming language has instructions for input and output, for calculations, for transfer of control, and for data movement, storage, and retrieval. In addition, most languages allow comments.

Levels of Language The four general categories of computer languages can be arranged hierarchically. From the lowest to the highest level, the classifications are machine languages, assembly languages, high-level languages, and application generators.

Machine Languages

A machine language consists of binary numbers that represent instructions, memory locations, and data so they can be processed by a specific computer model. Its own machine language is the only language that can be directly used by a computer.

Assembly Languages

An assembly language consists of mnemonic symbols that stand for the zeros and ones of machine language. An assembly language program is also machine-specific and must be translated into machine language by an assembler.

High-Level Languages

A high-level language consists of statements that are closer to human language or mathematical notation than are machine or assembly languages. High-level languages are machine-independent.

Compilers and Interpreters High-level languages must be translated into machine language by either compilers or interpreters. A compiler translates an entire program all at once; an interpreter translates and executes one statement at a time.

The Advantages of High-Level Languages High-level languages are easier to learn, write, correct, and revise than are assembly or machine languages. The programmer using a high-level language can pay more attention to the problem at hand and less attention to machine-specific details.

Major High-Level Languages

The most important high-level languages are those that are widely applicable and/or influential in the development of other languages.

FORTRAN FORTRAN is a popular language among scientists, engineers, and mathematicians because of its simplicity, conciseness, standardization, efficiency, and numerical precision.

COBOL COBOL has widespread application in businesses and is noted for its ability to handle the input and output of large volumes of alphanumeric data, its machine-independence, and its Englishlike statements.

BASIC BASIC is a notably simple language that is easy to learn and to use. It is the most widely used high-level language for microcomputers.

Pascal Pascal is a general-purpose, high-level language. Its simplicity, elegance, and embodiment of the concepts of structured programming and top-down design have made it extremely popular.

Modula-2 As Pascal's descendant, Modula-2 adds features for developing large software systems, team projects, and controlling low-level hardware functions.

C C is a concise, versatile, and portable general-purpose language. It is the language of choice for many operating system and application package programmers.

Ada Ada, commissioned by the Department of Defense, is a powerful language, applicable to a wide range of problems.

RPG III RPG III is a specialized language, designed to make it easy for users to handle common business tasks like report generation and file updating.

Other Important High-Level Languages ALGOL is a highly influential language noted for its clarity, elegance, and excellent control structures. APL is especially well suited to handling data arrays and performing mathematical computations quickly. APT is a specialized language used for programming automated machine tools. Forth is a powerful, flexible combination of programming language and operating system. LISP is designed to manipulate lists of abstract symbols. LOGO combines artificial intelligence and learning theories into an easy-to-use, interactive programming language. PL/I combines the best features of FORTRAN, COBOL, and ALGOL and is suited to both science and business applications. Prolog is a language used to develop artificial intelligence applications. Smalltalk is an object-oriented language that makes extensive use of the mouse. SNOBOL4 is widely used for processing character strings.

Application Generators

Application generators attempt to make it as easy as possible for users to tell the computer what they want instead of having to specify exactly how to do it. Query languages, which enable users to interrogate and access data bases, are in some ways similar to application generators.

What Makes a Language Good?

Suitability to the problem at hand, clarity and simplicity, efficiency, availability and support, and consistency are the criteria to be used when choosing a programming language.

Computer Concepts

As an extra review of the chapter, try defining the following terms. If you have trouble with any of them, refer to the page number listed.

programming language *243*
comments *244*
operation code (opcode) *244*
operand *244*
mnemonic symbols *245*
symbolic addressing *245*
assembler *245*
object code *245*

machine-independence *247*
portability *247*
compilers *247*
interpreters *247*
data types *248*
control statements *248*
subroutine *249*
function *249*

arrays *249*
reserved words *252*
compilation unit *260*
coroutine *260*
interrupt *260*
interrupt handler *260*
embedded computers *265*
application generators *271*
query languages *271*

Review Questions

1. What is the difference between human languages and computer languages?
2. Describe the four general classes of instructions found in all computer languages.
3. What are the four levels of programming languages?
4. What are the two parts of a machine language instruction?
5. Why is programming in machine language so difficult?

6. How do assembly languages differ from machine languages?
7. Why would a programmer want to use assembly language?
8. Why is machine-independence a desirable trait for a programming language to have?
9. What is the difference between a compiler and an interpreter?
10. What advantages do high-level languages have compared to low-level languages?
11. Give a short description of each of the major high-level languages covered in this chapter.
12. List and briefly characterize the other important high-level languages mentioned in this chapter.
13. How do application generators and query languages differ from high-level languages?
14. What are the criteria that should be applied when choosing a programming language?
15. Why is FORTRAN the top "number crunching" language?
16. What are FORTRAN's two types of subprograms? Describe.
17. What are some of the drawbacks of COBOL?
18. Which of the major high-level languages discussed is best for teaching structured programming? Why?
19. What high-level language is most popular for programmers who develop operating systems, compilers, and application packages for microcomputers?
20. Which language was designed for programming embedded computers? What capabilities and negative features does it have?

True or False

1. Programming languages have vast vocabularies and functions, similar to human languages.
2. Every machine language instruction consists of two parts, an operation code and an operand.
3. Assembly languages are more difficult to use than machine languages.
4. Assemblers perform a task similar to that performed by compilers.
5. FORTRAN was the first commercially available high-level language.
6. Reserved words are words reserved for a specific computer.
7. Of the major high-level languages discussed, BASIC is the most complex to learn and use.
8. RPG III was introduced by IBM as a general-purpose language.
9. LOGO was developed to control machine tools.
10. LISP is especially effective for robot control, pattern recognition, and artificial intelligence.

Multiple Choice

1. Assembly languages are written in:
   (a) zeros and ones   (b) mnemonics   (c) assemblers
2. A chief advantage of high-level language over assembly language is:
   (a) portability   (b) symbolic addressing   (c) octal numbers
3. The most widely used high-level language for microcomputers is:
   (a) COBOL   (b) C   (c) BASIC
4. The language developed to succeed Pascal for software developers is:
   (a) FORTRAN   (b) Modula-2   (c) Ada

5. A program which temporarily suspends one program to permit a high-priority one to run is:
   (a) a compilation unit   (b) a coroutine   (c) an interrupt handler

6. Key words in C must be written in:
   (a) lower-case letters   (b) mnemonics   (c) hexadecimal notation

7. The special-purpose language developed at MIT to control machine tools is:
   (a) APL   (b) Forth   (c) APT

8. The language which became the basis of the operating system of the Apple Macintosh is:
   (a) Smalltalk   (b) LISP   (c) LOGO

9. The most abstract programming languages are:
   (a) object-oriented   (b) application generators (c) arrays
       languages

10. A key advantage of query languages is:
    (a) economy of memory   (b) control of electronic   (c) ease of use
        and disk space   devices

A Sharper Focus

1. Do you think that learning a computer language is less difficult than learning a human language? Why?
2. Can you detect trends in the evolution of computer languages? What are they?

Projects

1. Many computer games are programmed in assembly language. Find out why this is so, and write up your findings in a report.

2. Programs written in a high-level language for a particular computer won't always run on another computer, even though the other computer has a compiler for the same language. In other words, high-level language programs sometimes do not have 100% portability. Write a report that explains why this happens. Include some specific examples of this type of incompatibility.

3. What programming languages are being used in the computer center at your school or office? Why were those languages chosen for their particular applications?

4. It has been reported that large bookstore chains sell more computer-related books than novels. From the titles of available books, it seems that a large percentage of the computer books sold are about programming languages. Survey local bookstores (and libraries) and report on the overall number of computer books available compared to the number on programming languages.

9

Application
Packages

In This Chapter

Focus On

Finding Inexpensive Software

Shareware, and software that is in the public domain, offer the computer user an inexpensive, yet often valuable, option from expensive commercial software packages. Finding the best package to solve a problem can be time-consuming given the enormous wealth of software available. In addition to the recommendations of your friends and colleagues, here are a few other sources for you to consider.

To find the best software package to satisfy your needs, your local computer user group (such as the Boston Computer Society) or professional society (such as your local ACM or DPMA chapter) can be a very valuable resource. Recommendations from members who may have dealt with a similar problem are always helpful. User groups may also have software reference libraries that members can access. In addition, user group newsletters may give reviews and recommendations for software, as well as instruction.

On-line commercial services such as CompuServe and GEnie and various bulletin boards offer another source for this software. The advantage of getting software in this manner is, of course, speed and efficiency. A user with a modem and a subscription can log onto a favorite information service or bulletin board, access the cata-

log of available programs, and download the desired files. The user should run error-checking software to make sure that the whole program was transmitted correctly.

Numerous catalogs are also available, offering a mind-numbing array of programs. For the well-informed user, these catalogs can prove a real gold mine.

For those with less time or experience, the mail order software house offers another option. Although these vary in quality and service, several that have been distributors of good quality programs include the Public Software Library (PSL) and PC-Software Interest Group (PC-SIG). Both of these commercial services offer proven and current packages for a modest price.

In the early days of computers, individuals, businesses, and other organizations all had to produce their own software. Just as the pioneers in this country had to grow their own food, build their own homes, and make their own clothes, the first computer users had to be completely self-sufficient as far as programming was concerned; no ready-made programs were available. Eventually, the hardware companies that produced computers began to offer software for their own customers. The programs provided by hardware manufacturers, however, were too general to meet all of their customers' software needs. As time passed and the number of computers grew, many users realized that they had common needs and that they were using computers to solve common problems. Soon, entrepreneurs started independent software firms to develop and sell programs with the end-user in mind. The software products offered by these vendors are called application packages. An **application package** is simply a single program or several related programs designed to accomplish some specific set of tasks. These packages put computers to practical use by helping people perform all kinds of workaday jobs. Literally thousands of application packages are now on the market for all kinds of computers and virtually everyone who uses computers uses them. This software is the primary reason most people learn, use, and buy computers, especially microcomputers. In this chapter we examine the most important types of application packages.

TYPES OF APPLICATION PACKAGES

Application packages are commonly purchased separately from computer hardware. Since the introduction of microcomputers, the number of companies developing application software has increased dramatically, and many different types of application packages are sold today. So many, in fact, that it would be impossible to mention them all. One way to classify application packages is by what they do, and three categories stand out clearly as the most prevalent types of application software: word processing, spreadsheet, and data base management. In addition, communications, graphics, integrated software, desktop publishing, business and finance, statistics and mathematics, education, entertainment, and hypertext packages are also commonly used.

Packages are classified by what they do

The most popular packages

WORD PROCESSING

Word-processing packages are perhaps the most popular type of application software. It's been estimated that over 90 percent of all computer owners have at least one word-processing program. Simply stated, a **word-processing package** helps you enter, store, modify, format, copy, and print text. Such software gives a computer and printer the power to do much more than an ordinary typewriter. Many of the tedious and time-consuming tasks associated with typing can be done automatically by word-processing packages. For example, most word processors can start a new line when you reach the margin, start a new page when you reach the bottom of a page, center titles, copy sections of text, alter line spacing, and even check for spelling errors. You can type, correct, and format your entire document on the computer display screen. Once you're satisfied that everything looks just right, you can print out any number of perfect copies on paper. Not only do word processors make it easy to enter and print text, but they allow you to store and update documents as well. We'll have more to say about this amazing tool in Chapter 14, but now let's examine the basic functions of a word-processing package and introduce a few of the most popular word processors being sold today.

The ultimate purpose of any word processor is the preparation of documents. Although today's word-processing programs are loaded with features, they all perform five basic functions: they create, edit, format, print, and manage documents.

Creating Documents

Whenever you start up a word-processing program, you initially have two choices: create a new document or work on an existing one. If you are creating a new document, the word processor asks you to supply a name for it and opens a new file on a disk. At first, this document file is empty and the word processor simply waits for you to enter text. Figure 9.1, for example, shows WordStar, a popular word-processing package for IBM-compatible microcomputers. Much of the screen is empty—reserved for the material you type. Depending on the word processor, a menu may appear across the top or bottom of the screen. In addition usually one or two more lines of information about your document are shown; for example, the name of the document file along with the page, line, and column numbers of your current location within the document. Sometimes a *ruler line* is also displayed to show your current margins and tab stop settings.

Features of word processors: the cursor, word-wrap, outlines, a thesaurus

Initially, the **cursor** is at the top left corner of the empty text area. This blinking underscore, vertical bar, or little box marks the exact position where text is to be inserted or where some other operation is to occur. To create a document, all you do is type the words and punctuation. Virtually all word processors have a feature called **word-wrap** that makes text entry easy and fast. Whenever you type a word that extends beyond the current right margin, that word is automatically "wrapped around," or moved down to the beginning of the next line. This allows you to type continuously without constantly checking to see if you're near the end of a line.

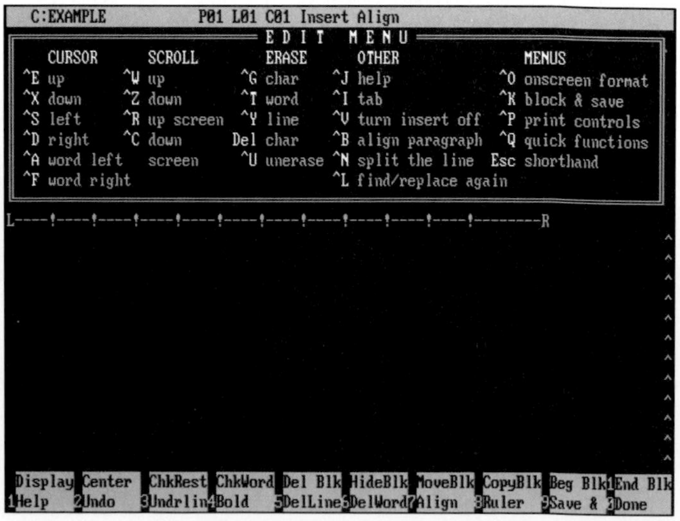

Figure 9.1 WordStar

This screen appears when you begin to create a document in WordStar. The top line lists the file name, page number, line number, column number, and indicators telling you that the insert mode and automatic right margin alignment are turned on. The box below the top line contains various commands you can execute while creating and editing a document (the ^ character means to press the Control key). The ruler line, which is directly below the Edit Menu, shows the positions of your left margin, tab stops, and right margin. Below the ruler line is the text area where you type your document. Finally, at the bottom of the screen is a menu that lists commands you can execute by pressing the function keys.

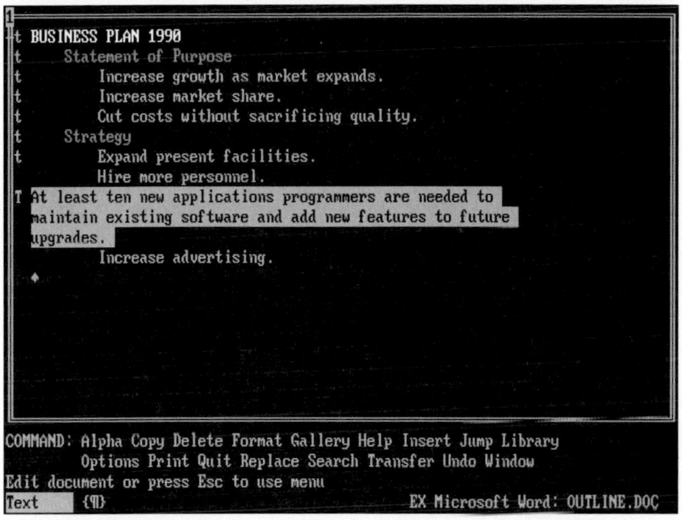

```
┌─────────────────────────────────────────┐
│1                                         │
│t BUSINESS PLAN 1990                      │
│t     Statement of Purpose                │
│t         Increase growth as market expands.│
│t         Increase market share.          │
│t         Cut costs without sacrificing quality.│
│t     Strategy                            │
│t         Expand present facilities.      │
│          Hire more personnel.            │
│T At least ten new applications programmers are needed to│
│  maintain existing software and add new features to future│
│  upgrades.                               │
│          Increase advertising.           │
│   ♦                                      │
│                                          │
│                                          │
│                                          │
│                                          │
│COMMAND: Alpha Copy Delete Format Gallery Help Insert Jump Library│
│        Options Print Quit Replace Search Transfer Undo Window│
│Edit document or press Esc to use menu    │
│Text    {¶}              EX Microsoft Word: OUTLINE.DOC│
└─────────────────────────────────────────┘
```

Figure 9.2 Outlining with Microsoft Word
This screen illustrates Microsoft Word's built-in outline processor. Headings can be typed and moved in or out to different levels. Text can be typed underneath the headings. When the text is "collapsed," as it is for the first seven headings, a t appears at the left edge of the screen to indicate that text appears beneath that heading. The text itself, however, disappears to reveal just the outline. If you want to see the text again, you can "expand" it as shown under the heading entitled *Hire more personnel.*

The carriage return (Enter key) need only be pressed to begin a new paragraph or to explicitly start a new line. Word-wrap is a great boon to typists because it increases both speed and accuracy.

Besides word-wrap, word-processing packages offer other aids to the creation of documents. For example, many high-level word processors have an **outline processor** that helps you design the structure of your document first and then fill in the details later. Figure 9.2 shows outline processing with Microsoft Word, a popular word-processing package with versions for both IBM-compatibles and Apple Macintosh microcomputers. You create an outline by typing headings and assigning levels to these headings. This outline then becomes the foundation for the rest of your document. Headings can be reordered, renumbered, and moved in or out to different levels. Text is inserted beneath each heading. You can collapse this text to view only your headings or expand headings to also display the text beneath them.

An **on-line thesaurus** is another word-processing feature that can come in handy when creating documents. Much easier and faster to use than an ordinary printed thesaurus, an on-line thesaurus gives you almost instant access to thousands of synonyms. All you have to do is place the cursor on the word you want to look up and press a certain combination of keys. As Figure 9.3 shows, the on-line thesaurus then presents on your screen any alternative terms it might contain. Press another keystroke combination and the alternative you select will immediately replace the original word. The Word Finder thesaurus shown in Figure 9.3, which comes with WordStar, contains nearly 220,000 synonyms

Editing Documents

Even the best typists make mistakes. Besides, many initially correct documents must frequently be updated, altered, or otherwise revised. Furthermore, word processors are extensively used to compose, and not just retype, written material. As any author will tell you, writing is a very dynamic process. Sentences are often changed many times before a document is finished. This constant editing may

Figure 9.3 Built-in Thesaurus

The screen shows Word Finder, a popular on-line thesaurus that comes with several word-processing programs (such as WordStar) and is also sold separately. Here it is being used to find synonyms for the word *beautiful.* To look up a word, all you do is place the cursor on the word, hold down the Alternate key, and type a 1. You can highlight any of the synonyms and press the Enter key to have it replace the original word.

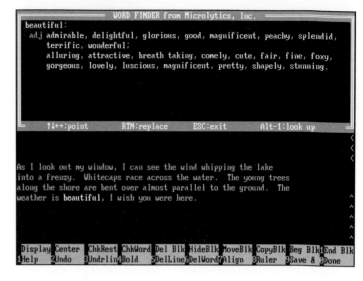

Insertions and deletions, cut-and-paste, spelling checkers include all kinds of activities that modify portions of text in various ways. Word processors are superb at performing a number of editing operations. For example, most word processors have editing features that let you view a document, insert text, delete text, cut-and-paste, search and replace, cancel commands, and check spelling.

View a Document

Documents are often too long to entirely fit on the display screen. A word-processing package must therefore provide some mechanism to view different parts of a document. This is usually done by pressing certain cursor movement keys to scroll through or jump to certain positions within a document. Commonly used keys

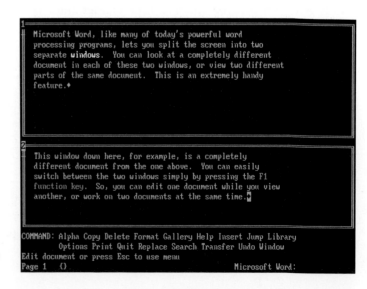

Figure 9.4 Split-Screen Word Processing

This figure illustrates the split-screen feature of Microsoft Word, which lets you edit two different documents or two different parts of the same document at the same time.

include arrow keys, Page Up and Page Down keys, and Home and End keys. Many word processors also let you use a mouse to move about within a document. Some packages even let you view two or more different parts of the same document, or completely different documents, on the screen at the same time in separate boxed-in areas called *windows*. As Figure 9.4 shows, Microsoft Word allows you to "split" your screen in this fashion.

Insert Text

Any amount of text from a single character to many pages may be inserted anywhere in a document. Word processing programs generally have two typing modes: insert and overwrite. When the **insert mode** is activated, all characters typed at the current cursor location simply push aside any text to the right. The opposite of the insert mode is the **overwrite mode,** in which characters typed at the current cursor location replace existing characters. Many word-processing programs operate in insert mode unless you explicitly switch to overwrite mode.

Delete Text

Text can be erased several different ways with a word-processing package. The simplest methods involve using the Backspace key, which usually erases the character to the left of the cursor, and the Delete key, which usually erases the character at the current cursor location. Word processors also have other operations for erasing entire words, lines, sentences, and paragraphs.

Cut-and-Paste

Most word-processing packages let you move existing text with a **cut-and-paste** operation. A segment of text is *marked* or *selected* in some fashion (see Figure 9.5). Then you can execute a special command to move it to a different location. **Copy-and-paste** is a similar editing operation in which the selected text is simply copied to the new location without deleting the original.

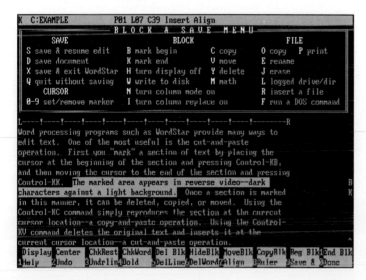

Figure 9.5 Cut-and-Paste

This screen shows a section of text that has been selected, or marked, in WordStar. Once the text has been highlighted in this manner, it can be moved (cut-and-paste operation) or copied (copy-and-paste operation) to some other part of the document.

Search and Replace

Most word processors can scan through an entire document to find a particular word or phrase (a *search* operation). A **search and replace** operation allows you to specify a substitute for the word or phrase being sought. For example, if you've consistently misspelled someone's name throughout an entire document, you can fix all the mistakes at once with a single repetitive search and replace operation.

Cancel Commands

Errors, of course, aren't limited to text entry. Sometimes you accidentally perform an editing procedure, such as deleting a line or doing a cut-and-paste. Maybe you've changed your mind and now want to cancel what you've just done. Fortunately, most word processors have an **undo** command that simply undoes whatever it was that you just did.

Check Spelling

A **spelling checker** is a standard feature in most of today's word-processing packages. Simply by executing a command, you can have the word-processing program automatically check every word in your document against a built-in spelling dictionary. Each word not found in this dictionary is then presented to you, and you can leave the word as it is, correct it yourself, or choose from a list of suggested corrections (see Figure 9.6). Some spelling checkers also let you look up specific words, or constantly check each word as you type, "beeping" whenever you enter a word that is not recognized.

Formatting Documents

Levels of formatting

Formatting a document involves arranging the text so that it looks nice when it is eventually printed. Formatting can be done on several different levels, and many features are available for controlling the appearance of text. Although different

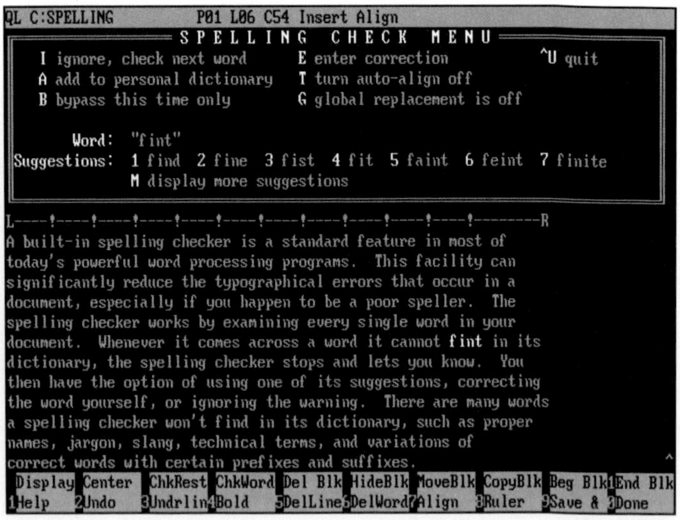

Figure 9.6 Spelling Checker

This screen illustrates WordStar's built-in spelling checker. To use it, all you do is move the cursor to the beginning of a document and press Control-QL. The program then checks the spelling of each word in the entire document against its internal spelling dictionary. Every time it finds a word it doesn't recognize, such as "fint" in this example, it lets you know. You can then substitute one of the suggested corrections, correct the word yourself, or ignore the warning.

word processors often use different terminology, the three basic levels used in document formatting are character, paragraph, and page.

Character Formatting

Character formatting allows you to vary the way individual letters or words are
presented. Most word-processing packages let you underline, use boldface or italic,
delete, and create superscript or subscript text within a document. Graphics-based
word-processing programs give you an even wider selection of character-format-
ting options. All word processors for the Apple Macintosh and a few for IBM-
compatible microcomputers, for example, let you have different type fonts, styles,
and sizes in your documents (see Figure 9.7). A **font** or **typeface** is a set of letters,
numbers, punctuation marks, and other symbols with a consistent appearance.
This appearance may be slightly altered by varying the character's style, such as
boldface or italic. The vertical size of characters is usually specified in **points,** a
typographical measure equal to 1/72 of an inch. Figure 9.7 shows some of these
character formats.

Paragraph Formatting

Paragraph formatting allows you to alter the appearance of individual blocks of text.
This usually involves controlling the alignment, indentation, and line spacing of a
paragraph.

Alignment refers to the way in which words are lined up within a paragraph.
There are four basic alignment variations: left, centered, right, and justified. Left
alignment is the most familiar; text is even along the left margin, while the right
margin is uneven or "ragged." Centered alignment puts each line midway between
the left and right margins. Right alignment is the opposite of left alignment. **Justified** alignment essentially combines both left and right alignment to create a
"block" look; spaces are inserted here and there so that every line is flush to both
the left and right margins. The paragraphs you see in this typeset book, for example, are justified.

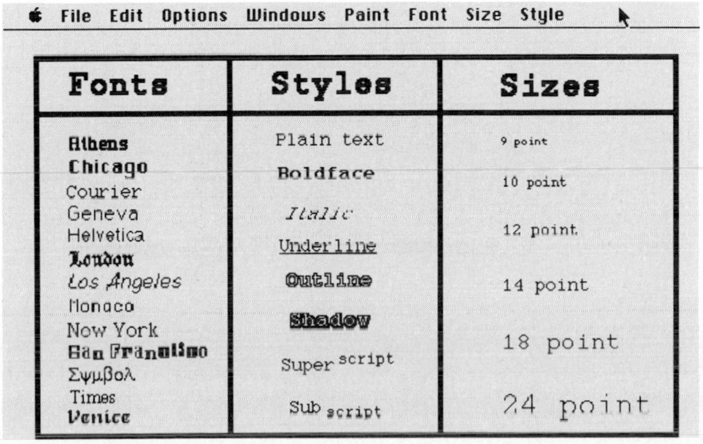

Figure 9.7 Fonts, Styles, and Sizes
This screen shows some of the fonts, styles, and typeface
sizes available in many word-processing programs for the
Apple Macintosh.

Indentation refers to how many spaces, if any, a paragraph is to be set in from the left or right margin. Most paragraphs simply have their first line indented several spaces to the right.

Spacing refers to the distance between the lines of text within a paragraph or the distance between the paragraphs. Single-spacing, for example, leaves no blank lines between adjacent lines of text, double-spacing leaves one blank line, and triple-spacing leaves two blank lines.

Page Formatting

Page formatting allows you to specify the general organization of an entire page of text. This can involve setting the left margin, right margin, and any tab stops. The number of lines to appear on each page can be specified, along with the position and format of page numbers. Many word processors let you put the same title, called a **running head,** at the top of every page. Many other formatting options are offered by today's word processors. Fortunately, you usually don't need to explicitly set them all. There are preprogrammed, or *default*, settings good enough for most situations. If you do need to specify a number of special settings for certain types of documents, many word-processing packages let you set up style sheets. A **style sheet** is a collection of formatting instructions that can be saved in a file and applied to different documents. Instead of respecifying each formatting instruction every time you create or edit a particular type of document, you can simply tell the word processor to use an existing style sheet. If you were writing a book, for example, you might create a style sheet that specifies the format for all chapters, including your settings for margins, line spacing, indentation, page length, page numbering, and a running head.

Printing Documents

Controlling the printer

The basic goal of every word processor is to produce documents on paper. So, an essential component of any system is a printer. The word-processing package takes charge of the printer and translates the document you see on the screen to pages formatted on paper. Most word processors provide facilities to help you control various aspects of this printing process (see Figure 9.8). For example, you can usually print parts of a document, print several copies, control the paper feed, specify the print quality, select between two printers, use print spooling, do print queuing, and mail-merge.

Printing Parts of a Document

Most of the time, you print an entire document when you are finished working on it. On occasion, however, you may only want to print a single page or a range of several pages from a document. Most word processors let you do this.

Printing Copies

When you need several copies of the same document, instead of waiting until each copy is finished and then initiating another print operation, most word processors will let you print several copies of a document with a single command.

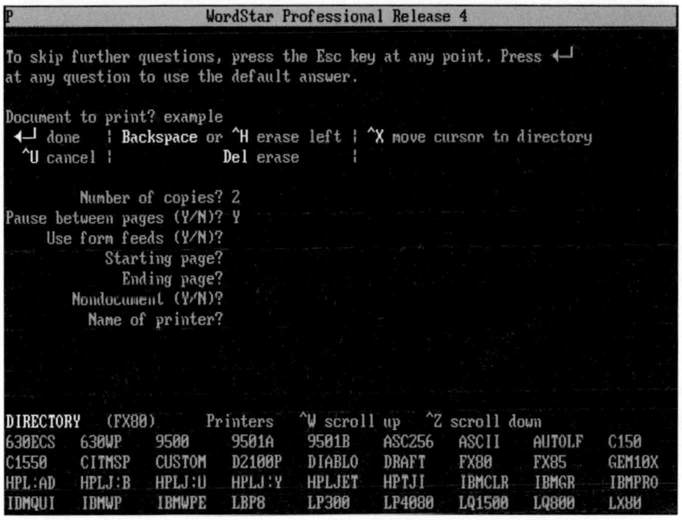

```
P              WordStar Professional Release 4

To skip further questions, press the Esc key at any point. Press ↵
at any question to use the default answer.

Document to print? example
 ↵ done     ¦ Backspace or ^H erase left ¦ ^X move cursor to directory
 ^U cancel              Del erase       ¦

       Number of copies? 2
Pause between pages (Y/N)? Y
   Use form feeds (Y/N)?
       Starting page?
         Ending page?
     Nondocument (Y/N)?
      Name of printer?




DIRECTORY   (FX80)     Printers   ^W scroll up  ^Z scroll down
630ECS  630WP   9500    9501A   9501B   ASC256  ASCII   AUTOLF  C150
C1550   CITMSP  CUSTOM  D2100P  DIABLO  DRAFT   FX80    FX85    GEM10X
HPL:AD  HPLJ:B  HPLJ:U  HPLJ:Y  HPLJET  HPTJI   IBMCLR  IBMGR   IBMPRO
IDMQUI  IDMWP   IBMWPE  LBP8    LP300   LP4000  LQ1500  LQ800   LX80
```

Figure 9.8 Printing

This screen illustrates the options you have when printing a document with WordStar.

Paper Feed

Many printers can use single sheets of paper, like preprinted letterhead, as well as continuous fan-fold computer paper. Some can even print on envelopes, gummed labels, and checks. Sheet feeders or paper trays can be attached to many printers so that you can put a whole stack of blank pages in the printer at once. This way, single sheets can be fed into the printer automatically. If you're going to use single sheet paper and your printer doesn't have a sheet feeder or paper tray, you will have to feed in each blank page by hand. In these cases, the word processor must be told to pause between pages so that a new sheet can be manually inserted each time.

Print Quality

Many word-processing packages offer several possible print modes. Dot-matrix printers may have a **draft mode** for quick, lower quality output; a medium-quality mode, which is a bit slower, but easier to read; and a true **letter-quality mode,** which looks as good or better than typewriter output, for final versions. Other printers, like daisy-wheel printers and laser printers, always produce letter-quality output. Some word processors and printers can use **proportional spacing,** which allots different amounts of space for different characters. For example, a proportionally spaced i takes up less space than a w. Proportional spacing makes the print look more professional and works better for justified text. Although it ultimately depends on your printer, most word processors give you some control over print quality features.

Printer Selection

It's not uncommon to connect two printers to the same computer. For example, you might use an inexpensive dot-matrix printer for everyday use and a laser printer for special projects. Many word processors can accommodate two printers by letting you select which one you want to use to print a particular document.

Print Spooling

Print spooling, also called **print buffering,** is the ability to print one document while you work on another. Once you initiate printing a document, it proceeds in the background, and you are free to use the word processor for something else. This is possible because most printers operate much more slowly than computers can send them data. Word processors that have print spooling can save you a great deal of time if you frequently print long documents.

Print Queuing

A queue is a first-come-first-served line, like a line you might stand in to buy movie tickets. Print queuing is the ability to specify a list of documents to be printed. Some word processors have this capability, which works especially well with print spooling.

Mail-Merge

Word processing is commonly used to create form letters. This process, often called **mail-merge,** involves combining a master document with a data file. The master document contains the main body of text along with instructions for merging the data file. The data file contains the variable information that will be used to "fill in the blanks" of the master document. For example, a form letter could be the master document, and a separate list of names and addresses could be the data file. A special print command is then used to merge the two and print out "personalized" form letters.

Managing Documents

Organizing files of documents

One of the most important advantages word processors have over ordinary type-writers is that they can store documents in disk files. Even after a document is printed, it's usually saved in secondary storage. Besides providing a compact method of keeping documents, disk storage allows you to quickly retrieve, view, and extract material from existing documents. Word processors help you organize your documents by offering several file management facilities (see Figure 9.9). You can save documents in their own disk files, load existing documents from their disk files into memory, combine files, delete files, copy files, rename files, and display directories of document files.

Popular Word-Processing Programs

The best-selling programs

Probably more microcomputer word-processing packages exist than any other single type of application software. For some reason, developers keep releasing word processors. It's unlikely that you'll find much consensus among users as to which word processor is the "best." Everybody seems to have their own particular favorite. So, there is no way that we could come up with a comprehensive list of all the popular microcomputer word processors. Three packages, however, stand out from the rest of the pack, even if only by a little bit: WordStar, WordPerfect, and Micro-

Figure 9.9 Managing Documents
This menu shows the document management options you have with WordStar.

soft Word—popular, powerful word processors with versions that run on a number of different computers.

WordStar

WordStar, from MicroPro International Corporation, is one of the best-known, most long-lived microcomputer application packages. Originally introduced in mid-1979, WordStar became the most popular program for early microcomputers, including the Apple II. When the IBM Personal Computer became a hit in 1981, MicroPro released an IBM-compatible version. It has been estimated that over a million copies of WordStar have been sold so far, and at least a million more illegal copies have been made. WordStar is the standard against which many other word processors are compared.

WordPerfect

WordPerfect from WordPerfect Corporation just might be the most widely used microcomputer word-processing package. Some industry experts estimate that WordPerfect has captured about 30 percent of the market, twice that of other popular word processors such as Microsoft Word. Since its introduction in October of 1982, WordPerfect has won the highest praise from both reviewers and users alike. A rich set of powerful new features seems to be added with every release. Versions have been developed to run on many different machines, including IBM, Apple II, Apple Macintosh, Commodore Amiga, Atari ST, and Digital VAX microcomputers.

Microsoft Word

Microsoft Word is a state-of-the-art word-processing package for both IBM-compatible and Apple Macintosh computers. First introduced in April 1983, Word became the program of choice for many people who own laser printers. Word is generally used with a graphics display and a mouse. Like WordPerfect, Microsoft Word includes many advanced word-processing features.

SPREADSHEET

Spreadsheet packages are a relatively new type of application software initially designed especially for microcomputers. A **spreadsheet package** allows you to enter, manipulate, and store tables of numbers and text. In 1978, an MIT graduate named Dan Bricklin, who was enrolled in Harvard Business School, believed that he was spending too much time laboring over the financial worksheets required for his accounting classes. (In accounting terminology, **worksheets,** also called **spreadsheets,** are tables of rows and columns of numerical data.) Bricklin had only two choices at the time: perform the many worksheet computations with a pocket calculator or make use of the school's mainframe computer. Neither of these alternatives particularly suited him. Because he couldn't store intermediate results except by writing them down, using a pocket calculator would be too time-consuming and error-prone. Gaining access to and programming the school's mainframe computer would be inconvenient. So Bricklin devised a microcomputer program that could easily manipulate tables of numbers and text. He and fellow MIT alumni Bob Frankston and Daniel Flystra formed a company called Software Arts in 1979 and sold the first spreadsheet program, called VisiCalc (short for Visible Calculator), which ran on Apple II microcomputers. Although VisiCalc is no longer sold, it paved the way for a whole new class of computer software.

Accounting programs for microcomputers; home applications

The spreadsheet program is an extremely flexible tool that can be applied to a wide range of common problems. Adept at manipulating tables of numbers, spreadsheet software is most often used to handle typical business accounting chores such as cash flow projections, depreciation calculations, balance sheets, and income statements. Spreadsheet programs can also be used to monitor investments, balance checkbooks, and work out home budgets. One of their most valuable features is that they allow users to ask ''what if'' questions about their data. This is possible because spreadsheet programs can automatically recalculate all entries whenever any single figure is changed. Once a worksheet has been set up, it's easy to alter values just to see what the results would be. The potential uses of spreadsheet programs are almost endless. In addition to the applications we've already mentioned, spreadsheet programs have also been used to create conversion tables, statistical analyses, financial models, and even games. This chapter's *A Closer Look* examines the use of today's most popular spreadsheet program, Lotus 1-2-3.

Worksheet Structure

Rows, columns, cells; size of the worksheet determined by amount of your computer's memory

When you start up a spreadsheet program, it presents you with a blank worksheet. Figure 9.10 shows a blank worksheet in Lotus 1-2-3. It consists of rows and columns of cells. A **cell** is simply the location at the intersection of a row and a column. Each cell in a worksheet is identified by its own **cell address,** a designation that specifies the cell's exact position within the worksheet. Most spreadsheet packages denote columns with letters (A, B, C, etc.) and rows with numbers (1, 2, 3, etc.). For example, the address of the upper left cell in a worksheet is A1.

The screen you see in Figure 9.10 shows only eight columns and 20 rows, but worksheets can be much larger than this. Just as a word processor lets you scroll the screen to work on long documents, spreadsheet programs let you do the same to work on truly massive worksheets. Spreadsheet programs not only let you scroll up and down, but also left and right. Many popular spreadsheet packages can address over 200 columns and more than 8000 rows. Lotus 1-2-3 Release 2.01, for

Figure 9.10 Lotus 1-2-3 Blank Worksheet
A blank worksheet appears when you start working with Lotus 1-2-3.

example, has 256 columns and 8192 rows. (The first 26 columns are labeled A to Z, the next 26 columns are labeled AA to AZ, the next 26 are labeled BA to BZ, and so on up to IV.) The actual number of cells that can be used, however, is dependent on the amount of memory installed in the computer.

Cell Contents

A worksheet cell is a place where you can put a piece of data. Three types of data can be entered into a cell: numbers, labels, and formulas.

Types of data included in a cell

Numbers

Numbers, of course, are simply quantities. They may be expressed as positive or negative values, with or without decimal points, and even in scientific notation. For example, all of the following numbers are valid cell entries: 10, -22, 1234, 0.5, -11.23, $4.32E+5$, and $-2.54E-5$. The last two numbers are given in scientific notation, which lets you compactly express very large and very small numbers. In other words, $4.32E+5$ is equal to 432,000 and $-2.54E-5$ is equal to -0.0000254.

Labels

A *label* is a textual heading, title, or other note that helps explain the contents of a worksheet. Labels are as essential to the usefulness of a spreadsheet program as numbers and formulas. In some cases, labels are not only used to annotate numbers, but are manipulated as textual data themselves. Most spreadsheet programs can be instructed to examine, select, and rearrange labels in various ways.

Formulas

If numbers and labels were all you could enter into cells, a spreadsheet program would be nothing but a primitive way to store data. You need formulas to tell the spreadsheet package what to do with your numbers and labels. A **formula** is an

Figure 9.11 Spreadsheet Formulas

This worksheet contains a very simple formula in cell C1: it tells the spreadsheet program to display the result of adding the contents of cells A1 and B1.

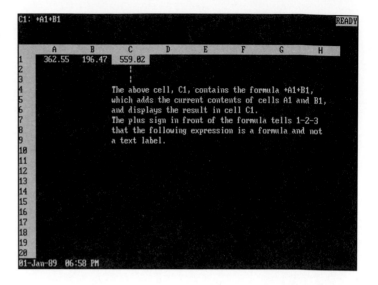

expression that instructs the spreadsheet program to perform calculations or other manipulations on the contents of specified cells. For example, the formula $+A1+B1$ tells the spreadsheet program to add the contents of cell A1 to the contents of cell B1, whatever those contents might be. The resulting sum is displayed in the cell containing the formula (see Figure 9.11).

Formulas are what make spreadsheet packages so powerful, flexible, and easy to use. Anyone with a basic understanding of arithmetic can learn how to construct all kinds of formulas. The notation used in constructing a formula is quite simple and is similar to that used in traditional mathematics. You've already seen that the plus sign (+) is used to symbolize addition, just as you would expect. Furthermore, the minus sign (−) represents subtraction, the asterisk (*) represents multiplication, and the forward slash (/) represents division. Besides these basic arithmetic operators, most spreadsheet programs also have symbols for raising a number to a power (exponentiation), combining text labels, and comparing numeric quantities.

Functions

Formulas can also contain special operations known as functions. A **function** is a ready-made procedure that performs tedious, complex, or often-used computations or other manipulations. A function is a shortcut that allows you to do an operation without specifying how it is done. All spreadsheet programs, for example, have a SUM function, which adds up the contents of a range of cells. All you have to do is supply the range of cells to be totaled, and the SUM function does the rest. For example, let's say that you wanted to total the contents of the first 10 cells in column B. In Lotus 1-2-3, you could do this with the formula $@SUM(B1..B10)$. The @ symbol indicates a function, and the B1..B10 designates the range of cells from B1 to B10. Many different functions are provided by most spreadsheet programs for all kinds of mathematical, statistical, financial, textual, logical, trigonometric, and logarithmic operations.

Entering and Editing Data

In many ways, a spreadsheet program is like a word-processing program that helps you work with numbers instead of words. You can enter, edit, format, calculate, copy, move, rearrange, print, and in some cases even graph data.

The numbers, labels, and formulas manipulated by a spreadsheet program don't just miraculously appear; one way or another, these entries must be typed at a keyboard. Although most spreadsheet programs can bring in data generated by other programs, such as word processors and data base managers, most worksheets are created by entering items directly into the spreadsheet program. Once data are entered, various editing features can be used to modify, insert, delete, select, copy, and move items.

Just as word-processing programs have a cursor to indicate where you can enter text, spreadsheet programs have a **cell pointer** that marks the location where you can enter data or initiate commands. The cell marked by the cell pointer is called the **current cell** or **active cell** and is shown on the screen as brightly lit, darkly outlined, or otherwise highlighted. Moving a cell pointer is similar to moving a word processor's cursor. Arrow keys, Page Up, Page Down, Home, End, and other combinations of keystrokes are used to move the cell pointer. A mouse is also used in many spreadsheet programs.

Cell pointers to enter data or give commands

When you begin a spreadsheet program, the cell pointer is initially at cell A1 and you can immediately enter data. You can, of course, move the cell pointer to any other cell before typing. In many spreadsheet programs, including Lotus 1-2-3, the characters you type appear at the top of the screen, above the worksheet in a place called the *control panel* (see Figure 9.12). Your entry isn't actually put into the cell until you press the Enter key or move the cell pointer to some other cell.

After you enter data, you can modify them, insert and delete rows and columns, and cut-and-paste and copy-and-paste ranges of cells within your worksheet. Spreadsheet programs provide a variety of commands to facilitate the editing of data within worksheets.

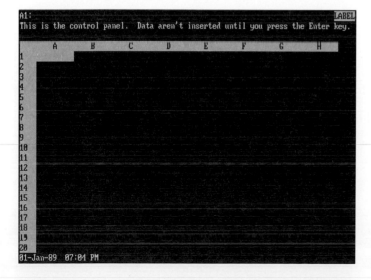

Figure 9.12 Control Panel

When you type data into a worksheet cell, it first appears up in the control panel. It isn't actually inserted into the cell until you press the Enter key.

Formatting Data

Different formats for different applications

Spreadsheet programs provide some of the same formatting capabilities as word-processing programs to make your worksheets easier to use and read. Since they are first and foremost number processors, spreadsheet programs can display and print numbers in a variety of ways. Although spreadsheet programs are most often used for manipulating monetary values, some are also used for scientific, engineering, and mathematical data processing. These different uses generally require different formats for the display of numbers in worksheets. Figure 9.13 shows some of the numeric formats common to spreadsheet programs.

Whichever numeric formats are used, you must make sure that numbers and formula results will completely fit into their cells. Unlike labels, numeric values cannot simply extend into empty adjacent cells. A number too long to fit into a cell will not be displayed. Most spreadsheet programs initially set the default width of all cells to 9 or 10 characters, but in some cases this isn't wide enough for long numbers. Fortunately, spreadsheet programs make it easy to change column widths. You can set a new default width for every column in the worksheet, or individually set the widths of particular columns. This lets you tailor your column widths for the best possible worksheet appearance.

Calculating Results

Changing the worksheet by changing a cell; automatic, manual, and smart recalculation

People use spreadsheet programs to perform calculations. The ease of use, power, and flexibility of these programs make them superior, in many situations, to other methods of calculation. In fact, spreadsheet programs are so easy to use that you usually don't even need to think at all about how they do what they do. Many spreadsheet programs, such as Lotus 1-2-3, have a feature called **automatic recalculation,** which updates the entire worksheet whenever you change the contents of a cell. This allows you to change existing figures to try out "what if" scenarios. If your worksheet is small, or doesn't have many formulas, automatic recalculation works quite nicely. The entire worksheet is updated so quickly that

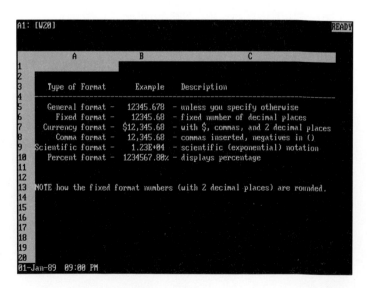

Figure 9.13 Numeric Formats

Spreadsheet programs can display numeric values in any one of several different formats.

you aren't even aware of the time it takes. Unfortunately, it can take several seconds to several minutes to recalculate every cell in a large or complex worksheet. Most spreadsheet programs with automatic recalculation also have a way to shut off this feature.

Manual recalculation is the alternative. This feature causes the formulas in a worksheet to be recalculated only when you explicitly tell the program to do so. When manual recalculation is turned on, you can enter values and formulas into your worksheet without having to wait for the program to update every cell after each entry. When you are finished editing, you press a special key or execute a command to tell the program to recalculate the worksheet. This can indeed save a lot of time and frustration when editing large or complex worksheets.

Although most spreadsheet programs have a manual recalculation feature, some programs don't have automatic recalculation as we've described it. Instead they use **smart recalculation.** This type of recalculation is performed automatically, unless you shut it off, but it doesn't update the entire worksheet every time you change a cell. When you enter new data or change the existing contents of a cell, smart recalculation only updates those cells, if any, that are affected by your entry. This is a good compromise between automatic and manual recalculation that can save time, yet always keep your worksheets updated.

Printing Worksheets

Worksheets, like documents produced with a word-processing program, are usually printed. Spreadsheet programs make it easy to produce professional-looking reports from your worksheets. Many worksheets can be printed in just one or two steps if you use the spreadsheet program's default print settings. On the other hand, you can play a more active role in designing page layouts by explicitly setting print-formatting options such as margins, page length, headings, and page numbering. With some spreadsheet programs, you can print the row numbers, column labels, and dividing lines. Even more useful, some programs can print a wide worksheet sideways on a page and continue it across several pages if necessary.

Default settings; designing page layouts; printing sideways.

Saving and Retrieving Worksheets

Most worksheets, like most documents, are saved on a disk even after they are printed. This allows you to go back and make updates or changes without having to re-enter the entire worksheet. Besides, it's often more compact and efficient to keep important documents and worksheets stored in disk files instead of ordinary paper files.

Storing documents for retrieving, editing, renaming

Typically, to save a worksheet you simply execute a File Save command or select the Save option from a File menu. The first time you save a worksheet, you may be required to enter a new name for its file. Otherwise, it may be given a default name such as *UNTITLED1* or *WORKSHEET1*. Once a worksheet has been named, it will always be saved under that name unless you specifically choose to rename it later.

Before you can change or update an existing worksheet, you must retrieve it from disk and load it into memory while you are running the spreadsheet program. This procedure is similar to saving a file. You either execute a File Retrieve command, or perhaps select the Open option from a File menu. In either case you'll probably be offered a list of names of worksheet files on your disk. After you choose a name from the list, or explicitly enter the name of a file, that worksheet will be loaded from the disk into memory, and you can then edit, format, print, and save the worksheet again.

Graphing

Producing a variety of graphs to display data

Ever since the introduction of Lotus 1-2-3, the ability to display and print graphs has been considered an essential feature of all but the most inexpensive spreadsheet programs. Bar graphs, pie charts, scatterplots, and line graphs can often communicate information much better than tables of numbers. Spreadsheet users, from business people to educators, frequently use such visual aids to help get their point across. Most spreadsheet programs make it easy to produce attractive graphs both on the display screen and printed on paper. These graphs can then be inserted into documents or photocopied onto transparency pages for use with an overhead projector. Figure 9.14 shows a graph on a display screen produced with Lotus 1-2-3.

Data Management

Organizing data in tables

One reason spreadsheet programs are so popular is that people understand them and feel comfortable using them. The tabular arrangement of data is well suited to a wide range of common tasks. It often makes sense to organize labels and numbers into rows and columns, even if you don't use a single formula. Consequently, many people use spreadsheet programs to store tables of data such as mailing lists, price lists, and inventories. Figure 9.15, for example, shows Lotus 1-2-3 being used to store a mailing list. Spreadsheet programs such as Lotus 1-2-3 typically include several features to help you create, maintain, search, and rearrange tables of data.

Figure 9.14 Spreadsheet Graph
Here is a simple graph produced with Lotus 1-2-3.

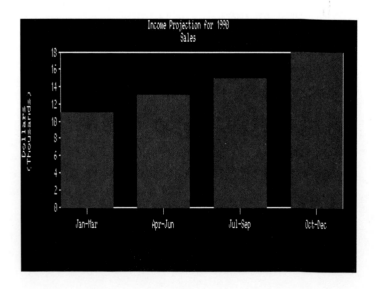

```
A3: [W15] 'Abel                                                   READY
          A          B            C              D      E    F
 1 Last Name    First Name   Street Address    City    State Zip
 2
 3 Abel         Larry        906 Busey #5      Urbana   IL   61801
 4 Alexander    Barbara      604 Armory        Champaign IL  61820
 5 Banks        David        1104 Grant Pl.    Champaign IL  61820
 6 Becker       Molly        310 W Paddock     Savoy    IL   61821
 7 Calhoon      Carrie       1007 Barclay      Tolono   IL   61880
 8 Carver       George       402 Main          Watseka  IL   60970
 9 Crawford     John         2012 Anderson     Urbana   IL   61801
10 Daily        Irene        2209 Philo        Urbana   IL   61801
11 Davis        Becky        2504 S Lynn       Urbana   IL   61801
12 Diamond      Jim          502 E Chalmers    Champaign IL  61820
13 Eaton        Candy        701 Dover Pl.     Champaign IL  61820
14 Edwards      Barbara      1721 Valley Rd    Paxton   IL   60957
15 Feldman      Francis      809 W Elm         Urbana   IL   61801
16 Franklin     Melissa      566 W Church      Champaign IL  61820
17 Garret       Gerald       1871 Parkdale     Rantoul  IL   61866
18 Griffith     Oscar        805 W Florida     Urbana   IL   61801
19 Hall         Robert       102 White         Pekin    IL   61554
20 Hudson       Henry        892 Bay Ave       Champaign IL  61820
01-Jan-89  09:09 PM
```

Figure 9.15 Spreadsheet Data Management

Spreadsheet programs are often used for simple data management tasks, such as maintaining a small mailing list. Data are simply entered as labels into cells. The spreadsheet program provides some commands for manipulating and rearranging the data.

Templates

Another reason spreadsheets are so popular is that general-purpose worksheets can be set up, saved, and used by many different people. A **template** is a worksheet that already contains labels, formulas, and perhaps some constant numbers. To use a template, all you have to do is fill in the blanks or change a few selected entries. Figure 9.16, for example, shows a simple template that computes the monthly payment on a loan, given the principal, interest rate, and term. This worksheet already has values filled in, but you can easily change them to compute the monthly payment for a different loan. Templates are a way for novices to use ready-made worksheets designed by experts to solve many different types of problems. In fact, over a thousand worksheet templates are commercially available; these work with the most popular spreadsheet programs to perform many common data analysis tasks, such as accounting, budgeting, investing, and tax planning.

Prelabeled worksheets

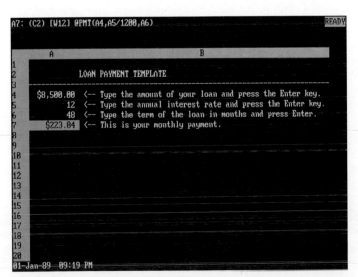

Figure 9.16 Spreadsheet Template

A template is a previously prepared worksheet that you can use to perform some task. All you have to do is fill in the blanks or change a few selected numbers. The labels and formulas are already in the template. This template computes the monthly payment on a loan, given the principal, interest rate, and term.

Popular Spreadsheet Programs

In the early 1980s, only a few really popular spreadsheet programs had been developed. The Apple II world was dominated by VisiCalc, and the IBM-compatible world was dominated by Lotus 1-2-3. When the Apple Macintosh came along in 1984, some spreadsheet programs were developed to run on it, but no single package was as popular as VisiCalc was on Apple IIs or as 1-2-3 was on IBM-compatibles. Today, VisiCalc is no longer sold, and a number of very popular spreadsheet programs are available. Besides Lotus 1-2-3, SuperCalc and Microsoft Excel are among the most noteworthy.

Lotus 1-2-3

Lotus 1-2-3 is almost synonymous with the word *spreadsheet*. It is probably the best-selling application package of all time. Ever since 1-2-3 was introduced in 1982, it has been the spreadsheet program against which all others are compared. This program not only has one of the most powerful spreadsheets in the business, it also includes graphing and data management capabilities. These three major components give 1-2-3 its name. Lotus 1-2-3 is still by far the most popular spreadsheet program for IBM-compatibles. It has an especially loyal following in corporate and business markets. Although Lotus has not yet released a version of 1-2-3 for Apple Macintosh computers as this book goes to press, it has announced its intention to do so. It will be interesting to see how 1-2-3 fares in the Macintosh arena.

SuperCalc

SuperCalc is a veteran spreadsheet, one of the few programs originally released before Lotus 1-2-3 that still survives. Now sold by Computer Associates International, SuperCalc began as a spreadsheet program for early microcomputers, including the Apple II. When IBM introduced its Personal Computer, SuperCalc was adapted to run on it. Soon, SuperCalc2 and SuperCalc3 were introduced. SuperCalc2 had improved formatting and other capabilities, while SuperCalc3 included graphing and data management. The latest incarnation is SuperCalc5, a powerful, well-designed program for IBM-compatibles that can easily hold its own against the likes of Lotus 1-2-3. Although it's not as popular as 1-2-3, SuperCalc5 is a fine product with a substantial following of fiercely loyal users.

Microsoft Excel

Microsoft Excel is an extremely flexible package that has become the top-selling spreadsheet for the Apple Macintosh. When Microsoft introduced an IBM-compatible version of Excel in 1987, *PC Magazine* declared it to be "unquestionably the most powerful PC spreadsheet you can buy." Like 1-2-3, Excel also offers data management, but its graphics abilities are more advanced and easier to use. Microsoft, arguably the leading microcomputer software developer, certainly has the technical know-how and marketing savvy to give the entrenched Lotus 1-2-3 a run for its money.

DATA BASE MANAGEMENT

One of the major jobs that we delegate to computers is managing huge quantities of data. Sometimes we don't need computers to actually compute anything—just store, sort, retrieve, print, or in some manner manipulate information. Large computers were doing this long before microcomputers came on the scene. Once microcomputers became so popular, however, it was only natural that they also be put to work managing data bases.

Managing large quantities of data

A **data base** is an organized collection of one or more files of interrelated data. A file, as we said in Chapter 5, is simply a mass of individual data items kept together in secondary storage. Computer files may contain programs, numeric data, or text. In general, data bases are made up of files containing numbers and text compiled for some specific purpose. For example, data bases are often used to store mailing lists, phone numbers, personnel files, customer accounts, credit records, inventories, bibliographies, and even entire reference works. A **data base management package** lets you create, add to, delete from, update, sort, rearrange, select from, print out, and otherwise administer data files. We'll have more to say about these sophisticated information storage and retrieval systems in Chapter 12, but for now let's examine some basic data base management features and introduce a few of the most popular packages.

Types of Data Base Managers

A data base can contain any type of data. This broad definition means that several different types of programs can be classified as data base managers, for example, flat-file, free-form, hypertext, relational, and programmable data base managers.

A variety of types to handle different kinds of data

Flat-File

A **flat-file data base manager** is a program that works with one file of structured data at a time. In other words, this type of program is designed to handle single files that are conveniently organized into regular-sized pieces of data, such as names, addresses, phone numbers, and price listings. Flat-file managers are generally simple, easy to use, and modestly priced. They are designed to do one basic job very well—accepting, reorganizing, and reporting information. Consequently, many individuals and small businesses find that a flat-file manager is more than adequate for their simple needs. Flat-file managers are ideal for maintaining mailing lists, addresses and phone numbers, personnel files, product price lists, and property inventories. Almost any sequential list of information can be kept with a flat-file manager. This type of program is often used as an electronic index like a computerized set of Rolodex cards.

Free-Form

In some cases, the information we want to organize with a computer cannot be conveniently broken down into regular-sized pieces of data. A **free-form data base manager** is a program designed to handle narrative text and irregular pieces of data, such as paragraphs, pages, articles, notes, discussions, and instructions. These programs generally allow you to index your information by choosing key words to locate sections of text. Some free-form data base managers allow you to search through your entire text for occurrences of any word or phrase. For example, if you use a free-form data base manager to organize recipes, you can attach key words like salad, entrée, beverage, and dessert to them. Then you can obtain a listing of just salads, for instance. If the program can search through all your data for any word or phrase, you could find all those recipes that include bananas. Free-form data base managers are usually relatively simple, easy to use, and inexpensive. They are used for applications like maintaining bibliographies, research observations, periodical abstracts, law listings, and even random, unrelated notes.

Hypertext

Hypertext is a term coined by Ted Nelson in 1965 to describe the nonsequential organization and presentation of information with a computer. Today, the term **hypermedia** is sometimes used as a more encompassing term than hypertext. In its purest form, a true hypermedia system would allow you to jump randomly from topic to related topic, accessing any kind of data the computer can store, including text, graphics, audio, and video. Since you can bypass intermediate topics, you need only extract what you specifically need from huge stores of information. Although we don't have any full hypermedia packages yet, a few hypertext products on the market can also store graphics and sound. The most notable of these is the immensely popular Hypercard, from Apple Computer.

Relational

Like a flat-file manager, a **relational data base manager** also allows you to create, maintain, reorganize, and print structured data, but it has the added ability to work with more than one file at a time. This sophisticated software can connect or relate data from two or more different files. For example, let's say that you have a personnel data base that consists of two files. One file contains each employee's name, social security number, address, and phone number. To help keep sensitive information private, the other file contains just the employees' social security numbers, current salaries, and performance evaluations. A relational data base management system can access both files at the same time to produce a report listing each employee's name and current salary, even though these two pieces of data reside in different files.

Relational data base managers are generally quite sophisticated and expensive. They may not be as easy to use as other types of data managers, but they are more flexible and more powerful. In general, a relational data base manager can do everything that a flat-file or spreadsheet data base manager can do, but they are usually not very well adapted to the kinds of tasks done by free-form data managers. Nevertheless, many businesses and organizations find that a relational data base management system is best for their needs.

Programmable

A **programmable data base manager** is a relational, flat-file, or hypertext data base manager that includes its own programming language or works with a standard programming language like C, COBOL, or Pascal. Although most average users never attempt to program a data base manager, this added feature gives experts the ability to customize the operation of the package for their own particular needs. For example, let's say that a mail-order company uses a programmable data base manager to keep track of all of the products it sells. At the end of every day, employees enter the number of each product that was sold that day. The data base manager can be programmed so that every Friday evening, a summary report is printed that lists the quantities of each product sold for the entire week, and other tasks can be automated and made easier for the workers. A simple menu system can be set up so that employees don't even have to know anything about the data base manager's commands to do their jobs. Programmable data base management systems are generally the most sophisticated, powerful, and expensive type of data base managers.

Creating a Data Base

Unfortunately, computers and software cannot do all the work. Although they can help a great deal, you must still plan your data base and collect the information to be stored inside. One way or another, data must be entered into the computer before it can be organized and stored on a disk. The two basic steps to creating a data base are defining its structure and entering the data records.

Defining the structure and entering the data

Defining the Structure

Except for free-form and hypertext programs, data base managers all require data to be structured in some regular manner. A data base is a collection of one or more files, each of which is a collection of records. A record is a sequence of *fields*, and a field is simply a single data item such as a number, character, or group of related characters such as a word or phrase. A field has two basic attributes: its length and the type of data it can hold. Generally, all the records in a file have the same structure. In other words, the number, type, and length of fields is the same for every record in a particular file. Different files, however, can have different record structures. A **relational data base** is a collection of files with different record structures, but every file contains at least one field that is duplicated in another file.

Before you can begin to enter records into a data base file, you must plan the structure and tell the data base manager how you want to organize the data. This consists of specifying the record structure. Then each field in the record structure must be given a name, length, and data type. The name of a field is usually a one- or two-word description of the contents of that field. The length of a field is the maximum number of characters it can hold. The data type specifies the kind of information that can be stored in a field. Most data base managers, for instance, can store at least the following data types: text, numbers, dates, logical values (true or false), and memos (longer segments of text). Figure 9.17 shows the process of defining the structure of a data base in a dBASE III PLUS, a popular data base management package for IBM-compatible microcomputers.

Entering Records

Once the structure of your data base file has been defined, you can actually begin entering data. This involves typing the contents of each field of each record into your file. For each new record, the data base program presents you with a blank

Figure 9.17 Data Base Structure

The first task in many data base management packages is to define the structure of your data records. This involves specifying the name, data type, and width in characters of each field in a record. Here is a typical mailing-list record structure created in dBASE III PLUS.

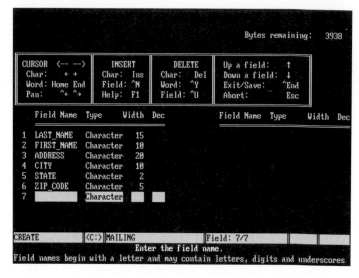

data entry form, which may look something like Figure 9.18. This form lists each field that you've defined along with an empty box for its contents. The size of the box indicates how much room you have by depicting the maximum length of that field. You usually begin typing with the first character of the first field. A cursor shows where you should type the characters. You key the entries for the fields in this record by pressing the Enter key after each one. You can correct mistakes by using the backspace key or by inserting and deleting selected characters within a field. When you are finished typing the last field of a record, the data base program may automatically go on to the next new record, or it may ask you if you want to enter a new record. After you have entered all of the records, you usually have to execute a command to tell the program to stop presenting new data entry forms and to return to the main menu.

Figure 9.18 Data Entry Form

Once the structure has been defined, you can begin entering the actual data. A blank data entry form, such as this one, is presented for you to fill in. The highlight blocks show the width of each field.

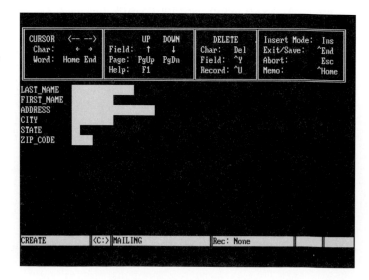

Viewing a Data Base

Let's assume that you have created and saved a data base. Now what do you do with it? Well, of the many reasons for keeping a data base, the simplest is that you store information so that you can look it up later. Perhaps the most common data base operation is viewing what has already been stored.

How to look at stored data

Browsing

If your data base file is small, and you are not looking for one particular record, the easiest way to view your data is to **browse.** This allows you to go through casually and view the records in your data base file. Typically, the data base manager lets you start with the first or last record in the file or with some record in between. It may present just one record on the screen in a filled data entry form or it may display several records in a table format, with one record per row (see Figure 9.19). You can usually go forward or backward to see additional records by pressing keys such as Page Up or Page Down.

Finding Records

Browsing is fine for examining short data base files, but it becomes impractical for files with many records. Besides, in many cases you may want to look at only one specific record or a selected set of records, not the entire data base. Data base management programs generally have several different ways to help you find the records you want to view. These programs let you search for only those records that meet one or more specific criteria. This is sometimes called **querying** a data base. The simplest type of query asks for only those records that contain a particular entry in one of their fields. For example, if you want to see Ellen McFall's record, you query the data base for the record that has *McFall* in its LAST_NAME field. Figure 9.20 shows the result. Finding Ellen McFall's record is a very simple search operation: only one field is searched for only one value. It is common, however, to formulate more complex queries that involve searching one or more additional

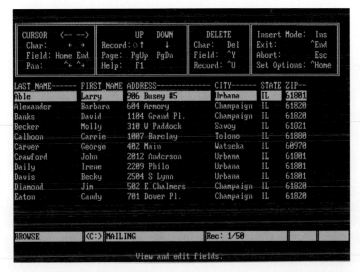

Figure 9.19 Browsing

Perhaps the easiest way to view the contents of a data base is to browse through the records. This is how dBASE III PLUS presents data records when you browse through them.

Figure 9.20 Querying

When you want to find a particular record or some set of related records in a large data base, the best way is to query the data base. This is what you see after asking dBASE III PLUS to locate a record with LAST_NAME equal to "McFall."

fields for other values. For example, you could search for those records with LAST_NAME equal to *McFall* and FIRST_NAME equal to *Ellen* and CITY equal to *Champaign*. Another example might be all those records with CITY equal to *Champaign* or CITY equal to *Urbana*. By stringing together search operations in this manner with AND and OR, you can construct very specific queries. This is especially helpful with very large data bases.

Updating a Data Base

Keeping data up-to-date

Most data bases must be changed over time. Some may be changed regularly, as often as several times a day. Other data bases may seldom need changing. One of the major functions of a data base management system is allowing you to keep your data bases up-to-date. This involves letting you add, delete, and modify records, as well as enabling you to change the existing structure of a data base.

Adding Records

New records must often be added to many data bases. Mailing lists, for example, are frequently expanded. The process of adding a new record to an existing data base file is very similar to entering a new record into a new data base file. Typically, you select an option from a menu or execute a command that presents a new blank data entry form on the screen. Then you simply enter the data for the new record.

Deleting Records

It is also necessary to be able to remove records from a data base. A mail-order company, for example, may decide not to send a new catalog to previous customers who placed their last order over three years ago. This company needs to periodically go through its data base and delete the records of inactive customers. The first step is to find the record to be removed. In this case you search the data base for a record with an order date over three years ago. Then you select an option from a menu or execute a command, often called DELETE, that removes the selected record from the data base file. In some data base programs, this removal is not actually finalized until you confirm your deletion or execute still another command. In dBASE III PLUS, for example, you need to execute a PACK command to permanently remove deleted records from a data base.

Modifying Records

Entirely removing a record from a data base is somewhat drastic. In many cases all you need to do is modify a record by changing the contents of selected fields. For example, let's say that a mail-order customer moves. The mail-order company doesn't want to remove this customer's record, just update the address. All data base management packages let you update existing records without removing them. Typically, you first find the record you want to change. When its filled data entry form is presented on the screen, you simply insert, delete, or overwrite characters to make your desired changes within the fields. For making small changes, modifying a record is much quicker than deleting it and adding a new one.

Changing the Structure

Adding, deleting, and modifying records are all common data base operations. Changing the existing structure of a data base is done less frequently. Nevertheless, you must occasionally change the name, length, or data type of a field; add new fields; or delete existing fields. Most data base managers let you perform all of these modifications.

Rearranging a Data Base

In general, data must be kept in some predictable order if they are to be useful. This becomes increasingly true the more data you have. Imagine trying to find one particular word in a dictionary if all words weren't alphabetized. The task would be so daunting that dictionaries would be practically useless. Keeping records organized is one of the most important jobs of a data base management package. As new records are added and old records deleted, a data base may have to be reorganized. You might also want to rearrange your data to see or use them in a different way. Instead of ordering your mailing-list by last name, for example, you might want to temporarily rearrange records into ZIP code order. By printing mailing labels for your letters in ZIP code order, you can take advantage of special discounts from the Post Office. Most data base managers offer two basic ways of rearranging records: sorting and indexing.

Keeping records organized

Sorting

The term **sorting** is generally used to mean rearranging the actual records of a data base into some particular order. Some data base management programs create a completely new file when records are sorted. The records in this new file are the same as the records in the original file, but they are arranged in a different order. Other data base management programs don't actually create a new file, they just rearrange the records in the original file. Either way, sorting results in a file with all records in a predictable order.

Figure 9.21 Sorting

Data bases are frequently rearranged on the basis of the contents of one or more fields. Here is the mailing-list data base sorted by ZIP code.

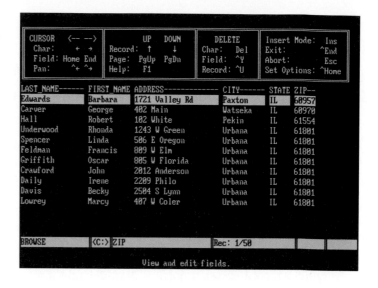

Before you can sort a data base you have to decide which field will be the *key*, the field used as the basis for the sort. If you want to alphabetically sort the records of a mailing list by last name, then the field that contains last names is the key. If you want to sort by ZIP code, then the field that contains ZIP codes is the key (see Figure 9.21).

Indexing

Indexing is a way to reorder the records of a data base without actually duplicating the data in a new file or rearranging the actual records in the original file. Every time you enter a record into a new data base file or append a record to an existing file, that record is assigned a unique record number, which the data base management system uses to identify it. When you index a data base file, you don't change the order of the records and the record numbers in the original file. Instead you create an index file that just lists the record numbers in the new order. With large data bases, the index file is usually much smaller than the data base file from which it was created. You can keep several different index files and use much less disk space than if you had performed several different sorts of the original file. Because indexing a file eliminates the need to copy or rearrange all of the data stored in the original file, it is also much quicker than sorting.

Generating Data Base Reports

Printing a formatted collection of fields

Like word-processing programs and spreadsheet programs, data base managers are frequently used to produce printed output. A **data base report** is simply a printed collection of record fields, usually formatted in some manner. Most data base managers give you a good deal of flexibility in specifying the layout of reports (see Figure 9.22). You can indicate the fields to be included, the order in which they are to appear, their positions on the page, their headings, and whether to sum numeric

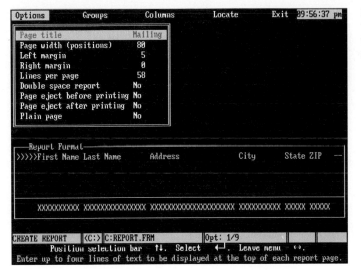

Figure 9.22 Generating Reports
To generate a data base report, you usually must specify the format of the report. This screen illustrates the process of specifying a report format in dBASE III PLUS.

fields. Margins, line spacing, page length, and page numbering can also be specified. Once you set up a report layout, many data base programs let you save this layout in a disk file so that you can use it again in the future without having to respecify all of the format settings.

Popular Data Base Managers

Many popular data base packages are currently available, from simple flat-file programs to fully programmable relational systems. Like Lotus 1-2-3 in the spreadsheet market, dBASE is the clear leader in the data base market. Singling out other data base packages is somewhat arbitrary, but R:base is one of the most frequently used competitors of dBASE. As the most popular hypertext program on the market, Hypercard is in a class by itself.

The most frequently used packages

dBASE

In the minds of many people, dBASE is synonymous with data base management. Sold by Ashton-Tate, dBASE is the most popular programmable relational data base management package for IBM-compatible computers. It is a very powerful, fast, feature-laden package that is the standard against which all other high-level data base managers are compared. Like other programs with a long history, various versions of dBASE have been released and the system has been consistently improved with each new version. Although dBASE has not always been known for user-friendliness, it is the program of choice for those needing power, speed, flexibility, and programmability in a data base management system. Recent versions of dBASE come with a menu system that makes them much easier to use than earlier command-oriented versions. In 1987, Ashton-Tate released an Apple Macintosh version that combines the power of the IBM-compatible dBASE with the ease of use and graphics ability of the Macintosh.

Figure 9.23 Hypertext

Hypertext packages promise to be one of the most useful and interesting types of data base software. This screen shows Hypercard, the most well-known hypertext package for Apple Macintosh computers.

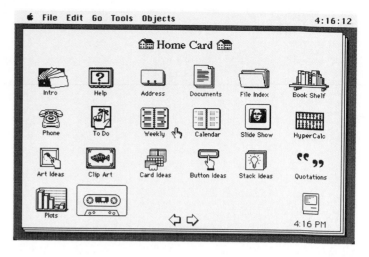

R:base

The R:base series of data base management systems, from Microrim Incorporated, has been one of the strongest contenders to the various versions of dBASE for IBM-compatible computers. R:base is a programmable relational data base management system that has just as many, if not more, features than dBASE. Some people think that R:base is significantly easier to use, even if it is somewhat slower, than dBASE. While dBASE seems more oriented to programmers who develop data base applications for other users, R:base caters more to end-users who need to occasionally customize data base applications.

Hypercard

This program from Apple Computer is by far the most well-known hypertext product on the market (see Figure 9.23). First introduced in August of 1987 for the Apple Macintosh, Hypercard lets you store information on computerized index cards. This information can be in the form of text, graphics, animations, sounds, or digitized voices. Individual index cards are grouped into stacks, usually reflecting some common theme. These stacks can be linked in many different ways, allowing the extremely rapid information retrieval characteristic of hypertext systems. Each index card can hold up to 32 kilobytes of information, and the theoretical maximum size of each stack is 500 megabytes. Stacks as large as 20 megabytes can be searched in about two seconds. What makes the program even more exciting is that Hypercard includes its own programming language, called Hypertalk, which is designed especially for nonprogrammers. Using Hypertalk, even novices can build their own customized information systems, called **stackware.** Thousands of stacks have been developed that are currently available commercially and in the public domain, covering almost every application imaginable, from storing addresses (and other traditional data storage capabilities), to animated games, illustrated miniencyclopedias, and educational tutorials.

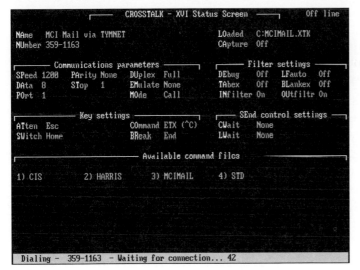

Figure 9.24 Communications Package

This screen shows Crosstalk, one of the most popular communications packages for IBM-compatible microcomputers.

COMMUNICATIONS

In Chapter 6 we saw how modems enable computers to transmit and receive data over telephone lines. Communications software, however, is just as important as hardware in the process of exchanging data and accessing remote computers. Figure 9.24, for example, shows Crosstalk, a popular communications package for IBM-compatible microcomputers. Communications programs such as Crosstalk help you perform the following essential tasks:

Exchanging data and accessing remote computers; dialing telephones, identifying users of a system, and transferring data from computer to computer

- *Set communications parameters.*   These are the settings that control the manner in which computers communicate. Communications parameters, which we discussed in Chapter 6, include the speed (in bits per second), the duplex setting (half or full), the type of parity (odd or even), and how many stop bits to be used. A communications package should make it easy for users to set up and modify these parameters.

- *Dial the phone.*   Today's communications packages enable users to dial the phone from their computer keyboards or automatically from phone directories stored on their disks. If a user has a modem compatible with such a feature, automatic dialing can make establishing communications fast and convenient. (Modem manufacturers sometimes supply free communications software with the purchase of a modem.)

- *Enter log-on information.*   Most multiuser computer systems allow access only to users who have an account or permission to use the facilities. The process by which users identify themselves as having a valid account is called **logging on,** or sometimes **signing on.** It usually involves supplying some combination of name, address, identification number, account number, and password. Many communications packages can do this automatically once the user has programmed in his or her individual log-on sequence.

- *Emulate a terminal.*   In multiuser computer systems, users work at their own terminals, which are input/output stations consisting of a keyboard and display. **Terminal emulation** is a feature of communications packages that lets you use a microcomputer as a remote terminal to some multiuser computer, usually a mainframe.

- *Capture incoming data.*   The communications package must allow a user's computer to receive and store data coming in from a remote computer. Transferring a file from a remote computer to your computer is called **downloading.**

- *Transmit data.*   Finally, the communications package must enable you to send messages, commands, and files to a remote computer. Transferring a file from your computer to a remote computer is called **uploading.**

Communications is one of the few reasonably standardized aspects of the computer industry (computers couldn't communicate at all if it weren't). Consequently, most communications packages are functionally quite similar. Almost all will provide the basic features we've outlined; their differences lie in their ease of use, speed, and number of extra features.

GRAPHICS

Creating pictures or other images

Graphics packages let users create pictures with their computers, and you know what they say about a picture being worth a thousand words. Computer-generated graphics can transform dull data into eye-catching informative images. Several different types of graphics application packages are commonly used, including charting, painting, drawing, computer-aided design, and slide show programs.

Charting

Programs to produce graphs and other charts

A **charting program** produces graphs, plots, and charts from data you enter directly or transfer from a worksheet or data base file. Although some application packages, such as spreadsheet programs, include a few basic chart-drawing features, *dedicated* charting programs typically provide a wide range of different kinds of charts and give you a great deal of control over a chart's final appearance. Figure 9.25 shows a chart on a screen from EnerGraphics, a popular dedicated charting program for IBM-compatible microcomputers. This particular package can do pie charts, bar graphs, several types of line plots, statistical graphs, scatter plots, and text charts. EnerGraphics also has some drawing tools to let you create organizational charts, flowcharts, logos, floor plans, electrical circuits, mechanical drawings, architectural drawings, musical scales, and advertising layouts.

Painting

Creating free-hand pictures

A **painting program** lets you create free-hand pictures with a mouse, graphics tablet, or trackball. Everything that you see on a computer display screen, including text, is composed of many tiny individual dots, called **pixels** (short for *picture*

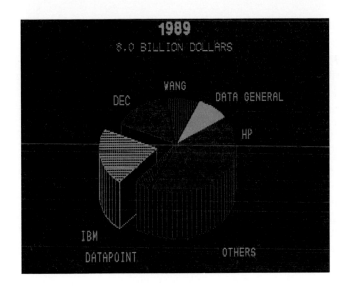

Figure 9.25 Charting Package
This three-dimensional pie chart was produced with EnerGraphics, a popular charting package for IBM-compatible computers.

elements). Painting programs give you ultimate control over every one of these dots and can produce an exact replica of the screen image (in black and white) on paper with your printer. For this reason, painting programs are often said to produce **pixel-based** or **bit-mapped graphics.**

Several predefined shapes such as lines, rectangles, ovals, and text can be incorporated into your creations, but you are not limited to these standard elements. You can draw your own shapes and use a variety of shading patterns. Many painting programs let you fully utilize the color capabilities of your computer display. Sections of the screen and individual shapes can be moved, copied, deleted, rotated, and "flipped over" horizontally or vertically. You can "zoom in" on parts of the screen to manipulate individual dots and edit images in great detail. You can also "zoom out" to see a preview of what the entire page will look like when it is printed. Text can be displayed in a wide range of fonts, styles, and sizes. Most

Figure 9.26 Painting Package
Painting programs, such as MacPaint for the Apple Macintosh, allow you to create all kinds of free-hand images. This particular picture is from T/Maker's Click Art Personal Graphics selection of clip art.

painting programs can even read in images from full-page or hand-held scanners. Completed pictures can be saved in disk files and faithfully reproduced on paper with a dot-matrix, ink-jet, or laser printer. Figure 9.26 shows one of the first and most popular painting programs, MacPaint for the Apple Macintosh.

Drawing

Constructing figures with discrete objects; making precise diagrams

A **drawing program** lets you construct figures composed of discrete graphic objects such as lines, squares, rectangles, circles, ovals, polygons, curves, and text. For this reason, drawing programs are often said to produce **object-oriented graphics.** Like painting programs, drawing programs usually employ a graphics input device such as a mouse, trackball, or graphics tablet. Drawing programs, however, are better than painting programs for making precise scaled diagrams. In addition, drawing programs usually take better advantage of high-resolution printers. For example, although MacPaint reproduces screen images on paper very well, these images have a resolution of only 72 dots per inch, even on a laser printer capable of 300 dots per inch. Drawing programs produce sharper output on paper with dot-matrix, ink-jet, and laser printers. Thus they are better suited than most painting programs for architectural renderings, layouts, blueprints, diagrams, charts, maps, mechanical drawings, and other technical illustrations. Figure 9.27 illustrates MacDraw, a popular drawing program for Apple Macintosh computers.

In short, drawing programs are good for making structured figures. They are easy-to-use tools for simple drafting applications. Drawing programs let you define on-screen rulers and accurately scale objects to metric or English measurements. Objects keep their individual identities, even if they are partially or completely obscured by other objects. Shapes can be selected, moved, stretched, duplicated, and deleted as needed. An on-screen *grid*, like the squares on graph paper, can be used to keep objects lined up with each other. Many drawing programs can create figures much larger than a single 8- by 10-inch page. Reduction, enlargement, and

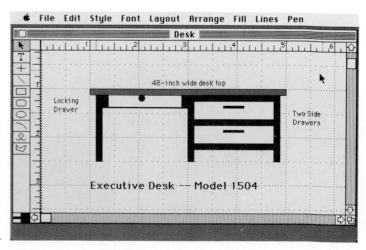

Figure 9.27 Drawing Package
Drawing programs allow you to manipulate graphic objects and are well suited to creating scaled figures, such as this desk plan made with MacDraw for the Macintosh.

scrolling features make it easier to work on drawings that are very detailed or too big to fit within a single screen. Although drawing programs don't let you erase parts of an object or edit individual pixels, they do let you change the way objects look by moving them, resizing them, and altering the patterns used to construct their borders and fill their interiors.

Computer-Aided Design

Drawing programs such as MacDraw are fine for relatively simple plans, diagrams, and blueprints. Although drawing programs can produce detailed figures, they are not powerful enough for many engineering, architectural, and technical illustrations. For truly complex drafting applications, **computer-aided design (CAD)** packages are much better. These packages have been used for years on mainframe and minicomputer systems and have become increasingly popular for use on microcomputers. Thanks to recent technological advances, microcomputer CAD packages offer much of the functionality of mainframe CAD packages at a fraction of the cost.

Creating engineering and architectural illustrations

Although CAD packages are generally more expensive and more difficult to learn than painting and drawing programs, they still have a wide range of potential users. Mechanical engineers, architects, circuit board designers, civil engineers, surveyors, interior planners, and graphic artists are but a few examples of the many diverse professionals who are using CAD packages. Consequently, tens of thousands of CAD systems are installed every year.

Figure 9.28 shows AutoCAD, the most popular CAD package for microcomputers. With over 100,000 copies sold, this software is used in some 55 percent of all microcomputer-based CAD installations. Like Lotus 1-2-3 and dBASE, AutoCAD has become the clear leader in its field. Originally designed for IBM-compatible microcomputers, AutoCAD was adapted in 1988 for use on Apple Macintoshes.

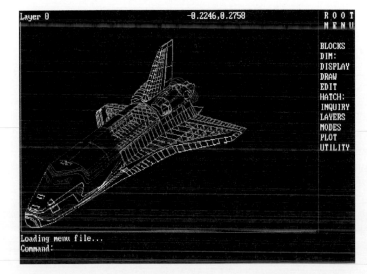

Figure 9.28 Computer-Aided Design Package
Computer-aided design (CAD) packages are the most sophisticated type of graphics package. They allow you to create complex engineering, mechanical, and architectural diagrams. This screen shows AutoCAD, the most popular CAD package for microcomputers, being used to edit a plan of the space shuttle Columbia.

Figure 9.29 Slide Show Package
A slide show package, such as IBM's PC StoryBoard, allows you to display a sequence of screen images, such as this one, for presentations, tutorials, and advertisements.

Slide Show

Creating visual displays to accompany oral presentations

A **slide show program** allows you to present a sequence of pictures on your computer screen, either automatically timed to go from picture to picture or directly controlled by you. These pictures are brought in from other graphics packages or produced within the slide show program itself. A host of special effects can be used to vary the visual transition from one picture to the next. For example, instead of instantly flipping from one picture to another, you can have the slide show program slowly "dissolve" the current image and fade into the succeeding picture. Text, numbers, graphs, charts, and free-hand drawings can be combined in stunning visual displays. This makes computer slide shows ideal for business presentations, educational demonstrations, tutorial lessons, traffic-stopping advertising pitches, and product descriptions. Figure 9.29 shows IBM's PC StoryBoard, a popular slide show program for IBM-compatible microcomputers.

INTEGRATED SOFTWARE

Combining the most commonly used packages

Most people who work with computers use several different types of application packages. The most commonly used packages are word processing, spreadsheet, data base management, communications, and graphics programs. A bewildering array of commercial packages are available in all of these categories. Why haven't software developers come up with packages that include all five of these major applications? They have: it's called **integrated software.**

The term *integrated software* has been applied to many packages that include more than one basic application. For example, Lotus 1-2-3 has often been categorized as integrated software because it includes spreadsheet, data base management, and graphics capabilities. These days, however, integrated software means packages that include at least word processing, spreadsheet, data base management, communications, and graphics functions. Several integrated software packages on the market fulfill these requirements, including Enable from The Software

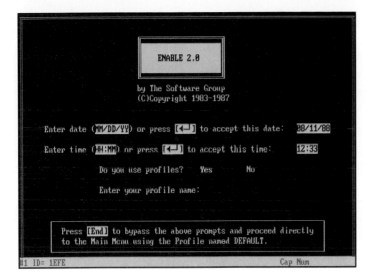

Figure 9.30 Integrated Software
Enable is a good example of an integrated software package that contains word processing, spreadsheet, data base management, graphics, and communications functions.

Group (see Figure 9.30), Symphony from Lotus Development Corporation, Framework from Ashton-Tate, and Microsoft Works.

The most important advantage of integrated software is that you learn a single set of consistent menus and commands for a wide range of tasks. It generally takes a good deal of time and effort to master any sophisticated application package. But because of its uniform approach to menus and commands, integrated software is usually much easier to learn and use than several separate application packages. Integrated software packages also make it easy to transfer data between the included applications, and they're usually less expensive than purchasing several individual programs.

DESKTOP PUBLISHING

Combine word processing and graphics capabilities with the beautiful output of a laser printer and you have the essence of desktop publishing. This type of application package can produce near typeset-quality printed material complete with illustrations, using microcomputers and laser printers at relatively low cost. Figure 9.31, for example, shows a newsletter being produced with Aldus PageMaker, a popular desktop publishing package for microcomputers. All kinds of organizations, from small clubs to multinational corporations, are using such packages to produce their own newsletters, advertisements, memos, contracts, documents, and even books. Chapter 14 will examine further the recent phenomenon of desktop publishing.

High-quality printed material produced at your desk

STATISTICS

With all that computers can do, it's easy to forget what they do best: work with numbers. Many professionals use computers to analyze all kinds of numeric data, from regional sales figures to rat reaction times in psychology experiments. Statis-

Figure 9.31 Desktop Publishing

Desktop publishing packages, such as Aldus PageMaker, allow you to create near-typeset-quality documents with a microcomputer and laser printer (or typesetter). Here, PageMaker is being used to combine text and graphics to create a newsletter.

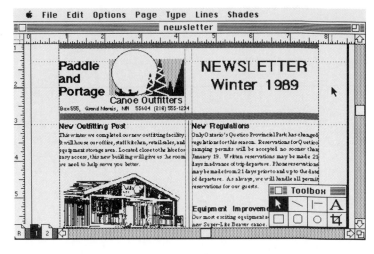

Producing statistical analyses with the microcomputer

tics is the branch of mathematics concerned with the collection, analysis, interpretation, and presentation of numeric data. In a variety of fields, statistical analysis is a critical tool. The Census Bureau uses it to monitor economic and social change. Manufacturers use it to maintain product quality controls. Public health officials use it to track infectious diseases. Agricultural scientists use it to study crop yields. Actuaries use it to set insurance premiums. Poll takers use it to gauge public opinion. The list of those who need statistics is almost endless.

If everyone who needed to do a statistical analysis had to write their own software, however, very few analyses would ever get done. Fortunately, a number of statistical packages on the market are able to do these analyses for you. All you have to do is supply the data, select the particular statistical procedure, and wait for the results. SYSTAT, from the company of the same name, is one example of a popular statistical package for both Apple Macintosh and IBM-compatible microcomputers. This particular program was modeled after SAS, a leading statistical package for mainframe computers. SYSTAT excels at handling large data bases with many different variables. Originally developed by a psychology professor at the University of Illinois, SYSTAT is especially well-suited to the advanced statistical techniques used in the behavioral and social sciences.

ACCOUNTING

Systems to help boost profits, pay bills, calculate earnings, and handle other bookkeeping chores

Despite the widespread acceptance of computers by virtually every segment of our society, they are still used by business most of all. So it's only natural that a large number of microcomputer application packages have been developed especially for businesses. This software basically consists of accounting systems designed to help boost profits, cut costs, improve cash flow, pay bills, calculate earnings, assemble marketing information, and explore operational alternatives. We'll have more to say about these electronic bookkeepers in Chapter 15.

PROJECT MANAGEMENT

More and more, computers are being used as organizational tools. All kinds of programs are now available for helping you outline, schedule, and chart your thoughts and activities. Project management software is one of the most popular and advanced categories of these various organizational programs. The purpose of a **project management package** is to help you formally plan and control complex undertakings, such as the construction of a new office building, the development of a new product, or the installation of a large computer system. Basically, a project management package lets you identify the individual tasks necessary to complete a project and calculate the time, money, and other resources each of these tasks will require. We'll have more to say about project management packages in Chapter 11.

Packages to handle large-scale tasks such as constructing a building or installing a large computer system

PERSONAL FINANCE AND TAX PREPARATION

On a more personal level, application software can help you organize your own finances, too. Some of the best-selling packages for microcomputers are personal finance programs. Whether you're struggling to balance your checkbook or trying to leverage your investments, a personal finance program can be a useful addition to your software library. One of the most popular, easy-to-use, and powerful personal finance packages is Andrew Tobias's Managing Your Money from MECA Ventures. This program contains financial advice and personal accounting procedures developed by the author of the perennial best-selling book *The Only Investment Guide You'll Ever Need*.

Managing investments, balancing checkbooks, calculating taxes with a personal computer

Although personal finance packages such as Managing Your Money can help you estimate your taxes, most cannot produce actual tax forms and schedules to submit to the IRS. For that, you need more specialized tax preparation software. Since the Tax Reform Act of 1986, this type of software has exploded into widespread use as confused taxpayers search for help. One of the best tax-preparation programs is Macintax Taxview (Federal Version) from Softview. This program, which comes in different versions for both the Apple Macintosh and IBM-compatible microcomputers, is easy to use and straightforward, yet surprisingly sophisticated. Macintax Taxview not only follows the structure of IRS tax forms, it exactly duplicates them on your computer screen (see Figure 9.32). Instead of writing your entries on paper forms, you type them right on the screen. If you need help or want to see the IRS instructions for an entry, you simply point to it and click the mouse button. All worksheets, forms, and schedules are automatically linked to each other and the main 1040 form. When you are finished filling out the necessary forms, all you have to do is print them, sign them, and send them to the IRS along with your earnings statement and possibly a check.

EDUCATION

Besides helping you with specific tasks such as managing your finances and preparing your taxes, application software can also teach you various subjects and skills; educational packages for microcomputers cover almost every topic imaginable. At

Programs that teach: from ABCs to thermodynamics

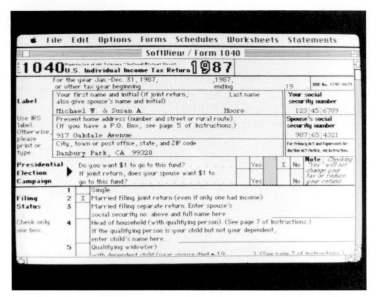

Figure 9.32 Tax Package

With the income-tax laws constantly changing, application packages that help you prepare your tax returns are becoming increasingly popular. This screen shows Macintax Taxview being used to fill out a 1040 Form.

one end of the spectrum are programs for young children, such as Alphabet Blocks from Bright Star Technology. This Macintosh program presents an on-screen elf who teaches prereaders the letters and sounds of the alphabet with a clear, digitized voice. At a more advanced level, Broderbund Software's Sensei Physics is a well-designed study aid that covers topics such as vectors, thermodynamics, and the nature of light. Students learn concepts of physics by designing their own animated experiments. Educational packages such as these are quite effective because they use graphics, sound, and student participation to make learning both interesting and fun.

ENTERTAINMENT

Games for children and would-be race car drivers

Computers can be enjoyable, even if you don't learn anything. An amazing variety of software has been developed with the primary intention of merely providing entertainment. Typically priced below $100, these entertainment packages range from simple childhood diversions such as ticktacktoe to sophisticated real-life simulations. You can find adventure games, strategy games, card games, board games, sports games, parlor games, game-show games, pinball games, arcade shoot-em-up games and programs that simulate operating a submarine, race car, airplane, jet, or spaceship. Even musical programs that range from simple computerized pianos to multi-instrument studio synthesizers and professional music composition tools have been created. And this just barely scratches the surface of the entertainment packages you can find for microcomputers.

Spreadsheet packages help users store, manipulate, analyze, and present data, most often numeric data. Many different kinds of tasks can be performed with a spreadsheet program. To give you an idea of what it's like to use this type of application software, let's create a simple income statement for an imaginary small business with Lotus 1-2-3, which is by far the most popular microcomputer spreadsheet package. An *income statement* is simply a report that lists the sources of income and expenses of a business over a given time period. The *bottom line* of an income statement shows the net profit earned, calculated by subtracting the total expenses from the total income. After we set up the income statement with Lotus 1-2-3, we will make a bar graph that shows the income for each quarter of the year.

First, to start up Lotus 1-2-3, you enter *123* into a computer that has the program installed on it. After an initial copyright screen, 1-2-3 presents a blank worksheet, like the one you see in Figure 9.10 of this chapter. At this point, it's best to take a few moments to plan the format of your worksheet. Ours will need six columns: one for the labels along the left side, one for each of the four quarters in a year, and one for the totals along the right side. The numbers in the income statement will all be currency values which could be as large as $100,000.00. The default column width in 1-2-3 is only nine characters and the default numeric format is general format (no dollar signs, no commas, and possibly more than two decimal places). This means that we have to change the column widths to 12 and the numeric format to currency format with two decimal places.

To change these settings, you have to use several 1-2-3 *commands*. In 1-2-3, commands are listed in *menus* that go across the top of the screen. Menus, however, are not present on the screen until you explicitly invoke them. This is done by typing the / (forward slash) character. When you type a /, 1-2-3 presents its main menu across the top of the screen, as shown at right.

You can select a command from this menu in either one of two ways: highlight it and press the Enter key, or type its first letter. You move the highlight bar by pressing the left or right arrow key. As the figure shows, right now the blue highlight bar is on the word Worksheet in the main menu. Because it's faster, most 1-2-3 users eventually select commands by typing their first letters.

Many 1-2-3 commands invoke another menu with still other options. These options are listed in the line directly below the command. For example, in the figure

A Closer Look

Using Lotus 1-2-3

below the Worksheet command is highlighted. The line below the word Worksheet shows the options you will have if you select the Worksheet command. To change the widths of all the columns in the worksheet to 12, you need to execute the Worksheet command, then the Global command, and finally the Column-Width option. In other words, from the start you would type

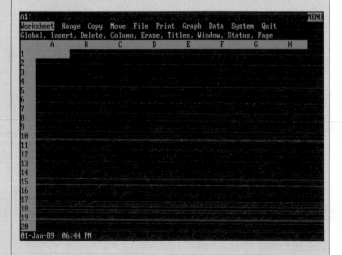

/WGC to change the worksheet global column width. The 1-2-3 program then asks you to specify the column width and you simply enter 12. All of the columns in the worksheet increase in width from 9 to 12 character spaces.

The process is similar for setting the global numeric format. The term *global*, which is commonly used in computer jargon, simply means something that applies everywhere. In this case, you want to change the global numeric format to currency so that every cell in the worksheet will display its numeric value as a dollar amount, complete with a dollar sign, commas separating thousands, and two places to the right of the decimal point. To do this you type */WGFC* and then enter a *2* for the number of decimal places. This executes the Worksheet Global Format Currency command.

Finally, you are ready to begin creating the actual worksheet. Most people begin by entering the text labels that will annotate the contents. All you have to do is move the cell pointer to the desired cell and begin typing. Long labels can overlap adjacent cells. For example, to enter the title of this worksheet, you move the cell pointer to cell C1 and enter *Income Statement 1989*. Because this entry begins with a letter, 1-2-3 knows that it is a label and not a number or formula. It is longer than 12 characters, but it simply overlaps part of cell D1. The second row in the worksheet is filled with dashes to form a dividing line. The third row contains column headings, as seen below.

These headings are centered within their cells by prefixing each one with a ˆ (carat) character. When a label begins with this prefix, 1-2-3 centers it within its cell. If you don't put anything before an entry, or if you use the ' (single quote) prefix character, 1-2-3 justifies

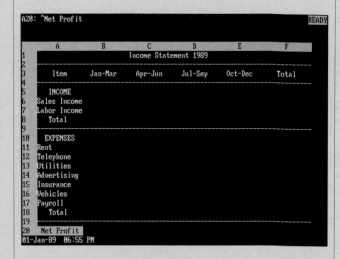

the label on the left within its cell. Finally, if you use the '' (double quote) prefix character before a label, it will be justified on the right within its cell.

Now you can go on to enter the rest of the labels that will identify the contents of this worksheet. The figure above shows the worksheet after you've finished.

The next step is to enter the actual data, the numbers that represent the various income and expense figures for the four quarters of 1989. Because this is an income statement for an imaginary business, we simply made up values. If this were a real business, however, these numbers would have to come from outside records. In other words, these numbers cannot be generated by the 1-2-3 program itself. When you enter a number, you type it without a dollar sign and commas separating thousands. These will be automatically displayed by 1-2-3. After the income and expenses numbers are entered, the worksheet looks like this:

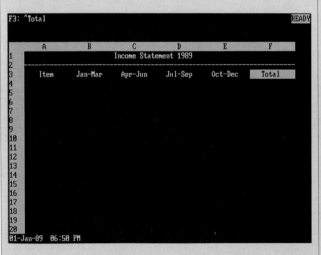

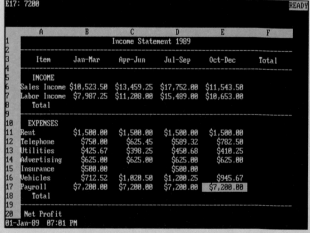

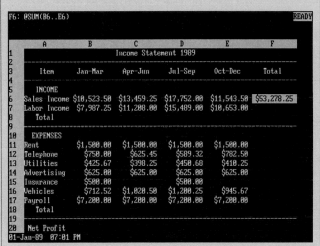

```
F6: @SUM(B6..E6)                                    READY
        A         B          C          D          E          F
 1                        Income Statement 1989
 2
 3      Item     Jan-Mar    Apr-Jun    Jul-Sep    Oct-Dec    Total
 4
 5      INCOME
 6   Sales Income $10,523.50 $13,459.25 $17,752.00 $11,543.50 $53,278.25
 7   Labor Income  $7,987.25 $11,208.00 $15,489.00 $10,653.00
 8      Total
 9
10      EXPENSES
11   Rent          $1,500.00  $1,500.00  $1,500.00  $1,500.00
12   Telephone       $750.00    $625.45    $589.32    $782.50
13   Utilities       $425.67    $398.25    $450.68    $410.25
14   Advertising     $625.00    $625.00    $625.00    $625.00
15   Insurance       $500.00               $500.00
16   Vehicles        $712.52  $1,020.50  $1,200.25    $945.67
17   Payroll       $7,200.00  $7,200.00  $7,200.00  $7,200.00
18      Total
19
20   Net Profit
01-Jan-89  07:01 PM
```

```
B8: +B6+B7                                          READY
        A         B          C          D          E          F
 1                        Income Statement 1989
 2
 3      Item     Jan-Mar    Apr-Jun    Jul-Sep    Oct-Dec    Total
 4
 5      INCOME
 6   Sales Income $10,523.50 $13,459.25 $17,752.00 $11,543.50 $53,278.25
 7   Labor Income  $7,987.25 $11,208.00 $15,489.00 $10,653.00 $45,337.75
 8      Total    $18,510.75
 9
10      EXPENSES
11   Rent          $1,500.00  $1,500.00  $1,500.00  $1,500.00  $6,000.00
12   Telephone       $750.00    $625.45    $589.32    $782.50  $2,747.27
13   Utilities       $425.67    $398.25    $450.68    $410.25  $1,684.85
14   Advertising     $625.00    $625.00    $625.00    $625.00  $2,500.00
15   Insurance       $500.00               $500.00             $1,000.00
16   Vehicles        $712.52  $1,020.50  $1,200.25    $945.67  $3,878.94
17   Payroll       $7,200.00  $7,200.00  $7,200.00  $7,200.00 $28,800.00
18      Total
19
20   Net Profit
01-Jan-89  07:02 PM
```

Once the data values have been entered, you can put in the formulas that will compute the totals and the net profit. For example, to total the sales income for the year, you enter this formula in cell F6: *@SUM(B6..E6)*. This formula uses the @SUM function to total the contents of cells B6, C6, D6, and E6 and display the result in cell F6. The figure above shows your screen at this point. Notice how the result $53,278.25 is displayed down in the worksheet cell F6, but the control panel at the top of the screen shows the actual contents of cell F6—the formula *@SUM(B6..E6)*.

You could manually enter similar formulas to compute the rest of the totals in column F, but there is an easier way. The Copy command can be used to replicate the formula from cell F6 into cells F7 and F11 through F17. To execute the Copy command, simply type */C*. The 1-2-3 program then asks you for the range of cells to copy from and you enter *F6*. Then it asks for the range of cells to copy to and you enter *F7*. The formula is reproduced in cell F7, but not as an exact copy. The cell references within the formula are adjusted to reflect the row to which you are copying the formula. In other words, the formula you copied from cell F6 is *@SUM(B6..E6)*, but the copy that is placed in cell F7 is *(@SUM(B7..E7)*. Since most worksheets contain many such similar formulas, the Copy command can save you a great deal of time. Using it, you can very easily copy the formula from cell F6 to the cells F11 through F17 as well.

The next set of formulas you must enter will sum the two income figures for each quarter. You move the cell pointer to cell B8 and enter this formula: *+B6+B7*. The leading plus sign tells 1-2-3 that the entry is a formula and not a label. Your screen will resemble the figure at top right.

Again, you could use the Copy command to reproduce the formula from cell B8 into cells C8 through F8. Similarly, you would then go on entering and copying formulas into the worksheet until all the totals are complete. The final set of formulas computes the net profit figures, which are simply the total income minus the total expenses for each column. When you are finished with all of the formulas, the worksheet looks like the figure below.

The great advantage of using a spreadsheet program instead of doing a worksheet by hand is the ease with which you can make changes. If you discover that you've made a mistake entering a number, or if certain figures must be updated, you simply change them. The entire worksheet automatically recalculates to display the new results. This feature also allows you to explore "what if" scenarios. For example, you can see what your total profit for the year would be if your rent were

```
F20: +F8-F18                                        READY
        A         B          C          D          E          F
 1                        Income Statement 1989
 2
 3      Item     Jan-Mar    Apr-Jun    Jul-Sep    Oct-Dec    Total
 4
 5      INCOME
 6   Sales Income $10,523.50 $13,459.25 $17,752.00 $11,543.50 $53,278.25
 7   Labor Income  $7,987.25 $11,208.00 $15,489.00 $10,653.00 $45,337.75
 8      Total    $18,510.75 $24,667.25 $33,241.50 $22,196.50 $98,616.00
 9
10      EXPENSES
11   Rent          $1,500.00  $1,500.00  $1,500.00  $1,500.00  $6,000.00
12   Telephone       $750.00    $625.45    $589.32    $782.50  $2,747.27
13   Utilities       $425.67    $398.25    $450.68    $410.25  $1,684.85
14   Advertising     $625.00    $625.00    $625.00    $625.00  $2,500.00
15   Insurance       $500.00               $500.00             $1,000.00
16   Vehicles        $712.52  $1,020.50  $1,200.25    $945.67  $3,878.94
17   Payroll       $7,200.00  $7,200.00  $7,200.00  $7,200.00 $28,800.00
18      Total    $11,713.19 $11,369.20 $12,065.25 $11,463.42 $46,611.06
19
20   Net Profit  $6,797.56 $13,298.05 $21,176.25 $10,733.08 $52,004.94
01-Jan-89  07:05 PM
```

increased by $50 per month. All you have to do is change the rent figures.

As a final sample of what you can do with a spreadsheet program, let's make a bar graph of the total income figures for each quarter. This is done by typing /G to execute the Graph command. There are a number of options you must then execute to set up the graph. First you tell the program that the type of graph you want to draw is a bar graph. Then you set the X-axis range to be cells B3 through E3. This will put the labels *Jan–Mar*, *Apr–Jun*, *Jul–Sep*, and *Oct–Dec* along the bottom of the graph. Next you set the first data range to be cells B8 through E8. This will use the total income figures to determine the height of each bar in the graph. Finally, you can then set the graph title to be *Income 1989* and the Y-axis title to be *Dollars*. Then you execute the View command from the Graph menu to actually display the graph on your screen, which looks like the figure at right.

This graph can be saved in a disk file and printed out later with a separate program called PrintGraph, which is included with the Lotus 1-2-3 package.

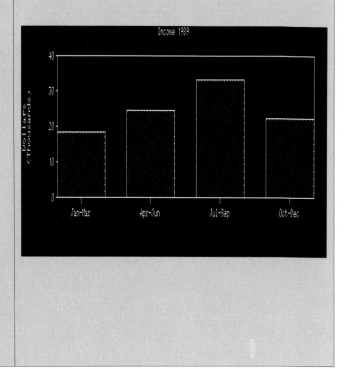

Summary

Types of Application Packages

An application package is a program or set of related programs that accomplish a specific set of tasks. The most prevalent types are word processors, spreadsheets, and data base managers.

Word Processing

The most popular of all packages, they give the user the power to enter, store, edit, format, copy, and print text.

Creating Documents The features common to most word processors include a cursor, word-wrap, a thesaurus, a spelling checker, and, in many, an outline processor.

Editing Documents Reworking text as it is composed is essential to writing and is one of the most important features of word processors. Some of the most important features of word processors are the ability to view a document, insert and delete text, cut-and-paste, search and replace, cancel commands, and check spelling.

Formatting Documents Word processors let the user arrange a document so it looks attractive when printed. The three levels of formatting are character formatting, paragraph formatting, and page formatting.

Printing Documents Word processors produce printed documents. Most packages allow the user to choose many different print options.

Managing Documents You can save and retrieve documents you have created.

Popular Word-Processing Programs There are many popular word-processing packages. The three most popular are WordStar, WordPerfect, and Microsoft Word.

Spreadsheet

These programs let the user enter, manipulate, and store tables of numbers and text. They are flexible enough to be applied to a variety of tasks.

Worksheet Structure   Data is entered into cells, each of which is identified by an address.

Cell Contents   Three types of data can be entered in a cell: numbers, labels, and formulas. Formulas can contain functions that perform tedious or often-used manipulations of data.

Entering and Editing Data   Spreadsheets have a cell pointer to enter data or give commands, similar to the cursor in word processors.

Formatting Data   As with word processors, spreadsheets offer a variety of ways to display and print numbers.

Calculating Results   Many spreadsheets have features to permit calculations in several ways such as automatic recalculation, manual recalculation, and smart recalculation.

Printing Worksheets   There are a number of default settings for printing reports. Users can also design their own layouts.

Saving and Retrieving Worksheets   Worksheets are usually saved for later retrieval and editing or printing.

Graphing   Instead of an entire worksheet, some users may prefer to print results in graphic form. Most programs permit the use of a variety of graphs including bar graphs, pie charts, scatterplots, and line graphs.

Data Management   A principal strength of spreadsheets is their ability to organize and display data of various types.

Templates   A template is a worksheet that contains labels, formulas and perhaps a few constants, enabling the user to just fill in the blanks.

Popular Spreadsheet Programs   Among the many spreadsheet programs, three stand out as the most widely used: Lotus 1-2-3, SuperCalc, and Microsoft Excel.

Data Base Management

One of the principal uses of computers is organizing and manipulating large collections of data called data bases.

Types of Data Base Managers   Types of managers include flat-file, free-form, hypertext, relational, and programmable managers.

Creating a Data Base   The user must create a format before the computer can handle the data.

Viewing a Data Base   Stored data can be reviewed.

Updating a Data Base   Data can be kept up-to-date by adding, deleting, and modifying records, and by changing the structure of the data base.

Rearranging a Data Base   For a number of reasons, a user may want to reorganize a data base by sorting or indexing the records.

Generating Data Base Reports   Just as with word processors and spreadsheets, data base managers are used to produce printed output, a report.

Popular Data Base Managers   Singling out the most popular packages is somewhat arbitrary but dBASE, R:base, and Hypercard stand out.

Communications

A variety of packages exist for accessing data computer-to-computer. The tasks these packages handle include setting communications parameters, dialing phones, entering log-on information, emulating a terminal, downloading, and uploading.

Graphics

Several types of graphics packages are commonly used to create images.

Charting   Programs can produce graphs, plots, and charts from data entered by the user or transferred from a worksheet or file.

Painting   You can create free-hand pictures with a mouse, graphics tablet, or trackball, using pre-defined shapes or creating your own.

Drawing   These packages produce object-oriented graphics for precise scaled diagrams such as architectural or engineering drawings.

Computer-Aided Design   Using CAD packages, engineers, architects, and other technical experts can create complicated illustrations of designs at their microcomputers.

Slide Show   This type of program permits the creation and use of slide presentations to accompany talks for more effective communication.

Integrated Software

Combining the most popular packages into one integrated package for microcomputers, software developers let users learn a uniform set of commands for a group of programs.

Desktop Publishing

Now microcomputer users with access to laser printers can produce high-quality printed matter complete with illustrations at a relatively modest cost.

Statistics

Back to basics—one of the most common uses of computers is to handle numbers. There are now packages that do statistical analyses using data supplied by the users.

Accounting

Packages can help boost profits, pay bills, calculate earnings, and explore alternative financial plans.

Project Management

Programs can help managers control complex undertakings such as large construction projects.

Personal Finance and Tax Preparation

With your microcomputer you can manage your money and calculate or even fill out your tax returns.

Education

Everything from the alphabet to languages and thermodynamics can be taught by computer programs.

Entertainment

When you finish your work, you can use your computer to play games ranging from ticktacktoe to sports or commanding spaceships.

As an extra review of the chapter, try defining the following terms. If you have trouble with any of them, refer to the page number listed.

application package *285*
word-processing package *285*
cursor *286*
word-wrap *286*
outline processor *287*
on-line thesaurus *287*
insert mode *289*
overwrite mode *289*
cut-and-paste *289*
copy-and-paste *289*
search and replace *290*
undo *290*
spelling checker *290*
font (typeface) *291*
points *291*
alignment *291*
justified *291*
running head *292*
style sheet *292*
draft mode *293*
letter-quality mode *293*
proportional spacing *293*
print spooling (print buffering) *294*
mail-merge *294*
spreadsheet package *296*

worksheets (spreadsheets) *296*
cell *296*
cell address *296*
formula *297*
function *298*
cell pointer *299*
current cell (active cell) *299*
automatic recalculation *300*
manual recalculation *301*
smart recalculation *301*
template *303*
data base *305*
data base management package *305*
flat-file data base manager *305*
free-form data base manager *305*
hypertext *306*
hypermedia *306*
relational data base manager *306*
programmable data base manager *306*

relational data base *307*
data entry form *308*
browse *309*
querying *309*
sorting *311*
indexing *312*
data base report *312*
stackware *314*
logging on (signing on) *315*
terminal emulation *316*
downloading *316*
uploading *316*
charting program *316*
painting program *316*
pixels *316*
pixel-based (bit-mapped) graphics *317*
drawing program *318*
object-oriented graphics *318*
computer-aided design (CAD) *319*
slide show program *320*
integrated software *320*
project management package *323*

1. What are the most prevalent types of application software?
2. List the five basic functions of all word processors.
3. What is the name for the word processing feature that permits the user to type past the existing right margin?
4. Name the feature of word processors, as well as other packages, that permits the user to view several areas of a document or different documents simultaneously.
5. List the facilities provided by most word processors that help control various aspects of the printing process.
6. What is the name given to the intersection for a row and a column of a spreadsheet and how is it identified?
7. What are the three types of data that can be entered into a cell?
8. Describe a function and name one common to all spreadsheet programs.
9. What is the spreadsheet feature that permits entry of values and formulas without waiting for updating of every cell in large worksheets?
10. Name five basic types of data base managers.
11. What are some of the features of a hypermedia system?
12. What is the term for transferring data from a remote computer to your own? For transferring data from your computer to another?

13. What are five commonly used types of graphic packages?
14. What is the term for the tiny individual dots on a computer display screen?
15. What name is given to packages that combine word processing, spreadsheet, data base management, communications, and graphics programs?
16. Name some of the capabilities of desktop publishing packages. For what are they especially useful?
17. Name a popular statistical package developed for microcomputers.
18. What is the term used to describe packages that help managers control large projects involving a number of complex tasks?
19. What is the best-selling software used for everything from balancing checkbooks to investing money?
20. What are some of the features that make educational packages useful and effective?

True or False

1. The word processing feature that sets margins is called word-wrap.
2. The operation that permits the movement of a segment of existing text from one location in a document to another is cut-and-paste.
3. A set of letters and other symbols with a consistent style is called a font.
4. The feature that permits printing one document while working on another is called print queuing.
5. A formula is an expression that instructs the spreadsheet program to perform calculations or other manipulations on the contents of specified cells.
6. Formulas can contain special operations known as functions.
7. The feature of a spreadsheet that is analogous to the cursor in a word processor is a cell pointer.
8. The most popular spreadsheet program for IBM compatibles is Lotus 1-2-3.
9. A relational data base manager can work with more than one file at a time.
10. Once entered, the structure of a data base cannot be changed.

Multiple Choice

1. Among the three most prevalent types of application software in use is:
   (a) mathematic   (b) word processing   (c) hypertext
2. The name given to the feature that permits replacing existing characters with new text is:
   (a) overwrite mode   (b) insert mode   (c) undo
3. The ability to specify a list of documents to be printed is called:
   (a) print spooling   (b) mail-merge   (c) print queuing
4. A software program that lets you store tables of numbers and text is called a:
   (a) word processor   (b) spreadsheet   (c) data base manager
5. The spreadsheet feature that updates the whole spreadsheet every time the contents of a cell are changed is called:
   (a) automatic recalculation (b) formatting   (c) a function
6. The name for a data base manager that handles only single files organized into regular-sized pieces of data is:
   (a) relational   (b) free-form   (c) flat-file

7. One way of updating a data base is:
   (a) adding records   (b) browsing   (c) querying

8. The process by which users of a multi-user system identify themselves is:
   (a) uploading   (b) logging on   (c) dialing

9. A program for producing complicated diagrams or illustrations for engineers, architects or scientists is:
   (a) MacPaint,   (b) pixel   (c) CAD

10. A package that combines word processing, spreadsheet, data base management, communications, and graphics is called:
    (a) a slide show program   (b) integrated software   (c) desktop publishing

A Sharper Focus

Now that you've completed this chapter, you should be able to answer the following questions.

1. Although you have not had hands-on experience with Mortgage Selector, can you tell what type of application package it is?

2. From its title, would you say it is a program for experts or for the end-user? Why? Relate this to an estimate of what the development and marketing costs for a typical package might be, thereby coming up with an estimate of what sales would have to be to break even or make a profit. Are software packages profitable in most cases, or are they just necessary in order to sell equipment?

Projects

1. Let's say that you have a Personal System/2 Model 50 computer and that you've been given $1000 with which to buy all the software you'll need as a student. Decide what kinds of application packages you require, investigate the products available from various manufacturers, and then choose which ones you want to purchase. Try to be a wise consumer by researching all possibilities and by striving to get the best value for your money. Prepare a report detailing your selections and the reasons behind them.

2. Although the number of different tasks to be done by a word-processing package is fairly small, dozens, perhaps even hundreds, of different packages are available for the most popular microcomputer models. Why? Do their features differ significantly? Investigate this question. Write a report with examples to illustrate your findings and include a table or chart summarizing them.

3. Small business owners are often told, "Find the application packages you want, then just buy a microcomputer that'll run them. They're all pretty much the same." What do you think of this advice, and why?

4. Many computer magazines carry monthly listings of the top 10 or 20 best-selling application packages for microcomputers. Compare older issues with more recent issues, and see what you can conclude about the average life of some of the packages mentioned in this chapter.

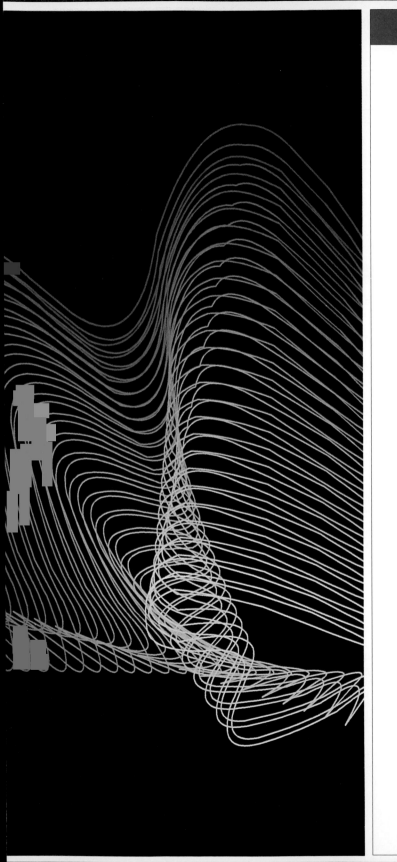

10

Operating Systems

In This Chapter

Focus On

UNIX

Work on [UNIX] started back in 1969 because Ken Thompson, 41, a bearded, long-haired programming pioneer who has been known to work 30 hours at a stretch, felt frustrated in constructing a computer game he called Space Travel.

Big operating systems of the sort that ran those computers are normally a product of hundreds of systems designers and programmers, and they incorporate many compromises. Thompson decided to strive for simplicity. . . . He wanted as much freedom and flexibility for users as possible.

Thompson was soon joined by another Bell Labs programmer, Dennis Ritchie, also bearded and inquisitive, and the two began incorporating into UNIX the best features they could find in various operating systems as well as contributing their own concepts. One of their most brilliant additions was the concept of "pipes," through which one command can be connected to another, allowing the user to create new applications programs by stringing together

UNIX "words" into "sentences." The UNIX language provides an unusually large number of preprogrammed commands—more than 200—for sorting data, manipulating text, or searching for information. These "utilities" can be used in thousands of combinations, offering the user a range of instruments of unusual . . . power. "UNIX," one user observed recently, "is the Swiss army knife of software."

A major virtue of UNIX is leverage—a little tapping on the keyboard can bring on a lot of action in the computer. As an example, people at Bell Laboratories point to the set of instructions below. They tell a computer to print out each word in a document, along with the number of times the word occurs, arranging the words in descending order of frequency. That may not be what you want from your computer, but it's a pretty good test of an operating system. A while back, a Bell Labs programmer asked outsiders to estimate how many lines of instructions the task would require—lines, in this sense, meaning commands—and most of the replies fell in the range of 100 to 1,000. With UNIX, just seven short commands do the trick.

```
tr [A-Z] [a-z] I
    Make capital letters lower case.
tr -d ''(.,;:\'''-_!?\)'' I
    Delete punctuation.
tr '' '' ''\012'' I
    Put each word on a separate line.
sed -e ''/^ *$/d'' I
    Delete blank lines.
sort I
    Sort words in alphabetical order.
uniq -c I
    Count occurrences of each word.
sort -nr
    Sort by frequency, in descending
    order.
```

Where does the leverage come from? Brian W. Kernighan, the Bell Labs programmer who coined the name UNIX, explains that pieces of the job are already done before the user taps a single key. Each of those seven brief directives begins with a general purpose command, such as "tr" or "sort," that is a program in itself. And UNIX is so designed that instructions to modify the general purpose command can readily be "glued on."

We've now covered almost all the basics: from input to output, from hardware to software. We've looked at how just about everything in a computer system works. Logically enough, we've saved for last the element that binds hardware and software together into an integrated, usable whole, capable of doing all the things for which its parts were designed. That element—the operating system—is easily the most important software a computer has. In most cases, the operating system is the first program executed when a computer is turned on, and the last program executed before it's shut down. No matter what you do with a computer, the operating system is behind it all.

In this chapter, we'll learn what operating systems do and how they do it, and we'll look at several of today's most widely used commercially available operating systems, from Apple's "user-cuddly" system for the Macintosh to IBM's powerful VM for mainframes.

FUNCTIONS OF OPERATING SYSTEMS

Operating systems are used on all types of general-purpose computers, from microcomputers to supercomputers. They are such an integral part of the computer that every user should have at least a general understanding of their functions. An **operating system (OS)** can be defined as a set of programs that controls, supervises, and supports a computer system's hardware and application packages. The fundamental task of an operating system is to manage the hardware carefully to achieve the best possible performance. To do this, the operating system controls and coordinates such resources as the central processing unit (CPU), other processing units, both primary memory and secondary storage, and all input/output devices. The hardware provides the raw computing power, and the operating system makes this power conveniently accessible to the application packages and ultimately to the user.

What operating systems do

Providing Services

By handling computer resources efficiently, so that users don't have to worry about every detail during processing, the operating system provides the following valuable services:

How operating systems help users

- *Sharing hardware among users.* In computer systems that can accommodate more than one user at a time, the operating system decides who gets what and when. For example, if there are five users and only one printer, the operating system must be prepared to accept and deal with five simultaneous printer requests. The operating system ensures that all users eventually get their turn with a shared hardware device.

- *Allowing users to share programs and data.* Systems that are simultaneously accessible to a number of users usually include some means by which programs and data can be shared among those users. Identical programs and data need not be duplicated for each user. In an airline reservation system, for example, the data base of flights, fares, and available seats and the programs that allow reservations to be made are shared by all travel agents who have access to the system.

- *Enabling users to protect their data.*   Computer systems with multiple users must provide measures by which users can be prevented from accessing or accidentally destroying one another's private data.

- *Scheduling resource use.*   Again, with several users, a computer's operating system must coordinate the use of all the available resources. A good operating system accomplishes this in the most efficient manner possible.

- *Facilitating input, output, and secondary storage operations.*   If a computer had no operating system, every application program would have to specify all the operating details of the input, output, and secondary storage devices. By taking care of such fundamental operations as reading characters from the keyboard, operating the display, sending characters to the printer, and writing records onto disks, the operating system frees users from worrying about low-level details.

- *Recovering from errors.*   Computer users (especially programmers) have an aptitude for "crashing" computers in any number of imaginative ways. They may write a program that accidentally branches to a memory location containing only garbage, or they may devise an infinite loop. Operating systems usually are capable of detecting errors such as these, informing users of their nature, and minimizing any damage to data. A good operating system can save the day in many cases and prevent the whole computer from coming to a grinding halt.

Acting as an Interface

The operating system as the user interface

The operating system functions as an *interface* (a shared boundary or connection) on two levels (see Figure 10.1). First, the operating system interfaces software with hardware. Application programs call the operating system to handle most of the details concerned with controlling the computer hardware. Thus, programs can utilize the services offered by the operating system without compromising its role as a resource manager. Second, the operating system interfaces users with the computer system. In Chapter 7, we said that a user interface specifies how a person communicates with a program. The operating system defines how users communicate with and control the computer system as a whole.

Who uses operating systems

There are various kinds of users, and each type interacts with the operating system in a slightly different way. *End users*—bank tellers, travel agents, authors, students, and so on—use a computer system in their day-to-day work. They rely on the operating system to run the application programs they need and to handle their storage, input, and output requests. *Novices* are beginning computer users. They often need extra help in learning how to use the computer, its operating system, and application packages. At the other end of the spectrum are the *experts*, sometimes called *power users*, who have a great deal of computer experience and who feel quite at home using computers.

Although programmers are generally experts, every expert is not necessarily a programmer. A person can become an expert at using an operating system or running particular application packages without knowing how to program a computer. In general, programmers fall into two categories: application programmers and systems programmers. *Application programmers* use the operating system to facilitate the entry, development, translation, and installation of application packages. *Systems programmers* are concerned with creating, installing, and maintaining the operating system itself.

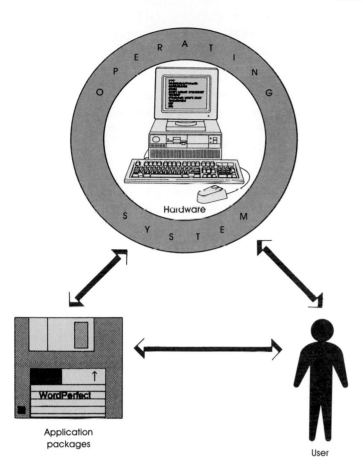

Figure 10.1 The Operating System as an Interface
The operating system insulates both users and application software from having to deal with low-level details of running computer hardware. Thus it acts as an interface between users and hardware, and application packages and hardware.

A SHORT HISTORY OF OPERATING SYSTEMS

In Chapter 2, we noted that the operating system emerged as a significant software development during the third generation of computers. Although primitive operating systems did exist before that, they didn't become a dominant force until the mid-1960s. The earliest computer systems had no operating systems; users had access to computer resources only via machine language programs. Programs were run one at a time by computer operators who manually entered the commands to initiate and complete each one. This technique wasted a great deal of computer time, since the CPU remained idle between the completion of one task and the initiation of the next.

How and why operating systems evolved

The 1950s were marked by the development of rudimentary operating systems designed to smooth the transitions between jobs (a **job** is any program or part of a program that is to be processed as a unit by a computer). This was the start of *batch processing,* in which programs to be executed were grouped into *batches.* While a particular program was running, it had total control of the computer. When it finished, however, control was returned to the operating system, which handled any necessary finalizations and started the next job. Letting the computer handle the transition between one job and the next instead of doing it manually took up less time, and more efficiently utilized the CPU.

During the 1960s, operating systems became much more sophisticated, leading up to the development of *shared systems.* These multitasking, time-sharing, and multiprocessing systems (which we will define and discuss in more detail later in this chapter) allowed several user programs to be run on a single computer system, seemingly at the same time. Additionally, these systems were the first to allow usage to take place in the *interactive,* or *conversational mode,* in which the user communicates directly with the computer, rather than submitting jobs and passively waiting for their completion. These developments made computer systems more widely accessible and easier to use. Instead of waiting for hours or even days for results from the batch processing of programs, users could get responses from the computer in seconds or minutes. This enhancement was a boon to programmers, who could more quickly locate and correct errors in their programs, and thus reduce the time it took to develop new software.

Real-time systems also emerged during the 1960s. These operating systems enabled computers to be used to control systems characterized by the need for immediate response, such as weapons systems or industrial plants. For example, if an oil refinery is being controlled by a real-time system, that system must respond immediately to temperature conditions that could cause an explosion.

In the late 1960s and the early 1970s, there was a trend toward *general-purpose operating systems.* These systems tried to be all things to all users. Often called **multimode systems,** some of them simultaneously supported batch processing, time sharing, real-time processing, and multiprocessing. They were large, expensive, and difficult to develop and maintain, but they helped sell a lot of computers. The prime example of this type of operating system was offered with the IBM System 360 family of mainframe computers first introduced in 1964. To get one of these monsters to perform even the simplest task, users had to learn a complex **job control language (JCL)** and employ it to specify how their programs were to be run and what resources they would need. Although multimode systems represented a great step forward, they reached no heights of user-friendliness.

The operating systems from the mid-1970s to the present cannot be characterized by a single, all-encompassing feature. The development of microcomputers and of simple, easy-to-use, single-user operating systems has had a profound effect on the newest systems being developed for all types of computers. The features most in demand are a high degree of user-friendliness and a computing environment that is *graphics-oriented* and *menu-driven* (refers to the use of graphic symbols and lists of options that aid users in selecting functions). Also, operating systems that support multitasking, computer networking, data security, and distributed data processing are the latest word. Modern operating systems create a **virtual machine,** an interface that relieves the user of any need to be concerned about most of the physical details of the computer system or the network being accessed. The virtual machine presented by the operating system lets users concentrate on getting their work done, without having to be familiar with the internal functioning of the actual hardware.

COMPONENTS OF OPERATING SYSTEMS

What makes up an operating system; where the system resides

An operating system consists of an integrated set of programs, each of which performs specific tasks. These component programs are expressly designed to work together as a team and can generally be categorized as either control programs or

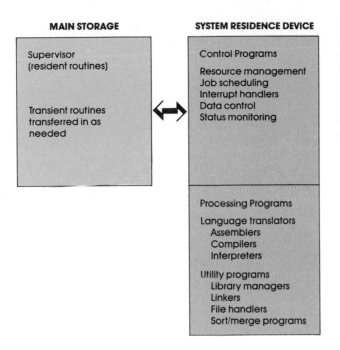

Figure 10.2   The Operating System
An operating system is a set of programs, which can be classified as either control programs or processing programs. These programs reside on the system residence device and are transferred into primary memory as needed. Some of them (the resident routines) are used so frequently that they are constantly held in primary memory.

processing programs. *Control programs* direct the operations of the computer system and perform such tasks as allocating resources, scheduling jobs, resolving interrupts, sending messages to users, and managing the fundamental workings of input, output, and secondary storage. *Processing programs* perform functions that aid programmers in the preparation and execution of system and application software.

The collection of programs that makes up an operating system is kept in secondary storage on the **system residence device,** the permanent home of the operating system. The control and processing programs are stored here, ready to be loaded into primary memory and executed whenever they are called on to perform their jobs (see Figure 10.2). In most cases, the system residence device is a disk (which led to the nickname *DOS,* or *disk operating system*). Read-only memory (ROM) chips are also frequently used to store parts of the operating system permanently inside the computer hardware.

Control Programs

The **supervisor** (also known as the **monitor** or **executive**) is the main control program of the operating system, responsible for coordinating the activities of all other parts of the operating system. When the computer is first turned on, the supervisor is the first program to be loaded from the system residence device into primary memory. The most frequently used components of the supervisor, **the resident routines** are kept in primary memory the entire time the computer is on. Portions used less frequently are known as the **transient routines;** they remain on the system residence device and are transferred into primary memory as needed. Tasks performed by the supervisor or by the other control programs it directs include managing system resources, scheduling jobs, handling interrupts, controlling the flow of data, and monitoring system status.

The routines that manage resources, schedule jobs, handle interrupts, control data, and monitor system status

Managing Resources

Control programs that manage computer resources basically govern who gets to use what and when. As we will see, this role is especially important when the operating system is servicing more than one user or program during the same time period. Primary memory and secondary storage must be managed so that they are utilized as efficiently as possible, while ensuring that no program destroys another's data. If there is more than one processing unit, control programs must assign which programs or parts of programs are run on which processors. If there is only one processing unit but more than one user or program to be serviced, control programs must divide up processing time. Conflicts must be resolved whenever more than one user or program needs to access the same input, output, or storage device at the same time.

Job Scheduling

Control programs for job scheduling establish the scheme by which multiple users or programs are serviced. This involves evaluating the resources needed for running jobs, assigning priorities, preparing jobs for execution, directing the flow of jobs through the computer system, and "cleaning up" after job completion (clearing memory locations, resetting input, output, and storage devices, and so on). On some mainframe computers, the performance of these activities may require interpreting job control language statements in order to determine the characteristics of a job to be run and which resources it will require. These statements, prepared by programmers for programs they want to run, are necessary for some operating systems, especially those that function in batch mode.

Handling Interrupts

Since a CPU performs arithmetic calculations much faster than most peripheral devices (terminals, disk drives, and printers) operate, most computer systems have adopted some form of interrupt scheme to reduce the time the CPU is idle. An **interrupt** is a temporary suspension of the running of a computer program so that another, higher-priority job can be handled immediately. For example, let's say that a particular program processes data that must be read from a disk drive or entered by a typist at a terminal keyboard. Instead of letting the CPU sit idly while this input is acquired, it is put to work on some other processing task that doesn't immediately require the requested data. When the data has been successfully read into primary memory, the CPU is interrupted, informed that the input is complete, and put back to work on the original task.

Although this switching back and forth from one job to another may seem like a complicated and hectic way to complete processing tasks, the more efficient utilization of the CPU's great speed dramatically increases the amount of work that can be accomplished. The operating system must be constantly ready to respond to interrupts triggered by internal or external events. When interrupts occur, control programs must coordinate the process of saving the current work, branching to the program that resolves the interrupt (the *interrupt service routine*) and returning to the previous task. This is a very important function of any operating system because interrupts are employed in computer systems of all sizes.

Controlling Data

Programs that control the input, output, and storage of data are an important part of any operating system. Processing tasks such as reading data from input devices, moving data between primary memory and secondary storage devices, and writing data to output devices must be performed by most application packages. It's more efficient to have the operating system handle the details of such tasks rather than to require every application program to specify them internally. This also simplifies the program development process by allowing programmers to avoid starting from scratch every time they must employ a common procedure. Data control programs consist of the low-level routines that drive the input, storage, and output devices. They are sometimes collectively known as the *input/output control system (IOCS)* or the *basic input/output system (BIOS)*.

In addition to directing these low-level activities, the data control programs of an operating system also control the use of such devices as buffers, channels, and spoolers. The concept of buffer storage was introduced in Chapter 3. To restate it in this context, buffers are commonly used for the temporary storage of data in order to reduce the demands on the CPU from operations of input, output, or data transfer. When buffers are used, the CPU can initiate an input, output, or data transfer operation and then return to other processing. After dumping the data to a buffer at high speed, the CPU is free to perform other tasks while the buffer transfers the data to the slower input, output, or storage device.

Large computer systems may utilize **channels** (not to be confused with communications channels): special-purpose microcomputers, minicomputers, or even mainframes that control the movement of data between the CPU and input/output devices. Once they have been invoked by the CPU, channels can control several input/output units simultaneously, and independently of the CPU.

Spooling (the word *spool* is an acronym for *simultaneous peripheral operating on line*) is an activity that enables several users to send output to a single printer while input and processing operations are also occurring. Each file to be printed is stored on an intermediate device (usually a disk) instead of being sent directly to the printer. The *spooler* handles the transfer of files from this intermediate storage device to the printer; the printing is carried out with no further involvement of the CPU. Users can continue with other work while their files are being printed via the spooler.

Monitoring System Status

Another important function of an operating system, especially of one for a large computer system, is monitoring its own operations. Control routines constantly check for errors or abnormal conditions and resolve these situations as smoothly as possible. A message may be output to the user, or the job causing the error condition may be aborted, before a **system crash** occurs. The dreaded system crash is essentially a run-time error in the operating system. Two common causes are branch instruction to some unintended memory location and an accidental erasure of part of the supervisor routine in primary storage. In general, the more complex the operating system, the more built-in safeguards it will have. Crashes do occasionally occur even with the best-protected systems, and their causes may be quite difficult to uncover.

System-monitoring routines also notify users when it is time to take care of manual tasks (such as loading a different disk into a disk drive), handle system security (for example, requiring users to log on), and compile statistics about system performance (the amount of CPU time used by each job, what computer resources are currently in use, how many lines of output have been printed, and so on). These job-accounting functions are especially important for large systems that service multiple users who must be billed correctly for the computer services they receive.

Processing Programs

The routines that aid the development and use of software by translating programs and providing utilities

In addition to control programs, operating systems also include processing programs. By aiding users in their preparation of programs and providing commonly used system functions, the processing programs simplify the development and execution of software. The two major classes of processing programs are language translators and utility programs.

Language Translators

In Chapter 8, we described the three major types of language translators: assemblers, compilers, and interpreters. These programs convert programming language instructions into machine language instructions. Because they're essential to the production of both system and application software, they are sometimes considered to be operating system components. Language translators primarily convert source code (instructions in an assembly or high-level language) into object code (instructions in machine language).

Besides the typical language translators such as assemblers, compilers, and interpreters, there are three special types: optimizing compilers, precompilers, and cross-compilers.

Optimizing compilers are translators expressly designed to produce highly efficient object code. Through the use of special techniques, these compilers yield translated programs that execute faster or require less storage than they would if they were translated with ordinary compilers. For the most part, optimizing compilers trade off storage space for execution speed, or vice versa. For example, if a certain program must run as quickly as possible, translating it with an optimizing compiler would, to some extent, make it take up more storage space to gain execution speed. On the other hand, a program could be made to require as little storage space as possible through the sacrifice of execution speed. Once a program has been fully developed and debugged, an optimizing compiler can be useful in cases that require high efficiency.

Precompilers, as their name implies, are translator programs that are employed before using a regular compiler. They translate some shorthand, enhanced, or otherwise modified version of a high-level language into a standard form. The output of a precompiler is standardized source code, which must then be translated by a compiler into machine language. What might be the purpose of introducing this additional step? The answer is that precompilers enable standard languages to be enhanced or customized for particular purposes. For example, before FORTRAN evolved its own built-in structured programming features, RATFOR (RATional FORtran) was a popular alternative language. Although similar to standard FORTRAN, RATFOR has additional features that are compatible with the principles of structured programming. RATFOR precompilers (which in many cases are actually written in RATFOR) are used to convert RATFOR programs into standard FOR-

TRAN programs, which are then translated by FORTRAN compilers into object code.

A **cross-compiler** is a translator that allows a programmer to develop a program on one computer with the intention of actually using it on another computer. With cross-compilers, programmers are able to "cross" their code from one computer to another. For example, let's say that a programmer has to write a complex program for a microcomputer and wants to develop it using a high-level language available only on a mainframe. The program can be developed and debugged using the superior facilities of the mainframe installation and then converted with a cross-compiler into object code that will run on the microcomputer.

Utility Programs

Utility programs (also known as **service programs**) are processing programs that provide users with common necessary functions. Included in this category of operating system components are library managers, linkers, file-handling programs, sort/merge programs, and a number of other programs that perform system "housekeeping" tasks.

Library managers are programs that allow users to build and use their own collections of frequently needed software modules. Such libraries must consist of manufacturer-supplied and user-written subroutines that can be called on by system or application software. By taking advantage of the capabilities of library managers, users can avoid having to rewrite routines they have previously developed. With library managers, users can add to, delete from, and catalog program modules kept in system libraries. Typical program modules kept in a library include those that compute mathematical functions, produce graphics, and interface peripheral devices (such as plotters and speech synthesizers).

Linkers (also called **linkage editors** or **linking loaders**) process the machine language code produced by assemblers or compilers and create the final *executable module*, which is ready to be run by the computer. A linker does this by adding the necessary subroutines from system libraries and by assigning actual storage addresses in primary memory to the components of the object code. In other words, the linker unifies the object code into a completely defined module, ready to be loaded into primary memory and executed by the computer.

File-handling programs perform a number of low-level tasks for users, for example, creating, deleting, moving, copying, and converting program and data files. *Sort/merge programs* enable users to rearrange and combine their data files without having to write their own software for this purpose. Since such file-associated tasks are so frequently required by all types of computer users, general utility programs for performing them are usually included in operating systems.

Finally, various other programs may also be included in operating system software. These perform such tasks as helping programmers debug their code, dumping the contents of memory into a file that can be output for examination, simple text editing, and informing the user about the current status of the system.

TYPES OF OPERATING SYSTEMS

Operating systems can be classified in a number of ways: by how they organize primary memory, by how many different programs they can execute concurrently, by how many users they can serve at the same time, by the setting in which they

Classifying operating systems

are to be used, or by the basic design of their components. We will describe eight types of operating systems: single-user, single-tasking; single-user, multitasking; multiuser, single-tasking; multiuser, multitasking; multiprocessing; virtual storage; real-time; and networking operating systems. Some of these categories are mutually exclusive. For example, an operating system is either single-user or it is multiuser. Other categories, however, do overlap to some extent. A single-user, multitasking operating system, for example, may also be a virtual storage operating system.

Single-User, Single-Tasking

Operating systems that let one person run one program at a time

The simplest type of operating system accommodates a single user at a time and is **single-tasking;** in other words, it can run only a single program at a time (see Figure 10.3). That program generally has access to all of the computer's resources, such as memory, disk storage, keyboard input, display output, and printer output. Once initiated, a program usually runs until it's finished or the user terminates execution. In reality, the program may be frequently interrupted for very short periods of time by the operating system to handle activities like updating the time of day and processing keyboard input.

This ability of operating systems to temporarily interrupt processing to handle some critical task has been put to some rather ingenious uses on some computers. **Memory-resident programs** have been developed for some operating systems that allow users to temporarily suspend what they're doing and switch to some other activity. For example, a program that simulates a hand-held calculator may be loaded into memory, but not executed, when the computer is turned on. By pressing some unique combination of keys, the user can activate this calculator. So, if you are using a word-processing program and you need to add several numbers, you can activate the calculator, temporarily suspend the word processor, compute

Figure 10.3   Single-User, Single-Tasking Operating System

This is the simplest type of operating system. Only one user and one program at a time can be serviced.

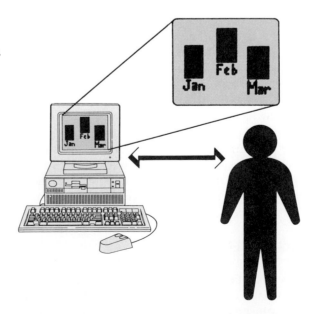

your sum, and then deactivate the calculator and return to word processing. Several different memory-resident programs may be installed and you may switch among them at will, but the computer is still only running a single program at a time. Most microcomputers have single-user, single-tasking operating systems, for example, MS-DOS.

Single-User, Multitasking

Most computer users probably get along quite well running only a single program at a time. For many computer applications, this is perfectly adequate. Often, however, running a single program at a time doesn't utilize the computer to its full potential. For example, most printers output characters much more slowly than computers can send characters over the cable. Depending on the word-processing or printing program, you might not be able to use your computer for other tasks while it prints a document. For long documents, this can tie up your computer for quite a while. This and many similar problems can be solved by multitasking operating systems.

Multitasking, also called **multiprogramming,** is the ability to run more than one program concurrently. This is similar to what a juggler does. First one ball is thrown up into the air, then another is caught and thrown up into the air, and so on. The juggler works so quickly that all the balls seem to be in the air at once. A single-user, multitasking operating system can juggle the execution of several programs (see Figure 10.4). The CPU very rapidly takes turns attending to each task so that it seems as if the programs are running simultaneously. For programs that use different computer resources, this works very well. For example, working with a spreadsheet program while printing a document would probably run just as quickly as it would if you weren't printing. Unless the CPU is powerful and fast, however, running several applications that utilize the same computer resources usually re-

Operating systems that let one person run several programs concurrently

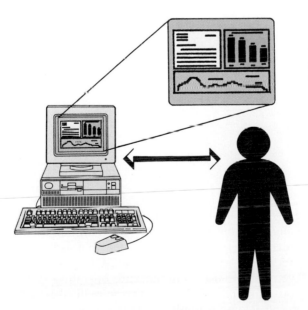

Figure 10.4 Single-User, Multitasking Operating System

These systems can execute several programs concurrently by switching the attention of the CPU back and forth among them.

Figure 10.5 Multiuser, Single-Tasking Operating System

Also called time sharing, this type of operating system can serve several users who are each running one program (not necessarily the same program) at a time.

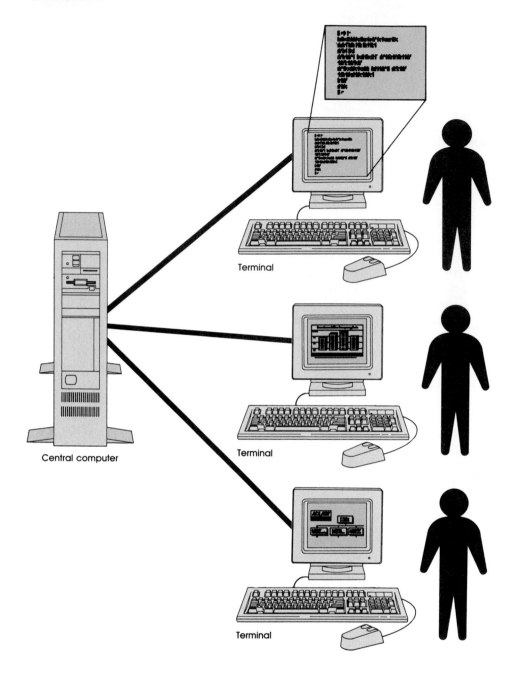

Central computer

Terminal

Terminal

Terminal

sults in some decrease in performance. For this reason, multitasking operating systems generally are implemented only on computers with fairly sophisticated CPUs. On microcomputers, this means models that use powerful microprocessors such as the Intel 80286 and 80386 and the Motorola MC68000, MC68020, and MC68030. Several single-user, multitasking operating systems are available for high-end microcomputers, and they are becoming increasingly popular. OS/2 from IBM and Microsoft is one example.

Multiuser, Single-Tasking

Another approach to solving the problem of underutilization of computer resources is to allow several users to access the same computer concurrently. Multiuser, single-tasking operating systems let several people each run one program at a time (see Figure 10.5). Each user is equipped with a *terminal,* or input/output station consisting of a keyboard and display, which is connected to the central computer. This arrangement is also called **time sharing,** because the operating system instructs the computer to switch rapidly among users at fixed intervals of time. These intervals, called *time slices,* are so short (typically a few thousandths of a second) that each user gets the illusion of having the computer's complete attention. As long as the CPU isn't saddled with more users than it can handle, its *response time* is quick enough to maintain this illusion. Consequently, time-sharing operating systems are generally implemented on computers with fast, powerful, and sophisticated CPUs. Although predominantly found on large computer systems, a few multiuser, single-tasking operating systems are available for some microcomputers.

Operating systems that let several people each run a single program at a time

Besides allowing several users to share the resources of a single computer, multiuser operating systems offer some other benefits. Thus, the cost per user for expensive hardware devices and software packages is reduced. Multiuser systems enable people to share data bases and send messages to one another easily. This can be especially useful in an office environment. One disadvantage of multiuser systems, however, is that if the central computer breaks down, everyone's work is brought to a halt.

Multiuser, Multitasking

Some sophisticated operating systems combine the concepts of time sharing and multitasking (see Figure 10.6). This allows each of several users to have more than one activity in progress at once. As you can imagine, multiuser, multitasking operating systems are quite sophisticated and generally require powerful computers. The UNIX operating system is often implemented as a multiuser, multitasking system on minicomputers, mainframes, and supercomputers.

Operating systems that let several people each run several programs concurrently

Multiprocessing

The operating systems we have discussed so far are generally used with computer systems that have one CPU. A multiprocessing operating system is used with a computer system that contains more than one CPU. **Multiprocessing** is the execution of several instructions in parallel fashion on a single computer system having several central processing units (see Figure 10.7). Multitasking and time-sharing systems run jobs concurrently, but multiprocessing systems truly run jobs simultaneously (at precisely the same instant). The main advantage to multiprocessing systems is speed; because more than one CPU is available, jobs can be processed faster than they can with only one CPU. Multiprocessing systems are high-performance operating systems, implemented mostly on mainframes and supercomputers. A few microprocessor-based multiprocessing computers, known as **transputers,** are available, however.

Operating systems that control more than one CPU to run several programs simultaneously

Multiprocessing systems can be subdivided into four general types, all of which have more than one processor:

Figure 10.6 Multiuser, Multitasking Operating System

This sophisticated type of operating system combines multitasking with time sharing to serve several users, each of whom may be running several concurrent programs.

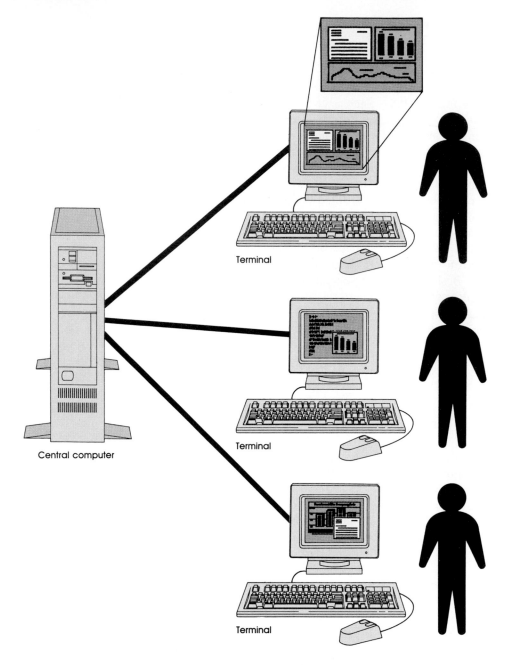

Central computer

Terminal

Terminal

Terminal

1. *Homogeneous multiprocessors.* These systems utilize multiple identical CPUs. The operating system coordinates the use of storage by the CPUs so that no unresolved conflicts occur. Homogeneous multiprocessors are commonly found in general-purpose mainframe computers used for business applications of data processing. Transputers are also homogeneous multiprocessors.

2. *Nonhomogeneous multiprocessors.* These systems utilize special-purpose processors in the computer unit, which are actually CPUs in their own right. Nonhomogeneous multiprocessors are found in general-purpose mainframe computers.

3. *Array processors.* These systems are composed of a set of identical processors (each is called a *processing element,* or *PE*) that are directed and synchronized by

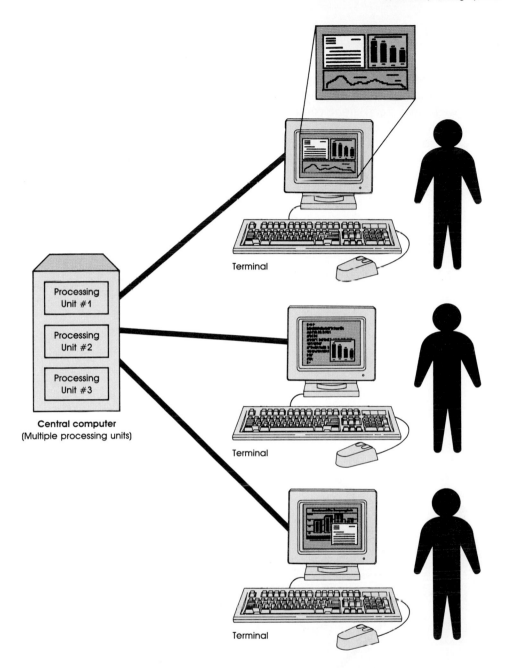

Figure 10.7 Multiprocessing Operating System

Multiprocessing operating systems achieve true simultaneity by executing several jobs on multiple processors. Usually, primary memory, secondary storage, and input/output channels are shared by all the CPUs.

Processing Unit #1

Processing Unit #2

Processing Unit #3

Central computer
(Multiple processing units)

Terminal

Terminal

Terminal

a single control unit. They are designed primarily for rapidly manipulating highly ordered sets of data, such as those encountered in scientific and mathematical applications.

4. *Pipeline processors.* In pipeline systems, multiple processors perform different stages of consecutive computer instructions simultaneously. The processors are arranged like a factory production line, which allows several operands to be in different stages of execution at the same time. Like array processor systems, these systems perform calculations very quickly and so are primarily used for scientific and mathematical applications.

Networking

Operating systems that control computer networks

A multiprocessing system may have many processing units, but it's still considered a single computer. Networking operating systems enable many individual computers to be connected together (see Figure 10.8). This gives users the advantages of having their own stand-alone computers, while allowing them to share hardware devices such as disk drives and laser printers, as well as software and data bases. They can also transmit and receive messages to others on the network. Networking all kinds of computers, especially microcomputers, has become extremely popular lately. Most major microcomputer operating systems either allow networking directly or can be equipped with extension software that makes it possible.

Figure 10.8 Networking Operating System

A networking operating system allows several stand-alone computers to be connected together to exchange messages and to share hardware, software, and data bases.

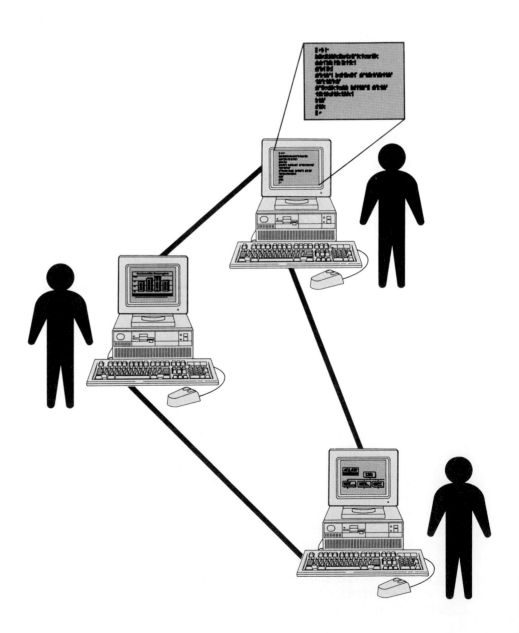

Virtual Storage

As you know, a program must be loaded into a computer's primary memory to be executed. What happens, however, if a program is too big to fit into the available memory or if several programs are competing for space in primary memory? Many operating systems can routinely resolve such situations, without user intervention, through the use of virtual storage techniques. **Virtual storage** (also called **virtual memory**) is a memory-management tactic that employs an area of rapidly accessible secondary storage (such as a hard disk) as an extension of primary memory. Portions of programs are swapped into real storage (the actual primary memory) from virtual storage as needed. This gives users the illusion that more primary memory is available than is actually the case. The operating system automatically handles this memory management, freeing users from worrying about how much memory their programs will require.

Operating systems that use memory-management techniques to overcome space limitations

Operating systems usually implement virtual storage by making use of segmentation, paging, or a combination of both. **Segmentation** is the process of dividing up a program into a number of chunks (or *segments*) of different sizes and placing these chunks in virtual memory wherever they fit. Segmentation is illustrated in Figure 10.9(a) on the following page. How a program is divided into segments usually depends on its internal logic. For example, a module, subroutine, or function might constitute a single segment. The areas of virtual memory into which the segments of a program are placed are not necessarily adjacent, so the operating system must keep track of the segments' locations by constructing a *segment table*. The operating system transfers segments into primary memory from virtual storage as needed, overwriting any old segments and eliminating the need for an entire program to be in primary memory at once. The price paid for this more efficient use of primary memory is the increased complexity and time it takes for the operating system to track and swap segments into real storage from virtual storage. In addition, the operating system must be able to pick out those segments that are presently needed in primary memory.

The process of **paging** resembles segmentation except that the program chunks (called *pages*) are all of the same, fixed size, as shown in Figure 10.9(b) on page 355; programs are chopped up and put into pages with no regard for the program logic. As with segmentation, the operating system keeps track of page locations by constructing a *page table*. Because of the pages' fixed size, paging can result in less waste of real storage space. With segments of different sizes, swapping in new segments from virtual storage can leave little fragments of unused space in real memory. By making all pages the same size, this type of waste is eliminated. Some memory, however, may still be wasted because not every program is exactly divisible into fixed-length pages. The last page may not be completely filled—the program may end before the page does. The unfilled page will still take up as much space in memory as a full page.

To combat the inefficiency inherent in both processes, a combination of segmentation and paging is frequently used to minimize the amount of wasted space in memory. In this combined process, a program is first broken into segments, and then the segments are broken into pages, as illustrated in Figure 10.9(c) on page 356. Both segment and page tables are needed to keep track of the various program pieces, which increases the complexity with which the operating system must deal. The result, however, is that fewer and smaller pieces of primary memory are left unused, thus increasing the overall efficiency of storage use.

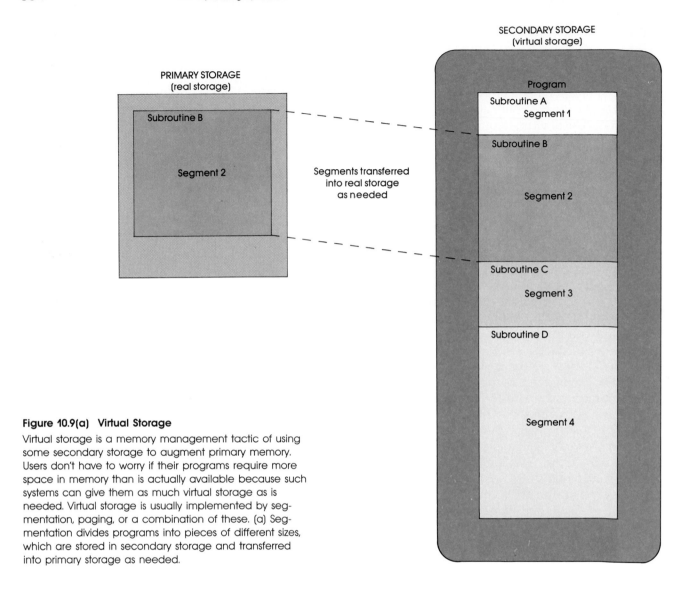

PRIMARY STORAGE
(real storage)

Subroutine B

Segment 2

Segments transferred
into real storage
as needed

SECONDARY STORAGE
(virtual storage)

Program

Subroutine A
Segment 1

Subroutine B

Segment 2

Subroutine C

Segment 3

Subroutine D

Segment 4

Figure 10.9(a) Virtual Storage
Virtual storage is a memory management tactic of using
some secondary storage to augment primary memory.
Users don't have to worry if their programs require more
space in memory than is actually available because such
systems can give them as much virtual storage as is
needed. Virtual storage is usually implemented by segmentation, paging, or a combination of these. (a) Segmentation divides programs into pieces of different sizes,
which are stored in secondary storage and transferred
into primary storage as needed.

Real-Time

*Operating systems that
control or monitor external
processes*

Real-time operating systems control computers that interact with their environments to perform work. The two major types are those that control processes
and those that merely monitor processes. **Process control systems** take input
data from sensors, analyze them, and then initiate actions that change the processes
that they control. **Process monitor systems** also take input data from sensors,
but they merely report this data without actually affecting the processes that they
are monitoring.

Both of these types of real-time operating systems are being used increasingly
in industrial and military applications. (We'll have more to say about some of these
applications in Part 6.) Examples of current use include automated environmental
monitoring for air and water pollution, microscopic assembly processes, medical

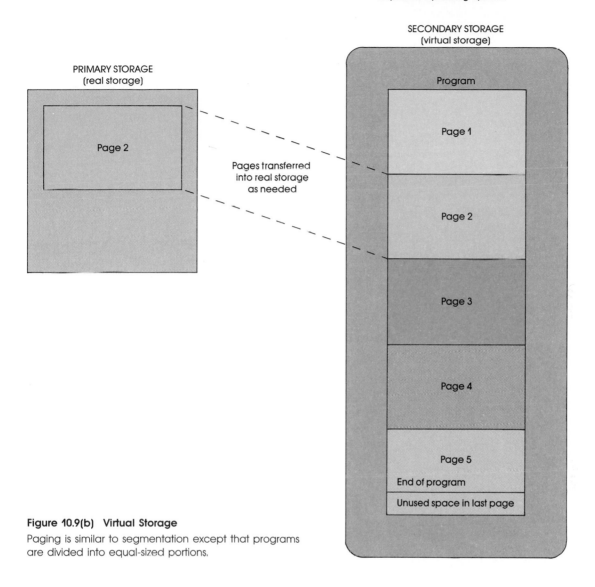

Figure 10.9(b) Virtual Storage
Paging is similar to segmentation except that programs
are divided into equal-sized portions.

analysis systems, air and automobile traffic control, factory production, and oil
pipeline regulation.

IMPORTANT OPERATING SYSTEMS

Like most of the hardware and software available these days, there may be several
operating systems from which to choose for a particular computer. Some of those
on the market are **generic operating systems**—that is, they can be installed in
various kinds of computers. Others are **proprietary operating systems,** specifically designed for a single type of computer. We've chosen a few of today's most
important operating systems for closer inspection: MS-DOS, OS/2, the Macintosh
operating system, UNIX, and IBM VM.

A few notable examples

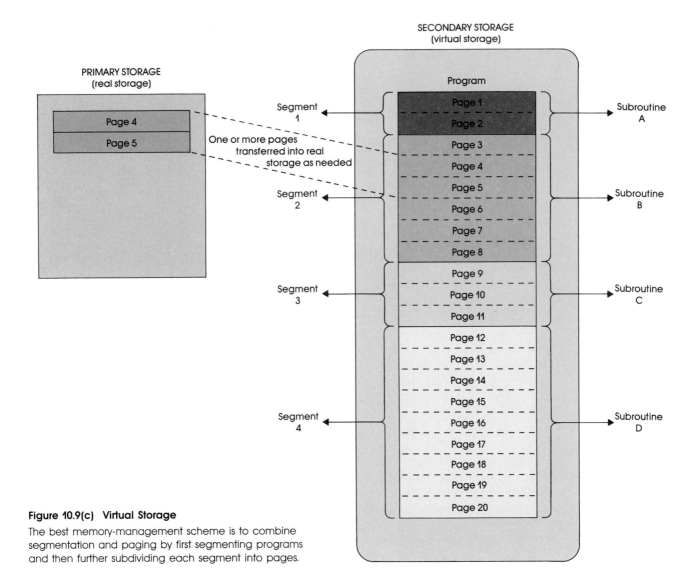

PRIMARY STORAGE
(real storage)

SECONDARY STORAGE
(virtual storage)

Program

Page 4

Page 5

One or more pages
transferred into real
storage as needed

Segment
1

Subroutine
A

Page 1

Page 2

Page 3

Page 4

Page 5

Segment
2

Subroutine
B

Page 6

Page 7

Page 8

Page 9

Segment
3

Subroutine
C

Page 10

Page 11

Page 12

Page 13

Page 14

Page 15

Segment
4

Subroutine
D

Page 16

Page 17

Page 18

Page 19

Page 20

Figure 10.9(c) Virtual Storage
The best memory-management scheme is to combine
segmentation and paging by first segmenting programs
and then further subdividing each segment into pages.

MS-DOS

*The most popular
microcomputer operating
system*

MS-DOS (the full name is Microsoft's Disk Operating System) is the dominant
operating system for IBM-compatible microcomputers. The nearly identical version
sold by IBM for its own microcomputers is called PC-DOS (Personal Computer
Disk Operating System). More microcomputers (at least 15 million in the United
States alone) use MS-DOS or PC-DOS than any other operating system, and the
number of application packages that run under this operating system is truly phenomenal. MS-DOS has become an overall industry standard and is by far the most
popular microcomputer operating system in the United States.

Originally somewhat similar to an earlier microcomputer operating system
called CP/M, MS-DOS also applies some concepts from the UNIX operating system,
which we will discuss shortly. In July of 1981, Microsoft bought an operating
system called QDOS (which is short for Quick and Dirty Operating System) from

Seattle Computer Products. Microsoft revised the system, renamed it, and licensed it to a number of firms, including IBM. IBM offered it as PC-DOS, the standard operating system on its family of microcomputers. When the original IBM Personal Computer became a runaway bestseller, MS-DOS rode with it to the top. The most recent versions of MS-DOS and PC-DOS have been codeveloped by IBM and Microsoft.

Although MS-DOS was originally a fairly primitive operating system, it has benefited from considerable improvements. The latest version is more powerful, easier to use, and handles errors better than previous versions. Because of this continual revision, MS-DOS is kept up to date with the latest hardware developments. MS-DOS commands are generally logical and straightforward. Earlier versions of MS-DOS were not particularly easy for novices to learn, and familiarity with the computer system on which it was installed was generally required before its full power could be realized. The most recent version, however, includes an optional menu-based interface that is much easier for novices to learn than the traditional MS-DOS commands. Nevertheless, MS-DOS remains a single-user, single-tasking operating system.

MS-DOS can be run on computers made by many different manufacturers, but it is not a true generic operating system. Controlled and licensed by IBM and Microsoft, it is designed to be used on computers built around the Intel 8086 family of microprocessors. These include the 8086, 8088, 80286, and the 80386 microprocessors. MS-DOS can sometimes be run on other types of computers, such as the high-end Apple Macintoshes, but a special circuit board is needed that includes one of the Intel 8086 family of microprocessors. Because MS-DOS is such an important operating system, we discuss more specifically how to use it in *A Closer Look* at the end of this chapter.

OS/2

In 1987, IBM and Microsoft joined forces again. They announced OS/2, a single-user, multitasking operating system designed for IBM and IBM-compatible microcomputers that use the Intel 80286 and 80386 microprocessors. OS/2 does not run on IBM and IBM-compatible machines that use the 8088 and 8086 chips. Nevertheless, this long-awaited operating system more fully utilizes the power of the 80286 and 80386 chips in ways that MS-DOS never could. OS/2 is a complex operating system that allows programs to access directly almost 16 megabytes of memory and that provides true multitasking. Although it requires software developers to write a new generation of application packages to fully utilize this power, OS/2 can run most existing MS-DOS programs in its *DOS Compatibility Box*. This is a special environment that can run a single MS-DOS application at a time. Other applications designed especially for OS/2 can be concurrently run as separate tasks while an MS-DOS program executes in the DOS Compatibility Box.

At its most basic level, OS/2 appears to be very similar to MS-DOS. It has the same command-oriented user interface and duplicates many of the existing MS-DOS commands. Applications are run from OS/2 just like they are from MS-DOS: by typing their name and pressing the Enter key. The difference is that with a special combination of keypresses you can switch the entire display screen to a different task and begin a new program before the other program is finished. Each of these different *screen groups*, as they are called, can run a single program or a group of programs. OS/2 can maintain perhaps 16 simultaneous screen groups,

Operating system for high-end IBM-compatibles

each running different programs. One special screen group is reserved for the DOS Compatibility Box we mentioned before, which can only run a single MS-DOS program at a time.

The first version of OS/2, called the Standard Edition, was released with only this basic command-oriented user interface. Subsequent versions of OS/2 Standard Edition, however, include a graphics-based windowing environment called the Presentation Manager. The Presentation Manager is itself a separate screen group that can run multiple programs. Although the simple command-oriented user interface is fine for full-screen programs that do not use graphics, the Presentation Manager is much better for graphics applications. In addition to the Standard Edition, IBM also offers an Extended Edition of OS/2. This version is similar to the Standard Edition, but includes two built-in applications: a communications manager and a data base manager.

Because OS/2 is a new operating system, relatively few applications have been written especially for it. It's also more expensive and requires much more memory than does ordinary MS-DOS. OS/2, however, is somewhat compatible with the huge base of existing MS-DOS applications. Furthermore, it has the potential to run extremely powerful application software. Although it's still too early to tell, IBM and Microsoft hope that OS/2 will become the standard operating system on 80286 and 80386 computers. The foundations established by OS/2 could carry such microcomputers through to almost the end of this century.

The Macintosh Operating System

User-friendly system for Apple Macintoshes

The original Apple Macintosh microcomputer, introduced in 1984, utilized a powerful 32-bit microprocessor, the Motorola 68000. This microcomputer, which evolved from the earlier Apple Lisa line, was revolutionary in design and achieved a high degree of user-friendliness. Most of this was due to its specially designed operating system, which had little in common with MS-DOS or any other existing microcomputer operating system. The advanced Macintosh operating system had its roots in the Smalltalk programming language developed at Xerox's Palo Alto Research Center in the 1970s (see Chapter 8) and borrowed many easy-to-use features originally included in the Xerox 8010 Star Information System. Early versions of the Macintosh operating system were strictly single-user, single-tasking. The most recent version, however, includes an accessory called the *MultiFinder*, which adds some multitasking capabilities to the newer Macintosh computers. These include the Macintosh Plus, the Macintosh SE, the Macintosh II, which has a Motorola 68020 microprocessor, and the Macintosh IIx, which has a 68030 chip.

The Macintosh operating system is made up of several levels. At the top level are the MultiFinder and the *Finder*. Both are system programs, each stored in its own disk file. They manage the Macintosh "desktop" (see Figure 10.10) by letting you run application programs, set up disks, and organize, copy, and delete files. Older Macintoshes came with just the Finder, which allows you to run only one application program at a time. The newest Macintoshes also include the Multi-Finder, which lets you open up several windows with a different program running in each one and rapidly switch between these windows. Although this sounds like multitasking, the current version of the MultiFinder isn't really a true multitasking system. Only the program in the currently selected window is fully active. Certain specially designed programs can run in the background, however, and perform unattended, time-consuming tasks such as printing documents, backing up disks, downloading files, recalculating worksheets, and sorting data bases.

Figure 10.10   The Macintosh Operating System

The user-friendly operating system of the Apple Macintosh microcomputer displays icons on the screen to represent files, file folders, activities, and application programs. You select actions to be performed with a mouse-directed pointer. The MultiFinder accessory allows you to switch rapidly between several programs that appear on the screen at the same time in different windows, and run certain tasks in the background.

Accompanying the MultiFinder and the Finder is the *System file*. It contains fonts, graphic images, text messages, and some of the program code that makes up the Macintosh operating system. At the lowest level of the Macintosh operating system is a powerful set of subprograms permanently encoded in a ROM chip that is built into the computer.

The main idea behind the Macintosh operating system is that the computer should adapt to the user instead of the other way around. It has an exceptional user interface that allows you to perform many tasks quickly and easily. You instruct the computer by using a mouse to manipulate graphic objects on the screen and select options from pull-down menus. These graphic objects, called **icons,** are symbols for files, file folders, actions to be performed, or application programs to be run. For example, to delete a file from a disk, you simply point to the icon representing that file, hold down the mouse button to capture the icon, drag the file icon over to a trash can symbol, and release the mouse button. With little instruction, most users can quickly learn to operate the Macintosh. This friendly operating system encourages experimentation and is just plain fun to use.

The Apple Macintosh and its operating system are a proprietary system. Apple holds and tightly controls the patents for many of the Macintosh hardware components and the copyrights for the system software. Apple has not licensed these patents and copyrights to other manufacturers, so there are no legal Macintosh clones. A few companies sell modified Macintoshes, but these are just Apple Macintoshes that have been taken apart and reassembled in a different form, such as a laptop. By keeping such tight controls over its microcomputers, Apple can maintain a high profit margin, but this means that the Macintosh operating system is not nearly as widespread as other operating systems, such as MS-DOS. Nevertheless, several million Apple Macintoshes are currently in use.

UNIX

UNIX is a multiuser, multitasking operating system originally developed by Bell Laboratories and promoted by AT&T. Ken Thompson and Dennis Ritchie, programmers at Bell Labs, wrote the first version in 1971. At the time, before the advent of microcomputers, UNIX was designed to run on minicomputers made by Digital Equipment Corporation. Since then, UNIX has been adapted to run on all kinds of computers, from microcomputers to supercomputers. It's perhaps the best example of a truly generic operating system. At first, UNIX was only implemented at colleges

Popular and portable operating system for all kinds of computers, from microcomputers to supercomputers

and universities because Bell Labs simply donated it to them. As those students and faculty members left school, however, they took their enthusiasm for UNIX with them. Consequently, UNIX has become increasingly popular with both scientists and business people.

The programs that comprise the UNIX operating system are written mostly in the high-level programming language C. For this reason, it's relatively easy to transport UNIX to any computer that can run C. This ability to run on almost any computer is one of the major attractions of UNIX. In addition, UNIX has many other desirable features. It can accommodate multiple users, each of whom can run several concurrent tasks. It is ideal for software developers because it usually provides hundreds of utility programs that perform many useful tasks and which can be easily incorporated into programs under development. In fact, many UNIX applications can be entirely constructed from this rich set of ready-made, built-in utilities.

Although UNIX is loved and cherished by many computer scientists and software developers, it also has its drawbacks as an operating system. Computer novices often find ordinary UNIX somewhat difficult to learn, but the operating system is so flexible that it can be enhanced to present a more friendly user interface. Perhaps the biggest problem people have with UNIX is that there are several different versions in common use, none of which are completely compatible. Even AT&T has a few distinct varieties of UNIX, although the major one is UNIX System V. One popular microcomputer version of UNIX, called Xenix, was written by Microsoft for IBM and IBM-compatible machines that use the 80286 and 80386 microprocessors. IBM also sells a version of UNIX known as AIX for its RT computer. Still another version of UNIX is A/UX, which is sold by Apple for its Macintosh computers and is based on the AT&T UNIX System V. Some versions of UNIX were designed for educational and scientific uses, so they may lack features important for business use. In addition, fewer application packages are available for UNIX systems than there are for other popular operating systems such as MS-DOS. Nevertheless, UNIX is an extremely influential operating system that is continually growing in popularity.

IBM VM

Large, powerful, and complex system for mainframes

The IBM VM (Virtual Machine) is a large, complex, multiuser, multitasking operating system used on mainframe computers. A virtual machine, as we mentioned earlier, is an illusion the user has that he or she is working with a real machine. VM can make a single computer appear to be several different computers to different users. Originally developed for the IBM 370 series of mainframe computers, VM has been adapted for use on a number of more recent systems.

VM manages the mainframe computer's hardware to create the illusion for each user operating from a terminal that he or she has an entire computer system, complete with a wide range of input/output devices. VM actually allows several different operating systems to be run at once, each of them creating its own virtual machine. Thus, each user can choose to run any of several different IBM operating systems or even a customized in-house system. Conventional multitasking operating systems share the resources of a single machine among several programs, but VM can simulate several machines by creating virtual processors, storage areas, and input/output devices. Because of this, VM is somewhat difficult to classify; it can concurrently be a multitasking, time-sharing, multiprocessing, and virtual-storage operating system.

VM offers users more power than any of the other systems we have discussed. This power is, of course, dependent on the power of the mainframe computer on which VM is run. Despite its size and complexity, or perhaps because of it, VM has been one of IBM's most successful mainframe operating systems.

WINDOWING ENVIRONMENTS

As we said in the previous chapter, integrated software packages provide several applications with a consistent user interface and an easy way to transfer data between them. Another approach is to use a special type of software that works very closely with the operating system called a **windowing environment.** It allows you to divide your screen into a number of different boxes, or windows, and run a separate program in each one (see Figure 10.11). Because Apple Macintosh computers that use the MultiFinder are by definition window-oriented, the term *windowing environment* is generally used to describe software that enhances the MS-DOS operating system used with IBM-compatible microcomputers.

Enhancements to existing operating systems that let you run several programs on the same screen

With a windowing environment, you can rapidly switch from one application to the next and easily transfer data between them. Furthermore, you aren't required to abandon your favorite application packages for new ones because most windowing environments generally work with existing software. As a particular windowing environment becomes accepted, however, software developers create special versions of their programs that abide by certain rules specified by that windowing system. Eventually, the windowing environment may lead to many independent software developers adopting a more uniform user interface for their programs. Thus, a windowing environment can provide most of the advantages of integrated software, without forcing you to buy and learn new application packages.

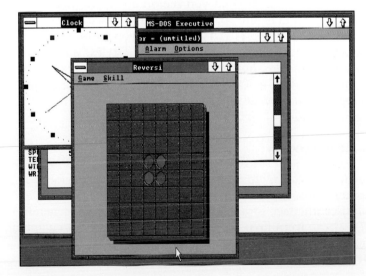

Figure 10.11 Microsoft Windows

Microsoft Windows is one of the most popular graphics-based multitasking windowing environments for IBM-compatible microcomputers. It enhances the MS-DOS operating system and lets you run several programs concurrently, each in its own window.

Types of Windowing Environments

Multitasking versus single-tasking, and text-based versus graphics-based

In many ways, windowing environments far surpass the capabilities of integrated software. First of all, a windowing environment lets you have several programs on your screen at the same time; the actual number of programs may only be limited by the number of windows you can fit on your screen and the amount of memory installed in your computer. You can run almost any program within any window—not just a word processor, spreadsheet, data base manager, communications program, or graphics program. You can even have the same program running separately in two or more different windows. For example, you could create two different windows on your screen, run your word processor separately in each window, and simultaneously edit two different documents. Furthermore, windowing environments often let you cut or copy material from one window and paste it into another window, thereby providing an easy way to transfer data between applications.

If you think this sounds like a single-user, multitasking operating system, you're absolutely right. In fact, many windowing environments are multitasking, allowing you to run several programs concurrently. For example, you could print a document from a word processor in one window, while a large and complicated spreadsheet recalculates in another window and you draw a chart with a graphics program in yet another window. This is true multitasking.

A few windowing environments, however, are not truly multitasking. These simpler systems allow you to switch between several windows on the screen, but only the program in your current active window is actually running. Each of the other programs on the screen is held in a kind of suspended animation, only to be revived when you switch to that window. The Apple MultiFinder, as we said before, operates in this fashion. So, one way to classify windowing environments is by whether they are truly multitasking.

The other major distinction between windowing systems is whether they are text-based or graphics-based. The simpler text-based windowing environments use only the standard character set built into the computer. Windows are enclosed in boxes constructed of special line characters. This type of system cannot display graphics within its windows.

The more popular graphics-based windowing environments, on the other hand, use a bit-mapped display similar to what you see on an Apple Macintosh screen. Microsoft Windows, shown in Figure 10.11, is a graphics-based windowing environment. This type of system is the most flexible, allowing you to run programs that deal with pictures and characters of all different sizes, styles, and fonts. Graphics-based windowing systems are, however, more complex than text-based systems. Consequently, they work best when used on computers that have a powerful microprocessor along with a good deal of memory.

Popular Windowing Environments

Microsoft Windows and DESQview are two multitasking enhancements to MS-DOS

A windowing environment offers a way to run a number of different programs on the screen at the same time while allowing you to easily transport data between them. Furthermore, the user interface of a windowing environment is generally menu-based and much easier to learn than ordinary operating system commands. Most popular windowing environments now use graphics and a mouse which help novices as well as experts.

Because of these advantages, there is a definite trend toward windowing and away from the original MS-DOS style commands in the operating systems of most mid- to high-end microcomputers. It's likely that in the near future most of these machines will come with an operating system that has a built-in windowing environment, such as the Presentation Manager of OS/2, which we discussed previously in this chapter. In the meantime, however, two very popular windowing environments on the market are available as enhancements to MS-DOS: Microsoft Windows and DESQView.

Microsoft Windows

Without a doubt, Microsoft Windows leads the pack of windowing environments for IBM-compatibles. One version is based on the Intel 8088, 8086, and 80286 microprocessors, and a special version is available for the more powerful 80386 chip. In addition, Microsoft Windows is the basis for the Presentation Manager of the OS/2 operating system. As Figure 10.11 shows, this software lets you run several different programs at the same time on the screen in overlapping windows. Microsoft Windows is a true multitasking, graphics-based windowing environment that uses a mouse and several features also found in the Macintosh operating system, such as icons and pull-down menus.

DESQview

This program from Quarterdeck Office Systems is another true multitasking windowing environment for all IBM-compatible computers. Originally a strictly text-based environment, the newest version of DESQview can now run most graphics programs in its windows. Unlike Microsoft Windows, DESQview doesn't simulate a desktop with little icons like the Apple Macintosh. Using DESQview is similar to using MS-DOS, except that you can open up several windows on your screen and run a different program in each one. In fact, DESQview can theoretically run up to 255 programs at the same time. Many experts consider DESQview the most elegant windowing environment for computers using MS-DOS and claim that its multitasking abilities are superior to those of Microsoft Windows.

MS-DOS is by far the most popular microcomputer operating system being used today. When we say MS-DOS, we also mean PC-DOS, which is virtually the same operating system released by IBM for its own microcomputers. (From now on, we'll refer to both MS-DOS and PC-DOS as just DOS.) It is run on at least 15 million IBM and IBM-compatible microcomputers in the United States alone.

Although DOS isn't really difficult to learn, it is not considered to be as user-friendly as the Apple Macintosh operating system, basically because DOS is a command-oriented operating system. In other words, you tell it what to do by typing a command and pressing the Enter key. This contrasts with a menu-oriented system in which you select options from a list of possible choices. Although the most recently announced version of DOS does include a menu-oriented user interface, this version was not yet available to us at the time this text was being written. In any case, most people are still using earlier versions of DOS, which operate only with commands. Even with the new version of DOS, the menu interface is only an option; you can still run it using the traditional commands.

In this section we take a closer look at using DOS. Specifically, we illustrate several of its most commonly used commands. To most people, a computer's operating system is primarily the means by which they start up and run application packages. Nevertheless, an operating system such as DOS performs many other important services. With today's sophisticated software, it is possible to use a computer without knowing too much about its operating system. Mastering a few basic operating system commands, however, can help you perform common tasks more easily, reduce the likelihood of making costly mistakes (such as accidentally erasing a disk full of vital data), and give you a better understanding of how the computer works. First, let's describe the process of starting up the operating system.

Booting Up

Before you can execute any commands you must first *boot up* the computer; this simply means to start the operating system. On a computer with a hard disk, all you generally have to do to boot up is turn it on. A special part of the operating system is automatically invoked to load the rest of the system from the disk into primary memory. Then the operating system simply waits for you to tell it what to do.

On computers that have only floppy disk drives, you have to put a floppy disk containing the operating sys-

Using MS-DOS

tem in the default disk drive before you turn on the power. This disk drive is labeled *A:* or simply called the A drive. If there is a second floppy disk drive present, it would be called the B drive. If there is a hard disk present, it is the C drive. This figure shows what you see on the screen when you boot up PC-DOS Version 3.30 from the A floppy drive of an IBM microcomputer:

```
Current date is Sun  1-01-1989
Enter new date (mm-dd-yy):
Current time is  9:19:39.63
Enter new time:


The IBM Personal Computer DOS
Version 3.30 (C)Copyright International Business Machines Corp 1981, 1987
                 (C)Copyright Microsoft Corp 1981, 1986

A>
```

This particular computer has a built-in automatic clock/calendar, so you don't have to type anything in response to its request for the new date and time. All you have to do is press the Enter key twice. On computers without a built-in clock/calendar, you would have to enter the current date and time. The *A>* you see on the screen is called the *DOS prompt*. This tells you that disk drive A is your current default drive and that DOS is waiting for you to enter a command. Note that DOS commands can be entered in either uppercase or lowercase letters.

DIR

DIR is one of the simplest and most commonly used DOS commands. It is an abbreviation of the word *directory*. A directory is a list of the files stored on a disk. To see a directory of your current disk displayed on your screen, you simply type *DIR* and press the Enter key. If you had the PC-DOS Version 3.30 Startup disk in drive A, you would see this on your screen after executing the DIR command:

```
COMMAND  COM    25307    3-17-87   12:00p
ANSI     SYS     1678    3-17-87   12:00p
COUNTRY  SYS    11285    3-17-87   12:00p
DISPLAY  SYS    11290    3-17-87   12:00p
DRIVER   SYS     1196    3-17-87   12:00p
FASTOPEN EXE     3919    3-17-87   12:00p
FDISK    COM    48216    3-18-87   12:00p
FORMAT   COM    11616    3-18-87   12:00p
KEYB     COM     9056    3-17-87   12:00p
KEYBOARD SYS    19766    3-17-87   12:00p
MODE     COM    15487    3-17-87   12:00p
NLSFUNC  EXE     3060    3-17-87   12:00p
PRINTER  SYS    13590    3-17-87   12:00p
REPLACE  EXE    11775    3-17-87   12:00p
SELECT   COM     4163    3-17-87   12:00p
SYS      COM     4766    3-17-87   12:00p
VDISK    SYS     3455    3-17-87   12:00p
XCOPY    EXE    11247    3-17-87   12:00p
EGA      CPI    49065    3-18-87   12:00p
LCD      CPI    10752    3-17-87   12:00p
4201     CPI    17089    3-18-87   12:00p
5202     CPI      459    3-17-87   12:00p
        22 File(s)     9216 bytes free

A>
```

The leftmost column lists the *primary file name* of each file on the disk. The second column lists the *file name extension* of each file. Under DOS, each file must have a name that can consist of these two parts. When written out, the primary file name and extension are usually given together but separated by a period. For example, the first file you see on the screen is named COMMAND.COM.

The column to the right of the file name extensions lists each file's size in bytes. COMMAND.COM, for example, contains 25,307 bytes of program code. The final two columns in the directory give the date and time each file was created or last modified. Just below the list the DIR command displays the number of files on the disk and how many bytes of empty space are still available.

CHKDSK

The DIR command is used to see what files are on a disk. Another DOS command, called CHKDSK (CHecK DiSK), displays a status report about a disk and the memory installed in your computer. This brief report contains some interesting and useful information. To execute the CHKDSK command, simply type *CHKDSK* and press the Enter key. Here is an example of what you might see:

```
A>chkdsk

  362496 bytes total disk space
       0 bytes in 1 hidden files
  307200 bytes in 31 user files
   55296 bytes available on disk

  524288 bytes total memory
  436432 bytes free

A>
```

In this figure and the rest of the figures in this section, we show what the user types in red characters. While the characters don't actually appear on the screen in red, we've colored them so you can distinguish what the user types from what DOS replies.

This report produced by the CHKDSK command reveals the total disk and memory capacities, along with numbers that reveal how much of this space is currently in use. The actual numbers produced by CHKDSK vary depending on how much memory is installed, what kind of disk drive is being checked, and what files are on that disk.

FORMAT

Before a new floppy disk can be used to store programs or data files, it must undergo an initial preparation known as *formatting*. Formatting is not usually done at the factory, so you must do it with your own computer for each new disk you are going to use. Generally you format a new disk only once, although you can reformat a previously formatted disk in order to clear it off completely. Whether the disk is new or not, formatting is a common DOS operation. During the formatting process, DOS performs the following procedures:

- Checks the disk for defective spots.
- Wipes out any files already on the disk.
- Builds a directory table that will hold information about the files that will be on the disk.
- Marks off the empty space into equal-sized chunks called *sectors*.
- Copies DOS onto the disk if specified to do so.

Let's say that you are working on a computer that has two floppy disk drives, A and B. The DOS disk is in drive A and you want to format a brand new floppy disk. To do this, you type *FORMAT B:* and press the Enter key. DOS prompts you to put the new disk into drive B and press the Enter key when you are ready (when the disk is in and the disk drive door or lever is closed). The formatting procedure takes about a minute or so. When it is complete, DOS tells you how much room is on the disk and if there were any defective spots detected. If there were no defects, your screen would look like this:

```
A>format b:
Insert new diskette for drive B:
and strike ENTER when ready

Format complete

    362496 bytes total disk space
    362496 bytes available on disk

Format another (Y/N)?n
A>
```

COPY

Once a disk has been formatted, it can be used to store program and data files. There are several ways to get files onto a disk, but one of the most common methods is the COPY command. This command can be used to duplicate one or more files on the same or on different disks. COPY is a versatile command that can be applied in a number of different ways. Perhaps the simplest application of the COPY command is to copy a single file from one disk to another. For example, let's say that you want to copy the file BASICA.COM from the disk in drive A to the disk in drive B. (This file contains the advanced Microsoft BASIC language interpreter that is included with DOS.) Assuming that drive A is your current default drive, you would type *COPY BASICA.COM B:*. Here is what your screen would look like (the DIR commands aren't strictly necessary; they are just used to show the contents of the disks and to confirm that the file has indeed been copied):

```
A>dir basica.com

 Volume in drive A has no label
 Directory of  A:\

BASICA   COM    36403   3-17-87  12:00p
        1 File(s)    55296 bytes free

A>copy basica.com b:
        1 File(s) copied

A>dir b:

 Volume in drive B has no label
 Directory of  B:\

BASICA   COM    36403   3-17-87  12:00p
        1 File(s)   325632 bytes free

A>
```

DEL

Just as you accumulate old memos, notes, letters, and other scraps of paper on your desk, disks can also become cluttered with unneeded files. Occasionally, you need to clean up a bit and discard those items you no longer need. Once you throw something away, however, you may have trouble retrieving it or may even find that you cannot get it back again. DOS makes it very easy to erase files but it has no built-in provision to *unerase*, or restore them. The DEL command (short for DELete), and the equivalent ERASE command, should be used with caution.

Let's say that you now want to delete the BASICA.COM file you just copied to the disk in drive B. All you do is enter *DEL B:BASICA.COM*. The *B:* preface tells DOS that the BASICA.COM file you want to delete is on the disk in drive B. This screen illustrates the process of deleting the file:

```
A>dir b:

Volume in drive B has no label
Directory of  B:\

BASICA   COM    36403   3-17-87  12:00p
         1 File(s)    325632 bytes free

A>del b:basica.com

A>dir b:

Volume in drive B has no label
Directory of  B:\

File not found

A>
```

Sometimes, there are several files you want to erase all at once. Perhaps you even want to delete every file on a disk. The DEL command can do this as well. For example, to erase every file on the disk in drive B, you could use this command: *DEL B:*.*.* The *.* designation means any file with any name and any extension. Because this is a potentially disastrous command if entered by mistake, DOS will ask you if you're sure you want to do this. If you enter Y for yes, DOS will go ahead and erase everything. If you enter N for no, DOS will immediately cancel the DEL command. The screen at top right illustrates using the DEL command to erase every file on the disk in drive B.

TYPE and PRINT

So far, we've described a few DOS commands for manipulating files, but we haven't yet looked inside a file. The TYPE command lets you display the contents of a text file on the screen. A *text file* is simply a file that contains only letters, numbers, punctuation marks, and other symbols that you see on the keyboard. A text file does not contain compiled object code or data stored in some special format. Text files can be created with word-processing and text-editing programs. For exam-

```
A>dir b:

Volume in drive B has no label
Directory of  B:\

BASICA   COM    36403   3-17-87  12:00p
MORTGAGE BAS     6251   3-17-87  12:00p
         2 File(s)    318464 bytes free

A>del b:*.*
Are you sure (Y/N)?y

A>dir b:

Volume in drive B has no label
Directory of  B:\

File not found

A>
```

ple, let's say that there is a file named README.TXT on the disk in drive B. To display the contents of this file on your screen, you would enter this command: *TYPE B:README.TXT*.

The PRINT command is similar to the TYPE command, except that it sends the specified text file to your printer. This screen illustrates the use of the TYPE and PRINT commands:

```
A>dir b:

Volume in drive B has no label
Directory of  B:\

README   TXT      259   1-01-89   9:35a
         1 File(s)    361472 bytes free

A>type b:readme.txt

This is an ordinary text file created with a word processor in non-document
mode.  It has been created to illustrate the use of the DOS commands TYPE and
PRINT.  TYPE lists text files on the display screen, while PRINT sends the
file to the printer.

A>print b:readme.txt
Name of list device [PRN]:
Resident part of PRINT installed

   B:\README.TXT is currently being printed

A>
```

Running an Application Package

Every time you enter a DOS command, you run a program designed to accomplish some very specific task. In the previous chapter we talked about many different kinds of application packages, which are programs for performing more general and complex tasks such as word processing, setting up worksheets, and managing data bases. The primary use of any operating system is to allow you to start up and run application packages. For example, to use Lotus 1-2-3, you first put the appropriate disk in the default disk drive, type the name of the program file, and press the Enter key. In this case, you would simply enter *123*. DOS would then load the 1-2-3 program from the disk into primary memory and begin its execution.

Summary

Functions of Operating Systems

An operating system is a set of programs that manages a computer system's hardware by controlling and coordinating such computer resources as the CPU, primary and secondary storage, and input/output devices.

Providing Services   Operating systems allow users to share hardware, programs, and data; enable users to protect their data; schedule resource use; facilitate input, output, and storage operations; and recover from errors.

Acting as an Interface   An operating system interfaces software with hardware and users with the computer system. Users can be classified as novices, experts, application programmers, and systems programmers.

A Short History of Operating Systems

Operating systems originated in the 1950s as a means of utilizing CPU time previously lost during job transitions. During the 1960s, more sophisticated operating systems were developed using multitasking, time-sharing, and multiprocessing techniques. Real-time systems were also developed in the 1960s, and multimode systems became popular in the early 1970s. Modern operating systems strive for user-friendliness while also incorporating features that allow users to utilize hardware capabilities fully.

Components of Operating Systems

Operating system programs are kept in secondary storage on the system residence device until they are needed.

Control Programs   Control programs are the routines that manage resources, schedule jobs, handle interrupts, control data, and monitor system status. The main control program is the supervisor. Resident routines are those that are most frequently used, so they remain in primary memory. Transient routines are transferred from the system residence device as needed.

Processing Programs   Processing programs simplify the development and use of software. Language translators and utility programs are the two major classes of processing programs.

Types of Operating Systems

Operating systems can be classified according to several criteria, such as the number of simultaneous users, the number of concurrent programs, how many processors they use, how memory is managed, and in what setting they are used.

Single-User, Single-Tasking   These operating systems serve only one user at a time and can only run one program at a time.

Single-User, Multitasking These operating systems serve only one user at a time, but the user can run several programs concurrently.

Multiuser, Single-Tasking These are time-sharing operating systems that allow each user to run one program at a time.

Multiuser, Multitasking These are time-sharing operating systems that allow each user to run several programs concurrently.

Multiprocessing These operating systems can execute several jobs simultaneously through the use of more than one processor.

Networking These operating systems control networks of connected computers.

Virtual Storage Virtual storage is a technique that uses some secondary storage, by employing segmentation and/or paging, to augment primary memory.

Real-Time Real-time operating systems either control or monitor external processes and are used in industrial and military applications.

Important Operating Systems

The following is a representative set of today's most important operating systems.

MS-DOS The leading microcomputer operating system, MS-DOS runs on millions of IBM-compatibles based on the Intel 8086 family of microprocessors. PC-DOS is the equivalent system from IBM for its own microcomputers.

OS/2 Another joint effort by IBM and Microsoft, OS/2 is a single-user, multitasking system for high-end IBM and IBM-compatible microcomputers.

The Macintosh Operating System Apple's operating system for its family of Macintosh microcomputers is renowned for its power and user-friendliness, but it cannot be used on any other computers.

UNIX UNIX is a popular generic operating system for all kinds of computers that is both multiuser and multitasking and is available in a number of slightly different versions.

IBM VM VM is a large, complex, and powerful operating system designed for use on mainframe computers.

Windowing Environments

A windowing environment is a special type of software that works very closely with the operating system. It allows you to divide your screen into a number of different boxes, or windows, and run a separate program in each one.

Types of Windowing Environments These environments may be classified as either truly multitasking or not and as either text-based or graphics-based.

Popular Windowing Environments The two leading windowing environments for MS-DOS are Microsoft Windows and DESQview.

As an extra review of this chapter, try defining the following terms. If you have trouble with any of them, refer to the page number listed.

Computer Concepts

Review Questions

1. What is the fundamental task of an operating system?
2. What are the key resources managed by an operating system?
3. What services do operating systems provide to users?
4. On what two levels does an operating system act as an interface?
5. What general types of users interact with operating systems?
6. What was the basic reason underlying the development of the first operating systems?
7. What are the two general categories of the component programs of an operating system?
8. What type of storage medium is most often used for the system residence device?
9. What coordinates the activities of all parts of an operating system?
10. What types of tasks are performed by an operating system's control programs?
11. Describe the two major classes of processing programs.
12. List seven different types of operating systems.
13. Which type of operating system permits one user to run more than one program at a time?
14. Which of the types indicated in question 12 is known also as time sharing?
15. What are the advantages and a disadvantage of multiuser systems?
16. What enables multiprocessing operating systems to execute several jobs simultaneously?
17. What are the three methods for implementing virtual storage?
18. What are the two types of real-time operating systems?
19. Describe the benefits to an individual user of VM.
20. List some advantages of a windowing environment.

True or False

1. The operating system functions as an interface between hardware and software.
2. Operating systems are always retained in primary storage.
3. Spooling is an activity involving only one user and a peripheral device.
4. Optimizing compilers are designed to produce efficient object code.
5. A library manager is a program that keeps track of books in a computer library.
6. An operating system can be both single-user and multiuser.
7. Most microcomputer operating systems do not allow networking.
8. Proprietary operating systems are designed for a specific type of computer.
9. UNIX is an example of a proprietary operating system.
10. A windowing environment permits a user to run several programs simultaneously and transfer data between them.

1. Computer users who are not necessarily computer specialists, but who routinely use computers in their daily work are called:
   (a) end users   (b) experts   (c) novices

2. An interface that permits a user to get work done on the computer without worrying about the machine's internal functions is:
   (a) a multimode system   (b) a virtual machine   (c) a real-time system

3. A system crash is an error:
   (a) caused by a careless user   (b) physical destruction of a computer   (c) a runtime error in the operating system

4. An operating system component that permits a program to be developed on one computer and used on another is called:
   (a) a utility program   (b) a linker   (c) a cross-compiler

5. The simplest type of operating system is:
   (a) single-user, single-tasking   (b) multiprogramming   (c) time sharing

6. A system that links a number of stand-alone computers together is:
   (a) multiprocessing   (b) a network   (c) a pipeline

7. A system that analyzes data from sensors and then causes actions to be taken is:
   (a) a process control system   (b) a process monitor system   (c) windowing

8. An operating system that allows a user to divide the screen into segments and permits the user to run several programs simultaneously is:
   (a) integrated   (b) windowing   (c) multiuser

9. A system for use on large mainframes that creates the illusion of a different computer system for each of a group of users is called:
   (a) multitasking   (b) a service program   (c) a virtual machine

10. The popular operating system that is truly generic is:
    (a) UNIX   (b) MultiFinder   (c) VM

1. Most supermarkets use bar code scanners at checkout stations to put data into their computers. In these systems what do you think are the user/computer system interfaces that must be managed by the operating system?
2. How do supermarket interfaces between users and computers differ from the interfaces in the travel industry, in health care and medicine? Do you think the same operating system could work well in all of these roles? Why?

1. Choose one of the specific operating systems we've discussed in this chapter and do some research on it. Learn how to use it if you can gain access to a computer system that runs it. Prepare a report that details the features it offers and describes how easy or difficult you found it to use and why.

2. Many campuses and offices find it efficient to use a time-sharing system rather than independent or linked microcomputers. Find out if there is such a system at your institution and discuss with a variety of users the advantages and problems they have encountered.

3. If your institution or local computer stores offer both IBM-compatible and Apple Macintosh microcomputers, compare the operating systems. Discuss the ease of learning each for a novice.

4. Contact a local industry (a utility company, for instance) which uses a process control system. Prepare a report on what tasks are controlled and how and what actions can be taken automatically.

4

SYSTEMS

In Parts 2 and 3, we looked at the two basic components of a computer system: hardware and software. In Part 4, we consider how to put together the right hardware and software to solve problems in business, industry, or any other area in which computers are utilized. The word *system* implies organization, and what is better suited than a computer to organize a jumble of data and functions into a smooth-running, efficient operation?

Chapter 11 introduces the systems analysts—and describes their pivotal role in the constructive application of technology to what are often complicated and demanding situations. Chapters 12 and 13 provide an in-depth look at three important kinds of computer systems: data base systems, management information systems, and decision support systems.

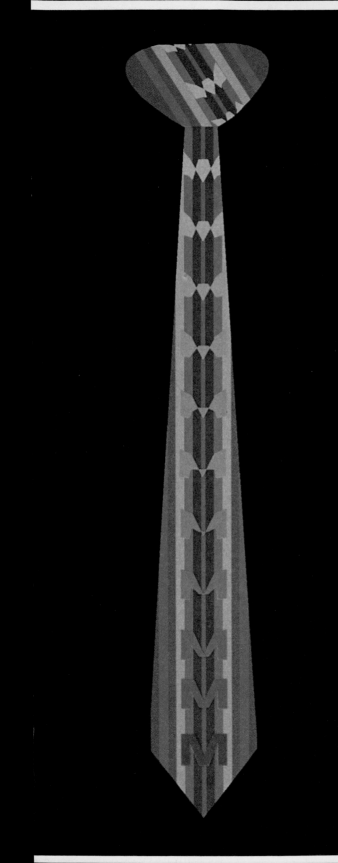

11

Systems Analysis and Design

The Systems Approach

    What Is a System?   *Defining the concept.*

    Why Systems Change   *The necessity for systems analysis and design.*

    The Role of the Systems Analyst   *What systems analysts do.*

Phase 1—Feasibility Study   *A look before leaping.*

    Defining the Problem   *What's wrong?*

    Estimating the Scope of the Project   *How hard will it be to fix?*

    Proposing Possible Solutions   *What can be done?*

    Reporting to Management   *Summarizing for the decision makers.*

Phase 2—Systems Analysis   *Find out how the old system works and what the new system must do.*

    Data Gathering   *Compile facts about the old system, using written documents, questionnaires, interviews, and observation.*

    Data Analysis   *Decide what functions the new system must include, using data flow diagrams, data dictionaries, and black box process descriptions.*

Phase 3—Systems Design   *Specify how to build the new system.*

    Review of Project Goals   *Reconsider the objectives of the system project.*

    Development of System Requirements *Detail exactly how the new system should work.*

    Presentation to Management   *Summarize once more.*

Phase 4—Systems Development   *Construct the new system.*

    Scheduling   *Prepare timetables*

    Programming   *Write the system programs.*

    Testing   *Confirm that the system works.*

    Documentation   *Explain how the system works.*

Phase 5—Implementation and Evaluation *Install and appraise the new system.*

    File Conversion   *Adapt data files so that the new system can use them*

    Personnel Training   *Teach users and operators how to run the system.*

    System Conversion   *Switch from the old system to the new one.*

    Evaluation   *Does it fulfill its requirements?*

    Maintenance   *Keep the system effective.*

Focus On

High Tech Traffic

Driving through the city of Baltimore, Maryland, especially during nonpeak hours, can make each motorist feel in control of the system of traffic lights as long as a speed equal to the posted limit is maintained. As you approach each intersection the light turns green, permitting you to go on to the next without excessive braking; at each successive light the same thing happens. This may continue for many lights until you either reach your destination or come to an intersection with a street that has equal or higher priority.

The city operates a Traffic Control Center whose functions include traffic signal control, traffic system surveillance and control of console and display devices. According to Carol Easton, Superintendent of Communications and Computers, there are at present about 900 signals on-line in the system and more are being added.

The systems were designed and installed by TRW, Inc. They include two MODCOMP IV computers and three MODCOMP II computers with associated peripheral equipment. There are three subsystems: Traffic Master A (TMA), Traffic Master B (TMB), and the Computer Communication Interface Unit (CCIU). The TMA subsystem supports detector data processing, an on-line data base update, data logging, and the map display which covers the critical control part of the metropolitan area. The TMB subsystem provides real-time control of the network. It analyzes status reports from the remote traffic controllers and selects and transmits new timing data to those controllers as required.

Prior to the morning rush hours, traffic flow and the timing of signals may be equal on two intersecting streets. However, as traffic builds up the timing can be changed to smooth the dominant flow in any direction. The CCIU coordinates communications between the TMB and the CCIU and between its own computers. If any signal goes out, it will show up immediately on the map and in the system, and it can then be put on its own local control system until the connections can be repaired. It won't be as automatically timed, but it will continue to function independently. Also, in the event of an emergency situation, such as a fire or road closure, a signal can immediately be changed to flash.

Baltimore's operation is the most advanced system of traffic control in the country. It is capable of handling up to 1200 of the city's signals. However, it is not the last word in computer hardware, and a new system is presently being installed that will greatly increase traffic control throughout the metropolitan area.

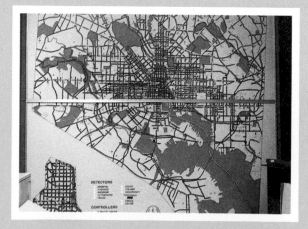

In this book, we've repeatedly stressed how computers make a process more efficient, how they speed operations and solve the problems that have plagued an organization or individual. But the fact of the matter is that an organization can't just bring an Apple or IBM machine back from the local computer store, plug it in, and expect that a bit of fancy keyboard tapping will make all their troubles disappear. An organization, large or small, that has a billing or personnel system or other system of any complexity will find that its problems and the solutions aren't all that easily isolated and fixed. Furthermore, replacing "the way it's always been done" with something new, strange, and untried can be a frustrating or even traumatic endeavor.

Here's where systems analysis and systems analysts come into the picture. A whole profession has emerged to develop appropriate solutions to individual problems and to make the transition from the old and cumbersome to the new and efficient smoother and more comfortable. In this chapter, we'll examine the step-by-step process of systems analysis and show how those professional troubleshooters—the systems analysts—save the day.

This chapter includes a six-part case study about a fictional dentist, Dr. Mary Parkley. As you read about each phase of a systems analysis project, you can refer to the corresponding section of the case study to see how the concepts are applied in a real-life situation.

THE SYSTEMS APPROACH

In Chapter 7, we described the process of developing a computer program. We focused primarily on the program as a single entity and on the process from the perspective of the programmer. In Chapter 9, we considered some particular application packages from the point of view of the user, who is seeking a solution to a specific problem. In this chapter, we'll take a more comprehensive view of the whole process by answering some crucial questions: Why are programs designed the way they are? What role is played by the elements supporting a particular program, such as the software, hardware, and peripheral devices and the users and other personnel? How do all of these things come together to produce a successful data-processing tool?

What Is a System?

Clearly, in answering the kind of questions listed above, we will deal with something much larger than a single program; we must deal with a complete, meticulously planned environment, in other words, with a system. We've used this word dozens of times throughout this book, and it's also used extensively in everyday life. We hear a lot about solar systems, circulatory systems, economic systems, communication systems, and of course, computer systems. To define the term formally in the context of data processing, we can use the words of the American National Standards Committee: a **system** is a "collection of people, machines, and methods organized to accomplish a set of specific functions." Note that this definition does not necessarily require that a system be computerized. Many small businesses and organizations run their affairs by means of manual systems, that is, without computers.

Defining the concept

Whether the paperwork is handled by people or computers, a number of attributes are common to most systems:

- *A system interacts with the environment.*   Systems receive input from and transmit output to their surroundings. Because they interact in this way with their environment, they are often called *open systems.*

- *A system has a purpose.*   Every system has some aim or objective that is fulfilled by the functions it carries out. For example, the purpose of the human circulatory system is to deliver oxygenated blood to all parts of the body so that life can be sustained, and the purpose of a firm's payroll system is to deliver salaries to employees.

- *A system is self-regulating.*   Systems should be able to maintain themselves in a steady state. In other words, they ought to be able to adjust their internal functions to accommodate externally imposed changes. For example, as a person exercises, the heart beats faster to supply the muscles' increased need for oxygenated blood.

- *A system is self-correcting.*   Finally, systems must also be able to respond to abnormal situations that cannot be controlled by routine self-regulation. Such occurrences should be handled in ways that won't jeopardize the system's whole purpose. To use the circulatory system as an example once more, when a blood vessel is cut or damaged, clotting takes place to minimize blood loss.

Why Systems Change

The necessity for systems analysis and design

We live in a world of constant change. The development of new systems or the modification of old systems may be necessary for any number of reasons. Businesses and organizations must stay abreast of ever-changing laws and regulations. The government may change the tax laws or require that businesses provide certain new data about their employees, which will prompt the modification of existing data-processing systems. Equipment may become obsolete or manufacturers may discontinue repair service and support, which will mean an investment in new hardware. A firm may reorganize and therefore require new or extensively modified accounting systems. Companies may be faced with increased competition or higher costs, which will compel them to streamline their data-processing systems to save time and money. Users may suddenly require new features and want to incorporate them into current systems. It's obvious that systems aren't static entities but are ongoing processes, constantly being created, updated, and transformed.

How do organizations and individuals cope with change, given that it's so prevalent? Unfortunately, all too often the answer to this question is "not very well." Users of data-processing systems are frequently resistant to change, regardless of whether it will make life easier. People sometimes feel that they will be replaced by computers if a new system is installed. Or they may dread the thought of learning how to use a different system, after having invested so much time and effort to master the old one. Users often believe, quite literally, that the new system will do no better than the old one and may even do worse. This attitude is particularly likely when system changes are called for by management rather than by the everyday users (who may be as fully aware of the system's deficiencies). Throughout this chapter, we'll pay attention to the role these "people" concerns play in the whole process of studying old systems and designing and implementing new ones.

The Role of the Systems Analyst

Systems analysis is the practice of evaluating an existing system to see how it works and how well it meets the users' needs. **Systems design** is the process of planning a new system based on the findings of a systems analysis. **Systems analysts** are normally involved in both of these activities; they are professionals whose basic responsibility consists of translating users' needs into technical specifications for programmers or buyers of software. Beginning with a logical description of the users' needs, the analyst designs a system that solves the problem. This design is then used as a basis for developing the software requirements. A search may be instigated for a software package that fulfills these requirements, or programmers may be given the task of writing new programs to perform the necessary functions. Sometimes software that is purchased must still be tailored to an organization's unique needs. Because computers, programmers, and systems analysts are quite expensive, management has a responsibility to control this whole development process. To an organization's managers, the data-processing system is an investment—the funds expended on it should be spent wisely. Thus, the systems analyst must ensure that the system allows management to exercise control efficiently and effectively.

What systems analysts do

Systems analysts have a difficult job. They must simultaneously deal with users, technicians, programmers, and managers. Each of these groups has different concerns and the expectation that the systems analyst will address them. Users want systems that are easy to work with, powerful, and fast. Technicians want the newest, glossiest, state-of-the-art equipment. Programmers are worried about bits, data flow, and control structures. Finally, managers are concerned with investment returns, cost/benefit ratios, and development schedules. Systems analysts must perform a juggling act—and do it with a smile. They are concerned not only with the development of software, but also with the hardware, the people who will operate that hardware, the methods of data entry and information output, system security, auditing, and every other aspect of the entire system.

The methodology by which systems analysts generally approach their task is the subject of the remainder of this chapter. This procedure is basically divided into five major phases and is often referred to as the **systems development life cycle.** It is important to note, however, that at any point along the way feedback from users, programmers, or managers may send the analyst back to a previous step. This continuous feedback and looping (see Figure 11.1) are essential to setting up a truly effective system.

PHASE 1—FEASIBILITY STUDY

The first step in any system project must be a **feasibility study** (also called a *preliminary investigation*). The nature and scope of the problem are examined to determine whether it's worthwhile to pursue the project further.

A look before leaping

Defining the Problem

Obviously, someone must recognize that a problem exists before a system project can be started. In addition, what is the source of the problem? Have users encountered difficulties and asked for help, or has management identified an area of poor

What's wrong?

Figure 11.1   The Systems Development Life Cycle

A system project is generally broken down into five major phases, often described as the systems development life cycle.

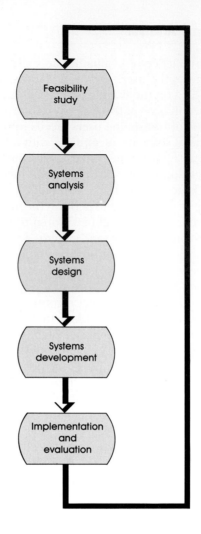

performance? Often, the systems analyst is the one who spots the problem. In this initial stage, informal discussions are held to try to reach a point where users, managers, and the systems analyst all agree that a problem exists.

Through interviews and conversations, the systems analyst tries to understand the organization, its history, and its current state of affairs. During this time, the analyst prepares a written statement explaining as clearly as possible his or her understanding of the problem. Ideally, this statement is then reviewed in a joint meeting with both users and managers so that obvious errors and misunderstandings can be corrected at an early stage. Although the time it takes to define the problem can be quite brief, perhaps only a single day or less, correctness of the definition is essential. Users, managers, and the systems analyst must agree on a general direction early in the project. If the problem is misunderstood and its definition is incorrect, the final system is almost certainly not going to solve that problem.

The Case of Dr. Mary Parkley, D.D.S.

Dr. Mary Parkley has run a successful dental practice in a college town for a number of years. She has about 2000 patients, one-fourth of whom are students. On an average day (except during college vacations), she sees between 15 and 25 patients. Billings, including dental insurance claims, average about $15,000 a month.

This might seem to be quite a profitable business, but Dr. Parkley doesn't pocket all the profits, not even a large portion of them. She must pay the salaries of her staff: a receptionist, an office manager, and two dental assistants. Other expenses include rent, malpractice insurance, equipment and supplies, continuing education for herself and her assistants, and, of course, subscriptions to all the magazines in the waiting room.

Until about six months ago, the office was managed by an old friend of Dr. Parkley's named Jerry Douglas. He ran things very smoothly and had become an indispensable employee. The rest of the staff trusted him, and he took care of all the necessary details to keep the office running efficiently. Unfortunately (for Dr. Parkley), Jerry won $40 million in the state lottery and decided to move to Alaska, where he'd always wanted to live (and which, incidentally, has no state income tax). Dr. Parkley suddenly found herself responsible for all those administrative tasks that Jerry had handled with his efficient, but undocumented, manual system.

Finding Jerry's replacement was difficult indeed. For a while, Dr. Parkley managed the office herself. However, she soon found that the work was too much and that the smooth functioning of the office had become just a pleasant memory. She did learn a lot about the business end of running a dental practice, but she vowed that she'd never again become so dependent on a single employee. Her experience enabled Dr. Parkley to come up with a more explicit job description for the position of office manager than "handling all the financial details," and she hired a recent graduate of the local business college, Elena Velasquez. It was apparent to Dr. Parkley that a business system should be set up so that Elena could follow predefined procedures instead of inventing her own unique ones. In several professional journals, Dr. Parkley had seen articles about the use of computers in dental offices; she thought perhaps a computer was the answer. One of her patients, Tom Washington, had his own firm called Central Systems Specialists (CSS). Dr. Parkley decided to call CSS and seek the help of a professional systems analyst.

Estimating the Scope of the Project

Once the problem has been defined, the systems analyst must estimate how big a job it will be to solve it. The scope of a project is generally a function of the type of problem that must be solved, how much time and money management is willing to spend, and how much change users and managers are willing to accept. This estimation is critical because project schedules and costs tend to expand indefinitely if no firm limits are set at the start. Also, a systems analyst should resist the temptation to recommend an entirely new system if users and managers will be satisfied with relatively simple alterations to the existing one.

How hard will it be to fix?

What management and users are looking for is the bottom line: How much will it cost and how long will it take? No one expects the systems analyst to predict exactly the final cost and schedule at this early stage, when so much is still unknown. As an expert, however, he or she must be able to come up with ballpark or order-of-magnitude figures. Before management can justifiably commit time and money to a project, it must have some idea of what the organization is getting into.

Proposing Possible Solutions

What can be done?

After the problem's nature and scope have been determined, a number of solutions may suggest themselves to the systems analyst. This isn't the time to work out the complete solution to the problem, but some preliminary ideas should be proposed. A relatively minor change might be in order, or an entirely new system might obviously be needed. It might be clear to the systems analyst that the functions of some manual system could be more conveniently and economically accomplished using a computer. The systems analyst should offer some suggestions that will

TECHNOLOGY CLOSEUP

Dr. Parkley's Project— Phase 1

Tom Washington, the senior analyst at CSS, decided that he would handle Dr. Parkley's case personally. They met briefly over lunch so that Dr. Parkley could outline her office's history and the current problems. Washington believed that he could help, and they agreed to go ahead with the first step, a feasibility study.

Later that week, Washington spent the better part of a day at Dr. Parkley's office. He talked to all the employees, but reserved most of his time for Dr. Parkley and Elena. The purpose of this visit was to form a clear definition of the problem at hand. Just what was it that Dr. Parkley hoped to solve? It seemed that generally what Dr. Parkley wanted was to be relieved of the responsibilities of managing her routine office finances. She did, however, want to remain in control and not to become totally dependent on any one employee. Through his conversations, Washington was able to identify two specific problem areas: billing and payroll.

A large part of the billing problem was due to the fact that about 50% of gross office earnings came from dental insurance carriers. Only half was paid directly by the patients. Insurance companies must receive completely filled-out forms before they will pay. Even slight errors can delay reimbursement for months. The result of inefficient and inaccurate billing procedures (the sorry state of affairs since Jerry's departure) was a serious cash flow problem. Dr. Parkley had actually borrowed money against her future insurance payments to pay her own bills. The extra money paid in interest on these loans (estimated at about $2500 per year), needless to say, could have been put to better use. Also, Dr. Parkley's professional image was being affected by billing errors. Both patients and insurance companies get upset when their bills are wrong.

The other key problem area was payroll. Dr. Parkley's employees trusted Jerry, and he knew the required procedures for figuring, withholding, and reporting income taxes. When Dr. Parkley took over the responsibility for payroll after Jerry left, the employees didn't mind, but it was a nightmare for her. She certainly hadn't learned much about tax law in dental school. Elena, on the other hand, was familiar with payroll procedures, but had not yet gained the confidence of her fellow workers. They all indicated that they would feel better if their paychecks were handled more automatically, say by computer.

Washington prepared a written statement summarizing his understanding of these two problem areas, and it was reviewed by Dr. Parkley. She agreed that he had correctly determined the major sources of her difficulties. She indicated that she might be interested in having CSS solve her problems, if it wouldn't cost too much or disrupt her office. Washington went on to prepare a report describing the scope of the problem as he saw it and suggesting two possible solutions. He estimated that his firm could set up a system for her at a total cost of about $15,000 and that it could be operating in about a month. Both possible solutions involved installing a computer system: the first proposed that CSS develop the required software; the other suggested purchasing a prewritten application package.

basically give users and managers an idea of how much change they should expect if the project is undertaken.

At this stage, a completely satisfactory solution to the problem may not be apparent. For example, it might be that a supermarket chain will just have to live with the fact that a certain percentage of perishable goods will spoil, given its distribution system. In such a case, the system project might attempt to minimize particularly undesirable circumstances instead of eliminating them altogether, for example, by more fully utilizing automated equipment and electronic "paper shuffling" to cut down on the time the food spends moving from warehouse to warehouse. In any case, the systems analyst must give management some assurance that something can be done about the problem before the system project can begin.

Reporting to Management

As the culmination of the feasibility study, the systems analyst submits a report to management summarizing his or her findings and recommendations. This report states the problem definition, project objectives and scope, and the preliminary ideas for solutions, along with estimated costs and benefits. The problem may be so simple that no further study is necessary, or it may require additional examination involving further costs. The central purpose of the report is to help management decide whether to continue with the project. Once the feasibility study is complete, management can better estimate if the work that lies ahead will be worth it. Many projects are in fact abandoned at this point; only those promising a good investment return should be pursued.

Summarizing for the decision makers

Careful consideration is important at this early stage because of the way costs rise sharply as projects proceed. Consequently, the formal presentation of the report to management marks a critical point in the life of a project. After this point, it becomes progressively more difficult to scrap the project without incurring significant losses.

If management approves the project, the feasibility report can stand as a model of the systems analyst's view of the project and can provide a picture of how subsequent development is likely to proceed.

PHASE 2—SYSTEMS ANALYSIS

Once management has officially decided to proceed with the project, the next phase is systems analysis. This is a logical process that determines exactly what must be done to solve the problem. The current system is studied in detail to find out what it does and how it works. This model of the existing system can then be compared to what users and managers agree the system should be doing. The process of systems analysis is usually broken down into two major activities: data gathering and data analysis.

Find out how the old system works and what the new system must do

Data Gathering

For an existing system to be understood, facts about that system must be compiled. The analyst must determine the exact inputs, operations, and outputs of the system. What is being done, who is doing it, how it is being done, and why it is being done

Compile facts about the old system, using written documents, questionnaires, interviews, and observation

Figure 11.2 An Organization Chart

This organization chart for a typical small manufacturing company illustrates the formal relationships among the employees and provides an overview of the administrative structure.

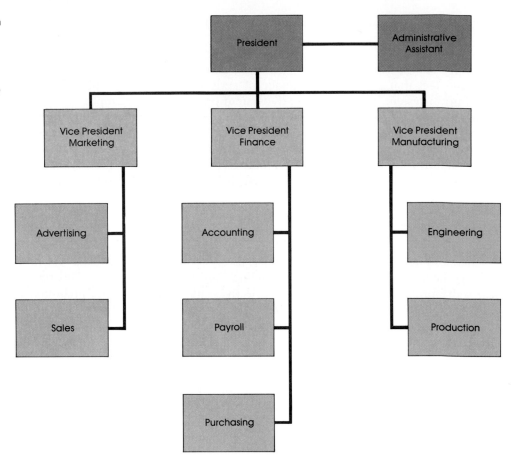

must all be determined accurately. Although the precise nature of the data that must be gathered and how they can best be obtained will vary from system to system, analysts frequently use four sources: written documents, questionnaires, interviews, and observation.

Written Documents

Written documents—forms, manuals, charts, diagrams, letters, and any other paperwork used by the organization—can yield insight into how the system works. Such materials contain a great deal of information about policies, procedures, and the nature of the relationship among the people in an organization. For example, a customer invoice form can reveal many facts about billing procedures. Organization charts can illustrate the formal relationships among personnel and can provide an overview of company operations (see Figure 11.2).

The systems analyst must exercise judgment in the selection of pertinent documents during the data gathering. A large organization will probably produce or process an almost overwhelming volume of paperwork every day. A systems analyst must be skilled at determining which documents tell the most about the workings of a system and which ones have a direct bearing on the problems at hand.

Questionnaires

Systems analysts frequently prepare and distribute questionnaires to the members of an organization as a means of rapidly and inexpensively gathering information. Questionnaires are especially applicable to large or geographically dispersed systems; they also permit anonymous responses. Ideally, a questionnaire consists of inquiries asking for short simple responses, such as checking off "yes" or "no" or rating agreement/disagreement on a scale from 1 to 10. Although not always easy to achieve, a balance should be struck between gathering as much information as possible and keeping the questionnaire easy to complete.

Questionnaires have several disadvantages, however, including the fact that many people will not take the time to fill them out, no matter what the incentive. In receiving responses only from a certain self-limited group within the organization, the analyst may be getting a biased view of the system. If management makes compliance with the systems analyst's requests mandatory, resentment may color the respondents' replies. Furthermore, some knowledge of statistics is usually required to interpret the results of a questionnaire accurately. Finally, many people are critical of questionnaires; they believe that they are rigid and impersonal and feel frustrated because they can't clarify and qualify their answers. These factors add to the difficulty of constructing a questionnaire. Psychologists have studied this problem for years, and systems analysts often take classes to learn how to create effective questionnaires.

Interviews

Interviews provide a flexibility that questionnaires lack, but are also more time-consuming. The systems analyst can gather a great deal of information by holding discussions with key personnel in an organization. Some people reveal more in discussions than they would in writing, and others feel that they are better able to express themselves when they are allowed to explain and qualify their answers the way they can in discussion. Also, the interviewer can observe voice inflections and emphases, which can reveal more than the words alone would. In a face-to-face talk, the interviewer is free to pursue different lines of investigation if a particularly interesting point comes up.

Interviews, however, also have their disadvantages. Some people are uncomfortable in such situations. Truths are sometimes distorted, or opinions are given instead of facts. In addition, questions or responses can be misinterpreted. Interview results, like questionnaire results, must be carefully scrutinized. And, like preparing successful questionnaires, effective interviewing is a skill that must be learned. Systems analysts can often acquire or improve interviewing techniques by taking special classes.

There are basically two types of interviews: structured and unstructured. *Structured interviews* include only questions that have been prepared ahead of time, and the interviewer asks no other questions. Although they are somewhat rigid, structured interviews are useful when the same set of questions must be asked of a number of people. *Unstructured interviews,* on the other hand, have a general goal and may include some questions chosen in advance, but the interviewer is free to pursue related topics and lines of inquiry if they seem appropriate. This additional flexibility generally requires the expense of more time and means that fewer people can be interviewed. Either type of interview is directed toward a particular goal and is further structured by some amount of advance preparation by the interviewer.

Observation

Simply observing the day-to-day operations of an organization is a useful activity for the systems analyst. By noting how data flow through the system, seeing how people and machines interact, and listening to what people say, the analyst can evaluate the accuracy of the information that was gathered via questionnaires or interviews. Furthermore, observation furnishes firsthand experience of what it's like within a system. Although people may at first be self-conscious in the analyst's presence, they usually become more relaxed and act more naturally after a short period of time. To facilitate this acceptance by the employees, the systems analyst may temporarily take part in the activities of the organization. Such *participant observation* can be especially productive if the system under study is complex.

Data Analysis

Decide what functions the new system must include, using data flow diagrams, data dictionaries, and black box process descriptions

Once information about the workings of the old system has been amassed, this collected data must be analyzed in order to define the logical functions that the new system should incorporate. During this data analysis, the objective is to develop a complete functional understanding of the proposed system. As you might expect, systems analysts can tackle this task in several ways. One popular structured method calls for the construction of three types of formally defined documents: data flow diagrams, data dictionaries, and black box process descriptions. These documents are then presented to management for an inspection and review.

Data Flow Diagrams

In analyzing the data for a system project, the analyst is concerned with summarizing the proposed system in a way that stresses function rather than physical implementation. In other words, in this phase, the analyst will consider *what* things need to be done instead of *how* they will be done. A **data flow diagram** is a tool well-suited to this purpose; it shows the sources, stores, and destinations of data, the directions of data flow, and the processes that transform data. It says nothing, however, about how any of these system elements are implemented. This contrasts with the flowcharts we introduced in Chapter 7. Flowcharts detail how functions are implemented; data flow diagrams show what functions are included and how they relate to one another.

A data flow diagram is constructed using four basic elements: data sources and destinations, data stores, processes, and data flows. Figure 11.3 shows the symbols for these elements, along with an example of a diagram. *Data sources and destinations* (symbolized by boxes) are the places data come from and go to. For example, in a payroll system, employee time records are a data source, and paychecks are a data destination. *Data stores* (symbolized by rectangles open on one side) are places where data are held for a time; for example, data stores may be files that reside on disk or in primary memory. *Processes* (symbolized by circles or round-cornered rectangles) are steps that change or move data; they can be program modules, whole programs, collections of programs, or even manual operations. Finally, *data flows* (symbolized by arrows) are the movements of data; they indicate how the data move among the other elements of the system.

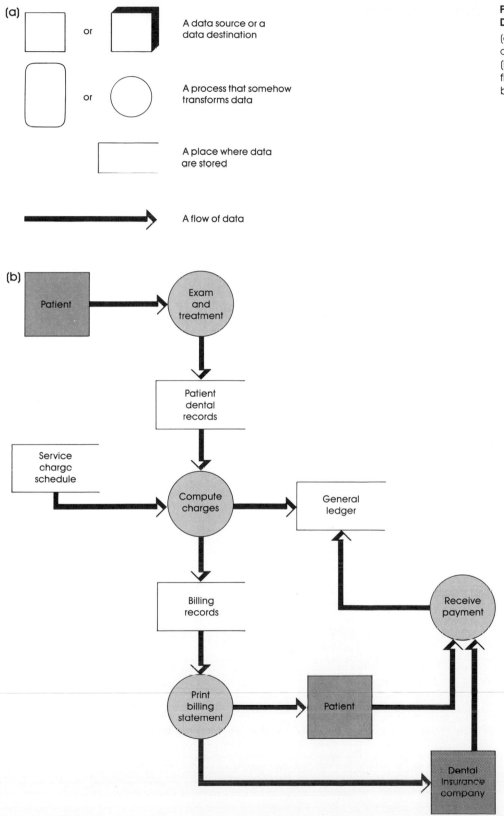

Figure 11.3 Data Flow Diagrams
(a) The four basic symbols of a data flow diagram.
(b) An example of a data flow diagram for a dentist's billing system.

(a)

A data source or a data destination

A process that somehow transforms data

A place where data are stored

A flow of data

(b)

Patient

Exam and treatment

Patient dental records

Service charge schedule

Compute charges

General ledger

Billing records

Receive payment

Print billing statement

Patient

Dental Insurance company

Data Dictionaries

A **data dictionary** is a collection of information about the data elements of a system. Typically, it contains the name, description, source, format, and use of each major category of data. Data dictionaries help analysts organize information about the data and can alert them to items that were somehow missed in the initial collection. In addition, the data dictionary is quite useful after the analysis phase is complete. It serves as valuable documentation during the succeeding phases of design, development, and implementation and evaluation by providing a reference source for all who must deal with the system.

At its simplest, a data dictionary can consist of a set of index cards, with one card for each data element (see Figure 11.4). A number of commercially available computerized data dictionaries allow analysts to enter information about data items into a data base. Such systems can be a valuable aid to analysts working on large or complex projects.

Black Box Process Descriptions

We have said that during the analysis phase of a system project the analyst is concerned with what functions are needed, not with how they will work. This means that the analyst must have some way to document the processes the system must perform, but only at a functional level. The concept of a **black box** is frequently encountered in computer science. Simply put, it is a piece of hardware or

Figure 11.4 A Data Dictionary

Here are three entries in a sample data dictionary for an employee payroll system.

NAME:	total-gross-pay
DESCRIPTION:	The total pay of an employee before taxes and other deductions have been withheld.
SOURCE:	Employee PAYROLL file.
FORMAT:	Positive, numeric; maximum value = 99999.00
USE:	Printed on checks and used for year-end totals.

NAME:	total-federal-tax
DESCRIPTION:	The total amount paid by an employee in federal income taxes.
SOURCE:	Employee PAYROLL file.
FORMAT:	Positive, numeric; maximum value = 99999.00
USE:	Printed on checks and used for year-end totals.

NAME:	employee-name
DESCRIPTION:	An employee's name in the form: last name, first name, middle initial.
SOURCE:	Employee timecards, PAYROLL file.
FORMAT:	Character
USE:	Printed on checks and used for PAYROLL file key.

Primarily through employee interviews, observation, and examining various written documents (like the dental insurance claim forms), Tom Washington gathered data about the present system. Since Dr. Parkley's office was a small operation, organization charts and questionnaires wouldn't be very helpful. Because the old system for billing and payroll was clearly inadequate (without Jerry, that is), it became evident to Washington that a completely new system would have to be prepared to handle both activities. Simply computerizing the current system wouldn't work.

By carrying out a data analysis, Washington established what the new system must do. To gain a complete understanding of the functions needed, he created a data flow diagram (see Figure 11.3), compiled a data dictionary (see Figure 11.4), and wrote black box process descriptions for the proposed new system. Keep in mind that what he did was describe **what** the new system must do, not **how** it was to be done. Systems design, the next phase, would establish the details of how the problem was to be solved.

Washington concluded this phase by submitting a report for Dr. Parkley and Elena to review. Their input was necessary at this point because it would be more difficult to add forgotten features once the actual work on the design had begun. They agreed with Washington's plans, and Dr. Parkley gave the go-ahead for the next step, systems design.

software that performs a specific function. How it performs this function is not known or is not specified in the context of the discussion; all that is known is that, given certain inputs, the black box will produce certain predictable outputs. A good example of a black box process is the square root function available on many calculators. You probably don't know how this works; all you need to know is that when you enter a number and press the square root key, you get the square root of that number. By viewing and describing system processes as black boxes, the analyst is able to show what should be done without detailing how it will be done.

Typically, the analyst documents black box processes by writing them out on index cards or sheets of paper (one per process). An overview of inputs and outputs can be sketched, and details can be added later as they become known. Another useful alternative is to use HIPO charts (see Chapter 7, particularly Figure 7.8), filling in minimal information. As the system project moves into the design phase, further details can be added to flesh out the diagrams. This reflects a structured methodology, which is worthwhile since the documentation produced in one step is directly relevant to future steps.

PHASE 3—SYSTEMS DESIGN

When the analysis phase of a system project has been completed, what must be done to solve the problem is usually known. The next step is to decide exactly how to implement a solution. Alternatives must be considered, and a single set of detailed specifications for the new system must be developed. In addition, the design that is chosen must reflect the previously established goals and scope of the project. Systems design thus consists of reviewing the project goals, developing the system requirements, and presenting a report to management.

Specify how to build the new system

Review of Project Goals

Reconsider the objectives of the system project

Throughout the design phase, the systems analyst is responsible for ensuring that the final product will be what users and managers need. To do this, the analyst should review the goals and scope of the system project before creating the actual design and should keep these items in mind as all subsequent work proceeds. Furthermore, as the design phase progresses, the systems analyst should consider the effects of certain important factors:

- *The long-range plans of the organization.*   Some organizations have plans for the eventual evolution of their data-processing systems. If this is so, the design of the current project must be compatible with these plans.

- *The user interface.*   Just as the user interface is an important consideration in the design of programs (see Chapter 7), human factors such as ease of use should be carefully monitored in the design of systems.

- *Economic trade-offs.*   Given that the money and time available for a project are finite, it cannot be perfect. It would be wonderful to produce a system that was completely flexible, extremely user-friendly, and able to recover from every possible error gracefully. This state, however, is seldom achieved in an actual system because it would cost too much. Priorities must be set and compromises made if a workable system is to be designed.

- *Availability of prewritten software.*   Careful evaluation must be made as to whether any off-the-shelf application package might be suitable. If a workable system can be purchased instead of being developed within an organization, a great deal of time, effort, and money can often be saved.

- *Applicability of design methods.*   In Chapter 7, we presented methods of designing programs. Most of these are applicable to systems design, as we'll see shortly. Before the design of a system begins in earnest, a consensus should be reached regarding which general method to use.

Development of System Requirements

Detail exactly how the new system should work

At this point in the system project, the analyst must detail exactly how the new system will work. Just as a program should be completely designed before coding begins, a new system should be comprehensively modeled before actual development work starts. Throughout the design phase, the analyst may employ tools like the program design aids we introduced in Chapter 7. The most popular aids for systems design are data flow diagrams and system flowcharts, but pseudocode, decision tables, structure charts, and HIPO charts are also often used. In addition, the concepts of structured programming, top-down design, modularity, egoless programming, and structured walkthroughs are all frequently employed in systems design.

The purpose of systems design is to document exactly how a new system should work. In essence, this means preparing a detailed set of specifications for the new system. These system requirements are very similar to the software requirements we talked about in Chapter 7. The design must address the following aspects of the proposed system, usually in this order:

1. Output requirements

2. Input requirements

3. File and storage requirements

4. Processing

5. Controls and backups

6. Personnel and procedures

Output Requirements

Before any other part of the system is designed, the analyst must specify exactly what must be produced, that is, the output. The output is what mainly interests users and managers and it dictates to a large extent how the input, processing, and storage are to be handled.

At the logical level, the analyst must decide what information users need, how detailed it should be, and how frequently it should be presented. At the physical level, the analyst must consider the hardware and media on which the output is to be presented, as well as the exact format. In other words, will the output be presented on a display screen, printer, plotter, or microfilm? Exactly how will it look on the output device or medium? The analyst may employ such aids as the **printer spacing chart** (see Figure 11.5), a formatting tool that enables one to plan how a printed report will look. **Display layout charts** are similar forms that are sometimes used to design the format of screen output.

Input Requirements

After the outputs have been fully specified, the analyst must determine what inputs are necessary for the system to produce them. How the inputs are formatted and entered, how often they should enter the system, and what media on which they will be presented must all be determined at this time. A systems analyst considers the following questions in order to establish the input requirements of a new system:

- *What data must be collected?* If a customer billing system is being designed, then the input must include the name, address, and phone number of the customer, the service rendered, the date, the charge, and so forth. These are the basic facts with which the system will work.

- *How should the data be formatted?* The analyst has to define how the data will be arranged so that the system can correctly identify, store, and process the input. A **record layout form** (see Figure 11.6) may be used to facilitate data formatting. At this point, the analyst may also have to design forms for people to fill out if the system will require written input from users. Like questionnaires, forms are not easy to construct well. Much thought and planning is necessary to design forms that are easy for people to use, yet collect the required information in a way that expedites later processing.

- *When will the data be input?* The analyst must determine whether data have to be input according to some schedule to coincide with processing needs. For example, if daily inventory reports are required as output, then daily inputs of inventory levels are necessary.

- *What input media and devices will be used?* Magnetic disks, computer terminals, and optical character recognition scanners are only a few of the alternatives the analyst must consider in deciding what input hardware and media fit in with the needs of the organization.

Printer Spacing Chart

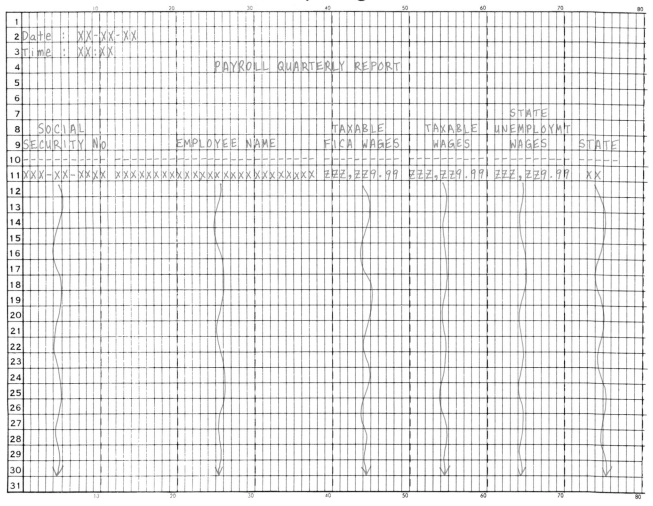

Figure 11.5 A Printer Spacing Chart

A printer spacing chart is used by the systems analyst to specify the format for a printed report.

File and Storage Requirements

The analyst must describe the data storage needs of the new system in detail. These include the sizes, contents, organization, media, devices, formats, access restrictions, and locations for all files the system will use. Record layout forms may be used to describe the content and format of files. Depending on how they are to be used, files may be organized as sequential, direct access, or indexed sequential files (see Chapter 5). Storage devices have to be chosen from such forms as floppy disk, hard disk, optical disk, or some combination of these. Also, decisions must be made regarding which devices will hold which files and which users should have access to which files.

Many large systems must interact extensively with data bases (we look at data base systems in Chapter 12). For such systems, the analyst has to decide whether a

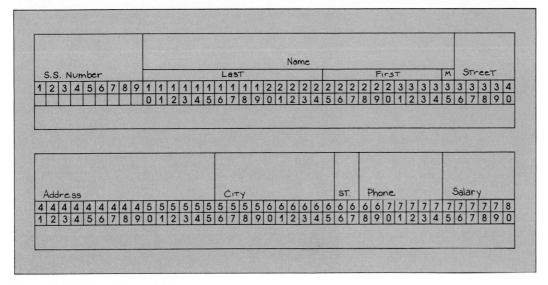

Figure 11.6 A Record Layout Form
The systems analyst can use a record layout form such as the one shown here for
setting up the formats for input and storage file records.

new data base needs to be established or if an existing one can be used. In either
case, careful planning of the new system's data storage must be done to ensure
compatibility with the organization of the data base.

Processing

The analyst must describe the processing steps that convert inputs to outputs. This
involves the use of data flow diagrams and the program design aids covered in
Chapter 7 to document fully the operation of the new system. At this time, the
analyst should also consider whether any special or new hardware is required to
perform the necessary processing. For example, if the new system will handle many
more computations than the former system did, acquiring a computer with a faster,
more powerful CPU may be necessary.

Controls and Backups

Vital to any organization are provisions to ensure the accuracy, security, and privacy of software and hardware resources. *System controls* are instituted to make sure
that data are input, processed, and output correctly and to prevent data destruction,
unauthorized program modifications, fraud, or any other tampering that might
occur. Such controls can be further subdivided into security and privacy controls,
accuracy controls, and audit controls.

Security and privacy controls include such things as putting locks and alarms on
computers and doors to computer rooms, requiring passwords for access to confidential programs and data, and applying data encryption to disguise secret data
(we'll go into more detail about such security measures in Chapter 17).

Accuracy controls are used to ensure that data remain correct and complete from
input through output. These measures are similar to software checks to ensure the

accuracy of input data (discussed in Chapter 4). The same techniques can be applied at various stages of system processing in an effort to keep errors from occurring.

Audit controls are used to certify that an organization's prescribed procedures are being followed, to check financial operations, and to establish the legitimacy of various external reports. Typically, audit controls trace specific outputs back to the inputs on which they are based. In a financial audit, an accounting firm traces a company's business transactions from source documents to final reports to determine how much money has been spent and how much has been earned. Similarly, data-processing systems often employ auditing techniques to make sure everything is going as it should and to trace the source of any problem that arises.

System backups are copies of essential data and program files that are made periodically to protect against inadvertent loss or malicious damage. A good analyst cannot overlook this important aspect of system design. An erasure of data might be the result of a power loss, an innocent but inappropriate user command, or a malicious attack by a discontented former employee—in any case, backup copies can save an organization from potential disaster. Imagine the chaos that would result if Social Security or Internal Revenue Service data files were destroyed and there were no backups!

Personnel and Procedures

The final aspect of the system the analyst must consider in preparing the design is the people who will make the system work. What personnel (operators, programmers, specialists, and so on) will be needed to run the system? What procedures will these people have to follow? A completely effective design must take such human factors into account.

Presentation to Management

Summarize once more

Up to this point, the analyst has been making plans for a proposed system but has yet to receive approval from management for the actual development. The considerations and plans of the design phase must be summarized for management in a *system design report* before the project can go any further. This report should contain all the facts management will need to make the best-informed decision. Specifically, the report should describe:

- *The problem.*   The nature of the current system and the problems it faces should be clearly presented.

- *The benefits.*   Why the new system has been proposed and how it specifically addresses the current system's problems should be explained.

- *The design.*   A design of the proposed system should be presented, but one that isn't overly detailed. Management is interested in the overall structure of the system but will not want to have to wade through highly technical specifications at this point. Relevant diagrams and design aids should be included.

- *The costs.*   An up-to-date estimate of the costs of the new system should be given. Any significant changes in the cost estimates since the completion of the feasibility study should be pointed out.

- *The schedule.*   How long it will take to develop and implement the new system must also be estimated.

Dr. Parkley's Project— Phase 3

Tom Washington began the design phase with a review of Dr. Parkley's goals in commissioning a new system. Along with considering her long-range plans and how Elena would interface with the system, he gave a lot of thought to whether the required software should be bought or written by his programming staff. He concluded that the software to handle payroll could be purchased right off the shelf because Dr. Parkley's personnel situation was not uncommon. However, her billing needs would have to be fulfilled with customized software—the special college-sponsored dental insurance many of her patients carried required certain additional information and special forms not called for by most other types of dental insurance.

Washington went on to specify the requirements of the new system in detail. He established the output requirements, input requirements, file and storage requirements, processing steps, controls and backups, and personnel and procedures (what Elena would have to do to operate the system). In this case, since Dr. Parkley's office previously had no computer system, he spent quite a bit of time investigating the hardware components he believed her system should include. Dr. Parkley knew almost nothing about the advantages and disadvantages of the wide array of computer hardware on the market, so this was a very important aspect of Washington's system design.

Before any further time or money was spent on the project, Washington prepared a report of his design recommendations for Dr. Parkley. Because she didn't want her staff to feel uneasy about the upcoming changes, she invited all of them to review this system design report and to offer their opinions in a meeting attended by Washington. Although they came up with a few suggestions that required some minor design changes, the staff was basically satisfied that the proposed system would work. Dr. Parkley was generally impressed with the report, which presented a thorough account of the problem, benefits, design, costs, and schedule of the new system, and she gave her approval for actual development to begin.

PHASE 4—SYSTEMS DEVELOPMENT

Once the final go-ahead has been given by management, the actual development of the proposed system can begin. This phase begins with the design specifications and ends when the system is ready for installation. Four general activities are carried out, to some extent concurrently, during this phase: scheduling, programming, testing, and documentation.

Construct the new system

Scheduling

The first step of the development phase is usually preparing a timetable to ensure that the system will be ready by a given date. Several schedules at various levels of detail may be prepared and further modified as the system development proceeds. One tool frequently used to diagram time spans and deadlines is the **Gantt chart,** or **milestone chart** (see Figure 11.7), a type of bar graph that shows how long it should take to complete various tasks within the complete schedule. The systems analyst typically prepares a Gantt chart showing the projected scheduling of all major development activities. Other members of the development team may construct more detailed Gantt charts covering the subtasks for which they are responsible.

Prepare timetables

Figure 11.7 The Gantt Chart

The Gantt chart is a convenient tool for keeping track of project schedules.

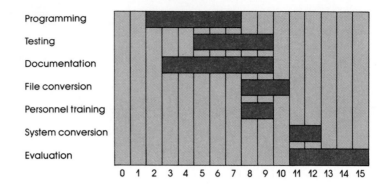

Other tools used in the scheduling of a project are the **critical path method (CPM)** and the **PERT chart** (see Figure 11.8), which stands for program evaluation and review technique. CPM is a scheduling method that focuses on the sequence of critical activities that must be performed to complete a project. Critical activities are those that must start after others are finished and must be completed before subsequent activities can begin. This sequence of activities is known as the *critical path*. There can be no slack time in completing the activities that comprise the critical path. CPM assumes that the time needed for individual activities can be estimated accurately, and it emphasizes the tradeoff between the cost of a project and the time needed to complete it.

The PERT approach was devised to schedule projects in which the completion times of individual tasks are difficult to estimate. Project schedules are developed for three possible scenarios: optimistic (earliest completion time), pessimistic (latest completion time), and most likely (expected duration). Today, CPM and PERT have become practically synonymous. The term *PERT* is generally used to describe a type of chart that graphically depicts a project as a network of interconnected activities, as shown in Figure 11.8. Basically, a PERT chart shows the order and interrelationship of a project's component tasks. The critical path through this network is usually highlighted in some manner. In Figure 11.8, for example, the critical path is shown by the dark arrows.

Both Gantt and PERT charts are often produced with a software tool called a **project management package** that is used extensively in many systems analysis and design projects. The purpose of a project management package is to help formally plan and control complex undertakings, such as the construction of a new office building, the development of a new product, or the installation of a new computer hardware and software system. This chapter's *A Closer Look* examines the use of Microsoft Project, a popular project management package for IBM-compatible microcomputers.

Programming

Write the system programs

We've barely mentioned programming in this chapter, but it does have its place in systems development. Just as coding can be the easiest and least time-consuming part of program development, programming is often the easiest part of systems development—that is, if the system design specifications have been properly

(a)

NOTATION

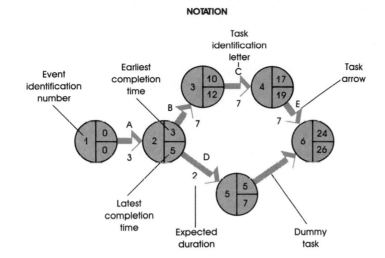

(b)

SAMPLE

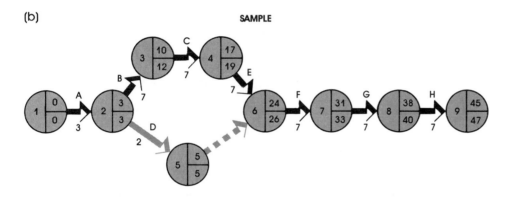

EVENT	DESCRIPTION	TASK	DESCRIPTION
1	Project approved		
2	Interview transcripts	A	Data gathering
3	Data flow diagrams, data dictionary, and black box descriptions	B	Data analysis
4	Systems requirements report	C	Develop systems requirements
5	Gantt and PERT charts	D	Scheduling
6	Hardware and software ordered	E	Select hardware and software
7	Hardware and software debugged	F	Testing
8	System implemented and converted	G	Training, file and system conversion
9	System appraisal	H	Evaluation

Figure 11.8 The PERT Chart

A PERT chart shows the order and interrelationship of a project's activities. (a) Notation. Circles (or *nodes*) represent events; arrows represent tasks. Each node contains an event identification number, earliest completion time (usually in days), and latest completion time (the absolute deadline). Each task arrow has a corresponding task identification letter and an expected duration. A dashed arrow represents a *dummy task,* which indicates a dependency between two events, although no time is required to go from one to the other. (b) Sample PERT chart that illustrates a systems development life cycle. Note that the table below the chart is essential for understanding the meaning of the chart. The darkest arrows represent the critical path.

prepared. It's essential that programming not be started too early in a system project because that can result in wasted effort (which translates into wasted time and money). If programming begins using incomplete or inadequate design specifications, the end-product is likely to be a system that neither meets user needs nor fulfills management expectations. Given detailed and thoughtfully prepared specifications, the programmer's job is straightforward, and the development of systems programs can proceed in a structured way (as outlined in Chapter 7). Furthermore, modern techniques such as prototyping and the use of application generators are often used in the programming of new systems, which can simplify and expedite the process of developing custom software.

Testing

Confirm that the system works

Before a system is put into operation, its component programs must be tested to make sure they work both individually and as a unit. As we mentioned in Chapter 7, desk checking should be done before programs are run on a computer. Comprehensive test data must be created so that programs can be thoroughly debugged. Bugs have a tendency to cost more the longer they are undiscovered, so rigorous testing is always a good practice. Errors caught in the development phase are much easier and less expensive to fix than those that come to light after the system is in daily operation.

TECHNOLOGY CLOSEUP

Dr. Parkley's Project— Phase 4

Tom Washington enjoyed this phase of the project the most. Because he'd done his job well in the earlier phases, development was fairly straightforward. Also, he always got excited seeing a new system come together. While he shopped around for suitable prewritten payroll packages, he set his programmers to work on the billing software he'd meticulously designed. Although he was always available in case they had questions, they seldom had anything to ask because his design specifications were so complete. His programmers were happy because they could concentrate on using their skills to produce the best possible software; they didn't have to spend time trying to figure out what Washington wanted.

The first step in this phase was preparing a schedule for the development work. Washington had his programming staff prepare a Gantt chart (see Figure 11.7) for their work, which he merged with one he'd prepared for his software search. Because Dr. Parkley's office required a new computer system, hardware on which the programming staff could develop the software had to be purchased. In addition, Washington needed to have access to the chosen computer so that he could test the payroll software that had to be purchased. In some cases, CSS programmers could write software on the firm's own computers, but the hardware chosen for Dr. Parkley's office wasn't compatible with these. Since they had to have access to the hardware on which the system would eventually run, the programmers had to wait for Washington to assemble it.

Once a suitable hardware configuration was available, the programming began. The programs written by the staff were tested and documented as they were developed, and Washington personally tested the software package he chose for handling Dr. Parkley's payroll. Finally, complete documentation was compiled to facilitate the next and final phase of the project, implementation and evaluation.

Documentation

Throughout the system project, documentation has been prepared in the form of reports to management, analysis and design aids, specifications, and charts. In Chapter 7, we pointed out the importance of documentation as an ongoing activity throughout the program development process. In addition to compiling documentation that describes the data and logic of the programs, a systems analyst must also arrange for the preparation of a comprehensive user manual. This manual is especially important for a large system because of the many potential users of the system. If user documentation is inadequate or poorly written because it has been prepared in a last-minute rush (which is, unfortunately, often the case), people will need more time to learn how to use the system and may never be able to take advantage of its full potential.

Explain how the system works

PHASE 5—IMPLEMENTATION AND EVALUATION

Even after the development phase is over, the system project isn't complete. The new system must be implemented, or installed, in the organization, and its operation must be evaluated to ensure that it fulfills its design specifications. Evaluation gives users another chance to provide constructive feedback. This final phase includes several activities that are necessary to make the new system successful and fully functional: file conversion, personnel training, system conversion, evaluation, and maintenance.

Install and appraise the new system

File Conversion

Computerized systems will usually require input data to be in some machine-readable form. This means that data previously handled manually must be entered into the computer system and stored in files. Data entry personnel may be temporarily employed if a large quantity of data must be keyed in initially. Even if the previous system was computerized, a new system may still require that files be modified to accommodate changes in the way in which data are stored or retrieved. Before a new system can be operational, the files it will utilize must be in formats that will be compatible with its programs.

Adapt data files so that the new system can use them

Personnel Training

We mentioned that the systems analyst should consider personnel aspects throughout the design phase of the project; the actual instruction of users, however, usually doesn't occur until implementation. Because the people who will be operating and using most systems aren't the same people who designed and developed them, training is a key factor in the success of any system project. A well-designed, full-featured system has little value if people don't know how to use it. Both end-user manuals and more technical programmer manuals are necessary learning and ref-

Teach users and operators how to run the system

erence aids, which should be prepared for any system of significant size or complexity. In addition, classes and hands-on training sessions are often held to familiarize users with system procedures and capabilities.

System Conversion

Switch from the old system to the new one

The moment of truth eventually arrives—the old system is shut down and the new one is turned on. This event, known as *system conversion,* may be handled in any of several ways. In **direct conversion,** the organization simply stops using the old system and immediately starts using the new one. Somewhat like diving courageously into a cold lake, direct conversion can be risky because it is too late to stop if something goes wrong. **Phased conversion** is like gradually wading in and getting used to the water at each level; all users ease into the new system one step at a time. With **pilot conversion,** only one department, plant, or branch office switches over to the new system, in a kind of trial run, before everyone changes. Finally, **parallel conversion** runs both systems simultaneously for a time until users are satisfied with the operation of the new system. Although it is the most expensive and prolonged approach, parallel conversion is also the safest because it leaves the old system intact until everyone is confident that the new system works.

TECHNOLOGY CLOSEUP

Dr. Parkley's Project— Phase 5

When development was complete, the new system had to be installed in Dr. Parkley's office. First, the new hardware had to be moved in and set up. After the hardware was checked out to ensure that it was not malfunctioning, the old billing and payroll files had to be entered into the new system. This was a big job since all the records had been kept manually. Tom Washington hired two temporary workers to enter the written records into the new system's storage files and verify them. For this project, file conversion was the most time-consuming of the implementation activities.

Next, Dr. Parkley and Elena were trained to use the new system. Since the other staff members wouldn't be using it, there was no need for them to receive training. Washington continually asked Dr. Parkley and Elena if there was anything they didn't understand or that they thought they'd be unable to teach someone else. He wanted to make sure that if Elena left, either she or Dr. Parkley could easily train her successor. This pleased Dr. Parkley because she could see that the running of her practice was no longer vulnerable to a single employee's sudden departure. The user documentation proved to be quite easy to follow, and the training was quickly completed.

In this case, converting from the old system to the new system could take place immediately and without any noticeable trauma. Direct conversion worked fine here because there was little risk involved in simply abandoning the old system in favor of the new. During a period of about a month following the conversion, the new system was on probation while it was evaluated by Elena and Dr. Parkley. Its performance was found to be superior to that of Jerry's manual system. Finally, Washington assured Dr. Parkley that his firm would be responsible for the maintenance of the new system. Any as yet undiscovered bugs would be promptly fixed, and future revisions or updates should present no major difficulties.

As Washington and his programmers rode off into the sunset, Dr. Parkley and her staff let out a collective sigh of relief. They could proceed to "drill 'em, fill 'em, and bill 'em," content in the knowledge that things should be running smoothly from then on.

Evaluation

During and after system conversion, the performance of the new system is appraised to see whether it fulfills all of the system requirements, which were developed in the systems design phase. Basically, the systems analyst will be interested in determining that the system is working as intended and that it is living up to the cost-benefit expectations outlined in the system design report. If the performance is inadequate in some way, the systems analyst must discover the source of the deficiency and fix it as best as possible. In addition, the entire system project may be evaluated at this time to verify that everything was completed on schedule and within budget.

Does it fulfill its requirements?

Maintenance

Even when a system is successfully installed and is operating as designed, the project is not quite completely finished. The program development process concludes with plans for handling future revisions, updates, additions, and undiscovered bugs; newly implemented systems usually require frequent monitoring and periodic adjustment. At some time, these changes may accumulate to the point of being beyond mere maintenance, and the entire systems analysis and design process has to begin anew.

Keep the system effective

A project management package is a program that helps you schedule and monitor the progress of complex undertakings, such as the development of a new product line, the construction of a building, or the installation of a sophisticated computer system. Basically, this type of software makes it easier to plan and control projects by carefully balancing tasks, time, and resources. Like spreadsheet packages, project management software lets you try out different scenarios with a computer before actually implementing them. This management tool also lets you change your plans once a project is underway. The major advantage project management software has over manual planning methods is that it facilitates the process of turning well-conceived plans into finished products more quickly and comprehensively. Once a plan has been formulated, a project management package makes it easy to enter changes, measure their effects, and track day-to-day performance.

Microsoft Project is one of the most popular project management packages for IBM-compatible microcomputers. The program is a solid performer that has been kept consistently up to date and is also straightforward and easy to use. When you start up Microsoft Project, this screen is displayed:

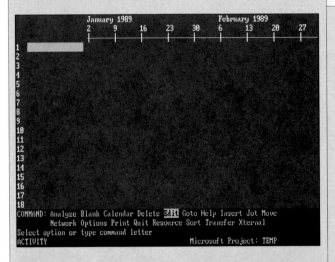

Let's illustrate project management software by using Microsoft Project to plan the development of a new product, a new line of designer wallpaper from a fictional company named Kreative Koverings.

As we mentioned on page 396, PERT (program evaluation and review technique) and CPM (critical path method) are two classic project-scheduling techniques. Both involve dividing a project into a series of distinct activities, each of which can be completed inde-

A Closer Look

Using Microsoft Project

pendently of the others. The timing of the activities must be analyzed to determine which ones are critical to the completion of the project. A delay in any of these critical tasks can set back the entire project. Microsoft Project, like most project management packages, incorporates elements of PERT and CPM to help you plan, schedule, and monitor all kinds of projects, from simple to complex.

The first step in the development of the new line of wallpaper is to schedule the basic activities by creating a Gantt chart. In the Gantt chart you enter a description of each activity, its start and finish dates, its *predecessors* (any activities that must come before), any resources required, and sometimes other information about the project. Before you begin entering activity information, however, you must tell Microsoft Project when the project itself will start. This is done by choosing the Options command from the Activity menu and then choosing the Project command. Now you can enter today's date and the project start date, as seen in the next screen.

Once the project start date has been entered, you can begin entering activities into the blank Gantt chart that appears on the screen. Before you can do this,

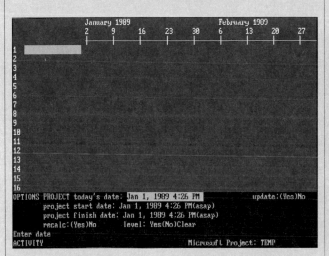

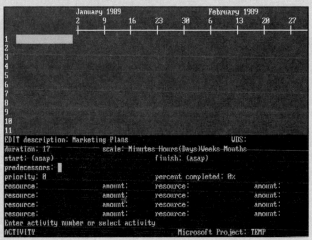

however, you need to ask the following questions about each activity:

- What is it? (a description)
- How long will it take? (its duration)
- What must be done beforehand? (its predecessors)
- When should it begin and end? (start date and finish date)

Sometimes, it helps to write down all of your activities with the answers to these questions before you enter the information into Microsoft Project's Gantt chart. For example, the table below demonstrates the activities for developing Kreative Koverings' new line of designer wallpaper. To schedule these activities with Microsoft Project, you choose the Edit command and then enter the information about each one. For example, when you enter the information about the first activity, you see the screen at top right.

Number	Description	Duration (days)	Predecessors (numbers)	Start Date
1	Marketing plans	17		ASAP
2	Assign duties	7	1	ASAP
3	Combine plans	7	1	ASAP
4	Review competition	17	3	ASAP
5	Hire sketch artist	14	2	ASAP
6	Preliminary designs	32	2, 3, 4, 5	ASAP
7	Hire layout artist	7	2	ASAP
8	Hire production staff	12	5	ASAP
9	Train production staff	22	8	ASAP
10	Review designs	7	6	ASAP
11	Final selection	0	4, 10	ASAP
12	Prepare ads	22	3, 7, 11	ASAP
13	Approve ads	7	11, 12	ASAP
14	Produce ads	17	12, 13	ASAP
15	Prepare press releases	12	11	ASAP
16	Approve press releases	7	15	ASAP
17	Final press releases	0	11, 14, 16, 16	ASAP

(Note: ASAP stands for as soon as possible.)

After you enter this information, Microsoft Project adds a horizontal bar to the Gantt chart. To complete the chart, you simply repeat the process for each activity. The critical path of activities is automatically shown by double-line bars. Here is what the completed Gantt chart looks like when the time scale is reduced to make it all fit on a single screen:

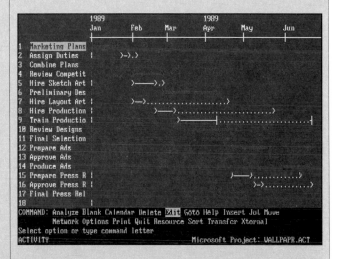

In this figure, the critical path is shown in red horizontal double-line bars. The yellow single-line bars show noncritical activities. Dotted lines represent the *slack time* of an activity, which is the amount of time the activity can be postponed without delaying the entire project. Activities with one or more predecessors begin with an arrow on the left side; activities with no predecessors begin with a vertical line. Similarly, activities with one or more successors end with an arrow, and activities with no successors end with a vertical line. Finally, the asterisks represent *milestones*, which are activities with a duration of zero time; they are informational markers that measure the progress of a project without affecting its scheduling.

A Gantt chart such as this one is *time-based;* it focuses on the dates of the activities that make up the critical path. You can also examine your project schedule in the form of a PERT chart, which is *order-based*. The PERT chart also identifies the activities along the critical path, but focuses on their relative order instead of their start and finish dates.

Microsoft Project calls PERT charts *network charts*. To create a network chart, you must select the Network command from the Activity menu. The following figure shows what you see on your screen:

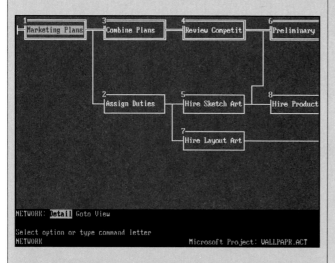

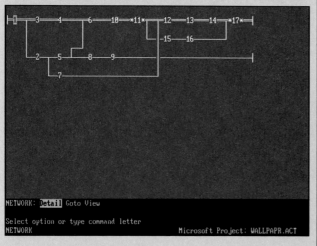

The chart consists of a network of interconnected activity boxes. The boxes that are outlined with double lines represent activities on the critical path. You can view different parts of the network by using Home, End, and the arrow keys on your keyboard. You can also "zoom out" to see the maximum amount of network chart on the screen, as seen in the bottom screen.

Finally, you can print the whole network chart or any part of it. In most cases, the printed version appears sideways on the paper and usually stretches across several pages. The network report contains the activity names, numbers, start and finish dates, durations, and slack times.

In addition to the creation of Gantt and PERT charts, an important part of any project management package is the allocation of resources to a project and the estimation of total cost. A *resource* is simply any equipment, supplies, or personnel needed to complete an activity. In Microsoft Project, you enter each activity's resources with the Edit command. When you are finished, you can display or print the resulting resource table, which shows each resource's description, capacity, cost per time unit, number of days needed, total cost per resource, and cost to complete the job. For example, here is a partial list of resources for the first six activities of the Kreative Koverings wallpaper project:

Number	Description	Resource	How Many
1	Marketing plans	Forecaster	2
2	Assign duties	Production manager	1
		Recruiter	1
3	Combine plans	Forecaster	1
		Production manager	1
		Word processor	1.5
4	Review competition	Production VP	1
		Production manager	1
5	Hire sketch artist	Recruiter	1
6	Preliminary designs	Sketch artist	1
		Graphic artist	1

To enter these resources, you highlight the particular activity in the Gantt chart and execute the Edit command from the Activity menu. The information you've already entered about that activity is displayed on the screen. All you have to do is enter the additional information about its resources, as seen in the next screen.

As you enter the activities' resources, Microsoft Project builds a resource table with this information. When you are finished, you can view this table by executing the Resource command. This brings up the Resource Screen, to which you can add the capacity and unit cost of each resource. Microsoft Project automatically com-

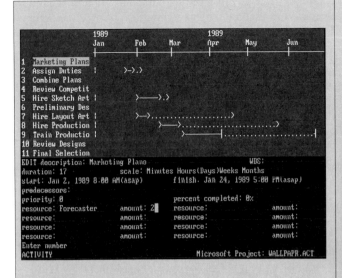

```
         1989              1989
         Jan     Feb    Mar    Apr    May    Jun
 1  Marketing Plans
 2  Assign Duties    |        )->.)
 3  Combine Plans
 4  Review Competit
 5  Hire Sketch Art  |        )———>.)
 6  Preliminary Des
 7  Hire Layout Art  |      )——>................)
 8  Hire Production  |         )——>................>
 9  Train Productio  |           )——>..........|
10  Review Designs   |                     |............)
11  Final Selection
EDIT description: Marketing Plans                WDS:
duration: 17              scale: Minutes Hours(Days)Weeks Months
start: Jan 2, 1989 8:00 AM(asap)      finish: Jan 24, 1989 5:00 PM(asap)
predecessors:
priority: 0                    percent completed: 0%
resource: Forecaster      amount: 2    resource:           amount:
resource:                 amount:      resource:           amount:
resource:                 amount:      resource:           amount:
resource:                 amount:      resource:           amount:
Enter number
ACTIVITY                               Microsoft Project: WALLPAPR.ACT
```

putes the current cost to complete the project and the total cost of the entire project. For example, the screen at right shows what the Resource Screen looks like after the costs have been entered.

Although we've only scratched the surface of what you can do with a project management package such as Microsoft Project, you should now understand some of the benefits this software can bring to the planning of complex undertakings.

Resource	Capacity	Unit Cost	Per	Days to Complete	Cost to Complete
1 Forecaster	No limit	1800.00	Month	41.00	3406.16
2 Production Mgr	No limit	2500.00	Month	31.00	3576.92
3 Recruiter	No limit	2200.00	Month	21.00	2132.31
4 Word Processor	No limit	8.00	Hour	10.50	672.00
5 Production VP	No limit	3000.00	Month	17.00	2981.54
6 Sketch Artist	No limit	250.00	Day	32.00	8000.00
7 Graphic Artist	No limit	250.00	Day	32.00	8000.00
8					
9					
10					
11					
12					
13					
14					
15					

```
Cost to complete 28768.93       Total cost of project 28768.93

COMMAND: Activity Blank Calendar Delete Edit Goto Help Insert
         Move Options Print Quit Sort Transfer View
Select option or type command letter
RESOURCE                               Microsoft Project: WALLPAPR.RES
```

Summary

The Systems Approach

A comprehensive view that considers more than the program development process must be taken to produce complex data-processing tools.

What Is a System?   According to the American National Standards Committee, a system is "a collection of people, machines, and methods organized to accomplish a set of specific functions." A system interacts with its environment, has a purpose, and is self-regulating and self-correcting.

Why Systems Change   Systems may need to change to adapt to new laws, to accommodate new technology, to service a reorganization, to compete more effectively, or to provide desired features.

The Role of the Systems Analyst   Systems analysts are involved in both the evaluation of existing systems and the planning of new systems.

Phase 1—Feasibility Study

The objective of a feasibility study is to determine if an existing system can be improved at a reasonable cost.

Defining the Problem   The first step is understanding and documenting the source of the current difficulties.

Estimating the Scope of the Project   The analyst must estimate how big a job it will be to solve the defined problem.

Proposing Possible Solutions   A number of potentially workable solutions will be offered by the systems analyst.

Reporting to Management   The feasibility study is concluded with the presentation of a report to management; this report explains the findings and recommendations of the systems analyst.

Phase 2—Systems Analysis

If management decides that a new system is warranted, the existing system is studied in depth so that specific improvements can be suggested.

Data Gathering   Facts are collected about the organization and its present system from written documents, questionnaires, structured and unstructured interviews, and direct observation.

Data Analysis   The analyst specifies in detail what the new system must do by preparing data flow diagrams, a data dictionary, and black box process descriptions.

Phase 3—Systems Design

In the design phase, the analyst develops the requirements of the new system and maps out its major components.

Review of Project Goals   Factors such as the long-range plans of the organization, the user interface, economic trade-offs, availability of prewritten software, and applicability of design methods must be considered by the systems analyst.

Development of System Requirements   The output requirements, input requirements, file and storage requirements, processing steps, controls and backups, and personnel and procedures must all be completely specified.

Presentation to Management   A system design report is prepared that describes the problem, benefits, design, costs, and schedule of the proposed system.

Phase 4—Systems Development

During the development phase, the new system is actually constructed.

Scheduling   Timetables must be prepared to ensure that the system will be ready by a given date. Sometimes these take the form of Gantt charts and PERT charts.

Programming   If the design has been properly carried out, programming for the new system is relatively fast and straightforward.

Testing   Before a system is put into operation, its various components must be thoroughly tested—alone and together—to make sure that they work as intended.

Documentation   Throughout the entire system project, but especially during the development phase, comprehensive documentation must be compiled.

Phase 5—Implementation and Evaluation

The newly constructed system is installed in the organization, and its operation is closely scrutinized.

File Conversion   Existing data files may have to be converted to different formats if required by the new system.

Personnel Training   Operators and users must be taught to use the new system to its full advantage.

System Conversion   The changeover from the old system to the new one is accomplished by direct, phased, pilot, or parallel conversion.

Evaluation   The new system is evaluated to see if it fulfills all requirements and lives up to cost and benefit expectations.

Maintenance   Even successfully installed systems usually need to be revised, updated, augmented, or fixed at some future time.

Computer Concepts

As an extra review of the chapter, try defining the following terms. If you have trouble with any of them, refer to the page number listed.

system *377*
systems analysis *379*
systems design *379*
systems analysts *379*
systems development life
 cycle *379*
feasibility study
 (preliminary
 investigation) *379*
data flow diagram *386*

data dictionary *388*
black box *388*
printer spacing chart *391*
display layout charts *391*
record layout form *391*
Gantt chart (milestone
 chart) *395*
critical path method
 (CPM) *396*

program evaluation and
 review technique (PERT)
 chart *396*
project management
 package *396*
direct conversion *400*
phased conversion *400*
pilot conversion *400*
parallel conversion *400*

Review Questions

1. List several attributes that are common to most systems.
2. What are some of the reasons systems need to change?
3. Briefly describe what a systems analyst does.
4. Describe the five major phases of the system's development life cycle.
5. What are four major aspects of a feasibility study?
6. What in general determines the scope of a project?
7. What are the four sources from which systems analysts most commonly collect data about a system?
8. What types of written documents may be used by systems analysts to yield insights into how the system works?
9. Describe the three types of formally defined documents that are often prepared during data analysis.
10. List some of the factors a systems analyst should consider when designing a new system.
11. What aspects of the system must an analyst be sure to address in the design of a new system?
12. What is a printer spacing chart?
13. What elements are usually described in a system design report?
14. Name several tools used in the scheduling of system development.
15. What software tool is used to produce Gantt and PERT charts?
16. What are the four general activities making up the systems development phase?
17. What document must the systems analyst prepare in addition to documentation describing data and logic of the new programs?
18. List the activities that must be performed during implementation and evaluation of a new system.
19. Describe several ways in which the old system may be converted to the new one.
20. Why is parallel conversion considered the safest conversion method?

True or False

1. A system refers only to the machines used to carry out a specific set of functions.
2. Systems design is the process of planning a new system based on the findings of a systems analyst.

3. The feasibility study examines the scope of a problem and whether it's worthwhile to pursue the project further.
4. As the central purpose of the systems analyst's report to management, the culminating phase of the feasibility study is to help management decide whether or not to continue with the project.
5. Systems analysis determines exactly what must be done to solve a problem.
6. The object of data analysis is to develop a complete functional understanding of the proposed system.
7. A data dictionary is useless after data analysis is complete.
8. The systems design phase begins by specifying the input requirements.
9. The systems development phase begins with design specifications and ends when the system is ready for installation.
10. When the new system is ready to be installed, the old one is shut down and the new one goes into use.

Multiple Choice

1. The culmination of a feasibility study is:
   (a) data gathering
   (b) estimating the cost of the project
   (c) reporting to management

2. Among the formally defined documents constructed during the data analysis process is:
   (a) a black box process description
   (b) a questionnaire
   (c) results of an interview

3. One of the tools used to diagram time spans in the scheduling of systems development is:
   (a) a black box
   (b) a Gantt chart
   (c) a management report

4. A project management package is:
   (a) a Gantt chart
   (b) a milestone chart
   (c) a software tool used to produce Gantt and PERT charts

5. The process of system conversion in which the old and new systems run simultaneously for a time is:
   (a) parallel conversion
   (b) direct conversion
   (c) pilot conversion

6. An important question for management in the first phase is:
   (a) How should the system be changed? (b) What will it cost? (c) What is a system?

7. In systems design the first aspect of the proposed system which must be addressed is:
   (a) processing
   (b) output requirements
   (c) personnel

8. The final phase in the systems development cycle is:
   (a) a feasibility study
   (b) systems analysis
   (c) implementation and evaluation

9. A key part of the final phase, which may require additional personnel, is:
   (a) file conversion
   (b) documentation
   (c) testing

10. Important learning and reference aids used in the process of training personnel to use the new system are:
    (a) CPM
    (b) end-user and technical programmer manuals
    (c) questionnaires

1. People in personnel departments often know little about what qualifications, background, education, or personal characteristics to look for when they are asked to recruit systems analysts, especially among candidates fresh out of school. What do you think some guidelines for a personnel department at a large public hospital ought to be? Why?
2. Outline specific potential consequences that might occur if a systems analysis is poorly done. What parts of a system project do you think are the most critical? Why?

Projects

1. For some system with which you deal at school or work, try to identify problems that could be solved by an approach like that outlined in this chapter for systems analysis and design. Perhaps the way classes are graded could be improved, or maybe you could come up with a better system for course registration. Choose some problem and carry out a system "mini project." You don't have to do any system development or implementation; just outline how these might be done. Try to achieve about the same level of detail as in this chapter's case study.
2. Look through your college course catalog and the catalogs of some other colleges. Prepare a list of courses you would take, if you were planning to become a systems analyst.
3. Have you ever filled out a state or federal income tax form and wondered who designed it? Systems analysts are often closely involved in activities like the design of forms. What specific recommendations would you make for the federal 1040 Form?
4. Try to find a business in your community that employs or has employed a systems analyst. Prepare a report on one of their projects.

12

Data Base Systems

In This Chapter

Fingering Data Bases

Ken Moses carried the fingerprint card with him for eight years.

The print belonged to a man who had shot and killed the resident of a house he was burglarizing. "It was one of those cases you really wanted to solve," Moses says.

From the time he lifted that latent print of the killer in 1978, Moses spent his spare hours trying to match it against thousands of other fingerprint cards in the department's files—to no avail.

Then, in early 1985, San Francisco installed an Automated Fingerprint Identification System (AFIS). The first thing Moses did was to put his pet fingerprint into this computer system. Four minutes and 10 seconds later, the computer had matched the print to another on file. The police arrested a suspect within 24 hours.

Eventually, law enforcement agencies envision a nationwide, computerized fingerprint network. It is a vision that even civil libertarians have few reservations about, since the accuracy of computerized fingerprint matching would reduce the chances that an innocent person would be arrested by mistake.

It will likely take two or three years to iron out the technological wrinkles in automated systems so that different states' computers can communicate with each other, says Mr. Wilson. Within five years, about two-thirds of the population will be covered by AFIS, he says.

Technology experts say it will take a long time for the biggest fingerprint repository of them all— the Federal Bureau of Investigation—to hook up with the states. The FBI has 20 million people on file for crimes, and, since most people have 10 fingers, that's 200 million prints. Sheer size is not the problem, however. Rather, the FBI's current system is not organized to conduct a "cold" search— that is, searching an unidentified, latent print. It can match a print only when the police have a suspect. The upshot is that the states currently have no centralized way of searching for, say, a serial killer who has crossed state lines.

Dennis Kurre, the head of the FBI's identification division, says the FBI wants to modernize its system so it can do "cold" searches for states by 1993.

The logical next step is for states to share information about suspects.

But there is a hitch. The three major companies that make automated fingerprint ID systems use different languages and measurements in computerizing the fingerprints.

In December 1986, the National Bureau of Standards approved a standard that would translate data into a format that the various machines could understand. All that was needed was for the vendors to agree on the standard.

Nick Williams at De La Rue Printrak, one of the vendors, concedes that vendors are reluctant to agree on a standard, "because it would mean disclosing proprietary information." But a little arm-twisting will probably solve the problem: "The law enforcement community will have to establish the standard and the vendors will follow," he says.

In Chapter 9, we said that a *data base* is an organized collection of one or more files of interrelated data, and a **data base management package** is a program used to create, maintain, manipulate, and access data bases. Another term, **data base management system,** or its abbreviation **DBMS,** is also commonly used. Originally developed for mainframe computers, data base management systems are now available for machines of all sizes. You once had to spend between $5000 and $50,000 for minicomputer data base systems and as much as $100,000 for mainframe systems. Today, data base management packages are available for popular microcomputers at prices ranging from around $40 to $4000. In fact, microcomputer software makes up the fastest growing segment of the market in data base management systems. Sales of data base management software for microcomputers have been steadily increasing and are now estimated to exceed $800 million per year. Although between 25 and 35 percent of all microcomputer users currently own data base software, some market analysts predict that the numbers will eventually increase to at least 50 percent.

Although we discussed some of the types and features of data base packages in Chapter 9, let's examine what they are and how they work from a more theoretical viewpoint. Then, in this chapter's *A Closer Look*, we'll cover some of the specific details of using a particular data base management package for microcomputers, Ashton-Tate's best-selling dBASE III PLUS.

BEFORE DATA BASE MANAGEMENT PACKAGES

Before the advent and popularity of prewritten data base management packages, the traditional approach to data storage was to custom-design files for each particular software application. For example, if a business decided to develop a program to handle accounts receivable, the systems analyst or programmer designed the data files that would hold the requisite data. The formats of the items in these files (customer names, addresses, account balances, and so on) were created especially for the program being developed. To this point, the traditional approach worked fine. Suppose, however, that another department in the same business also wanted to develop software that required some of the same data, or that the same department needed another new program that also required some of the same data in the accounts receivable files, for example, a mailing list program for sending out advertisements. Before data base management packages, completely new files had to be created or existing ones would be duplicated and restructured to fit the new application. Each department and each software application wound up having its own independent data files. As time passed, an organization was likely to accumulate several files holding the same data in different formats.

As you can imagine, this kind of approach resulted in some overall problems. Organizations that employed software applications that shared the same data had to deal with data redundancy, updating difficulties, data dependence, data dispersion, and underutilization of data.

The traditional method of file management

Data Redundancy

The duplication of files means that the same data are repeated in different files. This wastes storage space and the efforts of data entry personnel, who must enter new data into several different files. For example, suppose that the various departments

Duplication of effort

of a manufacturing company perform their respective data-processing functions without the benefit of a centralized data base. The accounting department maintains its own file of customer names and addresses for its accounts receivable software. The advertising department also keeps a file of active customers so that it can mail out such materials as announcements of new products. Finally, the sales department has yet another file containing the same customer names and addresses so that it can send salespeople to call periodically. Even though they were set up at different times and for different purposes, the three data files hold the same customer names and addresses. Entry time and data storage space are both triple what they would have to be, because each record was typed in three times and is held in three different locations.

Updating Difficulties

Changing every copy

Updating difficulties are related to data redundancy. Having a customer's address in several different files, for example, means that an address change must be reflected in each file. Not only is changing the address several times more work than changing it once, the likelihood of error increases. Also, confusion can occur later if the change isn't made in every file (an oversight that occurs all too often). If a customer moves, for instance, the accounting, advertising, and sales departments must all be notified so that they can update their respective address files. Obviously, it would be more efficient, economical, and accurate if address changes had to be made only once.

Data Dependence

Intertwining of programs and data

When data files are intended to be used by particular programs, the programs depend to some extent on the data formats and file organization methods used. If the format or organization of the data is altered, the programs that use those data will also have to be altered. Conversely, if an existing program must be changed, the format or organization of the data it uses may also have to be changed. This dependence substantially increases the cost of maintaining software.

Let's say that the advertising department of a company designed their customer address file specifically for a program that prints out mailing labels. This program is constructed to work with customer records that consist of name, street address, city, state, and zip code. If this record format were changed in some way, then the mailing list program would probably also have to be modified. Or if a new mailing list program were purchased, it might require the data to fit some slightly different format, and the customer address file itself would have to be changed. When files are designed specifically for particular programs, the resulting data dependence can cause difficulties if changes must be made to either the programs or the data formats.

Data Dispersion

Data, data everywhere

When the data items are stored in many different places and their organization and formats are so intimately tied to the programs for which they are intended, it's difficult for programs to share data. That is, it's hard to tie data together and make cross-references. For example, if the sales department wanted to know whether customers who received mailed advertisements subsequently placed orders for the advertised items, this would be difficult to determine. Since the advertising and accounting departments have separate files, each with a different format, answering even such a straightforward question would probably require developing a new, special-purpose computer program. The time and cost required for developing such a specific program would most likely be prohibitive.

Underutilization of Data

Because of data dispersion and the difficulties it causes, an organization often cannot take full advantage of its own data resources. The frequent need for special new programs means that users have little freedom to access existing data in ways not supported by current application programs. They are left with the frustration of knowing that the answers they want are stored in the files but that getting to them is too difficult. Clearly, it is advantageous if all the relevant data stored by an organization can be accessed by anyone who needs it. Any company, for example, would probably operate more efficiently if department managers could access and make use of pertinent information that has already been collected by other departments. Since writing a specific new computer program costs too much for most situations in which accessing data is the goal, some other approach must be used.

Being unable to do all that can be done

THE DATA BASE PHILOSOPHY

In an attempt to address such problems, software developers in the late 1960s and early 1970s began to design various packages to accept, organize, store, and retrieve data flexibly, quickly, and efficiently. These programs used collections of information, or data bases, organized according to some logical structure. As we said in Chapter 9, a data base consists of one or more files, the basic building block of which is the record. And records are further subdivided into fields. Fields consist of characters, which are themselves comprised of the elementary units of the computer world, binary zeros and ones. For example, a company's data base might include one file containing information about employees and another file about customers. The employee file might consist of records that hold the name, address, starting date, title, and salary for each employee.

The **data base philosophy** proposes the use of a single data base for all related information. This data base is controlled by a single software package, rather than having scattered collections of computer files maintained by individual groups of users. The ideals of the data base philosophy state that each piece of information be entered and stored just once and that every authorized user have quick and easy access to any of the stored data. The data are entered, maintained, and accessed in ways that are not dependent on any particular application program.

Of course, any ideal is difficult to achieve, and external factors will affect how closely it may be approached. The data base philosophy isn't practical unless some means exists for quickly accessing a great deal of information. Until the late 1960s and early 1970s, most data-processing installations used magnetic tape for on-line secondary storage, occasionally supplementing it with expensive hard disk systems.

Consolidation of data

Data access times were generally too slow and storage capabilities too limited to allow the creation of truly useful data bases. The further refinement of hard disk systems that improved the speed and efficiency of access to secondary storage and the development of fast, inexpensive semiconductor RAM chips for primary memory made the implementation of practical data base packages feasible.

DATA BASE MANAGEMENT OBJECTIVES

What a good DBMS should do

The designers of data base management systems face a number of challenges. Their software must provide users with concrete and worthwhile benefits to justify the expense and effort associated with installing and learning it. Ideally, a data base management system should exhibit the following attributes:

- *Efficient use of resources.*   A data base management system should function efficiently given the current or projected computer resources of the installation. It should not require the user to add expensive new hardware or software to make it work, and it should not waste storage space or processing time in the performance of designated tasks.

- *Speed.*   A data base management system must run fast enough to provide replies to users' questions within an acceptable time frame. Most systems are now interactive (the user types in a query and expects an immediate response), so speed is a primary objective.

- *Compatibility.*   A data base management system must interface smoothly with existing hardware, software, and data. If an organization has to buy a lot of new computer equipment or new software or have all its data reentered, it has probably chosen the wrong data base management system. Although some conversion of data and software is often required, it should be kept at a minimum.

- *Updatability.*   A data base management system must allow for the quick and efficient addition and deletion of data records and categories. It must also be flexible enough to handle changes to or rearrangement of the data in its data base.

- *Accessibility.*   Data base management system users should find it easy to interrogate the data base. Many systems now have query languages (first described in Chapter 8) that allow users to ask a wide variety of questions about the data without having to prepare specially designed application programs. We'll say more about query languages later in this chapter.

- *Data integrity.*   Since a particular data base may be the only place where vital information is stored, a very important attribute of a data base management system is how well it safeguards data integrity. In case something goes wrong (a power failure, for example), the data base management system should have backup measures to ensure that valuable data remain intact. Furthermore, the system should prevent users from making potentially disastrous mistakes. For example, requiring users to reconfirm data deletions can help to avert accidental erasures.

- *Privacy and security.*   One of the major concerns about data bases (which will be addressed further in Chapter 17) is the privacy and security of the information they contain. Medical records, bank records, credit files, and military information are but a few examples of the types of sensitive or confidential material kept in data bases. A major objective of any data base management system should be to limit access to only authorized users. Features such as passwords and access codes are often used to restrict unauthorized individuals from changing or viewing data.

ADVANTAGES AND DISADVANTAGES OF DATA BASE SYSTEMS

As shown in Figure 12.1, a **data base system** is an integrated set of computer hardware, software, and human users, that is, a working combination of a data base, a data base management package, and the people who use the data base. Given this general view of the data base system, what can an organization expect from one? As usual, data base systems offer both advantages and disadvantages. Their advantages include the following.

The pros and cons

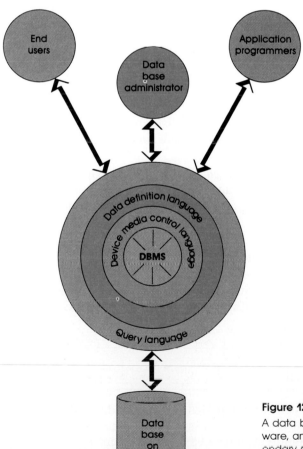

Figure 12.1 The Data Base System

A data base system is an integrated set of hardware, software, and human users. It consists of a data base in secondary storage, a data base management package, with all of its facilities, and the people who work with the data base, namely, end-users, application programmers, and data base administrators.

- *Reduction of data redundancy.*   Storing most data in one place means less duplication and less required space.

- *Enhancement of data integrity.*   Because data are centralized, fewer updating errors occur, and greater accuracy can be maintained.

- *Ensured data independence.*   Data are entered, stored, modified, and accessed by methods that are not affected by application programs. Also, changes made to data structures usually do not require changes in programs that access the data base.

- *Facilitation of data sharing and integration.*   Data base systems offer users the ability to combine or to cross-reference data in many different ways.

- *Improvement of access to data.*   Data base systems allow users to query the data base directly, without necessarily using an application program.

- *Centralization of security.*   It is easier to limit access to information if it is grouped together instead of being kept in several scattered files. Many data bases (see Chapter 17) must be protected and kept private.

- *Reduction of costs.*   Data entry, data storage, and the development of new application programs are all made more economical. By eliminating the duplication of data, many organizations can realize substantial savings.

Data base systems, however, also have certain disadvantages, such as:

- *Complexity.*   Data base systems include sophisticated software packages that may require special hardware. They are also difficult and time-consuming to develop.

- *Initial expense.*   Primarily because of their complexity and efficiency, data base systems can be expensive to set up.

- *Need for special training of users.*   The complexity and the many features offered mean that users must usually receive training before they can work with a data base.

- *Need for a substantial conversion effort.*   Changing from a traditional file-oriented system to a data base system can often involve large-scale reorganization of data and programs. This need can create user resistance, as we discussed in Chapter 11.

- *Vulnerability.*   Data in a data base may be more susceptible to sabotage, theft, or destruction. Although in one sense data bases are protected because of centralized security measures, in another sense they are vulnerable because all the eggs are in one basket. Unscrupulous users who gain access can wreak havoc, and hardware or software failures can possibly destroy vital data.

DATA MODELS

Approaches to data organization

A data base system can be designed in many different ways. Computer scientists have devoted whole careers to developing data base theories, and programmers have written hundreds of data base management packages. All data base systems are characterized by the way they structure, organize, and manipulate data items and by the relationships among the items. These design elements are reflected differently in the various **data models,** of which three are currently the most popular: the hierarchical model, the network model, and the relational model. Which of these three is the best is a fiercely debated issue. In fact, it depends on the situation, and, in practice, most systems combine features from each of the basic approaches.

The Hierarchical Model

Developed in the 1960s, the **hierarchical model** has been used primarily for large mainframe computer data base systems. It works best with data that fall naturally into some hierarchy; that is, groups of data items that can be arranged according to some ranking, similar to the organizational chart of a company. In a hierarchical data base system, such as the mainframe program Focus and its $1295 microcomputer offspring PC/Focus from Information Builders Corporation, information is expressed as a series of one-to-many relationships. Each item can have many subordinate items but at most only one item directly above it in the hierarchy. Graphically, the hierarchical model resembles a series of upside-down trees (see Figure 12.2). Subordinate items are often called *children*, superior items are called *parents*, and parents of parents are called *grandparents* or *ancestors*. In this model, a parent can have many children, but each child can have only one parent. For example, as shown in Figure 12.2, each part can have several suppliers, but each firm supplies only one part.

Ordering data by rank

The hierarchical model has the advantage of being relatively simple to implement, understand, and use, but it's not very flexible. Applications that aren't strictly hierarchical may be awkward to represent or may result in duplication of data. For instance, if a supplier is the source for more than one part, a SUPPLIER record will be required for each part finished. Furthermore, because of the strict hierarchical ordering of the data, certain types of queries aren't handled very efficiently. Since every record can only be accessed through its parent, such activities as finding out the total number of parts shipped by all suppliers, in this case, would require going through every record in the data base. To access each SHIPMENT record, the data base software would have to follow a path through all of its ancestors, which can be a rather time-consuming process. In addition, the user would have to be familiar with the hierarchical structure of data in the data base to even initiate the query.

The Network Model

The more general **network model** for data base systems consists of a set of records (also called *nodes*) and the links, or associations, between those records. It is most applicable if the records in a data base have *many-to-many relationships* (see Figure 12.3). The lines that represent links not only lead from parent to child, as they do in the hierarchical model, but also connect any two records in any direction. In other words, a given record may have any number of immediate superiors as well as any number of immediate subordinates. As you can see by the diagram in Figure 12.3, the records and their links form a *network*, or an interconnected system of nodes.

Interconnecting structure

Because a hierarchical data base can be seen as a restricted network with only single links between parents and children, the hierarchical model is often considered to be a special case of the network model. Although more complex than the hierarchical model, the network model has the advantage of also being more

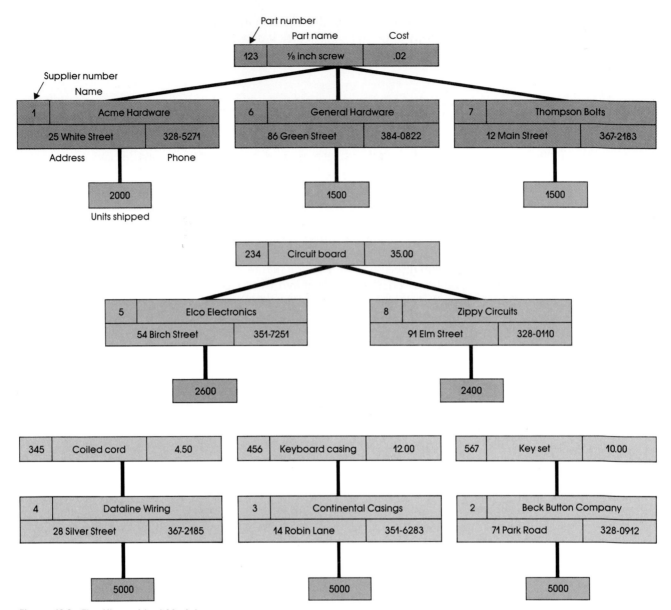

Figure 12.2 The Hierarchical Model
Here the structure of a simple hierarchical data base is illustrated by a parts data base for a fictional manufacturing company (of computer keyboards). Three types of records are used: (1) *PART records*, containing part number, part name, and cost; (2) *SUPPLIER records*, containing supplier number, name, address, and phone number; and (3) *SHIPMENT records*, containing how many units were shipped. The data are arranged in treelike structures in which PART records are the topmost items and SHIPMENT records the lowest.

general and is thus applicable to a wider range of situations. For instance, the network model works better for the manufacturing company's parts data base illustrated in Figures 12.2 and 12.3 since several suppliers do provide more than one part (many-to-many relationships). Furthermore, because sideways (horizontal) links are possible in a network data base, users aren't limited to accessing every record only through its ancestors, as is true with a hierarchical data base. Again, in

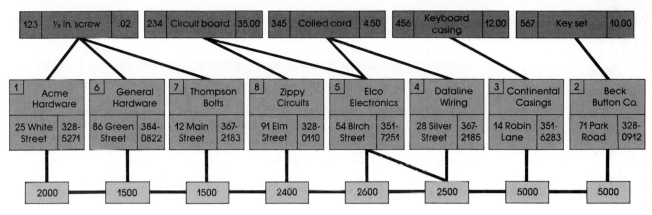

Figure 12.3 The Network Model

In this network model for a manufacturing company's parts data base, as in the hierarchical model, the data are represented by connected records. However, this model is more general because a given record may have any number of subordinates as well as any number of superiors. Thus, it allows for the fact that suppliers provide more than one part and for the horizontal linking of records of the same type. The basic record categories and contents are the same as those shown in Figure 12.2.

our example, since all of the SHIPMENT records are connected by sideways links, the data base management system can access them without having to go through all of the SUPPLIER and PART records. In many cases, records can be accessed quite efficiently with a network data base system.

Although the interconnecting links in a network data base allow quick and fairly flexible access to information, insertion and deletion of records are somewhat complicated by the fact that any new or broken links must be correctly updated. This means that network data base systems are most suitable when the relationships between records will remain relatively stable. For example, data bases for inventory and order entry are typically accessed in the same ways over a period of years. Because the data items and the relationships between them are well defined from the start, few occasions will arise when the network structure will need to be changed.

A common restricted form of the general network model, called the *CODASYL model*, is based on a set of standards established in 1971 by the Conference on Data System Languages (the model's name was taken from that of the conference), a group of computer industry and academic professionals that has been studying data base management systems since the late 1960s.

Network data base systems have been used extensively with mainframes and minicomputers but less frequently with microcomputers. A few microcomputer data base management packages, however, are based on the network model, such as the $3900 MDBS III from mdbs Inc.

The Relational Model

The **relational model** grew out of the work of Dr. Edgar F. Codd, a mathematician working as an IBM Fellow. First described in an internal IBM paper in August 1969, the relational model was slow to gain popularity. Only a few relational data base systems were implemented during the 1970s on mainframe computers. By the early 1980s, however, relational data base systems for microcomputers had flooded the market. Today, most microcomputer data base management systems are based, at least in part, on the relational model, and the model is also increasingly applied to systems for minicomputers and mainframes. R:base and dBASE III PLUS are examples of popular data base systems for microcomputers that are often described as relational.

Mathematically manipulated tables

Basically, the relational model allows concurrent access to multiple data files, as long as the data files are related through fields that they have in common. The relational model organizes all data into *flat* (or *two-way*) *tables*, each made up of rows and columns. The rows represent data records, and the columns represent fields within those records (see Figure 12.4). These tables (or *relations* in mathematical terms) are manipulated by the data base management system when storing and accessing information. The operations performed by true relational data base systems are all defined in strict mathematical terms, based on the theory proposed by Codd. In fact, using the term *relational* to describe most current microcomputer data base management packages is somewhat sloppy and misleading. Although these packages do allow access to multiple data files, Codd says that no currently available program fully meets all of his strict requirements of true relational data base

Figure 12.4 The Relational Model

By arranging records into tables, the relational data base provides a more flexible structure than do the other two data models. Without parents or children, relationships among records aren't predetermined by the data base structure. Here the manufacturing company's parts data base is structured as three tables: a PARTS table, a SUPPLIERS table, and a SHIPMENTS table.

PARTS TABLE

Number	Name	Cost
123	⅛ inch screw	.02
234	Circuit board	35.00
345	Coiled cord	4.50
456	Keyboard casing	12.00
567	Key set	10.00

SHIPMENTS TABLE

Supplier No.	Part No.	Quantity
1	123	2000
2	567	5000
3	456	5000
4	345	5000
5	234	2600
6	123	1500
7	123	1500
8	234	2400

SUPPLIERS TABLE

Supplier No.	Name	Address	Phone
1	Acme Hardware	25 White Street	328-5271
2	Beck Button Company	71 Park Road	328-0912
3	Continental Casings	14 Robin Lane	351-6283
4	Dataline Wiring	28 Silver Street	367-2185
5	Elco Electronics	54 Birch Street	351-7251
6	General Hardware	86 Green Street	384-0822
7	Thompson Bolts	12 Main Street	367-2183
8	Zippy Circuits	91 Elm Street	328-0110

management systems. In Figure 12.4, we've organized the data about parts, suppliers, and shipments into three tables according to the relational model. The significance of this model is not that data are arranged in tables, but that relationships between records are implied by the data values stored in common fields. For example, each part listed in the PARTS table is associated with its supplier in the SHIPMENTS table; the relationship between part and supplier is implied by the common field, Part Number. Part number 123 is also a field in a record in the SHIPMENTS table. Its supplier is number 1, and from the SUPPLIERS table we see that this number refers to Acme Hardware.

How does the user access a true relational data base? The software provides the user with a set of operations to manipulate data tables. Derived from mathematical set theory, these operations always result in a new data table being derived from one or more other tables. Here are the relational operations, briefly described in terms of rows, columns, and tables:

- *Selection.*   Gets a specified set of rows from a table.
- *Projection.*   Gets a specified set of columns from a table.
- *Product.*   Gets all possible combinations of one row from each of two tables.
- *Union.*   Gets all rows appearing in either or both of two tables.
- *Intersect.*   Gets only those rows that appear in both of two specified tables.
- *Difference.*   Gets all rows that appear in the first but not the second of two specified tables.
- *Join.*   Gets all possible pairs of rows, one from each of two specified tables, that both satisfy a particular condition.
- *Divide.*   Gets a set of rows built from two tables.

The relational model has some very appealing characteristics. It is conceptually quite simple; most people find it natural to organize and manipulate information in tables, since they are familiar with their use in everyday life. In a relational table, there are no parents or children; therefore, relationships among records in different tables aren't predetermined by the structure of the data base. Instead, they are specified by the user when data are retrieved. Consequently, relational data base systems provide a high degree of flexibility and data independence. Advance knowledge of what questions users might ask about information in the data base is unneccessary. Data files can be designed and set up and then perhaps used for purposes that hadn't been initially considered. Relational systems, in contrast to network and hierarchical systems, are therefore ideal for situations in which the types of user queries cannot be prespecified.

DATA DESCRIPTION

Every data base management system must provide procedures that allow users to describe information for the purposes of storage and display. Called **data description,** or **data definition,** this activity is often performed by specially trained *data base administrators* at large installations. Data description involves organizing how information will be stored in the data base to maintain accessibility, efficiency, and security. If you think of a data base as a filing cabinet, data description is like

Organizing the information

deciding how many folders are needed and what labels they should have, and then arranging the empty folders in the drawers.

In any case, data description requires some careful thought about the best ways to organize information for storage and retrieval. In general, storage in a data base is perceived as physical storage and as logical storage.

Physical Storage

Physical arrangement of data on the secondary storage device

One way to think about the arrangement of data in a data base is through the **physical** (or **external**) **storage,** which refers to how the data are actually placed on the secondary storage device (usually a magnetic disk). This physical arrangement is, for the most part, a concern of the designers, developers, and programmers of the data base management package. It is too low-level and too machine-oriented to interest the end-users and programmers who normally access the data base. Data base administrators, on the other hand, should have a basic understanding of how data are physically arranged in storage so that they can better comprehend how the system works and cope with problems that arise.

Logical Storage

Users' perception of data storage

Logical storage in a data base, in contrast to physical storage, is the end-users' view of how the data seem to be arranged. Logical storage is much more abstract and usually has nothing to do with how data are physically stored. For example, suppose you want to access a company's data base to extract the names and addresses of recent customers so that you can construct a mailing list for sending out advertisements. In this situation, it is more convenient for you to think of customer names and addresses as being stored together. Your *logical view* suggests that customer names and their full mailing addresses are stored in close proximity. In reality, the physical locations of these pieces of data may be anywhere on a magnetic disk, determined in some creative way so that the data base management system can handle updating, minimize storage space, and facilitate access. As long as the data base management software does its job in accessing the correct information, how or where the data are actually located in storage doesn't matter. The data base management system acts as an interface between the logical view the user employs and the true physical arrangement of the data in storage.

Many data base systems use different terms for the elements and concepts of logical storage, but a few common ones are worth noting here. A **data base record** (sometimes called a **segment**) is essentially the same as the traditional file record in that it consists of a collection of related fields. A **set** is a collection of records that have at least one attribute in common; in other words, they exhibit a *one-to-many relationship.* For example, for each customer record in a company's data base, there may exist a set containing one or more invoice records. These invoice records, each of which describes a purchasing transaction, are related by the fact that they all pertain to one customer.

At a more abstract level, the logical storage for a data base is often defined in terms of a **schema,** a global description of the conceptual organization of an entire data base. The organization of a specific portion of a data base is described by a **subschema.** Subschemas usually define cohesive subsets of the schema, such as all the data to be used by a specified group of programs or users. Subschemas are particularly useful for maintaining data base security and limiting access to authorized individuals. For example, in creating a customer mailing list, you would only need data from an accounts receivable subschema. You would have no business looking at, and would be denied access to, records concerning fellow employees' salaries (which would probably be in a personnel subschema).

Data Definition Language

In a standard high-level programming language, such as COBOL or Pascal, the declarations or descriptions of data items and the executable statements that actually process those data are all considered to be part of the same language. Most sophisticated data base management packages, however, separate the two functions of data description and data manipulation into two different languages. The primary reason for this difference is that in an ordinary program, data variables only exist while the program is running. A data base, on the other hand, is considered a more permanent data structure and so its definition may be declared once and for all.

A **data definition language (DDL)** is a notation for specifying the logical *Setting up the data base*
storage requirements of a data base. Data types, field widths, and field names, for example, are all declared with a data definition language. A data base management package may have its own unique DDL, or it may use one that has been standardized for use by other data base management packages. The DDL is only employed when the data base is initially designed or if its structure is subsequently modified.

Some mainframe computer data base management systems also include another type of data base language called a **device media control language (DMCL).** Unlike a DDL, however, a DMCL allows data base administrators to specify the physical storage requirements of a data base and thereby customize their data base systems to work more efficiently with the hardware at their particular installation.

DATA ENTRY AND UPDATING

Every data base management system obviously must include some means for entering *Inputting and modifying*
data, which can be accomplished in several different ways. The most common *data*
method is direct entry from a terminal or microcomputer keyboard. Data base management packages usually have built-in text editors to facilitate the data entry. Or, after the data descriptions are complete, the system might successively prompt users for each field of the input records (see Figure 12.5). Once all the fields have been filled with data, the entire record is usually displayed, giving the user a chance to correct any errors. When the user indicates that the record is correct and complete, it is entered into the data base, and the same prompts appear for typing in the next record.

Many data base systems allow users to design their own formats for data entry. Such systems have procedures that enable users to set up blank forms, which appear on the screen and are filled in with data. In Chapter 9, we saw that this feature is included in many data base management packages (see Figure 9.18 for an example of a data entry form). User-created forms can smooth the data entry process by customizing the way input information is typed in and displayed on the screen.

Figure 12.5 Prompting Data Entry
Some data base management packages prompt users
for data entry after the data descriptions are complete. In
this representation of a typical series of data entry
prompts, the information typed in by the user is highlighted in red.

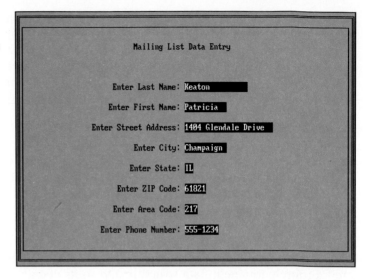

Every data base management system must also allow users to reaccess a previously entered record and to update any of its fields. In addition, some systems
provide a method for simultaneously changing a certain field of selected records in
the data base. With such a feature, for example, you could simultaneously decrease
the price of every item in an inventory data base by 10 percent for a storewide sale.

DATA MANIPULATION AND QUERYING

*Accessing data bases from
application programs*

Once information has been entered into a data base, there must be some means for
instructing the data base management system to rearrange, extract, or otherwise
manipulate data stored in the data files. A **data manipulation language (DML)**
is a specialized set of commands for rearranging or extracting data from data bases.
The same term also describes an interface between a standard high-level programming language (such as COBOL, Pascal, or C) and a data base management package. In either case, DMLs are employed to write programs that work with data base
management systems.

A *query language* (introduced in Chapter 8) is basically the same thing as a
DML, except that it is generally interactive. Any language that lets you directly
interrogate a data base management package about the contents of a data base can
be called a query language. Many different query languages have been used in
sophisticated data base management systems over the years. Today, the two major
rivals that have been somewhat standardized are SQL, or Structured Query Language, and QBE, or Query-by-Example. In addition, a considerable amount of
effort has been directed at using subsets of natural languages (such as ordinary
English) as relational data base query languages.

Structured Query Language

The work of Dr. Edgar F. Codd, who originally formulated the theory behind the
relational data base model in 1969, led to a great deal of research and experimentation. Some of this research concerned the development of query languages that

incorporated features of the relational model. One of these was SEQUEL (Structured English Query Language), defined in 1974 by D. D. Chamberlain and his colleagues at IBM's Research Laboratory in San Jose, California. Another version of SEQUEL created in 1976, dubbed SEQUEL/2, eventually became known as **Structured Query Language,** or simply **SQL.** In 1986, the American National Standards Institute (ANSI) accepted SQL as a standard query language for relational data base systems. Today, SQL is being adopted, or at least considered, by most major relational data base management package developers for use in their products.

SQL was developed to express in high-level form the operations on relational data bases (namely, selection, projection, product, union, intersect, difference, join, and divide). It is primarily used as an interactive language for extracting information from a data base. Although SQL does resemble general-purpose high-level programming languages in some ways, it has no built-in program control statements like IF-THEN-ELSE selections or WHILE loops. Consequently, SQL is sometimes combined with high-level programming languages such as COBOL or C when used to manipulate data bases in application packages. SQL does include its own DDL, its own DML, and facilities for controlling data base access privileges.

High-level data extraction

The SQL DDL is used to create and define data base tables. For example, the following DDL code would set up a data base table like the SUPPLIERS table shown in Figure 12.4:

```
(supplierno   CHAR(3)      NOT NULL,
 name         CHAR(20),
 address      CHAR(15),
 phone        CHAR(8),
 UNIQUE(supplierno))
```

The SQL DML's power comes from its ability to operate on entire sets of rows and not just on one row at a time. It includes statements for extracting and manipulating data stored in data base files. Suppose you had the tables shown in Figure 12.4 already defined in the SQL DDL, as we just did the SUPPLIERS table. Here are the SQL DML commands you would use to retrieve each supplier's name and the part they supply from the SUPPLIERS and SHIPMENTS tables:

```
SELECT    suppliers.name, shipments.part
FROM      suppliers, shipments
WHERE     suppliers.supplierno = shipments.supplierno
ORDER BY  suppliers.supplierno;
```

Several popular microcomputer data base management packages use SQL. The Extended Edition of IBM's OS/2 operating system includes an SQL-based data base management system, and the new dBASE IV from Ashton-Tate is also an SQL package.

Query-by-Example

Query-by-Example (QBE) is another one of IBM's data base contributions. This query "language" grew out of work done by M. M. Zloof at IBM's Research Laboratory in Yorktown Heights, New York, in 1977. QBE was designed from the start to be a highly interactive, easy way to extract information from a data base. The user seated at a terminal or a microcomputer runs a special screen editor to tell the system what to do. This screen editor displays a visual image of a single-row data base table, with one space for every field in the data base. The user simply moves

Asking questions with a screen editor

Figure 12.6   Query-by-Example

This screen illustrates the Query-by-Example (QBE) method of requesting information from a data base as it is used in the popular microcomputer package Paradox, from Ansa Software.

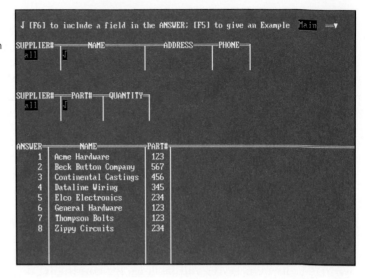

the cursor across the screen and leaves check marks in the fields where answers are desired. Figure 12.6, for example, shows a QBE query for the same list of suppliers' names and the parts they supply that we just did above in SQL. Paradox, from Ansa Software, is a popular data base management package for microcomputers that uses true QBE querying.

Natural Query Language

Software to interpret questions in normal English

Some query languages are designed to be as similar as possible to ordinary natural languages such as English. In reality, these so-called natural language interfaces generally have rather small vocabularies, and you may have to "teach" the system the English words that refer to your particular data base in order to subsequently query it in English. For example, Q&A from Symantec is a file manager that includes what it calls the Intelligent Assistant. The Intelligent Assistant comes with a

Figure 12.7   Natural Query Language

This screen is from Symantec's Q&A file manager package. It describes the natural query language used by this package to let you retrieve data from a file with ordinary English statements.

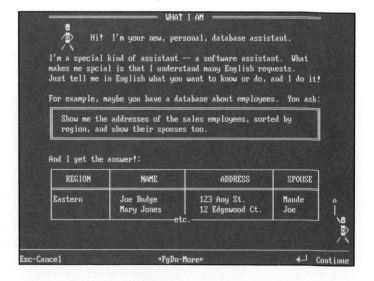

built-in vocabulary of 400 words and it automatically "knows" the words you use to name the fields in your file. You can personalize the Intelligent Assistant, but you have to give it certain lessons before you ask it any questions. During these lessons, you enter the words you want to use to refer to the different fields and data values in your file. Figure 12.7 shows a sample screen from Q&A that describes its natural query language. Although more sophisticated natural query languages are used in a few mainframe computer data base management systems, this type of query language does not approach the popularity of SQL and QBE.

REPORT GENERATION

Ultimately, all data base management systems must include certain features for outputting information. After selecting, sorting, combining, comparing, or otherwise manipulating items in a data base, a user frequently wants a printout of the results in an easy-to-understand format. Most data base systems provide a *report generator* that allows users to produce hard copy formatted according to their own design. Also, a report generator is often able to perform a few functions on its own, such as computing and printing out summary calculations.

Printing out the results

Sometimes included in a data base management package and sometimes sold separately, report generators vary greatly in their power and ease of use. A good report generator should be able to do the following:

- Print titles, headings, footers, and page numbers.
- Select, arrange, and rename fields for output.
- Set margins, page length, line spacing, and so on.
- Calculate and print counts, subtotals, averages, and grand totals.

DISTRIBUTED DATA BASES

Throughout this chapter, the data base has been discussed as if it were in one place on a single computer. However, just as computer systems can be arranged as local or wide area networks (see Chapter 6), data bases can also be distributed. In other words, a particular data base can be accessible to several computers concurrently. This may be accomplished by having the data base reside in a centralized host computer that is accessible to outlying computer sites. Another possible arrangement could have parts of the data base stored in different computers on a network, or a complete copy of the data base can exist at each remote location.

Accessibility to more than one computer

Distributed data bases offer the advantage of being available to more users; but, as a result of this increased accessibility, they must deal with *concurrent access*, which occurs when more than one user tries to access the same data at almost exactly the same time. Suppose, for example, that two travel agents are using a distributed data base to book flights for a commercial airline. If they both access the data base at nearly the same time and see that a particular seat is available, they may sell it to two different customers, which is certainly a problem. In addition, if one user is updating or deleting a record while another is trying to access it, entirely unpredictable results may occur. To deal with such situations, distributed data base systems usually have a feature that enables authorized users to "lock out" other users while certain operations are being performed.

Data base management packages basically let users create, add to, delete from, update, sort, rearrange, select from, print out, and otherwise manipulate data files. Since managing data is one of the most common tasks performed by computers, especially in businesses, data base management packages are an extremely important type of application software. To give you an idea what it's like to use this type of software, let's create a simple parts inventory data base for an imaginary small business with dBASE III PLUS, the most popular microcomputer data base management package. You'll recall that a *data base* is just an organized collection of one or more files of interrelated data, and a *file* is a mass of individual data items kept together in secondary storage, usually on a disk. Our simple example data base will consist of only one file. Once we set up this data base, we'll consider various ways of examining, querying, modifying, rearranging, and printing its contents.

First we must start up dBASE III PLUS. This is done by entering *dbase* into a computer that has the program installed on it. After an initial copyright message, dBASE III PLUS presents its Assistant menu system with the *Set Up* menu initially selected:

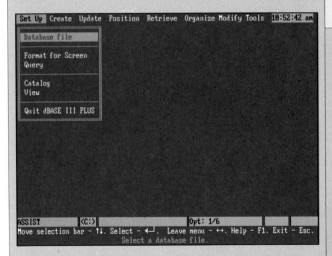

In dBASE III PLUS most simple functions can be executed by selecting options from the various menus of the Assistant. To select an option within a particular menu, you simply press the up or down arrow key to highlight that option and then press the Enter key. To display some other menu, you just press the left or right arrow key to highlight its title, which appears in the list of titles across the top of the screen. Another way to activate a different menu is to type the first letter of its title. For example, to go from the *Set Up* menu to the

A Closer Look

Using dBASE III PLUS

Create menu, you can either press the right arrow key once, or type *C*. The result is shown below.

Now we can begin to create our example parts inventory data base file. First, you highlight the *Database file* option (which should already be highlighted by default) and press the Enter key. Another little menu pops up showing a list of disk drive letters with your current

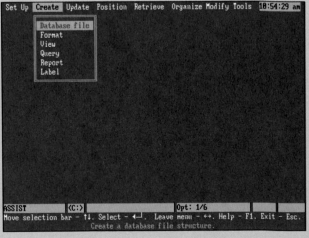

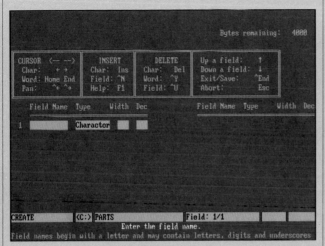

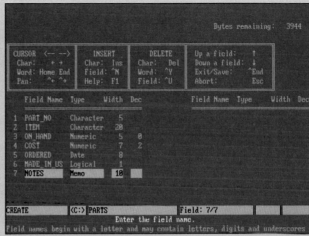

disk drive already highlighted. To choose your current disk drive, you press the Enter key. Because every file must have a name, you now need to name the data base. dBASE prompts you for a name, and you might enter one such as PARTS to identify the file's contents. After you enter an acceptable name, dBASE displays an empty data base file structure table on your screen as shown above.

Now you must tell dBASE how to structure the records of your data base. Recall that files are made up of *records*, each of which consists of a sequence of *fields*. Each field is simply a single data item such as a number, character, or group of related characters such as a word or phrase. In dBASE III PLUS, each field must have three attributes: a name, a type, and a width. The type of a field indicates what kind of data is to be stored within it. dBASE III PLUS has five types of data fields:

Character	up to 254 letters, digits, and symbols
Numeric	numbers used in calculations
Date	dates of the form mm/dd/yy (e.g., 01/01/89)
Logical	True or False, Yes or No
Memo	free-form text for notes

The width of a field is simply the maximum number of characters the field will take up. The maximum size of any single record in dBASE III PLUS is 4000 bytes. The message in the upper right corner of the screen tells you how many more bytes your record can hold. As you add fields to the record structure, the number in the upper right corner will decrease. In practice, most data base files use much fewer than 4000 bytes per record.

To define the structure of your data base file, you enter the name, data type, and width of each field in a record. First you must decide what fields to include in each record of your file; then for each field you have to enter its name, data type, and width in characters. If a field will contain a numeric value, you must also enter the number of digits that will appear to the right of the decimal point. This is put in the structure table under the column labeled *Dec*. The completed record structure table for our example PARTS data base file is shown above.

When you have finished defining the structure, dBASE asks you if you want to go ahead and immediately begin entering your records. In most cases, this is what you want to do. Now comes the most tedious part of creating a data base—entering the records. For huge data bases, this can involve a significant amount of time and effort. For our example PARTS data base, however, we will only enter a few records. At any rate, after telling dBASE you want to go ahead and enter your records, the program displays a blank data entry form on your screen, as shown on the following page.

This form represents a single record and displays a list of the names of the fields in that record. The reverse-video block to the right of each field name is where you enter the data for that field. The width of the block indicates the field width as you specified when you created the record structure. The cursor is initially placed at the first character of the first field in the first record. Since you can rearrange the file later, records can be entered in any order. You simply enter the data for each field in a record, resulting in the second screen on the following page.

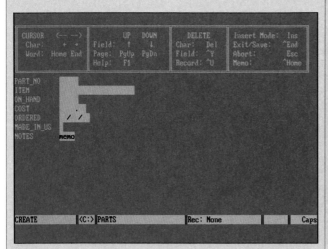

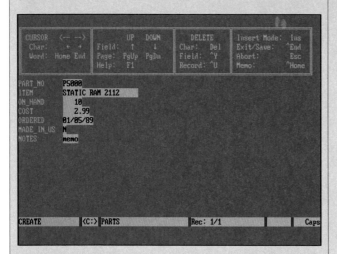

When you finish with one record, dBASE automatically advances to the next record, putting a new blank data entry form on your screen. When you are finished entering all the records in your file, you hold down the Control key and press the End key. The dBASE program saves your data base file on disk and returns to the *Create* menu.

One of the primary advantages of using a data base management package is the flexibility with which you can retrieve previously stored information. Most programs let you view records on the screen as well as produce formatted data base reports. You can examine several records presented in a table, or just look at one record at a time. In any case, you must first tell dBASE to retrieve the data base file you want to examine from the disk on which it is stored. This is accomplished by

selecting the *Database file* option from the *Set Up* menu. You can then select the disk drive and name of the data base file you want to retrieve.

If your data base is fairly small, or if you are not looking for a particular record, the easiest way to view the contents of a file is to *browse*. For example, you can select the *Browse* option from the *Update* menu. The result of executing a *Browse* command when our PARTS data base file has been retrieved from disk is shown in the next screen.

The first 11 records of the PARTS data base file are displayed on the screen in a table format. The very first record in the file is highlighted. You can see additional records by repeatedly pressing the down arrow key to move the highlight bar down. When you reach the bottom of the screen, the records scroll up, revealing the next record. Another way to see more records is to press the Page Down key, which reveals the next whole page of records. Similarly, you can use the up arrow key or the Page Up key to go back toward the beginning of the file. The *Browse* option of the *Update* menu can also be used to modify the contents of a data base file. The highlighted record can be changed by simply moving the cursor and inserting, overwriting, or deleting characters in any field. When you have finished using the *Browse* command, you press the Escape key, which returns you to the *Update* menu.

Browsing is fine for casually examining the contents of a small data base, but it isn't a very efficient method of locating one or more specific records in a large file. It is just too time consuming to scroll or page throughout a long file in search of a particular file. Besides, people cannot perform such tedious tasks very accurately. Fortunately, like all data base management packages, dBASE provides a better method of finding specific records.

A *query* is a request for information. A simple query would be asking to see the information on the part numbered P1234. A more complex query would be asking to see all parts that cost at least $1.00 and whose part numbers begin with "P1." As you can imagine, the greater the number of fields and records in a data base, the more complex your queries can be. Sophisticated data base management packages such as dBASE III PLUS provide many ways to search for records.

Let's pose a very simple query and find part P1234. Although this seems like a simple operation, to use the dBASE Assistant you must traverse several menus and a prompt to complete your task. Step-by-step, here is what you must do:

1. Activate the *Retrieve* menu by typing *R*.
2. Select the *Display* option by highlighting it and pressing Enter.
3. Select *Specify scope*.
4. Select *ALL*.
5. Select *Build a Search Condition*.
6. Select *PART_NO*.
7. Select *= Equal To*.
8. Enter the part number you want to find: *P1234*.
9. Select *No more conditions*.
10. Select *Execute the command*.

Here is the dBASE screen that results from these actions:

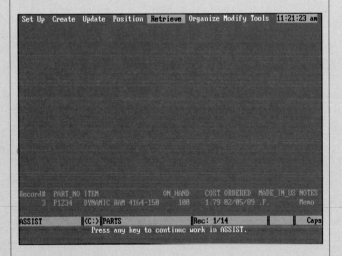

There is a quicker way to do this, but it requires using a powerful, but less user-friendly, feature of the dBASE program called the *dot-prompt*. This allows you to bypass the Assistant menus and enter commands directly to dBASE. These *dot-prompt commands* are essentially dBASE's own query language. For example, to perform the search for part P1234, you could also press the Escape key to switch to the dot-prompt and enter this command:

DISPLAY ALL FOR PART_NO = 'P1234'

This is equivalent to the 10 steps via the Assistant menu. When you are finished using the dot-prompt, you can reactivate the Assistant menu system by typing *ASSIST* and pressing the Enter key.

Besides querying, many other actions can be performed with a data base management package such as dBASE III PLUS. In addition to modifying existing records with the *Browse* command, you can update a data base by adding new records, deleting existing records, and changing the structure of records.

Perhaps the most common of these operations is adding new records. The process of adding a new record to an existing data base is practically identical to adding new records to a new file, as we've already done. All you have to do is execute the *Append* option from the *Update* menu, and a new blank data entry form appears on your screen. Any number of new records can then be added to the existing data base file.

Another common data base operation is to rearrange the contents of an existing data base. One way to do this is by *sorting*, which actually creates an alternate data base file with identical records listed in a different order. The records are arranged in this order on the basis of one or more *keys*. A key is simply a field that is used to order the records in a file. Let's say, for example, that the records of our PARTS data base were entered in random order. If we want our PARTS data base file to be sorted by part numbers, then the PART_NO field would be the primary key. To perform this action, you need to select the *Sort* option from the *Organize* menu. Then you can select the field you want to be the primary key and any other fields you want as secondary keys. Next you select the disk drive where you want to put the newly sorted file, and enter a new name for the newly sorted file, say SPARTS. dBASE performs the sort operation, informs you how many records were sorted, and tells you to press any key to return to the Assistant menu system. At this point there are two complete versions of the parts inventory data base file: PARTS and SPARTS. To see the new file you've created, you need to activate the *Set Up* menu, select the *Data-*

base file option, indicate the disk drive, and this time choose the SPARTS data base file. If you then select the *Browse* option from the *Update* menu, you'll see the screen at right.

Once you've created, updated, and sorted a data base file, you will likely want a printed listing of all or part of this file. Such listings, usually called *reports*, can be generated by dBASE according to instructions that you provide. The program gives you a great deal of flexibility in specifying report layouts. You can indicate the fields to include, the order in which they are to appear, where to put them on the page, what their headings should be, and whether to sum the contents of numeric fields. Once you set up a report layout, you can save it in a disk file and use it again later without having to respecify the format settings. We won't go through the details of specifying a dBASE report, but it is done via the *Report* option of the *Create* menu. Once you set up a report layout, you use the *Report* option from the *Retrieve* menu to actually send the formatted listing to your printer.

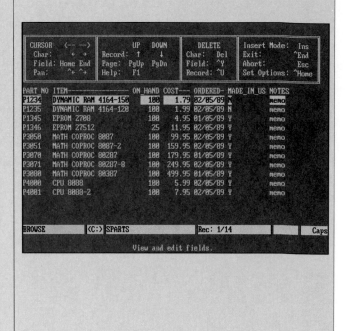

Summary

Before Data Management Packages

Traditionally, data files were custom-designed, created for specific software applications.

Data Redundancy Data are often repeated in more than one file.

Updating Difficulties Keeping all the files up to date can be problematic.

Data Dependence Programs may be dependent on the data formats and file organization methods used.

Data Dispersion Scattered data are difficult for programs to share.

Underutilization of Data Dispersed data cannot usually be used to full advantage.

The Data Base Philosophy

The data base philosophy is a view of data processing that proposes that a single data base be used for all related information.

Data Base Management Objectives

A DBMS should make efficient use of computer resources, be fast, interface smoothly with existing facilities, be updatable, provide easy access to authorized users, preserve data integrity, and ensure the privacy and security of data.

Advantages and Disadvantages of Data Base Systems

Data base systems reduce data redundancy, enhance data integrity, ensure data independence, facilitate the sharing and integrating of data, improve the access to data, centralize security for the data base, and reduce overall costs. However, they are complex and expensive to develop and set up, require special training of users and a substantial conversion effort, and are vulnerable to sabotage and intrusion (largely because of their centralized security).

Data Models

Data base systems are characterized by the way in which they structure, organize, and manipulate data items and by the relationships among these items.

The Hierarchical Model The hierarchical model arranges data according to some ranking, in a series of one-to-many relationships. Graphically, hierarchical data base systems resemble a series of upside-down trees. Data are divided into parents, children, and ancestors. Such systems are simple to implement, but somewhat inflexible.

The Network Model The network model is often used when the data exhibit many-to-many relationships. More flexible than the hierarchical model, the network model can be applied to a broader range of situations. But the large number of complex interconnections means that these systems do not allow for easy alteration of data.

The Relational Model The relational model organizes data into mathematically manipulated tables containing rows and columns. These systems are flexible and easy to use.

Data Description

Data must be defined in order to create, maintain, and update the DBMS. Data base administrators organize the data efficiently so that users can access the data easily.

Physical Storage Designers, developers, and programmers consider how the data are actually placed on the secondary storage device.

Logical Storage   Users may perceive related data as being stored near each other, although the actual location may be anywhere in secondary storage. Data base records and schemas logically define related data fields for the user.

Data Definition Language   Logical storage is defined using data definition languages. DDLs are used during the initial design and for modifications of a data base.

Data Entry and Updating

Data base systems may employ text editors, prompts, or user-defined forms for data entry.

Data Manipulation and Querying

Data manipulation languages allow programmers to access data bases from their application software.

Structured Query Language   Resembling a high-level language, SQL can extract a variety of information from the data base using predefined commands.

Query-by-Example   A screen editor gives the user a visual image of the data fields. The user chooses the fields from which answers are desired.

Natural Query Language   Companies have developed software that enables users to get information from the data base by asking questions in English.

Report Generation

Most data base systems provide a report generator that allows users to produce formatted hard copy.

Distributed Data Bases

Some data base systems are set up to be accessible to several computers concurrently.

Computer Concepts

As an extra review of the chapter, try defining the following terms. If you have trouble with any of them, refer to the page number listed.

Review Questions

1. What was the traditional approach to data storage before prewritten data base management packages were commonly used?
2. How is the duplication of files wasteful?
3. What is the data base philosophy?
4. What role did the refinement of hard disk systems play in the development of data base systems?
5. List the desirable attributes of a data base management system.
6. List some of the advantages and disadvantages of data base systems.
7. What characteristics are common to all data base systems?
8. What are an advantage and a disadvantage of a hierarchical model?
9. Of what does a network model for data based systems consist?
10. What are the general characteristics of the relational model?
11. What does the process of data description involve?
12. Contrast the physical storage of data in a data base with the logical storage.
13. What is a data base record? A set?
14. What expression is used to describe the conceptual organization of an entire data base? Of a specific portion of a data base?
15. Describe DDL and DMCL.
16. Describe several ways in which data entry into a DBMS can be accomplished.
17. What are the two major query languages used at the present time?
18. What kinds of things should a DBMS report generator be able to do?
19. In what ways can a particular data base be made accessible to several computers concurrently?
20. With what problem must distributed data bases deal? When does this occur?

True or False

1. Before data base management systems, an organization was likely to accumulate several files holding the same data.
2. Data dependence decreases the cost of software dependence.
3. One important attribute of an ideal data base sytem is quick and easy access to data.
4. A data base system is an integrated system of hardware, software, and users.
5. The most popular type of data model for microcomputers is the network model.
6. The end-users' view of how data are arranged in a data base is physical storage.
7. The global description of the conceptual organization of an entire data base is called a set.
8. A DML is a specialized set of commands for rearranging or extracting data from data bases.
9. Query languages are not interactive.
10. SQL is used primarily as an interactive language for extracting information from a data base

Multiple Choice

1. One of the ideal objectives of a data base management system is:
   (a) data dispersion
   (b) conservation of storage space
   (c) redundancy

2. The data model developed in the 1960s for large mainframe computer systems is:
   (a) the relational model
   (b) the network model
   (c) the hierarchical model

3. Today most microcomputer data base management systems are based, at least in part, on:
   (a) a network model
   (b) a relational model
   (c) a hierarchical model

4. When user queries cannot be prespecified, the best suited data base management system is:
   (a) relational
   (b) network
   (c) hierarchical

5. Most sophisticated data base management packages separate data description and data manipulation into two:
   (a) schemas
   (b) sets
   (c) languages

6. To facilitate data entry, data base management packages usually have built-in:
   (a) text editors
   (b) data manipulation languages
   (c) SQLs

7. SQL is being adopted or considered by most major developers of:
   (a) relational systems
   (b) network systems
   (c) hierarchical systems

8. The least popular of query languages is:
   (a) QBE
   (b) SQL
   (c) natural query language

9. A software package which permits the output of hard copy is:
   (a) DML
   (b) a report generator
   (c) DMCL

10. If a data base is accessible to several computers concurrently it is said to be:
    (a) dispersed
    (b) distributed
    (c) locked out

A Sharper Focus

1. Imagine that you are the data base administrator for your school's or company's mainframe computer system. How would you set up the data description for the data base? What security and privacy policies would you enact?

2. Consider the data base supporting a typical motel reservation system. Assume that the motel is a chain, with facilities in a number of cities. Do you think a hierarchical, network or relational data base structure would be best for this application? Why?

1. Prepare a list of ways in which you or your friends have been "victimized" by computer errors. Try to determine what role the data base management systems of the guilty computers may have played. What improvements could you suggest?

2. Investigate a situation in which improvements or changes have been made in a data base management system. Prepare a report on why the improvements or changes were needed.

3. It is often difficult to put a specific price tag on many of the benefits of a data base system (such as improved customer or student service). Prepare a plan on how you go about "selling" that data base concept to your school's administrators or your company's executives.

4. Your bank has "Kwik-Kash" automatic teller machines all over town which are operated by a data base system. One day, you stop at one and insert your card, intending to withdraw $100. What you don't know is that your spouse is doing the same thing, at the same time, at a mall on the other side of town. You both hit the ENTER button at the same time, both trying to withdraw $100 from an account containing only $125. Prepare a brief report on what happens. What can the bank do to prevent this sort of problem?

13

Management Information and Decision Support Systems

In This Chapter

Teaching Managers to Use an MIS

The head of a Fortune 500 company often spends 10 to 12 hours a day at his job and lugs home a briefcase full of work at night. Finding spare time to teach himself a new technology is almost impossible. So, most chief executives who use a personal computer began the learning process by attending an intensive hands-on class or by having a tutor available. . . .

Larry Burden, now the corporate vice-president of management information services at Firestone, has helped two CEOs [chief executive officers] through the initial stages. His first experience was with Ben Heineman, head of Northwest Industries. "Late in 1976, Heineman's assistant approached me with the idea of getting his boss and other lay executives at Northwest the ability to do financial analyses directly at a computer CRT," recalls Burden, then with Northwest. "I put together a prototype DSS (decision support system) for Heineman and three other senior executives. . . ."

With the system in place, Burden and other members of his management information staff acted as tutors on call. The prototype later became a formal system and many other executives at Northwest were trained. In the process Burden developed a programmed approach to teaching. "We hired people right out of MBA programs who understood financial analysis and showed a propensity for coaching," he explains. "We taught them to use the DSS system and made them available all day long to the CEO and other top executives." Heineman's usage flourished in the coaching environment and today he is an avid user of personal computers. . . .

His approach worked so well at Northwest that Burden used it again at Firestone. The only real differences were a full-day course he ran the executives through after an initial period of coaching, and the use of IBM Personal Computers from the beginning.

The first door Burden had to walk Firestone's CEO through was one labeled "Fear," he says. "Like most first-time users, John Nevin was afraid he was going to break the machine or destroy a file. The coaching helped him get past this computer mystique."

Fear of the machine is also the biggest problem Jim Alfaro faces in teaching CEOs. . . .

To break down the initial apprehensions, Alfaro starts his four- to eight-hour seminar with some simple financial routines that give the executives immediate screen successes. Each executive works at his own personal computer. "It's like teaching someone how to drive a car," he says. "You'd better start in a parking lot where the students won't get in an accident and they can forget about their fears by getting involved in something they can relate to." . . .

In the final analysis, teaching the CEO to compute is very much like teaching any other high-level executive, except his time is even more limited and his ego has to be treated a little more gingerly. Having someone on call for him who understands his very special needs and can still entice him forward is probably the single most important ingredient in a successful teaching program.

Throughout this part of this book, we have been examining computer-based systems. In this chapter, we look at business systems used to help management by providing information for decision making. Computers have, of course, been used in business since the 1950s. At that time, the prevailing buzzword was *electronic data processing (EDP)*. The primary purpose of early EDP systems was to reduce the costs of performing daily office work by computerizing many common business transactions. Each department of a company usually had its own set of software and data files which it maintained and operated independently of the other departments. As was the case with file processing before the development of data base systems, this arrangement resulted in significant duplication of efforts.

By the mid-1960s, many managers were convinced that these separate software systems could be tied together into a single integrated information system that would serve a whole organization. Ideally, such a system would provide managers with complete control of their businesses and considerable support for their decisions. Unfortunately, the computer hardware and software of the 1960s were not advanced enough to make such systems practical. Most data were kept in sequential files on magnetic tape; many were off-line and required minutes or even hours to locate, mount, and load into primary memory. In addition, data communications were rather slow, and data bases were quite expensive to implement. It wasn't feasible to set up on-line information systems to serve all parts of a geographically dispersed organization.

The 1970s and 1980s, however, brought dramatic advances in direct-access disk storage, data base systems, and data communications. These improvements made possible the development of the management information systems and decision support systems that we'll consider in this chapter.

WHAT IS AN MIS?

Management information system is one of those computer-industry labels that is widely used without having a universally accepted definition. In general, a **management information system (MIS)** is an organized means of providing managers with the information they need to do their jobs effectively. This includes internal and external information relating to an organization's past and present, as well as projections of what is likely to happen in the future. The purpose of an MIS is to furnish information within a workable time frame so that managers can make the best decisions concerning the planning, control, and operation of their organization's activities. Let's examine the important parts of this definition separately:

Defining the MIS concept

- *Organized means.* The parts of an MIS work together in well-coordinated fashion so that the system efficiently provides needed information.

- *Internal and external information.* An MIS must provide information about what's happening both inside and outside the organization (we'll have more to say about this later).

- *Past, present, and future.* The MIS must provide information that reveals where the firm has been, where it is now, and where it's likely to be in the future.

- *Workable time frame.* An MIS must be responsive, that is, provide its information quickly. A slow response can mean a missed opportunity.

- *Decision making.*   By providing needed information, the MIS helps managers make the decisions for which they are responsible.

- *Planning, control, and operation.*   An MIS helps managers manage. A manager's basic functions can be summarized as planning, control, and operation. Therefore, the MIS is an aid in planning what to do, executing plans, and controlling activities to ensure that plans are carried out.

WHAT IS MANAGEMENT?

Those who convert resources into results

To understand the importance of management information and decision support systems, we must start with a clear picture of what management is. In general, the job of management is to transform resources (such as money, property, labor, and information) in order to accomplish some desired results (such as producing a product or providing a service) and to do so profitably. This, of course, implies that managers must use available resources effectively if they are to fulfill their objectives. Since the resource we're primarily interested in here is information, our emphasis will be on what decisions managers must make and what kinds of information they need to make them.

What Managers Do

The five functions of management

One of the founders of the classic school of management theory, French theorist Henri Fayol, concisely described the functions of management, or the basic tasks that managers perform. According to Fayol, the following five functions are common to managers. Although not all managers perform all functions and although the functions aren't necessarily performed in this order, they are roughly chronological and representative (see Figure 13.1).

1. *Planning.*   Managers plan the activities of their organizations by establishing goals and developing policies, procedures, and programs to achieve them. To plan, they must forecast future conditions, set objectives, develop strategies, establish priorities, construct budgets, set procedures, and define policies.

2. *Organizing.*   Managers establish the organizational structures for utilizing resources to implement their plans. They must first identify and try to locate all of the resources needed to carry out their plans. Organizing can include, for example, setting up new departments, determining the chain of command, assigning responsibilities, and specifying division of labor.

3. *Staffing.*   Managers acquire the necessary resources to achieve their goals and objectives. Although staffing usually refers to the selection, orientation, and training of personnel, it is also used in a less limited sense to mean the acquisition of all required resources. Thus, staffing can include recruiting personnel, purchasing materials, raising capital, and procuring other necessary goods and services.

4. *Directing.*   Managers coordinate the actual execution of planned activities. As leaders, managers must ensure that resources are utilized in an efficient and cooperative manner. Directing includes delegating responsibility, as well as communicating with and motivating subordinates. Because of this, directing is sometimes described as getting things done by other people.

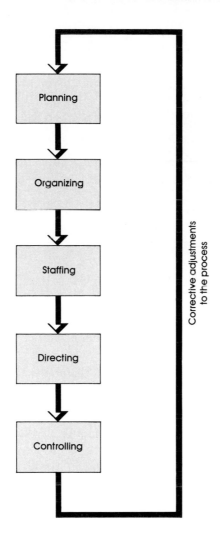

5. *Controlling.* Managers compare actual performance with planned performance and initiate actions to correct any shortcomings. Thus, controlling includes establishing a reporting system to monitor activities, developing performance standards, measuring results, rewarding good performance, and making corrective adjustments, which may mean starting a project over again from the planning stage.

Levels of Management

The five management functions just discussed are rather general because they are intended to apply to managers of all kinds. But just what kinds of managers are there? One approach views the composition of management as a hierarchy, which is traditionally organized into three levels: top, middle, and first-line. Of course, the actual number of managers in an organization depends on its size and complexity. A very small firm, such as a gas station, may have only a single manager (the sole proprietor). On the other hand, the largest corporations, such as General Motors, have thousands of managers. Regardless of the number of managers present in an

Three levels with distinct areas of responsibility

Figure 13.2 Management Levels

Management is usually organized into three hierarchical levels, reflecting different responsibilities, concerns, and needs for information.

Involved with

| Top management |
| Long-range strategic planning
The organization's future
Overall coordination
Community and business relations |

| Middle management |
| Short-range tactical planning
Performance management
Control activities
Personnel and training |

| First-line management |
| Daily operational planning
Work and employee supervision
Meeting schedules and deadlines
Cost and quality control |

organization, the three levels of management still apply. In a gas station, all three are embodied in the single owner; in General Motors, there are many managers at each level. The distinctions among the three levels can be explained in terms of their characteristic concerns and duties (see Figure 13.2).

Top management is concerned with long-range, strategic plans. This level of management is oriented toward the future of the organization and oversees the performance of the key personnel (middle management) who will carry out the plans. The duties of top management primarily involve planning the firm's activities for five or more years into the future, coordinating the overall efforts of the firm, establishing major policies, and dealing with external organizations and events. Examples of managers at this level are the chief executive officer, the president, the vice presidents, and the heads of major divisions.

Middle management is concerned with short-term, tactical plans—what the organization will be doing from one to five years into the future. Middle management's role is characterized by a fairly equal mix of planning and controlling. Managers at this level oversee the performance of first-line management and control the activities that move the organization toward the goals established by top management. Middle management typically takes responsiblity for such matters as plant layout, employee training and other personnel considerations, equipment and material acquisition, product improvement, and research and development. Examples of middle managers include plant managers, regional managers, directors of research laboratories, and retail managers.

First-line management is concerned with day-to-day, operational plans. The largest group of managers in a firm, first-line managers perform essentially supervisory functions and are more familiar with the technical skills of employees than either top or middle management. A first-line manager must ensure that employees follow established procedures in their work activities, that schedules are kept, and that deadlines and quality and cost control standards are met. Since first-line managers are closest to the workers and to the daily activities of the business, they also have the important task of providing feedback to the higher levels about how things are going "in the trenches." First-line management's main concern is with control; planning is performed on a very limited scale. Examples of first-line managers include department heads and plant supervisors.

INFORMATION NEEDS OF MANAGERS

Information—the output of an MIS—is vitally important to an organization's manager: it is essential for the achievement of short-term, intermediate, and long-range goals. Given adequate information, management can rely on deductive and analytical methods rather than on guesses and intuition, which are all that's possible if relevant facts are missing. Even though intuition based on experience can certainly be of value, many disastrous decisions have been based on insufficient or inaccurate information. As we have already noted, information forms one of the key resources of any organization. Many proficient managers believe that sound information is a major source of competitive power. It allows them to outmaneuver their rivals at critical times, such as when introducing new products or services. If managers don't have the information they need, they cannot effectively perform any of their functions. The result might well be an "out of control" firm that can neither gain the lead nor recover from setbacks.

A key resource

Given the importance of information to management, just what kinds do the different levels need? Figure 13.3 shows the general needs of the three management levels.

Strategic Information for Top Management

Just as managers at different levels have different concerns, they also have different information needs. **Strategic information** is used by top management in its long-range planning and for analysis of organizational problem areas. It usually consists in large part of material derived from or relating to areas of knowledge outside the organization. Sources of such *external information* can include governmental legislation, customer feedback, supplier reports, competitor announcements, labor union statements, and economic trends, forecasts, and indicators. Some strategic information is also derived from inside the organization. Such *internal information* typically includes forecasts and projections from various departments. Furthermore, it must be summarized—top management can't be concerned with every detail of the organization's operations.

Help in making long-range plans

Figure 13.3 Information Needs of Managers

Managers at different levels have information needs defined by their characteristic activities. This diagram shows the general types of information needed and used by managers at the three levels. For example, top management needs a higher percentage of external information than does middle or first-line management.

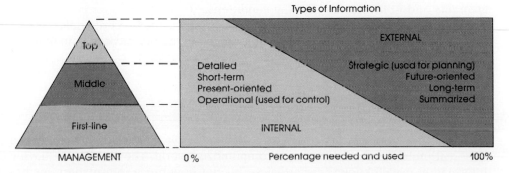

In most cases, strategic information is used to determine *why* rather than what, how, or where; it forms the basis of an organization's objectives, priorities, strategies, and policies. Examples of strategic information might be projected financial statements for the next five years, estimates of long-term capital need, present and projected personnel requirements, suggestions of potential new product lines and markets, long-range evaluations of research and development efforts, and investigations of alternative supply sources.

Tactical Information for Middle Management

Help in making short-term plans

Tactical information is used by middle management for relatively short-term planning (up to about a year in the future). This type of information is needed by middle management to implement the strategic plans made by top management and to allocate resources properly to attain organizational objectives. Unlike strategic information, tactical information is typically used by a large number of people in an organization. Also, tactical information is a fairly equal mix of summarized information for planning and detailed information for control; in contrast to strategic information, which is mainly directed toward planning activities. Thus, tactical information consists of roughly equal amounts of external and internal information.

As we mentioned earlier, the types of decisions made by middle management are likely to concern such areas as plant layout, personnel problems, product improvement, and research and development. Examples of tactical information include budget reports, shipping schedules, evaluations of sales department performance, periodic inventory summaries, engineering progress reports, research and development progress reports, and short-term market forecasts.

Operational Information for First-Line Management

Help in controlling routine activities

Operational information is used by first-line management to control the structured, repetitive, day-to-day activities of the organization and to ensure that specific tasks are implemented effectively. Since it is mostly concerned with control, it consists predominantly of detailed internal information. Operational information is used by the greatest number of people in a company, that is, by first-line managers and many nonmanagerial employees. Operational information makes it possible to measure actual performance against predetermined objectives and enables first-line managers to see whether operating standards and policies need improvement. This feedback from the workplace keeps higher levels of management aware of both favorable and unfavorable operating conditions.

Examples of operational information include personnel records, sales orders, engineering specifications, manufacturing orders, inventory records, purchase orders, shipping routes, and payroll and cash flow records.

Characteristics of Useful Information

Evaluating the quality of information: how true, up-to-date, pertinent, comprehensive, and succinct it is

As any student, businessperson, or professional knows, information overload is a very real problem in our fast-paced, computerized world. The necessity of having information is well known; nevertheless, it's not how much information one has that's important, it's how good that information is. Managers can easily be swamped by the deluge of information at their disposal. To be a real asset, an MIS must provide quality information. Generally, information that exhibits accuracy, timeliness, relevance, completeness, and conciseness is the most valuable.

Accuracy

Accuracy refers to how correct, true, or precise the information is, that is, whether the information represents the situation or event as it really is. Sometimes accuracy is expressed as a ratio (or a percentage) of correct information to total information during some period of time. For example, if 1000 payroll checks are produced each month and 980 of them are correct, the accuracy of the monthly payroll production is 0.98 (or 98%). The accuracy level that is acceptable depends on the activity and on an organization's standards. Issuing inaccurate checks to 20 employees each month is probably not acceptable; but if an inventory of inexpensive parts is 98 percent accurate, that might be good enough. As you can imagine, the accuracy of information is of paramount importance.

Timeliness

Timeliness refers to how current the information is. The most accurate information has little value if it is obtained too late to influence important decisions. The faster managers can receive the information they need, the better will be their ability to help their firms compete in the marketplace. Minimum acceptable response times from management information systems will vary, however, with the kind of information being provided. Some requests must be answered immediately, such as those for stock market figures, which can change hourly. On the other hand, some information, such as employee payroll reports, is only needed at certain regular intervals. Another important factor affecting response time is that computer resources that can produce immediate information generally cost more. Therefore, response times must be balanced against costs to ensure that information is obtained in time but not at excessive expense.

Relevance

Relevance refers to how applicable the information is to a given decision-making or problem-solving situation. An MIS cannot simply dump everything it has in a manager's lap—that leads back to the problem of information overload. The information that is provided should directly and conclusively pertain to the specific, well-defined issue. For example, if a manager is trying to determine whether to hire more people in the near future, he or she has no need to see every employee's personnel record. The relevant information in this case would be summary reports of present and projected personnel requirements.

Completeness

Completeness refers to whether the information tells all that is currently known about the subject at hand. Although managers can't afford to wade through reams of irrelevant material, they should have enough pertinent information to make informed decisions. If, after reading a report, a manager has a number of unanswered questions, the report is incomplete. For example, a research and development report that outlines current areas of investigation without summarizing the progress made so far is incomplete. Even though it is often impossible to achieve total completeness, information should be as complete as possible.

Conciseness

Conciseness refers to how compact the information is. As we have said, information should be relevant and complete, but it is also desirable that it be expressed as succinctly as possible. Extraneous and misleading details should be omitted. If a report that could take up five pages can be condensed to one or two pages, the shorter form is preferable. In many cases, graphs and charts present information more concisely and dramatically. This is one reason why computer-generated presentation graphics are so popular in the business community.

Output of Information

How an MIS presents information: printed summaries and fast answers

By now, you should have a fairly good idea of what makes information useful to management. But we must still discuss *how* information is presented to management by an MIS. The output of an MIS generally takes the form of reports or responses to inquiries.

Reports

Reports are the primary means by which an MIS presents information. They are usually classified according to how often they are output, how detailed they are, or the purpose for which they are used. In general, reports are produced more or less in batches. They fall into five general categories:

1. *Periodic reports.* Also called *scheduled reports,* these are produced at regular intervals (daily, weekly, monthly, etc.) and show routine information in detailed or summarized form. Examples include sales reports, financial statements, inventory records, and payroll reports.

2. *Demand reports.* Sometimes called *unscheduled reports,* these are produced only when called for (or on demand). Demand reports satisfy known, but not regularly recurring, information needs. They aren't prepared unless a manager makes a specific request. For example, a demand report listing employees' job skills might be requested by the personnel director when a vacancy must be filled.

3. *Exception reports.* These reports are automatically generated by an MIS when certain exceptional situations occur that require managerial attention. Exception reports are usually triggered by unsatisfactory or unusual conditions, for example, if actual costs are significantly greater than budgeted costs, or if production falls below levels that have been predetermined to be acceptable.

4. *Special reports.* Prepared to satisfy unanticipated informational needs, special reports are requested as a result of some significant but totally unforeseen turn of events. For example, the discovery of a hazardous substance in a manufacturing process might prompt managers to request a special report listing absenteeism and medical claims by personnel who have been exposed to the substance. Special reports differ from exception reports in that the exception reports are generated automatically by the MIS.

5. *Predictive reports.* These reports are prepared using techniques of statistical analysis, simulation, or modeling. Predictive reports attempt to forecast future trends. Examples are projections of personnel requirements, estimates of long-term capital needs, and projected financial statements.

Responses to Inquiries

As an alternative to reports, usually an MIS also allows users to submit direct requests for information, or *inquiries.* MIS inquiries enable managers to request information directly in an interactive fashion. Since, as we'll discuss later in this chapter, a data base system is an essential component of any MIS, addressing questions directly to an MIS is very similar to querying a data base.

Inquiries are answered in a matter of seconds or minutes, in contrast to the longer time periods usually associated with report generation. Even if a quick response isn't critical, inquiries are attractive because they allow greater freedom of expression on the part of the MIS user. Because inquiries are usually formulated in nonprocedural query languages (which we discussed in Chapters 8 and 12), little or no training is generally needed before managers are able to submit requests for information. Inquiry submission allows managers to experiment with different ideas, to follow up interesting answers with additional questions, and to utilize more fully their human capabilities of creativity, organization, analysis, and synthesis.

In contrast to reports, which often take up voluminous amounts of paper, inquiry responses are frequently limited to a size that will comfortably fit on a computer display screen. Inquiries tend to consist of quickly formulated questions that can be answered by a few lines or a page or two of displayed text. Sometimes responses include charts and graphs if the MIS software and hardware have graphics capabilities. If an inquiry requires a very long or overly specialized response (calling for hard-copy graphs, multiple copies, or wide-paper formats), then a special report would probably have been more appropriate.

Inquiry responses are used primarily to support planning and organizing, although their flexibility makes them applicable to most management functions. They are not generally relied on to support the directing and controlling of activities because those functions are already well serviced by report generation. Even though managers' use of inquiries is increasing dramatically, it is virtually certain that inquiry responses will never completely replace reports.

The ability to pose follow-up questions interactively is especially beneficial in the planning function. Planning is the least structured of all management functions, which means that managers are rarely able to anticipate completely all of the information that will be required to develop a plan. As plans begin to take shape, additional information needs often arise. A manager's planning abilities could be seriously impaired if information were available only in report form, or if applicable information were not considered simply because it would take too long to obtain.

In organizing, managers typically review many past and present situations in search of activities similar to those planned for the future. Inquiries can greatly aid this process by directing the MIS to search large volumes of data and select those elements that meet certain criteria. For example, a manager at an automobile plant who is organizing the production of a new model can ask the MIS to locate and present all previous cases of, say, front-wheel disc-brake assembly operations. This type of focused data gathering is extremely difficult and time-consuming to do manually, but is quite easy to do via inquiries to an MIS.

COMPONENTS OF AN MIS

It's rather difficult to describe management information systems in clear and unambiguous terms. Systems vary from one organization to another, reflecting different purposes, characteristics, information needs, and resources. You wouldn't expect the MIS of a large bank, for example, to be exactly like that of a major military installation. Also, management information systems are difficult to characterize because they are largely conceptual rather than physical. The information flows, functional relationships, and managerial decision-making processes central to such systems are less tangible than their computer hardware counterparts.

What an MIS is made of

An MIS can't be reduced to a collection of connected computer hardware or an application package. You can't go to your friendly neighborhood computer store and buy one. Unlike a data base management system, an MIS is not a discrete set of specially designed programs that are documented and packaged as a unit. Instead, an MIS consists of both computerized and noncomputerized parts, both hardware and software. The hardware can be almost any combination of those elements already covered in Part 2 of this book: a computer plus input, storage, output, and communications devices. Consequently, we will say almost nothing about the hardware components of management information systems. We will concentrate on the data management and functional subsystems that make up the typical MIS (see Figure 13.4).

To illustrate these subsystems, we've constructed a six-part case study about the MIS used at Keyboard Koncepts, a fictional firm that manufactures microcomputer and computer terminal keyboards. As you read about each subsystem, the corresponding part of the case study should give substance to the discussion. Although both the company and the MIS are fabricated, the example reflects what might be found in a typical manufacturing firm.

The Data Management Subsystem

The purpose of an MIS is to provide quality information to all three levels of management. Because this information is usually derived from massive quantities of stored data, the maintenance and use of data bases are central to all the activities of

TECHNOLOGY CLOSEUP

An MIS for Keyboard Koncepts

Keyboard Koncepts manufactures various models of electronic keyboards for both microcomputers and computer terminals. It has no retail outlets but sells its products to computer manufacturers using a network of sales personnel. The company owns three warehouses (in New York, Chicago, and Los Angeles) and one factory (in Chicago), where all the keyboards are produced. Keyboard Koncepts also has a central computing facility at its corporate headquarters (also in Chicago), which is used by the factory, warehouses, and sales personnel.

In many ways, Keyboard Koncepts is a typical manufacturing company. It advertises, solicits, receives, and fills orders, maintains warehouse inventories, manufactures its products to meet demand, carries out research and development, bills its customers, collects payments, and pays its employees, its suppliers, and its taxes. All these activities are documented in the detailed records maintained by the centralized computer system. Vice presidents in charge of marketing, finance, and manufacturing (production), along with their subordinate managers, must be able to access these records to run the company effectively. The MIS helps them do this.

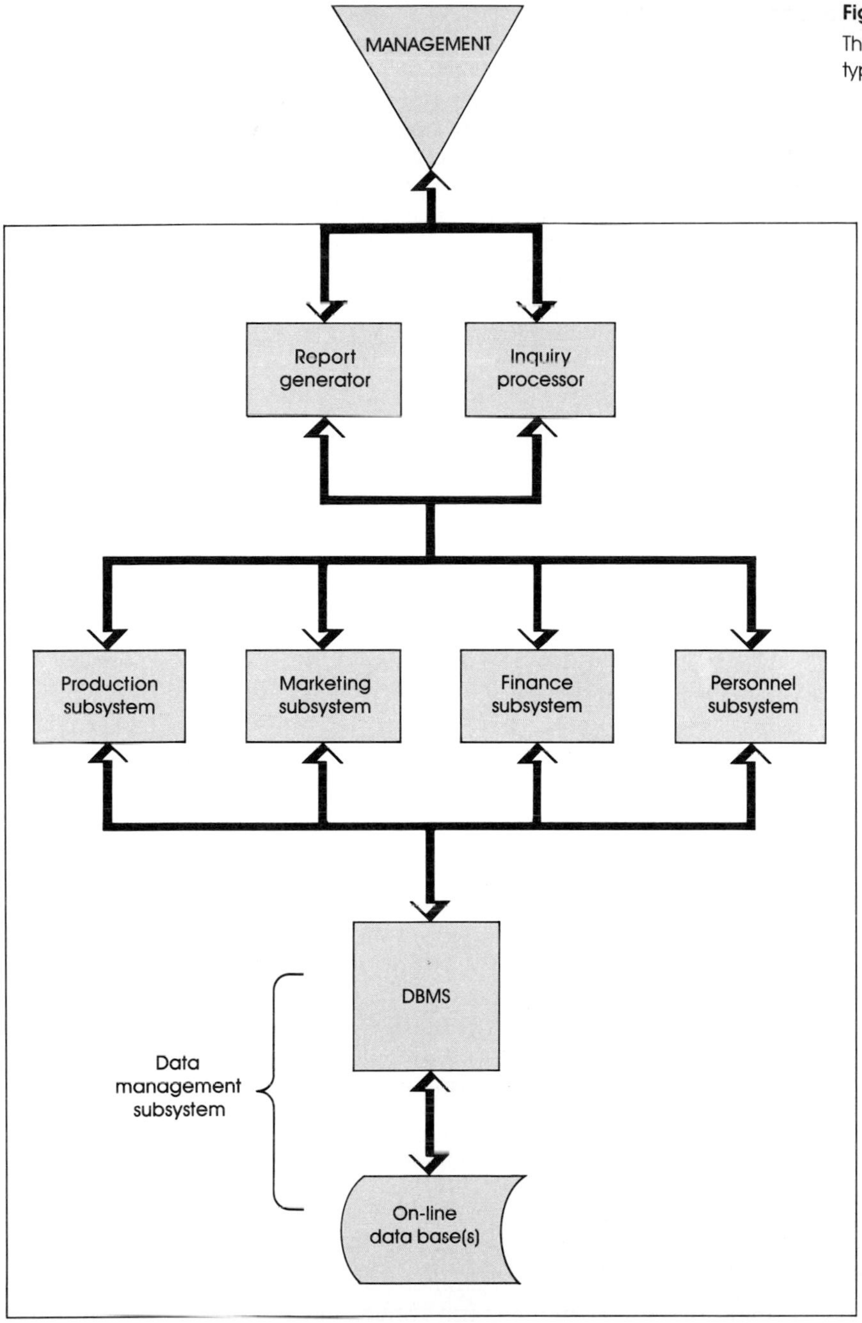

Figure 13.4 Components of a Typical MIS
The conceptual components of an MIS for a typical manufacturing firm.

---

an MIS. Therefore, the data management subsystem of an MIS consists of one or more data bases and a data base management system (see Chapter 12). This subsystem is perhaps the most important component of an MIS because proper data management is vital to the success of any computer-based system.

As a matter of fact, it's not uncommon to confuse the concepts of the MIS and the DBMS; in many instances, these two terms are treated as synonyms. Nevertheless, even though the two types of systems are clearly related to each other, they remain distinct from each other. A DBMS is concerned with the storage, updating,

Methods of information storage and use

Keyboard Koncepts has a central mainframe computer system, which it uses to maintain a single, fully integrated relational data base system (see Chapter 12). The DBMS includes a nonprocedural query language that lets users ask questions interactively. In addition, the DBMS has a data manipulation language and a report generator that are used by the functional subsystems of the MIS. The system also contains a local area network of microcomputers tied into the mainframe computer, through which managers can access the data base system. By organizing its data with such a system, Keyboard Koncepts can realize all the advantages associated with the use of a data base. Since the MIS gets all the data it needs from the DBMS, it is free to concentrate on producing the necessary answers and reports, without maintaining data files itself. The data base system is truly a central element of the MIS for Keyboard Koncepts.

and retrieval of data; an MIS concentrates instead on the *meaning* of those data. An MIS obtains appropriate data from data bases and processes them to produce information that has meaning for users. Thus, the DBMS provides the data, and the MIS provides the *meaning* through processing those data. An MIS selects the informational content for inclusion in reports and responses to inquiries; the DBMS provides that content. A DBMS is not the same as an MIS, but it's a central element of one.

Functional Subsystems

An MIS component for each department: production, marketing, finance, and personnel

Systems can be conceptually broken down into subsystems in any number of ways. For example, an organizational system could be divided into subsystems based on the flow of resources: labor, money, and materials. Management information systems, however, are typically viewed as collections of *functional subsystems*. This means that organizational activities (such as those of production or manufacturing, marketing, finance, and personnel) are grouped together into departments, with each department forming a subsystem. Not all organizations exhibit the same functions, of course, but the basic principles of functional organization apply in any case. For example, although a manufacturing firm typically has production, marketing, finance, and personnel subsystems, a governmental agency will have a different set of major departments. The discussion here will be based on the manufacturing firm.

The Production Subsystem

Production, or manufacturing, involves the conversion of resources (input) into goods or services (output). For example, an automobile manufacturer converts labor, capital, and raw materials into new cars. The most important production activities can be summarized as follows:

- *Inventory management* ensures that raw materials are on hand when they are needed and that enough finished goods are available to meet customers' demands.
- *Scheduling* attempts to achieve the most efficient use of production facilities.
- *Operations* are the processes by which the resources are actually converted into goods.

**Production at
Keyboard
Koncepts**

The production subsystem of the MIS for Keyboard Koncepts provides managers with various reports concerning the conversion of raw materials (keyboard casings, keysets, cords, circuit boards, screws, etc.) into finished products (fully assembled and tested keyboards). Inventory reports list the quantities and locations of both components and assembled keyboards in each of the firm's three warehouses. Production schedule reports show how many finished keyboards are being made each day, week, month, and year. Engineering reports give details about the design and specifications for each keyboard model the company offers. Order reports summarize how many of each type of keyboard will be needed to fill customers' requests. Purchasing reports show which raw materials must be ordered from which suppliers to fulfill production quotas. Finally, quality control reports indicate how successful the assembly line is at turning out keyboards that meet the design specifications.

- *Engineering* is responsible for the design of products and facilities.
- *Shipping and receiving* carry out shipping instructions from the finance department and process invoices from vendors.
- *Purchasing* involves the procurement of resources from suppliers.
- *Quality control* ensures that product standards are being upheld.

The production subsystem of an MIS serves these functions by supplying reports concerning such items as production schedules, inventories, suppliers' bills, customers' orders, forecasts of consumer demand, budgets, product specifications and designs, invoices, prices of materials, and quality control limits.

The Marketing Subsystem

Since the early 1950s, the marketing function has become increasingly important for companies. In very narrow terms, marketing consists of advertising and selling. However, marketing can also be defined as the performance of those business activities that direct the flow of goods from producer to consumer. Thus, it serves the two important functions of satisfying customer needs and accomplishing company objectives. Some of the following key activities come under the heading of marketing:

- *Market research* attempts to find out what the public wants and how much they are willing to pay for it.
- *Product development* is the link between market research and engineering, the translation of consumer preferences into product specifications.
- *Pricing* involves assigning an appropriate, competitive price for each product made by the firm.
- *Promotion,* one of the most important marketing activities, makes the public aware of products through advertising and other means.
- *Sales management* involves the administration of sales personnel.

The marketing subsystem of an MIS supports these activities by providing information on consumer preference surveys, product comparison tests, observations of buying habits, product warranties, competitors' prices, production costs, sales personnel performance ratings, sales budgets, and estimated sales figures.

The advertising and sales departments of Keyboard Koncepts depend heavily on the marketing subsystem of the company's MIS. The results of market research studies and customer preference questionnaires are processed at the central computing facility. The MIS prepares reports based on this market research, which are studied closely by the advertising and sales managers. The reports are then passed on to the engineering department, which in turn tries to incorporate any feasible suggestions into new keyboard specifications. Incorporating data about production costs and competitors' prices, the marketing subsystem generates reports that suggest the optimal amount to charge for each keyboard model. The advertising department uses the MIS to consolidate information about customers so that effective promotional campaigns can be developed and carried out. Finally, the sales department uses the marketing subsystem to administrate the activities of its mobile sales force. Through the use of laptop microcomputers with built-in modems, salespeople in the field can call headquarters daily to submit new customer orders and receive instructions and up-to-date market information.

The Finance Subsystem

The finance function comprises those activities that are concerned with the management of a firm's money. Since computer systems and data-processing techniques have been used in these areas for years, it's not surprising that the finance subsystem is often the most extensive subsystem of an organization's MIS. These are some of the most important finance activities:

- *Budgeting* makes possible managerial planning and control of the firm's financial resources.
- *Cost accounting* involves the determination of where money has actually been spent.
- *Funds management* ensures that enough money is available to meet the firm's ongoing financial obligations while maximizing the return on investments.
- *Financial accounting* is the classification, recording, and summarizing of monetary transactions for investors, creditors, and the government.
- *Accounts receivable* is the set of activities by which customers are billed and their payments processed.
- *Accounts payable* is the set of activities by which payments to vendors for materials are processed.

The finance subsystem of an MIS keeps managers on top of these activities by providing information such as projected cost and income figures, actual expenditures, investment opportunities, interest rates, balance sheets, income statements, and summaries of orders and invoices.

The Personnel Subsystem

Large organizations generally operate more economically if they maintain computerized personnel records. An additional benefit is that, when job openings occur, appropriately skilled individuals can often be found among current employees. Activities that fall under the personnel function are:

- *Labor relations*—interface between the firm and its employees.

The finance subsystem of the MIS for Keyboard Koncepts is the largest, most heavily used, and most indispensable of its subsystems. It processes the data and generates the reports that are used to manage the firm's financial resources. Cost-accounting reports show exactly how much money is spent and where it goes. These reports are extremely important to the managers involved in budgeting for payroll and for the purchase of materials and new assembly line equipment. Asset holdings and market analysis reports help funds managers keep Keyboard Koncepts in the black by providing the information needed to ensure that enough liquid capital is available to pay the bills. Financial accounting reports are generated to show investors, creditors, and the IRS how much money Keyboard Koncepts makes and spends. Finally, routine processing for both accounts receivable and accounts payable is completely handled by the finance subsystem of the MIS for Keyboard Koncepts.

- *Personnel actions*—such activities as hiring, promoting, keeping track of vacations and sick leave, and administering medical and life insurance programs.
- *Record maintenance*—the constant updating of all necessary data on all employees.
- *Payroll*—the process by which employees receive their wages.

The personnel subsystem of an MIS supplies information about these activities in such forms as employee contracts, wage scales, allowable fringe benefits, training provisions, wage rates, tax deductions and withholdings, paychecks, earnings statements, and payroll summary reports.

DECISION SUPPORT SYSTEMS

One of the more recent developments in computer-based information systems attempts to address the decision-making needs of the various levels of management. A **decision support system (DSS)** helps managers by giving them quick answers to interactively-asked "what if" questions. Decision support systems provide a basis for judging situations analytically; they do so by applying statistical and mathematical models and simulation. Decision support systems are intended to *help* managers make decisions, not to make decisions for managers. Furthermore, decision support systems generally are oriented toward dealing with relatively unstructured problems such as those concerning new products, policies, company mergers, and acquisitions.

Helping management make decisions

Like most companies with a lot of employees, Keyboard Koncepts has computerized its personnel operations. Records concerning the work history, job performance, skills, education, pay rate, accrued vacation time, benefits, and hours worked of each employee are kept in the centralized data base (subject to strict security measures). This information is used to process the payroll automatically and issue regular paychecks. The personnel subsystem of the MIS produces summary reports from these records and also helps to match up current employees with new positions that have opened up within the firm. By ensuring that payroll is accurately and rapidly processed and by pinpointing advancement opportunities for people already within the company, the personnel subsystem benefits both Keyboard Koncepts and its employees.

Decision support systems both complement and build on management information systems. Typically on-line and fully interactive, decision support systems are primarily designed for problems for which little or no precedent exists. Management information systems, on the other hand, generally are oriented toward collecting, organizing, and summarizing information to help managers deal with well-structured problems (such as where to locate plants and warehouses or the preparation of budgets, cost analyses, accounts payable, and payroll).

To be more specific, decision support systems are usually characterized by 10 essential qualities:

1. *A broad-based approach to the support of decision making.*   Decision support systems must directly relate to the goals and objectives that form the basis of corporate strategies. By providing flexible financial planning and budgeting models, for example, decision support systems encompass a broader view of organizations than management information systems typically do.

2. *Interaction between a person and a computer in which the person retains control over the decision-making process.*   The DSS is only a tool to be employed by managers in evaluating alternatives so that effective decisions can be made.

3. *Support for all types of decisions.*   Although decision support systems tend to be directed toward unstructured problem-solving, they can also be used to solve well-structured problems.

4. *Utilization of appropriate statistical and mathematical models.*   Decision support systems apply abstract models to approximate the real world so that inferences can be made about the effects of various courses of action.

5. *Output directed to all levels of organizational personnel.*   Effective decision support systems provide decision-making aids to managers at all levels, as well as to other operating employees.

6. *Interactive query capabilities.*   Decision support systems must allow on-line access so that users can obtain information on request.

7. *Integrated subsystems.*   All related functions must be well integrated into the overall system to allow management to retrieve and manipulate information for decision making.

8. *A comprehensive data base.*   As with management information systems, a complete data base and a DBMS are central to decision support systems.

9. *Ease of use.*   The hallmark of an effective DSS is its user-friendliness. A DSS should be a natural extension of the user's decision-making process.

10. *Adaptability.*   An effective DSS must allow for change over time. It should be a highly adaptive system that not only helps users confront new problems but can be modified to accommodate changing conditions.

The real key to the difference between a DSS and an MIS is the interaction between the person and the computer. The *human/machine interface,* as it's sometimes called, represents a step beyond the typical MIS in that it allows users to react immediately to the output. The decision maker can interact with the DSS by getting answers to a series of "what if" questions. That is, the DSS is geared toward fostering learning, creativity, and evaluation. More specifically, an MIS primarily helps managers quantify aspects of a problem, solve the problem, and produce output to aid in the decision-making process. In contrast, a DSS allows the decision maker to look inside a problem, discover previously hidden aspects, isolate certain parameters, and ask a series of "what if" questions involving these selected parameters.

This interplay between decision maker and computerized system helps uncover the essence of problems and often yields new ways of arriving at answers.

The following example should help clarify the basic difference between the typical MIS and DSS. A certain manager depends on an MIS in scheduling and controlling the day-to-day operations of a manufacturing plant. Although the system generally works well for these routine planning and controlling purposes, the special orders that are frequently received present a problem. These special orders request relatively small quantities of items that must be custom-designed and manufactured. Relying on the MIS, the plant manager has little choice but to decline these orders if the factory is busy because it would be too difficult to find out how each one would affect the existing production schedules. With a DSS, however, the manager can quickly and easily manipulate a mathematical scheduling model to work out on a display screen the effect of accommodating special orders. The human/machine interface makes it possible to establish the feasibility of accepting special orders by asking "what if we try to handle those orders?" Using the mathematical model, the manager is able to find out if shipping dates for regular orders can still be met and if the special orders can be profitably filled. Also, the DSS makes it possible to offer counterproposals to customers who place special orders, for example, if higher prices must be charged or if a later shipping date will be necessary. In this example, the DSS gives the plant manager complete control over the acceptance of special orders, an option that would be impossible with the typical MIS.

EXPERT SYSTEMS

An **expert system** or **knowledge-based system** is a computer program that contains a collection of facts and a list of rules for making inferences about those facts. The facts and rules usually concern one particular field and are generally contributed by experts in that field. Expert systems use the facts and rules to advise, analyze, categorize, diagnose, explain, identify, interpret, and teach. They attempt to address problems traditionally solved by human experts. Today numerous expert systems are being employed in all kinds of fields. A few of the most famous examples of expert systems are MYCIN, which helps doctors diagnose infections; PROSPECTOR, which aids geologists in evaluating mineral sites; and TAXADVISOR, which gives estate-planning advice. We'll have more to say about expert systems in Parts 5 and 6 of this book.

Computerized consultants

Like a DSS, an expert system can help managers make decisions. An expert system, however, is really a step beyond a DSS. The DSS is generally used by a manager who is playing out "what if" scenarios, and the system responds simply as it has been preprogrammed to do. The manager solves the problem by knowing how to best use the DSS.

An expert system, on the other hand, brings something new to the problem that the manager probably doesn't already have: in-depth knowledge about a particular field. Furthermore, the expert system has been programmed with artificial intelligence techniques to use logic in applying that knowledge to a particular problem-solving task. **Artificial intelligence,** or **AI** (about which we'll also have more to say in Parts 5 and 6), is a field of study that combines aspects of computer science, mathematics, philosophy, psychology, and linguistics. Its main goal is to endow computers with the ability to mimic certain aspects of human learning and decision making. So, the basic goal of an expert system is to provide the advice you might otherwise get from a human consultant about a specific topic.

Expert systems are among the most useful and marketable products of artificial intelligence. The three examples of expert systems we mentioned (MYCIN, PROSPECTOR, and TAXADVISOR) are quite specific. Many expert systems run only on minicomputers and mainframes, and special artificial intelligence programming languages, such as LISP, LOGO, and PROLOG, are frequently used to develop proprietary expert systems. There is, however, a relatively new class of software that runs on microcomputers and lets nonprogrammers set up their own expert systems. These programs are called **expert system shells.**

An expert system shell greatly simplifies the process of developing an expert system. You supply the facts to create the **knowledge base** and the rules to create the **rule base.** The expert system shell contains the **inference engine,** which actually applies *your* facts and rules to try and answer questions asked by end users (sometimes called *clients*). If necessary, the inference engine replies with further questions to get additional information. The inference engine then uses simple logic to draw conclusions from the details of a particular situation. Many expert system shells can also explain, with text and graphics, exactly how their conclusions have been reached. In *A Closer Look* later in this chapter we examine one of the most popular expert system shells for microcomputers, VP-Expert from Paperback Software International.

DESIGN AND IMPLEMENTATION OF AN MIS AND A DSS

Planning the MIS or DSS

You have probably realized by now that designing and implementing management information and decision support systems presents a tremendous challenge for systems analysts. The many issues that must be addressed and the difficult problems that must be solved to develop an effective MIS or DSS have been the subject of many recent articles and books. To give you an idea of what some of the important design and implementation questions are, we'll briefly consider a few specific ones.

Should a top-down or bottom-up design approach be followed? In Chapter 7, we defined top-down design as a hierarchical, divide-and-conquer approach. In the design of an MIS or DSS, this means first studying organizational goals and the types of problems managers face to develop a picture of how information flows through the firm. From this, the design specifications can be developed. A top-down design has the advantage of being a sensible way to solve such a big problem because it facilitates the integration of the various system elements. The disadvantage is that it's difficult to define goals and decision-making activities precisely enough so they can be translated fairly directly into detailed design specifications; if they are not, the building of an expensive yet ineffective system may result. The bottom-up approach to design, on the other hand, begins with low-level, day-to-day activities such as processing transactions and maintaining the data base. Higher

Issues in Technology

In this chapter, we have naturally emphasized managers' use of information. However, the most important resource with which managers work is people. Most managers would agree that dealing with and motivating employees is a major part of their job. A great deal of qualitative information is gathered by managers through interacting with their subordinates. Does the availability of an effective MIS encourage managers to spend less time in such interactions? Might a good MIS therefore create managers who are *less* in touch with the organizational atmosphere? What do you think?

level modules are then built and added on to support managerial functions such as planning, controlling, and decision making. The advantage of this approach is that smaller pieces of the whole are developed in detail, minimizing the likelihood of developing a complex but inadequate system. The disadvantage of a bottom-up design is that it's difficult to produce the type of overview information managers need, when systems are built up starting from low-level operational activities. Consequently, most systems designers use some combination of the two approaches.

How many data bases should be created? The designer of an MIS or DSS is faced with the problem of deciding on the organization of the data base(s). Should all three levels of management share a single data base, or should each level have its own? Or, should each functional subsystem have a separate data base? Since each management level has different information needs, it may be justifiable to have separate data bases to support the production of strategic, tactical, and operational information. Different functional subsystems also need different information, although usually a lot of data sharing takes place among departments. How the data items themselves are arranged is determined by the DBMS that is to be used, but the nature and number of data bases for the MIS or DSS must be decided by the designer.

How can external information be incorporated into the system? As we've already pointed out, the higher the managerial level, the greater the need for information about matters external to the organization. (Incorporating internal information into a system is much less problematic.) The systems designer is responsible for determining the methods by which information from external sources can be accessed and brought into the firm's data bases. Purchasing machine-readable data from outside organizations or arranging for direct access to outside data bases may be necessary.

ADVANTAGES OF AN MIS AND A DSS

Although they are usually expensive and often difficult to implement, management information systems and decision support systems offer several significant advantages to managers who use them:

How an MIS or DSS can help

- *Helping to diagnose problems and recognize opportunities.* By providing them with current internal and external information, these systems better equip managers to catch potentially troublesome conditions early and to spot ways to further organizational goals.
- *Saving time.* By summarizing mountains of data, these systems enable managers to spend more time performing high-level activities such as planning and organizing and less time searching through irrelevant material.
- *Clarifying complex relationships.* By providing quality information, these systems can help managers evaluate possible alternatives in complicated situations. For example, complex economic relationships can be more easily identified using these systems, which better equips managers to make their firms competitive in the marketplace.
- *Helping to implement plans.* By providing up-to-the-minute information, these systems help managers direct and control activities and thus implement their plans.
- *Centralizing decision making.* These systems help centralize decision making (and thus authority) by providing information that is effectively summarized.

A Closer Look

Using VP-Expert

An expert system is a computer program that gives advice by drawing on a store of knowledge, requesting specific information, and emulating certain aspects of human problem-solving abilities. Such systems use techniques of *artificial intelligence,* a field that encompasses computer science, mathematics, philosophy, psychology, and linguistics. Expert systems are among the most useful and marketable products of this exciting field of artificial intelligence. *Expert system shells* are application packages that contain everything you need to create your own expert systems. They are often designed especially for nonprogrammers.

Several expert system shells are currently available for microcomputers. One of the most notable and least expensive is VP-Expert from Paperback Software, which sells for $99.95. Despite its relatively low price, this program for IBM-compatible microcomputers is a sophisticated, powerful, yet easy-to-use, expert system development tool. VP-Expert contains the *inference engine* that applies rules from a *rule base* to facts from a *knowledge base* to answer a user's questions or to provide advice. With VP-Expert, all you have to do is construct the knowledge base and rule base with the provided tools. The inference engine does the rest. Although teaching you how to develop your own expert system is beyond the scope of this text, we can show you what it's like to use an existing system that has already been prepared with VP-Expert. The expert system we'll use as an example is the simple one included with the VP-Expert package to illustrate the consultation process. This sample system is a "cheese advisor" designed to recommend cheeses based on menu information and personal preferences supplied by the user during a consultation session.

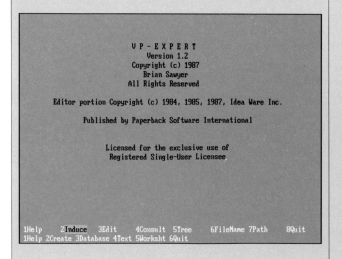

As usual, the first step is to start up the VP-Expert program. Enter *VPX* into a computer with the program installed on it, and VP-Expert will display its opening screen and Main Menu, which look like the screen at left.

The menus in VP-Expert work like the menus in other popular application packages. To select an option you can highlight it and press the Enter key or you can type its first letter. You can also press the Function key or number key corresponding to the number that immediately precedes the option. For example, we want to consult an existing expert system, so we need to execute the *Consult* option. This can be done by performing any one of the following actions: pressing the right arrow key twice and then pressing the Enter key, typing *C,* pressing the F4 function key, or typing *4.* The program then presents a list of existing knowledge base files, as the next screen illustrates.

To choose from this list, simply highlight the one you want and press the Enter key. The one we want to use is entitled *FROMAGE2.* After the knowledge base has been selected, VP-Expert then presents its Consult Menu, which looks like the middle screen.

To begin the consultation, you simply execute the Go option. The program then says, "Welcome to the

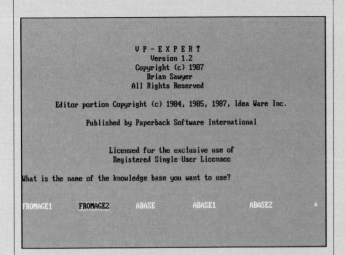

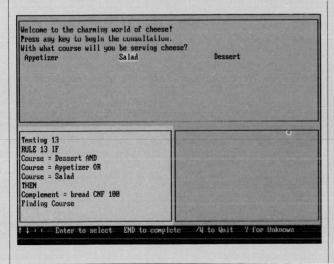

charming world of cheese!'' You are instructed to press any key to begin the consultation. After you do this, VP-Expert displays its first question along with the two possible answer choices (bottom left).

There are three separate windows on the screen. The big green one on top is the *consultation window,* which displays any messages, questions, and answer choices for the user. The gray box on the lower left side of the screen is the *rules window,* which allows you to observe the internal activity of the inference engine as it processes rules and interacts with the knowledge base. During a consultation, the rules being processed scroll by in this window. Finally, the blue box on the lower right side of the screen is the *results window,* which notes the intermediate and final conclusions made by the inference engine during the course of a consultation. As you can see, most of the messages are fairly self-explanatory. The abbreviation *CNF,* however, stands for *confidence factor.* It is followed by a number that indicates a relative degree of certainty. For example *CNF 100* attached to the conclusion of a rule means that there is an estimated 100% confidence level or 100% probability that the conclusion is correct. Similarly, *CNF 75* would indicate a conclusion drawn with 75% confidence.

Now let's try answering the questions posed by VP-Expert and see what cheese it recommends for a meal. The first question asks with what course the cheese will be served. To select one or more answers, you simply highlight each answer you want by using the left or right arrow key, and then press the Enter key. For our example, let's say that we are looking for a cheese to serve with salad. An arrow then appears next to the answer or answers that have been selected. To go on to the next question, you press the End key. Here is the next question displayed on the screen:

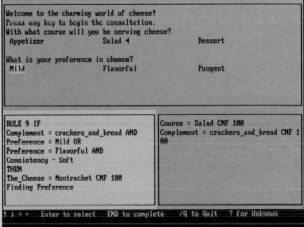

How about a mild cheese? Simply highlight the *Mild* option, press the Enter key, and then press the End key to go on to the next question:

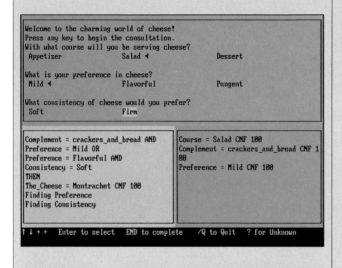

The final question asks for your preference in the consistency of a cheese. Let's answer *Firm* and see what happens (bottom left).

As you can see, the cheese expert system suggests that you serve Stilton with crackers and bread with your salad. (Stilton is a blue-veined cheese with a wrinkled rind made of whole cow's milk enriched with cream.) Furthermore, VP-Expert assigns a 100% confidence factor to the conclusions that Stilton and crackers and bread should be served with salad, based on your indicated preferences.

Although this "cheese advisor" is a rather trivial expert system application, you should now have some idea what it's like to use an expert system. These systems are likely to be used even more in the future as people become more familiar with the capabilities of expert system shells for microcomputers. Already, third-party knowledge bases created for VP-Expert can be purchased for advice and help with various specific problems. For example, Paperback Software also sells (for $39.95) an expert system built with VP-Expert called *Anthony Dias Blue Wines on Disk*. This knowledge base applies Mr. Blue's internationally renowned wine expertise to help you choose from over 600 top-rated American wines for any meal or occasion. *Wines on Disk* can recommend both popular wines and lesser-known varieties that are more difficult to find. Each wine entry includes comments that supply vineyard information, prices, ratings, and Mr. Blue's own tasting impressions. Despite our specific examples, other expert systems exist that have absolutely nothing to do with food and drink.

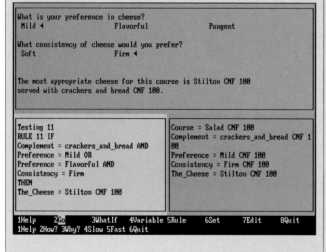

Summary

What Is an MIS?

A management information system is an organized means of providing managers with the information they need to do their jobs effectively.

What Is Management?

Management's job consists of converting resources in order to accomplish some desired results and doing so profitably.

What Managers Do   Managers basically plan, organize, staff, direct, and control.

Levels of Management   Management is traditionally organized into three levels. Top management is concerned with long-range plans; middle management is concerned with short-term plans; and first-line management is concerned with controlling day-to-day activities.

Information Needs of Managers

Without information, managers cannot effectively do their jobs. Different management levels have different information needs.

Strategic Information for Top Management   Strategic information helps top management make long-range plans and consists primarily of external information, along with some internal information.

Tactical Information for Middle Management   Tactical information helps middle management make short-term plans and implement the strategic plans made by top management; it consists (in fairly equal amounts) of internal and external, detailed and summarized information.

Operational Information for First-Line Management   Operational information is used by first-line management to control the structured, repetitive, day-to-day activities of the organization.

Characteristics of Useful Information   To be valuable, information must be accurate, timely, relevant, complete, and concise.

Output of Information   Management information systems generally provide output in the form of printed reports (periodic, demand, exception, special, or predictive) or on-line inquiry responses.

Components of an MIS

An MIS consists of both hardware and software.

The Data Management Subsystem   Central to all the activities of an MIS are one or more data bases and a data base management system.

Functional Subsystems   Management information systems are typically viewed as collections of functional subsystems, which correspond to organizational departments (for example, production, marketing, finance, and personnel).

Decision Support Systems

Decision support systems help managers by giving them quick answers to interactively-asked "what if" questions.

Expert Systems

An expert system is a program that uses artificial intelligence techniques to address problems that might otherwise be solved by a human consultant.

Design and Implementation of an MIS and a DSS

Issues that must be addressed in planning an MIS or DSS include whether a top-down or bottom-up approach should be used, how many data bases should be created, and how external information can be incorporated.

Advantages of an MIS and a DSS

An MIS and a DSS help diagnose problems and recognize opportunities, save time, clarify complex relationships, implement plans, and centralize decision making.

Computer Concepts

As an extra review of the chapter, try defining the following terms. If you have trouble with any of them, refer to the page number listed.

management information
  system (MIS) *443*
strategic information *447*
tactical information *448*
operational information
  448

decision support system
  (DSS) *457*
expert system (knowledge-
  based system) *459*
artificial intelligence (AI)
  459

expert system shells *460*
knowledge base *460*
rule base *460*
inference engine *460*

Review Questions

1. What is the purpose of an MIS?
2. What are the five functions of managers?
3. What are the three levels of management? With what is each concerned?
4. What level of management needs strategic information and of what does such information consist?
5. What type of information is used by middle management? By first-line management?
6. What characterizes valuable information?
7. What are the two basic forms of MIS output?
8. List and briefly describe the five types of MIS reports.
9. What advantages do inquiry responses offer over reports?
10. Why are management information systems difficult to characterize?
11. List and briefly describe the six most important production activities.
12. What are some of the key activities of the marketing department of a business?
13. What are some of the ways in which decision support systems help managers?
14. Compare MIS and DSS.
15. What are the 10 essential qualities of a DSS?
16. What is the real key to the difference between an MIS and a DSS?
17. Describe the characteristics of an expert system and explain how it differs from a DSS.
18. Describe the areas of study combined in AI.
19. What are three important questions to be considered when designing and implementing MIS and DSS?
20. List the advantages to managers of MIS and DSS.

True or False

1. An MIS must provide both internal and external information.
2. All five management functions apply only to top managers.
3. First-line are usually the smallest group of managers in a large firm.
4. Middle management oversees the performance of first-line managers.
5. The output of an MIS is essential only for the achievement of long-range goals.
6. An MIS system basically consists of a discrete set of specially designed programs.
7. MIS and DBMS are synonymous.
8. Usually the most extensive subsystem of an organization's MIS is the marketing subsystem.
9. In expert systems, the inference engine creates the rule base.
10. Top-down design of MIS facilitates the integration of the various system elements.

1. An example of top management would be a:
   (a) head of a major division   (b) plant manager   (c) plant supervisor

2. Ensuring that employees follow established procedures is the responsibility of:
   (a) top managers   (b) middle managers   (c) first-line managers

3. In an MIS, speed of information retrieval must be balanced against:
   (a) relevence   (b) cost   (c) conciseness

4. The primary means by which an MIS presents information is:
   (a) a report   (b) organizing   (c) modeling

5. The most important component of an MIS is perhaps:
   (a) the data management subsystem   (b) the production subsystem   (c) the personnel subsystem

6. The system that allows a decision-maker to ask "what if" questions is:
   (a) an MIS   (b) a data base   (c) a DSS

7. An expert system that helps doctors diagnose infections is:
   (a) PROSPECTOR   (b) AI   (c) MYCIN

8. Software which lets nonprogrammers set up their own expert systems is:
   (a) an expert system shell   (b) a knowledge base   (c) artificial intelligence

9. The most important resource with which managers work is:
   (a) MIS   (b) expert systems   (c) people

10. Bottom-up design begins with:
    (a) a hierarchical approach   (b) low-level day-to-day activities   (c) higher-level modules

1. Suppose you were head of a company that used MIS and DSS extensively and you were evaluating candidates for a position in top management. What experience, qualifications, and human qualities would you look for in the people who applied for the position? Why?

2. If you were offered a first-line management position by three different companies, would (or should) the quality of their management information systems affect your decision to accept one position over the other two? Why or why not?

1. Managers encounter two basic types of decision-making situations. The first type is routine in nature, recurs regularly, and is often called a *programmed decision situation*. The other type is nonroutine, nonrecurring, and might be encountered only once; it is described as a *nonprogrammed decision situation*. Investigate how management information systems and decision support systems can be used to assist managers in both these types of situations. Which system might be better for each type of situation, and why?

2. Management information systems are usually identified with large-scale computer systems. Consequently, many people think that an organization must own a mainframe computer to have an MIS. Investigate the feasibility of an MIS for an organization with a small computer. Is an MIS workable in such an environment? Do any management information systems exist for small computers? What might be the problems (if any) of using smaller computers?

3. Investigate some large businesses and organizations to find out if they have an MIS. Periodicals like *Computerworld* and *MIS Weekly* might be good places to start looking. Also, you can ask any people you know who work for such organizations. Write a report listing the organizations you uncover, and include whatever details you obtain about their systems.

4. Try to become familiar with a computer-based information system. Perhaps your school or company has such a system. Consider what would happen if this school or company did not use a computer. What sacrifices would have to be made in the types of information that would be available? What time delays would result? Be as specific as possible.

APPLICATIONS

Backed by a thorough understanding of computers—their history and hardware, software and systems—we can now turn our attention to the various ways we actually utilize them in everyday applications that are both vital and intriguing. This is the fruit of technology, the benefits that make computers worthwhile.

Chapter 14 explores the role computers play in modern offices, touching everything from word processing to teleconferencing. Chapter 15 introduces the "steel-collar worker" that is appearing in research laboratories and on assembly lines as major industries increasingly turn to computers for help in all areas of design and manufacturing. Chapter 15 also provides an overview of computers in the business world, exploring their applications in the commercial realm. Chapter 16 offers a brief, whirlwind tour of computer usage throughout our society, in education, entertainment, and government.

14

Computers in the
Office

In This Chapter

The Paper Revolution

The predictions of the paperless office, which at one time seemed so very reasonable, now appear more remote. A recent article by Paul Saffo in *Personal Computing* magazine reported that the use of paper was increasing at twice the rate of the Gross National Product. The traditional use of paper as a more permanent storage for the enormous quantity of information stored on computers does not seem to be changing. Let's look at other areas where the use of paper has persisted or increased.

Although personal computer displays have improved markedly, it is still difficult for the standard monitor to match the visual appeal of laser printer output that has been formatted with desktop publishing software. Since the visual impact of the document can sometimes be as important as the information it contains, paper may be the preferred alternative.

There is no doubt that specific items or groups of information and data can be accessed with tremendous speed and efficiency on a computer system. However, the scrolling speed of a computer, not to mention the sheer volume of information that can be stored and accessed, can easily overwhelm the reader. For longer documents, especially on microcomputers, some have argued that paper aids in the assimilation of the message.

In an environment where permanent storage is in electronic form, the ease of printing from this data and information resource often puts paper in the role of a temporary communication device, to be discarded once the message has been conveyed. Discarding paper, rather than saving it, because the permanent record has been stored electronically is a new phenomenon.

The ease of printing and improved data communications has also made possible the remote publishing of documents and newspapers such as *USA Today*.

The redefinition of office structure because of technological innovations has contributed to the increased use of paper. Our wonderful new office devices are so much faster and better at data and information processing that they are producing paper output at ever increasing rates. This improved efficiency in our photocopiers, printers, typewriters and other paper-consuming devices, as well as new uses and perceptions of paper documents, indicate that the paperless office is unlikely to be commonplace soon.

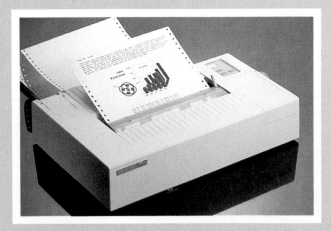

Bob Cratchit, Ebenezer Scrooge's clerk in "A Christmas Carol," scribbled away more than 12 hours a day, entering figures in ledgers and copying correspondence by candlelight in a cold, dim back room. Perched on a backless stool before a tiny desk, he's a well-known illustration, only somewhat exaggerated, of the office conditions under which most people worked in Dickens's London. Things were much the same in this country during the nineteenth century. The lighting was bad, the workload enormous, and the staffing, for the sake of economy, was as small as possible. The clerk, a sort of combination photocopier, secretary, and accountant, had too much to do, and most of the work was laborious, dull, and time-consuming. Imagine making 20 copies of this chapter by hand, each one identical, legible, and without scratch-outs, smudges, or erasures—and you've begun to imagine working in the old-style office.

By 1900, the typewriter was in general use. Its adoption in the workplace resembled the more recent integration of computers into the office, and the effect of its appearance was just as revolutionary. In the first half of the twentieth century, the office changed. Volume and productivity became the watchwords. The office was transformed into a giant manual processing system, and the clerks' cubbyholes gave way to warehouse-sized rooms full of rows of desks, with telephones, typewriters, and adding machines producing a deafening racket. The workplace for this sea of mechanized people was significantly brighter and more efficient than the Victorian office, but little more pleasant.

In the latter part of the twentieth century, the office has changed again. This chapter looks at the rise of the information age and its impact on how, and where, white-collar work is done.

THE DIMENSIONS OF OFFICE AUTOMATION

This chapter examines how computers are being used to improve the productivity and general environment of the modern office. This process, which has been going on since the early 1960s, has been directed at achieving the ultimate white-collar workplace, variously dubbed *the office of the future*, *the electronic office*, *the paperless office*, and *the integrated office*. Unfortunately, all of these terms are too optimistic and somewhat misleading. For example, it's doubtful that there will ever be a *paperless office*. Similarly, the term **office automation** has also been widely used to describe the conversion to this mythical perfect office of the future. Although offices will never be truly automated like a robot-run manufacturing assembly line, the term *office automation* has become an accepted buzzword. In general, it refers to the integration of computers, communications, and advanced office equipment to support the many activities that occur in an office environment.

Computers in the white-collar workplace

The Information Age

Basically, an office is a place where data are processed and information is managed. The growing importance of such places in today's society is at least partly due to the information explosion that has occurred for the past two decades. Over fifty percent of American workers are now employed in the information sector; the United States has progressed from having primarily an industrial economy (in which tangible goods like steel and automobiles are produced) to an information economy

Coping with paperwork and change

(in which data are processed into information). The salaries paid to office workers comprise a large percentage of many organizations' expenses, and they tend to increase every year. The application of new technology is one way in which existing staff can be made more productive while the chronic overflow of paperwork is reduced. In the information age, computers become more than just valuable; they are essential for handling vast quantities of data and keeping costs down to manageable levels.

Office Functions

In order to see how computers are being applied to office procedures, we need to start from some point of agreement about just what these functions are. This isn't as obvious as it might seem. Offices serve a variety of purposes, many of which aren't especially well defined. There are vast differences among the offices of various kinds of organizations, and modern offices in general are in a state of drastic change. Since the advent of data communications, it may not even be valid to impose geographical boundaries on offices; the activities and functions normally attributed to the office no longer necessarily have to occur in any particular location. There are, however, a few generalizations we can make about the nature of the office.

What goes on in the office

As we've already noted, offices process data and handle information. In general, the following functions are performed by the managers, professionals, and clerical staff who work in offices (see Figure 14.1):

- *Creation and input.*   Data and information must be originated or collected and brought into the organization. For example, a telephone company must assemble and input enormous quantity of data in order to publish its phone books each year. Office workers, especially managers and professionals, also create new information in the form of letters, memos, reports, and other documents.

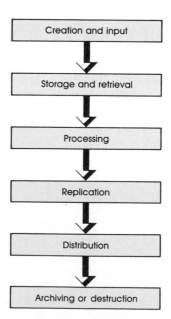

Figure 14.1 What Goes On in the Office
An office is a place where data and information are created and input, stored and retrieved, processed, replicated, distributed, and archived or destroyed.

- *Storage and retrieval.*   Data that have been gathered and information that has been generated must be held somewhere and obtained easily when needed. For a small business office, these functions might be accomplished by keeping folders in an ordinary filing cabinet. The Internal Revenue Service, on the other hand, maintains massive stores of data and information in electronic form on magnetic disks and tapes.

- *Processing.*   Data must be turned into information to be of use to an organization. The most common type of processing in most offices is word processing and desktop publishing, but other types of data processing are also done. For example, an accounting office naturally does a great deal of financial transaction processing.

- *Replication.*   In the office context, **replication** refers to a wide range of reproduction processes, from simply duplicating a document with a copy machine to full-fledged typesetting.

- *Distribution.*   A major activity in any office is communication, or the *distribution* of information both inside and outside the organization. There are many ways in which information is distributed by offices, from ordinary paper mail to electronic mail, and from telephone calls to video conferencing.

- *Archiving or destruction.*   Many records kept in offices are no longer needed frequently. **Archiving** is the process of preserving these relatively inactive, but still necessary, records in an economic and space-saving manner. When data and information completely outlive their usefulness, organizations must have procedures for destroying them, both for security and economic reasons.

The New Office Environment

Through history, the office environment has reflected the state of office technology. The Victorian scrivener needed only a pen and paper, and his "office" was accordingly small and self-contained—a stool, a desk, and a bottle of ink. The typewriter—noisy, sometimes messy, and unforgiving of error—created offices that were much the same. Today, high technology equipment demands a clean environment; the machines encourage speed, accuracy, efficiency, and streamlining of operations. Many of the office's traditionally repetitive, time-wasting tasks can be minimized or eliminated. Modern offices, as a result, are more pleasant places in which to work, and the work itself is more pleasant to do (see Figure 14.2). (We'll discuss some exceptions to this rule later, in Chapter 17.)

A more pleasant workplace

OFFICE INPUT

In an office, data and information must be created or collected and brought into the system before it can be stored, retrieved, processed, replicated, distributed, and archived. In general, office input can be subdivided into two major categories: original input and nonoriginal input.

Original input is data that comes into the office for the first time. It can consist of voice, text, and image input. Basically, original input includes raw data or ideas that are entered but not yet corrected, reviewed, or processed. In an office, this original input is refined into information that can be stored, analyzed, distributed,

Bringing data and information into the system

Figure 14.2 The Modern Office

The modern integrated office is a highly productive, yet pleasant place in which to work.

and hopefully put to good use. The ultimate form of the information produced from original input is often memos, letters, reports, presentations, and other publications.

Nonoriginal input, on the other hand, consists of data or information that already exists within an office. For example, *boilerplate* documents such as fill-in-the-blank forms, paragraphs that are frequently reused, and previously printed or type-set materials are all examples of nonoriginal input.

In either case, ideas are the most valuable input of office workers, especially workers at upper management levels. These ideas, however, must be entered and processed before they can translate into some kind of action. They can enter the information management system of an office in several ways. For example, long-hand text, shorthand text, direct dictation, machine dictation, direct keyboard entry, and scanning are all ways in which input can be generated inside an office. One recent survey of American executives revealed these input activities and the time spent on each:

Input activity	Percentage of time spent
Longhand text	75 %
Machine dictation	10 %
Shorthand	10 %
Other (scanning)	5 %

All of the various methods of office input can be grouped into three basic categories: voice, text, and image input.

Voice Input

For the most part, voice input consists of dictation, either directly to a secretary or indirectly with a *dictation machine* (see Figure 14.3). With the advent of voice recognition modules (discussed in Chapter 4), some computers can directly accept limited human speech as input. In offices, these voice recognition devices are being used in some computer systems for executives who either cannot or don't want to type.

Dictation and voice recognition

Text Input

Typing at a keyboard is the primary way original input is entered in most offices. Many office workers simply type their memos, letters, and other documents with a typewriter or computer word processor.

The primary type of office input

For those executives who cannot or do not wish to type, longhand text is the most frequently used form of original input. However, its slowness makes it a relatively inefficient means of entering input. While longhand writing averages around 10 or 15 words per minute, direct or machine dictation can proceed at an average of 80 words per minute.

Although its use has been declining in recent years, shorthand remains a helpful skill that allows an office worker to generate text or receive dictation at speeds much faster than longhand writing. Like longhand text, shorthand must eventually be typed or entered at a computer keyboard.

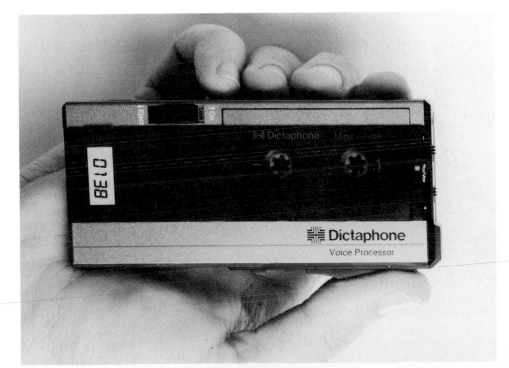

Figure 14.3 Dictation Machine

In an office, voice input often consists of dictation to a pocket-sized device such as this. A secretary can then enter the input later as text at a typewriter or word processor keyboard.

Finally, another form of text input is hard copy that has already been typed or printed, such as excerpts from magazines, books, and other documents. For offices that do not have a scanner that can read such materials, hard copy input is simply retyped with a typewriter or word processor.

Image Input

Materials such as typed or printed text and graphics are often called *image input* when they are entered by means of an optical scanner. Sometimes, input from video cameras, microfilm, and facsimile machines (which transmit and receive documents over phone lines) are also considered to be image input.

Scanned documents

The most significant kind of image input, however, is typewritten or typeset text that is read by a special type of scanner known as an **optical character recognition (OCR)** scanner. An OCR scanner has the ability to ''read'' text and convert it into digital form such as ASCII, the standard code that most computers use to represent characters. This text can then be imported into a word-processing program and further manipulated, reformatted, and printed out just as if it were directly typed. Many OCR scanners can also scan graphics, making them versatile tools for both office input and desktop publishing. Other OCR scanners can only read text that has been typewritten or printed in certain standard fonts and without proportional spacing. In contrast, many of the latest high-end models (see Figure 14.4) are capable of reading a wide range of fonts and have no problem with certain kinds of proportionally-spaced typeset text. OCR scanners are fast becoming almost standard office equipment, with sales now soaring. For example, the Gartner Group, a market researcher, predicts that scanner sales will top $400 million in 1989.

RECORDS MANAGEMENT

Storing and retrieving information

Offices are places where data and information are stored and retrieved, and ultimately are archived or destroyed. These are extremely critical office functions since information is one of an organization's most vital resources. Consequently, **records management** is an important aspect of office automation. ARMA (the Association of Records Managers and Administrators, Incorporated) defines records management as the systematic handling of documents from creation to destruction. In this sense, the term *record* is a unit of data or information that can be anything from a single character or code number up to an entire document. A record may be kept in any of the following basic forms:

- *Paper.* This is the most traditional and familiar media for keeping records. Paper is, however, the least flexible media for efficient retrieval unless records are extensively cross-referenced. It also requires a great deal of storage space and considerable labor to maintain.

- *Film.* Records in this form generally consist of microfilm and microfiche documents. They require much less space and can be generated, manipulated, stored, retrieved, and distributed with the help of computer technology. The disadvantage of film records is that they are somewhat expensive and require special equipment to create, store, and display.

Figure 14.4   OCR Scanner
Many offices now have optical scanners that can "read" printed or typeset text and convert it to digital ASCII codes that can be manipulated by word-processing computers. This Kurzweil Discover 7320 system, which sells for $9,950, scans many different character fonts and sizes, including most typeset material.

- *Digital.*   Records kept in digital form are compact, easy to store, can be quickly retrieved by computer, and are relatively inexpensive. Unfortunately, keeping digital records is almost synonymous with having a computer, as an organization must first install some kind of computer system before it can keep digital records. These records mostly consist of documents created with a word processor and stored on magnetic disk, magnetic tape, or optical disk. Nowadays, digital records can also consist of voice, music, charts, drawings, photographs, and even color video stored on these same media.

Paper Systems

Most offices have at least some of their data and information stored in traditional paper records. For the most part, paper record systems consist of file folders in either conventional vertical-drawer file cabinets or lateral files. A lateral file is simply a drawer file turned sideways with shelves instead of drawers (see Figure 14.5). Although lateral files make more efficient use of office space by allowing more records to be stored, they still consume a significant amount of room. A few mechanically driven paper filing systems, such as conveyers and motorized shelf files, allow an operator to sit at a control panel and retrieve records. Nevertheless, most paper filing systems are not automated at all and must be accessed manually by someone finding and physically retrieving records from drawers or shelves.

Traditional file folders

Film Systems

Film-based record systems have been adopted by many offices primarily because of the space they save. It has been estimated that every day U.S. businesses produce around 600 million pages of computer printouts, 235 million photocopies, and 76 million letters. In addition, at least 400 billion paper documents are stored in over 36 million four-drawer file cabinets. This paper deluge grows by approximately 20 percent every year, doubling the total volume of stored information every four years.

Figure 14.5 Paper File Systems

Many offices still use traditional paper records and storage systems such as this lateral file.

Microform documents

Micrographics help cope with this information overload in many offices. Basically, micrographics is the process of photographing, reducing, and recording paper documents and computer-generated output on **microforms,** or film such as microfilm and microfiche that can hold both text and graphics (see Figure 14.6). Many micrographic systems also include computer-assisted retrieval (CAR) mechanisms, which we first introduced in Chapter 4. Traditional film media, such as

Figure 14.6   Microforms

Microfilm and microfiche are the two most common types of microforms. They offer an alternative means for storing large quantities of information.

microfilm and microfiche, can reduce the size of reproduced documents 18 to 48 times, storing hundreds of images on the same film. **Ultrafiche,** a more compact form of microfiche, can reduce documents to less than 1/90th their original size and store thousands of images per film. Other types of microforms include film cartridges and aperture cards.

We briefly described the devices used in the production of computer output microfilm in Chapter 5. Other basic types of micrographics devices include microform recorders, microform retrievers, and microform readers. *Microform recorders* resemble copying machines, except that they produce tiny microform replicas instead of full-sized paper copies. Source pages are fed in, photographically reduced, and developed to form microimages on film. *Microform retrievers* locate and fetch desired images from stored microforms through the application of computer-assisted retrieval (CAR) techniques. Finally, *microform readers* magnify microform documents and project them onto display screens so that they can be easily viewed. Some readers can produce black on white, plain-paper copies of the screen from either positive or negative film images.

As we said, the main advantage to using micrographics is the space saved. With computer-assisted retrieval techniques, however, a micrographic system becomes much easier and more efficient to access. Access to any document is facilitated by an on-line index maintained by a microcomputer, minicomputer, or sometimes even a mainframe. The retrieval software in a CAR system typically allows complex searches based on combinations of criteria. For example, you could retrieve a letter that was written on a certain date to a particular person, all documents about a particular subject, or all correspondence from one particular person to another. The search process is usually interactive, allowing the user to narrow or broaden the query based on the computer's responses.

The use of micrographics can solve a significant problem in many offices, namely where to store large masses of paper documents. By replacing some of that paper and thereby greatly reducing the space required for storage, microforms provide a cost-effective means for keeping long-term or very voluminous records. Whether used alone or in conjunction with other office equipment, micrographic devices can significantly increase the productivity of information processing in the office.

Digital Systems

Throughout much of this book we have discussed digital computer storage and retrieval of all kinds of data and information. Now that microcomputers are relatively inexpensive, most offices keep some, if not most, of their records in the form of computer files. Hard disks are the most popular digital media for on-line storage. Floppy disks are employed for both on-line and archival storage. Magnetic tape is widely used as an inexpensive media for storing large quantities of off-line, archived data and information. Finally, optical disks such as CD-ROMs and WORMs (see Chapter 5) are gaining in popularity as inexpensive media for storing both on-line and archived records (see Figure 14.7). These storage devices, in conjunction with powerful software such as data base management systems, greatly increase the efficiency and reduce the costs of office records management.

Computer files

Figure 14.7   Computer-Assisted Retrieval
A CAR system such as this one is a very effective way to access huge stores of digitized documents that are stored on optical disks.

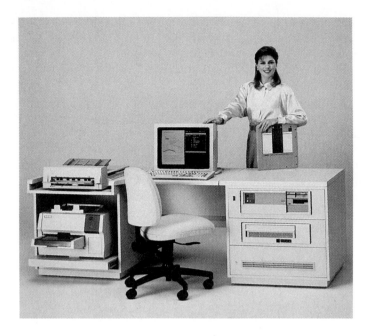

WORD PROCESSING

The cornerstone of office automation

All kinds of data processing are performed in offices. Office automation, however, is most closely associated with word processing. In fact, you might say that word processing is the cornerstone of office automation. In Chapter 9 we saw that word processing is essentially the application of computer technology to the input, editing, merging, storing, formatting, and printing of text. It evolved as a means to overcome the limitations associated with conventional typing. A *word processor* (the computer hardware and/or software) lets the user insert, delete, edit, rearrange, format, and merge textual material until a document appears exactly as it should. At that point, the document is ready to be stored, printed, copied, and distributed. In addition, stored text can be easily revised. Most word-processing systems can also do mail-merge (to produce personalized form letters), perform simple computations, check spelling, incorporate graphics, and print in a wide range of character fonts, styles, and sizes.

The Problem with Conventional Typing

As we mentioned at the start of this chapter, the introduction of the typewriter significantly affected the nature and productivity of office work. For most of this century, the typewritten document has been the primary vehicle of business communication. Yet, despite the typewriter's importance, analysts have long recognized that conventional typing has several inherent shortcomings:

- Repetitive text—such as the contents of form letters, report headings, standard contracts, and similar "boilerplate" material—must be retyped over and over to produce multiple originals. Such retyping is time-consuming and it carries with it the potential for introducing new errors each time and thus the necessity of proofreading each duplicate document.

- Even the most highly skilled typists make some keystroking errors. The usual correction methods (erasing, "whiting-out", or starting over) interrupt the typist, take time and may deface the document.

- Minor revisions or simple format changes often require retyping an entire document. Many documents—such as technical reports, proposals, and legal briefs—must be revised routinely as a result of content changes and/or rearrangements. Again, each time a document is retyped, the possibility exists for entering errors in portions that were initially typed correctly.

These shortcomings contribute to degraded work, low clerical productivity, and increased costs for document production. The major advantage of word processing as compared to conventional typing is that the operator doesn't have to retype corrected documents. Errors can be detected and easily corrected before documents are printed. Finished documents can be stored, and as many identical copies made as needed. If modifications are necessary, the entire document need not be retyped; instead, the stored text can be readily retrieved, altered, and reprinted.

Constant retyping and errors

A Brief History of Word Processing

Word processing evolved as a means to facilitate the input, editing, merging, storing, formatting, and printing of text, and to overcome the limitations associated with conventional typing.

In the early 1960s, automatic typewriters such as the Friden Flexowriter and the American Autotypist simplified the task of repetitious typing by storing keystrokes on punched paper tape that could be played back to create multiple typewritten originals. The era of word processing, however, actually began in 1964 with the introduction of IBM's Magnetic Tape Selectric Typewriter (MT/ST). This device, the first of its kind, recorded keystrokes simultaneously on paper and on an easily removable magnetic tape. Besides automatically producing typewritten copies of stored documents, the MT/ST made it easy for typists to correct errors and make changes in text. Although it seems crude by today's standards, the MT/ST set the stage for the use of computer technology and magnetic storage media in automated word processing.

From typewriters to computers

The next major development came with the introduction of CRT display screens, which allow operators to see and edit what they enter before it is printed on paper. As word processing became a common office practice, computer-based systems involving microcomputers, minicomputers, and mainframes were developed. Powerful and flexible user-friendly word-processing software packages (described in Chapter 9) became an important element in the continuing microcomputer revolution. Today, several categories of word processors are in widespread use.

Types of Word Processors

In Chapter 9, we covered the major functions and capabilities of word-processing software for microcomputers. Microcomputers, however, are not the only type of word processors used in today's offices. Although some of the categories overlap, most word-processing systems can be classified as one of four basic types: electronic typewriters, dedicated systems, microcomputer systems, and shared systems.

Electronic typewriters, dedicated systems, microcomputer systems, and shared systems

Figure 14.8 An Electronic Typewriter
The electronic typewriter is an electric typewriter with an embedded microprocessor.
Most models have at least a one-line display
screen, and some can store text on magnetic tapes, cards, or disks.

Electronic Typewriters

An **electronic typewriter** is essentially a typewriter with a microprocessor inside
(see Figure 14.8). More advanced than ordinary electric typewriters, these machines offer many features associated with word processing. Electronic typewriters
allow users to correct, insert, and delete words before the text is committed to
paper. Their keyboards usually include special keys to center titles, line up margins,
print in boldface and italics, and underscore words. Various printing mechanisms
are used, including dot-matrix, daisy-wheel, and removable-ball type elements.
Many companies offer interchangeable print elements that can be purchased to
equip their electronic typewriters with different typefaces.

Electronic typewriters are really very specialized computers. They have a CPU
(the microprocessor), as well as memory (ROM and RAM). Many electronic typewriters also have secondary storage in the form of magnetic tapes, cards, or disks.
Each tape, card, or disk can hold one or more pages of text which can be retrieved
to make updates or print additional copies. Most electronic typewriters have a
liquid crystal display (LCD) or light-emitting diode (LED) screen similar to those
found on calculators. Some models have a small screen that can display only a
portion of one line of text; other models are equipped with a larger screen that can
hold several complete lines of text. A few electronic typewriters can be equipped
with small, auxiliary CRT screens as well. Many of today's electronic typewriters
even have built-in dictionaries to detect and correct misspelled words automatically.

Electronic typewriters are well suited to repetitive tasks that don't require extensive editing and revision. These machines are particularly useful to good touch-
typists, who find that the advanced features can significantly speed up their work.
Electronic typewriters are generally more powerful and more reliable, yet they
often cost no more than electric typewriters. For these reasons, electronic typewriters have replaced electric typewriters in many organizations.

Dedicated Systems

A **dedicated word processor** is a microcomputer system expressly designed for
and solely devoted to the preparation, storage, and printing of documents. Out-
wardly, these dedicated systems are similar to ordinary microcomputers (see Figure
14.9). They typically include a system unit, CRT display, keyboard, floppy disk

Figure 14.9 A Dedicated Word Processor
The dedicated word processor is a specialized microcomputer system with a CRT display, a keyboard, one or two floppy disk drives, and a printer. Its sole function is word processing.

drives, and a letter-quality printer. Some models may also include a hard disk, and a few have built-in modems or circuit cards that allow them to communicate with other computers and word processors. The display screen, however, is often tall enough to present an entire 66-line page of text. Furthermore, the keyboard may include a number of special-purpose keys for common word-processing functions.

Dedicated word processors are single-user systems primarily designed for medium to large offices. They run on built-in word-processing software which usually cannot be replaced or supplemented by other application programs. Thus, unlike general-purpose microcomputers, dedicated word processors cannot run software such as spreadsheet programs and data base management packages. As complete systems designed purely for effective word processing, dedicated word processors are powerful, fast, and easy for office personnel to use. Nevertheless, dedicated systems have been steadily declining in popularity, chiefly due to our next category of word processors.

Microcomputer Systems

By far the most popular type of word processor is a general-purpose microcomputer system running a word-processing application program such as WordStar, WordPerfect, or Microsoft Word. Figure 14.10 illustrates a typical microcomputer system. Although an ordinary microcomputer may not be as efficient or quite as easy to use as a dedicated word processor, most people would rather have a

Figure 14.10   The Microcomputer as Word Processor

Any general-purpose microcomputer system becomes a word processor when it's running a word-processing application package.

computer that can be used to run other software, too. In many cases, microcomputer systems are also less expensive than dedicated word-processing systems.

Today's microcomputers offer sharp displays and well-designed keyboards. A wide variety of word-processing packages on the market ranges from the very simple to the very sophisticated. Much of this software is easy-to-learn and easy-to-use. Furthermore, microcomputers can be equipped with high-quality input and output devices, such as full-page displays, OCR and graphics scanners, and laser printers. With devices such as these, the combination of word processing, graphics, and desktop publishing software can be used to create near typeset-quality printed materials at a relatively low cost. So, microcomputer word-processing systems are potentially much more versatile and powerful than dedicated word processors.

Shared Systems

Word processing can also be done on larger multi-user minicomputers and mainframes. These systems are often called **shared word processors** (or **clustered word processors**) because they serve several users at once on a time-sharing basis (see Figure 14.11). Since large computers are already used in many offices and businesses for processing all kinds of data, it's often economical to run word-processing packages on existing facilities. The same software can be used by different people working at different computer terminals. Expensive peripheral devices such as scanners and laser printers can also be shared by many users.

Shared word processors, however, are now perhaps the least common of all types of word processors. In one sense, word processing "wastes" the time of extremely expensive large computers. These powerful machines are better suited to tasks involving complex calculations on large sets of data, which cannot be done on smaller computers in a reasonable amount of time. Dedicated systems and microcomputer systems are generally much easier to use for word processing than large computers. Most organizations, even those that already own big computers, have been purchasing microcomputers in large numbers. Given the popularity of microcomputer word processors, it's likely that shared systems will gradually become even less common.

Figure 14.11 Shared Word Processors
The shared word-processing system utilizes a powerful time-sharing computer, word-processing software, and multiple terminals to serve several users at once.

COMPUTER GRAPHICS

Word processing is one way to convert raw data (words, phrases, and sentences) into information (a finished document). Another way to process data into information involves computer graphics. In Chapter 9 we introduced various graphics application packages that let users create pictures with their computers. There are programs for creating charts, painting pictures, drawing figures, using computer-aided design (CAD), and generating slide shows. All of these types of graphics programs are commonly used in the modern office, but charting and slide show packages are probably the most popular (see Figure 14.12). Quite often, graphics are created for inclusion in text documents. (We'll have more to say about this use

Another way to process data into information

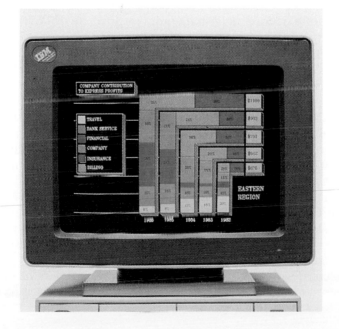

Figure 14.12 Office Graphics
Graphics software is increasingly used in the automated office environment to produce all types of graphs, charts, and drawings.

of graphics shortly, when we discuss desktop publishing.) In addition, graphics programs are frequently used for business presentations at meetings, seminars, and lectures. This method of replicating existing data into a more readily understood and attractive visual format has become extremely helpful in today's office. By allowing users to create their own graphs, charts, figures, and other visual aids, such business presentation software provides a cost-effective way to increase the impact of almost any message. Furthermore, computer graphics give the user increased control over the final product and usually take less time to prepare than having an outside artist do the work.

DESKTOP PUBLISHING

As we said previously, one of the major office functions is the replication of information. **Reprographics** is one type of replication that involves the reproduction of documents at or near full size. The primary goal of reprographics is the generation of additional hard copies of a document for physical distribution. There are several methods of preparing the original, or *master document*, from which the copies are to be made. In some cases, the master document can simply be typed or created with a word processor and printed with a letter-quality printer. This produces rather crude results. Today, most documents to be widely distributed are prepared with more sophisticated desktop publishing or typesetting methods. Once the master document has been prepared, multiple copies are usually made through photocopying, computer printing, or offset printing.

A combination of word processing and graphics

In Chapter 9 we said that **desktop publishing** combines word processing and graphics capabilities to produce high-quality documents with a laser printer. At least half of the 25,000 commercial, trade, and professional newsletters in the U.S. are produced with desktop publishing systems, and there are at least 200,000 laser printers being used for desktop publishing by corporations and government agencies across the country. Few advances in computer technology have enchanted users, especially office workers, like the recent phenomenon of desktop publishing. Perhaps it's because desktop publishing promises total control over a document's appearance. Who needs professional typesetters and graphic artists? You can write and edit your own text, draw figures, incorporate photos, design page layouts, and print completed documents on a high-resolution laser printer. Compared to traditional typesetting and printing, desktop publishing is flexible, quick, and inexpensive.

Unfortunately, desktop publishing is also not quite as wonderful as it sounds. First, a substantial hardware investment is necessary. Although a $5,000 to $10,000 microcomputer system is much less expensive than full-fledged typesetting equipment, the price tag is still too high for many potential users. Desktop publishing packages do offer a great deal of flexibility in document design, but you must first learn to use the software, a time-consuming process. Even if you have the hardware and software for desktop publishing, attractive results are not guaranteed. It also takes talent and skill to design and lay out pages that look good. Professional typesetters and graphic artists can still produce better results than most desktop publishers.

Nevertheless, desktop publishing does fill a very real need in the modern office. There is a huge market for hardware and software that can produce documents that look better than typewritten pages, even if they're not quite as good as true typeset printing. DataQuest, a San Jose, California market research firm, estimates that 400,000 desktop publishing systems will be sold in 1990 alone.

Components of a Desktop Publishing System

Desktop publishing generally requires a combination of fairly sophisticated hardware and software components. Figure 14.13 shows a typical system, which includes:

Microcomputer, graphics display, mouse, laser printer, scanner, word-processing software, graphics software, page layout software

- *A powerful microcomputer.*   Since desktop publishing involves manipulating both text and graphics on the display screen at the same time, you need a computer with a fast, powerful microprocessor and plenty of primary memory and secondary storage, such as high-end Apple Macintoshes and IBM Personal System/2 models.

- *Graphics display.*   True desktop publishing is impossible without a high-resolution graphics display adapter and monitor. Color capability is not really essential, at least not yet, since very few high-resolution printers can produce quality color output. Although desktop publishing often takes place on small monitors, large-screen models that can legibly display one or two full-size pages at once are clearly preferable.

- *A mouse.*   Most desktop publishing systems use a mouse to place text and graphics precisely on each page and to draw simple objects such as lines, boxes, and ovals.

- *Laser printer.*   Although dot-matrix or inkjet printers are sometimes used, the laser printer is by far the predominant hard-copy output device for desktop publishing. At speeds typically at least 6 pages per minute, these printers generally produce monochrome text and graphics at resolutions of at least 300 dots per inch.

Figure 14.13 Desktop Publishing System

This typical desktop publishing system consists of a powerful microcomputer, graphics display, mouse, laser printer, word-processing software, graphics software, and page layout software. Many systems also include an optical scanner (not shown here).

- *A scanner.*   Although a scanner is not strictly necessary, it's a popular option in many desktop publishing systems for reading in existing photographs and line drawings.

- *Word-processing software.*   A word-processing package is essential for entering and editing the text of a document to be produced with a desktop publishing system. High-end word-processing packages, such as WordPerfect, often include the ability to incorporate graphics and other page layout features.

- *Graphics software.*   One of the major reasons for using a desktop publishing system is to include drawings, diagrams, charts, and photographs in documents. Charting, painting, drawing, and CAD programs can all be used to generate images for desktop publishing.

- *Page layout software.*   A **page layout package** is neither a word processor nor a graphics package, but it lets you integrate the products of both packages into a single document. Separate page layout software may not be necessary for simple documents created with a word-processing package (such as WordPerfect) that includes some page layout features.

Page Layout

The page layout package represents the key to desktop publishing. An accurate visual representation of one or two entire pages is depicted on the screen at once (see Figure 14.14). Unlike many word processors, true desktop publishing systems have a **what-you-see-is-what-you-get (WYSIWYG)** display that closely, if not exactly, presents the appearance of the final printed output on the screen.

Designing the printed output

The page layout package lets you specify the number and width of columns on each page. Text from word-processed documents is placed on a page and can be easily arranged into columns. Empty blocks can be left for figures, and previously created graphics can be placed within these spaces. Text can even be made to "flow" automatically around embedded figures. Most page layout programs also allow you to crop, stretch, or compress graphics to fit within the blank spaces you've reserved.

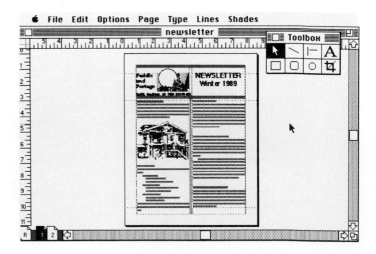

Figure 14.14   Page Layout Software
A page layout package, such as PageMaker, lets you combine text and graphics in the same document. This screen shows PageMaker being used to design a newsletter.

Headings, labels, and captions can be added in any number of character fonts, styles, and sizes. Imported text can also be reformatted and rearranged from within the page layout program. *Rules* can be placed to separate columns and offset blocks of text. These dividing lines can be drawn anywhere on a page in a number of different styles and thicknesses. Most page layout programs can also add boxes, ovals, shaded backgrounds, and reversed (white on black) text.

Finally, page layout programs are generally not limited to standard letter or legal size paper. You can work with documents of almost any size—from small $2 \times 3\frac{1}{2}$-inch business cards to large 17×22-inch newspaper pages. Once the pages have been designed, they can be sent directly to the printer from within the page layout program. Figure 14.15 shows a typical product of desktop publishing, a laser-printed newsletter.

Figure 14.15   Laser-Printed Newsletter

This shows a typical product of desktop publishing: a laser-printed newsletter.

Trips

This fall we took a trip into the Cherry Lake area for some lake trout fishing. We had our usual quota of rain, but did enjoy two beautiful crisp autumn days. Mornings we awoke to clear, deep blue skies with heavy, white steam rising from Cherry Lake. It was almost like being in a shaving commercial. On shore

Paddle and Portage

Canoe Outfitters

Box 555, Grand Marais, MN 55604 (218) 555-1234

NEWSLETTER
Winter 1989

...st year ever, we want to thank all ...endship and patronage and wish ...rosperous New Year. We look ...ou this spring, summer, or fall.

...nson, owners / operators ...Canoe Outfitters

Bulk Rate
Permit 555
Grand Marais, MN

New Outfitting Post

This winter we completed our new outfitting facility. It will house our office, staff kitchen, retail sales, and equipment storage area. Located close to the lake for easy access, this new building will give us the room we need to help serve you better.

Sport Shows

This year we will be attending the following sport shows:

    Jan 23 — Feb 1
        Chicagoland Show,
        O'Hare Exposition Center
    Feb 14 — Feb 22
        Greater Northwest Sport Show,
        Minneapolis Auditorium
    Mar 13 — Mar 22
        Milwaukee Sentinel Sport Show,
        MECCA Building

If you can, stop by and say "Hi." Remember our SPECIAL BONUS RATES for sport show reservations.

New Regulations

Only Ontario's Quetico Provincial Park has changed regulations for this season. Reservations for Quetico camping permits will be accepted no sooner than January 19. Written reservations may be made 21 days in advance of trip departure. Phone reservations may be made from 21 days prior to and up to the date of departure. As always, we will handle all permit reservations for our guests.

Equipment Improvements

Our most exciting equipment addition this year is a new Super-Lite Beaver canoe. It weighs, believe it or not, slightly over 40 pounds. We feel this new 17-foot Beaver canoe is ideal for wilderness tripping. It's stable, safe, and much easier to paddle and portage.

Last year we field tested several nylon packs and found one in particular that offered several advantages. Lighter and dryer than canvas Duluth packs, we will be incorporating these new nylon packs into our equipment line beginning this year. The Super Lite Beaver canoes and nylon packs will be available on a first-come, first-serve basis.

Trail Food Improvements

We have replaced the Ham and Potatoes with Meatballs and Gravy, the Beef Stromboli with Chicken Stew 'N Dumplings, and the Buttermilk Pancakes with Blueberry Pancakes. These are all taste improvements, not cost savings, so our Trail Food will be even better this year.

PageMaker and PostScript

In July of 1985, Aldus Corporation released a page layout program called PageMaker for the Apple Macintosh and LaserWriter printer (see Figure 14.14). Many experts consider this to be the real birth of desktop publishing. Available since 1987 for IBM and IBM-compatible microcomputers, more than twice as many copies of PageMaker have been sold than any of its competitors. This software truly sets the standard for page layout features, including simple pull-down menus, WYSIWYG page displays, the ability to incorporate text and graphics from many other programs, and support for popular high-resolution laser printers and some typesetters.

One of the attributes that gives PageMaker its power is its use of the PostScript page description language. In Chapter 4, we said that PostScript is a language used by printers that specifies what a page should look like. To be more precise, a **page description language** is a specialized computer programming language for defining the size, format, and position of text and graphic elements on a printed page. In other words, a page description language tells a printer how to reproduce a page on paper. PostScript, developed and licensed by Adobe Systems, is the most popular page description language used in desktop publishing systems. It's encoded into ROM chips inside several popular laser printers, including the Apple LaserWriter IINT and IBM's Personal Pageprinter. Starting at around $4,000, PostScript printers are somewhat expensive, but they include many fonts and provide a great deal of flexibility in specifying the size, shape, and orientation of printed objects. Since PostScript is a device-independent language, it is possible to design a document on one system and then print it on another system at higher resolution. For example, you can rough out a document with an Apple Macintosh and print a draft at 300 dots per inch on a LaserWriter IINT. When you are finished editing and making changes, you can produce the final version with a PostScript typesetter, such as the Allied Linotype Linotronic 100, at a resolution of at least 1270 dots per inch.

TYPESETTING

Most materials published for wide distribution, such as magazines and books, are created by **typesetting.** This process produces a master document for printing that achieves very high-quality, proportionally-spaced results. Years ago, documents to be printed were literally set in *type*—pieces of wood or metal each with a raised character in reverse on top. The type was composed into printing plates that were then inked and pressed against paper to make pages. Nowadays, the vast majority of typeset materials are created with **photocomposition** or **phototypesetting** equipment (see Figure 14.16). This equipment takes keyboarded text and digitized images and uses a photographic process to produce a master document on film or photosensitive paper. This film or paper is then developed and made into photographic plates for photocopying or offset printing. Typesetting results in documents printed at a resolution of at least 1270 dots per inch; many phototypesetting machines can easily achieve resolutions more than twice as sharp as this. Even under a powerful magnifying glass, it's difficult to see the individual dots that make up such high-resolution print.

Typesetting equipment was once much too expensive for most offices or businesses. Most materials to be typeset were sent out to professional printing shops.

Figure 14.16 A Phototypesetting Machine
A phototypesetting machine such as this accepts input text and graphics to produce a master document on film or repro paper, which can then be made into printing plates from which very attractive, high-quality documents can be reproduced.

Now, the distinction between desktop publishing and phototypesetting has blurred. For example, a microcomputer such as an IBM Personal System/2 Model 50 or an Apple Macintosh SE can produce page layouts using PageMaker. Since PageMaker produces output in the PostScript page description language, the page layouts can be fed into any one of several popular low-end PostScript typesetters, such as the Allied Linotype Linotronic 100, which achieves 1270 dots per inch and costs around $35,000. This typesetter produces pages on *repro paper* (sort of like high-contrast matte photographic paper) which is then photocopied or used to make plates for offset printing. While a laser printer produces copy directly on ordinary paper, a phototypesetter produces copy on film or repro paper.

COPYING AND PRINTING

For the most part, desktop publishing and typesetting are techniques used to create master documents that must be reproduced in some fashion before they can be widely distributed. There are two primary ways in which documents are reproduced by offices: photocopying and offset printing.

Reproducing the master document

Photocopying

Plain-paper copiers are now almost universal office equipment. At one end of the spectrum are the so-called *personal copiers* that can be purchased for as little as $500 (see Figure 14.17) and are generally used to make fewer than 3,000 copies per month. They are to high-volume copy machines what microcomputers are to mainframes—so small, so inexpensive, so convenient, and so reliable that they make it possible to have a copier on practically every desk.

Inexpensive, plain-paper reproduction

In mid-range are a relatively new breed of copiers that include either a laser printer or a facsimile machine in the same box and cost between $5,000 and $7,000. The copier/printer machines can be connected to a microcomputer and

Figure 14.17   Personal Copier
Inexpensive, small, reliable, and mainte-
nance-free personal copiers such as this one
have become extremely common in all kinds
of offices.

used for desktop publishing as well as for routine office copying. Copier/facsimile
machines can transmit and receive documents over the phone in addition to copying documents.

At the high end of the spectrum are large, high-volume copy machines. These
fast, powerful, and expensive machines, some of which can routinely produce
100,000 copies a month, incorporate many advanced features. For example, many
high-end copy machines have **electronic image editing** capabilities, which
allow you to modify copies instead of simply producing exact duplicates. Using an
electronic pen and tablet attached with a cable to the copier, you can delete or
rearrange portions of the original to create a new version. Certain areas can be
reduced or enlarged for emphasis while the rest of the original is left intact. Some
models can even print portions of a document in reverse (white on black) or in a
second color. Such **intelligent copiers** have embedded microprocessors that
allow them to be connected to computers as well as to be used as printers. Although they are still quite expensive (most are in the $30,000 to $60,000 range),
full-color copy machines are also available and are becoming increasingly popular.

Offset Printing

*High-quality, high-volume
reproduction*

Although photocopiers remain the most common reprographic machines, offset
equipment is often used for very high-volume printing. An **offset printer** (see
Figure 14.18) uses paper or metal plates to produce copies. The plates are usually
produced with a phototypesetting machine from the original master document. A
paper plate offset printer, sometimes called a *duplicator* or a *fast copier*, produces
high-quality results and is economical for relatively small runs of fewer than 2,500
copies. Metal plate offset printers are typically used for making many thousands of
copies because, unlike paper plates, metal plates are very durable and can be reused. Consequently, the cost per copy on very large runs will be quite low. Furthermore, offset printers can be extremely fast. There are models, for example, that can
print, sort, and collate 25,000 copies per hour. Since such equipment is quite ex-

Figure 14.18 Offset Printer
An offset printer uses paper or metal plates from a typesetter to produce high volume, high-quality copies.

pensive, most small offices simply send out documents for offset printing. Large companies and organizations often have their own print shops that are equipped with offset printers.

OFFICE COMMUNICATIONS

Information has little value if it isn't transmitted to those who have a use for it. The information that's generated, gathered, and analyzed in an office must also be distributed to various people, both inside and outside the organization. The methods and technologies of office communications are evolving rapidly. Although handwritten memos, intercoms, ordinary telephones, and messengers remain in use, a whole array of more advanced means of communication, including electronic mail, voice mail, facsimile transmission, local area networks, and remote conferencing, is now routinely offered in many of today's offices.

Distributing information

Electronic Mail

Electronic mail (or *E-mail*) systems are a fast, reliable, distance-independent means of moving information from one place to another. Relying on computers and telecommunications channels (see Chapter 6), they can transmit messages that would otherwise be sent by telephone call, interoffice memo, or the postal service. Unlike many other forms of communication, electronic mail automatically creates a permanent computer record of each transaction.

The cost of electronic mail systems has been steadily decreasing, and their popularity in offices has been increasing. Both trends are likely to continue. A recent study by Venture Development Corporation, a Wellesley, Massachusetts market research firm, forecasts that over 1.7 million electronic mail systems will be installed in offices by 1990.

The proliferation of these systems may be due to their superiority in certain respects over traditional channels for business communication. The postal service can be slow, letters are sometimes lost, and the mail usually takes longer the farther apart two places are. Telephone calls require both sender and receiver to be on the line at the same time or someone to take a message. Handwritten memos depend on some internal distribution process and are easily lost in the shuffle of paper. Electronic mail avoids all of these drawbacks.

Sending messages between computer users

An electronic mail system allows an authorized user to send a typed message to a specified recipient on the first try, at any time of the day or night. The message is held in the recipient's private *mailbox* (a sort of electronic in-basket) to be reviewed at his or her convenience. When users first join the system they receive a password to ensure that access is limited to authorized personnel. Messages can be sent to one person or to a group of people, who may or may not be using the computer system at the moment.

Terminals or microcomputers used for electronic mail are usually placed right on the desks of office personnel. The recipient can view incoming mail items on the display screen or print them out. After reviewing messages, the recipient can acknowledge their receipt, reply to them, store them for later action, forward them to others, or simply delete them. Messages can usually be sent and received from any remote terminal or from portable microcomputers. Electronic mail can be implemented on almost any computer system or network with multiple users. Many time-sharing computer systems have internal electronic mail facilities just for their own users. Many local area networks, which we discuss shortly, also have their own electronic mail facilities.

Some information services (such as CompuServe and The Source) provide electronic mail functions to widely distributed users of different computer systems. In addition, there are specialized services, such as MCI Mail, primarily devoted to

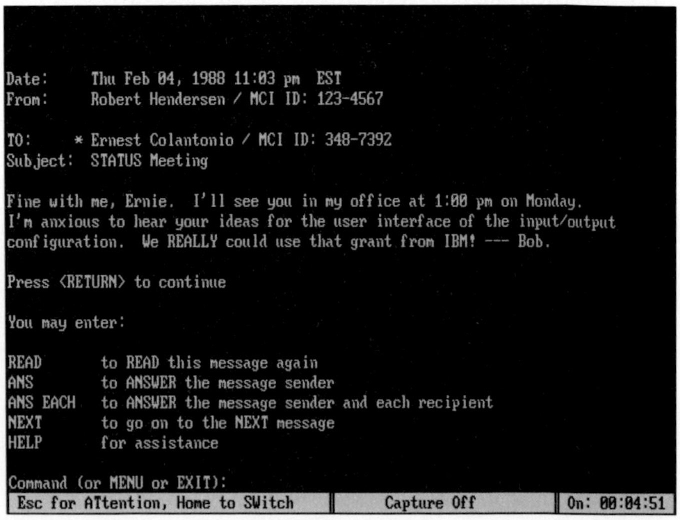

Figure 14.19 Electronic Mail

Electronic mail has emerged as an extremely popular means of office communication. This screen shows a session with MCI Mail, a public electronic mail service with over 140,000 subscribers.

electronic mail (see Figure 14.19). These companies offer public electronic mail services anywhere in the world to anyone who has a microcomputer or terminal and a modem and is willing to subscribe. Subscribers exchange messages by calling a central computer system. Many of these services also offer ways to print messages on paper and send them to nonsubscribers via regular mail, overnight mail, same-day mail, or telegram. Some can even print letters on registered letterhead stationery with reproduced signatures.

Voice Mail

Voice mail, sometimes called *voice store and forward*, is an electronic message system somewhat similar to electronic mail, except that the messages are vocal ones. Since most people find it easier to give a message verbally rather than to type it out, voice mail has an inherent advantage over electronic mail, at least from many users' standpoint. Furthermore, all the user needs for voice mail is an ordinary Touch-Tone telephone. Having or knowing how to use a microcomputer or terminal is not required. Current voice mail systems are designed to be easy to use, with spoken prompts that help users take full advantage of the features provided.

Recorded oral messages

The key to a voice mail system is a central computer that digitizes voice messages and stores them as disk files that can be copied, transmitted, and deleted. Likewise, this computer can convert stored or transmitted voice mail files back into vocal messages. Finally, the voice mail computer can recognize and respond to the telephone Touch-Tones used to command the system.

Instead of installing their own systems, many offices use an established voice mail service, such as the one offered by Voicemail International of Cupertino, California. Each subscriber to this particular service, which costs $20 per month and $0.50 per minute of connect time, is assigned a voice mailbox number and a personal identification number. To access the system, you dial the Voicemail 800 access number from a Touch-Tone phone. A pleasant voice prompts you to enter your "Identification number, please." Once you've entered your seven-digit personal identification number on the Touch-Tone telephone keypad, the Voicemail system automatically checks to see if you have any messages. If messages are waiting, you can listen to them simply by pressing the 8 button on your phone.

To send a message, you enter the intended recipient's mailbox number instead of your own identification number in response to the initial prompt. The system responds by identifying the name of the person associated with that mailbox, just to confirm that you've reached the correct mailbox. At that point, you can press the 1 button and begin talking. Pressing the 1 button again completes the message and sends it to the appropriate mailbox.

Messages are stored digitally on a magnetic disk until they are retrieved and replayed by the recipient. In fact, voice mail systems can do more than just record and replay messages on demand. Since they're computer-based and store messages in digital form, voice mail systems give users capabilities not found on basic telephone-answering machines. For example, a user can record a single message and distribute it to any number of recipients, request that the system confirm delivery to each recipient, and alert recipients if the message is urgent. Like electronic mail, voice mail can be sent from remote locations at any time of the day or night.

On the receiving end, users of a voice mail system can employ an ordinary Touch-Tone telephone to find out how many messages they have waiting and if any have been tagged as urgent. Routine messages can be held and listened to later;

once messages have been heard, they can be saved or discarded as desired. Messages can even be forwarded to others, with or without appended commentary.

Most voice mail users find that it is a sensible, practical office tool. It provides a more efficient method of communication than ordinary phone calls and produces tangible benefits. Furthermore, voice mail is typically easy to use and increases office productivity by eliminating "telephone tag."

Facsimile Transmission

Sending text and graphics over the phone

Facsimile transmission (or **fax**) is a way to send a copy of almost any kind of document over ordinary telephone lines. Basically, it involves sliding a sheet of paper into one fax machine and having a black and white duplicate emerge from another fax machine almost anywhere in the world in 40 seconds or less. Printed text, handwritten pages, pictures, maps, charts, and photographs can all be sent with a fax machine. Each page is optically scanned, converted into electronic signals, transmitted over telephone lines, and reproduced at a remote location by the receiving fax machine.

The invention of the facsimile machine can be traced back to Alexander Bain, who first developed a technique for sending crude images over telegraph lines in 1842. However, only after the telephone became popular did facsimile transmission really get its start. By 1965, more than 40,000 Bell Telephone facsimile machines had been installed. Today, much more sophisticated facsimile devices apply computer, copier, and communications technology to perform high-quality, high-speed, reliable image reproduction. Once considered too large and too expensive for most offices, many contemporary fax machines are not much bigger than telephone answering machines and can be purchased for less than $1,000. As a result, U.S. sales of fax machines are expected to top 400,000 units a year by 1990, pushing the industry's annual revenues to $1 billion. If prices continue to fall, fax machines could eventually become as common as microcomputers.

A fax machine is really part desktop copier and part telephone (see Figure 14.20). At one end, a document is fed into the machine and the built-in telephone is used to dial the number of the receiving fax machine. When the connection is made, the sending fax optically scans the document. As the scanner sweeps down the page, both text and graphics are converted into signals that are transmitted over the phone line. The receiving fax machine essentially reverses the process, ejecting a black and white duplicate of the original transmitted document.

Recently, a new type of facsimile machine has emerged as an alternative to this traditional arrangement. **PC fax** (personal computer facsimile) combines the capabilities of a microcomputer with the document transmission capabilities of ordinary fax machines. Text files and on-screen graphics are converted to fax format, then are compressed and transmitted over the phone line with a **fax board.** This circuit board fits into a microcomputer's expansion slot and acts as a specialized high-speed modem. At the other end of the line, an ordinary fax machine or another PC fax system captures the transmission. If the receiving machine is an ordinary fax, the document will be reproduced directly on paper. However, if the receiving machine is a PC fax, the document will appear displayed on the microcomputer display screen. It can then be stored in a disk file or sent to a dot-matrix or laser printer.

With a scanner for input and a printer for output, a microcomputer equipped with a fax board can substitute for a stand-alone fax machine. Although some PC

Figure 14.20   Fax Machine
A small, low-cost facsimile machine is a quick, inexpensive way to send almost any kind of document over the phone to another fax machine anywhere in the world.

fax boards are less expensive than stand-alone fax machines, a truly versatile microcomputer fax system will also require the added cost of a scanner and a printer. Furthermore, current PC fax systems are significantly more complex to operate than ordinary fax machines. The advantage to PC fax, however, is that text or graphics documents created on microcomputer can be sent directly to other fax machines without being printed first. In addition, if the receiving machine is a PC fax equipped with a laser printer, the resulting document will most likely be of higher quality.

The advantages of all fax machines are speed and cost. While Federal Express charges $14.00 to send an overnight letter, a fax machine can send the same letter in less than a minute for less than 50 cents. Fax machines now pose a serious threat to the likes of Federal Express and Western Union and could make telex messages and telegrams obsolete.

Local Area Networks

A key ingredient of office automation is the ability to communicate easily relevant data and information to every worker who needs it. Local area networks (LANs) have made this possible. In Chapter 6, we saw that a local area network allows individual computers and peripheral equipment to be linked together without employing modems or telephone lines. More and more offices are using LANs to implement private electronic mail systems and to share expensive computer resources, such as laser printers and high-capacity hard disk drives. Networks provide a way for every office worker to access a wide range of sophisticated equipment. Furthermore, a LAN can be expanded via a **gateway** to communicate with other networks in remote locations. In this sense, a gateway functions as a hardware and software system that allows two different networks to be connected together. The use of gateways can expand LANs into *WANs* (wide area networks) and even *global networks*.

Linking office equipment

LANs suit the office environment well. Since a local area network can be completely owned and operated by a single organization, it can help reduce the dependence on and the expense associated with an outside service like the telephone company. Furthermore, LANs are designed to operate within the confines of a relatively small geographic area, such as a single building or a closely grouped series of buildings. They allow very high rates of data transmission, are relatively inexpensive to install and maintain, and provide an effective interconnection for a large number of computers and computer-based devices.

Remote Conferencing

Organizations often have problems getting key members together for important conferences. Full work schedules, travel costs, and conflicting outside appointments make face-to-face meetings difficult to arrange for many managers. Computer conferencing and teleconferencing have recently emerged as viable alternatives to meeting in person. Usually easy to arrange on short notice once the systems are in place, computer conferences and teleconferences are particularly useful for crisis situations and the coordination of large and decentralized projects and in fast-moving markets and places that are isolated or difficult to reach through travel.

Computer Conferencing

On-line meetings

As we learned in Chapter 6, computer conferencing refers to the use of distributed computers and data communications networks to conduct on-line discussions among persons in remote locations. The participants don't even have to be on-line at the same time. Messages can be stored and displayed later. Because everyone doesn't have to participate at once, there's usually time to research and carefully prepare responses before they are entered on the system. Computer conferencing removes barriers of time and geography, allowing individuals to work at their own pace without the interruptions and digressions characteristic of conventional meetings.

Computer conferencing is frequently used to facilitate communication among groups of scattered individuals who must work together, such as researchers, scientists, and engineers working jointly on projects, editors and reviewers working on journals and books, and committee members drafting proposals.

Computer conferencing is also valuable for employees working at home (or telecommuting, introduced in Chapter 6). With access to computer conferencing facilities, some employees are able to work just as well at home as at an office. Many job activities can be performed practically anywhere on remote terminals or portable microcomputers. Computer conferences can link distributed workers so they can report on their progress or on problems they're encountering. Although it's similar in many ways to the use of electronic mail, telecommuting via computer conferencing is production-oriented rather than communication-oriented. Its purpose is to perform a particular job rather than to transmit routine messages.

Teleconferencing

Audio and video meetings

The term **teleconferencing** usually applies to audio and video meetings held by electronically linking geographically dispersed participants. This communication technique has been used successfully by such well-known organizations as IBM, AT&T, the Bank of America, and NASA. Teleconferencing is becoming a widespread business tool; at least 80% of the Fortune 500 companies have plans for the installation of some sort of teleconferencing system.

Audioconferencing in its simplest form is the conference call option offered by the telephone company by which several people in different places can talk to one another on the phone. More complex systems require special conference rooms equipped with microphones and loudspeakers. Although audioconferencing is quite economical and convenient, the lack of face-to-face interaction and the inability to transmit visual images such as graphs, charts, drawings, or photos limit its appeal and usefulness.

Videoconferencing involves holding a meeting using freeze-frame or full-motion color pictures over two-way, closed-circuit television (see Figure 14.21). It provides the face-to-face, visual interaction that audioconferencing and computer conferencing lack. Videoconferencing, however, requires that the conference rooms be studios equipped with highly sophisticated and expensive video and communications equipment, and sometimes fax machines and electronic chalkboards as well. The cost of today's systems can be as much as $450,000 per conference room in the standard two-room setup. A full-motion color system that links 25 locations by satellite costs around $6 million. Because of the high cost, most small organizations can't afford to have their own videoconferencing studios. To meet this demand, some companies such as AT&T maintain videoconferencing facilities in larger cities that they rent out by the hour. Many large companies, on the other hand, are finding that it can be worthwhile to install their own systems. According to a University of Wisconsin survey, 1,144 of the 4,400 largest North American companies (more than 25 percent) plan to install videoconferencing facilities on their own premises by 1990. This will result in an annual market of $1.6 billion.

THE OTHER OFFICE: TELECOMMUTING

As we said at the beginning of this chapter, office technology is rapidly breaking down the physical barriers of the modern office. Computer networks link the central office with its branches, and branch offices with each other; they bring on-line

Figure 14.21 Videoconferencing
Videoconferencing involves holding meetings via two-way closed-circuit television and is emerging as an efficient way for large companies to save time and travel costs.

information services and facsimile documents into the office from all over the country. And to a greater and greater extent they connect home and work for hundreds of thousands of people.

Working at home   **Telecommuting,** the practice of doing all or part of one's regular office work at home through a computer/modem link, is an attractive option for some workers, and for some employers, too. For one partner in a large Chicago law firm, telecommuting was the answer to urban burnout. He moved his practice to a small town in neighboring Indiana, where he set up a sophisticated electronic office in constant communication with his firm. He has access to legal data bases; associates and clerks do the usual research and mail it to him electronically rather than dropping it on his desk; and clients who call his old work number are automatically (and unknowingly) connected to his home. Because most of his work can be done over the phone or on the word processor, he commutes into the city only for occasional meetings. His clients can't tell the difference, and his firm has avoided the loss of a valuable partner.

Telecommuting is an option for virtually any professional who does most of his or her work at a keyboard or on the phone. Many workers (mostly women) split their time between telecommuting from home, where they can take care of young children, and the traditional office.

Other workers abandon the downtown office altogether in favor of entrepreneurial activities based in electronic home offices. These are the new small businesses, high-tech mom-and-pop operations, some of which have grown into very large and highly profitable companies run out of the PC in the family den. For example, one businessman moved his publishing company from a 10,000-square-foot building where he employed twenty people, to his home. He and his wife now run five businesses simultaneously, with four computers and eight phone lines keeping them in touch with what has grown into a nationwide publishing operation involving subcontracted writers, editors, artists, distributors, and printers. Retired couples have started second electronic careers from their living rooms; men and women disillusioned with high-pressure jobs have turned to the comfort and quiet of their apartments; home-working parents stuff the children's toys into cabinets in combination play/conference rooms.

Home-workers enjoy the enthusiasm that comes with entrepreneurship, citing a new-found sense of freedom and self-worth, greater control over their lives and career, and sometimes better money. These advantages tend to outweigh the obvious drawback: when you get out of bed in the morning, you're already at work.

A Closer Look

Using WordPerfect

The most common word-processing system consists of a general-purpose microcomputer running a word-processing application package. Simply stated, a word-processing package helps you enter, store, modify, format, copy, and print text. Most contemporary word-processing software goes beyond these basic functions to offer features such as a built-in spelling checker, an on-line thesaurus, and the ability to incorporate graphics in a document. To give you an idea of what it's like to use a modern word-processing program, let's create a simple report about the U.S. space shuttle with WordPerfect 5.0 on an IBM-compatible microcomputer. We cannot, of course, demonstrate every feature of this popular, powerful program. Nevertheless, we can go through the basic procedure of creating, editing, formatting, and printing a document that includes both text and graphics. Although WordPerfect is not a page layout program, it can be used for simple desktop publishing applications in which previously created charts, drawings, or diagrams are to appear inside documents.

The first step is to start up WordPerfect by entering *WP* into a computer that has the program installed on it. After an initial copyright screen, WordPerfect presents a blank *document editing screen*:

Doc 1 Pg 1 Ln 1" Pos 1"

The little underscore at the very top left of the screen is the *cursor*, which points to your current position and indicates where new text will be inserted. The bottom line on the screen is called the *status line*. It indicates your current document (*1 or 2*), page number, distance in inches from the top of the page (*Line*), and distance from the left edge of the page (*Position*).

Most commands in WordPerfect are executed by pressing one of the function keys (F1 through F10 or F12) by itself or in conjunction with another key such as Shift, Alternate (Alt), or Control (Ctrl). Most

WordPerfect users depend heavily, at least at first, on the printed *keyboard template* provided with the program. This guide lays on top of the keyboard and indicates which key combinations are used to invoke various menus and commands. You can even see an on-screen version of WordPerfect's keyboard template by pressing function key F3 (the Help key) twice:

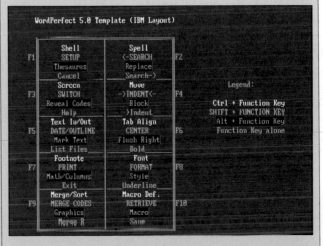

When you are finished using the Help facility, you press the Enter key or the space bar to return to the document editing screen.

It's actually very easy to use WordPerfect. Once you start up the program, you can simply begin typing. Screen formatting and paging are automatic. Initial formats such as line spacing, margins, justification, and tabs have already been set by default, although you can change these at any time. When typing text with a word processor, you don't even have to press the carriage return (Enter key) except at the end of a paragraph or to explicitly leave a blank line. Virtually all word processors have automatic *word wrap*, which drops the word you are typing down to a new line if the word extends past the right margin. If you make mistakes while typing, you can correct them right away by using the Backspace key to erase characters and then retyping them. It's also easy to go back and correct mistakes later by overwriting, deleting, and inserting characters anywhere in a document, so you don't have to worry about typing everything perfectly the first time. Let's begin our space shuttle document by typing the first paragraph, which looks like this:

```
During the height of the Apollo moon-landing program, NASA
officials came to the conclusion that a reusable space vehicle
would be necessary for future large-scale space operations.  On
January 5, 1972 President Richard M. Nixon formally authorized the
space shuttle program.  First flown in 1981, the space shuttle
became the principal U.S. launch vehicle, replacing the expendible
rockets used since the late 1950s.  This role has been questioned,
however, since the explosion of the space shuttle Challenger on
January 28, 1986.  Despite this serious setback to the U.S. space
program, the shuttle is still the primary American launch vehicle.




                                        Doc 1 Pg 1 Ln 2.5" Pos 7.6"
```

This paragraph looks fine, but we need a title at the top. With a word processor, it's easy to go back and insert text at any place in an existing document. In WordPerfect, you move to the beginning of a document by pressing the Home key twice and then pressing the up arrow key. The cursor jumps to the very first character position at the upper left corner of the document. To create a title for this report, all you have to do is type it and press the Enter key a couple of times to leave a blank line before the paragraph body. It would be nice, however, to emphasize the title in some way. For ex-

ample, you could boldface and underline the title. The ability to do such character formatting is also a basic function of any word processor. In WordPerfect, boldfacing is turned on by pressing the F6 function key and underlining is turned on by pressing the F8 function key. After pressing these two keys, you can then type the title: *The Space Shuttle*. To turn off boldfacing and underlining, the F6 and F8 keys are pressed again. Press the Enter key twice to leave a blank line between the title and first paragraph. This is what you see on the screen:

```
The Space Shuttle

During the height of the Apollo moon-landing program, NASA
officials came to the conclusion that a reusable space vehicle
would be necessary for future large-scale space operations.  On
January 5, 1972 President Richard M. Nixon formally authorized the
space shuttle program.  First flown in 1981, the space shuttle
became the principal U.S. launch vehicle, replacing the expendible
rockets used since the late 1950s.  This role has been questioned,
however, since the explosion of the space shuttle Challenger on
January 28, 1986.  Despite this serious setback to the U.S. space
program, the shuttle is still the primary American launch vehicle.


                                        Doc 1 Pg 1 Ln 1.33" Pos 1"
```

As you can see, WordPerfect displays boldfaced and underlined text in a different color from ordinary text. How text is actually printed on paper depends on the capabilities of your printer. Most printers can underline, boldface, and italicize text in at least two different sizes. Many printers, especially laser printers, have a wide range of different character fonts, styles, and sizes. WordPerfect can be set up to take advantage of all these printer capabilities.

At this point, you would probably take time to re-read the paragraph you've just entered. You might find a mistake or two and fix them by overtyping, deleting, and inserting characters. Or you might decide to rearrange or reword certain phrases. WordPerfect's on-line thesaurus can help. Nowadays, no serious word-processing package is considered complete without a thesaurus facility to search for and display synonyms (words with the same or similar meaning) for a word already in your document or a new word you enter at the keyboard. The thesaurus in WordPerfect also displays antonyms (words with the opposite meaning). For example, let's say that you want to find a better word than *necessary* in the third line. Position the cursor on the word *necessary* and press WordPerfect's thesaurus key combination, which is the Alt key pressed along with function key F1. This is what appears on your screen:

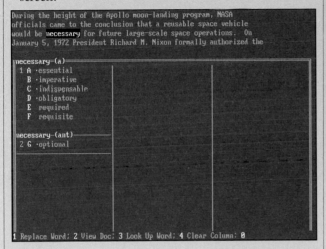

As you can see, WordPerfect presents several synonyms and one antonym choice as possible replacements for *necessary*. To choose one of these words, you type *1* and then the letter that appears in front of that word. For example, if you type *1* and then *A*, the word *necessary* will be automatically replaced with *essential*. An on-line thesaurus such as this can save you a great deal of time if you are in the habit of using an ordinary thesaurus when you write.

While an on-line thesaurus might be considered a luxury or even an unnecessary extravagance, a built-in spelling checker is practically essential in a word-processing program. Even those of us who are good spellers occasionally make mistakes. A computerized spelling checker lets you devote your proofreading attention to sentence structure, grammar, word choice, and points of fact instead of worrying about spelling. Consequently, people who use a spelling checker not only have significantly fewer spelling errors in their documents, they also tend to have fewer instances of other errors, too.

The procedure for using a spelling checker is similar in most word processors. If you want to check your whole document, you first move the cursor to the beginning of the file. In WordPerfect, the spelling checker is invoked by holding down the Ctrl key and pressing the F2 function key. The program then displays a menu of options. For example, you can check a single word, a single page, or your entire document. To check the entire document, you would type a *D* to choose this option. Here is the result:

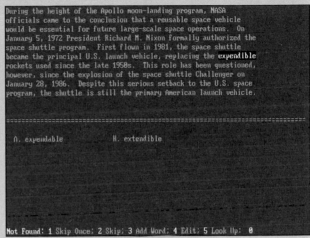

As you can see, we apparently spelled the word *expendable* incorrectly as *expendible*. Most spelling checkers can make one or more good suggestions of the intended word. If the word you meant to use is in this list of possible alternatives, you simply type the letter that precedes it. For example, to automatically replace *expendible* with *expendable*, you type *A*. Like most word-processor spelling checkers, the one in WordPerfect can also count the number of words in your document, and it allows you to set up your own supplementary spelling dictionaries for jargon, proper names, or technical terms unique to your own work.

With the advent of such useful microcomputer tools as graphics packages, optical scanners, and laser printers, many high-end word-processing programs have been given the capability to incorporate pictures along with text in documents. WordPerfect 5.0 is one of the best word-processing packages for mixing text and graphics together, without the need for a page layout program such as PageMaker. Charts, graphs, sketches, illustrations, and even scanned photographs from many different sources can be read directly by WordPerfect and inserted into documents. Furthermore, WordPerfect has an excellent facility for previewing and manipulating these graphic images on the display screen before they are printed on paper. A graphic image can be resized, cropped, moved, or rotated. A picture can be placed in a specific position anywhere on a page or tied to a particular paragraph. Finally, figures can also be outlined by a box, automatically numbered, or captioned.

As an example, let's insert a figure of the space shuttle orbiter at the end of our short document. This illustration was prepared beforehand with a painting program called PC Paint. More accurately, it originated as a sample drawing that came with the AutoCAD computer-aided design package. It was converted into PC Paint format and then slightly edited for inclusion in our WordPerfect document.

There are several steps to this procedure, so let's just list them (when actually performed, there are menus to guide you):

1. Move the cursor to the end of the document and press the Enter key.
2. Hold down the Alt key and press F9 to invoke the Graphics menu.
3. Type *U* to specify a user-defined box for the picture.
4. Type *C* to create a space for the figure.
5. Type *F* to specify the name of the file where the figure is stored.
6. Enter *SHUTTLE.PIC* as the name of our picture file.
7. Type *S* to specify the size and *W* to specify its width.
8. Enter 6.5 for the width in inches and WordPerfect will automatically calculate the appropriate height.
9. Press F7, the Exit key, to return to the document editing screen.

At this point, WordPerfect has inserted the figure in your document, but you cannot see it on the editing screen. If you would add more text, an outline box would appear. Since our figure is so wide, any new text you add would have to begin below the figure. With a smaller figure, however, WordPerfect would automatically wrap text around the figure. To actually see the figure you have inserted and get an idea of how your document will look when it is printed, you must use the View Document feature. This feature is invoked by pressing Shift-F7 to select the Print menu and then typing *V*. This is what appears on your screen:

WordPerfect displays a full-page view of your document on the screen, much like a page-layout program such as PageMaker. Although you cannot make out the details, this view gives you a good idea of what the entire page will look like when it is printed. You can also zoom in to see more detail, although less of the document will fit on the screen. For example, you can see an actual-size view of your document by typing *1* (for 100% view):

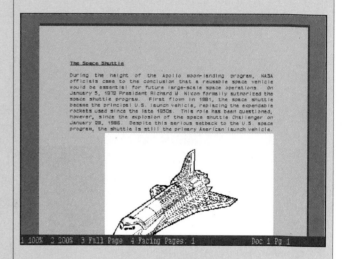

As you can see from the menu at the bottom of the screen, you can also zoom in to see a 200% view, which would make your document appear twice as large on the screen as it would be printed on paper:

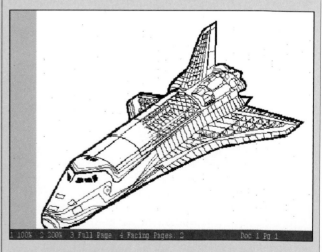

If you are satisfied with the way your document looks, you can proceed to print it. This is done by pressing the F7 (Exit) key to return to the document editing screen and then pressing Shift-F7 to bring up the Print menu again. To print the entire document, you type a *D*. The figure at right shows what the document looks like when printed on a Hewlett-Packard LaserJet laser printer.

Finally, if you are finished working on this document you can exit the WordPerfect program. This is done by pressing the F7 key. WordPerfect asks you if you want to save your document in a disk file. You type *Y* for yes and then enter a name for your document. Then WordPerfect will ask for confirmation that you really want to exit the word processor and return to the computer's operating system, and you would again type *Y* for yes.

The Space Shuttle

During the height of the Apollo moon-landing program, NASA officials came to the conclusion that a reusable space vehicle would be essential for future large-scale space operations. On January 5, 1972 President Richard M. Nixon formally authorized the space shuttle program. First flown in 1981, the space shuttle became the principal U.S. launch vehicle, replacing the expendable rockets used since the late 1950s. This role has been questioned, however, since the explosion of the space shuttle Challenger on January 28, 1986. Despite this serious setback to the U.S. space program, the shuttle is still the primary American launch vehicle.

Summary

The Dimensions of Office Automation

Office automation refers to the integration of computers, communications, and advanced office equipment to support the activities of the white-collar workplace.

The Information Age   Our economy is now based primarily on processing information. Office automation is necessary for coping with the glut of information and the state of rapid change.

Office Functions   The office is a place where data and information are created, input, stored, retrieved, processed, replicated, distributed, archived, and destroyed.

The New Office Environment   As a result of office automation, offices are much more pleasant places in which to work.

Office Input

Original input is data that comes into the office for the first time. Nonoriginal input consists of data or information that already exists within the office.

Voice Input   For the most part, voice input consists of dictation.

Text Input   Typing at a keyboard is the primary way that original input is entered in most offices.

Image Input   Image input comes from optical scanners, video cameras, microforms, and facsimile machines.

Records Management

Records management is the systematic handling of documents from creation to destruction.

Paper Systems   Most offices have some of their data and information stored in traditional paper files.

Film Systems   Micrographics is the process of photographing, reducing, and recording paper documents and computer-generated output on microforms such as microfilm, microfiche, and ultrafiche.

Digital Systems   Most offices keep some of their records in the form of computer files.

Word Processing

The cornerstone of office automation, word processing applies computer technology to the input, editing, merging, storing, formatting, and printing of text.

The Problem with Conventional Typing   Repetitive text must be retyped, errors are common and awkward to fix, and small revisions often require retyping an entire document.

A Brief History of Word Processing   Word processing began in 1964 with the introduction of the IBM MT/ST automatic typewriter, which stored text on magnetic tape. Further developments incorporated display screens and other advances in computer technology.

Types of Word Processors   An electronic typewriter has a microprocessor inside and a small display screen. A dedicated system is a specialized microcomputer solely devoted to word processing. A general-purpose microcomputer running a word-processing program is by far the most popular type of word processor. A shared word processor serves several users at once on a time-sharing basis.

Computer Graphics

Besides word processing, computer graphics offer another way to convert raw data into useful information. Charting, painting, drawing, CAD, and slide show programs all find uses in offices.

Desktop Publishing

Desktop publishing combines word processing and graphics to produce high-quality documents with a laser printer.

Components of a Desktop Publishing System   These include a powerful microcomputer, graphics display, mouse, laser printer, scanner (optional), word-processing software, graphics software, and page layout software.

Page Layout   Page layout software is the key to desktop publishing. It allows you to design the format, incorporate text and graphics, and use different character fonts, styles, and sizes in a document.

PageMaker and PostScript   PageMaker is the leading page layout package. It uses PostScript, the leading page description language for laser printers and some typesetters.

Typesetting

Typesetting is a method of producing a master document for printing that achieves very high-quality, proportionally-spaced results. Currently, most typeset materials are created with phototypesetting equipment.

Copying and Printing

Desktop publishing and typesetting are used to create master documents that must then be reproduced in quantity with methods such as photocopying and offset printing.

Photocopying   Plain-paper copiers are almost universal office equipment. Personal copiers are at the low end of the spectrum, and high-volume, intelligent copiers are at the high end.

Offset Printing   An offset printer uses paper or metal plates to produce high-quality, high-volume copies.

Office Communications

Information must be communicated to be useful; a wide range of modern office equipment is available to help distribute that information.

Electronic Mail   Electronic mail systems offer a fast, reliable, distance-independent means of moving information; they rely on computers and telecommunications channels.

Voice Mail   Voice mail resembles electronic mail except that messages are vocal and are stored digitally on computer disk. A user needs only a Touch-Tone telephone to use voice mail.

Facsimile Transmission   A fax machine can transmit a document containing text and graphics to another fax machine over ordinary telephone lines.

Local Area Networks   Many offices use local area networks to connect diverse office equipment.

Remote Conferencing   Computer conferencing refers to the use of distributed computers and communications networks to conduct on-line meetings. Teleconferencing refers to audio or video meetings held through electronically linking geographically dispersed participants.

The Other Office: Telecommuting

Office technology is rapidly breaking down physical communication barriers, allowing some people to telecommute, or work from their own homes through computer/modem links.

Computer Concepts

As an extra review of the chapter, try defining the following terms. If you have trouble with any of them, refer to the page number listed.

office automation *473*
replication *475*
archiving *475*
optical character recognition (OCR) *478*
records management *478*
micrographics *480*
microforms *480*
ultrafiche *481*
electronic typewriter *484*
dedicated word processor *484*

shared word processors (clustered word processors) *486*
reprographics *488*
desktop publishing *488*
page layout package *490*
what-you-see-is-what-you-get (WYSIWYG) *490*
page description language *492*
typesetting *492*
photocomposition (phototypesetting) *492*

electronic image editing *494*
intelligent copiers *494*
offset printer *494*
voice mail *497*
facsimile transmission (fax) *498*
PC fax *498*
fax board *498*
gateway *499*
teleconferencing *500*
telecommuting *502*

Review Questions

1. What is meant by "office automation" and what are some of the other terms used to describe it?
2. Why is office automation important in today's economy?
3. List some of the functions performed in offices. Briefly relate them to the basic operations of computers.
4. Essentially, what is word processing?
5. List the four basic types of word processors.
6. What kinds of advanced features are sometimes found in word processors?
7. Why has electronic mail become so popular?
8. What's the difference between voice mail and ordinary telephone answering machines?
9. What does a facsimile transceiver do?
10. How are local area networks used in offices?

11. What is computer conferencing?
12. What advantage does videoconferencing have over audioconferencing and computer conferencing? What are its disadvantages?
13. How can business graphics be used in the office?
14. What significant office problem can the use of micrographics help solve?
15. Enumerate some of the capabilities of intelligent copiers.
16. What are some reasons for interfacing word processors to phototypesetters?
17. What is a major advantage of desktop publishing?
18. How are LANs used in offices?
19. What is telecommuting?
20. What is the difference between telecommuting and working at home?

True or False

1. A dedicated word processor is a multipurpose microcomputer that is used mostly for word processing.
2. Clustered word processors are multiuser systems.
3. Mail-merge is an automated mail room.
4. Electronic mail systems automatically create a permanent computer record of what is transmitted.
5. Fax is a system which transmits facsimiles of voices.
6. Micrographics is concerned with production, handling, and use of small photographic images.
7. Desktop publishing is available only to a few large corporations with vast financial resources.
8. Voice mail does not require users to have a microcomputer.
9. Some phototypesetting machines can be directly linked to word processors.
10. Telecommuting brings the office into the home.

Multiple Choice

1. An electric typewriter with an embedded microprocessor is:
   (a) an electronic typewriter
   (b) a dedicated word processor
   (c) a shared word processor

2. A microcomputer with a display, keyboard, and printer that is used only for word processing is:
   (a) a clustered word processor
   (b) a dedicated word processor
   (c) a workstation

3. A system that uses computers to send typed messages electronically to specified recipients is:
   (a) mail-merge
   (b) electronic mail
   (c) teleconferencing

4. Systems that store voice messages digitally for later retrieval or transmittal to many recipients are:
   (a) fax
   (b) electronic answering machines
   (c) voice mail

5. Facsimile transmitters electronically send:
   (a) text and fixed graphic images
   (b) facsimiles of voices
   (c) moving images

6. A LAN links computers over a:
   (a) wide geographical area   (b) small geographical area   (c) state-wide network

7. A machine which can function as a copier or, linked to a computer, as a printer is:
   (a) a phototypesetter   (b) an intelligent copier   (c) a microform recorder

8. Desktop publishing requires an organization to have:
   (a) a phototypesetting machine
   (b) a large mainframe system
   (c) a computer, publishing software, and a laser printer

9. Which device produces the highest resolution output:
   (a) dot matrix printer   (b) laser printer   (c) typesetter

10. A system by which professionals can do most of their work at home using a computer/modem link is:
    (a) teleconferencing   (b) remote conferencing   (c) telecommuting

A Sharper Focus

1. Consider the general functions of an office. If you were starting a new ice cream business, how would you use automated office equipment to help your business survive and grow?
2. If you had a choice between working in an automated office and telecommuting, which would you choose? Why?

Projects

1. Many offices in large organizations use a mix of word-processing equipment. Try to find such a set-up locally (maybe on your campus or a local office equipment dealer) and ask to try a variety. Compare the ease of learning to use each type; discuss with the users (or salespeople in the dealership) what, if any, problems they had getting used to a particular system. You may be able to try one or two word-processing packages for comparison on a given system. Write a report on your findings, including a discussion of which type of system would be most useful to you in your present situation, future career, and for personal use.

2. What if an office worker chooses to telecommute? Consider the various functions performed by office workers and the various pieces of available hardware and software, and write a report about the factors associated with telecommuting. Mention not only the pros and cons, but also any special equipment and capabilities that would be needed. What sorts of office tasks would lend themselves to this environment? What couldn't be done? How would the use of at-home employees be controlled? What additional issues do you think should be raised about such an environment? Is it fair to employers?

3. Investigate what kinds of offices and businesses you think would use facsimile transmission technology extensively. What specific applications are used?

4. Desktop publishing is becoming more popular as microcomputers become more powerful, laser printers become better and more affordable, and software pours into the market. Contact several companies or professional firms who produce documents internally using such a system and prepare a report comparing the equipment and software used and the resulting text and graphics.

15

Computers in Industry

In This Chapter

Focus On

Automation in the Auto Industry

Although there has been much notice paid to the introduction of robots on the assembly lines of Detroit, artificial intelligence (AI) hasn't been utilized very much beyond the research stage. However, in the U.S. the research stage is very much alive and well, with over 100 vendors of AI systems trying to get a piece of the automotive market. Inference Corp., with partial backing from Ford, markets an expert system called Automated Reasoning Tool (ART) which is connected to a DEC VAX computer. Ford was also instrumental in the development of an expert system for assembly welding, together with Carnegie-Mellon University and the American Welding Institute.

The most popular areas for the use of AI are process control, diagnostics and maintenance. Some recent welding robots include rudimentary expert systems; for example, GM is working on controls that allow its robots to sense vibrations, temperature, and sounds that are generated during assembly and enable the robot to abort a job

that doesn't meet the normal criteria. The director of robotics for GM's Advanced Engineering Staff, Dick Beecher, notes that humans can use tools and can sense when things are going wrong. Robots aren't currently able to do that, and adding such a capability is costly.

Ford is a leader in developing expert systems for the industry and has been collaborating with Texas

Instruments, Boeing, DEC, and the Carnegie Group to develop such systems. One such effort is a program to cut warranty repair cost through a user-friendly diagnostic system. This would speed warranty repairs, a major expense even with increased quality control efforts. Other areas that are prime targets for AI systems include modeling and simulation for product planning, scheduling of plant operations, machine diagnostics, and shop floor maintenance.

Current systems in use are rule-based and contain only the intelligence that was programmed into them. The next generation will be programmable by the expert in the plant, rather than only by the programmer. These systems will consist of a series of definitions and descriptions of how a part works (as described by the user in the plant). They will then go on to solve manufacturing problems using that information.

New AI programs will not only aid in designing products, but they will also have their biggest role in designing manufacturing processes. Such programs already form a key part of the chemical and food industries which use precise controls for their processes. Manufacturing is more difficult because the parameters are not as well defined. GM has introduced one low-cost ($5500) system from Umecorp that detects problems on the plant floor, diagnoses their probable cause and assists in solving them. Such systems will rely more, rather than less, on human intelligence to guide them.

Before we get into this chapter's topic—the computer's applications in both new and old industries—let's consider the three main motivating forces behind the idea of industrial automation. The first and most basic motivation has been a desire to increase the productivity of labor. Since the Industrial Revolution's introduction of steam-powered machines into processes that had previously relied totally on human and animal muscle, increased productivity has been the primary goal. Today's computer-based automation takes another step toward that basic goal by being applied not only to physical labor, but also to certain jobs considered white collar—engineering, design, and project management.

The second motivation is quality. No one doubts that a bulldozer can move dirt faster than a person with a shovel, but emotions enter the picture when we try to judge the comparative quality of work. Although the machine's path may be uniform, the human's may be more precise or more aesthetically pleasing. Whether we're talking about construction or automobile assembly, or even the design of VLSI chips, the issue ultimately boils down to just what sort of quality is most profitable.

Finally, competition is a pressing reason for automation. If Company A switches over to an automated assembly line and produces a greater number of wooden boxes for a lower cost, then Company B may feel compelled to abandon its line of handcrafted boxes and get its own machines. Jobs are lost and jobs are gained through automation.

This is all part of what we'll call the *commercial network*, even though that may seem a somewhat fancy label for that familiar entity known as business. Unlike the word *business,* the concept of a network of commerce accurately describes what's going on out there. A business can be anything from a shoe store to a multinational corporation or a public utility; a network is a complex and interwoven system of buying and selling, shipping and receiving, manufacturing and storing, investing and banking, profit and loss.

The person who can understand and deal effectively with such a network is the person who will be a success in business. Those who try to do that—businesspeople—are discovering that they have an electronic helper that promises to make things simpler, more direct, faster, and much more profitable. What better device for harnessing the diverse and detailed information generated by the commercial network than the computer?

Our network contains two main elements. The first element is manufacturing, the second, business. The two parts are obviously mutually dependent. In this chapter, we'll see how computers play an increasingly vital role in this very important aspect of our national economy and our daily lives.

THE DESIGN/MANUFACTURING CYCLE

Until a few years ago, a relatively clear distinction existed between engineering and design. For one thing, engineering was done by trained engineers, and design was usually done by non–degree-holding designers or designer/draftspeople. For example, an electrical engineer would describe the components to be used in a circuit and would provide a rough sketch or description of how they were to be connected, but with no indication of the wiring pattern needed to produce the desired connections on the printed circuit board. A designer or designer/draftsperson would then carefully draw the components and their connections to scale and, by a trial-and-error process involving many redrawings, move them around until either an acceptable wiring pattern was produced or the problem was given up as unsolvable. In the latter case, it would be time for a conference with the engineer to find another approach. The engineering of an automobile would follow the same pattern. Teams of engineers would first design the subsystems to meet the product requirements for cost, performance, operating economy, weight, and safety. The job of the designers would then be to try to combine these subsystems all under the hood, which would sometimes mean redesigning them so they could all fit into the allocated space. The same sort of division between engineering and design existed in civil, industrial, and most other engineering fields.

The merging of engineering, design, and manufacturing into one continuous process

Today, particularly in electronics, the dividing line has become blurred. The computer-based *engineering workstation* now fills the engineer's need for a sketch pad, calculator, and computer, while at the same time its graphics software either directly converts sketches into precise final-design artwork displayed on its high-resolution screen or produces the input for specialized computer-based layout systems that display the artwork. The engineering workstation is a manifestation of a trend toward **computer-aided engineering (CAE),** that is, the application of computer programs that simulate complex electrical or mechanical systems for the design and development of products. The engineering workstation is also a manifestation of a similar growth in **computer-aided design (CAD),** which is primarily the application of interactive computer graphics to product design and drafting. The modern engineer's working environment now includes the hardware and software of both CAE and CAD systems. We will discuss both of these applications in the next section and will refer to them collectively as CAD.

Computer-aided manufacturing (CAM) can be characterized as the application of shared data bases and computers to all aspects of production, including the design of special tools and dies, the programming and use of computer-controlled machines, the monitoring and control of manufacturing processes, and the overall coordination of the manufacturing facility. Computer-aided manufacturing will be discussed in this chapter.

Figure 15.1 illustrates the place in the product cycle of CAE, CAD, and CAM.

COMPUTER-AIDED DESIGN

The linking of design and manufacturing

The two principal objectives of CAD are (1) to increase the productivity of product designers, and (2) to produce the information—graphic, numeric, and textual—required to manufacture the product. Achieving the first goal involves using the computer to simulate product designs so they can be analyzed and tested.

Interactive Graphics: The Geometric Model

In Chapter 4, we saw how users can input graphic information to computers from terminals. We learned how the digitizer, light pen, joystick, mouse, and touch panel work with the keyboard and screen to accomplish this. In CAD, an engineer uses one or more of these means to create a *geometric model* of a product on a

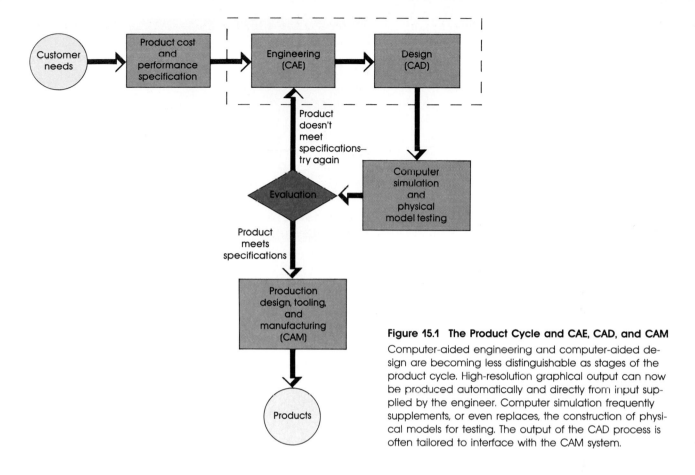

Figure 15.1 The Product Cycle and CAE, CAD, and CAM
Computer-aided engineering and computer-aided design are becoming less distinguishable as stages of the product cycle. High-resolution graphical output can now be produced automatically and directly from input supplied by the engineer. Computer simulation frequently supplements, or even replaces, the construction of physical models for testing. The output of the CAD process is often tailored to interface with the CAM system.

Letting the engineer see and manipulate the product

terminal screen. This model consists of a picture and an accompanying descriptive computer file, which together indicate all the constituent points, curves, and shapes. Curves may be lines, arcs of circles, or more complex curves; shapes may be two- or three-dimensional. Software then fills in these elements and connects them. It's becoming routine practice for the designs of all kinds of structures, from buildings to battleships, to go through a phase as a computerized geometric model. In fact, some architects now go directly from such a geometric model to building plans (see Figure 15.2).

Although we'll concentrate on areas of broader general concern, such as the strong interactions between CAD and CAM, it is important to note that once any geometric model exists in computer form, it has great potential to assist in the design process. For example, an engineer can manipulate the model by enlarging or reducing parts of it, and moving the pieces around. Three-dimensional images of geometric objects can be created on the display screen, with perspective, shading, and color automatically provided by the graphics software and hardware. These "solid" models can be "handled" by the engineer almost as if they were real. They can be turned about any axis or viewed from the back side. Obtaining each new view prior to the advent of computerized model-building might have taken weeks of drafting to produce a picture of comparable quality and value to the engineer.

**Figure 15.2 Three-Dimensional Geometric
Models Created Using CAD Systems**

Further, the image can be permanently stored, becoming part of a design data base, which can be searched when new parts are needed in the future. Figure 15.3 shows an example of the images that can be created with interactive graphics.

Analysis and Testing

Evaluating the computer model of a product

Using the geometric model, the design can be subjected to a variety of simulated testing using prepackaged or custom software. For example, structural analyses can be performed. Since all the dimensions of the product are completely specified and the properties of the materials of which it will be made are known, the engineer can determine the way it will respond to stresses. A *static analysis program* is used when the part will be in an environment in which the forces or loads on it are either constant or change very slowly with time. A *dynamic analysis program* is employed when the loads on the part will vary with time, as is the case for an aircraft in flight.

Figure 15.3 Interactive Graphics Facilitate Design

Figure 15.4 A "Driver" Tests a New Design
Here a computer does dynamic analysis interactively. A "driver" controls the simulated automobile by manipulating a joystick. With such a system, the performance effects of a new design can be tested without the cost and delay associated with building and assembling the parts. Only the most promising designs are actually built.

Using a CAD system, an engineer can retrieve a geometric model from the design data base, alter it if desired, specify the loads to be applied in a static or dynamic analysis, and then use the results to modify the geometric model before trying again. The engineer can accomplish in hours or days a job that only a few years ago involved many different skilled people (including designers, draftspeople, and model builders) and took weeks or months to complete. Computerized analysis and testing is being applied in the design of products from simple tools and appliances to ships, aircraft, and buildings.

For example, significant improvements in the performance and comfort of automobiles as well as in their fuel economy and engine emissions have resulted from the use of a dynamic analysis and testing system. For an automobile with electronic engine control, a major programming system in use at the Ford Motor Company simulates the interactions between the engine, the drive train (the mechanics that transmit the motion from the engine to the wheels), the electronic engine controls, and the driver (see Figure 15.4). Models of the various subsystems and their interactions are represented by subroutines, which are linked together by the overall program. This arrangement allows the engineers to alter an existing subsystem or insert a new subsystem without having to revise the overall program. The responses of the simulated driver can be programmed on the basis of known data about how drivers manipulate the gas and brake pedals to accomplish a desired change in speed. Alternatively, a person acting as "driver" may interact directly with the simulation program, using a joystick to simulate the pedal action. Clearly, the automobile industry, in the United States and abroad, is at the forefront in developing CAD and CAM systems.

The Manufacturing Interface

References to the acronym CAD/CAM are common, suggesting a single integrated process extending from the design to the manufacture of a product. In fact, the CAD systems that are used to design mechanical parts, for example, greatly facilitate the programming of the automatic cutting tools that manufacture the parts. The transition from a CAD system to a CAM system is even more direct in the production of electronic chips. (See Figure 15.5.)

CAD output as input to CAM

Figure 15.5 The Interface Between CAD and CAM
The results of the CAD phase are computer-analyzed and computer-tested products, represented by geometric models in the design data base. These models provide the input from which the detailed manufacturing plans are made.

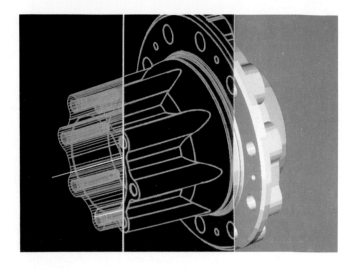

COMPUTER-AIDED MANUFACTURING

Two types of automation: programmable versus Detroit-type

It's common practice to distinguish two types of manufacturing automation: *Detroit-type automation*, an assembly line set up to achieve high-volume production of a single product, possibly with some limited range of variations; and what has come to be called **programmable automation.** In the first type, everything is geared for volume production at low cost. Production runs are assumed to have a reasonably long life; in Detroit, it is typically a year or more between major changes. The production process is relatively fixed, and changeover requires a major effort.

Computerized monitoring, control and integration of the manufacturing process from design to finished product

Programmable automation, on the other hand, is aimed at handling a more varied product environment. It employs tools that can be reprogrammed quickly and whose economic advantages can be secured over relatively short production runs. It is carried out primarily by numerically controlled machine tools but increasingly involves industrial robots. Foreign auto manufacturers have long relied on the speed, low cost, and efficiency of programmable automation, and this trend is growing in U.S. plants as well. We will concentrate on programmable automation, where the computer's role is clearly defined from the outset.

Programmable Industrial Machines

Turning a roughly shaped piece of metal into a precise machine-made part, for an aircraft or earth-mover engine, for example, was until the 1950s exclusively the job of highly skilled and experienced machinists. Today, more than 15 percent of the machine tools employed in U.S. industry can be programmed to grind, drill, shape, and, in general, work metal automatically. These are numerically controlled machine tools . Although their initial cost is higher than that of their manual counterparts, they can be quickly and economically reprogrammed and, of course, will work 24 hours a day under environmental conditions that a human couldn't tolerate.

Cousins to these programmable machines that work material are the programmable industrial robots that handle material and operate tools. These adaptable machines are used mostly in assembly operations, but they also do such jobs as welding and spray painting. Unlike computer-controlled machine tools, however, a robot can often be directly "taught" to do a job by being moved through the desired sequence of operations, which it stores in its memory.

Numerically Controlled Machine Tools

A **numerically controlled (NC) machine tool** is a power-driven mechanical device whose actions are determined by a program that describes, in detail, each step in the sequence of operations required to transform a piece of metal stock (the *workpiece*) into a finished, high-precision, machine-made product. To understand what this definition really means, it's best to start with a basic understanding of how a machine tool is manually operated and then contrast this with numerically controlled operation. Figure 15.6 shows the same basic machine tool in a manually controlled and a numerically controlled version. A skilled machinist, by turning the handwheels, can cut curved shapes with a precision of one thousandth of an inch. Numerically controlled machine tools are programmed to match the precision of a human operator.

Numerically controlled machine tools: turning rough stock into high precision products

In the early days of numeric control, these descriptions of the workpiece motions required to produce the part, collectively called the *part program*, were drawn up separately, one step at a time, from an engineering drawing. A numeric code representing each step was punched on a paper tape, which was then inserted in the electronic control unit. As you can imagine, this process was tedious and error-prone. A few years after the first numerically controlled machine tools were developed, a high-level programming language was created that greatly simplified part programming. Called APT (for Automatically Programmed Tools), it and its many related offshoots still dominate the field of programming industrial machines. An APT program consists of two sections. The first contains special geometric statements—for example, those defining points, lines, and circles—that describe the shape of the part. In the second section, the motion required to cut out the part is described, using a sequence of motion statements that refer to the part's geometric layout. Motion statements in an APT program look like these:

APT programs: defining the product's geometry and the required cutting path

```
FROM/STPT
GOFWD/L1
```

These statements translate to "from the starting point, go forward to line 1." Both the starting point and line 1 must be defined in earlier geometric statements. The APT program is compiled, and the control tape is generated by a computer. The entire process of producing a part in this fashion is summarized in Figure 15.7.

Another simplification, similar in spirit to the interface between CAD and CAM, has recently been made in this production process. Engineers use workstations where, with interactive graphics, they can create the geometric data base that describes a part. The engineer, or a part programmer, uses a light pen to trace out the cutter motion. After visually checking to see that the program produces the correct part, the control tape is created. Some programmable tools are controlled directly by a computer, eliminating the need for the tape, and some computers can control groups of such machines.

The basic principles of numerically controlled machine tools apply generally to controlling motion in two or three dimensions. The technology has been applied to build automatic plotters, wiring machines, drills, and numerous other devices.

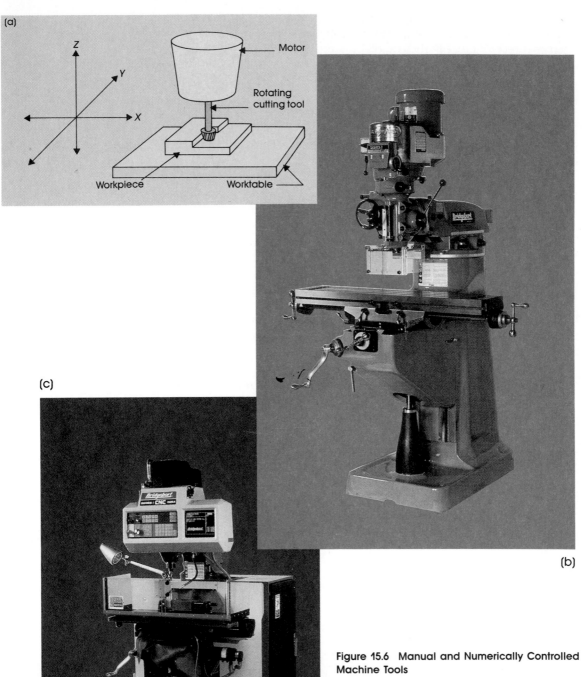

Figure 15.6   Manual and Numerically Controlled Machine Tools

(a) With the manually operated machine tool, the workpiece is first fastened to the worktable. The cutting tool is driven by a motor and can be lowered to the desired depth in the workpiece. The worktable (and with it the workpiece) is moved by turning the handwheels shown in (b), thereby cutting away metal to obtain the precise shape. (c) In the numerically controlled version, the worktable is moved not by manually operated handwheels but by special precision motors that are controlled by a tape in the electronic control unit at the right of the machine.

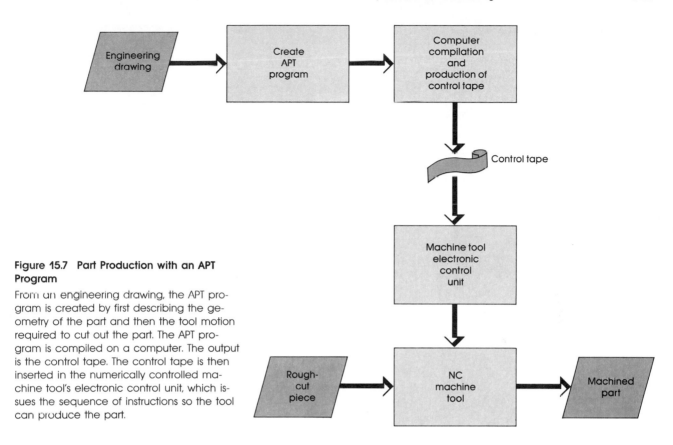

Figure 15.7 Part Production with an APT Program

From an engineering drawing, the APT program is created by first describing the geometry of the part and then the tool motion required to cut out the part. The APT program is compiled on a computer. The output is the control tape. The control tape is then inserted in the numerically controlled machine tool's electronic control unit, which issues the sequence of instructions so the tool can produce the part.

To be a machinist is to be a practitioner of an old and respected craft. As is the case with all true crafts, great satisfaction results from turning out an excellent piece of work using one's hands directly. Does a comparable satisfaction result when the work is "crafted" by an APT program? What determines a person's level of job satisfaction? In the case of working with machine tools, what has changed? What has remained the same?

Issues in Technology

Industrial Robots

An industrial robot is a general-purpose, programmable machine that has found a niche in a number of manufacturing processes. The number of industrial robots in current use is just beginning to become a significant part of the labor picture; about 60,000 are in use worldwide, and the population is increasing relatively rapidly. Almost all of these robots can only blindly repeat a task that they've been programmed or "taught" to do. That is, they can neither sense nor adjust to their environment; they don't have any means of observing the effect of their work. A robot will go on painting a fender even if, by some mistake, it isn't there. Figure 15.8 shows the set of movements of which the typical industrial robot is capable.

Robots are most frequently used for:

● Long sequences of absolutely repetitive mechanical tasks.

Industrial robots for boring or hazardous work environments and programmable production lines

Figure 15.8   An Industrial Robot's Range
The six program-controlled motions of which the typical industrial robot is capable. These robots can also be fitted with a variety of specialized "hands." [From Dan T. Moore, Jr., "Will Robots Save Democracy?" *The Futurist* **15** (August 1981): 17. Reprinted by permission of the publisher, World Future Society, 4916 St. Elmo Avenue, Washington, D.C. 20014.]

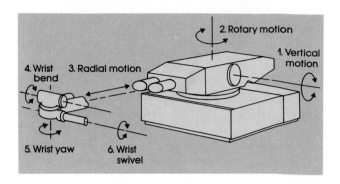

- Work in an environment that presents health hazards such as high temperatures, toxic byproducts, or fine paint or chemical sprays.
- Work that must continue at all hours.
- Work that involves lifting awkward or especially heavy loads.

As we mentioned earlier, a robot may be either programmed or taught to do a job, that is, to execute a precise sequence of the motions of which it's capable. Programs are usually written in a high-level language furnished by a robot's manufacturer. Although each manufacturer has its own proprietary language, these languages are rather similar, at least semantically. Newer robots have memories that can hold more than a thousand steps. Teaching a robot means using an auxiliary device called a *teach pedant,* which allows the robot to be taken manually through a sequence of moves and to store the data describing the physical aspects of each move so that the sequence can be repeated.

Robots can also be grouped to form reasonably flexible production lines for assembly or other operations. Figure 15.9 shows a robot line used in the manufacturing of automobiles. A robot line that paints automobiles or that does auto-body welding need not be set up all over again from scratch because of a moderate change in body style. Nothing more may be required than the reprogramming (or reteaching) of a few of the line's robots.

Process Monitoring and Control

Process monitoring: open-loop control, from the process to the computer

When a computer is used solely to observe, record, and display the state of a manufacturing system, it is called a **process monitor.** The information flow is one-way, from the process to the computer. A human operator reviews the displayed information and takes any required action to maintain or change the state of the process. This type of control is called **open-loop control** because there is no direct feedback from the computer to the process; the human operator provides the necessary link (see Figure 15.10).

Automatic process control: closed-loop control for continuous production processes

Automatic process control, on the other hand, operates without human intervention. The computer program, acting through specialized peripheral equipment, assesses the state of the process and operates controls so as to maintain it or, if it has gotten out of the desired state, to bring it back into line. Feedback moves both from process to computer and from computer to process, forming a closed loop, which gives the name **closed-loop control** to this type of process control.

Figure 15.9 A Robot Line
Unimate robots doing welding on an automobile production line.

The devices used to measure such parameters in a system's state as temperature, pressure, and electrical or chemical values are known as *sensors*. They measure practically any parameter and provide digital values to a computer. *Actuators* are controls, such as switches and valves, that operate the production system. The wide assortment of actuators operate by accepting digital values and responding appropriately (for example, a valve shuts off completely when an actuator receives a zero and opens fully at a one, with a range of intermediate states).

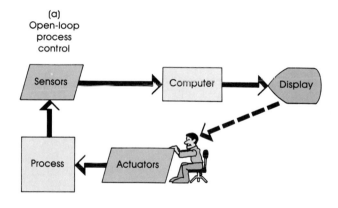

(a)
Open-loop
process
control

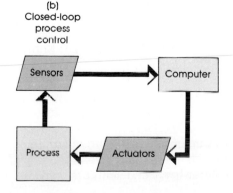

(b)
Closed-loop
process
control

Figure 15.10 Types of Process Control
(a) The computer displays the status of the process to an operator, who assesses the situation and responds by manipulating the actuators to maintain the process or to bring it to a desired state. This is open-loop control. (b) In closed-loop control, the assessment is made by the computer program, which controls the process directly.

Computer-based systems for process monitoring have some unique advantages. Even though a computer isn't being used to control the process, it can be programmed to increase the frequency with which it records certain conditions. This facility for extra vigilance is particularly useful for situations that threaten equipment or personnel because a detailed history leading up to the unsafe conditions can be recovered and the knowledge gained can be used to help prevent a recurrence. Of course, monitoring systems can and do display dangerous conditions, as well as indicating the appropriate steps to be taken by operating personnel. Monitoring systems are often used to track items through the manufacturing and testing stages. Pharmaceutical firms, for example, are required by federal law to keep records of materials used and products manufactured. By means of identification codes, batches can then be tracked automatically when needed, to determine which products used certain inputs and to which customers the products were shipped. Also, equipment is monitored to assess its reliability and performance, and the testing of products is monitored to assist in operation management and planning as well as in quality control.

Automatic process control is generally, but by no means exclusively, associated with continuous production processes such as electric-power generation, petroleum refining, and bulk production of chemicals and foodstuffs. The general trend in power production systems seems to be toward the incorporation of more automatic safety features in the context of increasingly automated process control. It isn't only in massive power plants that automatic process control is important. Food producers, for example, have relied on these production techniques for years. Even many of the most traditional food products, such as cookies and bread, are produced under a regime of automatic control. Daily or seasonal variations in the supplies of input materials and the demand for products are taken into account by computer programs that calculate the product mix that will produce the greatest profit at a given time. The bakery (or refinery or feed mill) is then controlled to produce that mix.

Manufacturing Support

So far, our discussion of CAM has emphasized its hardware aspects, by concentrating on the tools and robots that actually turn materials into products. Even though these machines are programmable, the output of the programs is actually the direct operation of this hardware that performs the production tasks. The hardware aspect of CAM takes precedence when the computer is used to control, or even to monitor, production machinery. In such a case, the computer remains physically attached to the machinery through sensors to which it directly responds.

Software-oriented applications to manufacturing

In contrast, manufacturing support, to which we now turn, is a predominantly software-oriented application. The hardware involved consists primarily of the standard data-processing variety we have already studied. **Manufacturing support** systems are used mainly to assist in the functions of production planning and control.

Inventory Management

The appropriate software can be immensely helpful in determining when to order parts or raw materials and how much to maintain on hand. The goal is to minimize the risk of shutting down a line because needed items are unavailable while, at the same time, not tying up cash and space by holding more inventory than is reasonably required. This procurement activity must be closely coordinated with production scheduling, which establishes when and where the given items will be needed and in what quantities.

Production Scheduling

Production scheduling is based on knowledge of the time and material requirements for each step in the production process. Gathering this data may involve doing time-and-motion studies for manual tasks and estimating or measuring the time required for the tasks that are to be performed automatically by machines. If past data are already on hand for some of the steps in the process, analyses of them may yield helpful information.

Production-Flow Simulation

When the time, material, equipment, and space requirements are known for each of the individual steps, the complete flow of production may be simulated. We've already noted the importance of computer simulation to CAD, but it is also important to CAM. Just as it's far less costly, and less dangerous, to detect an aircraft design flaw in a computer simulation than to discover it in the sky, it's also less costly to uncover a production bottleneck with a simulation program than to do so on the active production line. Production simulation systems run models of the production situation, sometimes incorporating information from statistical studies of the performance times of both humans and machines on given tasks. They help determine the mix of labor skills required to maintain a smooth flow in the production process.

Production Planning

The organization of any production process that involves the manufacturing and/or assembly of many different parts into more than one product presents so many possibilities that it is generally impossible to determine which production plan is best. For the typical factory situation, an acceptable plan can fall short of the best possible combination of labor, machines, and products, as long as it eliminates the major sources of delay and reduces inventory costs to a tolerable level.

A widely used and effective computerized method for preparing production plans was introduced by IBM in the late 1960s: **manufacturing resource planning** or **MRP.** Its technique is to begin with the required completion or delivery date for assembled products and to work back from there. When provided with all the necessary inputs concerning the time and materials requirements for individual production steps, the MRP program produces schedules for labor, machines, and materials. It is estimated that more than 10,000 manufacturing sites currently use MRP and most have achieved higher profitability as a result.

MRP: producing schedules that result in higher profits

BEYOND MANUFACTURING

Once a product is manufactured, it moves into the stream of commerce to be bought and sold in a series of numerous transactions before finally making its way to its ultimate destination. In fact, the buying and selling goes on even before a

The increasing cost and use of computers in business

product is made, as the raw materials are located, mined or produced, shipped, processed, shipped again, stored, and bought. The whole process is unimaginably vast, involving a wide diversity of business interests: owners, contractors, subcontractors, workers, bankers, investors, insurance companies, shippers—the list is endless. Each of these interests is touched by other, distinct business interests; the roads the shippers use are the end product of another series of commercial transactions, the trucks another, the warehouses and office buildings yet another.

Just as the diversity among types of businesses is infinitely complex, so are the applications of computers in this "business world." It has been estimated that businesses' expenditures on automation and computer technology will have long exceeded $1 trillion by the middle of the 1990s. Some claim the expenditures have reached that point already.

Let's turn our attention now, briefly, from the role of computers in manufacturing to their role in business.

Banking and Finance

The flow of personal and corporate money

Banking is a $15-trillion-a-year industry in the United States, and the Federal Reserve's computerized Fedwire system moves money around the country at a rate of $100 million per second. Aside from basic administrative operations, such as payroll and personnel, banks use computers for on-line savings and automation of check processing by means of MICR and OCR devices. Savings accounts are automatically updated when deposits or withdrawals take place, and interest is compounded electronically. Statements and analyses of loans, trusts, and investments are prepared with the help of computers. And one of the fastest growing applications of computers in banking is the use of the **automatic teller machine (ATM)** (see Figure 15.11). In 1985, there were fewer than 30,000 ATMs in the United States. Today, there are nearly half a million.

Every year in the United States, some 40 billion checks, representing more than $8 trillion, are passed between businesses, governments, and individuals. In fact, 90 percent of all financial transactions in this country are handled by check, and, if there were no computers to help process checks, as much as half of the entire population would be needed just to shuffle all the paper around to the right places. And the number of checks keeps rising; from 1940 to 1970, it increased by more than 1000 percent and has risen steadily at about 7 percent each year since then.

Plastic cards and electronic tellers

The enormous problem of moving the mountain of paper represented by all those checks and the somewhat smaller mountain of cash and coins may one day disappear. A vision of the future that has begun to seem more realistic is that of the *cashless society,* in which credit cards, ATMs, and the **electronic transfer of funds (EFT)** between bank accounts and creditors or between businesses will replace paper money.

Insurance

Managing and analyzing insurance data

Insurance companies use computers for figuring out premiums, billing, investment analysis, policy approval, keeping track of policyholders' records, and processing claims. Computers are used to set premium rates on the basis of *actuarial tables,*

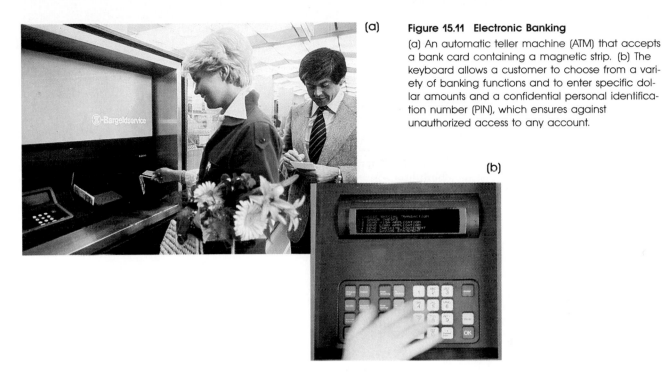

(a)

Figure 15.11 Electronic Banking
(a) An automatic teller machine (ATM) that accepts a bank card containing a magnetic strip. (b) The keyboard allows a customer to choose from a variety of banking functions and to enter specific dollar amounts and a confidential personal identification number (PIN), which ensures against unauthorized access to any account.

(b)

statistical analyses of the risks involved in insuring various groups (statistics on life expectancies or automobile accidents, for example). The data bases required to store and utilize this mass of data efficiently and effectively are necessarily enormous, so computers have become vital in the insurance industry.

Utilities

Public utilities—power, water, gas, and communications companies—use computers not only for running and monitoring the equipment that generates, distributes, and carries their commodities, but for billing, record keeping, and accounting. Rate schedules are set and state and local taxes are calculated with the aid of computers. Utilities also use computers to create **operational simulations,** models that project how a company's equipment will function under a hypothetical situation. A power company might want to know whether its generators could hold up at peak demand times during a long heat wave, or a long distance telephone company might want to know how many of its lines and switches are likely to be required on Mother's Day. Such computer simulations enable utilities to be prepared to meet their customers' needs.

From billing to simulations

Some power companies now use hand-held optical scanning devices to read the gas, electric, and water meters on or in customers' homes. Exterior meters can be read from across the yard or even as a truck containing electronic listening devices passes slowly down the block, "hearing" the usage data emitted by specially-equipped meters. Either way, the readings, which are far more accurate than a human's glance (and offer customers a higher level of personal security), are sent directly to the utility's billing computer (see Figure 15.12).

Transportation

In the air and on the ground

Airlines, bus companies, car rental agencies, trucking companies, and other businesses concerned with moving people and products from place to place also depend on computers. Rate calculations, tariff and regulation analyses, reservation systems, vehicle scheduling, purchasing and maintenance budgets, analyses of traffic patterns, and route selection are some of the tasks to which computers are applied.

Airline pilots and dispatchers receive accurate and up-to-date information about the weather, fuel consumption, and the flight plan from computers in the

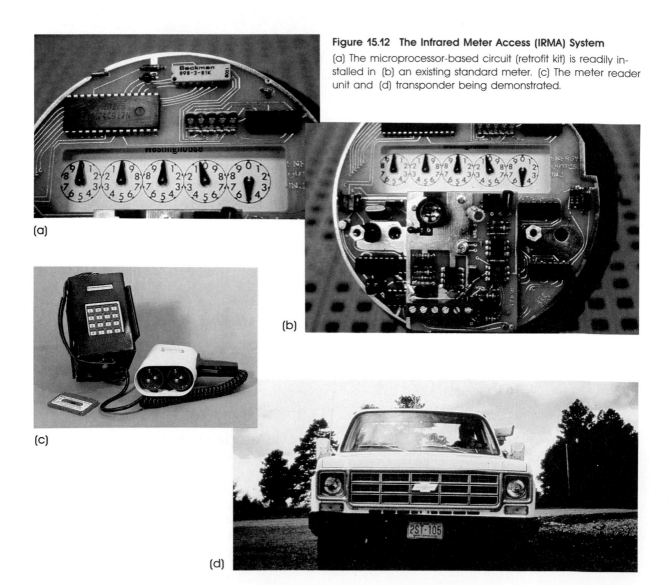

Figure 15.12 The Infrared Meter Access (IRMA) System
(a) The microprocessor-based circuit (retrofit kit) is readily installed in (b) an existing standard meter. (c) The meter reader unit and (d) transponder being demonstrated.

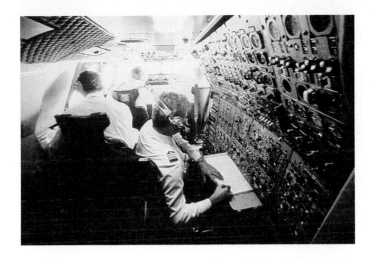

Figure 15.13 Computers in the Air
Electronic controls play a vital role in the flying of high-tech commercial aircraft such as the Concorde.

cockpit (see Figure 15.13). *Autoland computers* programmed with detailed data on airport locations and runway positions guide jumbo jets to safe "instrument" landings during periods of poor visibility. On the ground, air traffic controllers rely on computers to monitor landings and takeoffs, current flight locations, weather, and runway conditions. In the terminal, airline clerks use computers to make and cancel reservations, to assign seats and print tickets, and to keep track of requests for special meals, seating, or wheelchairs.

In the nation's travel agencies, a $20-billion-a-year service industry, computers are used to make hotel, train, airline, bus, ship, and rental car reservations. For example, American Airlines' SABRE system provides travel agents with the rates, flight schedules, and seating availability for most airlines and destinations. (American's own flights, of course, are displayed in the first positions of every listing.)

Hotels

Hotels and motels use computers (Holiday Inn's Holidex and Inn-Scan systems, for example) to make advance reservations within the chain, bill customers, and keep inventories. Computers also schedule maid service, monitor room schedules, and keep track of special requests for cribs, room service, wake-up calls, messages, and forwarding addresses and phone numbers. A subsystem of the Inn-Scan housekeeping system, Motorola's Maid-Aid, was designed specifically to streamline the cleaning of rooms. A maid simply calls the computer on the room telephone once a room has been cleaned, and the computer adds the room to the "open" list for the reservation system.

Electronic innkeeping

The Stock Market

Brokerage houses, investment firms, banks, and other organizations that have major funds invested in the stock market have been using computers in their activities for some time. The classic glass-domed ticker-tape machines have been replaced by CRT displays in brokers' offices. On the floor of the New York Stock

Brokers, bankers, investors, and the SEC

Exchange and on nearly 10,000 display boards worldwide, computers keep traders informed about international buying and selling activities as more than 100 million shares are traded every day. Besides minute-to-minute reporting applications, computers are also employed as links in financial information networks, which can provide instant data on the current financial condition of almost any company. Electronic information services are offered to amateur and professional investors alike by Dow Jones News/Retrieval, Standard and Poor's Compustat, Wharton Econometric, and Data Resources, Inc. (DRI). Financial news is available from UPI, *The Wall Street Journal, Forbes,* and *Barron's,* as well as from a number of sources in specific industries.

After the October 1987 stock market crash, a number of solutions to a too-active market were proposed. Chief among them was a reform in the use of *electronic trading*—the use by brokers of computers programmed to buy or sell stock automatically, with transactions triggered by a set of specific prices, activities among selected stocks or industries, or other conditions. Stock ownership thus shifted from holder to holder electronically, with money credited to or debited from accounts with little or no human intervention. The 1987 crash was, in fact, accelerated by uncontrolled electronic "panic selling" as the market indicators dropped lower and lower. After the crash, several large brokerage houses, such as Kidder, Peabody and Salomon Brothers, announced a suspension of such trading.

On the other hand, the Securities and Exchange Commission (SEC), in their study of the crash, recommended an increased use of computers to coordinate between regional markets. The General Accounting Office has also called for increased computer use to control the large volume of trading.

The SEC handles over 6 million pages of quarterly, annual, and other reports from companies every year. Information on a company's filings, earnings, or estimates of growth is vital both to brokers and investors and to the SEC, which examines the documents for discrepancies and for adherence to various laws and regulations. Every business day, express delivery trucks line up for blocks around the SEC's Washington, D.C. headquarters. In an effort to reduce the confusion and to streamline a cumbersome but essential regulatory process, the SEC introduced the EDGAR (Electronic Data Gathering And Retrieval) system, which allows companies to file their reports directly to the SEC, from computer to computer (see Figure 15.14). In addition to eliminating a great deal of paper, the system has established a valuable data base in which up-to-date information is available without the usual delay experienced with most financial data bases.

Figure 15.14 EDGAR

As well as providing an important data base for businesses, the Security and Exchange Commission's Electronic Data Gathering And Retrieval (EDGAR) system allows on-line preparation and filing of periodic financial reports.

Figure 15.15 Architectural Graphics
Programmers and animators at Omnibus Computer Graphics created this animated conception of Scotia Plaza, a building under construction in Toronto. Based on detailed architectural input, the images were generated in order to attract companies to buy office space in the uncompleted building.

Architecture

Architects can use computer models to run stress tests for buildings they're designing and computer graphics to create complete exterior and interior blueprints and sketches. Figure 15.15 shows the exterior view of such a computerized model. These computer graphics can even be animated so clients in the sales office can see what the building will look like as they walk around its base, fly around its upper stories, or stroll down a hallway. A computer can simulate and/or analyze earthquake resistance, the effects of wind, rain, snow, temperature, and age, and energy efficiency. Modifications can be made instantly. A single change in any part of a blueprint might affect the dimensions anywhere else, and subtle changes that a human might miss can be caught by the computer. The overall process of developing a building plan from generalized schematic sketches to detailed scale drawings can be shortened from three weeks to a day or two.

Computer-generated blueprints and models

BUSINESS APPLICATIONS PACKAGES

The cost of buying a small computer, peripheral devices, and accounting software is minimal in comparison with the cost (for salary, benefits, and facilities) of maintaining an accountant or two. Furthermore, the speed and convenience of keeping the books in-house using a computer far outweigh the difficulties of farming the job out to a CPA firm. A small business will spend only about $5,000 for a computer system that can handle most of its financial operations—an expenditure most small companies can afford. In fact, one South Carolina contractor's modest investment in computer technology saved his company $35,000 annually, paid for itself within four months, and increased his company's profit margin by 15 percent.

Software that contributes to growth and profitability

As the cost of computerizing financial functions falls, more medium and small businesses find it apparent that they're losing money by *not* buying their own computers. Once a company has made the investment in hardware, the use of the appropriate software in the form of *business application packages* enables the company to make drastic reductions in the amount of time and resources spent on mundane but crucial tasks, thus streamlining its operations. We discussed these application packages in detail in Chapter 9, but we will review some of them here.

Accounts and General Ledger

Doing an accountant's job

Computers, with their easily accessible memories and their ability to hold and organize vast quantities of data, are ideally suited to the task of keeping track of accounts, bills, and invoices. Efficient management of accounts helps ensure that customers are billed promptly, that credit is extended prudently (thus avoiding bad debts), and that invoices are paid on time (thus maintaining a good reputation with suppliers).

A *general ledger package* can assemble balance sheets, income statements, and reports that compare this year's financial situation with last year's (or with projections for upcoming months). It can also provide accurate and detailed breakdowns of all the significant information (see Figure 15.16).

Figure 15.16   Accounts and General Ledger Reports

(a) A computer-generated accounts receivable balance sheet and (b) a general ledger summary report.

(a)

```
                    ACCOUNTS  RECEIVABLE

   DATE 12-16-88
   _____

   _____
   CUSTOMER   CUSTOMER                    +30    +60    CREDIT   EXCEEDS
   NUMBER     NAME      BALANCE  CURRENT   DAYS   DAYS   LIMIT    LIMIT
   _____
   14332    ACRES INC    457.34   322.10  135.24                600.
   16734    BOOK CELLAR 1329.80   455.00  437.40  437.40       1500.
   23864    DELFI-CRAFT  152.00    27.00   96.      29.         100.      &
   39000    FITZ/TGNCO  5860.33  2257.00 3423.33               8000.
   57213    HART-PERM     22.00    22.00                       5000.
   78823    MERRICK INC 7833.25   568.20 5620.12 1644.93       6000.      &
   98652    SONDERBELT   745.23   700.00   45.23               1000.
   99455    INTERWHEEL   927.88   365.12  413.     149.76      2000.
   _____
```

(b)

```
                   HYTEK-DATAFLO  CORPORATION  (HDF)

                     SUMMARY   LEDGER   REPORT

                             2/14/89
   _____
                              ACCOUNT BALANCE     YEAR TO DATE
   ACCOUNT  DESCRIPTION         THIS YEAR          LAST YEAR
   _____
   CASH ON HAND & IN BANKS    344,584,904.32    253,452,143.60
   ACCOUNTS RECEIVABLE (NET)  655,473,321.08    527,004,321.97
   INVENTORIES                344,733,211.95    130,892,021.80
   LAND                           548,000.00       520,000.00
   BUILDINGS                  123,894,992.00       864,389.00
   EQUIPMENT/MACHINERY      1,448,993,406.00    894,600,000.00
   SALES                    5,945,652,870.00  1,236,772,345.00
   COST OF SALES GOODS        432,975,346.00    844,987,235.00
   _____
```

Payroll and Labor Analysis

A *payroll analysis* works with information such as pay scales, hours worked, tips, commissions, piecework done, and vacation and leave time owed. It calculates local, state, and federal taxes to be withheld. And it subtracts automatic deductions for Social Security payments, union dues, insurance, and charitable contributions, while simultaneously adding bonuses for holidays and profit-sharing or incentive programs. It even prints out paychecks and earnings statements (see Figure 15.17). All the payroll data can be incorporated into accounting programs that perform year-end calculations for tax filing and financial reports.

Paying employees

A *labor analysis package* is useful for examining worker productivity and cost-effectiveness, to determine whether a workforce should be expanded or diminished and how workers should be distributed throughout the business at any given time. By combining analyses of payroll and labor with information regarding sales volume and customers, an employer can determine the exact cost of providing some

Evaluating the workforce

Figure 15.17 Computerized Payroll

A computer produced this employee paycheck and earnings statement.

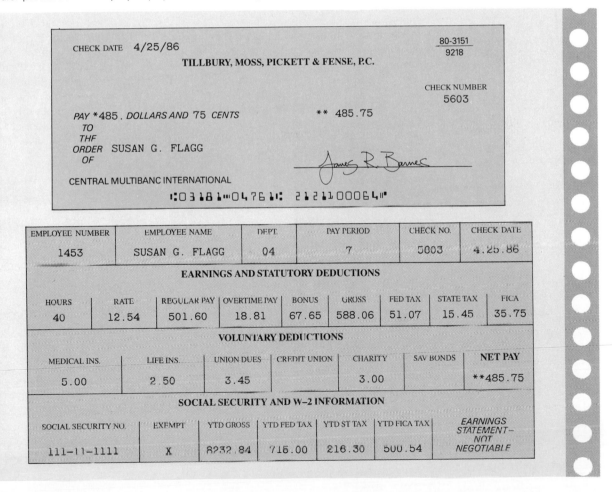

CHECK DATE 4/25/86

80-3151
9218

TILLBURY, MOSS, PICKETT & FENSE, P.C.

CHECK NUMBER
5603

PAY *485. DOLLARS AND 75 CENTS   ** 485.75
TO
THE
ORDER SUSAN G. FLAGG
OF

CENTRAL MULTIBANC INTERNATIONAL

EMPLOYEE NUMBER	EMPLOYEE NAME	DEPT.	PAY PERIOD	CHECK NO.	CHECK DATE
1453	SUSAN G. FLAGG	04	7	5603	4.25.86

EARNINGS AND STATUTORY DEDUCTIONS

HOURS	RATE	REGULAR PAY	OVERTIME PAY	BONUS	GROSS	FED TAX	STATE TAX	FICA
40	12.54	501.60	18.81	67.65	588.06	51.07	15.45	35.75

VOLUNTARY DEDUCTIONS

MEDICAL INS.	LIFE INS.	UNION DUES	CREDIT UNION	CHARITY	SAV BONDS	NET PAY
5.00	2.50	3.45		3.00		**485.75

SOCIAL SECURITY AND W-2 INFORMATION

SOCIAL SECURITY NO.	EXEMPT	YTD GROSS	YTD FED TAX	YTD ST TAX	YTD FICA TAX	EARNINGS STATEMENT— NOT NEGOTIABLE
111-11-1111	X	8232.84	716.00	216.30	500.54	

service to a customer and can therefore allocate employee time more efficiently. Some retail stores now display daily labor analyses on computer screens in the employee lounges, giving their workers greater incentive to produce.

Tax Planning

Paying the government

Information for tax forms, such as a company's quarterly estimates to the IRS and W-2 forms for employees, can also be calculated and then printed on the appropriate forms fairly easily by means of specialized business application packages. Programs for tax planning and preparation offer businesspeople the opportunity to enjoy the benefits of professional tax consultants without the costs. Such programs can project the future results of alternative tax plans and can demonstrate how a particular deduction or other scenario will affect the bottom line of profitability. Suppliers of tax-planning software generally sell updated versions that incorporate all the changes in federal and state tax laws for the past year, thus ensuring that businesses can take advantage of any beneficial new laws and avoid any accidental illegality.

Issues in Technology

Computers in business are only as effective as the businesspeople who run them. A number of studies have shown that in many companies the use of popular business application packages and expensive computer systems resulted in *lower* profits. The reason is that the companies were initially weak, and their management practices failed to keep up with the technology. In these cases, computers only served to make poor business practices worse and did it with the same dramatic efficiency with which they can help sound practices work better. Is there a risk that businesses will expect computers to solve all their problems, will interpret manufacturers' promises of increased profitability as meaning ''just plug it in and watch it go''? How can this risk be avoided? What kind of retraining or restructuring is necessary if management is to avoid the perils of GIGO?

RETAIL APPLICATIONS

Point of Sale

Systems to speed up retail transactions

Today **point-of-sale (POS) systems** are found in grocery stores, pharmacies, department stores, record shops, shoe stores, book stores, video rental outlets—anywhere you can imagine. A POS system consists of one or more terminals connected either to a local minicomputer or to a storage unit that transmits data to a large central computer located elsewhere. Data are entered at the terminal through a keyboard very similar to a cash register's or through OCR or MICR devices, such as hand-held wands or the optical scanners used in many grocery stores.

Although POS terminals cost between 20% and 25% more than conventional cash registers, transactions that take nearly three minutes on those registers are completed in less than 40 seconds with a POS system. POS systems are more accurate and more convenient for customers (aside from their speed, they produce detailed receipts) and cut employee training time in half. The installation of POS systems also allows the number of check-out stations and personnel to be reduced by 25%–50%.

Inventory

Before the advent of computers, retail stores would close down for a day or two to take inventory, that is, to go through the store and stockroom and count how many of each item were present. The process was costly (since the store would lose two days' sales), time-consuming, and subject to errors. Furthermore, since it was only an annual or semiannual event, the numbers weren't current enough to be useful much of the time. With POS systems, stores keep track of their inventories with up-to-the-minute accuracy, and current data are available to managers whenever they need them. Hand-held OCR wands (see Figure 15.18) can be used to enter inventory counts and also to change prices of items electronically. The printed bar codes remain the same, but the computer's interpretation of a code is altered—a much more efficient process than changing thousands of price tags.

Instant performance of a tedious job

Order Processing

The data collected through POS systems can be used in a third way. Not only can a store's computer deduct items from its inventory record with each sale (or add them with each delivery or return), it can be programmed to reorder items automatically when specified inventory threshholds are reached. Computers can be directly connected with regular suppliers, and the ordering, shipping, and payment are all accomplished in a single electronic transaction. This helps avoid costly overstocking or, worse, losing customers because an item has not been ordered in time. Many stores now use automatic order-processing systems for a few items for which sales are generally predictable and for which there is always a demand. In most cases, managers use the detailed inventory data provided by their computer to

Electronic restocking

(a)

(b)

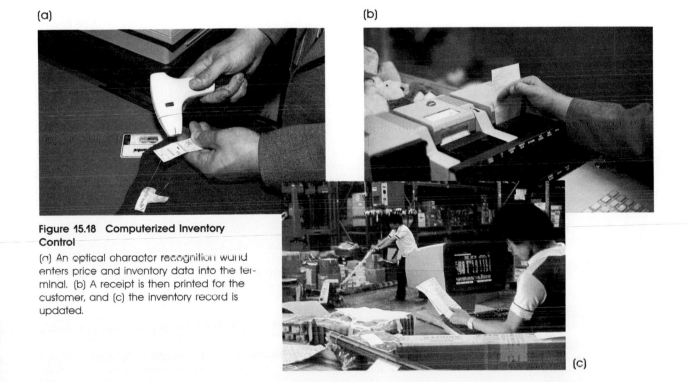

Figure 15.18 Computerized Inventory Control

(a) An optical character recognition wand enters price and inventory data into the terminal. (b) A receipt is then printed for the customer, and (c) the inventory record is updated.

(c)

make informed decisions about whether to reorder. The computer provides the information; the manager still makes the decision. A professional's business sense and good judgement are still necessary, even in this age of computerized business systems.

THE COMMERCIAL NETWORK: PUTTING IT ALL TOGETHER

A summary of computers' roles in business

We've looked now at the various parts of the complicated system we've called the commercial network, from the manufacturing end to the point of sale. Let's take one last look, now, at how it all fits together, with computers every step of the way.

- From the initial conception of a product, to the communication of the idea, to its manufacture, the computer is a tool that insures that the final product reflects the designer's vision and is of superior quality.

- When the product leaves the manufacturing site, computers continue to monitor and assist in the distribution and inventory control functions.

- Behind the scenes, the firm uses computers and application software to maintain its own financial health and to protect its workers, as well as to increase their efficiency.

- When a customer purchases a product, it is both the end and the beginning of our commercial network.

Summary

The Design/Manufacturing Cycle

For many classes of products, the separations among engineering conception (CAE), design (CAD), and detailed specification and drawing are breaking down. Engineering workstations are accelerating the merging of these parts of product development into one continuous process whose output feeds directly into the manufacturing process.

Computer-Aided Design

The main objectives of computer-aided design (CAD) are to increase the productivity of product designers and to produce the required interface to computer-aided manufacturing.

Interactive Graphics: The Geometric Model The engineer creates a geometric model of a product on the screen of an interactive terminal, utilizing any of a variety of input means. The product can then be viewed from different angles and "handled" almost as if it were real. The computer file describing the product also serves as input to analysis and testing programs.

Analysis and Testing Structural and other types of simulated analyses can be performed on a geometric model. Analysis programs can accomplish in hours or days what used to take weeks or months to complete. In addition to saving time and money, this software allows many more design alternatives to be investigated.

The Manufacturing Interface CAD systems automatically produce much of the data required to manufacture a product.

Computer-Aided Manufacturing

Detroit-type automation is geared to the high-volume production of a single product over a relatively long period of time. Programmable automation, using computer-based numerically controlled machine tools and industrial robots, is aimed at increasing the efficiency of more frequently modified or shorter production runs. A major use of the computer in all types of industry, whether automated or not, is the planning, management, and operation of manufacturing.

Programmable Industrial Machines Numerically controlled machine tools turn rough stock into precise machine-made parts. Industrial robots do assembly operations as well as such jobs as welding and spray painting. In numerically controlled machine tools, computer-controlled motors move the material past a cutting tool. The sequence of motions required to cut a given shape is derived from a program written in the specialized high-level programming language APT. Industrial robots can execute a large repertoire of motions and are used for a variety of repetitious, unsafe, or difficult tasks. Robots can be programmed using special languages. They can also be "taught" to do a sequence of operations by moving them manually through the desired sequence. In many applications, robots are grouped into flexible, completely automated production lines.

Process Monitoring and Control When a computer is used as a process monitor, information flows only one way, from sensors measuring physical characteristics of the process to the computer. The computer simply displays information concerning the state of the process, and a human operator takes any necessary action. In automatic process control, which is used mainly in continuous production processes, no human intervention is required.

Manufacturing Support Manufacturing support is a primarily software-oriented application of computer technology in the areas of production planning and control. Inventory management and production scheduling are two main functions that are supported. Computers are sometimes used to simulate production flow in order to detect potential bottlenecks. MRP is a widely used computerized method for generating manufacturing plans; it works backwards from desired completion dates, providing detailed production schedules.

Beyond Manufacturing

Computers are vital to the smooth functioning of a variety of industries.

Banking and Finance On the financial side of the commercial network, computers are not only increasingly convenient, but increasingly necessary. Automatic teller machines (ATMs), which provide basic banking services at diverse locations, and electronic funds transfer (EFT) systems, which allow even wider computer application in financial transactions, may well be the start of the cashless society.

Insurance Insurance companies have huge data bases, containing premiums, policies, actuarial tables, and a host of other statistics, which require the help of computers.

Utilities Running and monitoring equipment, billing, record keeping, rate setting, and operational simulation are some of the principal computer applications on which public utilities rely.

Transportation Rate calculations, reservation systems, and route selection are some of the important tasks to which computers are put by airlines, bus and trucking companies, and car rental agencies. In the airline industry, computers are especially important for inflight control and air traffic control.

Hotels Hotels and motels use computers to streamline reservations, billing, inventory, housekeeping, and special services.

The Stock Market Brokers, investors, and banks use computers when they invest funds in the stock market. The SEC's EDGAR system delivers complete, up-to-date financial data on companies. Electronic information systems provide financial news and market performance information.

Architecture Architects use computers to run stress tests, design buildings, produce blueprints, and sell their designs to customers by using computer-generated (sometimes animated) graphics.

Business Application Packages

Computerizing a business can greatly reduce expenditures, but software is necessary to make a system work. It is largely through the use of business application packages that businesses save time and money.

Accounts and General Ledger Computers help companies keep track of money they owe and money owed to them. Efficient account management ensures prompt billing and payments. A general ledger package uses sales, profit, loss, and expense data and assembles it into coherent records and reports.

Payroll and Labor Analysis Working with such data as pay scales, hours worked, tax rates, and payroll deductions, payroll analysis packages produce paychecks, earning statements, and accounting documents. A labor analysis package can help raise productivity and lower costs by evaluating a company's workforce.

Tax Planning Tax planning programs calculate a company's tax payments by taking profits, expenses, deductions, and tax laws into account. They can prepare the forms and the appropriate documentation.

Retail Applications

From the factory to the check-out aisle, computers help move products, money, and ideas throughout the commercial network. Even the smallest purchase has a significant impact.

Point of Sale POS systems help stores complete sales transactions more quickly and accurately and reduce overhead costs significantly.

Inventory Some of the benefits of a POS system are accurate, updated inventory records, automatic reorders, and information on the current status of the stock.

Order Processing The detailed information produced by a POS system lets managers make informed decisions on what, when, and how much to reorder. Suppliers and manufacturers use computers to process and fill orders.

Computer Concepts

As an extra review of the chapter, try defining the following terms. If you have trouble with any of them, refer to the page number listed.

computer-aided
  engineering (CAE) *516*
computer-aided design
  (CAD) *516*
computer-aided
  manufacturing (CAM)
  516
programmable automation
  520
numerically controlled
  (NC) machine tool *521*

process monitor *524*
open-loop control *524*
automatic process control
  524
closed-loop control *524*
manufacturing support
  526
manufacturing resource
  planning (MRP) *527*

automatic teller machine
  (ATM) *528*
electronic funds transfer
  (EFT) *528*
operational simulations
  529
point-of-sale (POS)
  systems *536*

Review Questions

1. What is computer-aided engineering?
2. What are the two principal objectives of computer-aided design?
3. What is a geometric model? How is it used?

4. What is the difference between dynamic analysis and static analysis?
5. Describe the interactions simulated by Ford Motor Company's automobile simulation system.
6. Distinguish between Detroit-type automation and programmable automation.
7. What are two important types of programmable industrial machines? What is the basic difference between numerically controlled machine tools and programmable industrial robots?
8. Why are most common types of industrial robots referred to as "blind"?
9. What is the main function of a machine tool?
10. What is APT?
11. List six movement capabilities of the typical industrial robot.
12. What is a teach pedant?
13. What are the advantages of a robot-operated production line?
14. Distinguish between process monitoring and automatic process control, and between open-loop control and closed-loop control.
15. With what type of production process do we generally associate automatic process control? Give some examples.
16. What are the major applications of computer-based manufacturing support?
17. What are operational simulations?
18. What is an autoland computer?
19. What is a POS system? What advantages does it have for a business and for a consumer?

True or False

1. A modern engineer's working environment includes CAE and CAD systems.
2. Once a geometric model is in the design data base, it cannot be altered.
3. A dynamic analysis program is used when the loads on a part will be constant.
4. Industrial robots can be reprogrammed to accommodate moderate changes in their tasks.
5. Automatic process control operates only with human intervention.
6. After the October 1987 stock market plunge, an SEC study recommended an increased use of computers to coordinate among regional markets.
7. Credit cards, ATMS, and electronic transfer of funds may replace paper money in the future.
8. A labor analysis package calculates pay scales, tips, commissions, and so forth.
9. Business applications packages are available only for very large companies with large mainframe systems.
10. POS terminals cost slightly less than conventional cash registers because they function more slowly.

Multiple Choice

1. The application of computer programs to simulate electrical or mechanical systems for the design and development of products is:
   (a) CAE   (b) CAD   (c) CAM

2. An assembly line set up to achieve high-volume production of a single product is called:
   (a) programmable   (b) CAD/CAM   (c) Detroit-type
       automation   automation

3. The programming language developed to control part production is:
   (a) APT   (b) workpiece   (c) NC

4. A computer system which relays information about a process to a person who then takes action is:
   - (a) an open-loop control
   - (b) a closed-loop control
   - (c) an actuator

5. The name given to a computerized method developed by IBM for preparing production plans is called:
   - (a) process monitor
   - (b) automatic process control
   - (c) MRP

6. One of the fastest growing applications of computers in banking is the use of:
   - (a) administrative operations
   - (b) ATMs
   - (c) actuarial tables

7. Computers in the insurance industry set rates based on:
   - (a) actuarial tables
   - (b) data bases
   - (c) EFT

8. Computers that guide large jetliners to safe instrument landings are:
   - (a) operational simulators
   - (b) SABRE computers
   - (c) autoland computers

9. A regulatory system that permits the direct filing of company reports with the SEC is called:
   - (a) SABRE
   - (b) EDGAR
   - (c) Inn-Scan

10. A system found in many retail stores that uses local minicomputer terminals connected to a central computer elsewhere is:
   - (a) POS
   - (b) OCR
   - (c) MICR

A Sharper Focus

1. Suppose you had to design a safe and portable container for a toxic waste that remained toxic for 100 years. How would you use CAD to help you test and analyze your product? Do you think you would need to use both static and dynamic analysis programs? Why?

2. How would you describe the advantages and disadvantages of living in a "cashless society?"

Projects

1. Look through the advertisements in several popular magazines. Make a list of products that you think may have been designed and manufactured using CAD/CAM technology. Look through the yellow pages of your phone book. Make a list of businesses you think may use CAD/CAM technology.

2. How many of the business applications of computers discussed in this chapter can you locate in your community? Prepare a brief report in which you document the locations and functions of as many different business applications as you can. Also, suggest what the advantages of each application might be for managers, employees, and consumers.

3. Two students are talking. One says, "Why should I have to learn anything about data processing? I'll be going to work for my father in our funeral parlor." The other replies, "I know. My mom and dad are farmers, and I'm going to work on their farm once I get my degree in agriculture. Computers have nothing to do with me." Are they right? Do some businesses have nothing to gain from adapting a computer to their operations?

Can these two students avoid learning about data processing and still expect their businesses to thrive in today's environment? Support your answer with careful research and cite your sources.

4. One of the cost-saving aspects of POS systems to stores is the fact that they need no longer price each item individually—a big factor in a large grocery store with thousands of items on display, and prices changing from week to week. Prices are simply posted on cards affixed to the display shelves. In the District of Columbia, however, a number of local politicians have become so concerned about the possibility that grocery stores using POS terminals may be programming their computers to charge prices higher than those posted, that they have passed legislation requiring stores to price individually, regardless of whether or not they use POS systems. Write a letter to the editor of your local paper in which you argue one side or the other: Are consumers' interests really threatened by POS?

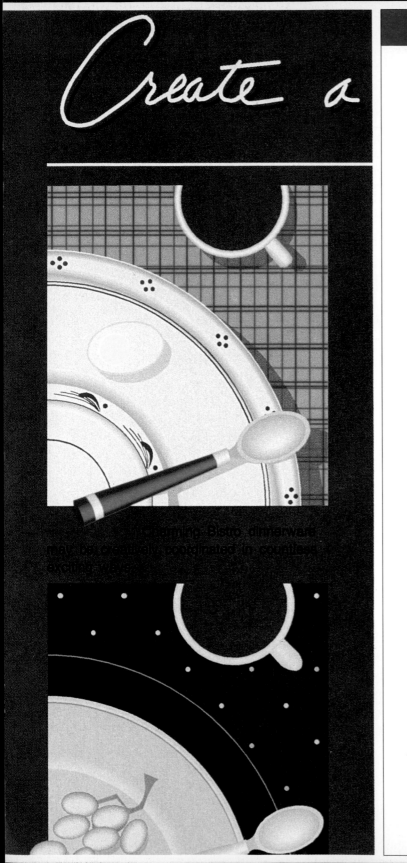

Create a

Whether formal or charming, Bistro dinnerware may be creatively coordinated in countless exciting ways.

16

Computers In Society

In This Chapter

Focus On

Posting Climate Notes on an Electronic Bulletin Board

American, European, and Soviet scientists, acting privately, have gone where their governments, acting officially, might be unable to tread. They have found an electronic meeting place within an American communications system where they can conduct an ongoing dialogue about climatic change.

Normally, such a system would be off limits to the Soviets. It is one of the computer-based networks people use to tap information data banks and communicate using desktop and portable computers. The United States government is skittish about foreign access—especially East-bloc access—to such a system even when it is entirely civilian and open.

Thanks to the good offices of the European Space Agency (ESA), this privately funded venture has managed to allay security concerns. It's a minor communications breakthrough that should benefit the whole world.

For the next year, the scientists involved will be discussing one of the most important of global environmental problems—the prospects for, and possible effects of, a so-called greenhouse climatic warming. This is the warming expected as carbon dioxide, produced by burning fossil fuels, and other heat-trapping gases accumulate in the atmosphere.

A number of national and international programs are already studying such global climate questions. The electronic linkup provides a kind of electronic lounge where experts from three major fuel-burning regions can talk about their work informally. It would be impossible to do this on a face-to-face basis when the participants are scattered across the Northern Hemisphere. This way, two or more of them can converse daily and leave messages on what amounts to a community bulletin board.

They will tackle many aspects of the warming question, including possible effects on agriculture. They can share ideas, speculate, and explore possible solutions to problems they perceive. Any suggestions for action can then be fed back to their governments and into their formal research programs.

Roald Sagdeyev, head of the Institute for Space Research of the Soviet Union, chairs the Soviet panel. Walter Orr Roberts, president emeritus of the University Corporation for Atmospheric Research, and Russell Schweikert, a former astronaut, chair the American group. ESA ties bring the two groups and some European scientists together.

ESA supplied computers to the Soviets in a way that meets export restrictions. With these, Soviet scientists can go through an ESA communications line to tap into a segment of the electronic mail system of the Telenet network. That's all they can do, Schweikert explains. They don't even know the procedure to log on to the network. So American security needs are satisfied.

It's an ingenious way to make connections from which everyone profits.

"Society," in its broadest sense, is nothing more than the way in which individuals relate to one another. Specifically, it is a group of human beings distinguished from other groups by mutual interests, shared institutions, and a common culture. In our society, people teach and learn, they cure illness, they entertain themselves, and they protect one another—through laws and, sometimes, through force. (That's hardly an exhaustive list, but it will do for now.) We pay for the privileges of our society by paying taxes. In all of these activities, in which we build and maintain a livable society for ourselves, computers are a rapidly growing influence. Teachers, artists, doctors, policemen, soldiers, and politicians all use the same tool, in its various incarnations, to achieve their different goals.

In this chapter, we'll look at some of the applications of computer technology used in a wide range of fields. We'll begin with a common starting point for everyone—education—and then turn to the fascinating, ground-breaking, creative, and controversial applications of computers in the arts, medicine, law enforcement, and defense.

COMPUTERS AND EDUCATION

Nearly two million computers can be found in U.S. schools, helping administrators keep track of the business of education, helping teachers improve their students' progress, and helping students learn. It's an $800 million-a-year investment. Most of the applications are still confined to computer classes, though, with the most exciting possibilities only just being tapped. For example, a 1988 study by the National Assessment of Educational Progress showed that while 60 percent of eleventh graders knew that computers were good for word processing and games, they were unfamiliar with graphics applications or data bases—some of the areas just now being explored by educators. But computer manufacturers are finding that worthwhile tax breaks and other incentives are available from federal, state, and local governments in return for the donation of computers to financially stressed public schools. With a growing quantity of computers being used in schools, the number of educational applications of computers is likely to increase significantly.

Improving students' performance

Educators, once wary of their electronic teaching assistants, are finding computers are not threats to their own jobs but rather are valuable learning tools for students. In an age increasingly affected by computer technology, the absence of terminals in a school may prove to be as devastating to a student's potential as would be the absence of instruction in reading or arithmetic (see Figure 16.1). Studies have revealed that students in high schools where computers are available score from 13 to 16 points more on the SAT exam, particularly on the math section, than students in computerless schools. One Maryland county required computer-assisted instruction in its classrooms in 1983, and five years later student test scores elevated the county's schools from 13th place to third in the state. In Florida high schools, interactive computers have helped curb the growing flood of dropouts. Some studies report that one of the major contributing factors to a student's dropping out is pressure from peers to work beyond the student's ability: a student with fourth-grade reading skills in a tenth-grade classroom quickly lost confidence and, in large part to avoid ridicule, left. With computers, no one but the student and teacher know at what level the high-risk student is working; confidence and enthusiasm, followed by real educational progress, result.

Figure 16.1 Computer-Assisted Instruction
Learning to read isn't just a simple matter of opening books anymore. Here, a young reader is learning to spell *elephant* with the help of a voice-recognition system and computer graphics.

At the college level, students spend more than $1 billion a year on personal computing products. But even at the elementary level, teachers are using computers with remarkable success to teach children in kindergarten how to read. Even earlier, education-minded parents with home computers have access to a wide variety of software designed with preschoolers in mind—Cookie Monster helps three-year-olds learn to count; elephants and bears demonstrate shapes. And while most students' subsequent use of computers is restricted to either programming classes, computer labs, or drills and tutorials in language and math, the possibilities presented by modeling, graphics, simulation, and interactivity are endless as shown in Figure 16.2.

In special education classes, teachers are discovering that use of computers can improve the reading skills of learning-impaired children by more than 70 percent. Physically and mentally disabled students are able to use computers to manipulate their environment in ways they never could before. Students with cerebral palsy, for example, who can't use their hands to draw on paper, can create pictures on a computer screen by keying in a program. That such activities perform an instructional and therapeutic function is obvious. That computers have opened up careers previously closed to the disabled, such as architecture and design, is perhaps less

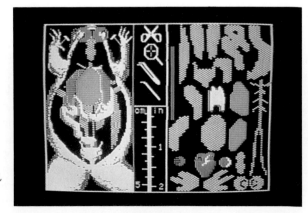

Figure 16.2 Educational Stimulation
Scholastic Inc.'s *Operation: Frog* is an excellent example of an educational simulation package. With this program, a microcomputer user can perform a realistic dissection of a frog.

apparent, but no less appreciated by educators. In all special education classes, computers have demonstrated convincingly that they are an asset, not just a distraction.

Computer-Assisted Instruction

Computer-assisted instruction, or **CAI,** is the use of computers to assist in the process of learning. CAI is derived from the work in *behavior modification* done by B. F. Skinner. Educators were quick to see the possible classroom applications of his theories of reward and punishment. If students receive an immediate positive response to their work, they tend to learn material more rapidly and to retain information longer. Although instant feedback can be virtually impossible for one teacher faced with 30 students, it's a piece of cake for a computer. Thus the development of computer-assisted instruction.

Helping teachers provide individualized attention

Initially, computer-assisted instruction consisted of quizzing, or "drill-and-practice," routines. The computer presented a question to the student, who responded. If the student's answer was correct, the computer displayed "yes" or some similar positive message and went on to the next question. If the student was wrong, the computer indicated that, gave the right answer, and presented another question similar to the first. Although such simple formats are still in use today, for example, in the kindergarten reading program we described above, more intriguing and sophisticated educational uses of computers are being developed every day. Computers are used for foreign language drills (in which the student and computer engage in a Spanish, French, or German dialog), tutoring (in which concepts are explained and wrong answers are corrected at length), and problem solving in physics and higher mathematics. Computers can provide students with realistic decision-making scenarios (as we'll see in a later section of this chapter on physician training) or engage them in complex *Socratic dialogs* (interchanges in which questions and answers, from both student and computer, run along a logical line to a clear conclusion). In history classes, students can refight the Battle of Gettysburg or rule a feudal manor, in which case the computer will inform them of the effects of their decrees on the economy, agriculture, or political climate of their fiefdom.

Math teachers have found that computers perform a doubly valuable role in their classrooms, since writing a program to solve a problem requires that a student be completely comfortable not only with programming techniques but also with the basic mathematical concepts represented by the problem (see Figure 16.3). Some high school students have become such practiced programmers that they have produced customized software for their teachers in geography, economics, calculus, and history. One of these precocious programmers made over $40,000 his first year out of high school by writing a game for an Apple computer.

Some colleges and universities, such as Carnegie-Mellon, Drexel, Boston College, and Dartmouth, require some or all of their entering students to purchase a personal computer along with their textbooks and notepads. More and more college libraries are installing catalog search computer systems to replace bulky and unmanageable files of index cards. In addition to traditional fields of computer-based instruction (math and science), CAI programs teach subjects as diverse as expository writing, poetry, physics, logic, foreign languages, business, economics, and sociology. Business students can create and operate electronic businesses, create whole chains of suppliers and customers, and experiment with different management techniques in the face of shortages, labor disputes, or rapid market expansion.

Figure 16.3 The Math Utilities
An excellent example of software used in mathematics
instruction.

Some college departments across the country are participating in programs in which professors are loaned personal computers that they can keep if they develop an application appropriate to their discipline. The benefits are threefold: increased production of home-generated software for colleges, innovative course material for students, and personal computers for professors' use.

For example, Professor Alfred Kern, a professor at Allegheny College in Pennsylvania, teaches a class called ''BASIC Poetry.'' Professor Kern wrote a program that produces poetry, and uses it to demonstrate to students the mathematical properties of classic poetic forms such as the sonnet. Armed with a list of 600 words and instructions on grammar, syntax, line length, meter, and stanza forms, the computer randomly selects words from its dictionary and assembles them into the appropriate format:

Diary Excerpt: Emeritus

The sunset is leaving, shouting but silent
Singing or crying its joy or anger
The sun's whim was this afternoon's season:
Beautiful, cruel, worldly, now forgotten, now cherished,
Sometimes feared, sometimes invented, always grasping
As we were demanding earths and legs and continents of orchids
And the intention and the life of our own raucous blood;
For this sunset is ours, our curse, our home,
Rushing but staying, enduring time glacial and quick.

Computer-Managed Instruction

All CAI applications represent ways in which computers are used primarily to help students. **Computer-managed instruction,** or **CMI,** on the other hand, is the use of computers to help teachers. Although they are different, CAI and CMI are

Figure 16.4 Archive 2
An electronic test banking, construction, and printing system for instructors.

often used together. CMI systems allow teachers to monitor students' progress in CAI programs and to diagnose their strengths and weaknesses (see Figure 16.4). CMI systems can graphically display a student's performance over a given period, illustrate overall progress, or output detailed breakdowns and analyses of problem areas. In addition, as a sort of electronic attendance-keeper, the CMI system can keep track of how often and for how long each student was at the terminal, which lets the teacher know whether students have been conscientious about their assignments and reveals whether more or less computer-assisted instruction is required.

Monitoring students' progress

What happens to students who attend financially strapped inner-city or isolated rural schools that can't afford to purchase expensive computer equipment? Manufacturers can't be expected to donate computers to every school in the country, but schools that can get computers have a clear advantage. Might our democratic public education system soon begin to produce two distinct "classes" of students: the computer-literate, who have higher test scores and a clearer shot at success in a high-tech job market; and the computer-illiterate, who are as unfairly deprived of a complete education as if they were denied math books? What is the answer, if any?

Issues in Technology

COMPUTERS AND ENTERTAINMENT

The word *entertainment* encompasses a far broader range of endeavors than we'll be able to discuss here. However, whether the field is music, literature, dance, sculpture, painting, photography, cinematography, or even the language arts, computers are playing an ever-expanding role in all kinds of creative, and entertaining, expressions.

Music

Computer-generated music and computer-assisted composition

The first song actually played on a computer was "A Bicycle Built for Two" at Bell Laboratories in 1932, and computers have, in effect, been humming away ever since. For a computer to produce music, just as for a computer to do anything, its input must be converted to numbers, processed, and then converted into human-understandable output. Because music's tonal and rhythmical qualities are mathematically based (it was the Greek mathematician Pythagoras who, in the sixth century B.C., invented the seven-tone *diatonic scale* still used in Western music), converting a melody's "formula" into computerese is a fairly straightforward operation.

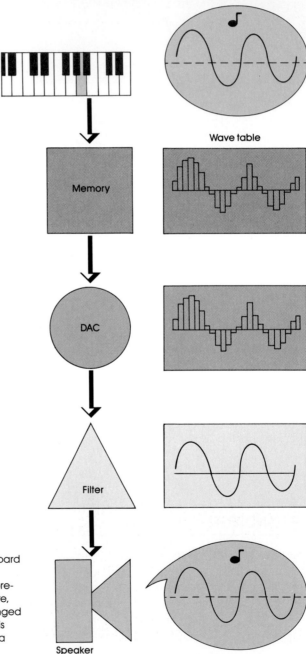

Figure 16.5 Pulse Code Modulation

A computer produces sound by matching each keyboard instruction (or note) to a sequence of binary numbers stored in its memory. The sequence, a *wave table* representing a sound wave that will produce a musical note, goes to a digital-to-analog converter, where it is changed into a series of electrical pulses. This "stair-step" wave is then smoothed by a filter into a wave that can drive a speaker.

Pulse Code Modulation

Electronic music is the result when the conversion of a melodic formula into binary form is made through **pulse code modulation (PCM).** Simply stated, pulse code modulation is the assigning of binary values to tonal input—that is, a sound wave receives its own digital description (B-flat becomes, for example, 00001101). A sound wave is a series of fluctuations in the air pressure measured over time. These fluctuations are assigned a digital value, called a **sample,** that is stored in a computer's memory. The computer displays the sound wave graphically as a series of "stair-step" bars called a **waveform.** A **digital-to-analog converter (DAC)** is a device that translates the binary word representing a sound into a voltage signal, and a *filter* smooths the computer's stair-step sound wave into a curve, which is then amplified through a speaker so it becomes audible sound. Figure 16.5 illustrates this process.

In the old days (15 years ago) generating computer music required tape recorders and a lot of time. Today, the whole process can be completed in real time: an on-stage computer can process and manipulate a soloist's or even a whole orchestra's sound even as it is produced, mixing instrumental, choral, and "processed" sounds to achieve new and frequently beautiful effects. A computer for such a concert must be very fast, such as the French SOGITEC 4X, which performs 200 million operations per second and stores 1,032 different waveforms. The mixing of sound and routing among speakers is the job of a computer like the IRCAM Matrix 32, which is capable of totally reconfiguring sounds in one-tenth of a second.

Composition

Composers from Phillip Glass to virtually any current pop group are also aided by the use of computer hardware and software. Composers can use systems produced by Yamaha, IBM, Apple, and dozens of smaller companies, to compose music at a keyboard; the notes they play are displayed on a screen in standard sheet-music format as seen in Figure 16.6. The composition can be edited, the notes can be printed on sheet-music paper, and the musical data can be stored on diskettes. A software-drive synthesizer will play back the composition for the composer, simulating as many as 100 different musical instruments from French horns to kazoos. Figure 16.7 shows some of the components of a computerized music system.

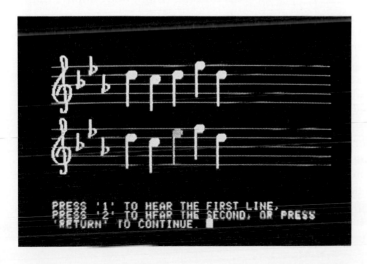

Figure 16.6 Music System Components
An Apple music composition system.

Figure 16.7 Electronic Music
As computer-based electronics flood the music world, it's becoming increasingly difficult to tell the performers from the engineers. For this musician, the piano keyboard and the computer keyboard are equally important instruments.

With music software and a synthesizer, composers can alter a work's rhythm and tempo at will. The computer automatically stores the input notes according to the desired time, regardless of the speed at which the musician plays them. Melodies, harmonies, and intricate variations can be mixed and altered with a few simple commands. Many popular musicians can't read music, but such musical computer systems allow them to compose by ear as well as to produce copies of their musical creations so other musicians can perform them. Computers may thus serve to democratize music by opening up composition and performance to people who possess natural musical talent, but lack the years of training traditionally required.

Creative Graphics

We've already seen some applications of computer graphics to video games, product design, and business presentations. Now we consider the use of the computer by artists who create original images for films and television, and simply for art's sake.

Computer images can not only mimic reality but also create original pictures and impossible and otherworldly scenes with a startling realism and mathematical precision. Remember that computers can deal only with numbers, and the production of graphics is no exception to that rule. The delicate Japanese teapots in Figure 16.8 are simply the end-product of complex mathematical equations to the computer that created them. They result from calculations just like those performed by a hand-held calculator, only many degrees more complicated.

Analyzing and manipulating pixels to generate art

A graphic simulator "sees" and reproduces the world as a sort of jigsaw puzzle of *pixels*, or *picture elements*. Computers, of course, are not the only devices that break images up into pieces. Look closely at a newspaper picture—it's actually just a collection of shaded dots, a form of pixels. About 25,000 dots are contained in a 2-inch by 3-inch newspaper photograph. A television picture is also a collection of pixels, about 281,000 on a 19-inch screen. The 35-mm motion picture film used for

Figure 16.8 A Computer-Generated Still Life
This image was developed and produced by a Lucasfilm computer, with some help from programmer Alvy Ray Smith. Using a process called ray tracing, the computer "traces" an imaginary ray of light from each pixel point on its screen to an "object," the objects surrounding it, and finally to the light source. By thus "tracing" a ray of light backward, the computer collects detailed data on the object's color and reflective properties, as well as the location, brightness, and color of the light source. Painstaking and strange, the process results in astoundingly realistic images, such as these teapots.

most movies has about 9 million pixels per frame. The more pixels, or *dots per inch (DPI)*, the better will be the picture's clarity, or *resolution.*

For a computer to generate graphic images like those shown here, it first reads an artist's program, which mathematically describes the dimensions, shape, and configuration of the image to be generated. In an alternative method, analog-to-digital conversion hardware (similar to the digital-to-analog converters we described in the section on music) scans photographs or drawings and converts the images to binary digits, which the computer can store and which can be called up later for alteration or printing. A third method involves the use of a special graphics tablet, or digitizer, and a light pen, with which the artist directly inputs the lines forming the image into the computer.

In any case, the picture is transformed into pixels, which the computer then fills in. First each pixel is assigned a multidigit code. This code describes the shade of the pixel's color and the intensity with which it reflects the light (which determines the material of which the object will appear to be made) and is based on knowledge of the laws of optics stored in the computer's memory. Then each pixel is compared with all the others, which can number from 9 million to more than 100 million, to achieve the proper relationships of shape and texture, light and shadow, color and reflection.

An image composed of 9 million pixels can take a computer nearly 20 hours to generate. When this technology is applied, whether commercially or artistically, the entire process can take months to complete. But all the time, effort and expense required to produce "computer art" hasn't dissuaded artists, filmmakers, advertising agencies, television networks, and a wide variety of others striving for striking visual presentations from turning to computers for artistic assistance (see Figure 16.9).

Recreating Reality

A technique called **ray tracing** allows the computer to recreate the effects of individual rays of light reflected off of smooth surfaces and entering an observer's eye. Combined with a more recent technique, **radiosity,** which quantifies the way light is diffused by highly textured or translucent objects, algorithms can accurately

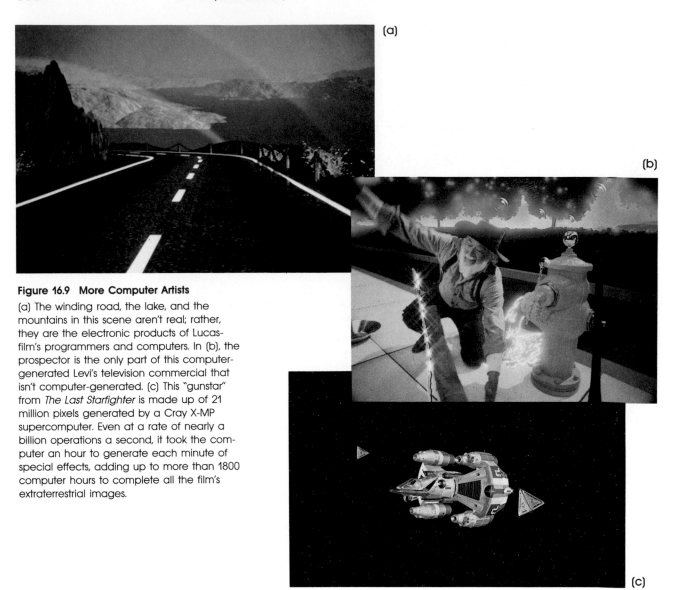

Figure 16.9 More Computer Artists

(a) The winding road, the lake, and the mountains in this scene aren't real; rather, they are the electronic products of Lucasfilm's programmers and computers. In (b), the prospector is the only part of this computer-generated Levi's television commercial that isn't computer-generated. (c) This "gunstar" from *The Last Starfighter* is made up of 21 million pixels generated by a Cray X-MP supercomputer. Even at a rate of nearly a billion operations a second, it took the computer an hour to generate each minute of special effects, adding up to more than 1800 computer hours to complete all the film's extraterrestrial images.

simulate the visual look and "feel" of an object. Experiments with a new technique called a **rendering equation,** that shows how light is refracted by a transparent medium onto another surface, have been encouraging. Nonetheless, the shimmering of sunlight on the bottom of a swimming pool is hard for a computer, bound by mathematics and geometry, to recreate. Through **fractal geometry** (algorithms that can generate seemingly random structures and objects), computer artists can create mountain ranges, forests, and ocean waves. But truly complex, textured, idiosyncratic images that defy reduction to polygons—faces, animals, a quilt tossed over the back of a sofa—are still impossible for a computer to recreate with any level of convincing realism. But computer programmer–artists keep trying.

The Movies

Of all the arts, film is the most modern, the most mechanical, and the most dependent on technological advances. A piece of charcoal and a fairly clean cave wall are the only necessary components of painting, and all a musician really needs is a voice, but film is essentially a technological art form. Before Thomas Edison and William Dickson invented the kinetograph around 1890, there simply were no movies. Since then, whenever an applicable technological advance was made, whether it was sound recording (also an Edison invention, intended to help the hearing impaired), or cameras that could take pictures in existing light, the movie industry quickly embraced it. Computers are no exception. Today, some avant-garde filmmakers are producing short movies that are entirely composed of computer-generated images. In the mainstream, the application of computers in two areas of filmmaking, editing and special effects, is particularly significant.

A technology-dependent medium, from editing and sound mixing to special effects

Editing

The two-hour movie you see at your local cinema was recorded on more than 10,000 feet of celluloid held on six reels; more than 1000 individual still pictures (*frames*) are required for each minute of action. The movie was composed of an average of 2000 separate pieces of film, painstakingly strung together, resorted, and respliced (taped and cut and taped again). Many months of work (that sometimes takes longer than the filming itself) are needed before those assorted bits of celluloid will wind up telling a story. That's the way most movies are made.

By capitalizing on the speedy and efficient organizational and cataloging abilities of computers, filmmakers can both shorten and improve the editing process. *Star Wars* director George Lucas has an advanced editing computer called EditDroid at his northern California studio that edits film in a fraction of the time. EditDroid scans unedited pieces of film and transfers the images to videodisks, assigning a number value to each frame. With EditDroid's help, the editor can then mark the beginnings and ends of sequences and move them around the same way a word processor moves blocks of text.

Special Effects

The production of new and original images or photographic effects is becoming increasingly important to movies. As audiences become more sophisticated, the old techniques of painted backdrops, models "flying" on wires, stop-action gorillas, and men in monster suits stomping little cardboard cities no longer packs them in. Traditional *matte effects* (Figure 16.10) produced shadowless, disproportioned images with blue-ringed silhouettes. The whole point of a special effect is to convince the audience that what they're seeing is "real." In a world where films boast a new special effect every 11 minutes (such as Lucas's 1988 film *Willow*), computers, again, are the filmmakers' answer.

A computer simply scans the film and "reads" the images not as pictures but as numeric values. The computer can then be programmed to remove all the blue or red or green values of a particular shade or any combination of shades, and replace them, precisely, with values from the desired background or object. People can be "inserted" convincingly into unexpected locations, cities can be transformed—anything can happen. The resultant image is as precise as numbers can be.

(a)

(b)

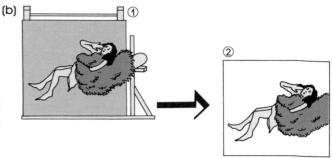

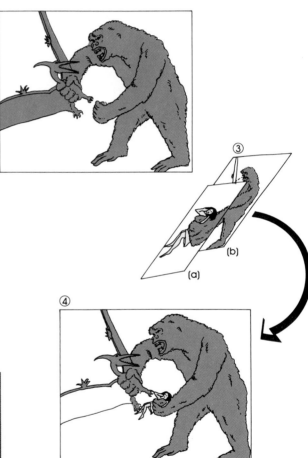

Figure 16.10   The Matte Effect

(a) The matte effect was used extensively (along with other manually-produced photographic effects) in movies such as 1933's *King Kong*. In this still, the ape and pterodactyl, the woman, and the background were all filmed separately, then combined. (b) Traditionally, a matte effect is achieved by (1) filming an image in front of a blue screen, then (2) photographically reprocessing the image to remove the blue elements, leaving only a figure on a transparent field. When that print is physically overlaid onto another (3), the result is a matte image (4). The first image blocks out part of the second, and the two appear to be in the same place. Exact synchronization of camera and model movements, as well as a steady, expert hand in the photo lab, are vital if the effect is to be convincing. (c) This special effects scene from 1983's *Return of the Jedi* far surpasses the quality of computer images of earlier films.

(c)

COMPUTERS AND MEDICINE

Education and entertainment aren't the only areas in which the power of computers to manage data, to simulate, and to model is revolutionizing the way things are done. The cost of health services in the United States exceeds $300 billion annually. This is more than the defense budget or the cost of all food sold at the retail level; it's about 10 percent of the annual gross national product. Computers play a significant and growing part in virtually all aspects of the health services industry. Although they contribute positively to the quality of medical education, instrumentation, diagnosis, and treatment, they may also contribute to the increased cost of health care. In this section, we'll study the role of the computer in medical advances from the points of view of both patient and practitioner.

Physician Training

Even before they become M.D.'s, today's medical students are exposed to computers. At New York University's School of Medicine, for example, computer-generated graphics allows students to "operate" repeatedly on a simulated patient, practicing different techniques and surgical strategies that would otherwise require hundreds of cadavers. A three-dimensional perspective can be viewed from any angle; unexpected (but preprogrammed) complications can arise; and the healing process takes place in minutes, allowing the prospective surgeons to observe their success.

Simulating the patient's response to treatment

At the University of Illinois Medical Center in Chicago, students practice diagnosis with the help of a computer-simulated "patient." Students ask questions in conversational English and receive responses. They can call up stored medical records concerning the case and consult with programmed "specialists" before diagnosing the problem and prescribing a cure. The correct diagnosis is provided immediately, as well as the results of the selected treatment. If they get it wrong, they can try again—an option that won't necessarily be open to them in real practice, of course.

Decision Making

Since the late 1950s, ongoing attempts have been made to use medical data bases to make diagnoses by relating sets of symptoms to specific diseases through the use of various inference techniques. (Some of these techniques can be classified as artificial intelligence, which we'll discuss in Chapter 18.) The largest of these systems is the University of Pittsburgh's CADUCEUS (formerly known as INTERNIST), a program that cross-indexes 500 disease profiles with more than 3000 separate symptoms. When provided with a patient's medical records and current complaints, it can diagnose the patient's problem, recommend further tests (including a consideration of costs and discomfort factors), and suggest treatment. The program was designed to follow the diagnostic strategies of an eminent physician at the university and has passed the board examinations in internal medicine. Similar programs include Stanford's MYCIN, which diagnoses blood infections, and PUFF, which analyzes data from breath samples to diagnose cardiopulmonary problems.

Computer-generated diagnoses

Medical Imaging

*X-rays, CAT scans,
ultrasound, and other
imaging techniques*

The medical applications we've discussed so far work with data that consist of either alphanumeric text or digitized (one-dimensional) curves, requiring no more than several thousand bytes of storage for each record. Now we turn to the two- and three-dimensional images produced by medical imaging systems. More than 20,000 traditional X-ray machines are in use in the United States and another 10,000 fluorographic X-ray units. Some hospitals currently digitize X-ray films by a variety of means and maintain them in a computer-accessed data base. Since an average X-ray machine produces 50 films per day, and each digitized film requires a million bytes of storage, this is no small job. Another problem is that the digitizing methods aren't uniformly good at preserving the high resolution required for making difficult diagnoses.

It seems entirely possible that conventional X-ray machines will, over the long run, be displaced by recently developed units that produce digital images directly. A conventional X-ray machine works by exposing a film plate to a beam of X-rays. A new system, developed by Fuji, exposes a phosphor plate to the X-rays. When scanned by a laser, this plate produces light output that can be digitally recorded. The phosphor plates are packaged in cassettes of the same size as the film cassettes that fit into the existing machines. Moreover, they require shorter exposure times. This new system, as well as other direct digital X-ray techniques, is currently being evaluated at several major U.S. hospitals.

A complicating factor in X-ray diagnosis is that the more dense a region of the body, the higher its rate of absorption of X-rays. As a result, all dense regions show up on X-ray images as shadows, and it's often difficult to distinguish overlapping structures, particularly when they have comparable densities. **Computerized axial tomography (CAT)** scanners solve this problem by taking X-rays through the body at many different angles. The various images obtained this way are then

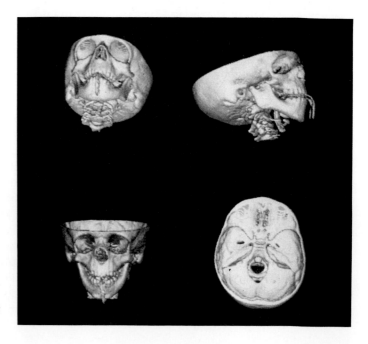

Figure 16.11 Computerized Axial Tomography
Data from a CAT scan or NMR scan can be manipulated, in real time, by the examining physician. Using controls such as trackballs and cursors, they can be rotated or cut away to show what lies beneath.

recombined by a sophisticated computer program into images of horizontal sections of the body. These "slices," when stacked up, show the internal structures in three dimensions. More than 2000 CAT scanners are currently in use in the United States.

A comparable imaging technique employs ultrasound; this technique is like radar in the sense that it reconstructs information on the basis of the returning echoes of transmitted pulses. These pulses, however, are at ultrasonic, rather than radio, frequencies. Ultrasound systems primarily employ analog computers for the reconstruction and storing of images on videocassette recorders. They are particularly safe to use since they use acoustic radiation, and they are also relatively inexpensive. As a result, more than 10,000 of these systems have been installed in the United States.

Other computerized imaging techniques are **positron emission transaxial tomography (PETT)** and **nuclear magnetic resonance (NMR)** scans. Doctors who want to avoid exploratory brain surgery can employ PETT or NMR scans to observe chemical reactions and metabolic functions in the brain to locate tumors or discern brain damage. PETT scans use a radioactive substance that is injected into the patient's brain. NMR scans represent the newest technology in imaging. They are carried out not with X-rays or with radioactive injections, but with magnetic fields produced by a large circular magnet that surrounds the patient. A radio-frequency energy source is coupled with this magnetic field to create a computer-generated image more accurate than that of a CAT scan. While doctors watch, the NMR scanner can produce "motion pictures" showing the movement of blood or the reaction of a tumor to treatment.

An excellent example of the merging of computerized medical imaging techniques with advanced computer display systems is shown in Figure 16.11.

Prosthetics and Beyond

Microelectronics has brought amazing advances to the field of prosthesis (the replacement of limbs and organs with artificial devices). Over 100,000 electronic pacemakers are implanted every year in the United States alone. Researchers at the Illinois Institute of Technology have invented a microelectronic system by which artificial limbs can be moved by the brain's own electrical impulses, just like natural limbs—a sort of "thought control." Electrodes convert neural signals into electricity, which a microprocessor in the artificial limb interprets to activate an electromechanical movement system. Similar systems are used to exercise and control paralyzed limbs. Pressure-sensitive silicon sensors arrayed on the tips of prosthetic fingers can give people an artificial sense of touch.

Tiny, surgically-embedded computers can also stimulate auditory and optical nerve signals, bypassing damaged or malfunctioning inner ears or optical nerves, allowing the deaf to hear and the blind to see: such experimental microsystems are now in the late stages of development (Figure 16.12). Artificial hearts controlled by microprocessors have the potential to prolong life for years (although doctors at the Humana hospitals more frequently rely on them not as permanent replacements, but rather as short-term, interim measures). Computers that perform fetal monitoring can warn doctors of health problems in patients still unborn, and computerized devices that detect brain waves are accepted in many states as the final authority in pronouncing death. From *before* the cradle to the grave, physicians now rely on computers to help them observe, analyze, monitor, treat, and cure their patients.

Microprocessor-driven systems to replace injured limbs and organs

Figure 16.12 Hopkins/NASA "Spaceglasses"

Technology provides new hope for the visually impaired.

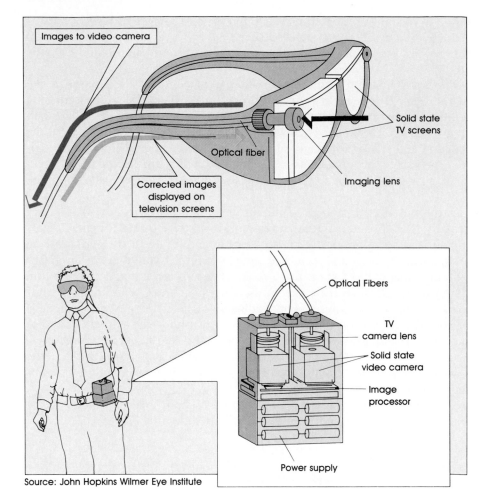

Source: John Hopkins Wilmer Eye Institute

COMPUTERS AND GOVERNMENT

Let's turn our attention now from the use of computers in the private sector to their use in the public sector, in some of our governmental institutions. We'll look at three areas in particular: law enforcement; the Internal Revenue Service; and defense. Law, taxes, and war may hardly seem to be the most pleasant topics; but government use of computers is hardly limited to these sometimes unpopular applications—these are just the largest, most pervasive, and, in the case of defense, most technologically innovative.

The Big Picture

More than 100,000 local, county, and state government bodies in the United States use computers to do everything from counting votes in school referenda to capturing criminals. On the national level, more than 4 billion personal files are stored in computer systems by the federal government—15 or 20 files on each and every citizen. The information is vital to the government's ability to provide benefits from the whole range of social programs, for the enforcement of tax laws, and for letting legislators know just what the voters want.

In Congress, those legislators use computers to cast votes and track legislative bills as they make their way through a labyrinth of committees and subcommittees, and to personalize correspondence with constituents (see Figure 16.13). Lobbyists and other groups use computers to track legislation of interest to them, and to keep track of voting records. And in the White House, the Executive Office of the Presidency Computer Center (EOPCC) has more than quadrupled in size since 1980. Computers in local, state, and federal governments work together in areas such as welfare and taxation, saving time, money, and mountains of paper. The governmental applications of computer technology are as extensive as the bureaucracy itself; the computers' software and circuitry are working tirelessly, night and day, to "preserve and protect."

Law Enforcement

Many of the newest computer applications in government are in law enforcement. The Want and Warrant System of Los Angeles County, the Law Enforcement Information Network (LEIN) of the Michigan state police, and the New York Statewide Police Information Network (NYSPIN) are just three examples of the increasing use of computer networks by the police. By storing criminal and arrest records and crime reports in computers, law enforcement personnel can more readily identify stolen property and suspected criminals. When local computers are linked with county and state data bases, and states or regions cooperatively set up computer-

Finding, capturing, and monitoring criminals

(a)

(b)

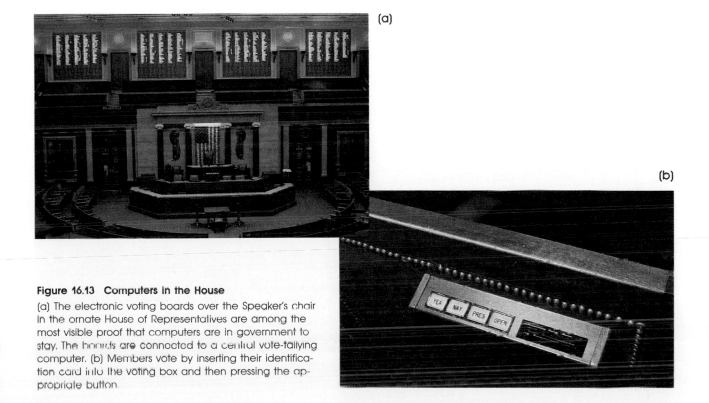

Figure 16.13 Computers in the House

(a) The electronic voting boards over the Speaker's chair in the ornate House of Representatives are among the most visible proof that computers are in government to stay. The boards are connected to a central vote-tallying computer. (b) Members vote by inserting their identification card into the voting box and then pressing the appropriate button.

ized dragnets, law enforcement becomes much more efficient. In most major cities, police squad cars are equipped with portable computer terminals for quickly checking license plates, car registrations, and driver's licenses against a central data base (see Figure 16.14). In New York, a hand-held computer called SIDNEY (short for Summons-Issuing Device for New York) helps traffic police identify drivers who habitually neglect to pay their parking tickets. When an officer enters the license plate number on SIDNEY's tiny keyboard, a small printer strapped to his or her belt prints the ticket, and SIDNEY's screen displays any prior unpaid violations. The car can then be towed away if necessary.

The National Crime Information Center

Established in 1967, the FBI's **National Crime Information Center (NCIC)** is a central data repository used by law enforcement agencies all over North America and in Europe. Its computers store over 8 million active records of arrests and convictions and are accessed by local police more than 275,000 times every day. Fingerprint records have been digitized and are now accessible through NCIC computers as well. NCIC's responses are sent back in less than two seconds and result in roughly a thousand arrests or return of stolen property daily (see Figure 16.15).

For example, suppose that a local police officer in a tiny Iowa town stops a speeding auto. The officer, before leaving her car, routinely radios the license plate number to the state police, who check with computers at the National Crime Information Center (NCIC). In two minutes, the police officer approaches the stopped car cautiously, with her gun out, because she knows that the car's license plates were stolen in Nebraska, the car was stolen in Florida, and the driver is a man on the FBI's most-wanted list for murder in Kentucky. Before the advent of computer-assisted law enforcement, the driver might have simply paid his fine and gone free.

Collecting Debts to Society

Other examples are less dramatic but equally effective. For instance, the California Department of Social Services collected the names of 117,000 parents from all over the state who had neglected to make child support payments. These names were

Figure 16.14 Computers on Patrol
In Chicago, and on the streets of many other cities as well, police cars come equipped with their own on-board computers. These mobile systems allow officers instant access to car and driver registration records, arrest histories, and the FBI's National Crime Information Center computers.

Figure 16.15 NCIC
The records contained in the FBI's National Crime Information Center computer system provide police departments across the country and around the world with fast, up-to-date information on crimes, criminals, and investigations. Such sharing of information helps law enforcement agencies do their jobs more effectively.

sent to the tax board, and $10 million in tax refunds due to those persons were held back to offset the costs to the state of supporting their dependents. The whole process required such enormous quantities of data—legal records, tax returns, and addresses—and such immense requirements of time and energy that it would have been an impossible task without computers. This system is now widely used across the country in child-support cases, and some legislators suggest that it might be used to enforce other delinquent bills as well, such as unpaid student loans.

The Internal Revenue Service

The Internal Revenue Service is the federal government's largest computer user. The IRS uses computers to record and store the information sent in by taxpayers on their returns and to send out forms and notices (see Figure 16.16). Its tax return files, over 95 million individual returns annually, are stored in 1500 reels of magnetic tape. The average taxpayer's complete tax history for the last five years takes up only about a quarter inch of such tape.

Collecting taxes

Because the IRS needs to know who does and doesn't owe taxes, and whether anyone has neglected to pay in the past, the volume of paperwork used to be (and, to a large extent, still is) mind-boggling. Computers have become absolutely essential to the maintenance of the huge data bases on which the functioning of the tax system depends.

Tax Collection

Computers are involved in all stages of the tax-paying and tax-collecting process, beginning with the calculator or personal computer you use in preparing your return. When a 1040 Form arrives at the IRS regional center, it is sorted by bar code readers that can handle 30,000 returns an hour. The form then passes through human sorters, who write special codes on it that stand for tax bracket, exemptions and deductions claimed, and other key information. The codes are entered into another computer, which checks them for legal and mathematical consistency and then transfers the data to magnetic tape. The tape eventually ends up at the IRS

Figure 16.16   The IRS

The IRS's computer system is one of the most complex, extensive, and efficient systems in the country. At tax time, virtually unimaginable quantities of data are entered into the IRS's regional and national computers.

National Center in Martinsburg, West Virginia, where yet another computer compares the return's data against the information supplied by banks and employers (for example, on a W-2 Form) and determines such things as whether a refund is due and whether the check enclosed does in fact represent the correct amount of tax owed.

A recent mass acquisition of portable laptop computers (Figure 16.17) by the IRS now lets revenue agents carrying out audits confirm return and accounting information by simply connecting their laptop to the Martinsburg facility over the phone. Thus, agents can not only verify the taxpayer's records provided at the audit, but instantly inform the taxpayer of the exact amount of back taxes owed, if any. This speeds up an auditing process that used to take weeks, at best, and years in some cases.

Sample Audits

Since 1962, the IRS has annually selected a random sample of 30,000 taxpayers for intense 200-question audits as part of the **Taxpayer Compliance Measurement Program (TCMP).** The TCMP computer analyzes the answers and projects, on the basis of income and region, the statistical probabilities that any taxpayer will commit fraud. IRS auditing policies and decisions are made on the basis of this computer model. By the mid-1990s, the IRS hopes to have new computer systems installed in a dozen regional centers that will be capable of performing instant

Figure 16.17 Lap-top Computers
Revenue agents can now access the IRS's mainframe computer records from remote locations.

audits on *all* returns, thus further increasing the Service's efficiency while discouraging taxpayer cheating.

Defense

Computer-based weaponry

In fiscal year 1987, the Department of Defense (DOD) spent over $2.25 billion on computer hardware and support systems and some $200 million on software. The DOD is no different from any other bureaucratic agency or giant corporation in one respect: with millions of employees and contractors and programs, mountains of paper and data are generated daily. As a result, many of the DOD's computers are used for word processing, data management, and accounting, just as with any other business.

Some of the DOD's other applications of computers are on the cutting-edge of not just defense technology, but just about any technology. We will now examine some of these functions.

Missile Guidance Systems

The **Terrain Contour Matching (TERCOM) System** developed by McDonnell-Douglas weighs only 82 pounds yet can guide a Cruise missile to within about 60 feet of its target. The TERCOM computer is a specialized image-processing system. The images it examines are elevation maps of areas that the Cruise will fly over en route to its target. Each pixel on a map represents the elevation of one of the small squares into which an area is divided, as illustrated in Figure 16.18. The computer's memory contains the elevation of each square. A radar altimeter aboard the Cruise constantly reports the altitudes of the areas beneath the missile. As the missile enters one of the mapped areas, the computer recognizes the pattern of elevations, identifying them with a particular map in its memory, which also contains the desired course through that area. The sequence of elevations it is flying over gives its actual course. If the missile gets off course, it is a straightforward matter to compute and execute the corrections required to restore it to its planned flight path. The computer provides the means to transform a collection of low-cost subsystems into a high-precision weapon. Each Cruise missile costs only $750,000, which is a bargain compared to the enormous costs of the fleets of "look-down" radar planes and long-range intercept aircraft required to defend against it.

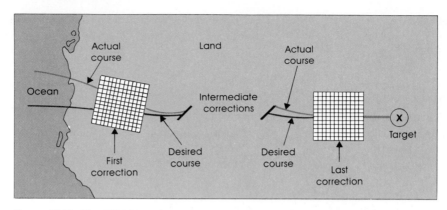

Figure 16.18 The TERCOM System
When the cruise missile gets over land, the TERCOM computer starts comparing the patterns of elevations observed beneath to its stored landfall maps. When the pattern matches, it checks to see if the current course is correct and computes any needed correction to bring it back to the desired flight path. It repeats this process periodically over successive mapped areas. The computer accurately guides the Cruise missile to its target, despite the lack of precision of its low-cost subsystems.

Matching observed real terrain against a set of stored elevation maps, as the Cruise does, is one example from a general class of image-matching techniques used to guide weapons to their targets. **Template matching** is the technique of comparing what's actually there against a predefined pattern, in this case a specific arrangement of pixels that defines the target. When the target is matched, the weapon is directed against it. (This same pattern-recognition technique forms the basis for numerous nonmilitary industrial applications.)

Another application of computer technology to missile guidance is found in MIRVs (Multiple Independently Targeted Reentry Vehicles). Guided by an on-board computer, the "MIRVed" missile—that is, a missile equipped with several nuclear warheads—can release its smaller bombs with deadly accuracy. An on-board guidance computer makes adjustments in the course, speed, and direction of each warhead, allowing for wind resistance, terrain, and weather conditions, and sends them directly to their assigned target.

C³I System

The **Command, Control, Communications, and Intelligence (C³I) System** is an integrated network of computers, telecommunications systems, Airborne Warning and Control Systems aircraft (or AWACS, the "look-down" radar planes previously mentioned), satellites, ground radar, and flying command centers on board modified commercial aircraft (see Figure 16.19). The U.S. government spends more than $1 billion annually to maintain this huge system, employing more than 90,000 people just to keep the equipment operational. The system gives the National Command Authority (the president, secretary of defense, and chief cabinet and Pentagon officials) direct control of all strategic forces at all levels, enabling them to receive intelligence information, issue commands, and keep up-to-date on a situation. In an age of complex, accurate, and very fast weapons, such a computer-centered network is essential to maintaining control of the defense efforts. Without computers, such control would be impossible.

Figure 16.19 AWACS
The Airborne Warning and Control Systems aircraft.

The SDI Computers

On March 23, 1983, President Reagan announced his plan for the federal government to undertake a program he called the **Strategic Defense Initiative (SDI),** a research and development project that would surpass, both in cost and in the production of new technology, the Manhattan Project of the 1940s and the Apollo space program of the 1960s and 1970s: $12 billion was spent from 1983 to 1988 on SDI research and development, and the total cost of the program has been estimated at anywhere between $60 billion to $1 trillion. Because of its reliance on space-based weapons and computer technology just slightly ahead of the state of the art, SDI quickly became known as the "Star Wars" program.

A computer-based defense system

Essentially, SDI is projected as a three-tier system composed of both space-based and ground-based antimissile defensive weapons. **Kinetic-energy weapons (KEWs)** would provide the first layer. KEWs are armed missiles, heavy, self-guided projectiles (*"smart bullets"*), or even 15-foot umbrella-frame weighted nets (Figure 16.20). Launched from space platforms and guided by sophisticated on-board computers and heat-seeking guidance systems, KEWs would crash into the oncoming missiles during their initial launch phase, before they deploy their multiple warheads.

The second tier, **directed-energy weapons (DEWs),** would involve huge space-based mirrors, 30 feet in diameter, that would direct laser beans generated on the ground toward any missiles or warheads that escaped the first tier. The final level, designed to destroy any stragglers, relies on ground-launched missiles, computer-piloted drones, and rockets fired from bombers and jet fighters.

Every phase of this controversial defense system relies on computers, from the detection of a missile launch to the identification of decoys, the assignment of targets, the arming, firing, and guiding of the drones and projectiles, the verification of strikes, and the operation of communications and command systems. The analysis of virtually unimaginable amounts of diverse data, as well as the split-second speed with which it must be done, when combined with the essential element of absolute fail-safe accuracy, are well beyond the capabilities both of humans and of existing supercomputers. Although some existing computer programs are more massive than those required by SDI, such as the one used by AT&T to run its national telecommunications network, the failure of a telephone call to go through

Figure 16.20   Strategic Defense Initiative (SDI)
Computers and programs more sophisticated than any
now in use are the critical element of this program.

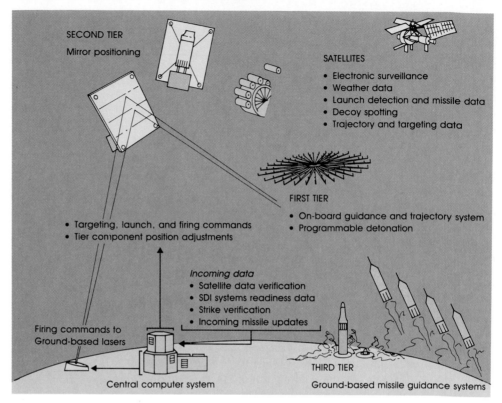

on the first try hardly has the same disastrous consequences as a failure of a nation's defense against incoming nuclear attack. SDI programs have to be written and debugged by artificial intelligence systems still to be invented. State-of-the-art image-analyzing computers, such as NASA's Massively Parallel Processor (MPP) (which was used to convert the signals from the Viking probes into pictures), can perform 6.5 billion operations per second. Such computers only anticipate SDI's minimum requirements.

Civilian Satellites

Private projects on government rockets

In addition to their numerous military applications (surveillance, tracking, reconnaissance, detection of communications signals, military activity, and weapons testing), satellites have a wide variety of peaceful applications. But the government is still closely involved when private enterprise goes into space. Most obviously, the launch vehicles that lift commercial and experimental satellites into orbit are still almost exclusively government-owned and -operated, although a fledgling private rocket-launching industry is slowly developing. As the commercial applications of satellites increase, however, it is likely that the government's role will diminish and the number (and success rate) of private rocket entrepreneurs will grow.

In general, nonmilitary satellites are employed to:

- aid sea and air navigation,
- map the atmosphere as input to numerical weather prediction,
- provide economical telephone links for long-distance voice or data communications,
- relay television signals,
- map the earth's resources, and
- monitor crop and environmental conditions

It is even conceivable that satellites 25 miles wide will one day convert solar radiation into microwave energy, which could then be transmitted to earth and turned into electricity. There are more than a billion dollars' worth of commercial satellites in orbit, and probably more than that amount of military satellites. When you talk to someone overseas on the telephone or when you watch Alpine skiing or network news on television, you are on the receiving end of signals that were transmitted via satellite. Satellites use computers to receive and transmit signals, to analyze data, and to maintain or alter their orbital paths.

Intelsat (short for International Telecommunications Satellite), for example, is part of an international network linking more than 100 nations and 20,000 telephone circuits. Two-thirds of the world's transoceanic communications travel across the seas by being bounced off the Intelsat satellite. Intelsat, like all other communications satellites, is in geosynchronous orbit at an altitude of 22,300 miles.

Other satellite systems, Landsat and Thematic Mapper, locate water and mineral deposits and monitor soil erosion and pollution. They are used for mapping, evaluating crop and soil conditions, and monitoring snowfall and flooding.

We saw in Chapter 6 how satellites are used to link distant computers with each other. That application is becoming more important as computers become more numerous.

Summary

Computers and Education

When computers are introduced into the educational process, students' interest, comprehension, and test scores have been shown to rise considerably. Computers also open up new possibilities for disabled students.

Computer-Assisted Instruction Computer-assisted instruction has grown from simple quizzing routines to an interactive educational tool, involving students in individualized instructional efforts.

Computer-Managed Instruction Computer-managed instruction helps teachers keep track of students' progress, maintain class records, and pinpoint problem areas.

Computers and Entertainment

Computers are assisting artists of all kinds in their creative expression.

Music Music is a mathematical art form, perfectly suited to computers. Musicians can compose, revise, orchestrate, print, and perform their works with help from computers.

Creative Graphics By breaking a picture down into pixels, a computer can generate, alter, and create images for movies or television commercials, or simply for art's sake.

The Movies Filmmaking is essentially a technological art form and has made extensive use of new developments since its inception. By converting sound and images to machine-readable binary digits, editing machines cut the time and costs involved in assembling scenes into a movie. And computerized mattes and computer-generated graphics are dramatically changing movies' special effects.

Computers and Medicine

Computers play a vital part in medical education, instrumentation, diagnosis, and treatment, as well as contributing to the costs of modern medical care.

Physician Training Simulation systems permit medical students to practice their skills and observe the effects of their treatment on a varied group of "patients."

Decision Making Medical data bases and expert systems help doctors make the most informed decisions possible.

Medical Imaging Two- and three-dimensional images of the interior of the body are produced by computer-driven X-ray units, CAT scanners, PETT scanners, and NMR scanners. They are already an indispensable part of the diagnostic process.

Prosthetics and Beyond Microprocessors are being used to provide complex interfaces between the brain and artificial limbs and organs.

Computers and Government

The Big Picture Computers are used in local, county, state and national government bodies for a wide variety of functions.

Law Enforcement Most government computer applications are in the area of crime control and law enforcement: criminal record clearinghouses and crime information systems.

The Internal Revenue Service The Internal Revenue Service is the federal government's largest computer user. Tax returns are processed and audited, reports are compiled, and taxpayer histories are updated by IRS computers.

Defense Computers are, in general, indispensable to the rapid assessment and action that are demanded in modern warfare. In missile guidance systems, the Cruise missile uses a computer to guide it to its target, turning low-cost subsystems into a high-precision weapon. Perhaps more important than the weapons themselves is the computer's role in the Command, Control, Communications, and Intelligence System (C^3I) and in the National Security Agency's collection of intelligence and surveillance data. The Strategic Defense Initiative (SDI) depends on the development of futuristic computerized satellite weapons and the computers that would control them. Civilian satellites are used for many nonmilitary applications, including relaying television signals, and transoceanic telephone calls, monitoring atmospheric and environmental conditions, and mapping the earth's resources.

As an extra review of the chapter, try defining the following terms. If you have trouble with any of them, refer to the page number listed.

computer-assisted instruction (CAI) *549*
computer-managed instruction (CMI) *550*
pulse code modulation (PCM) *553*
sample waveform *553*
digital-to-analog converter (DAC) *553*
ray tracing *555*
radiosity *555*
rendering equation *556*
fractal geometry *556*
computerized axial tomography (CAT) *560*

positron emission transaxial tomography (PETT) *561*
nuclear magnetic resonance (NMR) *561*
National Crime Information Center (NCIC) *564*
Taxpayer Compliance Measurement program (TCMP) *566*
Terrain Contour Matching (TERCOM) System *567*
template matching *568*

Command, Control, Communications, and Intelligence (C^3I) System *568*
Strategic Defense Initiative (SDI) *569*
kinetic-energy weapons (KEW) *569*
directed-energy weapons (DEW) *569*
Intelsat *571*

1. What is CAI?
2. What were the initial applications of computer-assisted instruction, and what is CAI like today?
3. What are the advantages of computer-managed instruction for teachers and for students?
4. How do computers aid musicians?
5. What techniques permit computer programmers to simulate the visual look and feel of an object?
6. What is the name of the computer used by George Lucas to edit film in a manner similar to word processing and how does it operate?
7. What is a major advantage of using computers to train physicians?
8. What does the CADUCEUS system do?
9. Contrast the operation of the new Fuji system with that of a conventional X-ray machine.
10. How does a CAT scanner work?
11. How is ultrasound used to produce images?
12. Contrast PETT and NMR scans.
13. What is the role of microprocessors in artificial limbs?
14. What are two areas in which state, local, and federal governments use computers to work together?
15. What are the advantages to law enforcement of systems such as SIDNEY and the NCIC?
16. Describe the use of computers in the processing of income tax returns. How else does the IRS use computers?
17. What is the TERCOM computer?
18. What are the three tiers of the SDI defense system?
19. What do the letters in C^3I stand for? What are the elements of this integrated network?

True or False

1. Computers do not appear to have had a noticeable effect on students' progress in schools.
2. CAI is derived from work in behavior modification.
3. Computers have been used to demonstrate the mathematical properties of classical poetic forms.
4. Computer music today cannot be created in real time; it requires a long time to generate.
5. Computers can imitate real images but cannot create anything original.
6. Sophisticated special effects in modern movies are created with the aid of computers.
7. A medical scanning technique that produces images more accurate than CAT scans is NMR.
8. The federal government's largest computer user is the FBI.
9. The technique of comparing actual terrain against a computerized image is template matching.
10. The Strategic Defense Initiative (SDI) is based on a system of ground-based and space-based defensive weapons controlled by computers.

Multiple Choice

1. Systems which help teachers monitor students' progress and diagnose performance are known as:
   (a) CMI   (b) CAI   (c) behavior modification

2. A system which assigns binary values to tonal input is:
   (a) DAC   (b) diatonic scale   (c) PCM

3. The elements of a picture that we see on a video or computer display screen are called:
   (a) DPI   (b) pixels   (c) resolution

4. An artistic technique using algorithms to create realistic mountains, forests, and ocean waves is:
   (a) rendering equation   (b) picture elements   (c) fractal geometry

5. The name given to a medical diagnosis system developed at the University of Pittsburgh is:
   (a) NMR   (b) PETT   (c) CADUCEUS

6. Imaging systems which use echoes of transmitted pulses are called:
   (a) CAT scans   (b) ultrasound systems   (c) X-ray scans

7. The name given to the FBI's central data base on crime is:
   (a) LEIN   (b) SIDNEY   (c) NCIC

8. The largest computer user in the federal government is:
   (a) the Social Security system   (b) the IRS   (c) the FBI

9. The anagram for the integrated network of computers, telecommunications, AWACS, satellites, ground radar, and flying command systems is:
   (a) C^3I (b) TERCOM   (c) SDI

10. The second tier, space-based phase of the SDI system is composed of:
    (a) TERCOM   (b) DEWs   (c) Cruise missiles

1. Do you think computers could be used to teach art and music? How?
2. If you were ill and had to choose either CADUCEUS or a qualified physician to make your diagnosis and recommend treatment, which would you choose? Why? If you chose the physician, give some reasons why someone might choose CADUCEUS.

Projects

1. Using your own college as an example, and your past educational experience, discuss your own contacts with CAI. Did you like it? Do you think it was better, worse, or the same as human instruction? Research the ways in which schools and parents are using computers to educate children and students in new and original ways.

2. Choose a rock group or other musician who uses a computer-based electronic instrument of any sort (instruments are often identified on album covers). Find out more about the particular instrument by consulting retailers, manufacturers' literature, or publications such as *Modern Recording and Music*. Prepare a report describing the instrument, its properties and capabilities, its cost, its sound quality compared to that of other similar instruments, and its role in a particular piece of music.

3. Visit your local hospital and list the computer applications you find. Discuss their costs and benefits with hospital personnel. You might choose to concentrate just on imaging systems. Prepare a report on your findings.

4. Contact your local police department and ask if they use the NCIC network. Find out from them what they think of the application of the computer in law enforcement, and how technology has helped or hindered them.

6

IMPLICATIONS

What are the possibilities, good and bad, rasied by the technology we've been studying? Just because we ask this question near the end of this book doesn't mean that the answer is somehow of secondary importance and should be treated lightly. Actually, what better time to question the impact of facts than once those facts are all finally understood?

In Chapter 17, we'll cover the major areas of social unease related to the computer applications we've discussed, looking at some very real problems and suggesting possible solutions. We'll also illustrate the point that change is not only essential, but unavoidable. Chapter 18 picks up on that point and takes a realistic look at the inevitable changes that will occur during the next 20 years in the way we live and work.

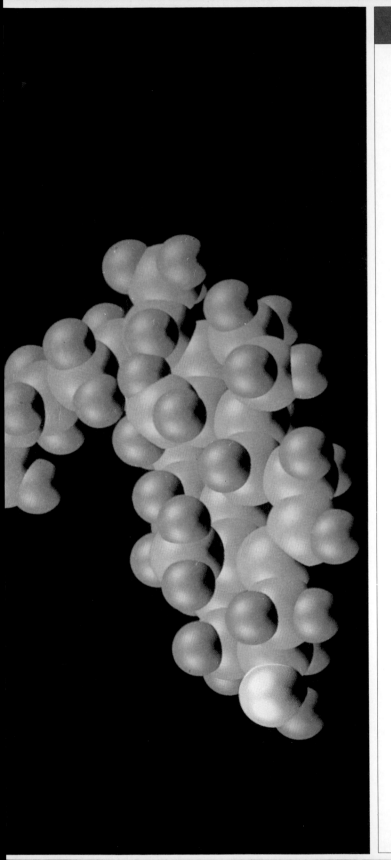

17

Privacy, Security, and Other Concerns

In This Chapter

Focus On

Computers in Planned Societies

When Mikhail Gorbachev announced perestroika in the Soviet Union, it was to include a speeding up of scientific and technical progress. However, there are fundamental problems in how (and whether) to introduce computers in Soviet industry, schools, and homes.

While western Europe, the United States, and Japan were rapidly moving ahead with computers, especially personal computers, East European governments considered the personal computer an unnecessary luxury, not to mention a possible source of subversion.

There are many problems in bringing these societies into the computerized world. First, there are questions about whether to develop home-grown industries that may be 10 to 20 years behind current technology or to import the latest products. Currently, home computers are exceedingly rare in East Europe. The Soviet Union offers the fewest. Poles can get personal computers on the black market, but they start at the equivalent of $10,000 at the offi-

cial rate. However, in East Germany, Czechoslovakia, and Hungary, the possibility of having a personal computer is realistic. Czechoslovakia imports Sharp personal computers for home use at a cost of about $600 (average monthly income is $184).

In 1985 prime ministers from the Eastern bloc Council for Mutual Economic Assistance countries met in Moscow to sign a plan for the development of science and

technology to the year 2000. The idea was to avoid duplication of research and development while keeping up with technological developments elsewhere.

The results have been successful in certain areas such as biotechnology and robotics. The Soviet Union has set up robotics projects with Bulgaria, Czechoslovakia and East Germany, enabling it to keep control on the industry. In other areas, particularly in developing computers, things haven't gone so smoothly. The East European countries, except for Romania, are developing computer systems in competition with each other. Hungary is the leading producer of software in the region. It produces games and spreadsheets that sell in western Europe. Bulgaria has had problems producing software because it sets project targets that ignore the fact that technology elsewhere may be overtaking those targets. Add to that the fact that Hungary would rather sell its games for hard currencies than data bases for Bulgarian leva. In addition, products imported from another Eastern country may be unreliable, and parts may be unavailable.

East Germany is the area's leading producer of computers. It is not clear how willing they will be to cooperate with other Eastern bloc countries. East Germany already produces a 32-bit computer while the others are having problems with 16-bit machines.

There has been some progress, however. Chips are becoming available from several countries. As a result, Bulgaria may be the first to export to western Europe in quantity. Bulgarian officials say they expect that by 1990 a private citizen can walk into a computer store and buy a 20-megabyte hard disk over the counter.

Technology has always aroused controversy. In early nineteenth-century England, the Luddites tried (without much success) to stop the Industrial Revolution by breaking into factories and smashing machines. They believed the new devices threatened their jobs, their health, and their way of life. Later in that century, similar movements arose in the United States as industrialization spread unchecked. Recent technological advances—especially machines that seem somehow to think for themselves—have stirred up similar fears and concerns.

We will examine some of the most controversial questions raised by the use of this new technology to encourage a healthy awareness of the dilemmas that face us.

PRIVACY

In Chapter 16, we noted that the federal government maintains an average of 17 separate computer files on each of the 234 million U.S. citizens, or 4 billion files. More than 200,000 times every day, one credit company based in southern California supplies a client with the name, address, telephone number, place of employment, salary, marital status, and credit history of one of the 86 million individuals recorded in its computer files. Nearly half of the nation's population is included in the computer records of only five credit companies.

Maintaining privacy in the information age

If you're married, a marriage license bureau somewhere has a record of the occasion. If you're not, you may be on file with a computer dating service. Your doctor may have your medical history and payment record on disk, and your hospital's computer stores a record of your visits. Hotels and stores have your name, address, and credit card numbers; telephone companies know who you called and how long you talked; and mail-order houses use computers to send you sales brochures and contest flyers. If you pay taxes, drive a car, vote, own a gun, or travel abroad, there are computer records about you. Little wonder that nearly half of all U.S. citizens say they are concerned about violations of their personal privacy.

Matching

Computers' speed and accuracy and the ways in which they shorten lines, hasten deliveries, organize inventories, and improve product quality are well known and are generally appreciated. What worries some people is that personal information kept in computer systems can be so quickly retrieved, so widely accessed, and so easily cross-referenced with other personal data to paint a potentially damaging portrait.

In the 1960s, the Kennedy and Johnson administrations considered creating a national "central data bank" that would consolidate all the information held by various government agencies. The public outcry against this project was so loud and the task itself so enormous that it was never undertaken. During the late 1970s and early 1980s, however, in the Carter and Reagan administrations, comparisons of federal computer files were widely used to detect fraud in government programs. **Matching,** as this practice is called, uses computers to compare records from government or private information systems to find individuals who are common to more than one set. This simple procedure has an enormous number of diverse applications. Social Security employment records, for example, can be compared

What happens when government agencies share data

with food-stamp rolls to find people who are earning more than the minimum allowed. Tax returns can be matched to student assistance records to find those graduates who have neglected to repay their loans. Those who fail to pay alimony or register with the Selective Service at age 18 can also be located through computerized matching.

A special committee was established by President Reagan to encourage such data matching by federal agencies because the Department of Labor estimated that the government could retrieve billions of dollars every year previously lost to fraud or error. A public outcry was raised again, however, when it turned out that a number of people were removed from welfare and child-support rolls on the basis of incorrect income data.

Legal Protection

Legislation to protect the individual's right to privacy

U.S. citizens are not explicitly guaranteed a right to privacy by the Constitution, although many legal experts have concluded that the right is implied in the document. The Fourth Amendment protects citizens against "unreasonable searches and seizures" of "person, house, papers, and effects," but whether those effects include credit ratings and checking account histories is problematic. The best protection against unwarranted distribution of computerized personal information or against the perpetuation of damaging misinformation lies outside the Constitution, in four acts of Congress.

The Fair Credit Reporting Act of 1970

The Fair Credit Reporting Act of 1970 guarantees your legal right to have free access to your credit records. If you find a mistake, you also have the right to challenge the accuracy of the data. The credit agency may charge a fee for access and correction unless you've been denied credit for any reason, in which case you have the right to examine your records free of charge.

The Freedom of Information Act of 1970

The Freedom of Information Act of 1970 guarantees citizens the right of access to all personal data gathered by any agency of the federal government. Any government agency, from the Department of the Navy to the IRS, the FBI, and the CIA, if requested in writing, must turn over copies of any records they are keeping, unless that information is vital to the national security or represents an invasion of someone else's privacy.

The Crime Control Act of 1973

Because arrest records can be very damaging, it is especially important that they be accurate. The Crime Control Act of 1973 requires that when arrest histories are distributed by agencies such as the FBI or the NCIC the data must show not only that an arrest took place, but whether prosecution and conviction followed. It also provides that "an individual who believes that information concerning him (*sic*) in an automated system is inaccurate, incomplete or maintained in violation of this (Act)" has access to the records "for the purpose of challenge or correction."

The Federal Privacy Act of 1974

The Federal Privacy Act of 1974 limits the activities of the federal government in gathering information about citizens to "relevant and necessary" information that is obtained, whenever possible, directly from the person being investigated. The subject must be informed of why the information is needed, how it will be used, and what legal right the government has to ask for it. Further, agencies are prohibited from disclosing personally identifiable information without the subject's consent, except in cases of "routine use." These requirements are intended to protect people from mysterious interrogations or surveillance based on gossip, hearsay, and false reports. The "routine use" exception, however, is cited as a justification for interagency sharing and matching of data.

Further efforts to prevent invasion of the individual's privacy continue. The Computer Systems Protection Act, introduced in 1977, would have provided further protection. It declared that unauthorized access, alteration, or destruction of computers, programs, and data was a federal crime punishable by fines and imprisonment. The bill, however, was never passed.

COMPUTER CRIME

The laws and protections set up to secure privacy have little effect on some people. The average **computer crime**—that is, the unauthorized manipulation of computers, computer programs, or data for inappropriate or unlawful purposes (generally for personal profit)—nets its perpetrator about $500,000. Compare that with the $15,000 taken in an average armed bank robbery, even with the $25,000 from the average embezzlement, and you can see why computer crime is on the increase. It has been estimated that anywhere from $100 million to $5 billion is lost every year to computer-related crime. The perpetrators range from high school hackers to white collar embezzlers or industrial and political spies. Their activities range from simple unauthorized access and data destruction to the wholesale theft of ideas, software, data, and money.

Unauthorized access for unlawful purposes

Viruses

A recently publicized innovation in the field of computer crime is the **virus**: hidden programs-within-programs that spread, like a biological disease, by contact: they clone themselves by various methods including being passed through shareware, "infecting" primary storage systems, or spreading through a network of linked computers. In the space of only a few hundred characters, the virus will instruct the computer to see if the software is already infected. If not, it then tells the computer to make and hide copies of the virus, omitting its name from the index of programs (see Figure 17.1). Usually the work of knowledgeable programmers (who should know better), viruses can modify a program's operation, causing a computer to malfunction or crash, creating costly delays, or even destroying vital data, such as patient records or credit histories.

Some viruses are ostensibly harmless, like the 1987 Christmas greeting that was started by a student in West Germany and sent to his friends. It spread through

Illicit, infectious programs

IS YOUR MACHINE AT RISK?

(1)   Computer "viruses" are actually miniature computer programs. Most were written by malicious programmers intent on destroying information in computers for fun.

(2)   Those who write virus programs often conceal them on floppy disks that are inserted in the computer. The disks contain all programs needed to run the machine, such as word processing programs, drawing programs or spreadsheet programs.

(3)   A malicious programmer makes the disk available to others, saying it contains a useful program or game. These programs can be lent to others or put onto computerized "bulletin boards" where anyone can copy them for personal use.

(4)   A computer receiving the programs will "read" the disk and the tiny virus program at the same time. The virus may then order the computer to do a number of things:
• Tell it to read the virus and follow instructions.
• Tell it to make a copy of the virus and place it on any disk inserted in the machine today
• Tell it to check the computer's clock, and on a certain date destroy all information that tells where data is stored on any disk; if an operator has no way of retrieving information, it is destroyed.

• Tell it not to list the virus programs when the computer is asked for an index of programs.

(5)   In this way, the computer will copy the virus onto many disks— perhaps all or nearly all the disks used in the infected machine.The virus may also be passed over the telephone, when one computer sends or receives data from another.

(6)   Ultimately hundreds or thousands of people may have infected disks and potential time bombs in their systems.

◀ **Figure 17.1 Line drawing-and adaptatical of attached line**
© The Washington Post

IBM's electronic mail network, causing general delays in the system. In 1988, a virus in Israel was set to destroy all data in any computer it could reach. It would have caused massive chaos had its author not made a mistake: by failing to check for prior infection, the virus made multiple copies of itself and noticeably filled computer memories. Programmers scrambled to erase it and to warn users, and catastrophe was averted. Communist insurgents in the Phillipines inadvertently passed a data-destroying virus through their portable computers.

More than 30 viruses were reported in the United States in 1988, infecting tens of thousands of computers. Half the Macintoshes at NASA have malfunctioned or crashed due to a virus, and computers in the House of Representatives, six universities, CompuServe, and Electronic Data Systems (EDS) have fallen victim to viruses. Five thousand copies of an infected drawing program for the Macintosh, called Freehand, were packaged and sold in stores. A few months later, a "universal message of peace" flashed on users' screens.

Viruses evolved from **worms**—errors or instructions intentionally written into a program either to harass unauthorized users or to ensure against copying. A user who copied a friend's software, for example, might suddenly find his or her entire disk erased, with a scolding message flashing on the screen. The public and commercial outrage against worms was so intense that manufacturers sought less harsh methods of protection and abandoned the practice.

Software disinfecting programs, with names like Vaccine, Syringe, or Flu Shot, can be used to search out and destroy viruses. The wary user should avoid programs copied from electronic bulletin boards or made at the end of a long chain of copies. Other than that, no general antidote is in sight because new virus programs are being written to thwart the cures.

Other Access Methods

Viruses are mostly intended to destroy data or interfere with systems. They are thus of limited use to an ambitious computer criminal planning to profit from their electronic crimes. Intruders use four common procedures to gain access to computer systems.

How it's done: the trapdoor, the Trojan horse, the time bomb, and the salami slice

The **trapdoor** is a set of program instructions that allows the perpetrator to bypass the computer's normal internal security systems. Once inside, the invader may just want to "look around"—discover and steal data for use in other criminal activities.

Another access method is a **Trojan horse,** named for the hollow wooden horse in which invading Greek warriors hid. The perpetrator, usually a computer programmer, develops a useful program which is installed in the system and used by other employees to conduct legitimate operations; for example, a program that computes interest for a bank. Embedded in the program, however, is a set of instructions (an electronic Greek soldier) that can detect when a "privileged" user (the criminal) is running the program and that can provide access to otherwise inaccessible data. Once in the system, the criminal can sack the data at will—changing balances, transferring interests to their own accounts, and otherwise disrupting the normal course of business.

A variant on the Trojan horse is the **time bomb,** used by computer criminals not so much for personal gain as to damage data or to cover their tracks. A time bomb is a coded section of a program that initiates some event C after other events A and B have occurred. For example, assume that for two years Paula X has been using a Trojan horse to alter her company's financial records for her own profit. She adds a time bomb to the program and gives a week's notice, saying she's found a new job. A week later, her name is deleted from the company's active personnel list (event A). Two weeks after that, her final paycheck is processed and her name is taken off the payroll (event B). Then the time bomb goes into effect. Its "fuse" slowly burns away over a week's time, and then the bomb "explodes," destroying incriminating data, crashing the system, and leaving no evidence of itself. Paula has been gone for three weeks.

Closely related to viruses, time bombs are intended for one-time use in a single system, while viruses are passed around among machines. In 1988, a Texas programmer was charged with sabotage and burglary for using both time bomb and Trojan horse methods to enter a former employer's computer system, where he deleted thousands of employees' sales commission records and instructed the computer to delete any further sales commission entries. The program had the ability to alter its file name and location in the system. The programmer was found guilty in a civil action and fined $12,000 in damages, and he now faces a lengthy prison term. This case represents one of the first such prosecutions of a computer criminal. The reason for the scarcity of prosecutions is simple: few financial institutions want to admit that there has been any sort of lapse in their security.

A slower, less direct method of committing computer crime is via the **salami slice,** in which small amounts of money are diverted during normal processing to a separate place; for example, fractions are "sliced" off all the accounts in a bank file every time interest is compounded. The pennies, or even fractions of pennies (the tenths of a cent deleted in rounding off), are transferred from many thousands of accounts to a dummy account which the criminal later closes out as if it were legitimate. In 1975, a computer programmer "sliced" fractions from employees' accounts in a company investment plan and absconded with $385,000, which had automatically accrued for him while he went about his normal business.

Computer Vandalism

Hackers' pranks as serious crimes carrying heavy penalties

Another type of computer crime is not robbery or even massive virus infection. Rather, it is a small-scale, yet serious, sort of high-tech vandalism. For example, four 13-year-old students in New York tapped into the Telenet data network and accessed the data bases of 19 different Canadian companies (including PepsiCo, Honeywell, and Bell-Canada) in an attempt to have a few free cases of Pepsi delivered to their school. That lark destroyed 20 percent of the data in one company's computers. A 17-year-old student in California gained access to U.S. Leasing's computer system and filled the files with obscenities, which came streaming out of printers every time inventory was called up. Also in California, 26 college students used Cal Tech's IBM 370/158 to print up 1.2 million entry forms for a McDonald's contest and won $40,000 in prizes. And a reporter for *Newsweek* magazine found that his credit card numbers, as well as his address, phone number, and wife's name, had been stolen from a credit company computer and his telephone and power service were being disrupted by young *hackers* (computer-programming enthusiasts) across the country who had been annoyed by an article he'd written exposing their antics. Once they managed to get access to his credit card and utility account numbers and post them on electronic bulletin boards, there was virtually no limit to the damage they could do to his credit rating, finances, and peace of mind.

In the early 1980s, a flurry of reports surfaced about hackers accessing commercial, Department of Defense, and NASA computers. Even in 1987, a young West German hacker was discovered to have accessed Department of Defense computers for at least five years, gaining entry into a vast network of sensitive data in the United States, Europe, and Japan. Apparently in search of data on SDI, the hacker managed to gain access to only unclassified material. Although most the stories of large quantities of sensitive data being blipped out of existence like Space Invaders are mostly fictional and greatly exaggerated, this kind of unauthorized and malicious access is a bothersome problem, certainly irresponsible, sometimes criminal, and in any case a disturbing suggestion of the possibility of more sinister tampering (see Figure 17.2).

Often the search for computer vandals is so expensive that companies prefer simply to take their losses. In the Telenet case, the search for the four schoolboys cost $250,000, and no charges were filed against them. The obscene inventory file at U.S. Leasing cost that company $60,000 to repair plus $200,000 to find the culprit, who was then subject only to charges of making an obscene phone call.

Old laws, new crimes

This type of computer tampering is so new that it is difficult to make the old laws effectively fit the new crimes. No federal laws prohibit unauthorized entry into computers, although Congress is currently considering such legislation. Most computer vandals are prosecuted under section 1343 of Title XVII of the U.S. Code, which forbids unlawful use of telephone lines. However, laws specifically governing computer crime have been enacted in a number of states. In 1984, for example, a 19-year-old college sophomore in Los Angeles used his $200 home computer to break into the Department of Defense's communications network. He was caught and charged with 12 felony counts of "malicious access to a computer system" and one count of receiving stolen property (the data he'd removed). Those charges could lead to six years in prison.

Industrial Espionage

There is another sort of computer crime, in which a computer or software manufacturer, rather than an individual, is the victim. **Industrial espionage,** the cloak-and-dagger spying activities between corporations intent on stealing one another's ideas, designs, or trade secrets, is becoming more common as the computer and software industries become not only more lucrative, but also more competitive. In

Competition leading to spying and theft

A number of computer vandals have claimed that they were actually performing a valuable public service by revealing weaknesses in computer security systems, which could be exploited by people less honest and responsible than themselves. In light of what you know about computer crimes, does this plea hold any water? What really compels such wayward hackers to invade computer systems and destroy or steal valuable or sensitive data?

Issues in Technology

Figure 17.2 "Syscruncher" and "Vladimir"

In 1980, hackers calling themselves "Syscruncher" and "Vladimir" invaded the computer system of Chicago's DePaul University. They locked out authorized users, accessed the school's master account file, and crashed the entire system twice. Two high school students were eventually arrested on charges of "theft of services" and were sentenced to a year's probation, despite their mothers' pleas that they were just "exuberant, innocent pranksters." It took nearly 200 hours to repair the damage they'd caused. (Donn B. Parker, excerpted from *Fighting Computer Crime.* Copyright 1983. Reprinted with permission of Charles Scribner's Sons.)

```
**LOGOFF E110 1218 #20
**LOGON  B999 1218 #18
03  HELLO, THIS IS THE 'SYSCRUNCHER'  (REMEMBER ME? I BROUGHT YOUR SYSTEM
03  DOWN LAST WEEK?)
**LOGOFF  D204 1219 #05
03 ATTENTION.................................................
03 IS THERE ANYONE THERE, I WANT TO TALK TO YOU N O W !
**LOGON  D204 1219 #05
03 €€€€€€€€€€€€€€€€€€€€€33333333333333333333##############>>>>>>>>>>>>>>>>>
03 AAAAAAAAAAAAAAAAAAAAAAAASSSSSSSSSSSSSSSSSSSSDDDDDDDDDDDDDDDFFFFFFFFFFFFF
03 >>>>>>>>>>>>>>>>>>>((((((((((((((((((.......................///////////
03
03 IF YOU GIVE ME A LISTING OF YOUR 'MIX' ASSEMBLY PROGRAM, I WILL
03 LEAVE YOUR SYSTEM ALONE
03 HELLO, ARE YOU THERE
03 YOUR ATTENTION PLEASE
03
03 BEEP     B E E P
03 BBBBBBBBBBBBBBEEEEEEEEEEEEEEEEEEEEEEEEEEEPPPPPPPPPPPPPPPPPP
03 I WILL BE BACK A LITTLE LATER TO TALK TO YOU, OR EVEN BETTER,
03 IF YOU LEAVE ME A PHONE #, I'LL CALL YOU INSTEAD
03 BYE NOW
03
03
03                         SYSCRUNCHER
**LOGOFF M209 1224 #04
**LOGON  M209 1224 #04

PLEASE LOG IN
HELLOO--X999,XXX999
ILLEGAL FORMAT
BYER
PLEASE LOG IN
BYE
PLEASE LOG IN
BYE
PLEASE LOG IN
HEL-X999,XXX9999
ILLEGAL ACCESS
HEL-D200,320

WELCOME TO VLADIMIR'S NEWLY CONQUERED
HP 2000 TIMESHARING SYSTEM. IF YOU
WANT TO CONTACT VLADIMIR, PLEASE LEAVE
A MESSAGE ON PBBS PHONE #359-9450
```

```
203:                              CAVEMAN DAVE
204:                           ALIAS: THE GAME PLAYER
205:
206: JAMES T. KIRK
207: VLADIMIR
208: DE PAUL
209: SEP. 25, 1980
210: VIRGIN
211: VLAD: CONGRATULATIONS.  WE MUST GET TOGETHER TO DISCUSS
212: HOW YOU ACCOMPLISHED THE GREAT DEED.  BEING DISGRUNTLED
213: WITH THIS              UNIVERSITY MYSELF. I GOT A BIG KICK
214: OUT OF HAVING IT BROUGHT TO ITS KNEES.  GET BACK TO ME.
215:
216: VLADIMIR & SYSCRUNCHER
217: JAMES T. KIRK
218: DE PAUL
219: SEP. 26, 1980
220: ORBY
221: HI ! THIS IS SYSCRUNCHER
222: ACTUALLY, VLAD HAD VERY LITTLE TO DO WITH THE DOWN FALL
223: AND EVENTUAL DESTRUCTION OF YOUR MIGHTY (COUGH) HP (SNICKER!)
224: IT WAS V E R Y SIMPLE TO READ YOUR PASSWORD FILE ON A000
225: ESPECIALLY SINCE THE FILES ITSELF WAS LOCKED, AND
226: THERE JUST HAPPENED TO BE A LOCKED FILE READING PROGRAM
227: ALSO ON A000.  THEN IT WAS A SIMPLE MATTER TO EXE*OUT = x THE
228: FILE PROGRAM SO IT WOULD PRINT IT INTO THE FILE. I DID THIS
229: SINCE THE LINES IN THE FILE WERE 250 CHARACTERS ACROSS
230: I THEN READ THE FILE AND B I N G O ! THERE WERE YOUR PASSWORDS
231: WE USED A OSI MICRO TO GET A000 SINCE YOU NEGLECTED TO PLACE
232: IT IN A FILE. AFTER WE KNEW THE FORM OF YOUR PASSWORDS
233: (3 LETTERS) IT WAS SIMPLE !!!
234: DO NOT FEEL BAD, ESPECIALLY SINCE YOURS IS NOT THE FIRST
235: SYSTEM TO FALL BEFORE ME, NOR WILL IT BE THE LAST !
236: THE SYSTEMS TO MY CREDIT ARE:
237: D211
238: D214
239: DE PAUL
240: GAMEMASTER
241: AND OTHER LESSER SYSTEMS THAT NEED NOT BE MENTIONED
242: IF YOU NEED HELP IN RESTRUCTURING YOUR ID SYSTEM, LEAVE
243: ME A MESSAGE. OTHER WISE, WATCH OUT,
244: SYSCRUNCHER IS ALIVE AND WELL !!!
245:
246: VLADIMIR
247: JAMES T. KIRK
248: DE PAUL
249: SEP. 26, 1980
250: O
251: HELLO THERE!! I THOUGHT SOMEONE WOULD
252: APPRECIATE MY DEED, I'M A SENIOR IN HIGH SCHOOL
253: AND HAVE SOME QUESTIONS ABOUT YOUR SYSTEM,
254: I WOULD LIKE TO CONTACT YOU BUT IF YOUR ON THE
255: STAFF
256: MY NUMBER IF YOU REPLY.
257: DESTRUCTIVELY YOURS
258: VLADIMIR
```

1971, the plans for IBM's 330 disk file system were stolen by a group of IBM employees. The plans were worth $160 million to competitors, who wanted to produce identical or compatible products of their own. The thieves were caught in 1973 and charged with felony theft of trade secrets, receipt of stolen property, conspiracy, and offering or accepting inducement to steal trade secrets.

In 1983, in the largest industrial espionage case to date, two Hitachi employees paid $622,000 for the plans of a then-experimental IBM computer, the 3081. Unfortunately for them, they paid the money to an FBI sting operation and were charged with industrial espionage. Hitachi settled with IBM out of court for $300 million, and Mitsubishi Electrical Corp., which was also involved in the theft, was fined $10,000. An American company, National Semiconductor, which markets Hitachi's IBM-compatible products through its subsidiary National Advanced Systems, was accused by IBM of conspiring with the Japanese companies to obtain trade secrets. Although denying the charges, National Semiconductor settled with IBM for $3 million.

In 1984, Congress passed the Semiconductor Chip Protection Act, which makes it illegal to reproduce any chip pattern for 10 years after the design is registered with the Library of Congress. The law imposes fines of up to $250,000 for copyright infringement. However, *reverse engineering* (taking something apart to see how it was put together) is allowed as long as the intention is to improve the chip, not just reproduce it.

Software Piracy

The threat from users who copy rather than buy

If any industry is growing more rapidly than the manufacturing of computer hardware, it's the production of computer software. In 1982, total software sales totaled $1 billion. By the end of 1985, that figure was $5 billion. More than $12 billion in software sales is projected for 1990. But analysts and software companies suspect that for every program purchased as many as 10 illegitimate copies exist. Just as unauthorized cassette recordings crippled the record industry, and just as home videotaping poses a serious threat to Hollywood, piracy of software may be equally dangerous to the software industry. A 1984 Supreme Court decision that home videotaping of copyrighted materials for personal use was not illegal did not calm the software manufacturers' fears. They saw a clear similarity between copying a studio's movie or a network's television show onto a blank videotape and copying computer programs onto blank diskettes.

Despite the **Copyright Act of 1980,** which grants software programs the same protections afforded other creative products (and allows fines of $50,000 for willful illegal duplication other than for a single backup copy), software manufacturers have sought a variety of means to protect their intellectual property against theft. As we've discussed, worms were a favorite, and effective, software protection for a few years. A current widespread technique is to use **software licensing,** rather than selling the product outright. That is, the disks are sealed in plastic, with labels stating that once the seal is broken, the purchaser has entered into a legal and binding contract that gives the purchaser alone the right to use the software (see Figure 17.3). The manufacturers theorize that, if copies are made, a contract has been broken, and the user can be sued in court. The legal consensus, however, is that these licensing agreements are hollow scare tactics with no binding authority; the software is really sold, and so recourse to the courts is unlikely.

International Business Machines Corporation   Boca Raton, Florida 33432

IBM Program License Agreement

YOU SHOULD CAREFULLY READ THE FOLLOWING TERMS AND CONDITIONS BEFORE OPENING THIS DISKETTE(S) OR CASSETTE(S) PACKAGE. OPENING THIS DISKETTE(S) OR CASSETTE(S) PACKAGE INDICATES YOUR ACCEPTANCE OF THESE TERMS AND CONDITIONS. IF YOU DO NOT AGREE WITH THEM, YOU SHOULD PROMPTLY RETURN THE PACKAGE UNOPENED; AND YOUR MONEY WILL BE REFUNDED.

IBM provides this program and licenses its use in the United States and Puerto Rico. You assume responsibility for the selection of the program to achieve your intended results, and for the installation, use and results obtained from the program.

LICENSE

You may:

a. use the program on a single machine;

b. copy the program into any machine readable or printed form for backup or modification purposes in support of your use of the program on the single machine (Certain programs, however, may include mechanisms to limit or inhibit copying. They are marked "copy protected.");

c. modify the program and/or merge it into another program for your use on the single machine (Any portion of this program merged into another program will continue to be subject to the terms and conditions of this Agreement.); and,

d. transfer the program and license to another party if the other party agrees to accept the terms and conditions of this Agreement. If you transfer the program, you must at the same time either transfer all copies whether in printed or machine-readable form to the same party or destroy any copies not transferred; this includes all modifications and portions of the program contained or merged into other programs.

You must reproduce and include the copyright notice on any copy, modification or portion merged into another program.

YOU MAY NOT USE, COPY, MODIFY, OR TRANSFER THE PROGRAM, OR ANY COPY, MODIFICATION OR MERGED PORTION, IN WHOLE OR IN PART, EXCEPT AS EXPRESSLY PROVIDED FOR IN THIS LICENSE.

IF YOU TRANSFER POSSESSION OF ANY COPY, MODIFICATION OR MERGED PORTION OF THE PROGRAM TO ANOTHER PARTY, YOUR LICENSE IS AUTOMATICALLY TERMINATED.

TERM

The license is effective until terminated. You may terminate it at any other time by destroying the program together with all copies, modifications and merged portions in any form. It will also terminate upon conditions set forth elsewhere in this Agreement or if you fail to comply with any term or condition of this Agreement. You agree upon such termination to destroy the program together with all copies, modifications and merged portions in any form.

LIMITED WARRANTY

THE PROGRAM IS PROVIDED "AS IS" WITHOUT WARRANTY OF ANY KIND, EITHER EXPRESSED OR IMPLIED, INCLUDING, BUT NOT LIMITED TO THE IMPLIED WARRANTIES OF MERCHANTABILITY AND FITNESS FOR A PARTICULAR PURPOSE. THE ENTIRE RISK AS TO THE QUALITY AND PERFORMANCE OF THE PROGRAM IS WITH YOU. SHOULD THE PROGRAM PROVE DEFECTIVE, YOU (AND NOT IBM OR AN AUTHORIZED PERSONAL COMPUTER DEALER) ASSUME THE ENTIRE COST OF ALL NECESSARY SERVICING, REPAIR OR CORRECTION.

Continued on inside back cover

Figure 17.3

This license agreement accompanies IBM's Easywriter software. Like other software licensing agreements, it stipulates that only the purchaser is entitled to use the software under a contract that is "signed" by breaking the package seal. The contract is terminated only if the original program and all copies are destroyed. This is one way software manufacturers provide themselves with legal protection. (Reproduced by permission of IBM.)

SECURING THE SYSTEM

Computers themselves are not without defenses to keep vital personal information from being stolen or destroyed. A number of measures can be taken to ensure the integrity of computer systems and protect them from improper access.

Controlling Personnel

Avoiding unauthorized use

Because many invasions of data files and abuses of computer systems are performed by the people who are employed to work with them, limiting access to a few carefully screened and authorized individuals is one measure that can improve security. If programmers are also computer operators, then they can not only write illegitimate programs but can conveniently run them as well. However, if programmers work in their offices and operators in the computer room, and management keeps track of their activities, then opportunities for covert electronic embezzlement decrease significantly. Such separation of functions is, of course, easy for a firm with a large data-processing staff but it may be impossible for a small company with only two or three computer professionals, each of whom must each handle several overlapping jobs. In any case, careful screening of job applicants—checking their references and looking closely at their backgrounds—is vital to any system's security. If someone lies on a resume or has a history of committing computer crimes, that person is obviously not a good risk.

Figure 17.4 shows two devices used to physically limit access to computer systems to authorized personnel.

Passwords and Access Logs

Guaranteeing authorized access

Passwords and **access logs** are two means of ensuring that all users are identified before they can enter the system. Supplying the correct password gets a user into the system, and an access log keeps track of who "passed" in, when they entered, and when they left. Frequent examination of programs and access logs by professional auditors is another commonly used security method. If there has been a great deal of activity on the computer system during what should be off-hours, an auditor who inspects the log thoroughly may be able to stop a computer crime before it starts.

Passwords or account numbers are an attempt to provide access to the computer only to authorized users. If Sam, a bona fide computer user, can gain access to the system by simply entering his name, an unauthorized person who knows that Sam has access can key in SAM and enter the system. Instead, Sam should use something else that is unlikely that another person would easily guess.

Cryptography

Disguising data via ciphers

Cryptography is the practice of transcribing a message from its *plaintext*, or original form, into a secret code or cipher. The original meaning can supposedly be recovered only by an authorized recipient who holds the *key*, or system of retranscription. With a *code*, some predetermined substitution is made for words, phrases, or other meaningful parts of a sentence. A **cipher,** on the other hand,

Figure 17.4 On-the-Job Security

(a) At this factory, only authorized workers are able to enter a particular area. The security system functions as a guard against improper access and as a time clock, recording who entered, and when. (b) These security terminals, manufactured by SecuraKey, help organizations keep certain areas "off limits." The stand-alone ENTRACOMP 2100 access control computer (left) can keep up to 8000 authorized card numbers in its memory, and can print out the date, time, and card number of each attempted entry. The Data Logger L-2 (right) sounds an alarm if an unauthorized entry attempt is made. (c) Fingerprints can be digitalized and used as an effective and secure means of worker identification.

makes a substitution for each letter (or sometimes each fixed group of letters). That is, each letter in the plaintext is replaced by a different letter or symbol. The sentence *Eagle buys the laundry* is a code in which *Eagle* stands for Agent X, *buys* for steals, and *laundry* for the secret plans. Enciphered, with its letters altered and regrouped into new blocks, the same message might read *DZB.FH DJXHMF ?ZKJRFJ.*

In 1977, the National Bureau of Standards (NBS), in cooperation with IBM, designed the **Data Encryption Standard (DES),** a standard public cipher for senders and receivers of data. The National Security Agency (NSA) has endorsed this cipher, which the NBS claims would cost over $200 million and take more than 3000 years to crack (or 571 years, if, with the help of a supercomputer, one attempt were made every microsecond). The DES is a *block cipher;* that is, it breaks up the text to be coded into groups (or blocks) of 8 bytes (64 bits) and uses a 7-byte key to transform those blocks into new 8-byte groupings. There are over 70 quadrillion (70,000,000,000,000,000) possible combinations of digits. Here's an example:

Plaintext: THIS IS A SECRET MESSAGE

DES cipher: I,R.[-C.*Q = W.,S9GE9.3---N.,!.3,[

Inexpensive commercial software packages (such as Standard Software's The Protector of *K & L* N-Code) designed solely to encrypt microcomputer programs are also available. Although all ciphers are made to be broken, the enciphering of programs provides substantial protection against invasion.

HAZARDS AND SAFEGUARDS

Of course, people aren't the only serious threat to the security of a computer system's data. A variety of environmental perils create serious problems for computers—everything from fire and water to cockroaches and nuclear war.

Heat

Guarding against overheating and moisture

Computer rooms must be kept cool because a computer's circuits can generate enough heat to keep several offices warm. (In fact, the home office of the Hartford Insurance Group saved over 81,000 gallons of oil the first year it used its computer facilities as a heat source.) Computer components that get hot fail more often than ones that remain cool. This has prompted computer manufacturers to install fans in many of their units, even in small desktop computers that use only about 100 watts of power. Larger (and therefore hotter) computer systems come equipped with liquid refrigeration units (you've no doubt noticed that computer rooms are often very chilly).

Smoke and Steam

Damage to magnetic storage media

Steam, or even just very high humidity, can short out circuits, while the particles suspended in smoke and dust can scratch and permanently damage the magnetic surfaces of tapes and disks or clog ventilation systems. For example, the fine volcanic ash from the 1980 eruption of Mount St. Helens brought down a number of computer systems in the state of Washington. Filtered ventilation systems and moisture detectors are therefore common safeguards in computer rooms.

Electricity

Protecting against power failures

A common computer-related concern is that if the electricity surges or fails, all human knowledge (or at least our bank accounts) could be lost. To some extent, this concern is justified; a loss of electricity, even for a sixtieth of a second, can cause the destruction of data. As a rule, however, most major systems have banks of batteries that can sustain the power supply long enough (usually a few minutes)

Figure 17.5 Surge Protector
Surge protectors prevent damage to computers and data caused by fluctuations in the power supply.

to unload the contents of all volatile memory onto nonvolatile magnetic storage media. If a computer's function is so vital that it simply can't be left sitting idle until power is restored (air traffic control computers, for example), large diesel- or gas-powered generators can be employed to provide emergency power. For microcomputers, there are dozens of surge-protection devices (see Figure 17.5) that sell for under $20 and small stand-by generators that cost between $300 and $500.

A less dramatic form of electrical threat is caused by static electricity, which can damage tapes and disks. Grounded wire woven into the computer room carpeting or special antistatic slippers worn by computer operators help prevent the generation of this static electricity.

Wildlife

On an even smaller scale, mice can nibble the insulation around wiring or even gnaw through live cables (which tends to crash both computer and mouse). Insects and small animals have, from time to time, managed to block off ventilation ducts with their nests, causing dust and overheating in computer rooms. Even a tiny insect on a disk represents an enormous obstacle to read/write head. Clearly, those in charge of maintaining the computer's environment must occasionally be prepared to go on safari.

Insects and mice can raise havoc

Earthquakes

In 1985, a large earthquake in Mexico City caused dozens of computer systems to be down for several days. Most of the damage came not from gaping cracks in the earth, but from hardware units crashing into each other. Anchoring cabinets and consoles is a simple precaution against such damage. Earthquakes have secondary effects, though, including fires and smoke, steam from broken pipes, power failures, and debris, as well as the complete destruction of the facility itself.

Seismic catastrophes

Terrorism

Computers as targets

In 1987, 24 West European computer centers were bombed by political terrorists. In the information age, computers have joined politicians and business leaders as targets of terrorism. The FBI believes that a terrorist attack on a hundred select computers could bring the U.S. economy to a halt and seriously impair national security. Although it is impossible to completely shield any target from a sufficiently determined fanatic, government and private computer centers considered at risk are frequently barricaded behind multilayer, blastproof, reinforced fire walls, or even buried deep in subbasements. Limited access and independent power sources are additional means of ensuring security against a literal attack on the system.

Electromagnetic Pulse

Computers and nuclear war

One further threat to computer systems exists. A single megaton nuclear warhead, detonated in the upper atmosphere over the United States, would create an *electromagnetic pulse (EMP)*, like a giant bolt of lightning, that would effectively black out all computerized communications systems for several hours, days, or even longer. In the event of a nuclear war, the difficulty of placing a long-distance call might seem minor, but consider the more serious effects. Conventional military command, control, and communications systems; incoming warhead detection; and television, radio, and civil defense communications would also be silenced. Organization of coordinated relief and rescue efforts would be made very difficult since no one would be able to talk to anyone else over any distance. The Department of Defense has studied the potential effects of an EMP and ways to avoid its consequences, but its findings are classified. The mobile and largely airborne C^{3}I System discussed in Chapter 16, however, is considered one possible safeguard against such catastrophic disruption.

Disaster Recovery Teams

Preparation for catastrophes

The establishment of a **disaster recovery team** can help minimize damage to a company's computer system. Particularly common in earthquake-prone regions, a team composed of systems analysts, disaster recovery experts, and employees carefully plans which programs are most essential and need to be reinstalled immediately after the disaster. They decide what equipment, facilities, and supplies will be required right away and which employees are essential. Dry runs and drills keep the plan operational, but the adoption of new equipment, software, or management objectives can send the team back to the planning stages. Cooperative agreements are often worked out with competing companies nearby to share personnel and facilities in the event of a disaster. Off-site storage of spare parts, copies of data and programs, and even backup hardware can also help soften the blow.

HEALTH

The health problems associated with computer use can be divided into four categories: radiation-linked problems, visual disturbances, musculoskeletal difficulties, and stress. Even before they reach homes and offices, computers may pose dangers to their builders. Some of these health problems have been investigated and either dismissed as baseless or are in the process of being resolved; others have just been discovered.

Radiation and VDTs

Within a year after the installation of video display terminals (VDTs) in the editorial offices of *The New York Times*, two editors developed cataracts. Since 1980, there have been reports of clusters of miscarriages and birth defects in the United States and Canada among women who operated VDTs for long periods of time. These and similar reports have given rise to concerns that VDTs emit radiation that causes cataracts, birth defects, sterility, blindness, cancer, or other less-specific complaints. But, in fact, no epidemics of cataracts or birth defects have occurred, as might have been expected after the widespread adoption of VDTs. The March of Dimes Birth Defects Foundation observed that the increased numbers of women who work with VDTs has itself raised the statistical probability of "chance clusters" of problem pregnancies.

Public concern about radiation leakage from terminal screens

Public concern, however, prompted extensive studies by the Food and Drug Administration's Bureau of Radiological Health (FDA-BRH), the Occupational Safety and Health Administration (OSHA), the National Institute of Occupational Safety and Health (NIOSH), and the Canadian Radiation Protection Bureau, all of which found no detectable radiation hazard from VDTs. (In Canada, however, VDT operators who become pregnant are now regularly transferred to other duties.) In the FDA-BRH study, for example, 125 different VDT units were examined under worst-case conditions, and only eight emitted more X-ray radiation than is allowed for televisions. Those eight models were withdrawn from the market.

Computer-Chip Toxins

Real problems similar to those claimed by VDT workers are being found among workers in computer-chip manufacturing plants. The production process involves a number of toxic chemicals, including arsenic, cadmium, gallium, and glycol ether. Federal, state, and corporate studies at individual plants have found rates of miscarriage among women workers nearly twice the national average, and fertility problems among men.

Manufacturing workers are exposed to harmful chemicals

In response to these findings, Digital Equipment Corporation (DEC) and AT&T urge pregnant women to transfer to comparable "clean" jobs, and other manufacturers are adopting similar policies. Labor and civil rights activists, however, point out that removing pregnant women does not solve the problem of other workers' exposure to known toxins. The Semiconductor Industry Association maintains that manufacturers' standards for chemical exposure fall within government limits, and that the toxic effect of such new uses of chemicals has yet to be established.

Physical Complaints

The extensive tests for radiation uncovered other problems with VDTs in the workplace. Eyestrain, neck pains, backaches, and fatigue were common operator complaints. The source of these physical problems was clear: traditional office design

Aches and pains from poorly designed workstations

Figure 17.6 Operator Posture

NOSH recommended that the center of the VDT screen should be no more than 10°–20° below the operator's eye level, at a distance of no more than 19¾ inches. The keyboard's home row should be no higher than 31 inches from the floor.

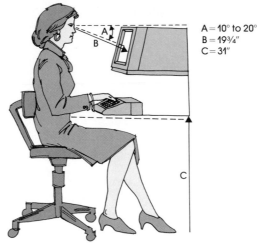

A = 10° to 20°
B = 19¾″
C = 31″

and furniture simply do not comfortably accommodate the new technology. Glare, flickering images, heat, noise, and poor posture frequently cause discomfort among VDT operators.

To alleviate such problems, NIOSH made a number of recommendations for safer, more comfortable workstations (see Figure 17.6):

- Screen hoods to block glare from light sources
- Antiglare filters on screens
- Indirect lighting in offices
- Recessed work-area lighting fixtures with downward (rather than outward) deflectors
- Adjustable blinds or curtains on windows to block glare from direct sunlight
- Screen brightness of 500 to 700 *lux* (luminous flux, the international unit of illumination)
- 5 × 7 dot matrix to form characters 2.6 mm to 4.2 mm high
- Keyboard home-row height of 720 mm and 790 mm (28¼ inches and 31 inches), that is, at about elbow height
- Screen at 10° to 20° below the horizontal plane of the operator's eyes, at a distance of 450 to 500 mm (17¾—19¾ inches)
- Upright copyholders
- Adjustable chairs with lower back rests

Furthermore, the "reassuring click" of keyboard keys and the clatter of printers could become an annoyance. The office environment should also be closely monitored to prevent the heat generated by desktop computer hardware from becoming uncomfortable.

Ergonomics

A science to answer workers' complaints

Ergonomics is the study of how people's living and working conditions can be adapted to the technology around them, whether it's making tractor seats more comfortable or computer workstations more pleasant. It is closely related to

ERGONOMICS-ADDRESSING THE HUMAN VARIABLES

Top view of BIOTEC fully adjustable base unit illustrates 360° rotation of VDT surface and the adjustable keyboard surface with standard palm support.

Ergonomics: "...a science that seeks to adapt working conditions to suit the worker."

The term "Ergonomics" as it applies to office furniture is relatively new in the United States. However, Ergonomics and ergonomically designed furniture have been key issues in Europe for several years. The improved physical well being of VDT operators and its effect on productivity has sparked the growth of ergonomic furniture in most European industrialized countries. Today, the majority of European companies will not even consider VDT furniture unless it is "ergonomically designed."

The recent emphasis on ergonomics in the United States is due to the rapid growth of office automation and the discovery of physical and physiological problems of individuals working with the equipment and its effect on productivity. As a result, the office automation industry and its users in this country have become aware of the critical need for ergonomically designed VDT furniture.

Taking Ergonomics one step further we have:

BIOTECHNOLOGY: the aspect of technology concerned with the application of biological engineering data to problems relating to the mutual adjustment of man and machine.

BIOTEC combines "Ergonomics" and "Biotechnology" and the end result:

BIOTEC:* Ergonomically designed VDT furniture which through the recognition of individual operator physiological and physical needs improves VDT operator productivity.

BIOTEC is a complete line of VDT furniture with an aesthetic design that will enhance any office environment. Base units are available in 72", 60", 48" and 36" widths. A 32" wide base unit is available for corner applications. Free standing returns can be added to any base unit using 90°, 120°, 150° cluster or square corner connectors.

Whether you're designing an automated office system layout for a small cluster, a department, or an entire floor, BIOTEC is your answer to the Ergonomic question.

Figure 17.7 The Ergonomics Industry

A whole new business has grown up around the need to adapt the workplace to the new tools, as this advertisement for the Biotec line of office equipment demonstrates. It emphasizes the timeliness, decreased health risks, greater worker productivity, and the aesthetic appeal of the work stations.

BIOTEC caters to people of different sizes. A keyboard and screen position which is comfortable for one operator may not be for another. The operator on the left is 4'11" and the operator on the right is 5'10" tall.

Each is shown using an identical base unit adjusted to suit their particular body dimensions and posture.

*Patent Pending

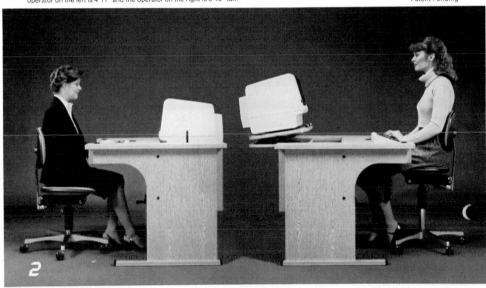

biotechnology, which is that aspect of technological research concerned with the problems posed by the interaction of human beings and machines. Studies such as those conducted by NIOSH (which was an ergonomic study, since it was aimed at adjusting the working environment to the workers' requirements) have resulted in a number of intriguing changes in the workplace. Several companies have begun to market "ergonomically-designed" workstations and office furniture (see Figure 17.7). Swiveling or tilting terminal bases, recessed keyboards, adjustable chairs, wrist rests, convenient and compact storage devices, and **acoustical enclosure units** (cabinets that muffle printer noise) are only a few of the specially designed furnishings available from ergonomically-minded manufacturers.

Figure 17.8 Worker Isolation
As fewer people are needed to operate increasingly self-sufficient computers, the potential emotional problems created by worker isolation and lonely, sterile working conditions must be faced.

Stress

Psychological consequences of overwork

The technological improvement of work conditions, however, can lead to another problem for computer workers—stress. A person working at a word processor can produce twice the material he or she could type on a typewriter. This potential gain in productivity has made many employers expect greater efficiency from their operators. Also, because material can be called up, assigned, corrected, stored, printed, and forwarded from one workstation, social isolation can become another problem (see Figure 17.8). An operator may begin to feel pushed or harassed by the seemingly insatiable computer, separated from coworkers, and generally overworked. Morale may decline, and job-induced illness result. The very tools introduced to increase productivity have proven in a number of cases to be the source of increased tardiness, sick leave, absenteeism, slow-downs, errors, and turnovers.

Related to the stress caused by increased work demands is the stress resulting from **computer-based monitoring,** constant electronic evaluation of an employee's performance in terms of time, quantity, and quality. The Congressional Office of Technology Assessment estimates that 6 million workers in telecommunications, financial services, and airlines are evaluated on the basis of computer monitoring of their work. The same study found some evidence but no clear links suggesting that monitoring leads to high stress levels. To employers, computer-based monitoring (discussed earlier), is just another evaluation method. They argue that worker competitiveness and productivity increases when their strengths and weaknesses are pinpointed and management feedback on performance is fast and specific. Unions disagree, calling computer-based monitoring a high-pressure invasion of employee privacy.

On the other hand, word processors and other pieces of electronic equipment in the office are often greeted with delight and relief by office workers. The speed and efficiency they bring to formerly time-consuming and monotonous typing and filing chores generally make secretarial and clerical functions lighter and more pleasant. Most typists, for example, have found the opportunity to be trained on and work with high-tech equipment improves not only their job performance but also their opportunities for advancement.

Many European and American companies, as a result of either management initiative or union contract, have set specific limits on the amount of time their workers should spend operating VDTs and have taken advantage of higher productivity to upgrade and expand workers' other administrative and clerical responsibilities. As a result, computers in such workplaces have led to higher morale and greater feelings of self-esteem, as well as reducing "intensity anxiety," or stress caused by feelings of being overworked. The FDA-BRH report mentioned earlier found "that efforts expended to reduce stress would also reduce the adverse impact on health," and other studies have found that positive attention to the ergonomics affecting office workers can increase their productivity by 13 to 15 percent. Everybody gains from a comfortable, healthy environment.

Isolation

The advent of personal computers that can be linked to large central systems has offered employers the option of enlarging a workforce without expanding facilities. There is no longer any reason why a number of jobs, particularly some secretarial and clerical work, can't be performed just as efficiently at home as in the office (see Figure 17.9). The University of Southern California's Center for Futures Research estimates that 10 million people will work at home with computers by the year 2000. However, many of those workers whose job functions are well suited to telecommuting are afraid that they will become trapped in the home. Their concern is that at-home workers will be paid less and will have fewer benefits than full-time office workers, that they will miss out on the social aspects of the office environment and be stuck in a low-prestige semicareer. Other workers, particularly those with small children, and a growing number of professionals such as attorneys, welcome the opportunity to be a full-time parent and a wage-earner as well.

Isolation in the workplace isn't the only concern. There is a growing fear that, as society becomes increasingly linked together by computers, people will hide away by themselves, endlessly tapping away at keyboards, living their lives by computer. A similar fear, interestingly enough, was expressed following the invention of the telephone: that people would no longer talk face-to-face but would

Telecommuting and social isolation

Figure 17.9 Home Work
The advent of the personal and portable computer has made it possible for much office work to be done at home. While working at home may be attractive for some, isolation, lack of benefits, and less than ideal working conditions are drawbacks to such arrangements that need to be considered.

instead converse exclusively over wires. Conversation has certainly not decreased in the years since Bell's invention, and the more people talked, the more lingering nineteenth-century social barriers were broken down. Computer linkage may have a similar effect, opening new avenues of communication among more people.

ETHICS AND RESPONSIBILITY

Most professions have a code of ethics or ethical guidelines, a set of general principles by which the people in that profession are expected to behave. The doctor's Hippocratic oath and the attorney's Canon of Ethics are two such standards, and doctors or lawyers who violate them are subject to reprimand, suspension, or expulsion from their profession. With so many sensitive issues facing professionals in the fields of computer science and data processing, it seems reasonable to expect some standard for their behavior. In fact, there are several. The *American Federation of Information-Processing Societies (AFIPS)* is an umbrella organization that includes most computer societies, such as the Association for Computing Machinery (ACM), the Data Processing Management Association (DPMA), and the Institute of Electrical and Electronic Engineers (IEEE), all organizations devoted to the advancement and effectiveness of their professions. (See Figure 17.10.)

A new sense of professional responsibility

AFIPS recognized the need for a formal code of ethics in 1970. Since then, many of its affiliates have developed standards of ethical behavior for their members. Violations include falsifying data, using a company computer for personal projects, taking advantage of a known vulnerability in a system to gain unauthorized access, obtaining records or data without permission, or assisting anyone else to do so. The *Institute for Certification of Computer Professionals (ICCP)* oversees a certification process that requires five years of experience and passing an examination on data-processing equipment, management principles, accounting, finance, mathematics, statistics, and systems analysis and design. The ICCP awards the *Certificate in Data Processing (CDP)* in recognition of a person's experience and competence, and binding him or her to its ethical standard. There would seem to be little

Figure 17.10 DPMA Code of Ethics
(Reprint permission granted. Data Processing Management Association. 1988. All rights reserved.)

Code of Ethics

I acknowledge:

That I have an obligation to management, therefore, I shall promote the understanding of information processing methods and procedures to management using every resource at my command.

That I have an obligation to my fellow members, therefore, I shall uphold the high ideals of DPMA as outlined in its Association Bylaws. Further, I shall cooperate with my fellow members and shall treat them with honesty and respect at all times.

That I have an obligation to society and will participate to the best of my ability in the dissemination of knowledge pertaining to the general development and understanding of information processing. Further, I shall not use knowledge of a confidential nature to further my personal interest, nor shall I violate the privacy and confidentiality of information entrusted to me or to which I may gain access.

That I have an obligation to my employer whose trust I hold, therefore, I shall endeavor to discharge this obligation to the best of my ability, to guard my employer's interests, and to advise him or her wisely and honestly.

That I have an obligation to my country, therefore, in my personal, business and social contacts, I shall uphold my nation and shall honor the chosen way of life of my fellow citizens.

I accept these obligations as a personal responsibility and as a member of this Association. I shall actively discharge these obligations and I dedicate myself to that end.

reason, however, for the AFIPS code of ethics not to be adopted unofficially by casual, nonprofessional users.

THE DISPLACING TECHNOLOGY

According to the Congressional Budget Office, in any year since 1984 between 450,000 and 750,000 people lost their jobs because of technological advances. A private study commissioned by the W. E. Upjohn Institute for Employment Research found that, by 1990, from 100,000 to 200,000 more jobs will be eliminated because of technology, largely in the auto industry. The same study projects that from 32,000 to 64,000 new jobs will be created in robotics, but the new jobs will be for highly skilled workers. Researchers at Carnegie-Mellon University estimate that 4 million manufacturing workers could be displaced by robots by the turn of the century. By 2025, they say, it is conceivable that nearly all current blue collar jobs could be eliminated. Thus, in the ideal future we will all be freed from drudgery and repetitive and heavy labor by technology, and will be free to explore our interests, with plenty of leisure time on our hands.

The new technologies both create and destroy jobs

Retooling programs are necessary to retrain industrial workers in technologically useful skills. A joint study conducted by the state of Michigan and IBM calls on states to teach blue collar workers about computers and math. Simple literacy, the report said, is no longer enough. Workers need to be able to read and understand computer manuals and operate sensitive, complex equipment. In the future, we may all work part-time at two or three different jobs in order to make room for each other, which in turn means practically lifelong education and training for everyone. Dramatic changes in our whole society may very well be inevitable. And technology doesn't stand still. The computer and electronics industries are undergoing rapid changes, and today's high-tech professionals will need to retool themselves as the technology becomes more advanced. We're all going to have to face a lot of change.

Summary

Privacy

We are becoming increasingly dependent on the wide dispersal and easy accessibility of personal data. Greater convenience and efficiency may lead to greater intrusions into personal privacy.

Matching   The idea of matching different data bases dates from as early as 1960. The practice is now commonly used to spot fraud and mismanagement, particularly in welfare and tax evasion, saving taxpayers billions of dollars every year.

Legal Protection   Although there is no clear constitutional guarantee of a "right to privacy," the Fourth Amendment may apply. Four acts of Congress definitely do: the Fair Credit Reporting Act of 1970 (free access to credit records); the Freedom of Information Act of 1970 (free access to personal data gathered by the U.S. government); the Crime Control Act of 1973 (arrest histories must be kept current and complete); and the Federal Privacy Act of 1974 (investigations must be justified).

Computer Crime

Computer crime is the unauthorized manipulation of computers, computer programs, or data for inappropriate or unlawful purposes.

Viruses   Illicit programs infect programs through sharing or copying software and cause damage from minor delays to destruction of data.

Other Access Methods   The four most common methods for committing computer crime are the trapdoor, the Trojan horse, the time bomb, and the salami slice.

Computer Vandalism   High-tech vandalism by hackers destroys data, creates inconvenience, and costs money. The high cost and low probability of locating computer vandals make many companies unwilling to pursue them. Laws are only recently being written or updated to apply specifically to computer vandalism.

Industrial Espionage   As the computer and software industries become more lucrative and competitive, engaging in cloak-and-dagger spying activities becomes more tempting.

Software Piracy   Software manufacturers need to take precautions to protect themselves against the pirating of copies of their merchandise. ''Hidden'' program segments and software licensing agreements with customers are two such precautions.

Securing the System

A number of measures can be taken to ensure the integrity and security of computer systems.

Controlling Personnel   Screening employees and limiting access to computer equipment are examples of worthwhile security measures.

Passwords and Access Logs   The use of secret user codes and accurate access logs is a comparatively simple technique for securing data against unauthorized intruders.

Cryptography   The use of enciphering can protect sensitive data from unauthorized access or use. The Data Encryption Standard (DES) developed by the National Bureau of Standards may be the most secure cipher.

Hazards and Safeguards

Perils other than those posed by criminals threaten the security of data.

Heat   Computer circuitry converts most of the electricity it consumes into heat, and the warmer the circuitry, the greater is the chance of malfunction. Built-in fans and cooling systems and air-conditioning of facilities are solutions to overheating. Excess humidity can short out circuitry, so moisture detectors are also needed.

Smoke and Steam   High levels of smoke, dust, or ash may scratch and damage tapes and disks or clog vents. Filtered ventilation systems and smoke detectors are common in computer rooms.

Electricity   Computers can be protected against power surges and failures by surge-protection devices and backup sources of power such as batteries or generators. Static electricity can be controlled by using grounded carpets and special slippers.

Wildlife   Mice and insects can be a problem. They can gnaw through wiring or nest in vents, causing shorts, fires, dust, or overheating.

Earthquakes   Earthquakes' primary hazard is that unanchored hardware units can crash into each other. The secondary effects—fire, smoke, steam, power failures, and debris—can also be devastating to an organization.

Terrorism   Computers are increasingly becoming targets of political terror.

Electromagnetic Pulse   An electromagnetic pulse from the detonation of a nuclear warhead would black out computerized communications systems nationwide. Airborne communications centers may be one possible safeguard.

Disaster Recovery Teams   Disaster recovery teams are established to create and implement workable plans for returning computer systems to normal operation following a disaster.

Health

Health problems reported to be associated with the use of computers, specifically with the use of video display terminals (VDTs), include radiation-linked problems, visual disturbances, musculoskeletal difficulties, and stress.

Radiation and VDTs Despite concerns about the incidence of cataracts, miscarriages, birth defects, sterility, and cancer, studies by the U.S. and Canadian governments and private research groups have found no link between VDT radiation and disease.

Computer-Chip Toxins Workers in the computer-chip manufacturing industry are exposed to toxic chemicals that may pose health threats similar to those feared from VDTs.

Physical Complaints Studies have shown that computer users may develop eyestrain, neck pains, backaches, and fatigue as a result of a poor working environment. Such workstation improvements as screen hoods, filters, indirect lighting, adjustable chairs, and specific changes in screen brightness, character size, and keyboard height can alleviate these problems.

Ergonomics Ergonomics is the study of how living and working conditions can be adapted to technology; biotechnology is research into the problems posed by the interaction of humans and machines. The need for better working environments has resulted in the marketing of specially designed furniture: adjustable chairs, terminal bases, wrist rests, and acoustical enclosure units.

Stress Because computers are so fast, VDT operators may feel compelled to work faster. Tension, isolation, and pressure can sometimes result in decreases in productivity and morale. Some companies limit the amount of time their workers will spend operating VDTs.

Isolation Although computer networks and personal computers may make life more efficient, their impact on the overall quality of living may not be entirely positive. Loss of job benefits and isolation of telecommuters are some of the issues that will need to be faced.

Ethics and Responsibility

Ethical standards adopted by the affiliates of American Federation of Information Processing Societies (AFIPS) and by the Institute for Certification of Computer Professionals (ICCP) for its requirements for the certificate in data processing (CDP) are designed to guide the professional ethics of computer professionals.

The Displacing Technology

With the possibility of one million people being out of work by 1990 due to technological advances, and 4 million more jobs eliminated by the year 2000, our society faces some serious questions about how it will change and what all of those people will do. Retooling, retraining, and job sharing are possible solutions.

Computer Concepts

As an extra review of the chapter, try defining the following terms. If you have trouble with any of them, refer to the page number listed.

matching *581*
computer crime *583*
virus *583*
worm *585*
trapdoor *585*
Trojan horse *585*
time bomb *586*
salami slice *586*

industrial espionage *587*
Copyright Act of 1980 *590*
software licensing *590*
passwords *592*
access logs *592*
cryptography *592*
cipher *592*
Data Encryption Standard (DES) *593*

disaster recovery team *596*
ergonomics *598*
biotechnology *599*
acoustical enclosure units *599*
computer-based monitoring *600*
retooling *603*

Review Questions

1. Name some of the different places in which computer files on an individual may be kept.
2. Why do some people feel that personal information kept in computer systems is potentially damaging?
3. What Acts of Congress protect a U.S. citizen against misuse of and inaccuracies in personal computer records on file with the government and other agencies?
4. What are the guarantees of the Fair Credit Reporting Act of 1970?
5. What is computer crime?
6. What is a trapdoor?
7. What was made illegal by the Semiconductor Chip Protection Act?
8. What is the current technique used to protect software from piracy? How effective can it be?
9. What are some of the possible penalties for computer vandals?
10. What are the ways computer systems can be safeguarded against unauthorized intrusion?
11. What types of personnel generally make up a disaster recovery team?
12. Explain the effects of each of the following on computer systems: heat, humidity, smoke, dust, earthquakes, mice, terrorists, and an EMP. How can computers be protected from each?
13. What are the four categories of health problems associated with the use of computers?
14. What are two health problems associated with workers involved in the manufacturing of computer chips?
15. What is computer-based monitoring?
16. How have most typists reacted to the opportunity to work with high-tech equipment?
17. Describe some of the concerns people have about telecommuting.
18. What are some violations of ethics as outlined by the AFIPS?
19. How might the problem of worker displacement be partly solved?
20. What skills, beyond basic computer literacy, do workers need, according to a joint study by the State of Michigan and IBM?

True or False

1. The process of comparing records of government and private data systems is called matching.
2. The U.S. Constitution guarantees citizens the right to privacy.
3. Congress enacted a law limiting the information-gathering activities of federal agencies.
4. The average computer crime nets perpetrators less than the average white collar crime.
5. A computer program that modifies a computer's operation by replicating itself in software causing system malfunctions is a virus.
6. Licensing of software is generally conceded to be an effective means to prevent unauthorized copying of software.
7. One method for securing a computer system from unauthorized users is the use of access logs.
8. One low-tech threat to computer systems is mice.
9. One computer-related cause of stress in the workplace is ergonomics.
10. Concern about isolation resulting from the proliferation of personal computers is new in the history of technology.

Multiple Choice

1. A program hidden within a program in a computer which modifies a program's operation, causing malfunctions, is:

    (a) a match   (b) a virus   (c) a trapdoor

2. A drastic technique used to discourage software users from making copies of a program is:
   (a) a worm   (b) a Trojan horse   (c) a virus

3. One form of crime which victimizes a manufacturer of computer hardware or software is:
   (a) a Trojan horse   (b) vandalism   (c) industrial espionage

4. One means of identifying users of computer systems is:
   (a) cryptography   (b) ciphers   (c) passwords

5. A device for protecting personal computers from temporary loss of electrical power is:
   (a) a bank of batteries   (b) EMP   (c) a cipher

6. The study of adapting living or working conditions to new technology is called:
   (a) matching   (b) ergonomics   (c) computer-based monitoring

7. One concern mentioned as possibly resulting from telecommuting is:
   (a) isolation   (b) monitoring   (c) matching

8. This same concern was voiced following the invention of the:
   (a) automobile   (b) telephone   (c) radio

9. One solution to the potential problem of having millions of unemployed workers around the world is:
   (a) CAD/CAM   (b) industrialization   (c) retooling programs

A Sharper Focus

1. If you were offered a telecommuting position and were told by the company that you would be paid less than those who did the same job but worked in the office, how would you respond? Do you think it's fair to pay telecommuters less? If you were the employer, how would you argue for your policy?

2. Do you think it is easier for computer professionals to be unethical than it is for other professionals like lawyers and doctors? Why or why not?

Projects

1. Find out more about one of the computer crimes described in this chapter. How (and why) did the perpetrators do it? What did they get? Where are they now?

2. Laws and penalties for computer crimes vary from state to state. Some states have very specific and very strict laws; others attempt to apply existing laws to computer crimes. Find out about the laws regarding computer crime that have been enacted or are under consideration in your state. When were they passed, what do they say, and what are the possible penalties? If your state has no specific law on computer crime, should it, or is the current arrangement sufficient? Finally, find out if any significant computer crimes have been committed in your state.

3. Talk with an official in your school's computer center or in a local company. How is the system safeguarded against unauthorized access? Find out if there have ever been any attempts to gain access.

4. Perform an ergonomic study of places in which VDTs are in use in your school, library, offices, or home. Determine, as best you can, whether or not the work areas comply with the NIOSH recommendations.

18

The Next Twenty Years

Focus On

Neural Networks

One of the key areas of research in artificial intelligence just being explored currently is the area of neural networks. That is, how does the human brain (or any animal brain, for that matter) store and retrieve information? This research actually started in the 1960s but until now models were loosely based on biological data. These models have produced some results with voice recognition, face and fingerprint recognition. However, they give no help to biologists who want to know how the brain learns, remembers, and recalls.

Recently, a group of neurobiologists and computer scientists at the University of California described what they knew about neurons in rat brains that are linked to sorting and storage of smells. They then added a set of stimuli representing odors and input all of it into a computer. Rather than asking specific questions or presenting a specific problem, they watched to see what happened with this simulation.

The result was that the computer organized the data in unexpected ways and predicted a number of phenomena, which have since been confirmed in the laboratory with live rats. Basically, what the computer did is analogous with linking a city, for example Rome, with other large cities such as Los Angeles, rather than with Italy.

Examining the patterns of neurons after the computer "sniffs" an odor, the scientists discovered that similarities among odors were emphasized by the computer. What the computer did on repeated sniffs was to identify smells first by their similarities, then on subsequent sniffs by highlighting their differences. This turned out to be how the rats learn to distinguish odors. The simulation also illustrates how the brain uses a specific rhythm of electrical activity to orchestrate the biological events involved in learning.

The researchers believe that using such biologically-based computer simulations they will start to understand the neocortex—the area of the human brain (80% of the whole brain) which is believed to play a role in everything from handling language to spatial relations.

Predicting the future isn't very difficult: just sit down and dream up some sleek, high-tech scenario out of a science fiction movie, and call it "A Look Ahead" or even "The Next Twenty Years." On the other hand, it's much harder to predict the future *accurately*. A world exposition in the early part of this century tried to predict life in the 1960s and envisioned four-mile-high skyscrapers with businesspeople ferried between them in biplanes and gliders. In the early 1950s, another prophetic exposition foresaw cities of the 1980s full of moving sidewalks, wheelless cars that floated above the streets on a cushion of air, and buildings that looked more like plumbing fixtures than architectural structures. George Orwell and H. G. Wells made their predictions several decades ago; Arthur C. Clarke and Isaac Asimov do so today.

Of course, we can't predict the future with any certainty, and trying to predict the way people will live 20 years from now is a risky undertaking. After all, so many variables besides technological innovation have an influence: political, economic, social, commercial, and artistic. What we can do is try to take a look ahead at what is *reasonably* likely to happen within a *reasonable* period of time. All through this book we've been considering today's technology. Here, we'll look at what today's developments seem to suggest for the near future, that is, somewhere around the end of the first decade of the next century. Don't expect predictions of colonies on Jupiter or humanlike robots running for president; instead, you'll see what changes your home, or your children's homes, may undergo during the course of the next two decades. We'll discuss artificial intelligence and advanced robotics, but we'll also talk about homes and cars and work. In short, we're looking for the *real* future, the future whose foundation is already laid today.

Before we look at some ways computers will change our lives, let's look at how the machines themselves will be changing over the next 20 years.

ARTIFICIAL INTELLIGENCE

For application after application, we've seen how difficult it is to distinguish what computers produce from what humans produce. And we've learned that all any computer really does is to perform a very long and highly branched sequence of operations on binary numbers. Nonetheless, the results can be astonishing. If computers can so accurately perform basic humanlike operations, from calculation to welding, are there any limitations to their ability to simulate the products and processes of human intelligence? This is the question posed by researchers in a field called **artificial intelligence (AI).** Two approaches have characterized this 20-year-old field. One approach imitates human thought processes as closely as possible in the hope of producing intelligent results; the other attempts to produce those end results.

Computer simulation of human intelligence

But where, exactly, is the dividing line between a machine that simply does what a program specifies and one that very clearly demonstrates those qualities that we associate with intelligence? Debate rages over whether machines are capable of crossing that line. The British mathematician Alan Turing, who made lasting contributions to theoretical computer science, suggested a neat answer to this question. He proposed that a human submit typed questions to a computer and to another human, both unseen by the questioner. The human's responses would be typed back in such a way as to demonstrate his or her human identity most convincingly, while the computer would be programmed to do as convincing a job as possible of

Alan Turing's test

answering as a human would. Turing said that the machine would demonstrate intelligence if the questioner had a 50:50 chance of guessing the identities of the two respondents incorrectly, that is, of being fooled by the computer half the time. Think about the complexity of the program: for a chess-playing computer to "converse" about chess is quite an achievement; for a computer to be able to chat in an unstructured, humanlike way about recent movies, favorite restaurants, quantum physics, and its best bowling score is an almost unimaginable programming feat.

Knowledge-Based Systems

We are confronted every day with decisions that must be made without the benefit of precise mathematical algorithms:

"Do I have a cold or is my allergy acting up?"

"Is that my bus coming?"

"Should I put my money in a savings account or a money market fund, or spend it all on software?"

We apply experience and intuition to such problems, perhaps of greater or lesser importance, many times each day. We may seek the advice of experts about the more important ones; but, although we feel our decisions are better for having their advice and we often act on it, we don't expect it to be absolutely correct all of the time. This is true for a wide range of problems, from medical diagnosis and financial advice to deciding where to drill for oil. Computers involved in AI research often employ **heuristic algorithms** to simulate human thought processes. Heuristic algorithms, like humans, employ intuition and common sense to solve problems. They don't necessarily produce perfect solutions, or even the best possible ones. Rather, these algorithms rely on strategies that select good or adequate solutions from a huge, unwieldy set of possibilities.

Systems that simulate intuition and common sense

Just as we don't expect a physician to make a diagnosis without adequate knowledge of symptoms, treatments, and cures—a specific decision environment called *domain knowledge*—we can't expect a computer to help in problem solving unless a similarly adequate knowledge base is available. And such a knowledge base, unlike the conventional data bases we've discussed previously in this book, must include diverse kinds of knowledge, for example, knowledge about objects and processes, about goals and actions, and about cause-and-effect relationships. Such knowledge will often involve intuition or common sense, judgment that is generally difficult to represent in a satisfactory way in a computer system. For this reason, researchers in AI are deeply concerned with the subject of *knowledge representation* as it pertains to **knowledge-based systems.** Such systems attempt to program computers to make deductions from a stored base of facts and experience, rather than through execution of a precise algorithm that is mathematically guaranteed to solve a problem.

PROLOG's rules for making inferences

AI researchers are also concerned with the closely related questions of how to manipulate stored knowledge: how to draw inferences, how to deal with incomplete knowledge, and how to extract the knowledge of human experts to set up a knowledge base. The programming language that most AI researchers currently prefer to use in dealing with such questions is called PROLOG. Using PROLOG, one can express both information and rules for making inferences based on the information. The information that John likes Mary, for example, is represented as

```
likes(John, Mary)
```

The information that Mary is very popular can be expressed as

```
likes(y, Mary)
```

where y is anyone. Rules in PROLOG have the form

```
P₁ if (P₂ and P₃ and P₄)
```

where P_1, P_2, P_3, and P_4 are items of information, such as that John likes Mary. If we want to state the rule that children like their mothers, we first express that z is the mother of y by writing

```
mother(z, y)
```

Then we write the rule

```
likes(y, z) if mother(z, y)
```

The rule that John likes anyone who likes him is written

```
likes(John, x) if likes(x, John)
```

where x is anyone.

PROLOG can be used to determine new inferences from given information and rules or to verify if some assumption is consistent with a given set of rules and facts. It has been used to develop many expert systems.

Expert Systems

Expert systems are frameworks that allow for the incorporation and organization of the knowledge of human experts in specific subject areas. They are used much like human experts are—to render assistance in fields as diverse as medicine and mineral prospecting. To create an expert system, the *knowledge engineer* (AI programmer) interviews human experts in a field and distills their collective expertise into a series of if/then equations like those previously discussed. AI researchers have found that it is frequently more important to amass a sufficiently large knowledge base than to discover and incorporate more complex rules and relationships. This finding has led to a recognition of the real importance of human experts in developing expert systems. First, there must be reasonable agreement about who is an expert. Second, the experts must be able to communicate their decision methods and the knowledge on which those decisions are based.

Furthermore, many investigators have found that systems using only simple PROLOG-type rules for making inferences don't necessarily produce the best results. When empirical information, acquired from the experience of experts, is the only information available, basing a system on such rules is a useful and practical alternative. However, when causal or functional relationships are known, their inclusion will improve the results. In Chapter 16, we mentioned three expert systems currently used in medical diagnosis: MYCIN and PUFF, which deal with relatively narrow areas of knowledge about specific diseases, and CADUCEUS. CADUCEUS achieves its great generality (it can deal with about 500 diseases) by incorporating some knowledge beyond empirical rules: it uses a model of the human body and the relationships between its organs to construct inferences. It makes inferences on the basis of the timing of symptoms as a disease progresses.

Rules and relationships applied to specific subject areas

Figure 18.1 CADUCEUS

Interactive expert systems use a series of
questions to solve problems. Here, two doctors use the CADUCEUS medical expert system to help them quickly diagnose a patient's illness.

CADUCEUS, like many expert systems, is interactive; that is, the user works with
the system to solve a problem through a series of questions, the answers to which
lead to further questions, and ultimately to a solution. A physician communicates
with CADUCEUS using a special vocabulary, as shown in Figure 18.1.

Expert systems are actually quite elementary, when you consider that AI researchers are trying to develop computers that mimic human thought processes.
But for the most part, as AI has emerged from university labs and into the real
world, business and industry have found the mundane utility of expert systems a
most attractive aspect of AI; so attractive, in fact, that AI and expert systems are
used synonymously in the marketplace, although expert systems are only a subcat-
egory of AI. Today, expert system software that runs on the personal, mini-, and
mainframe computers already used in businesses is finding an expanding market.
Annual sales of AI hardware and software (software companies generally sell **expert system shells,** which are software "skeletons" fleshed out with expert data
by the purchaser), are expected to exceed $1.7 billion by 1990—four times the
1986 level (see Figure 18.2).

Figure 18.2 VP-Expert

A popular and inexpensive expert system application
program.

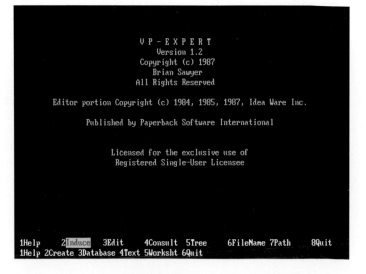

The rapidly growing list of areas in which expert systems are already available includes self-help (how to maintain a car engine or plant a successful garden), taxes, investments, real estate, accounting, law, and management, as well as electronic circuit design, mineral prospecting, chemical analysis, computer system configuring, robotics, and, naturally, the design of expert systems.

Natural-Language Programs

A second category of AI, more advanced than expert systems, is the **natural-language program.** While expert systems simply provide access to "encyclopedias" of topic-specific knowledge, natural-language programs come closer to mimicking human cognitive processes. Used in conjunction with expert systems, natural-language programs make the expert systems more accessible. Essentially a result of AI research into how meaning is derived from language (for example, how we understand from context whether someone is saying "there," "their," or "they're"), natural-language programs let users access expert data bases with plain English commands such as "How do I change the oil in my Taurus?" or "Which new high-tech companies in Minnesota are the most profitable investments?"

Communicating with expert systems in plain English

Speech

Natural-language programs are still largely limited to keyboard input, but AI research has, since its inception, been active in trying to achieve more natural human communication with computers. The recognition of speech by machines remains a high-priority objective for computer scientists in this field. Although progress has unquestionably been made, and some machines can be directed by humans using restricted vocabularies and speaking with special emphasis, the goal of a machine that accepts and transcribes natural, continuous speech has yet to be achieved.

Speaking to machines and applying speech recognition

When you speak into a telephone, your voice causes a diaphragm to vibrate. This vibration produces a corresponding variation in an electric current, that is, an analog waveform. At the receiving end, the current flows through an electromagnet. As the strength of this magnet varies with the magnitude of the current, so does its attraction for a steel diaphragm, which vibrates accordingly to produce sound.

Many developments have resulted from the digital revolution in telephone communications. Transforming speech into binary digits rather than just analog waveforms made many new functions possible, as seen in Figure 18.3. Speech may be more readily "compressed" to reduce the storage space required for messages, and improved security is made possible through encryption. Vocalized words and phrases that have been stored are readily manipulated by computers to produce the familiar recorded messages, from time-and-temperature reports to directory assistance, talking registers in grocery stores, and chatty Coke machines. Spoken messages can be stored and forwarded at a time specified by the caller. These and many other now-routine digital speech-processing functions have also helped pave the way for AI investigators working on the automatic recognition and understanding of speech.

Considerable progress has been made in getting computers to recognize special vocabularies of isolated words. As their label implies, these are words that are surrounded by pauses or intervals of silence. The computer is thus not faced with the formidable job of distinguishing the individual words among the continuously

Figure 18.3 A Typewriter That Takes Dictation

spoken phrases of normal speech. No computer will have that capacity in the near future unless progress takes place at an unforeseen rate. However, even computers' current capability to recognize isolated words is producing a growing number of significant applications. For example, an existing limited-vocabulary system permits physicians to call in 24 hours a day to match organs with transplant recipients. Executive telephone terminals that can, via speaker phones, respond to a set of voice commands such as ''Call Henry'' have been developed. As we'll see shortly, some computers that run household appliances can be told to dim the lights or put on a record.

Neural Networks

Simulating human brain activity

A third form of AI, **neural networks,** is the most advanced and is still largely experimental. Developers at Princeton and at the California Institute of Technology are trying to simulate the human brain's complex of neural pathways in silicon. The goal is a familiar one: to build a computer capable of actually engaging in humanlike thought. Although the technology is far from ready for general use, some successes have been recorded. Researchers have simulated the nerve structure of the retina and inner ear, and AT&T has managed to simulate the brain of a garden slug. While of limited application, it's certainly a start.

AI at Work and Play

Beyond knowledge-based systems, AI is in the forefront of research into industrial technologies. In addition, attempts to endow computers with humanlike logical and cognitive skills have long been made in the context of chess.

Vision and Advanced Robotics

In Chapter 15, we discussed the current generation of industrial robots, almost all of which are insensate; that is, the locations of all components and subassemblies must be controlled very accurately so that the ''blind'' robots can find them exactly where they're supposed to be. This requirement can add considerably to the cost of industrial automation. More than 30 years ago, AI scientists began research aimed at producing more flexible robots that could sense important aspects of their environment. As a result, a few robots with limited vision and tactile feedback to their computer controls have made their commercial debut. These sensor-based robots are at the center of much of the excitement and promise of the next generation of robots. They promise to revolutionize not only manufacturing, but space exploration, undersea mining, and the development of entirely new classes of prosthetic devices.

Robots that sense their environment

A welding robot being tested at General Electric's Evandale, Ohio, aircraft engine plant, welds together the curved edges of two steel plates. A vision subsystem consisting of a laser illumination source and a video camera monitors the position of the path to be welded, feeds out the proper amount of welding wire, and controls the welding torch. In robot systems such as this, the vision subsystem is necessary because the pieces being worked on are large and heavy and consequently are difficult to position accurately. The robot must be able to make the required adjustments and execute different welding paths for pieces of different shapes. The General Electric robot does high-quality work at a speed about twice as fast as an average human operator, using the image-processing techniques described in Chapter 16.

Although robotics has been moving ahead rapidly in the automation of work done with heavy pieces in difficult environments, it has progressed slowly in light assembly, such as in electronics manufacturing where the most important requirements are speed and dexterity. Meaningful robot penetration into this area can result only if there is substantial simultaneous progress in the development of more sophisticated and less costly manipulators, vision sensors, and controls.

AI and Chess

For over a thousand years, chess has enjoyed a unique place among intellectual recreations. It has long attracted AI researchers, because it is one arena where results can readily be measured against human performance. These results clearly demonstrate both the progress that has been made in developing AI and the distance yet to go.

The classic test of progress in artificial intelligence

Numerous chess-playing programs have at one time or another used all the AI techniques: heuristic and nonheuristic algorithms, knowledge bases containing move-by-move example games, and learning schemes that improve the program's play on the basis of both winning and losing experience. The complexity and variety of the possible moves make chess particularly challenging for programmers. Figure 18.4 will give you an idea of exactly how challenging chess is by examining a much simpler game's programming structure.

Among the techniques used to develop good to excellent chess-playing programs are combinations of knowledge bases, including stored actual games. These help the computer avoid moves that have previously resulted in losses and encourage those that have produced wins. Heuristic algorithms that apply numeric scores to board positions and produce good, if not optimal, moves are also used, as well as schemes for projecting a few plays ahead (to avoid making moves that can lead to vulnerable positions).

How good are chess programs? The best of them, running on supercomputers, play very respectable games. The United States Chess Federation groups chess players into various categories: international grand masters, international masters,

Figure 18.4 Game Tree for Tic-Tac-Toe

Many games are best represented for computers as tree-like data structures. The set of game positions that can result from the possible moves at a turn is called a *ply*. The branches of the tree are the moves, and the leaves (called *nodes*) are the resulting game positions. The game tree for tic-tac-toe can't be any deeper than 9 plies (since there are only nine squares in the game), and covering the 3 basic moves (corner, center, and side) brings the total number of possible game positions to about 300. This number of alternatives can be easily searched by a program to select the move at each turn that will lead to a win or a draw. It isn't that easy with chess, however. An average game between good players involves about 45 moves for each, or 90 plies. For each position on the board, there are an average of 35 possible moves, which means that the bottom ply of the game tree for chess contains 35^{90} nodes.

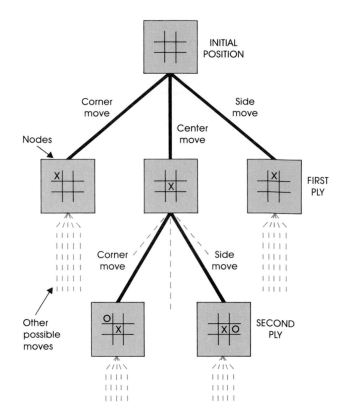

American masters, expert players, and average to strong amateurs. The best chess programs are in the American master range. And it seems that not only can some computers play chess better than many humans, they are increasingly able to talk about it, too, with their newly advanced speech capabilities.

A NEW WORLD

A boom in the sales and use of computers

From the beginning of time until 1980 or so, maybe a million computers were produced. Since then, more than that have been sold every year. Some 20,000 Apple units alone have been delivered each month. By 1990, computers may be selling at the rate of nearly 11 million a year, and International Data Corporation estimates that there will be 400 million computers in the United States by the turn of the century. But such growth has not been without setbacks. In a single week early in 1985, IBM ended production of the failed PCjr, Apple temporarily closed down its Macintosh production facilities due to massive overstocks, and Wang also declared a one-month halt in production. It looked as if the bubble had burst, and indeed, many analysts believe that the computer industry had banked too heavily on a computer in every living room. Then the industry turned to the business sector, and, with the introduction of the IBM PC/AT, and the realignment of the Apple Macintosh toward business applications, new and expanding markets re-opened.

That's not to say that only corporations are buying computers—far from it. The growing emphasis on computer literacy at all levels of elementary and secondary education makes them highly desirable in homes with children. To increasing numbers of people doing at least part of their work at home, a personal computer is

Figure 18.5   An On-line Family
This family uses computers for everything from schoolwork to running the family business.

indispensable. And a lot of folks just like computers (see Figure 18.5). However, the transition from a computerless society to one in which computers are found in most people's homes will be slower than once thought.

THE IMPACT ON DAILY LIFE

The increasing use of computers in our society isn't just idle conjecture. New York's Citibank plans to have more than half of its 2.5 million account-holders on-line by 1995. Major retail chains like J. C. Penney's are experimenting with at-home shopping systems. A shopping mall near Washington, D.C., offers shoppers a "window shopping" service accessible through a modem. The service lists sales and specials in a store-by-store index. Users can call up price comparisons of particular items, place orders, and request gift suggestions for women, men, children, pets, older relatives, secretaries, or a variety of other recipient categories.

The present trends that will shape the future

A wide availability of inexpensive computers could have a dramatic impact on our society. Sociologists once worried about the American culture becoming rootless and too mobile; the personal computer might well bring everyone back home. It isn't unreasonable to suggest that 10 million people may be telecommuting full-time from their homes by the turn of the century, and that another 25 million could be telecommuting half of each week and spending the other half in the office. Men and women could pursue domestic and professional careers simultaneously; parents could spend more time with their children. With computers completely taking over some mundane and repetitive household chores and expediting many others, there will be increased time to work out any new stress created in family life.

Don't be surprised to find future store shelves stocked with smart blow-dryers, toasters, and toothbrushes (which may remind you to brush up and down rather than from side to side or warn you of impending cavities while simultaneously scheduling your next appointment with the dentist). Don't laugh: before 1983 it would have been silly to suggest that microprocessors could be put in greeting cards to sing happy birthday, or in story-telling teddy bears to babysit high-tech toddlers.

It's now undeniable that computers are going to become increasingly embedded in the least computerlike aspects of our day-to-day existence, whether or not there's a personal computer in every den. Many of these systems and devices have been recently introduced. As the number of users grows, and as access to these applications becomes virtually unlimited, these now isolated examples will cease to be merely interesting anecdotes or conveniences for a privileged few. It's at that point in time, when navigation systems in cars and computers that run whole households have become as common as pocket calculators or telephones, that our look at the future begins.

At Home: The Smart House

Computer-based systems taking care of routine domestic chores

Computer-based systems that operate most household appliances are already available (see Figure 18.6). Heating, air-conditioning, lights, stereos, CD-players, VCRs, and kitchen appliances can be monitored, controlled, and timed by the computer to ensure safe, convenient, and energy-efficient operation. Controlled by voice, touchscreen, remote keypad, or telephone, the systems respond instantly to a wide range of preprogrammed commands. Not only do such systems lower utility bills, but their vigilance also reduces the hazards of fire or explosion. Sensor devices at doors and windows, activated by unauthorized pressure or the breaking of a beam of light, can alert the local police station of a break-in, while at the same time sounding a general alarm. Unlike traditional burglar alarm/security systems, some of the **home automation** systems can differentiate between a prowler in the dining room and Mom going to the kitchen for a midnight snack.

Home automation is an expensive proposition today. Basic smart security devices start at around $2200, but whole home-automating systems can cost more than $200,000. The cost is expected to drop by the early 1990s, however, when as many as half of all new homes built will have some degree of home automation built in. The National Association of Homebuilders, in conjunction with its members, utility companies, and electronics manufacturers, has built a prototype "Smart House," accepted by industry and government regulatory authorities as the standard in home automation technology (see Figure 18.7). Most current homes form the hub for a multitude of incoming gas, electrical, telephone, and cable

(a)

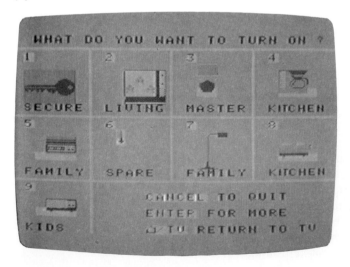

Figure 18.6 Today's Computer-Based House

General Electric's HomeMinder system is a step toward computerized housekeeping, turning the home's electrical wiring into a computer-controlled network. (a) The family television serves as the central command point, displaying HomeMinder's functions and locations around the house. (b) At the left, the adaptor wall plugs that link appliances and the computer (center). On the right, the hand-held keypad onto which commands are entered.

(b)

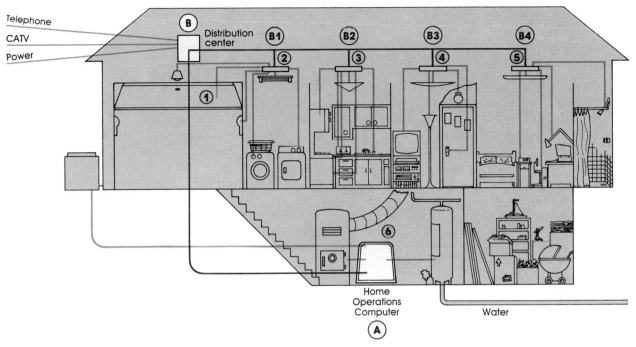

Figure 18.7 Smart House

In the computer-based home of the future, normal household functions will be monitored and controlled by a central home operations computer (A). Incoming lines (telephone, power, and cable television) are consolidated in the main distribution center (B) into a single cable running throughout the six zones of this house—garage/security (1), laundry room (2), kitchen (3), living room/entertainment center (4), bedroom/office/bathroom (5), and environmental appliances (6). Each zone has its own branch circuit controller to provide distributed intelligence and power, data, and audio/visual signals to its zone. The computer may be programmed to operate the house on a fixed timetable ("turn the porch light on at 5:30 P.M." "maintain zones 4 and 5 at 75°F"), or any appliance or function may be operated from any point in the house through a control module. Power is used in each zone only as it is needed; that is, there will be no current in the toaster's outlet until the toaster is plugged in. Even then, the toaster will "know" the precise amount of electricity required to lightly brown a muffin and will ask for, and receive, only that amount.

Legend:
- ——— High-speed data link
- ——— Incoming lines
- ——— Appliance/service control

television lines. The interior consists of a tangle of a.c. power cables, low-voltage wiring, thermostat wiring, alarm system wiring, television antenna and cable wires, speaker wires, and telephone wires. In the Smart House, a single cable integrates power distribution; audio, video, and telephone lines; and data signal distribution. A central computer distributes power to the toaster outlet only when the toaster's microprocessor announces that it is turned on—and even then provides only the power needed. This limits fire hazards and is a safety feature for families with young, inquisitive children. An infant can stick a screwdriver into a wall socket for hours, and, because the screwdriver sends no signal to the central computer, no current will flow. The computer maintains temperatures in a constant and economical way, makes coffee, turns the VCR on and off, locks the doors, turns on the yard light, and answers the phone.

The Smart House project inspired numerous small home automation companies. Systems with names like Jeeves, HomeBrain, and Home Manager generated

Figure 18.8 Home Appliances Containing Microprocessors

more than $350 million in sales in 1987; conservative projections put sales in excess of $30 billion by 1993. The biggest cost today is in refitting existing homes with the specialized cables. That cost is significantly lowered when the cables are installed as the house is built. So, over the years to come, as old houses fade away and new ones take their place, look for greater and greater levels of automation right in your own living room.

Appliance manufacturers have already started creating the automated home. Microprocessors are found in dishwashers, food processors, washing machines, dryers, color televisions, and microwave ovens. A new refrigerator by Whirlpool adjusts its interior temperature when food is added or the kitchen warms up, and General Electric's 24E refrigerator boasts ''brilliant little microchip computers'' that beep if the door is left open (and probably ensure that the light goes out inside). (See Figure 18.8.) Dryers containing moisture sensors that end the cycle when the clothes are actually dry and dishwashers that alert users when the drain is clogged and can display specific mechanical failures requiring a service call are currently available as top-of-the-line models. A more mundane application in widespread use is the embedding of microprocessors to control appliances' mechanical parts to increase their efficient use of energy. In the developmental stages are microwave ovens that respond to voice commands and washing machines that sense how dirty the clothes are and measure the precise amount of detergent needed to clean them.

Shopping, working, and playing while at home

Imagine that it's the middle of a cold winter 15 years from now, and that you are expecting guests for dinner. You order groceries using your personal computer, and they're delivered to your home (delivery is inexpensive, since home shopping has eliminated many of the costs of maintaining attractive, service-oriented super-markets, which have given way to low-cost, mechanized warehouses). When you place an order, the store's computer enters the items' bar code data into your personal computer via microwave transmissions received by the dish antenna on your roof (see Figure 18.9). Billing and payment are also, of course, done through your home computer.

The bar code contains not only price and inventory data, but also cooking instructions for frozen and packaged foods. You read the OCR code number from a gourmet frozen dinner to your microwave oven in order to call up the instructions,

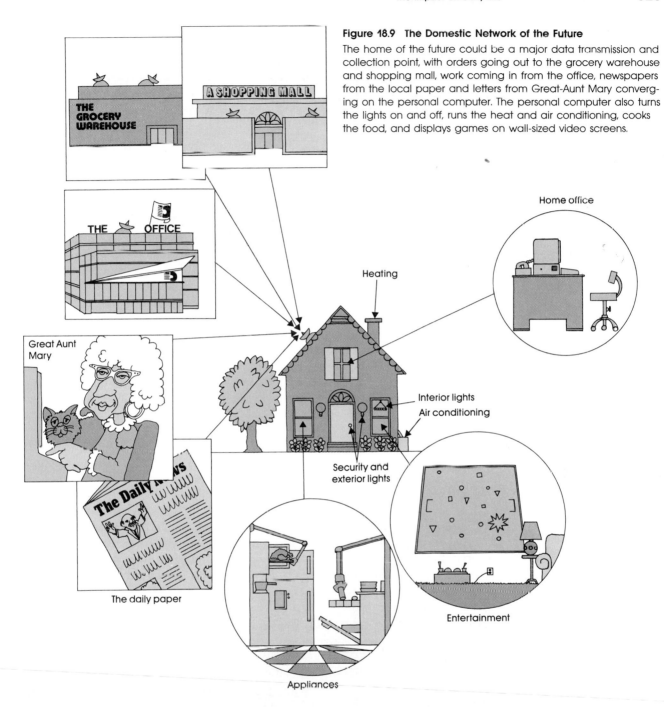

Figure 18.9 The Domestic Network of the Future
The home of the future could be a major data transmission and collection point, with orders going out to the grocery warehouse and shopping mall, work coming in from the office, newspapers from the local paper and letters from Great-Aunt Mary converging on the personal computer. The personal computer also turns the lights on and off, runs the heat and air conditioning, cooks the food, and displays games on wall-sized video screens.

THE GROCERY WAREHOUSE

A SHOPPING MALL

THE OFFICE

Great Aunt Mary

The Daily News

The daily paper

Heating

Home office

Interior lights
Air conditioning

Security and exterior lights

Entertainment

Appliances

pop the dinner in, say "defrost," and the oven sets the correct time and temperature. If you feel more ambitious, you can put a duck in your gas-microwave oven, announce the product code, and clean the house while the duck is microwaved to perfection, then gas-flamed to a crispy brown. When cooking is complete, the oven gently tells you so. If you prefer a more exotic recipe than that included in the product code, you can simply replace it with the appropriate code from your personal computer's recipe file. You'll still have to peel potatoes and make the salad, but a large part of the work of cooking will be done for you.

You're vacuuming when your guests arrive (computers still can't do everything, although some very wealthy neighbors own a vacuum-robot: they vacuumed the house with it once, to store the pattern in its memory, and now it vacuums three times a week without being asked), so you don't hear the doorbell the first time. Your home controller signals the vacuum to shut off so you can hear the bell and tell the door to unlock. When the duck is done, the central computer turns off the oven and dims the dining room lights. You tell it to put on some soft music and then serve dinner.

After the meal, while you and your friends relax, a small robot arm looks at the dirty dishes in the dining room, reaches out to clear the table, and loads them into the dishwasher. The robot then sprays the countertop with cleaning fluid and wipes it dry. This was one of the first domestic applications of industrial robotics, and your friends already call you old-fashioned because you don't have similar robots for putting food in the oven and cleaning the bathroom. You do have a new computerized video system that lets you put yourself into the movies you watch on your wall-sized television (so *you* can say "Play it again, Sam"). Your personal computer is a master chess player and not bad at Monopoly. Optical sensors brighten or dim the panels of your ceiling lights depending on how much light is coming in the window, where in the room you're sitting, and what you're doing—providing more light for reading, dimmer and less direct light for word processing, and a soft amber glow first thing in the morning.

On (and Off) the Road

Smart cars with built-in electronic navigation systems

When you leave your home in the not-so-distant future, driving may be a lot easier. Today, microprocessors scan a car's major systems and alert the driver to problems as they develop (see Figure 18.10). Automobile manufacturers plan to expand their applications of computers and are already testing systems that not only monitor interior temperature shifts and adjust the heat or air conditioning accordingly, but also operate defrosters, demisters, and windshield wipers. Experimental systems project holographs showing speed, mileage, and engine data onto the windshield in the driver's line of sight, where they appear to hover inconspicuously outside, just

Figure 18.10 Computer-Controlled Cars

Ford Motor Company's fourth-generation electronic engine control system (EEC-IV) is used in most Ford vehicles for engine control. Of its components, MROM is the read-only memory that stores the program and data. KAM (keep-alive memory) is a low-power, read-write memory that maintains its needed information even when engine power is off. The driver controls fuel injection, and QDD controls the car's many small electric motors. The CPU runs the whole show. All this computer hardware and associated electronic devices—with more power than two UNIVACs—help you operate your car!

over the hood ornament. Other automotive systems in development include an automatic transmission controlled by touch-sensitive spots on the steering wheel and voice-activated ignition systems, door locks, trunk and hood latches, and lights (your mislaid car keys can already beep at you if you clap in their vicinity). The latter systems will increase both convenience and security—the days of lost or locked-in keys will end, and voice-print security systems will ensure against theft.

Other systems being developed include obstacle-detecting radar connected to computer-controlled brakes and electronic navigation systems. One such system, called the Navigator, can generate street maps of all major cities in the United States. When provided with the car's current location and destination, the Navigator can chart the best course, illustrate the car's location on it at all times, and detect wrong turns. If tied into the computer systems of local traffic control and emergency authorities, such navigating devices could keep drivers updated on road and traffic conditions and could alter suggested routes to avoid traffic jams, icy patches, or construction. Drivers could also override the normal selection criteria by requesting scenic drives in the autumn or sight-seeing routes in historic cities. Chrysler's experimental navigation system, called Class, uses signals from navigation satellites to compute the car's location and stores maps on a digital laser disk.

For longer trips, you might someday take a train that runs by **magnetic levitation** (or **maglev**). Today, the world's fastest trains are the French TGV and the Japanese bullet train, or *skinkansen*, both of which depend on computers for navigation and control as they speed along at 125 miles per hour (see Figure 18.11). Maglev trains, however, could leave them far behind. A system of charged electromagnets mounted on the rails and on the train provides a frictionless propulsion that can produce speeds of over 250 miles per hour while treating passengers to a silent, vibrationless ride. At such speeds, trackside signals and conventional controls are rendered obsolete: the signals would be blurs, and the operator's reaction times too slow to be effective. Instead, on-board computers will control speed, guidance, and the electrical current to the magnets to maintain the proper gap between rail and train. The maglev train's "engineer" will be a computer that monitors weather, position, and track conditions; operates acceleration and braking devices; and lowers the train gently onto the tracks at the station. All along the route, the train's computer will be constantly communicating with a central routing computer that will ensure that schedules are kept and safety requirements met. Experimental maglev systems are currently being developed in the United States,

Magnetic levitation for trains

Figure 18.11 French TGV Train

*Computerized air traffic
control*

the Soviet Union, France, Germany, and Japan. Routes between Frankfurt and Paris and along the Boston–Washington, D.C. corridor are planned.

Computerized air traffic control has already been tested in several airports, resulting in a lower incidence of near accidents. Computers on the ground, linked with computers in planes, combine with radar and sonar devices to keep track of the location and speed of each plane at all times. A human air traffic controller can watch only one flight closely at a time, but a computerized system can monitor all incoming flights essentially simultaneously. The increased use of computers to perform tasks in which human error is both possible and disastrous can free humans to exercise their professional judgment and to do other things that computers—at least for now—can't do.

At the Office

*A future day's work: an
office that turns itself on;
extensive management
information systems; flexible
work schedules through
telecommuting*

The manager of the future is coaxed awake by an alarm clock, which also automatically triggers the shower, the coffee maker, and the toaster. In the study, an agenda of the day's activities and a memo from the company's vice-president start printing. After breakfast, the dishes are left for the kitchen robot to clear away. About the size of a beer keg, the robot is the end result of work started in 1988 to modify an automated floor-scrubber used in some hospitals. The robot moves about the kitchen and dining room gathering dishes, vacuuming the carpet and washing the floor as it goes, and puts them in the dishwasher. The machine senses the weight and distribution of the dirty dishes and releases the precise amount of detergent required, then turns itself on, carefully regulating water consumption.

Our manager gets into her car and tells its navigational computer the address of the downtown parking lot nearest her office. Because of a stalled car on the freeway, the computer charts the best alternate route through town, adjusting the car's speed to the timing of the city's computerized traffic light system. Arriving at her office building just on time, she announces her floor to the elevator, which takes her there. Meanwhile, a voice-recognition device in her office senses her in the lobby and turns on the lights, adjusts the blinds, and activates the computer terminal on her desk, which immediately displays the vice president's memo—just in case she hasn't read it yet.

Down the hall, three operators in the word-processing room are already at work. This same room used to house seven of the company's 15 typists; now it holds the operators and several laser printers, and twice the workload is handled in a fraction of the time it used to take. The machines print out clean copies quickly, with errors in spelling and grammar all corrected. Every two hours, each of the operators takes a 45-minute break in the gym, working through exercise routines designed by a computer to meet that individual's health needs. The computer monitors these sessions and prints out a daily report on calories burned, repetitions performed, and general progress over the past months. Other breaks are taken in the coffee room, but in either case productivity remains high, as the daily labor analyses show. The other clerical personnel, as well as the managers, also take an exercise break during the day in addition to lunch. While they're out, their desktop computers work on compiling statistics, organizing data, or printing reports and correspondence.

The manager has to make several decisions based on data from a number of field offices. Her computer gathers the material, and an expert system produces five different practical alternatives for solving the problem. She selects one, and the computer shows her that it will have a slightly negative impact on the company's profits for the next five years but will broaden its base of customers and streamline production. She instructs the computer to print out the data in the form of colorful bar graphs, which she will incorporate into a presentation for the company president.

The rest of her day's work involves reading the daily reports from the field offices, which she can just as easily do at home. By 2:30 in the afternoon, she's back in her own apartment, wearing comfortable clothes. As the daily reports come into her office via the Intelpost electronic mail network (set up in the early 1980s by the U.S. Postal Service), they are retransmitted to her personal computer. Her machine reads them aloud to her as she tidies the house and starts the kitchen cooking the dinner she's planned for a little party that evening.

Clearly, not everyone's professional life will be as high-tech as this example, and there's no guarantee that all computer applications will be this humane—there's always the potential for isolation and overwork, for lower benefits and the exploitation of telecommuters (as we discussed in Chapter 17). But all the technology we've described exists to some degree in offices today. The only things missing are its unified application and the existence of the necessary complex networks. As computers become less expensive, easier to use, and more vital to the successful operation of businesses, the more likely it is that they will become as much of an everyday fixture in most offices as the current coffee machine. Once that happens and computerized contact among clients, competitors, field workers, managers, and support staff is as easy and as accessible as it is via telephone now, an amazing variety of work schedules, office designs, and professional relationships will be possible. The result for everyone could be a streamlined, more pleasant, more productive place to work, with the opportunity not only for advancement and success but for increased leisure time as well.

Summary

Artificial Intelligence

Artificial intelligence (AI) is the computer simulation of human intelligence. The research in the field includes the study of knowledge-based systems, which use inference rules to provide assistance in applications for which exact algorithms are not known or are not computationally practical. Applications of knowledge-based systems to specific fields are called expert systems.

Knowledge-Based Systems Knowledge-based systems simulate the results of human intuition and common sense; knowledge representation is a key element. The computer language PROLOG is the basis of many current efforts to create rule-based systems.

Expert Systems Expert systems provide frameworks for the incorporation and organization of the knowledge of human experts about specific subject areas. Commercial systems exist in a growing number of fields, including medicine, circuit design, mineral prospecting, chemical analysis, and robotics.

Natural-Language Programs Natural-language programs allow users to interact with computers in plain English. Used in conjunction with expert systems, they make knowledge data bases readily and conveniently available even to novices.

Speech The understanding of human speech by machines is a principal goal of research in AI. Developments were hastened by the representation of speech in digital form for telephone communications.

Neural Networks   Researchers are trying, with some limited successes, to simulate the neural structure and functioning of the human brain in silicon.

AI at Work and Play   AI research is concerned with robots that can sense some aspects of their environment, principally through the use of vision subsystems. Such robots, now in the development stage, don't require the precise positioning of parts to do their tasks, making their application more flexible. AI and chess have had a long relationship. Chess programs have been the historic testing ground for progress in AI, because they rely on knowledge bases and learning schemes. The best chess-playing programs currently play at the level of American masters.

A New World

More computers have been sold every year since 1980 than were sold in the whole history of the world until then. As the cost of computers drops, their role as permanent, everyday fixtures in our lives increases dramatically.

The Impact on Daily Life

The future is approaching with surprising speed, as the growing number of personal computers and microprocessor applications have dramatic effects on our society.

At Home: The Smart House   Microprocessors embedded in appliances are already a reality; linked into a home computer system, they'll help relieve domestic life of much of its drudgery. Computer-based systems such as GE's HomeMinder will use a central computer to control the lights, heat, air-conditioning, and appliances and to coordinate home entertainment, telecommuting, housekeeping, shopping, information transmission, and correspondence.

On (and Off) the Road   Cars of the future will feature a variety of computerized systems, including electronic navigation systems. Maglev trains will make extensive use of computers for safety, guidance, and other functions as they travel at high speeds. Computerized assisted air traffic control will further reduce accidents and near-misses.

At the Office   Computer technology can link the workplace and the home, blurring the distinctions between the two. Clerical work is faster and more efficient when computers are employed, and managers can benefit from extensive information regarding their business decisions. If used wisely, computers can make work more pleasant, as well as faster and more efficient, resulting in healthier, more productive, and happier employees who have more leisure time.

Computer Concepts

As an extra review of the chapter, try defining the following terms. If you have trouble with any of them, refer to the page number listed.

1. What was Alan Turing's proposed test for whether a computer system possessed intelligence?
2. What are knowledge-based systems?
3. In addition to information, what can be expressed by PROLOG?
4. Name some of the fields in which expert systems currently exist.
5. What are the advantages of natural-language programs?
6. What has resulted from the digital revolution in telephone communications?
7. What are some applications of speech-recognition abilities in computers?
8. What is the goal of research into neural networks?
9. What neural structures have researchers been able to simulate?
10. Distinguish between insensate robots and sensor-based robots.
11. Why is a vision system essential in the welding robot being tested at the GE plant in Evandale, Ohio?
12. In what way has chess played an important role in AI?
13. What techniques are used by AI investigators to develop computer chess games?
14. What makes chess particularly challenging for programmers?
15. Describe the "window shopping" service offered by a shopping mall near Washington, D.C.
16. What appliances in your home currently have embedded microprocessors?
17. Describe some likely future applications of computer technology in the home.
18. When tied into systems of local traffic control and emergency authorities, how could navigating devices help drivers?
19. What will the maglev train's "engineer" do?
20. In addition to computer technology, what is necessary to the evolution of the professional and personal "high-tech life?"

1. The two approaches taken by AI research are to imitate human thought processes to produce intelligent results and to produce those results using any means.
2. Human common sense is easily represented in computer systems.
3. Heuristics is a programming language used in AI research to deal with questions of how to manipulate stored knowledge.
4. Systems that incorporate and organize the knowledge of human people skilled in specific subject areas are called expert systems.
5. Natural-language programs are largely limited to voice input.
6. A welding robot developed at General Electric contains a neural network.
7. Expert system software for personal computers is not yet available.
8. Automobile manufacturers are developing voice-activated ignition systems, door locks, and lights.
9. The fastest trains in use today travel at over 250 miles per hour.
10. Computerized air traffic control systems can handle more air traffic with lower rates of near-misses.

Multiple Choice

1. The area of research into developing computers that perform humanlike operations is:
   (a) robotics (b) domain knowledge (c) artificial intelligence

2. Sets of rules developed by AI researchers using human intuition and common sense are called:
   (a) heuristic algorithms (b) domain knowledge (c) neural networks

3. The software skeletons sold with the expectation that the expert user will fill in the data are called:
   (a) expert system shells (b) natural language programs (c) PROLOG

4. Voices stored in message recorders for later computer transmittal are in the form of:
   (a) analog waveforms (b) binary digits (c) heuristics

5. The most advanced area of AI research currently is:
   (a) natural language (b) expert systems (c) neural networks

6. The best computer chess programs are at the level of:
   (a) American masters (b) strong amateurs (c) international grand masters

7. In early 1985 it appeared that:
   (a) there would be a computer in every home
   (b) sales were increasing at least as steadily as before
   (c) the bottom dropped out of the computer industry

8. Computer-based systems to operate home security, lighting, heating and air conditioning are:
   (a) available now (b) far in the future (c) likely to appear in the 1990s

9. Trains that operate on frictionless propulsion systems are called:
   (a) TGV (b) maglev (c) skinkansen

10. A system of electronic navigation for cars which can generate street maps of all cities in the United States is called:
    (a) Navigator (b) TGV (c) obstacle-detecting radar

A Sharper Focus

1. A large number of high school and college math teachers have complained that the introduction of the pocket calculator "destroyed" mathematics. They believe that today's students can't do even simple arithmetic problems without consulting their calculators. Do you agree? Why or why not? Think about what might be the result of the introduction of an inexpensive textbook-sized computer with a word processor and a spelling checker. Would this similarly "destroy" other disciplines? What do your teachers think?

2. Assuming that the computer technology were available, how would you design your own "smart house?" What would your choices of systems be in order of priority?

1. If you were called on to take part in one of Alan Turing's experiments as a questioner, how would you prepare? Make a list of 10 questions that would enable you tell the difference between a computer's response and a human's. Explain why you think your questions would trip up the machine.

2. Is the technology of artificial intelligence being used on your campus? If it is, write a report describing how AI is being used. If not, write a report describing how you would use it to improve one aspect of campus life.

3. Considering recent problems with conventional engineers on trains in the U.S., maglev trains with computer controls might seem to be the answer to the traveler's prayers. Draw up a list of advantages over the current railroad system in this, and most other, countries. Can you envision any drawbacks to such a system?

4. Computer-managed systems may change the environment of the manager of future homes, removing many of the problems and annoyances faced by present-day members of the household. How comfortable would you feel with a system that anticipates your every move and is immediately ready with a response? Write a report outlining your day with such systems, discussing the general effects of this type of automation on work and leisure activities.

Data Representation

The CPU in any contemporary computer system deals only with the zeros and ones of the binary system, which correspond to the on and off states of an electronic switch. People, however, find data more readable when they're presented as **alphanumeric characters** (letters, numbers, and punctuation marks). This difference raises the problem of how to get from the alphanumeric representations that are convenient for people to the binary ones and zeros that are necessary for computers.

Various number systems and coding schemes have been employed to address this problem. Let's examine the most common ones in use today.

BINARY NUMBERS

The number system with which we are most familiar, the decimal system, uses 10 symbols (the digits 0 through 9) to represent numerical quantities; single digits represent quantities smaller than 10, and groups of two or more digits represent quantities larger than 9. A digit's position in a group and its value contribute to the overall value of the group. Since each position stands for a certain power of 10, the decimal system is said to have a *base* of 10.

The binary system, with a base of 2, uses the symbols 0 and 1 to represent values less than 2, in the same way that the decimal system uses 0 through 9 for values less than 10. Quantities larger than 1 are represented by groups of zeros and ones. The digit positions in these groups represent successive powers of 2, rather than powers of 10. For example, in the decimal system, the number 57 is a shorthand expression meaning

5   7

$$7 \times 1 = (7 \times 10^0) = 7$$

$$5 \times 10 = (5 \times 10^1) = \underline{50+}$$
$$57$$

In the binary system, the decimal number 57 is expressed as 111001:

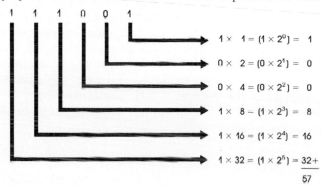

$$1 \times 1 = (1 \times 2^0) = 1$$

$$0 \times 2 = (0 \times 2^1) = 0$$

$$0 \times 4 = (0 \times 2^2) = 0$$

$$1 \times 8 = (1 \times 2^3) = 8$$

$$1 \times 16 = (1 \times 2^4) = 16$$

$$1 \times 32 = (1 \times 2^5) = \underline{32+}$$
$$57$$

2^0	=	1
2^1	=	2
2^2	=	4
2^3	=	8
2^4	=	16
2^5	=	32
2^6	=	64
2^7	=	128
2^8	=	256
2^9	=	512
2^{10}	=	1024
2^{11}	=	2048
2^{12}	=	4096
2^{13}	=	8192
2^{14}	=	16,384
2^{15}	=	32,768
2^{16}	=	65,536

Figure A.1   Powers of 2

Just as the decimal number system uses successive powers of 10 (that is, 1, 10, 100, 1000, . . .), the binary number system uses successive powers of 2. Some of these powers and their decimal equivalents are listed here.

Figure A.1 lists the decimal values of the powers of 2. If you work around computers intimately, like an assembly language programmer, you'll soon become as familiar with these as you are with the powers of 10. Note that a 10-digit decimal number can represent any of 10 billion values (from 0,000,000,000 or just 0, through 9,999,999,999), while a 10-digit binary number can only represent 1024 different values (0000000000 through 1111111111). It may clarify this to note that 9,999,999,999 is 1 less than 10,000,000,000 and similarly, 1111111111 is 1 less than 10000000000 (which is 2^{10}, or 1024). (It is customary to use no commas or spaces when writing binary numbers.) Binary numbers can be used to represent fractions and mixed numbers as well as whole numbers (integers). For example, let's examine the decimal number 43.75. Its whole number or integer part is 43; the period is called the decimal point; its fractional part is 75. Figure A.2(a) shows how this number breaks down in the decimal system, and Figure A.2(b) shows how it breaks down in the binary system. In the second case, the period is called the **binary point** (instead of the decimal point). The binary digits to the left of it represent positive powers of 2, and the binary digits to the right of it represent negative powers of 2.

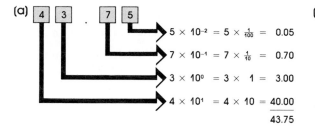

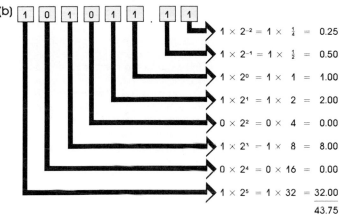

Figure A.2   Decimal and Binary Mixed Numbers
(a) Breaking down the decimal number 43.75 into its powers of 10 demonstrates what the digits and positions really mean. (b) Similarly, the binary number equal to 43.75 can be broken down into powers of 2.

FIXED-POINT AND FLOATING-POINT NUMBERS

There are two main types of numbers that computers can handle: fixed-point numbers and floating-point numbers. A **fixed-point number** is one whose point (decimal or binary) is in a fixed place in relation to the digits. For example, both integers and fractions can be represented as fixed-point numbers. For integers, the point is fixed at the extreme right; for fractions, the point is fixed at the extreme left. Since the point position is fixed and predefined, it does not have to be stored in memory with the value.

A **floating-point number** (also called a **real number,** one in which the position of the point can vary from number to number), in contrast, can be used to represent a mixed number (integer part plus fractional part). You may already be familiar with this concept in its application known as *scientific notation*, since it's used with most pocket calculators. One number is used for the fractional part, called the *mantissa*, and another number is used for the power of the base, or the *exponent*. For example, the mixed number 43.75 can't be stored as a fixed-point number because it has both an integer part and a fractional part. It can, however, be stored as a floating-point number like this:

        4375   2
     mantissa   exponent

The decimal point in the mantissa is assumed to be at the extreme left, and thus is not explicitly stored. The exponent indicates that the decimal point is really located two positions from the left of the mantissa. In other words, the exponent indicates that the mantissa (.4375) is to be multiplied by 10^2 to get the actual value. Most of the time, it is desirable to have the mantissa shifted all the way to the left, that is, to have a mantissa with no leading zeros. A floating point number stored in this way is said to be *normalized*. Figure A.3 on the following page illustrates these concepts for binary numbers.

Figure A.3 Fixed-Point and Floating-Point Binary Numbers

(a) Fixed-point binary numbers can express either integers or fractions. The binary point is assumed to be at the extreme right in the case of an integer, and at the extreme left in the case of a fraction. (Subscripts show the base of the number system used, as in $10_2 + 10_2 = 4_{10}$.) (b) Floating-point binary numbers can represent mixed numbers. The mantissa holds the digits of the number as a fraction, with the binary point assumed to be at the extreme left. The exponent holds the power of 2 by which the mantissa must be multiplied. In this case, the mantissa, which is normalized (meaning there are no leading zeros), must be multiplied by 2^6 ($110_2 = 6_{10}$) to get the actual value, 101011.11. Another way to look at this is to see that the binary point, assumed to be at the extreme left of the mantissa, must be shifted six places to the right to get the correct value.

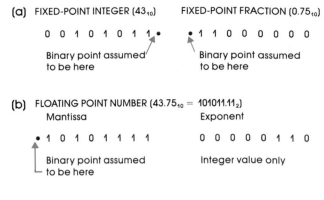

OCTAL AND HEXADECIMAL NUMBERS

You've probably realized from the few examples given here how unsuited people are to the routine handling of binary numbers. Their length (six digits to represent the decimal value 43) and their monotony (nothing but zeros and ones) make dealing with them tedious and error-prone for humans. Two compromises between binary and decimal—the **octal system** (base 8) and the **hexadecimal system** (base 16)—are often employed by programmers and other users who work with low-level details of a computer (see Figure A.4).

The octal system uses eight symbols: 0, 1, 2, 3, 4, 5, 6, and 7. Since 2^3 is equal to 8, the octal system offers a convenient shorthand for binary; each octal digit is equivalent to three binary digits. Figure A.5 illustrates this more graphically by showing how each digit of an octal number can stand for three binary digits.

The hexadecimal number system uses 16 symbols, which are listed in Figure A.6(a) with their decimal system equivalents. Although using letters as numbers might seem strange, it is necessary in order to have a single character to represent

Figure A.4 Powers of 8 and 16

(a) Octal numbers are based on successive powers of 8. (b) Hexadecimal numbers are based on successive powers of 16.

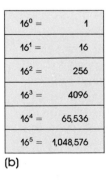

Figure A.5 Octal Numbers

Octal numbers, consisting of successive powers of 8, are a convenient shorthand for binary numbers.

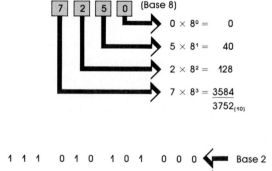

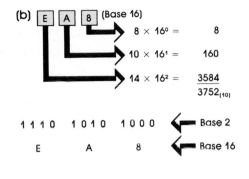

(a)

Base 16	Base 10
0	0
1	1
2	2
3	3
4	4
5	5
6	6
7	7
8	8
9	9
A	10
B	11
C	12
D	13
E	14
F	15

Figure A.6 Hexadecimal Numbers

(a) Because it must represent values from 10 through 15 with single "digits," the hexadecimal number system employs six letters as symbols. (b) Hexadecimal numbers are built up of successive powers of 16 and are a convenient shorthand for binary numbers.

each value from 10 to 15. Since each hexadecimal digit is equivalent to four binary digits (2^4 is equal to 16), the hexadecimal system is also a shorthand way to express binary numbers, as illustrated in Figure A.6(b).

CODING SYSTEMS TO REPRESENT ALPHANUMERIC CHARACTERS

Generally, computers use the binary number system to store and manipulate numeric data. In order to store and represent text in a computer, some scheme must be employed to convert letters, punctuation marks, and special characters to binary numbers. In fact, one way to think of octal numbers is as a set of 3-bit codes that represent the characters 0 through 7. Similarly, the hexadecimal system can be thought of as a 4-bit system for representing the characters 0 through 9 and A through F. These codes can only represent decimal and binary values, however. To represent more than 16 characters, some scheme is required that uses codes of more than 4 bits. Various coding systems have been developed over the years using 6-bit, 7-bit, and 8-bit codes. Of these, two are common today: ASCII and EBCDIC.

The ASCII System

The **ASCII (American Standard Code for Information Interchange) system** is a 7-bit code cooperatively developed by several computer manufacturers whose objective was to produce a standard code for all computers. That objective has been accomplished, at least for microcomputers—virtually every such machine marketed today uses some variant of the ASCII code. Although ASCII is officially a 7-bit code (see Figure A.7) with 128 different characters and control codes, there is an 8-bit version dubbed ASCII-8. In practice, some manufacturers such as IBM also extend standard 7-bit ASCII with another bit to include 127 additional special-purpose characters (see Figure A.8).

Figure A.7 Table of Standard ASCII Codes

This table shows the 128 standard ASCII codes. The first column shows the character itself or an abbreviation of a control code. The second column gives the ASCII code for that character or control code in decimal (base 10). The third column gives the same ASCII code in hexadecimal (base 16) and the fourth column gives it in binary (base 2). ASCII codes from 0 to 31 are not actually characters that can appear on the screen or be printed. They are control codes for actions such as carriage return, backspace, line feed, form feed, and other signals for coordinating communication between a computer and a display screen, printer, modem, or some other input/output device.

Char	Dec	Hex	Binary
NUL	0	00	00000000
SOH	1	01	00000001
STX	2	02	00000010
ETX	3	03	00000011
EOT	4	04	00000100
ENQ	5	05	00000101
ACK	6	06	00000110
BEL	7	07	00000111
BS	8	08	00001000
HT	9	09	00001001
LF	10	0A	00001010
VT	11	0B	00001011
FF	12	0C	00001100
CR	13	0D	00001101
SO	14	0E	00001110
SI	15	0F	00001111
DLE	16	10	00010000
DC1	17	11	00010001
DC2	18	12	00010010
DC3	19	13	00010011
DC4	20	14	00010100
NAK	21	15	00010101
SYN	22	16	00010110
ETB	23	17	00010111
CAN	24	18	00011000
EM	25	19	00011001
SUB	26	1A	00011010
ESC	27	1B	00011011
FS	28	1C	00011100
GS	29	1D	00011101
RS	30	1E	00011110
US	31	1F	00011111
	32	20	00100000
!	33	21	00100001
"	34	22	00100010
#	35	23	00100011
$	36	24	00100100
%	37	25	00100101
&	38	26	00100110
'	39	27	00100111
(	40	28	00101000
)	41	29	00101001
*	42	2A	00101010
+	43	2B	00101011
,	44	2C	00101100
-	45	2D	00101101
.	46	2E	00101110
/	47	2F	00101111
0	48	30	00110000
1	49	31	00110001
2	50	32	00110010
3	51	33	00110011
4	52	34	00110100
5	53	35	00110101
6	54	36	00110110
7	55	37	00110111
8	56	38	00111000
9	57	39	00111001
:	58	3A	00111010
;	59	3B	00111011
<	60	3C	00111100
=	61	3D	00111101
>	62	3E	00111110
?	63	3F	00111111

Char	Dec	Hex	Binary
@	64	40	01000000
A	65	41	01000001
B	66	42	01000010
C	67	43	01000011
D	68	44	01000100
E	69	45	01000101
F	70	46	01000110
G	71	47	01000111
H	72	48	01001000
I	73	49	01001001
J	74	4A	01001010
K	75	4B	01001011
L	76	4C	01001100
M	77	4D	01001101
N	78	4E	01001110
O	79	4F	01001111
P	80	50	01010000
Q	81	51	01010001
R	82	52	01010010
S	83	53	01010011
T	84	54	01010100
U	85	55	01010101
V	86	56	01010110
W	87	57	01010111
X	88	58	01011000
Y	89	59	01011001
Z	90	5A	01011010
[	91	5B	01011011
\	92	5C	01011100
]	93	5D	01011101
^	94	5E	01011110
_	95	5F	01011111
`	96	60	01100000
a	97	61	01100001
b	98	62	01100010
c	99	63	01100011
d	100	64	01100100
e	101	65	01100101
f	102	66	01100110
g	103	67	01100111
h	104	68	01101000
i	105	69	01101001
j	106	6A	01101010
k	107	6B	01101011
l	108	6C	01101100
m	109	6D	01101101
n	110	6E	01101110
o	111	6F	01101111
p	112	70	01110000
q	113	71	01110001
r	114	72	01110010
s	115	73	01110011
t	116	74	01110100
u	117	75	01110101
v	118	76	01110110
w	119	77	01110111
x	120	78	01111000
y	121	79	01111001
z	122	7A	01111010
{	123	7B	01111011
¦	124	7C	01111100
}	125	7D	01111101
~	126	7E	01111110
	127	7F	01111111

The EBCDIC System

The **EBCDIC (Extended Binary Code Decimal Interchange Code) system** is an 8-bit code that allows 256 (2^8) possible bit combinations. This code can be used to represent uppercase and lowercase letters, decimal digits, punctuation marks, and special characters. The four leftmost bits are called the *zone bits,* and the four rightmost bits are called the *numeric bits.* A unique combination of the zone and numeric bits represents each character. This code was established by IBM and is used primarily in IBM mainframe computers and peripheral devices. Figure A.9 shows some alphanumeric characters encoded in both EBCDIC and ASCII binary numbers for comparison.

Figure A.8   IBM Extended ASCII Codes

This screen shows the extended ASCII code system used by IBM microcomputers. These include special characters that appear on the screen for the first 32 ASCII codes, and an additional 128 characters that are encoded by using the eighth (leftmost) bit in an 8-bit byte (normally unused in standard 7-bit ASCII). In this figure, the decimal ASCII codes appear in black numbers and the characters themselves are white.

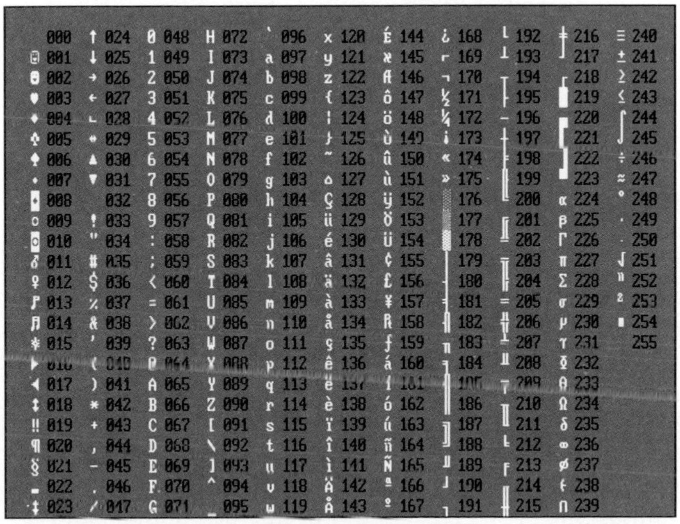

Figure A.9   EBCDIC Codes

This table shows some alphanumeric characters encoded in both binary EBCDIC and ASCII for comparison.

CHARACTER	EBCDIC	ASCII
A	1100 0001	100 0001
B	1100 0010	100 0010
C	1100 0011	100 0011
D	1100 0100	100 0100
E	1100 0101	100 0101
F	1100 0110	100 0110
G	1100 0111	100 0111
H	1100 1000	100 1000
I	1100 1001	100 1001
J	1101 0001	100 1010
K	1101 0010	100 1011
L	1101 0011	100 1100
M	1101 0100	100 1101
N	1101 0101	100 1110
O	1101 0110	100 1111
P	1101 0111	101 0000
Q	1101 1000	101 0001
R	1101 1001	101 0010
S	1110 0010	101 0011
T	1110 0011	101 0100
U	1110 0100	101 0101
V	1110 0101	101 0110
W	1110 0110	101 0111
X	1110 0111	101 1000
Y	1110 1000	101 1001
Z	1110 1001	101 1010
0	1110 0000	011 0000
1	1110 0001	011 0001
2	1111 0010	011 0010
3	1111 0011	011 0011
4	1111 0100	011 0100
5	1111 0101	011 0101
6	1111 0110	011 0110
7	1111 0111	011 0111
8	1111 1000	011 1000
9	1111 1001	011 1001

Careers in Technology: Computer-Related Employment Opportunities

INTRODUCTION

For those of you who will be looking for employment in the computer field, the news is good. In fact, prospects for employment are generally better in that field than in just about any other.

Much of this book is devoted to showing how pervasive computers are, how they touch virtually every aspect of our lives. It's hard to think of any job that does not, somehow, at some point, rely on a computer for something. But lines can still be drawn; there are some jobs that are computer jobs (programmers, word processors) and some that aren't (policeman, lawyer, dentist). Here we'll consider the history, present state, and potential of computer employment.

The Big Picture

By 1990 well over two million people will hold jobs directly associated with computer operation, computer maintenance, and systems analysis. That number doesn't include the millions more in retailing, manufacturing, and service industries who will use computers daily or those who will make, market, and sell computer hardware and software. Despite a general leveling-off after the big boom of the early 1980s, the expected growth rate for computer-related jobs is still three times that for all other jobs in the nation.

Furthermore, computer-related jobs will be available nearly everywhere. In the late 1970s and early 1980s, more than two-thirds of computer jobs were in major metropolitan areas, where the money and facilities to support computer systems were more likely to be found. But the increasing use of microcomputers and distributed data processing is rapidly decentralizing computer systems thus creating more opportunities for high-technology employment in all geographic regions, particularly in the West and South.

More than 80% of all data-processing personnel are employed in only five fields. In descending order of numbers employed, these are data-processing service organizations (over half of all computer professionals are employed by such companies, which provide computing services to business and industry); manufacturing firms; insurance, finance, and real estate companies; banking; and wholesale or retail trade. Transportation, communications, chemical and pharmaceutical companies, public utilities, petroleum and gas companies, government, mining, construction, and agriculture together account for only about 20% of computer-related employment. The highest salaries are paid by manufacturing firms, with public utilities a close second. In 1988, a graduate with a B.A. in computer science could look forward to the second-highest average starting salary of all degree-holders. Only engineering graduates earned more.

Beyond Data Processing

The growing use of computer systems makes a background in data processing (such as you have chosen to receive) a valuable asset even in job markets not directly related to computer operations. Secretaries, typists, and file clerks are finding that experience in word processing is increasingly important, that many employers do in fact already require it. Lawyers, doctors, business managers, accountants—all are finding they use computer skills to a greater and greater degree.

According to the U.S. Department of Labor, as new applications are developed for computers, more and more workers in noncomputer jobs will have to adapt to using computers. This, of course, means that some background in computers will prove valuable to almost every job seeker. While computer literacy is clearly not the key hiring factor for noncomputer jobs—experience, leadership skills, and personality are still the main considerations—data processing skills are frequently cited by recruiters and employers as a tie-breaking consideration between otherwise equally qualified applicants. Studies show that 70% of recently-hired college graduates in a variety of fields believe their computer skills helped them get the job and salary they wanted.

Among the occupations expected to be most affected by computers in the next decade are journalist, editor, real estate broker and agent, actuary, and stock broker; banker, loan officer, accountant, accounting clerk, auditor, and bank teller; doctor, lawyer, scientist, teacher, librarian, pilot, and engineer. Also, in a competitive employment market for teachers, those trained in computer science, mathematics, and natural sciences have particularly favorable employment prospects.

In recognition of the growing pervasiveness of computers throughout society, high schools and colleges are adding new computer courses and utilizing computers across their curricula. Nearly half of current college undergraduates use computers in their course work, and this number is increasing.

Today's Uncertain Market

Long-term, even short-term, employment projections can only be educated guesses based on an analysis of past economic, employment, and business forces; they are a prediction of things that *might* be, not of things that will be. In fact, what looks like an exciting prospect one day may look really dismal the next. In the middle of 1985, for example, the experts who had assured everyone of the computer industry's unlimited profitability and employment prospects got a big surprise. In the space of only a few weeks, IBM stopped producing the PCjr, and both Apple and Wang announced temporary factory shut-downs. A number of once-booming small computer and software manufacturers folded. There was new talk of limited markets for computers, suggestions that perhaps a computer in every home and office was an unrealistic goal. And it was discovered that unemployment could exist in Silicon Valley as well as in Detroit.

Four years later, realignment in the industry, an emphasis on business applications, and the development of new technologies seem, by most indicators, to have turned things around. The 1985 slump may have been a freak, or it may have been part of a recurring cycle. Still, the U.S. Bureau of Labor Statistics continues to project a near doubling of employment in computer fields between now and the year 2000.

COMPUTER-RELATED JOBS

To illustrate not only what jobs are available in the computer industry, but also what the people who have them do, we've selected seven points in the process of a company's acquisition and use of a computer system. These seven job areas are also those projected to hold the greatest opportunities over the next ten years.

The process of acquisition and use of a computer begins with a **systems analyst**, who determines how the company might best use a computer. The company then consults with **computer sales personnel** to decide what equipment to buy. Once the hardware is in place, **programmers, software designers,** and **systems programmers** go to work. The **computer operator** manages the equipment, and the **service technician** repairs it when necessary.

Now let's take a closer look at these jobs.

Systems Analyst

Job Description

Systems analysts isolate, analyze, and solve problems in business, science, and engineering and develop methods of applying their findings to data-processing systems. Systems analysts are problem solvers working at all levels of an organization. Developing a more complete management information system, finding a better way to calculate payroll and benefits, or working out a more cost-effective and labor-efficient manufacturing sytem—wherever there's a system that can be improved is where a systems analyst can work.

Business systems analysts work on the problems of commercial organizations, for example, inventory control or production efficiency. The scientific systems analyst (or technical systems analyst) performs logical analyses of scientific or engineering problems and formulates a mathematical model that is made into a program and solved by a computer. System engineers determine what hardware will be necessary to run a particular program or to serve an individual client and also plan how the system should be physically laid out to achieve the most efficient operation.

Qualifications

Systems analysts must have a bachelor's degree in computer science, business administration, or systems analysis. Business specialists need a strong background in accounting, business, economics, and information systems. Scientific or technical analysts must have a degree in physical science, computer science, math, or engineering. Many organizations like candidates to have experience or background in management science or industrial engineering, as well as familiarity with on-line systems design and software. Finally, organizational, management, and communications skills are certainly among the most important assets of a good systems analyst. A familiarity with computer programming is certainly a plus, since it enables the analyst to understand his or her tools. However, employers seem to be about equally divided on the question of whether management or computer skills are more important. An entry-level systems analyst can expect a salary in the $20,000 range, depending on his or her background and skills, and the employers assets and policies.

Outlook

As companies acquire their own computer systems, employment of people who can help them adapt to the new technology with the least trouble is expected to increase. In 1971, there were 93,000 systems analysts; in the early 1980s, there were approximately 250,000. Most projections say that the number of employed systems analysts will increase by as much as 75% by the turn of the century. Most of the growth will be in urban manufacturing companies, where most of the changeover to computers is expected to occur. However, wholesale businesses, data-processing services, banks, and insurance companies will also provide more job opportunities. It is important to note, however, that seven out of ten job openings in this field are filled by in-house programmers, not recent graduates.

Computer Sales Personnel

Job Description

A computer salesperson in a retail showroom should know more than just the price of a personal computer and whether there's one in stock. He or she needs to understand how different systems operate, what their strengths and weaknesses are, and which ones are compatible. Salespeople also have to be able to answer more formal requests for proposals (or RFPs) from potential large-scale clients (corporate or individual users) who are planning to make a significant investment in computers. The salesperson must be able to put together the most reasonably priced and best-suited system for a particular client, while at the same time ensuring a maximum profit for his or her own company.

Marketing or customer support representatives are highly trained salespeople who travel a geographical region selling new equipment and servicing existing accounts. They commonly work for computer manufacturers or distributors rather than for retailers. Market representatives must also be able to offer proposals to potential clients and must have a strong understanding of the technical aspects of their company's equipment.

Both retail salespeople and marketing representatives usually work on a commission basis in addition to their base salary. The bulk of a successful salesperson's income derives from commissions. Companies set annual sales quotas (generally expressed in points, with, say, 10 points given for a disk drive and 30 points for a laser printer) and offer bonuses or vacations as incentives.

Qualifications

Marketing representatives generally must have a B.S. in computer science or electrical engineering, with a strong background in business and marketing, or a B.A. in marketing with considerable training in computer science. Requirements vary from company to company. Salespeople in retail stores, whether local branches of the Computerland chain or manufacturers' outlets like the Radio Shack stores, don't necessarily need a college degree. What they do need are a basic knowledge of data processing and a sound technical proficiency gained either from college and vocational courses or from hands-on experience with a variety of systems. Communication and selling skills are clearly essential, and again, either direct experience in sales or substantial marketing coursework is often required. Most organizations offer their own training courses for sales personnel.

Outlook

The job prospects in the field of computer sales are excellent, although competition is increasing and standards are getting higher all the time.

Computer Programmer

Job Description

A computer programmer writes the computer programs to solve problems in business, science, and engineering as defined by a systems analyst. A simple program may take a few hours to create, but a more complex program, using complicated mathematical formulas or numerous data files, may occupy a whole team of programmers for more than a year.

In many organizations, a programmer is responsible for both the analysis of problems and the creation of appropriate programs. Such a person is called a *programmer analyst,* and he or she fulfills the roles of both programmer and systems analyst, working on developing new programs or extending and maintaining existing ones—thus analyzing *and* solving problems.

Qualifications

Most employers require a bachelor's degree with a data-processing background. Scientific or technological research organizations, however, may require a graduate-level degree in some scientific field, along with a background in advanced mathematics and computer programming. A knowledge of some specific programming language, such as COBOL, RPG, Ada, or C, and familiarity with data base management systems are often required, as is some experience with the particular hardware and systems used by the employer. Well-developed communication and administrative skills, as well as the ability to function efficiently both independently and as part of a team, are considered valuable assets.

Outlook

The number of people employed as computer programmers is expected to rise by about 70%, or 335,000 jobs, by the year 2000, with most of the increase concentrated in manufacturing firms, data-processing services, government agencies, and insurance companies. As a rule, more programmers are hired by large firms, which can afford their own systems, than by smaller firms, which either use a data-processing service or have a simpler system running packaged software. Entry-level programmers can expect to earn from $24,000 to $34,000 a year.

The widespread shortage of qualified programmers of a few years ago is disappearing rapidly. Despite the projected increases in job opportunities, many experts believe that there may be an oversupply of programmers in the not-too-distant future.

Applications Software Designer

Job Description

An applications software designer (or applications software engineer) is a specialized computer programmer. He or she designs, codes, and documents applications programs (a payroll processing program, for example). Applications software designers usually work for software vendors such as Microsoft or for large corporations that need and can afford to develop their own customized applications software. In working for a software vendor, the emphasis will be on testing and compatibility, since the program will be widely marketed. Smaller vendors may call on their designers to provide field support and customer training as well. On the other hand, if a designer works developing in-house software for a large company, wide compatibility and diversity of application are less likely to be issues.

Qualifications

A B.S. degree with an emphasis in computers is a basic requirement, and many firms prefer to hire people with an M.S. degree in computer science. In either case, two to four years of experience as a programmer in a business or scientific environment is required before one can specialize in applications design. Some familiarity with accounting principles is also beneficial. Excellent programming skills coupled with an ability to work well under deadline pressure, are the qualities most sought by employers.

Outlook

Applications software design is a specialized aspect of programming, so the career outlook is closely linked to that of programmers in general. Programmers who move into software design are choosing programming as a career, as opposed to other data-processing fields such as systems analysis. In any case, all areas of programming have excellent job prospects for the next decade.

Systems Programmer

Job Description

Systems programmers create, test, and document software for a computer's operating system and compilers, as well as for its sorting and data communications programs. They advise systems analysts who are developing new systems or modifying old ones to meet fresh needs. A systems programmer's work is oriented toward the internal operating efficiency of the computer, as compared to that of an application programmer, who is concerned with computer input and output. A systems programmer writes and revises the programs that make the computer operate and spends a great deal of time working with the computer's code. Systems programmers must sometimes help repair a system that goes down because of a problem with its operating software and must often serve as consultants to in-house users. A systems programmer's work may need to be done at night and on weekends when the computer isn't in use, and, of course, emergencies can arise at any time.

Qualifications

Experience is currently a more important factor than education in qualifying for this position. However, as the job market becomes more competitive, employers are likely to set higher academic standards and requirements at all levels. Right now, basic academic requirements include a bachelor's or associate's degree in computer science with a heavy emphasis on assembly language, compiler design, and operating systems. A proven technical aptitude and expertise in systems software gained from at least two years in application programming are the qualifications most frequently sought. Furthermore, a systems programmer must be able to work alone for long periods of time isolated from other people by the off-peak hours the job requires.

Outlook

Because the work is demanding and highly technical and the hours and isolation discourage many candidates, the employment outlook is good for someone with the particular skills and self-discipline this position requires. Since several years of experience are needed before entering this specialty, prospective systems programmers have plenty of time to survey potential openings. The market is larger than the pool of applicants, putting those planning to change jobs in a strong position. Those programmers who plan to enter the field later in their careers have the advantage of being able to tailor their résumé to fit a goal they have an excellent chance of achieving. Because of continued shortages of qualified people, new openings, and attrition, the outlook for this career is bright.

Computer Operator

Job Description

Computer operators are responsible for the actual processing of data. They prepare the computer for operation by testing the equipment and loading the input and output units (for example, putting a disk pack in the disk drive and paper in the printer). Then they run the programs. While programs are running, they must monitor the system for malfunctions and be able to diagnose, locate, and attempt to correct problems as they arise. Computer operators are responsible for the stability of the computer's environment, which means seeing that proper conditions of temperature, ventilation, and humidity are maintained in the computer room (see Chapter 17). Finally, computer operators must be able to write clear and well-documented reports describing operations activities.

Qualifications

Most organizations want job applicants to have a degree or certificate in data processing or computer operations, and many also require a familiarity with one or two programming languages (such as RPG, JCL, or COBOL), since operators should be able to read the programs they run. Some employers, however (the Federal Civil Service among them), require only a high school diploma and some specialized training or on-the-job experience in data processing. Prospective employees are almost invariably given logical reasoning and aptitude tests. Newly hired candidates must often undergo a probationary training period of several months before taking on the full responsibilities of the position.

Outlook

In 1970, there were 117,222 computer and peripheral equipment operators, accounting for less than one-fifth of total computer industry employment. By 1984, that number rose to well over 500,000. Within four years, 263,000 new jobs appeared, and the Bureau of Labor Statistics forecasts another 387,000 by the year 2000. In short, more than 1 million people will be employed as computer operators by the end of this century. Out of every ten openings, four are filled by people who have had no hands-on experience with the equipment used by a particular company. College courses (along with vocational, military, and in-house training) are the primary sources of experience in computer operations.

Computer Service Technician

Job Description

Also known as a field engineer or a customer engineer, the computer service technician is responsible for scheduled or unscheduled computer hardware maintenance. IBM had the first service representatives, whose navy blue suits and ties set standards that still apply to this position and gave IBM its nickname Big Blue.

Although computer service technicians must be able to perform relatively simple repairs such as adjusting, lubricating, and cleaning mechanical and electromechanical parts, they also must have sufficient advanced general knowledge to troubleshoot efficiently. They must have the technical and analytical skills to diagnose the often mysterious causes of equipment failure. Computer service technicians are also called on to run diagnostic programs, lay cables, hook up connections between machines, and install new equipment. If a systems analyst designs a new configuration for a company's computer system, the service technician must set it up.

Most service technicians work for firms that specialize in computer maintenance and repair services or as part of the computer equipment vendor's customer service department. Generally, a technician is assigned a specific geographical area and is responsible for answering all repair calls from clients within that region.

Qualifications

A computer service technician must have a high school diploma, and two years of post-high school study of basic electronics and electrical engineering at a college or vocational school or in the military. Good hearing (to identify and locate "funny" noises) and color perception (to differentiate color-coded wiring) are essential. Finally, computer service technicians must possess good communications skills, to assist the customer in identifying the exact nature of the problem, answer questions, and offer maintenance advice, generally to people who may be unfamiliar with technical jargon.

A newly hired technician should expect to enter a three- to six-month period of course work in computer theory, math, circuitry, and electronics, followed by from six months to two years of on-the-job apprenticeship. Entry-level technicians earn salaries around $15,000, and experienced technicians can expect to receive at least $25,000 a year.

Outlook

In 1971, there were 30,000 computer service technicians. By 1980, that number had increased to over 83,000. Current projections indicate that there may be an increase of more than an 80% in employment of service technicians over the next ten years.

FOR MORE INFORMATION

We've given you an overview of only a few of the employment opportunities available in computer-related occupations. We've provided some general job descriptions, projections, and statistics, but where do you go for more specific information? The following is a list of some of the larger manufacturers of computers and peripheral equipment. We also include the addresses of some manufacturers of automobiles, aircraft, and electronic equipment. These are some of the largest private-sector employers of computer professionals outside the computer industry itself. We're also including corporate addresses, so you can write to any of these firms for information on their products, employment practices, and personnel requirements.

Apple Computer
Professional Staffing
20525 Mariani Avenue
MS-9C
Cupertino, CA 95014

Ashton-Tate
Human Resources Department
20101 Hamilton Avenue
Torrance, CA 90502-1319

AT&T Information Systems
Mr. Robert Bohan
50 Boston Post Road
Orange, CT 06477

Bendix Allied Corporation
Manager—Employer Relations
Allied Signal Automotive World
   Headquarters
20650 Civic Center Drive
Southfield, MI 48086

Boeing Company, Incorporated
P.O. Box 3707
MS 31-11
Seattle, WA 98124
Attn: Personnel

Control Data Corporation
Human Resources Department
8100 34th Avenue South
Minneapolis, MN 55440

Data General Corporation
4400 Computer Drive
Westborough, MA 01580

Digital Equipment Corporation
Corporate Employment
150 Coulter Drive
Concord, MA 01752

Ford Motor Company
The American Road
Dearborn, MI 48121
Attn: Central Placement Office

General Dynamics Corporation
Electronics Division
Human Resources P.O. Box 85227
San Diego, CA 92138-5227

General Motors Corporation
EDS Staffing
700 Tower Drive
P.O. Box 7019
Troy, MI 48007-7019

Grumman Corporation
1111 Stewart Avenue
Bethpage, NY 11714
Attn: New Graduate Department

Hewlett-Packard Company
3000 Hanover Street
Palo Alto, CA 94304
Attn: Computer Staffing

Honeywell, Inc.
Honeywell Plaza
Minneapolis, MN 55408

IBM
IBM Employment Office
12 Water Street
White Plains, NY 10601

Intel Corporation
P.O. Box 58119
Santa Clara, CA 95052-8119

Lockheed Electronics Corporation
1501 U.S. Highway 22
Plainfield, NJ 07061

Lotus Development Corporation
Human Resources Department
55 Cambridge Parkway
Cambridge, MA 02142

McDonnell-Douglas Corporation
5701 Pitella Avenue
Cypress, CA 90630
Attn: Personnel

Memorex Corporation
Front Lobby
461 South Milipites Boulevard
Milipites, CA 95035

Microsoft
16011 North East 36th Way
P.O. Box 97017
Redmond, WA 98073-9717

Motorola Corporation
1301 East Algonquin Road
Schaumburg, IL 60195

NCR Corporate Personnel
1700 South Patterson Boulevard
Dayton, OH 45479

Raytheon Corporation
Employment Department
141 Spring Street
Lexington, MA 02173

RCA Corporation
Personnel
Building 2-2
Front and Cooper Streets
Camden, NJ 08102

Rockwell International
Employment Division
3370 Miraloma Avenue
Anaheim, CA 92803

Storage Technology Corporation
2270 South 88th Street
Louisville, CO 80028

Tandy Corporation
500 One Tandy Center
Fort Worth, TX 76012

Texas Instruments, Inc.
P.O. Box 655474
MS 67
Dallas, TX 75265

3M
3M Center
Staffing Department
Building 224-1W-02
St. Paul, MN 55144-1000

TRW, Inc.
Human Relations Department
1900 Richmond Drive
Cleveland, OH 44124

UNISYS Corporation
World Headquarters
One Unisys Place
Detroit, MI 48232
Attn: Corporate Personnel

United Technologies Corporation
Personnel
United Technologies Building
One Financial Plaza
Hartford, CT 06101

Wang Laboratories, Inc.
Corporate Headquarters Building
One Industrial Avenue
Lowell, MA 01851
Attn: Personnel

LOOKING FOR A JOB

The Résumé

Of course, you don't get a computer job just by walking in the door; you need to apply. Your chance of getting the job you want is improved by preparing a good résumé. Here are a few tips on putting together an effective résumé, based on advice from placement professionals, teachers, and job seekers themselves.

- Make your résumé short, inclusive, and assertive, but not "bossy" or commercial-like. While some experts suggest an enthusiastic sales pitch across the top of your résumé, proclaiming yourself "brilliant, aggressive, and challenge-seeking." This may be a turn-off to some employers. The often-recommended career goal or job objective line may be superfluous or even self-defeating unless you are very certain of a specific goal.

- Emphasize your academic background if you have no prior experience, with special attention to career-related coursework, programming languages learned, number of programs written, and types of hardware used. Applicable coursework is a strong selling point for an entry-level job, but lists of courses should be limited to the higher-level and most relevant classes. Include your overall grade average only if it's good.

- Include previous work experience. Emphasize internship, summer or apprenticeship programs in your field. If a nonrelated job seems applicable, mention it: a clerical job that included operating a word processor is a type of computer experience. However, even if all your jobs have been totally unrelated to computers, consistent employment is a positive attribute. If you lack prior employment experience, you'll need to emphasize academic work all the more. In either case mention of involvement in school or civic organizations related to your ultimate career goals is helpful for demonstrating real interest and leadership.

- Avoid both controversy and filler. Listing work experience for a special interest group or a political party may not be good in some cases. A gold star for attendance is not serious enough material for a résumé. Use good judgment.

- Do not provide references. Not including them makes a second contact necessary if the employer is interested. Unimpressive references (a relative or your fourth grade teacher) can sour your whole résumé. On the other hand, if your personal references include professionals in the field, or employees of the company where you're applying, it might be wise to include them. Consider including a line that says that references are available on request.

- Don't include a salary requirement in your résumé. Like the career goal, it can prove limiting.

- Leave out personal data not directly related to the job. It is illegal for employers to discriminate against an applicant on account of age, sex, race, physical disability, or military service so don't put employers in a potentially awkward position by including such information. Photographs are unwise unless specifically requested. Even then, you should ask yourself why this employer requests a photograph.

- Have your résumé professionally typeset or produced on a letter-quality printer (a laser printer is recommended), and then printed or photocopied on attractive, heavy-stock paper.

- Your résumé is your first contact with a potential employer, and just as you need to make a good impression in person, your résumé needs to make a good impression as well. Figure B.1 shows a good sample format.

The Cover Letter

Your résumé should be accompanied by a brief letter that fills in the sketch your résumé provides.

- Try not to repeat information stated on your résumé. The cover letter is the place to state your career goal and your interest in the particular position.

- Sell yourself in the cover letter. Phrases such as "I am a dedicated and responsible individual eager to apply my outstanding skills for your company" are perfectly acceptable here.

- Be polite but sure of yourself. Your résumé provides the dry details; your cover letter should demonstrate what makes you special, interesting, and worth interviewing. At the same time, be sure to be respectful and courteous.

- Be direct and to the point. Clearly state in the first paragraph where you heard about the job—an advertisement, the placement office, or some other source. If you are not answering an ad, say that you're writing "regarding the possibility of employment" with the organization. In either case, make it clear exactly what sort of position you're interested in. In the second paragraph, cover the highlights of your résumé, adding interesting or significant details of your experience and qualifications. The third paragraph should emphasize your availability for an interview and your strong interest in the position, while the final paragraph closes your letter on a polite and professional note, thanking prospective employers for their time and consideration.

Figure B.2 illustrates a traditional format and style for a cover letter.

Figure B.1 The Résumé
Here's a sample résumé, prepared for a person applying for a position as a customer support representative for a major supplier of business computers. The format is generally applicable. Note that only *essential* information is included on a *single* page, and that references to coursework and experience are tailored to fit a position that combines marketing and computers. The numbers in brackets refer to the notes that follow the résumé.

NANCY EBERT   [1]
384 K Street
Silicon, California 90000
(110) 011-1011

EDUCATION   West College; B.A., 1986   [2]
               Major: Sales and Marketing
               Minor: Computer Information Systems
               Grade-Point Average: 3.9/4.0

               Coursework included: Market Analysis, Contract Administra-   [3]
               tion, Financial Analysis; Information Systems Planning, Of-
               fice Automation, Software and Hardware Concepts.

               Hardware used: Radio Shack Model II for BASIC language   [4]
               course and CRT training. System 3031, IBM/370 OS/MV JES
               2 IMS/VS; JDS OS/COBOL for COBOL language courses. IBM
               PC/AT.

               Programming Experience: (860 hours) 18 BASIC, 26 COBOL,
               2 major projects in Advanced COBOL.

EXPERIENCE   1984–1986   Trusty Sam's A-1 Computer Shoppe   [5]
               Part-time salesperson: handled customer requests for prod-
               uct information (IBM, Apple, Sam's Own A-1), sold recrea-
               tional software on a commission basis.

               1982–1984   The Book Cellar
               Summer sales clerk: processed credit charges, operated
               MISOCS register.

ACTIVITIES   Vice-President, West College Marketing Club   [6]
               Advertising Manager, West Daily Output
               Member, Data Marketing Association
               CRT Operator/Data Control Certified

References and transcript available upon request.   [7]

---

[1] **Personal data:** name, address, and telephone number.
[2] **Academic history:** college, degree (if any), and major. Minor, GPA, and class rank optional. List last college attended first.
[3] **Coursework:** *short* list of appropriate classes.
[4] **Technical experience** (optional): list hardware, programming experience.
[5] **Employment history:** start with most recent employer; list job title and responsibilities.
[6] **Etc.:** memberships, certifications, prizes (add AND AWARDS to heading) and other appropriate responsibilities.
[7] **Employer option:** if they want more information, they'll ask for it; don't overwhelm them with paper they don't need.

[1]

N. G. Ebert
384 K Street
Silicon, California 90000
(110) 011-1011

March 4, 1990

[2] Director of Personnel
International TechSystems Corporation
1 MIS Plaza
Cobol, New Jersey 87654

[3] Dear Sir or Madam,

[4] I am writing in regard to your advertisement in *Computerworld* magazine seeking an entry-level customer support representative for your western regional office. I will receive my B.A. in business next month and am currently seeking a position such as that you describe.

My enclosed résumé demonstrates a successful academic background combining a traditional sales and marketing curriculum with a strong emphasis in computers, data processing, and business systems. My work as a salesperson for a local computer vendor has provided me with professional hands-on experience in the preparation of RFPs for corporations as well as matching individual end users with computer systems appropriate for their needs. Coupled with my extensive programming experience and extracurricular pursuits, my background has been specifically structured for the type of position you advertise. My communications skills, research and analytical abilities, and willingness to take on responsibility and initiative are all equally strong. I think you will agree that my experience and training are exactly what you're looking for.

I am eager to discuss this matter with you further, and am available for an interview at your earliest convenience. I can be reached at the address and telephone number provided above.

Thank you for your time and consideration.

Yours sincerely,

Nancy G. Ebert

encl.

Figure B.2 The Cover Letter
The traditional business letter has six parts: the heading, inside address, salutation, body, closing, and notations. Most businesses use a modified block style, such as that shown here: the heading and closing are indented to a center margin, while the rest of the letter is single-spaced against the left margin with no paragraph indention (paragraphs are double-spaced). Like a résumé, the cover letter should be no more than one page long.

[1] **Heading:** your name, address, telephone number, and the date.
[2] **Inside address:** where the letter is going.
[3] **Salutation:** A gender-neutral greeting, unless you know the recipient is a Mr. or a Ms.
[4] **Body:** The first paragraph tells where you heard about the job.
[5] The second paragraph expands on your résumé, and sells your skills.
[6] The third paragraph re-emphasizes your interest.
[7] **Complimentary close**
[8] **Signature:** Your name should be both signed and typed.
[9] **Notation:** "encl." (enclosure) lets the employer know there's a résumé attached.

The Search

Now you have your résumé, but how do you go about finding a place to send it? Here's a list of potential sources of information regarding job openings for entry-level computer professionals.

- Consult the placement advisor at your school. He or she has access to a variety of employment sources and is there to help you.

- Join a local data processing organization (such as a branch of the Data Processing Management Association) to make professional contacts.

- Join the American Society for Information Science (ASIS), which operates a placement service for its members.

- Consult *Computerworld* or a similar publication for classified job ads.

- Attend a job fair. These trade shows for jobs offer applicants instant interviews and the chance to talk with as many as sixty different companies in a single day.

- Hire an employment agency. While their assistance can be expensive, they have a 90 to 92% average success rate.

- Contact the nearest U.S. Office of Personnel Management (OPM) for a list of government agencies with openings, and for a copy of Standard Form 171, the government-wide application form.

The Interview

Now it's time to talk. Most initial interviews last about 30 minutes, and it's possible that it will seem to be little more than a chat about what you like to do. Don't be discouraged. Interviewers often use first interviews to get to know an applicant's personality: make sure yours is interesting, diverse, and open to challenges.

Here are some suggestions for a successful interview. While following them won't guarantee you a job, it might help you guard against common mistakes.

- Be on time.

- Dress neatly and conservatively to demonstrate your respect for the job, the interviewer, and yourself.

- Don't smoke (even if you normally do, and even if the interviewer does); don't drink alchoholic beverages; don't chew gum. Some interviews take place over lunch: don't eat anything messy.

- Be cheerful, but not giddy; be relaxed, but not informal; be positive and assertive about yourself, but not aggressive or dishonest.

- Be courteous to the receptionist, the secretary, the office manager, the personnel director, the department head, and the vice-president alike. You can never tell who influences whom.

- Do your homework. Know what the job entails and how you qualify. Have some idea of the general salary range for the position (consult the Bureau of Labor Statistics), so you can give a specific answer to the question of how much money you want. A range, such as "high teens" or "low twenties," is almost always acceptable, but be ready with a specific number in case you're pressed. Don't be vague, evasive, or humorous in your response.

- Have your references' names, addresses, and phone numbers with you. Three are generally requested, but you should have five ready.

- Practice a good response to the following often-asked questions:
  "So tell me about yourself."
  "What can you contribute to the company?"
  "What do you see yourself doing five years from now?"
  "Why did you go into (your field)?"
  "Do you have any questions?" (Have some.)

- Know your résumé. Don't rehash information you've already provided the interviewer, except to emphasize some particularly pertinent point. Bring extra copies.

- Do four things when you leave. First, assure the interviewer of your continued interest. Ask when a decision will be made (and say that you hope it will be in your favor). Thank him or her by name—"Bob" if first names have been used, "Ms. Brown" if the interview was more formal. Shake hands firmly and cordially, but don't be brutal (be sure to do this at the start of the interview, too.)

- Write a formal thank-you letter as soon as you get home, re-affirming your interest, suggesting how your skills clearly meet the position's needs, and expressing your enthusiasm about joining their organization. Try to mention some specific, positive incident from the meeting, both to show that you paid attention and to remind the interviewer, who has probably talked to many people already, who you were. Figure B.3 on the following page suggests a possible thank-you letter.

A Final Note

No matter what career path you follow, computers are bound to be a major force in your future. We wish you success in your professional endeavors, whatever they may be.

Figure B.3 The Follow-Up

As soon as you get home from an interview, follow up with a thank-you letter. It should be very short, but should serve to reinforce the good impression you've made. Modified block form is still appropriate.

Nancy G. Ebert
384 K Street
Silicon, CA 90000
(110) 011-1011

March 20, 1990

Mr. Robert Ortega,
Vice-President, Systems Sales
International TechSystems Corporation
1 MIS Plaza
Cobol, New Jersey 87654

Dear Mr. Ortega:

Thank you for taking the time to talk with me about the sales position. The job sounds both challenging and rewarding, and is exactly the sort of career opportunity I'm looking for. As you pointed out during our discussion, the position demands someone who is willing to travel extensively and to devote a great deal of personal time to the work. Let me emphasize that I am that person.

I look forward to your decision, and remain enthusiastic about the possibility of joining the ITC team.

Yours sincerely,

Nancy G. Ebert

Photo Credits

Chapter 1

Opener Crosfield Dicomed, Inc.; *Focus* Dan Nerney/Dot; *1.1* IBM; *1.3* Stan Smith/University of Illinois; *1.5* IBM; *1.6* Sun Microsystems, Inc.; *1.7* Digital Equipment Corp; *1.8* IBM; *1.9* Cray Research, Inc.; *1.11* IBM; *1.12* Intel Corp.; *1.13* IBM; *1.14* (left) Memorex; *1.14* (right) IBM; *1.23(a)* MSI Data Corp.; *1.23(b)* Chuck O'Rear/Woodfin Camp & Associates; *1.23(c)* MSI Data Corp.; *1.24 (all)* General Motors

Chapter 2

Opener Pat LaCroix/The Image Bank; *Focus* Daniel Kottke; *2.1(a)* Languepin/Rapho/Photo Researchers, Inc.; *2.2* Smithsonian Institution; *2.3* Dr. E. R. Degginger; *2.4* Smithsonian Institution; *2.5(a)* Seth Thomas; *2.5(b)* Seth Thomas; *2.5(c)* Dr. E. R. Degginger; *2.5(d)* Joe Demaio/Picture Cube; *2.6* IBM; *2.7(a)* IBM; *2.7(b)* Smithsonian Institution; *2.8* Smithsonian Institution; *2.9* Smithsonian Institution; *2.10 (both)* Smithsonian Institution; *2.11* Smithsonian Institution; *2.12* Sperry Corp.; *2.13* Erik Anderson; *2.14* AT&T Archives; *2.15 (both)* IBM; *2.16 (all)* Intel Corp.; *2.17 (both)* Apple Computer, Inc.; *2.18 (both)* IBM; *2.19* Motorola Inc.; *2.20* Cray Research, Inc.; *2.21(a)* Toshiba; *2.21(b)* Radio Shack, A Tandy Corp.; *2.22* Apple Computer, Inc.

Chapter 3

Opener Motorola Inc.; *Focus* Motorola Inc.; *3.1(a)* Thom O'Connor; *3.1(b)* IBM; *3.11* Intel Corp.

Chapter 4

Opener Microsoft; *Focus* Apple Computer, Inc.; *4.1(a)* Apple Computer, Inc.; *4.1(b)* Apple Computer, Inc.; *4.1(c)* IBM; *4.1(d)* IBM; *4.2* Zenith; *4.3(a)* Apple Computer, Inc.; *4.3(b)* IBM; *4.3(c)* Apple Computer, Inc.; *4.3(d)* Apple Computer, Inc.; *4.4* Hewlett Packard; *4.6(b)* Melchior Gigacacomo/The Image Bank; *4.7(a)* Bay Bank Boston; *4.7(b)* NCR Corp.; *4.8(b)* National Computer Systems; *4.10* Hewlett Packard; *4.11* Hewlett Packard; *4.12* Burroughs Corp.; *4.14(a)* Dataproducts; *4.15(a)* Dataproducts; *4.17(a)* Diablo; *4.17(b)* Epson; *4.17(c)* Hewlett Packard; *4.18* Hewlett Packard; *4.19* Ken Whitmore/BASF; *4.20(b)* Hewlett Packard; *4.21(b)* Calcomp; *4.21(c)* Hewlett Packard; *4.22* Kodak

Chapter 5

Opener Sepp Seitz/Woodfin Camp & Associates; *Focus* Robert Llewellyn; *5.1(a)* 3M; *5.1(b)* 3M; *5.1(c)* Memorex; *5.6(c)* Seagate Technology; *5.8* NEC; *5.12* AT&T; *5.13* 3M; *5.14* Hitachi

Chapter 6

Opener Evans & Sutherland; *6.1* Compuserve; *6.4* Hayes Microcomputer; *6.9* AT&T; *6.10(a)* D. McCoy/Rainbow; *6.10(b)* NASA; *6.10(c)* Peter Menzel/Stock, Boston; *6.11* Howard Sochurek/Woodfin Camp & Associates

Chapter 7

Opener Crosfield Dicomed Inc.; *Focus* Fairchild Camera and Instrument Corporation; *7.11* John Terrance/The Image Bank

Chapter 8

Opener IBM; *Focus* IBM

Chapter 9

Opener Crosfield Dicomed Inc.; *Focus* IBM; *9.32* Softview

Chapter 10

Opener Crosfield Dicomed Inc.; *Focus* AT&T Archives; *10.10* Apple Computer, Inc.

Chapter 11

Opener Crosfield Dicomed Inc.; *Focus* Baltimore Police Dept.

Chapter 12

Opener Crosfield Dicomed Inc.

Chapter 13

Opener Crosfield Dicomed Inc.; *Focus* IBM

Chapter 14

Opener IBM; *Focus* Hewlett Packard; *14.2* Steelcase Inc.; *14.3* Dictaphone Corp.; *14.4* Kurzweil Computer Products, a Xerox Company; *14.5* Tab Products Co.; *14.6* Association of Information and Image Management; *14.7* Tab Products Co.; *14.8* Xerox Corp.; *14.9* Raytheon; *14.10* IBM; *14.11* Datapoint; *14.12* IBM; *14.13* IBM; *14.16* AM Varityper; *14.17* Xerox Corp.; *14.18* ATF Davidson Co.; *14.20* Sharp; *14.21* AT&T

Chapter 15

Opener Crosfield Dicomed Inc.; *Focus* Unimation; *15.2* Ford Motor Co.; *15.3* Ford Motor Co.; *15.4* Ford Motor Co.; *15.5* Applicon; *15.6(b)* Bridgeport Textron; *15.6(c)* Bridgeport Textron; *15.9* Dick Durrance/Woodfin Camp & Associates; *15.11(a)* IBM; *15.11(b)* IBM; *15.12(a)* Navopache Labs; *15.12(b)* Navopache Labs; *15.12(c)* Energy Optics Inc.; *15.12(d)* Navopache Labs; *15.13* Air France; *15.14* The EDGAR System, US Securities and Exchange Commission; *15.15* Omnibus Computer Graphics; *15.18(a)* Jeffrey Mark Dunn; *15.18(b)* Jeffrey Mark Dunn; *15.18(c)* Hewlett Packard

Chapter 16

Opener Crosfield Dicomed Inc.; *Focus* Peter Menzel/Stock, Boston; *16.1* Hank Morgan/Rainbow; *16.2* © 1984 Interactive Pictures Systems, Inc. Published by Scholastic, Inc.; *16.6* Apple Computer, Inc.; *16.7* Cameramann International Ltd.; *16.8* © Lucasfilm Ltd. (LFL) 1982. All rights reserved. *16.9(a)* © Lucasfilm Ltd. (LFL) 1983. All rights reserved. *16.9(b)* Robert Abel & Associates; *16.9(c)* Digital scene simulation (sm) by Digital Productions, Los Angeles, CA © copyright 1985. All rights reserved. *16.10(a)* Museum of Modern Art/Film Stills Archive; *16.10(b)* © Lucasfilm Ltd. (LFL) 1983. All rights reserved. *16.11* Dept. of Neurology, University of Wisconsin; *16.13(a)* Keith Jewell/Office of Photography, U.S. Congress; *16.13(b)* Keith Jewell/Office of Photography, U.S. Congress; *16.14* Cameramann International Ltd.; *16.17* Zenith; *16.19* Boeing

Chapter 17

Opener Evans & Sutherland; *Focus* Tass from Sovfoto; *17.4(a)* NCR Corp.; *17.4(b)* Secura Key, a Division of Soundcraft, Inc.; *17.4(c)* De Le Rue Printak, Inc.; *17.5* Radio Shack, A Tandy Corp.; *17.7* Biotec Systems, A Division of Hamilton Sorter Co., Inc.; *17.8* Cameramann International Ltd.; *17.9* Hewlett Packard

Chapter 18

Opener Crosfield Dicomed Inc.; *Focus* Carolina Biological, *18.1* Dept. of News and Publication, University of Pittsburgh; *18.3* Hank Morgan/Rainbow; *18.5* Michael Datoli; *18.6(a)* General Electric; *18.6(b)* Buick/General Motors Corp.; *18.8* Raytheon; *18.10* Ford Motor Co.; *18.11* SNCF

Text Credits

Credit lines refer to *Focus* features.

Chapter 1
Adapted from "Sail Wars" by Michael Levitt, pp. 93–103. Reprinted from *PC Computing*, September, 1988. Copyright © 1988 Ziff Communications Company.

Chapter 2
From "Early Days of Computers" by Stephen Gray, pp. 6–14. Reprinted from *Creative Computing*, November, 1984. Copyright © 1984 Ziff Communications Company.

Chapter 4
From "High Powered Presentation Graphics" by Charles Rubin. Reprinted with permission from *Personal Computing*, April 1984, pp. 65–74. Copyright 1984 Hayden Publishing Company.

Chapter 5
Adapted from "The Death of the Library Tradition Is In the Cards" by Mitch Betts, p. 1. Copyright 1988 by CW Publishing Inc., Framingham, MA 01701. Reprinted from *Computerworld*.

Chapter 6
Adapted from "On-line Chat Services Rekindle CB Spirit, Bring PC Users Together" from After Hours section, p. 440. Reprinted from *PC Magazine*, June 14, 1988. Copyright © 1988 Ziff Communications Company.

Chapter 7
Adapted from "Gambling on the New Frontier," pp. 20–21, *Cray Channels*, Fall 1986 by permission of Cray Research, Inc.

Chapter 10
Adapted from "The Holes in AT&T's Computer Strategy" by Gene Bylinsky, *Fortune*, September 17, 1984, pp. 68–82. Courtesy of FORTUNE, © 1984 Time Inc. All rights reserved.

Chapter 12
Adapted from "Fingered by the Police Computer" by Barbara Bradley, Thursday, June 9, 1988. Reprinted by permission from *The Christian Science Monitor*. Copyright © 1988 Christian Science Publishing Society. All right reserved.

Chapter 13
From "Teaching CEOs to Use Personal Computers." Reprinted with permission from *Personal Computing*, March 1985, p. 70. Copyright 1985 Hayden Publishing Company.

Chapter 15
Adapted from "Artificial Intelligence Eases into Automaking" by Bill Kalb, *Automotive Industries*, July 1987, pp. 58–60. Reprinted by permission of Chilton's Automotive Industries.

Chapter 16
From "World scientists post climate notes on an electronic 'bulletin board'" by Robert C. Cowan, May 3, 1988. Reprinted by permission from *The Christian Science Monitor*. © 1988 The Christian Science Publishing Society. All rights reserved.

Chapter 17
Adapted from "Perestroika and the Personal Computer" by Misha Glenny, p. 28. Reprinted by permission of *New Scientist*, February 1988.

Glossary

access arms mechanisms that move read/write heads in and out across the surface of a magnetic disk (Ch. 5)

access log a computer-security technique for keeping track of the users who enter a system or program, when they enter, and when they exit (Ch. 17)

access time the amount of time it takes for data to be written on or read from a given storage medium (Ch. 5)

accounting package application software that manages finances (Ch. 1)

accumulator a register in the CPU that holds the results of ALU operations (Chs. 3 & 7)

acoustical enclosure units cabinets used to muffle printer noise (Ch. 17)

acoustic modem a modulator/demodulator that transfers audio signals via telephone lines (Ch. 6)

active cell see *current cell* (Ch. 9)

adapter see *expansion board* (Ch. 3)

address a unique number in the computer instruction that specifies the memory location of a data value (Ch. 3)

address register indicates the location of data to be stored or retrieved from primary storage (Ch. 3)

AI acronym for *artificial intelligence* (Chs. 13 & 18)

algorithm a step-by-step method for getting from input (data) to output (results) (Ch. 7)

ALU acronym for *arithmetic and logic unit* (Ch. 3)

American Standard Code for Information Interchange system see *ASCII system* (Ch. 3)

analog having a continuous range of possible values (Ch. 2)

application generators the most abstract type of programming languages (Ch. 8)

application package see *application software* (Chs. 1, 2, & 9)

application software (application package) a collection of related programs or subprograms designed to accomplish some specified set of tasks (Chs. 1, 2, & 9)

architecture the logical design of the CPU or computer system (Ch. 3)

archiving the process of economically storing records needed infrequently (Ch. 14)

arithmetic and logic unit (ALU) the part of a CPU that performs mathematical and logical operations and manipulates values based on logical comparisons (Ch. 3)

arithmetic operations addition, subtraction, multiplication, division, and comparison performed by the ALU (Ch. 3)

arrays ordered sets or lists of data items identified by a single name (Ch. 8)

artificial intelligence (AI) the branch of computer science concerned with building systems that imitate human thought processes or decision making (Chs. 13 & 18)

ASCII (American Standard Code for Information Interchange) system a 7 or 8-bit code cooperatively developed by several computer manufacturers for representing characters (Ch. 3)

assembler a special program that converts assembly-language instructions into machine language (the strings of zeros and ones that the computer can manipulate) (Chs. 2 & 8)

assembly language a low-level, machine-specific programming language that allows programmers to use mnemonics for operations and symbols for variables (Ch. 2)

asynchronous transmission the sending of one character at a time over communications channels (Ch. 6)

ATM acronym for *automated teller machine* (Chs. 6 & 15)

automated teller machine (ATM) a remote terminal programmed to perform many of the functions of human bank tellers, such as dispensing cash, receiving deposits and payments, and reporting account balances (Chs. 6 & 15)

automatic process control a type of regulation of any manufacturing process in which a computer program, acting through specialized peripheral equipment, assesses the state of the process and operates controls so as to maintain it, or, if it has gotten out of the desired state, to bring it back within the limits (Ch. 15)

automatic recalculation a feature of spreadsheet programs that updates the entire worksheet whenever the contents of a cell is changed (Ch. 9)

auxiliary storage see *secondary storage* (Chs. 2, 3, & 5)

back plane a bus implemented on a separate circuit board from the CPU and memory (Ch. 3)

band printer line printers having a printing mechanism consisting of a scalloped steel band with five sections of 48 characters each, and an array of hammers, one for each position in the line (Ch. 4)

bandwidth the range of frequencies that can be accurately transmitted over a communications channel (Ch. 6)

bar codes a means of representing data as a series of machine-readable white and black marks (Ch. 4)

baud a unit used to measure transmission speed, equivalent to bits per second (Ch. 6)

BBS acronym for *electronic bulletin boards* (Ch. 6)

binary system a number system in which the digits of each number indicate what powers of 2 (1, 2, 4, 8, 16, etc.) it contains (Ch. 2)

biotechnology an area of scientific research concerned with the problems posed by the interactions of human beings and machines (Ch. 17)

bit one binary digit, either a 0 or a 1 (Ch. 2)

bit-mapped graphics see *pixel-based graphics* (Ch. 9)

black box a symbol used to designate a piece of hardware or software that performs a certain function in an unknown or unspecified manner (Ch. 11)

blocking factor the fixed number of logical records that make up a block (Ch. 5)

blocks (physical records) groups of records (Ch. 5)

bpi abbreviated form of the unit *bytes per inch* (Ch. 5)

branch a transfer to different sequences of instructions that are executed based on the data or results (Ch. 3)

bridge a device that connects two local area networks (Ch. 6)

broadband channels communications pathways with a bandwidth greater than 3000 hertz and a transmission rate as high as several million characters per second (Ch. 6)

browse a feature of data base software programs that allows the user to view all the records in the data base (Ch. 9)

buffer storage a unit inserted between two different forms of storage in order to synchronize their activities efficiently (Ch. 3)

bulk memory a type of supplemental memory with a size and an access speed intermediate between those of primary and secondary storage (Ch. 3)

bus a group of wires that connect the various internal and external components of a computer system with its CPU (Ch. 3)

byte a group of 8 bits (Ch. 3)

bytes per inch (bpi) a unit used to measure the data density on a storage medium such as magnetic tape (Ch. 5)

CAD acronym for *computer-aided design* (Chs. 9 & 18)

CAE acronym for *computer-aided engineering* (Ch. 18)

CAI acronym for *computer-assisted instruction* (Ch. 16)

CAM acronym for *computer-aided manufacturing* (Ch. 15)

card see *expansion board* (Ch. 3)

carrier sense multiple access (CSMA) a protocol that requires each workstation to listen before sending messages (Ch. 6)

CAT see *computerized axial tomography* (Ch. 16)

catalog see *directory* (Ch. 5)

cathode ray tube (CRT) a device in which a raster scan technique produces images on a screen; the basis of the majority of computer displays now in use (Ch. 4)

CD-ROM read-only optical disks used for information that is not volatile (Ch. 5)

C³I System abbreviated form of *Command, Control, Communications, and Intelligence System* (Ch. 16)

cell each usable position in an electronic spreadsheet identified by its row and column (Ch. 9)

cell address a designation that specifies the cell's exact position in a worksheet (Ch. 9)

cell pointer marks the location in an electronic spreadsheet where data can be entered or commands initiated (Ch. 9)

central processing unit (CPU) the collective name for the registers, the arithmetic and logic unit, and the main control unit of a computer system (Ch. 1)

channels special-purpose microcomputers or minicomputers that control the movement of data between a CPU and input/output devices (Ch. 10)

character printers machines that print a single character at a time, one after another, across the paper from margin to margin (Ch. 4)

charting program a program that produces graphs, plots and charts from numeric data transferred from a spreadsheet or data base file (Ch. 9)

chassis the frame that houses all of the computer's internal components (Ch. 3)

check digit a single number used for error checking that is based on an input number, calculated through the use of some predefined mathematical formula, then appended to the input number (Ch. 4)

chief programmer team a collection of specialized personnel directed by a chief programmer who prepares the software requirements, designs the overall structure of the program, and oversees all of the lower-level activities of the program development process (Ch. 7)

cipher a method of concealing the meaning of a message by making a substitution for each letter or for a fixed number of letters (Ch. 17)

CISC acronym for *complex instruction set computer* (Ch. 3)

clock cycle one oscillation of the system clock (Ch. 3)

clones see *IBM-compatibles* (Ch. 2)

closed-loop control a type of regulation of any manufacturing process in which feedback flows both from process to computer and from computer to process (Ch. 15)

clustered word processors see *shared word processors* (Ch. 14)

CMI acronym for *computer-managed instruction* (Ch. 16)

coaxial cables communications lines consisting of a central wire or wires completely surrounded by, but insulated from, a layer of outer wires that help to reduce electromagnetic interference (Ch. 6)

coding the process of expressing a fully detailed algorithm in some standard programming language (Ch. 7)

cohesion a structured programming term used to describe the closeness of the relationships among the elements within a module (Ch. 7)

COM acronym for *computer output microfilm* (Ch. 4)

Command, Control, Communications, and Intelligence (C³I) System an integrated defense network of computers, telecommunications systems, airborne warning and control systems aircraft (AWACS), satellites, ground radar, and flying command centers (Ch. 16)

comments explanatory notes inserted within a program's source code to help clarify its operation; ignored by the computer during program translation and execution (Ch. 8)

common carrier a company licensed or regulated by a state or the federal government to carry the property of others at approved rates (Ch. 6)

communications channels the pathways over which data are sent (Ch. 6)

communications package software that allows one computer to "talk" to another (Ch. 1)

communications server a workstation that lets network users communicate with computers outside the network (Ch. 6)

compilation unit a program or a piece of a program that must be compiled all at once (Ch. 8)

compiler (translator) a special program that translates a high-level language program into a machine language program (Chs. 2 & 8)

complex instruction set computer (CISC) a type of CPU architecture that requires several clock cycles to complete most of its instructions (Ch. 3)

computer an electronic device, made up of several distinct components, that can be instructed to process or manipulate data in some manner (Ch. 1)

computer-aided design (CAD) the application of interactive computer graphics to product design (Chs. 9 & 15)

computer-aided engineering (CAE) the application of computer programs that simulate complex electrical or mechanical systems to the design and development of products (Ch. 15)

computer-aided manufacturing (CAM) the application of shared data bases and computers to all aspects of production (Ch. 15)

computer-assisted instruction (CAI) the use of computers to facilitate the process of learning (Ch. 16)

computer-based monitoring constant evaluation by computer of an employee's performance in terms of time, quantity, and quality (Ch. 17)

computer conferencing the use of a telecommunications link to join distant computers and terminals so that users can exchange information or messages immediately and directly (Ch. 6)

computer crime the unauthorized manipulation of computers, computer programs, or data for inappropriate or unlawful purposes (generally for personal profit) (Ch. 17)

computerized axial tomography (CAT) the process where scanners take X-ray pictures of the body from many angles, then recombine them into a three-dimensional image (Ch. 16)

computer-managed instruction (CMI) using computers to help teachers monitor their students' progress (Ch. 16)

computer output microfilm (COM, microfilm) rolls or sheets of thin plastic film (microfiche) on which output text is reproduced photographically at greatly reduced size (Ch. 4)

computer program a precise, ordered group of statements that specifies how a computer is to execute a well-defined task (Ch. 7)

computer system a CPU, its peripheral equipment, and software (Ch. 1)

computer terminal any of a wide variety of devices that collects and sends input to a computer and receives and displays output (Ch. 4)

concentrator a minicomputer or microcomputer that combines the data from a number of terminals onto a single high speed transmission line connected to a central computer (Ch. 6)

contention a technique for maintaining smooth flow of data in a data communications system; each terminal is instructed to "listen" to see if any other terminal is transmitting and, if so, to wait (Ch. 6)

control statements high-level language statements that show how the flow of program logic proceeds (Ch. 8)

control structure a framework that indicates the order in which the operations of a program are performed (Ch. 7)

control totals sums that are computed by hand before input, recomputed by the computer afterward, then compared as a check for input errors (Ch. 4)

control unit directs the operation of the CPU (Ch. 3)

copy-and-paste a word-processing feature that lets the user select part of a document and copy it somewhere else without erasing the original (Ch. 9)

Copyright Act of 1980 grants software programs the same protections afforded other creative works (Ch. 17)

coroutine a subprogram that can execute concurrently with another coroutine (Ch. 8)

coupling a measure of the strength of interconnection between two modules of a computer program (Ch. 7)

CPM acronym for *critical path method* (Ch. 11)

CPU acronym for *central processing unit* (Ch. 1)

critical path method (CPM) a scheduling method that focuses on the sequence of critical activities (Ch. 11)

cryptography the practice of transcribing a message from its original form into a secret code or cipher (Ch. 17)

cross-compiler a translator that allows a programmer to develop a program on one computer with the intention of using it on another computer (Ch. 10)

CRT acronym for *cathode ray tube* (Ch. 4)

CSMA acronym for *carrier sense multiple access* (Ch. 6)

current cell (active cell) the cell marked by the pointer in a spreadsheet program (Ch. 9)

cursor a blinking underscore, vertical bar, or box that marks the exact position on a screen where text is to be inserted or where some other operation is to occur (Ch. 9)

cut-and-paste a word-processing feature that lets the user select a part of a document and move it somewhere else in the document (Ch. 9)

cylinder method an approach to the organization of data on disks in disk packs in which each track on the surface of one disk lines up with the corresponding track on all the other disks, creating a set of nested cylinders (Ch. 5)

DAC acronym for *digital-to-analog converter* (Ch. 16)

daisy wheel printers character printers with raised characters on the ends of arms that are arranged like the spokes of a wheel or the petals of a daisy (Ch. 4)

data the raw materials of a problem that are input into a computer for processing (Ch. 1)

data base an organized collection of one or more files of interrelated or interdependent data (Ch. 9)

data base management package software that allows the user to organize and access large quantities of information (Chs. 1, 9, & 12)

data base management systems (DBMS) software used to create, maintain, and access data bases (Ch. 12)

data base philosophy a data processing view that proposes a single data base for all related information (Ch. 12)

data base record (segment) a collection of related fields; essentially the same as a file record (Ch. 12)

data base report a printed collection of data base record fields (Ch. 9)

data base system a working combination of a data base, a data base management system, and the people who use the data base (Ch. 12)

data communications the transmission of data between geographically separated computers (Ch. 6)

data definition language (DDL) a set of commands with a formal syntax that enables users to create logical descriptions of the contents of a data base (Ch. 12)

data density the number of bytes of data stored per given area on a storage medium (Ch. 5)

data dictionary a collection of information about the data elements of a computer system; typically contains the name, description, source, format, and use of each major category of data (Ch. 11)

Data Encryption Standard (DES) a standard block cipher designed by the National Bureau of Standards for use by senders and receivers of data (Ch. 17)

data entry form a blank form presented by data base software that lists each predefined field (Ch. 9)

data flow diagram a systems analysis tool that shows the sources, storage locations, and destinations of data as well as the directions of data flow and the processes that transform data (Ch. 11)

data manipulation language (DML) an interface between a programming language and a data base management system (Ch. 12)

data models the means by which data base systems structure, organize, and manipulate data items (Ch. 12)

data register holds data just transferred to or from primary storage (Ch. 3)

data transfer time the amount of time it takes for a data item to be transmitted from secondary storage to the CPU or vice versa (Ch. 5)

data types the kinds of data that can be processed using a particular programming language (Ch. 8)

DBMS acronym for *data base management system* (Ch. 12)

DDL acronym for *data definition language* (Ch. 12)

DDP see *distributed data-processing networks* (Ch. 6)

debugging the process of detecting, locating, and correcting logic errors (or bugs) in a computer program (Ch. 7)

decision support system (DSS) a computer-based information system that applies statistical and mathematical models and simulation techniques to provide a basis for judging situations analytically, thereby giving quick answers to interactively asked ''what if'' questions (Ch. 13)

decision table a program design aid used for specifying complex logical conditions and the actions to be taken in response (Ch. 7)

dedicated server a workstation that is reserved for one specific chore (Ch. 6)

dedicated word processors systems used solely for word processing, consisting of a microcomputer with a large CRT display screen, a full keyboard, one or two floppy disk drives, and a letter-quality printer (Ch. 14)

demodulation the conversion of analog signals into digital signals (Ch. 6)

DES acronym for *Data Encryption Standard* (Ch. 17)

desk checking (hand checking) the process of proofreading source code for obvious syntax errors as well as for not-so-obvious logic errors (Ch. 7)

desktop publishing the process that combines the results of word processing and graphics to produce near typeset quality hard copy, commonly by using special software, a microcomputer and a laser printer (Chs. 1 & 14)

device controller a set of chips or a circuit board that operates a piece of computer equipment (Ch. 3)

device media control language (DMCL) a facility that may be included in a DBMS to allow users to define how data are to be stored physically (Ch. 12)

diagnostic programs special software that tests computer hardware and locates faulty parts quickly (Ch. 2)

dialects versions of a high-level programming language (Ch. 2)

digital having only a discrete set of predefined values, for example, the digits 0 through 9 (Ch. 2)

digital-to-analog converter (DAC) a device that translates a discrete data value into an electrical signal of a certain voltage (Ch. 16)

digitizer (graphic tablet) a flat input device on which the user draws with a special stylus and which produces signals communicating the x-y coordinates of the contact points to the computer (Ch. 4)

direct access file (random access file) a group of records stored on a direct access medium, such as a disk, according to some addressing scheme (Ch. 5)

direct access medium a storage medium that allows any particular item to be read at any time without having to go through all of the preceding items (Ch. 5)

direct-connect modems modulating/demodulating devices that plug into standard phone jacks (Ch. 6)

direct conversion a changeover from an old computer system to a new one in which an organization simply stops using the old system and immediately starts using the new one (Ch. 11)

directed-energy weapons (DEWs) laser beams on the ground in the second phase of the SDI program that would fire at any enemy missiles that escaped the kinetic-energy weapons (Ch. 16)

directory (catalog) the place on the disk where the names of files and information about them are stored (Ch. 5)

disaster recovery team a group composed of systems analysts, disaster recovery experts, and company or agency employees that carefully plans which programs and devices are most essential and need to be reinstalled immediately if a disaster should crash the system (Ch. 17)

disk (diskette) see *floppy disk, hard disk* (Ch. 1)

disk cache bulk memory that is set aside for temporarily holding data and computer instructions on magnetic disks (Ch. 3)

disk drive the part of the computer system that reads and writes data and computer instructions on magnetic disks (Ch. 1)

disk packs sets of magnetic disks connected in tandem that can be removed from a disk drive and stored elsewhere (Ch. 2)

display an output device, similar to a television screen, that presents text and graphics (Ch. 1)

display layout charts a formatting tool that is used to design the format of a screen (Ch. 11)

distributed data-processing hierarchical network computers that are connected to each other in a pyramid-like arrangement (Ch. 6)

distributed data-processing (DDP) networks data communications systems consisting of several widely dispersed, but interconnected, computers (Ch. 6)

distributed data-processing ring network several computers connected directly to each other (Ch. 6)

distributed data-processing star network several computers connected to a central computer (Ch. 6)

DMCL acronym for *device media control language* (Ch. 12)

DML acronym for *data manipulation language* (Ch. 12)

documentation a detailed written description of a computer program's algorithm, design, coding method, testing, and proper usage (Ch. 7)

dot matrix printers character printers with a printhead that constructs character images by striking a vertical column of eight or more pins repeatedly against the ribbon and paper, forming successive columns of dots that make up the characters (Ch. 4)

double-density diskettes floppy disks that can hold 6400 bits of data per inch (Ch. 5)

downloading the process of transferring a file from a remote computer to the user's computer (Ch. 9)

draft mode a dot-matrix print mode that quickly prints low-quality output (Ch. 9)

DRAM acronym for *dynamic random access memory* (Ch. 3)

drawing program a program that allows the user to compose graphic objects such as lines, circles, polygons, and text (Ch. 9)

drum plotters graphic output devices in which a continuous sheet of paper rolls over a cylinder beneath one or more pens (Ch. 4)

drum printers line printers having a solid metal cylinder embossed across its outside surface with a row of characters for each character position on a line of text (Ch. 4)

DSS acronym for *decision support system* (Ch. 13)

dumb terminal an on-line peripheral device, usually consisting of a keyboard and CRT display, that can only be used to send data to and receive data from a computer (Ch. 4)

dynamic random access memory (DRAM) primary storage that must be periodically refreshed with additional boosts of electricity to retain its contents (Ch. 3)

EBCDIC (Extended Binary Coded Decimal Interchange Code) system an 8-bit (4 zone bits and 4 numeric bits) code developed for mainframes that represents 256 (2^8) different characters (Ch. 3)

EEPROM acronym for *electrically erasable programmable read-only memory* (Ch. 3)

EFT acronym for *electronic funds transfer* (Chs. 6 & 15)

egoless programming a model that sees the creation of programs as a social activity, open to and benefiting from the feedback of colleagues, who check each other's work for errors in a constructive, rather than a negative, manner (Ch. 7)

ELD acronym for *electroluminescent display* (Ch. 4)

electrically erasable programmable read-only memory (EEPROM) a read-only memory chip that can be erased with an electrical charge while it is still in the computer, then can be reprogrammed (Ch. 3)

electroluminescent display (ELD) a flat-panel screen consisting of a thin layer of zinc sulfide and manganese sandwiched between glass panels containing an embedded network of wires that produce an image composed of orange and yellow dots (Ch. 4)

electronic bulletin boards (BBS) data communications networks that provide a means for their users to exchange messages, programming tips, advice, comments, and software (Ch. 6)

electronic funds transfer (EFT) the movement of money into, out of, and between bank accounts by means of computers and telecommunications technology (Chs. 6 & 15)

electronic image editing the capability of some photocopiers to let the user alter copies rather than just reproduce them (Ch. 14)

electronic mail a data communications service that employs computers and telecommunications lines to send and store messages that would otherwise take the form of a phone call, memo, or letter (Chs. 1 & 6)

electronic typewriter an electric typewriter that contains an embedded microprocessor (Ch. 14)

electrostatic printers character printers that employ sparks of static electricity to burn aluminum off special aluminum coated, black-backed paper (Ch. 4)

embedded computers computers that are part of larger electromechanical systems (Ch. 8)

end-of-file (EOF) a special marker between files stored on magnetic tape (Ch. 5)

end-user see *user* (Ch. 1)

EOF acronym for *end-of-file* (Ch. 5)

EPROM acronym for *erasable programmable read-only memory* (Ch. 3)

erasable programmable read-only memory (EPROM) a read-only memory chip that can be erased by exposing it to ultra-violet light and then can be reprogrammed (Ch. 3)

ergonomics the study of people's physical, psychological, and anatomical relationship to their working environment (Ch. 17)

escape sequence a set of characters that specify some action of the display screen (Ch. 4)

execution cycle the second part of the machine cycle where the instruction is carried out (Ch. 3)

executive see *supervisor* (Ch. 10)

expansion board (card, adapter) a circuit board that plugs into an expansion slot (Ch. 3)

expansion slot an internal connector that allows additional circuit boards containing extra components to be plugged in (Ch. 3)

expert (power user) someone who is very comfortable using a computer and who knows how to manipulate software to produce desired results (Ch. 1)

expert system (knowledge-based system) complex software designed to imitate the thought processes and decision-making patterns of human experts in a given field (Chs. 13 & 18)

expert system shells programs that let nonprogrammers set up their own expert systems (Chs. 13 & 18)

Extended Binary Coded Decimal Interchange Code system see *EBCDIC system* (Ch. 3)

external storage see *physical storage* (Ch. 12)

facsimile transmission (fax) a process by which text and fixed graphic images are optically scanned, converted into electronic signals, sent over communications lines, and reproduced at a remote location (Ch. 14)

fax abbreviated form of *facsimile transmission* (Ch. 14)

fax board a circuit board that fits into a microcomputer's expansion slot and acts as a specialized high-speed modem (Ch. 14))

feasibility study (preliminary investigation) the first step in any system project, in which the nature and scope of the problem are examined to determine whether the project should be undertaken (Ch. 11)

fetch cycle the first part of the machine cycle where the computer instruction is retrieved from primary storage (Ch. 3)

fiber optic cables communications lines consisting of very thin glass filaments that transmit data and information as light (Ch. 6)

fields groups of characters that are somehow related (Ch. 5)

files collections of data records that need to be maintained outside of a computer's primary memory (Ch. 5)

file server a workstation that stores shared program and data files on a large-capacity, high-speed hard disk (Ch. 6)

file system a method of accessing and creating names for files stored on disks (Ch. 5)

fixed bar code readers stationary peripheral devices for reading bar codes such as the UPC (Ch. 4)

flags individual bits contained in status registers that indicate computer conditions (Ch. 3)

flatbed plotters graphic output devices that have a pen or pens suspended from a moveable carriage above paper placed on a horizontal surface (Ch. 4)

flat-file data base manager data base software that handles one file of data at a time (Ch. 9)

flat-panel screen a computer display screen popular in portable computers (Ch. 4)

floppy disk a thin, circular sheet of flexible plastic coated on one or both sides with a magnetizable substance and enclosed in a plastic envelope or case (Ch. 1)

flowchart a graphic depiction of an algorithm in which standard symbols represent the necessary operations and indicate the order in which they are to be performed (Ch. 7)

font (typeface) a set of letters, numbers, punctuation marks, and other symbols with a consistent appearance (Ch. 9)

formula an expression that instructs a spreadsheet program to perform calculations or other manipulations on the contents of specified cells (Ch. 9)

fractal geometry algorithms that generate seemingly random structures and objects (Ch. 16)

frame buffer a computer device that captures a video image and processes it as a string of numbers (Ch. 4)

free-form data base manager data base software that handles text and irregular pieces of data such as paragraphs, articles, and instructions (Ch. 9)

front-end processor a computer, usually located at the same site as the central computer in a data communications system, whose function is to relieve the central computer of routine transmission-oriented tasks (Ch. 6)

full-duplex channels communications pathways that allow transmission in both directions simultaneously (Ch. 6)

function a subroutine that returns a single value (for example, the square root of a number) to the main program; also used in spreadsheet programs (Chs. 8 & 9)

function keys special keys on a personal computer's keyboard that reduce certain often-used commands to single keystrokes (Ch. 4)

Gantt chart (milestone chart) a type of bar graph that shows how long various tasks are expected to take to complete in the context of an entire schedule (Ch. 11)

gateway a device that transports messages from computers on one network to computers on another network (Chs. 6 & 14)

general-purpose registers used by programmers to store instructions, data, memory, addresses, and intermediate results (Ch. 3)

generic operating systems operating systems that can be installed in various computer models (Ch. 10)

gigabyte a unit equal to 2^{30} (approximately one billion bytes); used to measure storage capacity (Ch. 3)

GOTO statement a programming language instruction that causes an unconditional jump from one part of a program to another (Ch. 7)

graphic input data that describe a pictorial image or a particular place on a display screen (Ch. 4)

graphics any kind of pictures, drawings, charts, or diagrams (Ch. 1)

graphics package software that produces pictures and charts (Ch. 1)

graphic tablet see *digitizer* (Ch. 4)

half-duplex channels communications pathways that allow transmission in either direction, but not simultaneously (Ch. 6)

hand checking see *desk checking* (Ch. 7)

hard copy any form of permanent computer output that a user can read (Ch. 1)

hard disk drive a disk drive with vast, high-capacity, rigid magnetic disks (Ch. 3)

hard-sectored floppy disks with a fixed number and size of sectors (Ch. 5)

hardware the electrical and mechanical components that make up a computer system (Ch. 1)

hashing (randomizing) a transformation of a record key into an address to be used for direct access storage (Ch. 5)

head crash a collision between a disk drive's read/write head and any obstruction on the surface of a disk (Ch. 5)

hierarchical model a data model for expressing information as a series of one-to-many relationships; each data item can have many subordinate items but only one item directly above it in the hierarchy (Ch. 12)

high-level languages machine-independent programming languages that allow users to express problem solutions in abstract terms (Ch. 2)

highlighting emphasizing particular sections of text on a display screen by means of underlining, increased intensity, blinking, or reverse video (Ch. 4)

HIPO (Hierarchy plus Input-Process-Output) chart a tool for designing programs that clearly displays what a program does, what data it uses, and what output it creates (Ch. 7)

home automation computer systems in the home that monitor and control lights, stereos, kitchen appliances, and security devices (Ch. 18)

host communications software a program that enables the host computer to establish, coordinate, monitor, and control the flow of data through data communications systems (Ch. 6)

host computer the machine that is designated as the central controlling unit of a data communications system (Ch. 6)

hypermedia a program that allows the user to jump from topic to topic and access any data the computer has stored, including text, graphics, video and audio (Ch. 9)

hypertext the nonsequential organization and presentation of information with a computer (Ch. 9)

IBG acronym for *interblock gap* (Ch. 5)

IBM-compatibles (clones) microcomputers made by companies other than IBM that can run software and use hardware made for IBM microcomputers (Ch. 2)

icons graphic objects symbolizing options or actions to be performed (Ch. 10)

impact methods a printing technique in which an object is struck against an inked ribbon and a paper surface to produce an image of a character (Ch. 4)

index a table of selected record keys and their addresses that is stored on the same disk as the file of records to which it refers (Ch. 5)

indexed sequential file a group of records that is kept sorted so that transactions can be processed in batches (Ch. 5)

indexing a method of reordering data base records without duplicating the data in a new file or physically rearranging the records (Ch. 9)

industrial espionage spying activities engaged in by corporations intent on stealing one another's ideas, designs, or trade secrets (Ch. 17)

inference engine an analytic device or method that uses logic to apply the facts and rules designed by the user to answer questions posed to it (Ch. 13)

information the answer to a problem, the result of computer processing, or the human-usable output of a computer program (Ch. 1)

information services organizations that offer interactive networking to users who have terminals or personal computers (Ch. 6)

inkjet plotters computer-controlled output devices that produce images by spraying droplets of colored inks on paper rolled over a rotating drum (Ch. 4)

inkjet printers character printers with a printing mechanism that shoots tiny electrically charged droplets of ink out of a nozzle; the droplets are guided to their proper positions by electrically charged deflection plates (Ch. 4)

input data entered into a computer (Ch. 1)

insert mode when activated in word processing, all characters keyed in at the current cursor position push any text to the right (Ch. 9)

instruction register holds the instruction about to be executed (Ch. 3)

instruction set all the op-codes of a computer (Ch. 3)

integrated circuits small solid pieces of silicon containing the equivalent of many discrete electronic components (Ch. 2)

integrated software a software package that combines more than one application (Ch. 9)

intelligent copiers photocopiers with imbedded microprocessors that allow them to be connected to computers and to be used as printers (Ch. 14)

intelligent modems a modulator/demodulator that can simultaneously transmit both voice and data, automatically answer incoming calls, and test and select telephone transmission lines (Ch. 6)

intelligent terminal a smart terminal that can be programmed by the user to perform simple processing tasks independently of the computer to which it is connected (Ch. 4)

Intelsat the International Telecommunications Satellite, part of an international network linking more than 100 nations and 20,000 telephone circuits (Ch. 16)

interblock gap (IBG) a blank space separating one block of records from the next on magnetic tape (Ch. 5)

interpreters special programs that translate a high-level language into machine language, one statement at a time (Ch. 8)

interrecord gap a blank space that separates adjacent records on magnetic tape (Ch. 5)

interrupt a signal generated by hardware that indicates a high-priority job for the computer (Ch. 8)

interrupt handler a program that temporarily suspends the current program to process a higher-priority job (Ch. 8)

iteration control structure a loop, or pattern of program statements, that causes the repeated processing of a set of operations (Ch. 7)

JCL acronym for *job control language* (Ch. 10)

job any program or part of a program that is to be processed as a unit by a computer (Ch. 10)

job control language (JCL) special language used with multimode operating systems to specify how programs are to be run and what computer resources they will need (Ch. 10)

justified spaces are inserted in each line of text so that every line is flush left and flush right (Ch. 9)

key the data item on which the sorting of records is to be based (Ch. 5)

keyboard the primary device for entering data and telling the computer what to do (Ch. 1)

kilobyte a unit equal to 1024 bytes (Ch. 3)

kinetic-energy weapons (KEW) missiles in the first phase of the proposed SDI program that would seek out and destroy enemy missiles (Ch. 16)

knowledge-based system see *expert system* (Chs. 13 & 18)

label the first part of a magnetic tape that gives information describing the tape (Ch. 5)

LAN acronym for *local area network* (Ch. 6)

LAN bus network a local area network in which each workstation is connected to a single cable running past the workstations (Ch. 6)

LAN ring network a local area network similar to a bus network, except the two ends of the cable are connected (Ch. 6)

LAN star network a local area network in which each workstation has its own cable connecting it to the central server (Ch. 6)

laser disk see *optical disk* (Ch. 5)

laser printers page printers in which laser beams reflected from spinning disks onto electrically charged paper form electrostatic images that attract the oppositely charged particles of an ink toner (Ch. 4)

LCD acronym for *liquid crystal display* (Ch. 4)

leased lines telecommunications links that connect computers with fixed destinations (Ch. 6)

letter-quality mode a printer mode that produces output that looks as good as or better than electric typewriter output (Ch. 9)

library managers utility programs that allow users to build and use their own collections of frequently needed modules (Ch. 10)

light pen a light-sensitive pen used with special graphics terminals (Ch. 4)

line printers machines that print an entire line at a time (Ch. 4)

linkage editors see *linkers* (Ch. 10)

linkers (linkage editors, linking loaders) utility programs that process the machine language code produced by assemblers or compilers and create executable modules (Ch. 10)

linking loaders see *linkers* (Ch. 10)

liquid crystal display (LCD) a flat-panel screen made of a thin layer of a liquid crystalline material between two polarized sheets of glass in which thin wires are embedded (Ch. 4)

local area network (LAN) a data communications system consisting of two or more microcomputers physically connected together by some type of wire or cable which forms a pathway over which data are transmitted (Ch. 6)

logging on (signing on) the process by which users of time-sharing systems identify themselves as being authorized to gain access (Ch. 9)

logical connectives words such as AND and OR used to combine statements (Ch. 3)

logical expressions statements constructed by connecting simpler statements with the logical connectives AND, NOT, and OR (Ch. 3)

logical record a record stored on tape or disk in a block, reflecting the fact that there is some intrinsic relationship among the records' fields (Ch. 5)

logical storage the users' view of how stored data seem to be arranged (Ch. 12)

logic operations comparing or combining numbers in some manner (Ch. 3)

loop the repetition of a sequence of instructions in a program (Ch. 7)

machine cycle the two major phases, the fetch cycle and the execution cycle, of carrying out a computer instruction (Ch. 3)

machine code see *object code* (Chs. 2 & 8)

machine-independence (portability) the characteristic of a programming language that allows it to be used on any computer as long as that computer has the applicable translator program (compiler) (Ch. 8)

machine language strings of binary digits providing program instructions and data to the computer (Ch. 2)

maglev abbreviated form of *magnetic levitation* (Ch. 18)

magnetic bubble storage a form of computer memory that utilizes tiny spherical magnetized areas induced on chips of synthetic garnet (Ch. 5)

magnetic cores tiny doughnut shapes pressed from powdered magnetic material and strung together on wires to form the primary memory of second-generation computers (Ch. 2)

magnetic disk a large, flat, round secondary storage medium first utilized in second-generation computers (Chs. 1 & 2)

magnetic drums cylinders with a magnetizable outer surface; used as internal memory for many first-generation computers (Ch. 2)

magnetic ink character recognition (MICR) an input method by which characters printed with magnetizable ink are automatically entered into the computer (Ch. 4)

magnetic levitation (maglev) a method of train propulsion employing a system of charged electromagnets mounted on the rails and on the train to provide a frictionless, vibrationless, high-speed ride (Ch. 18)

magnetic strips short lengths of plastic-covered, magnetizable coating that can hold data; often found on the backs of credit cards, bank cards, identification cards, and security badges (Ch. 4)

magnetic tape a recording medium used extensively for computer batch input and back-up storage; consists of a long, thin strip of Mylar plastic coated on one side with a film of an easily magnetizable substance, such as iron oxide (Ch. 5)

mail-merge a word-processing feature that allows the user to merge a file of names from a mailing list with the text of a form letter (Ch. 9)

mainframe a large-scale, high-speed computer that usually serves hundreds of users at the same time and is principally used by large organizations and government agencies (Ch. 1)

main memory see *primary storage* (Chs. 2 & 3)

management information system (MIS) an organized means of providing managers with the information they need to do their jobs effectively (Ch. 13)

manual recalculation an electronic spreadsheet feature that recalculates the formulas of a spreadsheet only when instructed to do so (Ch. 9)

manufacturing resource planning (MRP) a computerized technique for preparing production plans by working backwards from the required completion or delivery date for assembled products (Ch. 15)

manufacturing support application systems used mainly to assist in production planning and control (Ch. 15)

mark sensing see *optical mark recognition* (Ch. 4)

master files files of records that are updated periodically using transaction files (Ch. 5)

matching a process by which a computer is used to compare records from government or private information systems in order to find names that are common to more than one set (Ch. 17)

megabyte a unit equal to 2^{20} or approximately one million bytes; used to measure storage capacity (Ch. 3)

megahertz one million clock cycles per second (Ch. 3)

memory the place in a computer system where data and programs are stored temporarily (Ch. 1)

memory cache holds on to the contents of the memory location most frequently used by the CPU; the CPU can access this information more quickly than information in primary storage (Ch. 3)

memory-resident programs programs that allow users to suspend what they are doing temporarily and switch to some other activity (Ch. 10)

message switcher a device that receives all transmissions from all terminals in a data communications system, analyzes them to determine their destinations and proper routing, and forwards them to the appropriate locations (Ch. 6)

MICR acronym for *magnetic ink character recognition* (Ch. 4)

microcode a sequence of electrical signals that causes the ALU to execute a particular operation (Ch. 3)

microcomputers (personal computers) the smallest and least expensive computer systems (Ch. 1)

microfiche sheets of film holding very small photographic images (Ch. 4)

microfilm see *computer-output microfilm* (Ch. 4)

microforms very small photographic images used to store both text and graphics (Ch. 14)

micrographics the area of information processing concerned with the production, handling, and use of microforms (Ch. 14)

microinstructions the instructions needed to perform an operation for the CPU (Ch. 3)

microprocessor the entire CPU of a microcomputer on a single integrated circuit chip (Chs. 1 & 2)

microwaves radio signals with very high frequencies; used to transmit all kinds of data (Ch. 6)

MICR reader-sorter unit a device that automatically records the data from bank checks and then sorts them by means of the special characters printed on them with magnetic ink (Ch. 4)

milestone chart see *Gantt chart* (Ch. 10)

minicomputers computers in the middle range of size and power (Ch. 1)

MIS acronym for *management information system* (Ch. 13)

mnemonic symbols easy-to-remember abbreviations for computer operations (Ch. 8)

modem a modulator/demodulator, or an interface unit that enables a computer or terminal to transmit and receive data via telephone lines (Chs. 1 & 6)

modulation the conversion of digital signals into analog signals (Ch. 6)

module a relatively independent, identifiable group of related program statements that can be treated as a unit (Ch. 7)

monitor a unit consisting solely of a display screen (Ch. 4)

monitor see *supervisor* (Ch. 10)

monochrome of one color (Ch. 4)

motherboard (system board) the main circuit board of the computer holding the CPU, some memory, and control circuitry (Ch. 3)

mouse an input device consisting of a small plastic box with either wheels or a ball roller that produces electrical pulses when rolled on a flat surface; it allows the user to manipulate objects on the display screen (Chs. 1 & 4)

MRP acronym for *manufacturing resource planning* (Ch. 15)

multidrop lines a system of wires or cables that connects several terminals to a computer via a single channel (Ch. 6)

multimode systems large, general-purpose operating systems that simultaneously support batch processing, time sharing, real-time processing, etc. (Ch. 10)

multiplexer a device that combines the signals from several terminals into a single transmission that can be carried by one communications channel (Ch. 6)

multiprocessing the ability of a computer with more than one CPU to run several programs truly simultaneously (Ch. 10)

multiprogramming see *multitasking* (Ch. 10)

multitasking the ability of an operating system to run more than one program concurrently by rapidly switching between them (Ch. 10)

nanosecond one billionth of a second (Ch. 3)

narrowband channels communications pathways with a bandwidth of less than 3000 hertz and a transmission rate between 5 and 30 characters per second (Ch. 6)

National Crime Information Center (NCIC) a central data repository maintained by the FBI and accessed by law enforcement agencies all over North America, as well as in Europe (Ch. 16)

natural-language program programs that mimic human cognitive processes and allow users to access complex data bases with plain English commands (Ch. 18)

NC acronym for *numerically controlled* (Ch. 15)

NCIC acronym for *National Crime Information Center* (Ch. 16)

network interface an adapter that links workstations to a network (Ch. 6)

network media the cables and other hardware that connect various workstations (Ch. 6)

network model a data model that specifies a set of records (also called nodes) and the links, or associations, between those records (Ch. 12)

network server a workstation that handles special chores (Ch. 6)

network workstation a microcomputer connected to a local area network used to run software, transfer files, and send messages (Ch. 6)

neural networks a field of AI where programmers are attempting to make a computer simulate the human brain's complex of neural pathways (Ch. 18)

newline a character that tells the computer to begin a new line on the display or printer (Ch. 4)

nibble (nybble) one-half of a byte, or 4 bits (Ch. 3)

NMR acronym for *nuclear magnetic resonance* (Ch. 16)

nonimpact methods printing techniques employing inkjet, thermal, or electrostatic processes to form character images on paper (Ch. 4)

novice a beginning user (Ch. 1)

nuclear magnetic resonance (NMR) a computerized imaging technique that uses magnetic fields coupled with a radio-frequency energy source to produce moving pictures of the patient's brain (Ch. 16)

numerically controlled (NC) machine tool a power-driven mechanical device whose actions are determined by a program that describes, in detail, each step in the sequence of operations required to transform a piece of metal stock into a finished, high-precision, machined product (Ch. 15)

nybble see *nibble* (Ch. 3)

object code (object program, machine code) machine-language code resulting from a compiler's translation of a source program (Chs. 2 & 8)

object-oriented graphics output produced by drawing programs (Ch. 9)

object program see *object code* (Chs. 2 & 8)

OCR acronym for *optical character recognition* (Chs. 4 & 14)

OCR-A typeface a standard typeface designed to be read easily by optical character recognition techniques (Ch. 4)

office automation the application of new electronic, telecommunications, and computer technology in the white-collar workplace (Ch. 14)

off-line having no permanent physical connection to the CPU; requiring manual connection before accessing (Ch. 5)

offset printer a reprographic device that uses a master document on paper or a metal plate to produce copies (Ch. 14)

OMR acronym for *optical mark recognition* (Ch. 4)

on-line physically connected to and controlled by the CPU (Ch. 5)

on-line information services services that allow users to perform a variety of everyday tasks via computer (Ch. 1)

on-line thesaurus a feature of some word-processing packages that lets the user instantly look up synonyms to any word in the document (Ch. 9)

op-code see *operation code* (Chs. 3 & 8)

open-loop control a type of regulation of any manufacturing process in which information flows from the process to a monitoring computer, but no direct feedback returns from the computer to the process (Ch. 15)

operand the number on which an operation is to be performed (Chs. 3 & 8)

operating system (OS) a set of programs that controls, supervises, and supports a computer system's hardware by matching jobs that need to be done with the equipment that is available (Chs. 2 & 10)

operation the part of a computer instruction that specifies what is to be done with the data value stored at the memory location specified by the address (Ch. 3)

operational information information used by first-line management to control the repetitive, day-to-day activities of an organization (Ch. 13)

operational simulations computerized models that project how equipment will function in any of a number of hypothetical situations (Ch. 15)

operation code (op-code) a binary code representing an elementary computer operation to be performed (Chs. 3 & 8)

operation decoder a read-only memory that stores all the sets of signals that can be sent to the ALU to cause operations to be executed (Ch. 3)

optical character recognition (OCR) an input technique that employs a light beam to read alphanumeric characters (Chs. 4 & 14)

optical disk (laser disk) a circular platter of a thin metal beneath a layer of glass or plastic on which data are written and read by lasers (Ch. 5)

optical mark recognition (OMR, mark sensing) an input technique widely used in the scoring of test forms; employs light beams to convert the pencil marks on forms into electrical signals that can be entered into a computer (Ch. 4)

optimizing compilers translators expressly designed to produce highly efficient object code (Ch. 10)

OS acronym for *operating system* (Chs. 2 & 10)

outline processor a feature of some word-processing programs that lets the user design the structure of a document first and fill in the details later (Ch. 9)

output printed or otherwise displayed information that has been processed or stored by computer (Ch. 1)

overwrite mode in word processing, a condition in which characters typed at the current cursor position replace existing characters (Ch. 9)

page description language a specialized computer programming language for defining the size, format, and position of text and graphics on the printed page (Ch. 14)

page layout package software that allows the user to integrate graphics and text into a single document (Ch. 14)

page printers devices that print entire pages at a time (Ch. 4)

page scanners devices that convert an image from a printed page into computer-readable digital representation (Ch. 4)

paging the process of dividing a program that is to be run into chunks of a fixed size and placing these chunks into virtual memory (Ch. 10)

painting program a graphics package that allows the user to use a mouse to draw pictures on the display screen (Chs. 1 & 9)

parallel conversion a changeover from an old computer system to a new one in which both systems are run simultaneously for a time until users are satisfied with the operation of the new system (Ch. 11)

parity bit an extra binary digit that is added to a byte for error-detecting purposes (Ch. 4)

password a specific sequence of letters and/or numbers that must be supplied by a user in order to gain access to a computer program or system (Ch. 17)

PC acronym for *personal computer* (Ch. 1)

PC fax (personal computer facsimile) a computer that combines the capabilities of a microcomputer and a fax machine (Ch. 14)

PCM acronym for *pulse code modulation* (Ch. 16)

PDP acronym for *plasma display panel* (Ch. 4)

pen plotters computer-controlled drawing machines that produce images by moving a pen or pens across the surface of paper (Ch. 4)

personal computer (PC) see *microcomputer* (Ch. 1)

PERT (program evaluation and review technique) chart a method used for scheduling projects when the completion times are difficult to estimate (Ch. 11)

PETT acronym for *positron emission transaxial tomography* (Ch. 16)

phased conversion a changeover from an old computer system to a new one in which users ease into the new system one step at a time (Ch. 11)

photocomposition (phototypesetting) equipment that uses a photographic process to merge keyboarded text and digitized images to produce a master document on film or photosensitive paper (Ch. 14)

phototypesetting see *photocomposition* (Ch. 14)

physical records see *blocks* (Ch. 5)

physical storage (external storage) how the data are actually placed on a secondary storage device (Ch. 12)

pilot conversion a changeover from an old computer system to a new one in which only one department, plant, or branch office switches over to the new system for a trial run, before everyone changes (Ch. 11)

pixel-based (bit-mapped) graphics output composed of tiny individual dots called pixels (Ch. 9)

pixels short for "picture elements;" the tiny dots of light making up the images on computer display screens (Ch. 9)

plasma display panel (PDP) a flat-panel screen consisting of a neon gas mixture sandwiched between glass sheets criss-crossed with wires that glow orange at the points where current flows through two intersecting wires (Ch. 4)

plotters computer-controlled drawing machines used to produce paper output in the form of maps, graphs, charts, or illustrations (Ch. 4)

point-of-sale (POS) systems one or more intelligent terminals located at check-out counters in stores used to pass inventory information to the store's central computer (Chs. 4 & 15)

point-to-point lines communications pathways that connect each terminal directly to the central computer by a separate line (Ch. 6)

points a typographical measurement for the vertical size of characters; equal to $\frac{1}{72}$ of an inch (Ch. 9)

polling a technique for maintaining smooth flow of data in a data communications system; each connected terminal, in turn, is "asked" if it has data to send (Ch. 6)

portability see *machine-independence* (Chs. 2 & 8)

POS acronym for *point-of-sale* (Chs. 4 & 15)

positron emission transaxial tomography (PETT) a computerized imaging technique that allows doctors to observe metabolic functions or to locate tumors in the brain by injecting a radioactive substance into the brain (Ch. 16)

power supply a computer's source of electrical power; it contains a transformer to lower and regulate the voltage level of electricity provided to the computer (Ch. 3)

power user see *expert* (Ch. 1)

precompilers translator programs that are employed to preprocess source code before a regular compiler is used (Ch. 10)

preliminary investigation see *feasibility study* (Ch. 10)

primary memory see *primary storage* (Ch. 2)

primary storage (primary memory, main memory) the place where input, program instructions, intermediate calculations, and output are held just before and after they are processed by the CPU (Chs. 2 & 3)

print buffering see *print spooling* (Ch. 9)

printed circuit board a removable assembly in second-generation computers on which the electronic components were mounted (Ch. 2)

printer a piece of peripheral equipment that produces hard copy of text and graphics (Chs. 1 & 4)

printer spacing chart a formatting tool that is used to specify the appearance of a printed report (Ch. 11)

print server a workstation that controls a printer shared by other workstations on a network (Ch. 6)

print spooling (print buffering) a word-processing feature that lets the user print one document while working on another (Ch. 9)

process control systems real-time systems that take input data from sensors, perform some analysis, then initiate actions that will change the process that is being regulated (Ch. 10)

process monitor a computer that observes, records, and displays the state of a manufacturing system (Ch. 15)

process monitor systems real-time operating systems that take input data from sensors and report this data without affecting the process that is being monitored (Ch. 10)

program the step-by-step list of instructions that tells a computer how to solve a problem or perform a task (Ch. 1)

program counter a register that holds the primary storage address of the next instruction to be executed (Ch. 3)

program design aid a tool for constructing computer programs that either outlines a program's overall organization or gives some of its specific steps (Ch. 7)

program development process the series of activities necessary for the creation of a successful computer program (Ch. 7)

programmable automation in manufacturing facilities, the use of tools that can be reprogrammed, such as numerically controlled machine tools and industrial robots (Ch. 15)

programmable data base manager data base software that works with a standard, high-level programming language (Ch. 9)

programmable read-only memory (PROM) a primary storage device that is loaded only once by the user (Ch. 3)

program maintenance an ongoing process of correcting any bugs found in a program during operation, upgrading the program to accommodate new hardware or software, and introducing minor improvements (Ch. 7)

programmer a person who develops computer programs (Ch. 1)

programming language a set of symbols and usage rules employed to direct the operations of a computer (Chs. 1 & 8)

project management package software that aids the user in planning and controlling complex undertakings (Chs. 9 & 11)

PROM acronym for *programmable read-only memory* (Ch. 3)

proportional spacing allowing different amounts of space for different characters (Ch. 9)

proprietary operating system an operating system specifically designed for a single type of computer (Ch. 10)

protocols sets of rules or procedures spelling out how to initiate and maintain data communications (Ch. 6)

prototyping a method of specifying the software requirements of a program by demonstrating what the screen will look like when the program is finished (Ch. 7)

pseudocode an informal expression of a program's algorithm using words and mathematical symbols to represent the elements and flow of the program (Ch. 7)

pulse code modulation (PCM) the assigning of binary values to tonal output (Ch. 16)

quad-density floppy disks that hold more data per inch than double-density disks (Ch. 5)

QBE acronym for *Query-by-Example* (Ch. 12)

Query-by-Example (QBE) a highly interactive language developed to extract information from a data base (Ch. 12)

querying a feature of data base software that allows the user to look for records that meet certain criteria (Ch. 9)

query languages nonprocedural languages that enable users to access and interrogate data bases by means of Englishlike statements (Ch. 8)

radiosity a technique that quantifies the way light is diffused by highly textured or translucent objects (Ch. 16)

RAM acronym for *random access memory* (Ch. 3)

RAM disk extended memory treated as a very fast disk drive (Ch. 5)

random access file see *direct access file* (Ch. 5)

random access memory (RAM) primary storage in which any randomly selected location can be accessed in the same amount of time (Ch. 3)

randomizing see *hashing* (Ch. 5)

ray tracing a technique that allows a computer to recreate the effects of individual rays of light reflected off smooth surfaces (Ch. 16)

read-only memory (ROM) a type of primary storage written to only once as it is manufactured; after that its contents cannot be altered (Ch. 3)

real-time operating systems operating systems that control computers that interact with their environments to perform work; often used to control systems characterized by the need for immediate response, such as weapons systems or industrial plants (Ch. 10)

record layout form a tool used to facilitate data formatting (Ch. 11)

records groups of fields (Ch. 5)

records management the systematic handling of documents from creation to destruction (Ch. 14)

reduced instruction set computer (RISC) a type of CPU architecture that keeps the number of fundamental instructions to a minimum and usually needs only one clock cycle to complete each instruction (Ch. 3)

redundancy codes extra binary digits that are added to codes to aid in detecting errors (Ch. 4)

register a special high-speed storage location that temporarily holds inputs and outputs for the ALU (Ch. 3)

relational data base a collection of files with different record structures, but with at least one field that is duplicated in another file (Ch. 9)

relational data base manager data base software that can work with more than one file at a time (Ch. 9)

relational model a data model that organizes data into flat (or two way) tables, each made up of rows (representing data records) and columns (representing fields within the records) (Ch. 12)

relays electromechanical switches

remote job entry systems teleprocessing systems in which the host computer receives tasks to be processed from distant terminals and batches them (Ch. 6)

rendering equation a technique that shows how light is refracted by a transparent medium onto another surface (Ch. 16)

replication the wide range of reproduction processes in the modern office (Ch. 14)

reprographics the area of information processing concerned with the reproduction of documents, mainly at, or near, full size (Ch. 14)

reserved words words that have set meanings in a programming language and that are not available for programmers to use as file or variable names (Ch. 8)

resident routines the most frequently used components of the operating system supervisor that are always kept in memory (Ch. 10)

retooling the retraining of industrial workers in technologically useful skills (Ch. 17)

RISC acronym for *reduced instruction set computer* (Ch. 3)

ROM acronym for *read-only memory* (Ch. 3)

rotational delay the time it takes for the turning motion of a magnetic disk to bring the desired record under the read/write head once the access arm is in position (Ch. 5)

rule base the set of conditions or rules installed in an expert system (Ch. 13)

running head a title printed at the top of every page (Ch. 9)

salami slice a computer-crime technique by which small amounts of money are regularly diverted to a non-authorized account during normal processing (Ch. 17)

sample a digital value, stored in a computer's memory, assigned to a series of fluctuations in a sound wave (Ch. 16)

scanner an input device that optically reads text directly from a printed page (Ch. 1)

schema a global description of the conceptual organization of an entire data base (Ch. 12)

scrolling the ability to move lines of text up or down on a display screen (Ch. 4)

SDI acronym for *Strategic Defense Initiative* (Ch. 16)

search and replace a word-processing feature that lets the user search for a character, word, or phrase and replace it with something else (Ch. 9)

secondary storage (auxiliary storage) memory with a higher capacity but a longer access time than primary storage; programs and data are kept here when the computer is not processing them (Chs. 2, 3, & 5)

sector method an approach to data organization in which the disk surface is divided into shapes like slices of a pie, called sectors; used on virtually all floppy disks (Ch. 5)

seek time the amount of time it takes for an access arm to position its read/write head over the proper track or at the proper cylinder (Ch. 5)

segment see *data base record* (Ch. 12)

segmentation process of dividing up a program that is to be run into a number of chunks of different sizes and placing these chunks in virtual memory (Ch. 10)

selection control structure a two-path pattern of computer program statements that reflect the IF-THEN or the IF-THEN ELSE logical structure of pseudocode (Ch. 7)

sequence control structure a pattern of computer program statements that specifies one step after another in a straightforward, linear fashion (Ch. 7)

sequential access code a characteristic of some secondary storage media where the time required to retrieve data depends on the location of that data (Ch. 3)

sequential access medium any means for the storage of data from which the items must be accessed in the order in which they were recorded (Ch. 5)

sequential file a collection of data organized so that one record follows another in some fixed succession (Ch. 5)

service programs see *utility programs* (Ch. 10)

set a collection of records that have at least one attribute in common (Ch. 12)

shared word processors (clustered word processors) powerful word-processing systems based on a minicomputer or a mainframe and capable of serving multiple users on a time-sharing basis (Ch. 14)

signing on see *logging on* (Ch. 9)

simplex channels communications pathways that allow transmission in one direction only (Ch. 6)

single-density diskettes floppy disks that can hold 3200 bits of data per inch (Ch. 5)

single-tasking an operating system that can run only a single program at a single time (Ch. 10)

slide show program a program that allows the user to present a series of pictures on a display screen (Ch. 9)

smart recalculation an electronic spreadsheet feature that recalculates only those cells affected by a change to the worksheet (Ch. 9)

smart terminal a terminal with an embedded microprocessor and some internal storage, enabling it to do some data editing prior to transmission (Ch. 4)

soft-sectored floppy disks with only one index hole so that the number and size of the sectors can be readjusted by reformatting (Ch. 5)

software controlling programs that tell the hardware comprising a computer system what to do (Ch. 1)

software licensing a method for protecting a software manufacturer's intellectual property (the program) against theft by copying; disks are sealed in plastic, with labels stating that once the seal is broken, the purchaser has entered into a legal and binding contract giving him or her the sole right of use of the software (Ch. 17)

software requirements specifications that define what a computer program is to do, without giving any details concerning how this will be done (Ch. 7)

source code (source program) a high-level language computer program expressed in some programming language other than machine language (Chs. 2 & 7)

source program see *source code* (Chs. 2 & 7)

speaker-dependent systems the most prevalent type of voice recognition modules, that recognize only words that have been recorded on a template (Ch. 4)

speaker-independent systems voice recognition modules that can recognize the words in their vocabularies on their built-in templates (Ch. 4)

specialized common carriers companies that offer a limited number of data communications services in and between selected metropolitan areas (Ch. 6)

spelling checker a word-processing feature that checks every word in a document against a built-in spelling dictionary and flags misspelled words for the user (Ch. 9)

spooling an activity that enables several users to send output to the same printer while input and processing operations are also occurring (Ch. 10)

spreadsheet see *worksheet* (Ch. 9)

spreadsheet package a software package that manipulates tables of numbers (Chs. 1 & 9)

SQL acronym for *Structured Query Language* (Ch. 12)

SRAM acronym for *static random access memory* (Ch. 3)

stack a central data structure that stores both data and results (Ch. 3)

stackware customized information systems (Ch. 9)

static random access memory (SRAM) memory that must constantly be supplied with an electrical charge to retain its contents (Ch. 3)

status register contains flags that indicate computer conditions (Ch. 3)

Strategic Defense Initiative (SDI) a U.S. defense project under development (Ch. 16)

strategic information information used by top management for long-range planning (Ch. 13)

structure chart a program design aid that helps programmers organize large, multipart programs (Ch. 7)

structured flowcharts flowcharts that use only the three basic control structures (Ch. 7)

structured programming a set of software development techniques aimed at the standardization of programming teams' efforts (Chs. 2 & 7)

structured pseudocode pseudocode that uses only the three basic control structures (Ch. 7)

Structured Query Language (SQL) a language that was developed to express in high-level form the operations on relational data bases (Ch. 12)

structured walkthroughs reviews by a group of peers of the design and/or coding of a computer program (Ch. 7)

style sheet a collection of formatting instructions that can be saved in a file and applied to different documents (Ch. 9)

subroutine a module, or a sequence of statements that performs a particular processing task and that can be called on from various locations in the main program (Ch. 8)

subschema the description of the organization of a specific portion of a data base (Ch. 12)

supercomputers the fastest and most powerful mainframe computers (Ch. 1)

supermicro see *workstation* (Ch. 1)

supervisor (monitor, executive) the main control program of an operating system (Ch. 11)

switched line a communications link that can connect a computer through switching centers to any of a number of destinations (Ch. 6)

symbolic addressing the practice of using representative names in program statements instead of numeric memory addresses (Ch. 8)

synchronous transmission the rapid sending of data as blocks of characters (Ch. 6)

syntax the vocabulary, grammar, and punctuation of programming language (Ch. 7)

system "a collection of people, machines, and methods organized to accomplish a set of specific functions" (from the American National Standards Committee) (Ch. 11)

system board see *motherboard* (Ch. 3)

system clock a chip that vibrates or "ticks" at a certain frequency to synchronize the operation of the computer components (Ch. 3)

system crash a shutdown of a computer system as a result of equipment or software failure (Ch. 10)

system residence device the permanent home of the operating system within on-line secondary storage (Ch. 10)

systems analysis the practice of evaluating an existing system to see how it works and how well it meets the users' needs (Ch. 11)

systems analysts professionals whose basic responsibility consists of evaluating existing manual and computer systems and planning new ones by translating users' needs into technical specifications (Ch. 11)

systems design the process of planning a new system based on the findings from a systems analysis (Ch. 11)

systems development life cycle the methodology by which systems analysts approach the task of evaluating and planning computer systems (Ch. 11)

system software software that handles the details of managing a computer system (Ch. 1)

system unit the central component of a microcomputer system; it houses the CPU (Ch. 1)

tactical information information used by middle management for relatively short-term planning (Ch. 13)

tape cartridges plastic cases enclosing small reels that hold 140–150 feet of ¼-inch magnetic tape; commonly used with minicomputer systems (Ch. 5)

tape cassettes plastic cases similar to regular audio cassettes and holding tape for microcomputer secondary storage (Ch. 5)

tape reels large spools of magnetic tape commonly used with mainframes and some minicomputers (Ch. 5)

Taxpayer Compliance Measurement program (TCMP) a method of using a computer to analyze answers to taxpayer surveys and give the statistical probability that a taxpayer will commit fraud (Ch. 16)

telecommuting working at home using a computer linked to an office via telecommunications lines (Chs. 6 & 14)

teleconferences an interactive electronic meeting (Ch. 1)

teleconferencing holding audio and/or video meetings by electronically linking geographically dispersed participants (Ch. 14)

teleprocessing systems data communications systems consisting of remote terminals connected via channels to a central host computer (Ch. 6)

template matching in pattern recognition, the technique of comparing what is actually present against a predefined pattern (Ch. 16)

templates in a voice-recognition module, the speech patterns against which the computer compares all subsequent voice commands; also, in electronic spreadsheets, a worksheet that already contains labels, formulas, and constants (Chs. 4 & 9)

terabyte a unit equal to 2^{40} (approximately one trillion) bytes; used to measure storage capacity (Ch. 3)

TERCOM System acronym for *Terrain Contour Matching System* (Ch. 16)

terminal a display screen with an attached keyboard used to enter data and display data and programs; the most popular on-line input device (Ch. 1)

terminal emulation a feature of communications packages that uses a microcomputer as a terminal to a multiuser computer (Ch. 9)

terminal emulator software that performs some of the same tasks as an ordinary terminal (Ch. 6)

Terrain Contour Matching (TERCOM) System a specialized image-processing system that uses elevation maps to guide a Cruise missile on its planned flight path (Ch. 16)

thermal printers character printers that employ heat to produce characters resembling dot matrix ones on special heat-sensitive paper (Ch. 4)

time bomb a coded section of a program that initiates some event after certain other specified events have occurred; used by computer criminals to damage data for vindictive reasons or to destroy evidence of crimes (Ch. 17)

time sharing the parceling out by an operating system of successive connection times of a few milliseconds' duration to several users, creating the illusion for each user of having sole and immediate access to the computer (Chs. 2 & 10)

token-passing a protocol that uses a signal (token) to determine which workstation is allowed to transmit data (Ch. 6)

top-down design an approach to program design that involves breaking down a large task into successively smaller subtasks, that are organized hierarchically (Ch. 7)

topology the arrangement of hardware in a network (Ch. 6)

touch-panel screens input devices employing either a pressure-sensitive surface or crisscrossing beams of infrared light to enable users to enter data by simply touching a display screen (Ch. 4)

touch-tone devices input devices that send input data, in the form of sounds of varying pitches, over telephone lines from remote locations to a central computer (Ch. 4)

trackball an input device consisting of a rolling ball in a stationary housing; it allows the user to manipulate objects on the screen (Ch. 4)

transaction files collections of additions, deletions, and changes to be made to sequential files (Ch. 5)

transient routines the less frequently used portions of the operating system supervisor (Ch. 10)

transistor an electronic device made of solid material that functions like a vacuum tube (Ch. 2)

translation the conversion of source code into machine-language instructions (Ch. 7)

translator see *compiler* (Chs. 2 & 8)

transputers microprocessor-based multiprocessing computers (Ch. 10)

trapdoor a set of program instructions that allows the perpetrator of a computer crime to bypass a computer's normal internal security systems (Ch. 17)

Trojan horse a set of program instructions embedded in a legitimate operational program by a computer criminal in order to access otherwise inaccessible data (Ch. 17)

truth table a table that gives all possible results of applying logic operations to binary inputs (Ch. 3)

twisted pairs pairs of copper wires in bundles that carry information in telegraph and telephone lines (Ch. 6)

typeface see *font* (Ch. 9)

typesetting the process of producing a master document that achieves high-quality, proportionally-spaced results (Ch. 14)

ultrafiche a compact form of microfiche that can reduce documents to ¹/₉₀th of their original size (Ch. 14)

undo a word-processing command that undoes whatever function the user just performed (Ch. 9)

Universal Product Code (UPC) a bar code identifying the manufacturer and the product; appears on most supermarket items and on books and magazines (Ch. 4)

UPC acronym for *Universal Product Code* (Ch. 4)

uploading the process of transferring a file from the user's computer to a remote computer (Ch. 9)

upward compatibility a characteristic of a family of computers (a product line) that allows a program written for one machine to run on any larger machine in the series (Ch. 2)

user (end-user) a person who runs software on a computer to accomplish a task (Ch. 1)

user-friendly the characteristic of software that makes it easy to use; instructions and answers to questions are built-in to guide the user (Chs. 1 & 7)

user interface the means by which the people using a computer program communicate with it (Ch. 7)

utility (service) programs processing programs that provide users with common, necessary functions (Ch. 10)

vacuum tube an electronic switch that sends electrons over a finite distance in a matter of microseconds; employed in the first electronic computers (Ch. 2)

value-added carriers companies that lease communications channels from common carriers and add extra services beyond the basic ones provided (Ch. 6)

value-added network (VAN) a data communications system that offers some extra service to its users (Ch. 6)

VAN acronym for *value-added network* (Ch. 6)

virtual machine an interface that relieves the user of any need to be concerned about most of the physical details of the computer system or network being accessed (Ch. 10)

virtual memory see *virtual storage* (Ch. 10)

virtual storage (virtual memory) a memory management tactic that employs an area of rapidly accessible secondary storage (such as a hard disk) as an extension of primary memory (Ch. 10)

virus a hidden program-within-a-program that often clones itself and can destroy data and cause delays (Ch. 17)

voiceband channels communications pathways with a bandwidth of about 3000 hertz and transmission rates as high as 960 characters per second; commonly used for voice communications (Ch. 6)

voice mail an electronic message-transmitting system similar to electronic mail except that the messages are vocal ones (Ch. 14)

voice recognition module (VRM) an input device that can recognize from 40 to 200 isolated sounds, words, and phrases (Chs. 1 & 4)

volume table of contents (VTOC) the second part of magnetic tape that holds information about all the files recorded on the tape (Ch. 5)

VRM acronym for *voice recognition module* (Chs. 1 & 4)

VTOC acronym for *volume table of contents* (Ch. 5)

waveform a graphic display of a sound wave (Ch. 16)

what-you-see-is-what-you-get (WYSIWYG) desktop publishing systems that present the appearance of the final printed output on the display screen (Ch. 14)

Winchester disk drive a device that has access arms, read/write heads, and a hard disk or disks completely enclosed in a sealed, airtight housing; originally developed by IBM (Ch. 5)

windowing environment a type of software that allows the user to divide the display screen into "windows" with an application program running in each one (Ch. 10)

word a group of adjacent bits that are manipulated and stored as a unit (Ch. 3)

word-processing package software package that enables the user to enter, store, modify, format, copy, and print text (Chs. 1 & 9)

word-wrap in word processing, when a word is keyed in that extends beyond the right margin, it is automatically moved down to the next line (Ch. 9)

workstation (supermicro) a powerful desktop computer (Ch. 1)

worksheet (spreadsheet) tables of rows and columns of numerical data (Ch. 9)

WORM acronym for *write once read many* (Ch. 5)

worm an error or instruction written into a program to harass unauthorized users or to protect against copying (Ch. 17)

write once read many (WORM) optical disks that can be used to read stored data and write new data but from which data cannot be erased (Ch. 5)

write-protect a mechanism that protects secondary storage media from being altered (Ch. 5)

WYSIWYG acronym for *what-you-see-is-what-you-get* (Ch. 14)

Answers to Selected Exercises

Chapter 1

True or False

1. T
2. T
3. F
4. T
5. T
6. T
7. F
8. T
9. F
10. T

Multiple Choice

1. b
2. c
3. c
4. c
5. a
6. b
7. c
8. b
9. c
10. b

Chapter 2

True or False

1. T
2. F
3. T
4. T
5. T
6. T
7. F
8. T
9. T
10. T

Multiple Choice

1. b
2. c
3. b
4. b
5. c
6. a
7. a

8. a
9. c
10. a

Chapter 3

True or False

1. F
2. T
3. F
4. T
5. F
6. T
7. T
8. F
9. T
10. T

Multiple Choice

1. b
2. c
3. a
4. a
5. c
6. b
7. c
8. b
9. a
10. c

Chapter 4

True or False

1. F
2. T
3. T
4. T
5. F
6. F
7. T
8. F
9. F
10. T

Multiple Choice

1. b
2. a

3. c
4. b
5. a
6. c
7. b
8. a
9. c
10. b

Chapter 5

True or False

1. T
2. F
3. F
4. T
5. F
6. T
7. T
8. F
9. T
10. T

Multiple Choice

1. c
2. b
3. c
4. a
5. b
6. b
7. b
8. c
9. b
10. a

Chapter 6

True or False

1. T
2. T
3. F
4. T
5. T
6. F
7. F
8. T
9. F
10. T

Multiple Choice

1. b
2. c
3. b
4. a
5. c
6. a
7. c
8. c
9. b
10. b

Chapter 7

True or False

1. T
2. F
3. T
4. T
5. T
6. F
7. F
8. F
9. T
10. T

Multiple Choice

1. c
2. a
3. b
4. b
5. a
6. b
7. c
8. c
9. a
10. c

Chapter 8

True or False

1. F
2. T
3. F
4. T
5. T
6. F

7. F	7. F	7. F	7. F
8. F	8. T	8. T	8. T
9. F	9. F	9. F	9. F
10. T	10. T	10. T	10. T

Multiple Choice	Multiple Choice	Multiple Choice	Multiple Choice
1. b	1. a	1. b	1. a
2. a	2. b	2. c	2. b
3. c	3. c	3. b	3. b
4. b	4. c	4. a	4. c
5. c	5. a	5. c	5. a
6. a	6. b	6. a	6. b
7. c	7. a	7. a	7. b
8. a	8. b	8. c	8. c
9. b	9. c	9. b	9. a
10. c	10. a	10. b	10. c

Chapter 9	Chapter 11	Chapter 13	Chapter 15

True or False	True or False	True or False	True or False
1. F	1. F	1. T	1. T
2. T	2. T	2. F	2. F
3. T	3. T	3. F	3. F
4. F	4. T	4. T	4. T
5. T	5. T	5. F	5. F
6. T	6. T	6. F	6. T
7. T	7. F	7. F	7. T
8. T	8. F	8. F	8. F
9. T	9. T	9. F	9. F
10. F	10. F	10. T	10. F

Multiple Choice	Multiple Choice	Multiple Choice	Multiple Choice
1. b	1. c	1. a	1. a
2. a	2. a	2. c	2. c
3. c	3. b	3. b	3. a
4. b	4. c	4. b	4. a
5. a	5. a	5. a	5. c
6. c	6. b	6. c	6. b
7. a	7. b	7. c	7. a
8. b	8. c	8. a	8. c
9. c	9. a	9. c	9. b
10. a	10. b	10. b	10. a

Chapter 10	Chapter 12	Chapter 14	Chapter 16

True or False	True or False	True or False	True or False
1. T	1. T	1. T	1. F
2. F	2. F	2. F	2. T
3. F	3. T	3. T	3. T
4. T	4. T	4. T	4. F
5. F	5. F	5. T	5. F
6. F	6. F	6. T	6. T

7. T
8. F
9. T
10. T

Multiple Choice

1. a
2. c
3. b
4. c
5. c
6. b
7. c
8. b
9. a
10. b

Chapter 17

True or False

1. T
2. F
3. T
4. F
5. T
6. F
7. T
8. T
9. F
10. F

Multiple Choice

1. b
2. a
3. c
4. c
5. a
6. b
7. a
8. b
9. c

Chapter 18

True or False

1. T
2. F
3. F
4. T
5. F
6. F
7. F
8. T
9. F
10. T

Multiple Choice

1. c
2. a
3. a
4. b
5. c
6. a
7. c
8. a
9. b
10. a

Index